Plenty of varietas
Something that ...

CLARENDON ANCIENT

General Editors

Brian Bosworth   Miriam Griffin
David Whitehead   Susan Treggiari

The aim of the CLARENDON ANCIENT HISTORY SERIES is to provide authoritative translations, introductions, and commentaries to a wide range of Greek and Latin texts studied by ancient historians. The books will be of interest to scholars, graduate students, and advanced undergraduates.

THE ELDER PLINY ON THE HUMAN ANIMAL

Natural History

BOOK 7

Translated
with Introduction and Historical Commentary by

Mary Beagon

CLARENDON PRESS · OXFORD

OXFORD
UNIVERSITY PRESS

Great Clarendon Street, Oxford OX2 6DP

Oxford University Press is a department of the University of Oxford.
It furthers the University's objective of excellence in research, scholarship,
and education by publishing worldwide in

Oxford New York

Auckland Cape Town Dar es Salaam Hong Kong Karachi
Kuala Lumpur Madrid Melbourne Mexico City Nairobi
New Delhi Shanghai Taipei Toronto

With offices in

Argentina Austria Brazil Chile Czech Republic France Greece
Guatemala Hungary Italy Japan South Korea Poland Portugal
Singapore Switzerland Thailand Turkey Ukraine Vietnam

Oxford is a registered trade mark of Oxford University Press
in the UK and in certain other countries

Published in the United States
by Oxford University Press Inc., New York

British Library Cataloguing in Publication Data
Data available

Library of Congress Cataloging-in-Publication Data
Pliny, the Elder.
[Naturalis historia. Liber 7. English]
The elder Pliny on the human animal : Natural history, book 7 / translated
with introduction and historical commentary by Mary Beagon.
p. cm.—(Clarendon ancient history series)
Includes bibliographical references (p.   ) and index.
1. Human physiology—Early works to 1800. 2. Medicine,
Greek and Roman. I. Beagon, Mary. II. Title. III. Series.
QP29.P6813 2005   610—dc22   2004027969

ISBN 0-19-815065-2 (acid-free paper)
ISBN 0-19-927701-X (pbk.:acid-free paper)

1 3 5 7 9 10 8 6 4 2

Typeset by Regent Typesetting, London
Printed in Great Britain
on acid-free paper by
Biddles Ltd, King's Lynn, Norfolk

For James and Timothy
Fortes fortuna iuvat.

PREFACE

CHOOSING a small part of a very large work for treatment in a detailed commentary inevitably requires some justification. Book 7 of Pliny's *Natural History* is, however, in many respects an ideal candidate for such analysis. It contains his discussion of the human race, the first of four books devoted to the animal kingdom in Pliny's magisterial survey of nature and all its parts. As the creature 'for whose sake nature appears to have created everything else' (*HN* 7. 1), the human animal's position at the top of the *scala naturae* justifies the dedication of a complete book to its natural history. Book 7 is thus at once an integral part of Pliny's overall enterprise, but, as an in-depth treatment of matters human, it is also relatively self-contained. Moreover, the readers who take up *HN* 7 do not automatically cut themselves off from the other 36 books, since the human animal, as the quotation above suggests, is in fact crucial to the understanding of Pliny's view of nature as a whole. The centrality of the human race in the Plinian universe and the teleological emphasis ('*for whose sake* nature appears to have created everything else . . .) imply that, without an understanding of man in nature, we cannot hope to understand nature itself.

The philosophical antecedents of Pliny's anthropocentric universe and its impact on the *HN* as a whole are discussed in the Introduction. For the moment, emphasis should be placed on the symbiotic relationship between nature and humanity in the *HN*. For Pliny, 'nature' is essentially 'man in nature' and, when he describes the subject of the *HN* as 'nature, that is, life' (pref. 13) he effectively means human life. Bearing this in mind, not only does *HN* 7 assume an importance in its own right, but it also emerges as the key to Pliny's treatment of the rest of the natural world in the *HN* as a whole. Viewed from a human perspective, and with a view to human needs, nature is assimilated to culture. Descriptions of plants centre on their roles in medicine or agriculture, while those of minerals take manufacture, architecture, or art as their starting-point, to the extent that we habitually speak of 'Pliny on art' or 'Pliny on remedies'.

Although this assimilation of nature and culture had its roots in Pliny's Stoic-influenced philosophical background, it had no obvious literary antecedents. Even the title, *Historia Naturalis*, hinted at a combination of normally distinct traditions. Greek *historie*, or inquiry, while by no means limited to 'history' in the sense of civil, political, and military developments, tended at least to use the *res gestae* of humanity as its focal point. Ancient historians varied in the degree to which they pursued the ripples emanating from this point. Herodotus had ventured far both literally and metaphorically by including descriptions of exotic peoples, their customs and their natural habitats in his *Histories*. By declaring nature to be the focus of his inquiries, however, Pliny expands them into the domain of the natural philosophers and cosmologists, and the framework of the *HN*, in which cosmology (book 2) is followed by the geographical divisions of the world (3–6) and then by the world's component parts (7–37), is dictated by nature, not humanity. Yet Pliny's anthropocentric view of nature means that, within this framework, the actual treatment of nature and its parts is dictated by human interests, whether in the utilization of nature's products, the (re)construction of landscape or the interpretation and effects of celestial, meteorological, and subterranean phenomena. The focus of this history remains human, but its scope, embracing every possible sphere of human interest and activity, is unparalleled.

I have laid stress on this symbiosis of nature and culture in the *Natural History*, since it not only underpins Pliny's treatment of the human animal in book 7, but has also provided a rationale for the emphases of the present commentary. The variety and density of material in book 7 can be overwhelming and commentators have frequently clung to those passages which offer material for what might, for want of a better phrase, be termed mainstream historical analysis. Thus, the names of the famous and not so famous present opportunities for prosopographical study, and historical commentators find themselves on firm ground with the details of Pompey's career (7. 95–9), the chequered fortunes of Agrippa (45–6) or Augustus (147–50), or developments in navigation (206–9). Much of this is of indisputable value. The discussion of Augustus, for example, raises the question of a source, or sources, other than the largely eulogizing and upbeat 'official' line on the first emperor; while Pliny's discussion of Pompey includes epigraphical material unknown from other sources. It may be that such passages on their own would justify a commentary on *HN* 7, but to concentrate on these alone is to fail to recognize where the true value of the text lies. Pliny's enterprise is nothing less than a cultural/natural history of the human race, in accordance with the common knowledge of his era. Within the natural framework of the human lifespan, the ambiguous relationship of nature and nature's prodigy is played out before the reader in the variety of human attainment, physiological, intellectual, moral, and emotional.

This natural history of humanity reveals the cultural belief system of the first century AD with a detail and variety unmatched by any other ancient record. Thus, while it is important for the commentator on Pliny to point out the new light thrown by the author on familiar areas of political or social history, it is equally important to highlight the ideas underpinning Pliny's cultural construct. The most rewarding approach to *HN* 7 lies in the investigation of those odd and puzzling comments normally sidestepped by the commentator. Why are seven-months' births confined to those conceived on the day before or after the full moon, or at the beginning of the month? Why was a breech birth unlucky? What beliefs lay behind tales of apparent deaths? Why was king Pyrrhus' toe thought to have healing properties? What was the rationale behind the belief in sex changes? What might have caused the symptoms of precocious development and premature death described in 7. 75–6? In each case, we find ourselves tapping into a complex network of beliefs, an accumulated wisdom deriving in the first instance from the many written sources consulted by Pliny, but also reflecting non-literary traditions, often of considerable antiquity. An apparently simple statement proves upon further investigation to rely on a much broader substructure of thought regarding, for example, the evil eye, lunar influences, rituals of birth and death, the properties of male and female, or the nature of disease. Much of the material reaches beyond the confines of first-century AD Rome. Folklorists, anthropologists, and social historians will find echoes and parallels, similarities, variants, and differences, in other times and places up to the present day. The present commentary has been written with the interdisciplinary appeal of Pliny's material in mind. Untranslated Greek and Latin phrases and unexplained technical terms are avoided as far as is practicable, while the general Introduction offers an account of Pliny's life and times which aims to provide a basic outline for the non-specialist, as well as general orientation for the classical reader. While every effort has been made to ensure that due note has been taken of the most significant recent scholarship on relevant issues, it is inevitable that a work such as this can never be fully up to date in this respect. Two substantial contributions to Plinian studies, Sorcha Carey's *Pliny's Catalogue of Culture: Art and Empire in the Natural History* (Oxford, 2003) and Valérie Naas' *Le Projet encyclopédique de Pline l'Ancien* (Rome, 2002), which only became available when the manuscript was at the point of completion, are particularly worthy of mention in this respect. Although both are referred to in the general Introduction, I have not been able to give them the attention they deserve in the context of this commentary.

The vast and complex nature of the cultural tradition drawn on by Pliny means that the interpretations offered in the commentary can by no means claim to provide complete, definitive, or 'correct' answers to the sort of questions posed by Pliny's text. At the very least, however, it is hoped that they will initiate discussion of, and instigate further inquiry into, a relatively neglected treasure-trove of ancient common wisdom. *HN* 7 deserves to rekindle today the same intellectual curiosity which led to its composition over two thousand years ago by an author intent on exploring the most obscure byways of human knowledge.

If the days when much of Pliny's material could be pushed to one side by 'serious' historians are behind us, commentators on such topics may yet be deterred by more prosaic considerations. As I suggested earlier, apparently simple statements may turn out to conceal a more complex substructure of ideas beneath their surface, requiring substantial exposition. I am therefore very grateful to the editors of the Clarendon Ancient History series not only for commissioning this commentary, but also for allowing it to be of a length which makes such exposition possible. I would particularly like to thank Miriam Griffin for all her helpful suggestions and comments on the final draft. Thanks are also due to all those who have responded to my inquiries on Plinian problems and obscurities over the last few years. Colleagues at Manchester were particularly susceptible in this respect, and I am very grateful to David Bain, John Briscoe, Tim Cornell, David Langslow, and John Prag for their suggestions on various topics. Valérie Naas and John Patterson came to my rescue when I was in the final stages of preparing the manuscript by tracking down elusive bibliographic references. Any errors and omissions remaining are, of course, entirely my own responsibility, but they would have been considerably greater in number had it not been for the assistance of the above-mentioned colleagues. Many of the ideas now incorporated into the commentary were first aired in student seminars at Manchester and benefited from the ensuing discussions. Nils Mason kindly read a draft of the general Introduction. Finally, I am indebted to the AHRB for funding a period of research leave in 2002–3, thereby enabling this long-standing project to be completed. My thanks are offered to all concerned.

M.B

CONTENTS

ABBREVIATIONS

ACD	*Acta Classica Universitatis Scientiarum Debreceniensis.*
AJA	*American Journal of Archaeology*
AJAH	*American Journal of Ancient History*
Ajasson de Grandsagne	J. B. F. S. Ajasson de Grandsagne, *Caii Plinii Secundi Libri de Animalibus I, cum notis variorum: notas et excursus Zoologici Argumenti adiecit G. Cuvier*, Lemaire edn. (Paris, 1827)
Am. J. Obstet. Gyn.	*American Journal of Obstetrics and Gynecology*
Anat. Stud.	*Anatolian Studies*
Ann. N. Y. Ac. Sci.	*Annals of the New York Academy of Sciences*
ANRW	H. Temporini and W. Haase (eds.), *Aufstieg und Niedergang der römischen Welt* (Berlin and New York, 1972–)
Bard (1999)	Bard, K. A. (ed.), *Encyclopaedia of the Archaeology of Ancient Egypt*, (London, 1999)
BHM	*Bulletin of the History of Medicine*
Broughton, *MRR*	T. R. S. Broughton, *The Magistrates of the Roman Republic*, 3 vols. (Philological Monographs 15; New York, 1951–60)
CAH	*The Cambridge Ancient History* (Cambridge, 1st and 2nd edns. 1923–2000; 3rd edn. 1970–)
C&M	*Classica et Mediaevalia*
CIL	Th. Mommsen et al. (eds.), *Corpus Inscriptionum Latinarum* (Berlin, 1863–)
CJ	*Classical Journal*
CMG	*Corpus Medicorum Graecorum* (Berlin, 1908–)
CPh.	*Classical Philology*
CQ	*Classical Quarterly*
CR	*Classical Review*
CRAI	*Comptes Rendus de l'Académie des Inscriptions et Belles-Lettres*
CSCA	*California Studies in Classical Antiquity*
CSHB	W. Dindorf, I. Bekker, et al. (eds.), *Corpus Scriptorum Historiae Byzantinae*, 49 vols. (Bonn, 1828–78)

Dessau	H. Dessau (ed.), *Inscriptiones Latinae Selectae*, 3 vols. (Berlin, 1892–1916)
Detlefsen	D. Detlefsen, *Historia Naturalis Libri XXXVII*, 6 vols. (Berlin, 1866–82)
DK	H. Diels and W. Kranz, *Fragmente der Vorsokratiker*, 6th edn. (Berlin, 1959–60)
DS	C. Daremberg and E. Saglio, *Dictionnaire des antiquités grecques et romains d'après les textes et les monuments* (Paris, 1877–1919)
EAA	*Enciclopedia dell'arte antica, classica e orientale* (Rome, 1958–84)
Dundes (1980)	Dundes, A. (ed.), *Interpreting Folklore* (Indiana U.P., 1980)
FGH	F. Jacoby, *Die Fragmente der griechischen Historiker*, 14 vols. (pts. 1–4 and indices) (Berlin and Leiden, 1923–99)
FHG	C. Müller, *Fragmenta Historicorum Graecorum* (Paris, 1841–70)
French and Greenaway (1986)	R. French and F. Greenaway (eds.), *Science in the early Roman Empire: Pliny the Elder, his Sources and Influence* (London, 1986)
G&R	*Greece and Rome*
GGM	C. Muller (ed.), *Geographi Graeci Minores*, 3 vols. (Paris, 1855–61)
Giannini	A. Giannini, *Paradoxographorum Graecorum Reliquiae* (Milan, 1965)
GIF	*Giornale Italiano di Filologia*
GRBS	*Greek, Roman and Byzantine Studies*
Griffin and Barnes (1989)	Griffin, M. T., and Barnes, J. (eds.), *Philosophia Togata* (Oxford, 1989)
Hardouin	J. Hardouin (ed.), *Plinius, Naturalis Historia*, 3rd edn. (Paris, 1741)
Hastings	J. Hastings (ed.), *Encyclopaedia of Religion and Ethics*, 12 vols. and index (Edinburgh, 1908–26)
Hope and Marshall (2000)	Hope, V. M. and Marshall, E. (eds.), *Death and Disease in the Ancient City*, (London, 2000)
HSCP	*Harvard Studies in Classical Philology*
H. Th. R.	*Harvard Theological Review*
IG	A. Kirchoff and D. Lewis *et al.* (eds.), *Inscriptiones Graecae*, 3rd edn. (Berlin and New York, 1872–)

IGR	R. Cagnat, J. Toutain, and P. Jouguet (eds.), *Inscriptiones Graecae ad res Romanas pertinentes* (Paris, 1906–)
ILS	H. Dessau (ed.), *Inscriptiones Latinae Selectae*, 3 vols. (Berlin, 1892–1916)
Inscr. It. xiii. 1, xiii. 2	A. Degrassi (ed.), *Inscriptiones Italiae*, xiii. 1: *Fasti Consulares et Triumphales* (Rome, 1947); xiii. 2: *Fasti Anni Numani et Iuliani* (Rome, 1963)
Ist. Lomb. Rend. Lett.	*Istituto Lombardo di Scienze e Lettere Rendiconti: classe di lettere e scienze morali e storiche*
JHM	*Journal of the History of Medicine and Allied Sciences*
JHS	*Journal of Hellenic Studies*
JRA	*Journal of Roman Archaeology*
JRS	*Journal of Roman Studies*
JWCI	*Journal of the Warburg and Courtauld Institute*
Keeling (1992)	Keeling, J. W. (ed.), *Fetal and Neo-natal Pathology* [2] (London, 1992).
König and Winckler	R. König and G. Winckler, *C. Plinius der Ältere, Naturkunde VII*, Tusculum Bücherei edn. (Munich, 1975)
KRS	G. S. Kirk, J. E. Raven, and M. Schofield, *The Presocratic Philosophers: A Critical History with a Selection of Texts*, 2nd edn. (Cambridge, 1983)
Loeb	*see below*, Rackham
MAAR	*Memoirs of the American Academy in Rome*
Maloney (1976)	C. Maloney, (ed.), *The Evil Eye* (Colombia, 1976)
Mayhoff	C. Mayhoff, *Historia Naturalis Libri XXXVII*, Teubner edn., 6 vols. (Leipzig, 1892–1906)
MEFRA	*Mélanges d'Archéologie et d'Histoire de l'École Française de Rome*
Migne, PG	J.-P. Migne (ed.), *Patrologiae Cursus, series Graeca* (Paris, 1857–1978)
Migne, PL	J.-P. Migne (ed.), *Patrologiae Cursus, series Latina* (Paris, 1855–1960)
Mus. Helv.	*Museum Helveticum*
NP	H. Cancik and H. Schneider (eds.), *Der neue Pauly: English* (Leiden, 2002–)

OCD³   S. Hornblower and A. Spawforth (eds.), *The Oxford Classical Dictionary*, 3rd edn. (Oxford, 1996)

OGIS   W. Dittenberger, *Orientis Graeci Inscriptiones Selectae*, 2 vols. (Lipsiae, 1903–5)

OJA   *Oxford Journal of Archaeology*

OLD   *Oxford Latin Dictionary* (Oxford, 1968)

Olympia V   W. Dittenberger and K. Purgold (eds.), *Die Inschriften von Olympia*, vol. v (Amsterdam, 1966)

ORF²   H. Malcovati (ed.), *Oratorum Romanorum Fragmenta*, 2nd edn. (1955)

P&P   *Past and Present*

PBSR   *Papers of the British School at Rome*

PCPS   *Proceedings of the Cambridge Philological Society*

Peter   H. Peter (ed.), *Historicorum Romanorum Reliquiae*, 2 vols. (Leipzig, 1906 and 1914)

PGM   K. Preisendanz and A. Henrichs (eds.), *Papyri Graecae Magicae: Die griechischen Zauberpapyri*, 2 vols., 2nd edn. (Stuttgart, 1973–4)

Philol.   *Philologus*

Pigeaud and Oroz (1987)   J. Pigeaud and J. Oroz (eds.), *Pline l'Ancien: temoin de sa temps*, Conventus Pliniani Internationalis, Nantes, 22–26 Octobre 1985 (Salamanca/Nantes, 1987)

PIR   E. Klebs and H. Dessau (eds.), *Prosopographia Imperii Romani Saeculi*¹ I, II, III (Berlin, 1897–8); 2nd edn. by E. Groag, A. Stein *et al.* (Berlin, 1933–)

Plinio il Vecchio   *Plinio il Vecchio sotto il profilo storico e letterario: atti del convegno di Como 5–7 ottobre, 1979* (Como, 1982)

Pomeroy (1991)   S. B. Pomeroy (ed.), *Women's History and Ancient History* (Chapel Hill, N. Carolina, 1991)

Proc. Roy. Soc. B.   *Proceedings of the Royal Society of London series B: biological sciences*

Rackham   H. Rackham (ed. and trans.), *Pliny Natural History: Libri III–VII* (Cambridge, Mass., and London, 1969): vol. II in H. Rackham and W. H. S. Jones (eds.),

	Pliny, Natural History, Loeb Classical Library, 10 vols. (Cambridge, Mass., 1938–83); other volumes = Loeb
RE	A. Pauly, G. Wissowa, and W. Kroll, *Real-Encyclopädie der classischen Altertumswissenschaft* (Stuttgart, 1893–1980)
REA	*Revue des Études Anciennes*
Reece (1977)	R. Reece (ed.), *Burial in the Roman world*, CBA report 22 (London, 1977)
Rend. Pont.	*Rendiconti della Pontificia Accademia Romana di Archeologia*
Rev. Phil.	*Revue de Philologie* (NS 1877–)
RHR	*Revue de l'Histoire des Religions*
RM	*Rheinisches Museum für Philologie* (1827– ; NS 1842–)
Roscher *Lexikon*	W. H. Roscher, *Ausführliches Lexicon der griechischen und römischen Mythologie*, 12 vols. (parts 1–5 and supplements) (Leipzig, 1884–1924)
Schilling	R. Schilling, texte établi, traduit et commenté par, *Pline l'Ancien Histoire Naturelle livre VII*, Collection des Universités de France, Budé edn. (Paris, 1977)
SHA	*Scriptores Historiae Augustae*
SIG³	W. Dittenberger, *Sylloge Inscriptionum Graecorum*, 3rd edn. (Lipsiae, 1915–24)
Sillig	J. Sillig (ed.), *Plinius, Naturalis Historia* (Hamburg and Gotha, 1851)
SVF	H. von Arnim, *Stoicorum Veterum Fragmenta*, 4 vols. (Leipzig, 1903–24)
TAPA	*Transactions of the American Philological Association*
Thes. Ling. Graec.	*Thesaurus Linguae Graecae*
Thes. Ling. Lat.	*Thesaurus Linguae Latinae*, 16 vols., (Lipsiae, 1900–)
Thompson	Stith Thompson, *Motif Index of Folk-Literature*, 6 vols. (Bloomington, Indiana U. P., 1955–8)
Urlichs	L. Urlichs, *Chrestomathia Pliniana* (Berlin, 1857)
Westermann	A. Westermann, *Vitarum Scriptores Graeci Minores* (Braunschweig, 1845; repr. Amsterdam, 1964)

WS	*Wiener Studien*
YCS	*Yale Classical Studies*
ZPE	*Zeitschrift für Papyrologie und Epigraphik*

A CHRONOLOGY OF PLINY'S
LIFE AND TIMES

14	Death of Augustus; accession of Tiberius
23	Birth of Pliny into an equestrian family of Novum Comum
37	Death of Tiberius; accession of Gaius Caligula
39	Birth of Titus
41	Death of Caligula; accession of Claudius
c.46–59 (or 60 and after?)	Pliny holds military posts in Upper and Lower Germany. Becomes friendly with future emperor Titus? Composes treatise *On Throwing the Javelin from Horseback* and a biography of his patron, Pomponius Secundus. Starts a twenty-volume history of Rome's German Wars
54	Death of Claudius; accession of Nero
59 and after	Pliny engaged on grammatical and rhetorical works. Official post under Nero?
65	Pisonian conspiracy
67	Titus joins his father Vespasian in the suppression of the Jewish revolt
68	Death of Nero. Pliny starts his continuation of the history of Aufudius Bassus, in thirty-one volumes?
68–9	'Year of Four Emperors'
69	July 1: Vespasian acclaimed emperor by troops in Egypt.
70	Vespasian returns to Italy. Titus captures Jerusalem
71 and after	Titus becomes Vespasian's consular colleague
70–6	Pliny holds series of Procuratorships. Working on the *Natural History*
73–4	Pliny Procurator of Hispania Tarraconensis. Offered 400,000 sesterces for his notebooks, according to his nephew. Censorship of Vespasian and Titus
75	Dedication of Temple of Peace
77 and after	Pliny holds equestrian posts in Rome, including ?command of the *vigiles*; and, finally, command of the fleet at Misenum. The *Natural History* is finished
79	Death of Vespasian on 23 June; accession of Titus Pliny dies in the eruption of Vesuvius on 24 August
80	Fire and plague at Rome
81	Death of Titus, on 13 September

A NOTE ON WEIGHTS AND MEASURES IN *HN* 7

The terms 'pounds', 'inches', and 'miles' in the translation refer to Roman weights and measures. They are normally followed by metric equivalences in parentheses. A more detailed key is provided below.

Length

12 *unciae* (inches) = 1 *pes* (Roman foot).
I Roman foot = .296 m., or 11.65 imperial inches.
5 *pedes* = 1 *passus* (pace), and 125 paces = 1 *stadium* (stade).
1 stade (originally the length of the track in a stadium) = approx. 185 m., or just over 200 yards.
1,000 paces or 8 stades = 1 Roman mile.
1 Roman mile = 1,480 m., or 1,618.5 yards. (The imperial mile = 1,760 yards or 1.609 km. There are about 8.7 stades to an imperial mile.)
Some smaller lengths are measured in cubits (.444 m., roughly 18 imperial inches), spans (.222 m., roughly 9 imperial inches), and palms (.074 m., roughly 3 imperial inches).

Weight

1 *libra* (Roman pound) = 327.45 grammes, or .721 of the pound avoirdupois.

INTRODUCTION
PLINY AND THE *HISTORIA NATURALIS*

I. THE AUTHOR: PLINY'S CAREER AND ITS PROBLEMS

The elder Pliny (AD 23–79) came from Novum Comum in northern Italy, and was a member of the equestrian order, a section of the Roman elite second only to the senatorial order in social standing. His life and career is tantalizingly sketched for us in a letter written by his nephew (*Ep.* 3. 5). As the younger Pliny's emphasis is on the extraordinary capacity of his uncle for work, the letter presents us with a fascinating account of a typical day in the latter's life. Unfortunately, only the haziest outline of his career as a whole is given, in incidental comments on a chronological list of his writings. We are told that he had practised at the bar in his younger days and that his earliest compositions, a treatise on throwing the javelin from horseback, a biography of his patron Pomponius Secundus and the beginnings, at least, of a twenty-volume history of Rome's German wars, were produced during military service as a cavalry officer in Germany. Grammatical and rhetorical works followed, the latter, according to the younger Pliny, being regarded as a safe occupation in the politically dangerous atmosphere of Nero's last years. After Nero's death (we can probably assume), a thirty-one-volume continuation of the history of Aufidius Bassus was produced. Its chronological scope is unclear. Pliny writes to the dedicatee of the *Natural History*, the future emperor Titus, that he has dealt in the *Histories* with Titus himself and his father and brother (pref. 20), which gives us a finale in the Vespasianic present.[1] Its beginning is more conjectural; we do not know when Aufidius, who was still alive in the early 60s (Seneca, *Ep.* 30. 1), had ended his history, but it continued to at least AD 31.[2] Pliny's last work was the *Historia Naturalis* in thirty-seven volumes, 'learned and comprehensive and as varied as nature herself' (Pliny, *Ep.* 3. 5. 3). It

---

[1] Titus is called six-times consul in pref. 3, giving a date of AD 77 for the final stages of the *HN*.

[2] It was cited this far by Cassiodorus: see von Rohden, *RE* 2. 2, Aufidius Bassus (15), 2290–1.

was finished around AD 77,[3] less than two years before Pliny met his death, at the age of 55, in the great eruption of Vesuvius on 24 August AD 79, a martyr to his spirit of scientific inquiry and ultimately to his humanitarian attempts to rescue others, as described by his nephew in a famous letter to the historian Tacitus (*Ep.* 6. 16). Between his early years at the bar and his death, we are told only that Pliny was greatly preoccupied with important offices and his friendship with the emperors. From Suetonius,[4] we can adduce that the offices included a 'continuous series of distinguished procuratorships' (*procurationes splendidissimae et continuae*). His remarkable combination of such duties with his voluminous literary output is illustrated by his nephew's description of a typical working day in the reign of Vespasian, in which a visit to the emperor in the early hours preceded attention to his official duties. These were followed by study in any spare time remaining, with all periods of potential inactivity, such as eating, travelling, or bathing, being converted to study time by judicious use of readers and secretaries (below, 4.5.2).

If his nephew has left us with an abiding image of Pliny's ingenious methods of squeezing every opportunity for study out of an action-packed day, modern scholars have been equally ingenious in attempting to fill in the details of the official duties with which the studies competed, including the 'continuous series of distinguished procuratorships' (prime administrative posts for equestrians), mentioned by Suetonius. Ronald Syme, developing a prototype of Münzer's, produced the most elaborate reconstruction,[5] building on clues in the *HN* itself, particularly passages where Pliny states or implies personal experience or an eyewitness account of a particular person, place, object, or phenomenon. As relatively few of these are totally unambiguous references to authorial presence or autopsy, however, the result remains necessarily hypothetical, if broadly plausible.

---

[3] Above, n. 1.

[4] *De Illustr.* p. 300 (Roth).

[5] R. Syme, 'Pliny the Procurator', *HSCP* 73 (1969), 201–36 (= *Roman Papers*, ed. E. Badian, ii (Oxford, 1979), 742–73); 'Carrière et amis consulaires de Pline', in J. Pigeaud and J. Oroz (eds.), *Pline d'Ancien: Temoin de sa Temps* (Salamanca and Nantes, 1987), 539–47; 'Consular friends of the Elder Pliny', in A. R. Birley (ed.), *Roman Papers*, vii (Oxford, 1991), 496–511, and cf. also *Tacitus* (Oxford, 1958), 60–3, 291–3; F. Münzer, *Beiträge zur Quellenkritik der Naturgeschichte des Plinius* (Berlin, 1897). Other discussions by Ziegler, *RE* 21. 1, Plinius (5), 271–85, H. G. Pflaum, *Les Carrières procuratoriènnes Equestres sous le Haut-Empire Romain* (Paris, 1960), 105ff. and A.N. Sherwin-White, *The Letters of Pliny* (Oxford, 1966), 219ff. cf. also refs. below, n.10.

For Pliny's military posts in Germany, Syme outlined three distinct periods of service: in Lower Germany, *circa* 46–7, under the famous general Domitius Corbulo, as cohort commander (*praefectus cohortis*); in Upper Germany, under his patron Pomponius Secundus, as military tribune; and, finally, back in Lower Germany, as *praefectus alae*, or commander of a cavalry squadron. This last posting has been given some material basis by the discovery of a *phalera*, an equestrian decoration, inscribed *Plin. praef. eq.* at Vetera (Xanten in west Germany). This schedule for Pliny's military service is of more than theoretical interest with regard to the *HN*, for it is the most likely setting for Pliny's 'comradeship' (*contubernium*, pref. 3) with the work's dedicatee, Titus.[6] Titus served as military tribune in Germany and Britain,[7] but there is no clear indication of date or whether he was in Upper or Lower Germany.[8] A period on the Lower Rhine in the late 50s was suggested by Syme,[9] Pliny apparently being back in Italy in 59, if a vivid account of a solar eclipse in Campania (*HN* 2. 80) is indeed an eyewitness account. Others have not been convinced, and it has more recently been suggested that it was not inconceivable that they were together in Germany after 60,[10] at the commencement of what Syme called an 'obscure decade' in Pliny's official career.

The obscurity is not brightened by Suetonius' biographical fragment mentioning the continuous sequence of distinguished procuratorships.[11] Of those conjectured, only one is based on firm evidence and is in fact to be dated to 73–4: it was while Pliny was serving as procurator in Hispania Tarraconensis that a certain Larcius Licinus, probably *iuridicus* (judge) of the province, wished to buy his voluminous notebooks. The date is suggested by Pliny's

---

[6] The other scenario, that Pliny accompanied Titus on the Judaean campaign, is unlikely. There is no indication that Pliny was there; nor, if he was, is he likely to have been *contubernalis*, literally 'tent-companion' (cf. *HN* pref. 3), to Titus when the latter was commander, since this implies equal rank, according to B. Jones, *The Emperor Titus* (London, 1984), 15. However, Titus had a reputation for friendliness and approachability as commander-in-chief in Judaea (Tac. *Hist.* 5. 1). But cf. also Syme (1991), 497, on the unlikelihood of Pliny being the ']inius Secun[dus' who was at the siege of Jerusalem according to the Aradus inscription (*OGIS* 586=*IGR* iii 1015).

[7] Suetonus, *Titus* 4; cf. Tacitus, *Hist.* 2. 77.

[8] Syme (1991), 500; Jones (1984), 14–15, 28–9 n. 77, 30 n. 92.

[9] Syme (1991), 500–1.

[10] See Jones (1984), 15–16; and P. Maxwell-Stuart, 'Studies in the Career of Pliny the Elder and the Composition of his *Naturalis Historia*' (Ph.D. diss., St Andrews, 1996=1996a), 1–103, taken up by J. Healy, *Pliny the Elder on Science and Technology* (Oxford, 1999), 5–7.

[11] Above, n. 4.

inclusion in the *HN* (3. 28) of census figures for the north-west regions of Tarraconensis. For the 60s, in contrast, Pliny's letter suggests that his uncle may have been in semi-retirement, keeping to his estates and writing grammatical treatises unlikely to cause offence or draw undue attention to himself. References to Nero in the *HN* are invariably and vehemently hostile.[12] Such evidence is not conclusive: the career of the future emperor Vespasian himself was impeded, according to Suetonius, not by his antagonism towards Nero, but by the antagonism of the emperor's mother, Agrippina, towards surviving friends and protégés of Claudius' freedman Narcissus, who had previously promoted Vespasian's interests. Although personal relations between Nero and Vespasian were not good (Suetonius records the former's resentment at the latter's lack of appreciation of his singing performances in Greece in AD 66!), the value of Vespasian's military experience, together with his lack of noble birth, which presented less of a threat to the emperor, ensured that he and other members of his family enjoyed revived careers after Agrippina's death. In AD 62 or 63 he governed Africa as proconsul and three or four years later, only months after the Greek episode, was in charge of the suppression of the Jewish revolt (Suetonius, *Vesp.* 4). Pliny, too, may have been more politically active than his nephew was later to imply.[13] His later vehemence may have been an exaggerated reaction in tune with Flavian ideology (below, 2.1), tinged with a certain amount of guilt at earlier compromising behaviour. However, his literary prudence may well have extended to the political sphere, a stance vindicated by the spate of condemnations following the conspiracy of Piso in AD 65, including that of Thrasea Paetus, a friend of his patron Pomponius Secundus (below, 2.2).

In addition to Tarraconensis, three other procuratorships were postulated by Münzer and Syme: Gallia Narbonensis, Africa, and Gallia Belgica, all of them based on instances of autopsy and other internal evidence in the *HN*. Of the three, Africa seems to be the most convincing, while the evidence for the Gallic posts is sparser and less conclusive. If all three are accepted, they are probably to

---

[12] See e.g. M. Beagon, *Roman Nature: The Thought of Pliny the Elder* (Oxford, 1992), 17–18; F. Ripoll, 'Aspects et function de Néron dans la propagande imperiale Flavienne', in J. M. Croisille, R. Martin, and Y. Perrin (eds.), *Néron: Histoire et légende: Notes du Ve Colloque International 2–6 Novembre 1994* (Brussels, 1999), 137–51; and below, 2.1.

[13] See M. T. Griffin, *Seneca: A Philosopher in Politics*, rev. edn. (Oxford, 1992), 438–9.

be fitted into the years 70–6, a crowded, though not impossible career.[14] Finally, the younger Pliny's letter clearly depicts his uncle carrying out official duties for Vespasian at Rome. It would seem that his final years were spent in domestic equestrian posts, possibly the command of the *vigiles* (the city watchmen) and certainly the command of the fleet at Misenum, the post in which he died. The latter may not have required the permanent presence in person of the admiral (Pliny, *Ep.* 6. 16. 4).

Apart from his sister and his nephew, his adopted heir, Pliny's family remains something of a mystery. Syme's prosopographical study found a number of Plinii in Comum and the surrounding area who were possibly descendants or else clients, dependants of the Plinii, who customarily took the family name after manumission or acquisition of citizenship.[15] A wife who died in childbirth or in the plague of AD 65 is a possibility. Syme ventured to suggest a marriage link to Verginius Rufus, the younger Pliny's guardian (Pliny, *Ep.* 2. 1. 8), or Vestricius Spurinna whose wife, Cottia, is the only female recipient of the nephew's letters not otherwise known to be a relative.[16] However, Pliny's historical significance does not rest on family connections or even on his distinguished, action-packed equestrian career, but rather in the principle behind the astonishing energy and dynamism which inspired his whole life and outlook and the awe behind his nephew's eulogizing description. 'Life is being awake', he states in the preface to the *HN*. This principle led to the successful completion of an equally awe-inspiring project: a magisterial thirty-seven-volume summation of culture in his era, in effect a microcosmic reflection of the Roman world of the first century AD.

---

[14] See Syme (1991), 502–5. Considerations include making the posts *continuae* and assuming that they were held under Vespasian rather than Nero; though if Pliny was not wholly in retirement under Nero, Africa and/or Narbonensis could possibly be placed earlier (Syme 505; Griffin (1992), 438–9). Allowance must also be made for the final stage of his career, back in Rome. For scepticism, particularly about the Gallic posts, see Maxwell-Stuart (1996a), 1–103 and Healy (1999), 7–23.

[15] Syme (1991), 510 nn. 103–4.

[16] Syme (1991), 510; 'Correspondents of Pliny', *Historia*, 34 (1985), 351 (= *Roman Papers*, v (1988), 468).

2. THE FLAVIAN BACKGROUND

2.1. Pliny and the New Dynasty

In dedicating the *HN* to Vespasian's son and heir Titus, Pliny, as we saw, incidentally provides us with the date (AD 77, pref. 3) at which he was putting the finishing touches and composing the preface to his work. As we shall see, composition had spanned the 70s, but the raw material of the *HN* was probably the result of Pliny's scholarly activities over an even longer period (below, 4.5.1).

In its final form, however, the *HN* is in many ways a product of the Flavian era, the work of an author in sympathy with the general tone of imperial policies.[17] In his comments on the Flavians and their imperial predecessors, Pliny articulates the emphases and attitudes promulgated by the new regime. Thus, for example, Augustus and Claudius get a generally good press. Both were regarded by Vespasian, who had had a successful career under the latter, as models and exemplars for his own rule.[18] Nero, by contrast, was the antithesis of the comparatively humbly born, down-to-earth Vespasian and his portrayal in the *HN* is consistently negative (above, Sect. 1). He was, moreover, the antithesis of nature herself, having been born feet first (7. 46 and comm. ad loc.) and, since his savagery (*saevitia*) makes him an enemy of the human race (*hostis humani generis*), the antithesis of the *HN*'s Stoic humanitarian ideal.[19] In contrast, Vespasian was renowned for his affability and common touch[20] and this, together with his 'Augustan' restoration of peace and stability after civil war, allows of his portrayal as the Stoic ideal ruler, labouring on behalf of his people (*HN* 2. 18; below,

[17] The tone of the preface goes beyond the formal requirements of such dedications and its genuine enthusiasm absolves it of the flattering excesses of Velleius Paterculus towards the emperor Tiberius. The illustrious position of power to which fortune has elevated Titus has made no change to Pliny's agreeable comrade in Germany, other than offering him unlimited opportunities to display his benevolence.

[18] For Vespasian's career, see e.g. Jones (1984), 7. For the Flavian rehabilitation of Claudius, see B. Levick, *Claudius* (London, 1990), 190–3; although not all aspects of Claudius' reign were to be regarded as models, as Pliny himself recognized: see M. T. Griffin, 'The Flavians', in A. K. Bowman, P. Garnsey, and D. Rathbone (eds.) *The Cambridge Ancient History*², xi (Cambridge, 2000), 23–5. Both Augustus and Claudius are cited as precedents in the *Lex de Imperio Vespasiani*.

[19] Beagon (1992), 18. See below, 3.1.1–3; 4.4.

[20] This gave him another link with Claudius: see Levick (1990), 112, 190.

this section and 3.1.1). Vespasian's coins, with such inscriptions as *pax populi Romani* 'the peace of the Roman people', *Pax orbis terrarum Augusta*, 'world-wide Augustan peace', *ob cives servatos*, 'for saving the lives of citizens', etc., implicitly enforced the contrast with his predecessor and invited comparison with his chosen models.[21] Claudius, indeed, could, with his murdered son Britannicus, be depicted as the rightful dynastic progression, violently usurped by Nero, but now restored in the persons of Vespasian and his son and heir Titus.[22] Titus had been educated with Britannicus and was, as emperor, to revere the memory of his dead friend (Suet. *Titus* 2). In addition, the emphasis Vespasian placed on his dynastic intentions was remarkable. Titus held nearly all the imperial offices in partnership with his father. In June AD 70 this partnership was self-consciously paraded in their elaborate double Jewish triumph (Josephus, *BJ* 7. 121) and all imperial acclamations were addressed to them jointly thereafter. Even if Titus' power was not, strictly speaking, equal to Vespasian's,[23] it was to all appearances a joint rule. This emphasis is not lost on Pliny: three times in the first six sections of the preface Titus is either addressed as *imperator* or reference is made to his *imperium*. His father and his brother Domitian are woven into the opening encomium (pref. 1 and 5; cf. 20), so that the personal dedication to Titus becomes a celebration of the whole dynasty. Elsewhere in the *HN*, Vespasian and Titus are addressed as a duo of *imperatores*.[24]

The link with Vespasian's chosen Julio-Claudian predecessor, Claudius, was enhanced by the completion of the huge unfinished temple dedicated to him, thus emphasizing and confirming his divine status. In other areas, too, Vespasian's policy reflected the ideals of the new dynasty and this too was not lost on Pliny. The writer deplores private luxury and its exhibition in houses and the

---

[21] See E. S. Ramage, 'Denigration of Predecessor under Claudius, Galba and Vespasian', *Historia*, 32 (1983), 211. However, coins also show that the importance attached to continuity could in some cases override the wish to break entirely from a 'bad' predecessor. Some of Nero's early coins showed deference to Claudius (see M. T. Griffin, *Nero: The End of a Dynasty* (London, 1984), 58–9 and n. 26). Above all, the political necessity for Nero to be seen as Claudius' rightful heir, 'son of the deified Claudius', ensured the latter's deification in 54.

[22] Levick (1990), 190–3; R. Darwall-Smith, *Emperors and Architecture: A Study of Flavian Rome* (Brussels, 1996), 52–5.

[23] Jones (1984), 79.

[24] See **162** comm. On the use of the terms *princeps* and *imperator* of Titus, see F. de Oliveira, *Les Idées politiques et morales de Pline l'Ancien*, Estudos de Cultura Clássica, 5 (Coimbra, 1992), 97–9.

art collections hidden within them (*HN* 36. 101–25).[25] In contrast, buildings with a public and/or utilitarian function are applauded. The former vice is epitomized by the private palaces of Gaius and Nero, the latter ideal by the grand engineering works initiated by Claudius and the 'most beautiful buildings ever built' the Basilica Aemilia, the forum of Augustus, and Vespasian's own temple of Peace. In this temple, Vespasian had redeployed for public viewing precious artworks previously 'imprisoned' in the Golden House of Nero (*HN* 35. 120).[26] In addition, the temple may also have been publicly utilized as a venue for the teaching of rhetoric, which the emperor also sponsored.[27]

The practical euergetism articulated by the temple's public function was complemented by the symbolism of its dedication to Peace. Together they endorse Pliny's specific identification of the Flavian father and son with the selfless Stoic humanitarian ideal in *HN* 2. 18 (below, 4.4). In Nero's case, by contrast, euergetism had been self-centred, his self-indulgent artistic interests frequently taking on the role of public entertainment, literally so in the case of his appearances on the stage or in the circus. Vespasian's and Titus' paternalistic benevolence was exemplified in Vespasian's careful generosity to gifted individuals (Suet. *Vesp.* 18–19) and in the public amenities of the temple of Peace and the Colosseum begun by Titus. The common touch was displayed to perfection by Titus at public games.[28] Their protective attitude towards their subjects was epitomized in Vespasian's case by Suetonius' famous anecdote about his desire to provide for the plebs and by Titus' reaction to the fire of 80, where he is reported to have behaved as though it were a personal tragedy to be made good from his own private possessions. When, in the same year, plague struck Rome, he personally instigated a search for remedies.[29]

---

[25] A traditional Roman prejudice: Tiberius' removal of Lysippus' *apoxyomenos* from the baths of Agrippa into his private palace had caused a public outcry, *HN* 34. 62; cf. 35. 26 and P. Zanker, *The Power of Images in the Age of Augustus* (Ann Arbor, 1988), 140–1. The younger Pliny comments in his obituary of the dubious Domitius Tullus that he had large quantities of valuable works of art stored out of view and forgotten (*Ep.* 8. 18. 11).

[26] On this and other aspects of Vespasian's building policy, see Darwall-Smith (1996), 35–74, esp. 58–61; J. Isager, *Pliny on Art and Society: The Elder Pliny's Chapters on the History of Art* (London, 1991), 103, 131, 133, 183, 209, 223–9.

[27] See A. Woodside, 'Vespasian's Patronage of Education', *TAPA* 73 (1942), 123–9.

[28] Without Claudius' loss of dignity: see Suet. *Titus* 2 and contrast *Claudius* 21.

[29] *Vesp.* 18; *Titus* 8. 4. For paternalistic benevolence as a governmental ideal in the *HN*, see de Oliveira (1992), *passim*, esp. 333–6.

It was to Titus, of course, rather than Vespasian, that the *HN* was dedicated. The shared military service had undoubtedly created a genuine friendship: while the elder *imperator* is to be addressed as 'greatest' (*maximus*), Titus is apostrophized as 'most pleasant/charming (*iucundissime) emperor*' (pref. 1). In addition, the sources depict him as a cultured individual. According to Suetonius, he composed speeches and wrote poetry in both Greek and Latin, as well as being an accomplished musician;[30] all of which may have given him a desire to patronize the arts more spontaneous than that of his father whose attitude has been described as more calculated.[31] The friendship with Pliny, then, may have blossomed on a cultural level. Pliny talks of previous exchanges between them on the subject of his literary output and indulges in literary pleasantries with his patron (pref. 1–2). Titus may even have taken an interest in the practicalities of Pliny's scholarship, with its voluminous note-taking: he was adept at shorthand, reputedly engaging in contests with his own secretaries, according to Suetonius (*Titus* 3). Above all, it is probably Titus' combination of the qualities of statesmanship and culture which make him the ideal dedicatee of the *HN*. Suetonius talks of 'his aptitude for almost all the arts of war and peace'. A similar point is made in Tacitus' *Histories*.[32] Pliny combines Titus' intellectual and political achievements in an elaborate rhetorical compliment, praising the *fasces* of his genius, the dictatorial power of his eloquence, and the tribunician authority of his wit (pref. 5). Apart from the mention of their comradeship in arms, the specifically military side of Titus' talents is of less interest to Pliny in this literary context. The ideal Roman combination of political, military, and rhetorical qualities attributed to the elder Cato (7. 100) could well have described Titus. Instead, it is in the scholar Pliny's lengthy and enthusiastic encomium of his preferred *vir bonus*, Cicero, the great Republican statesman and intellectual, that we find a closer parallel to his portrayal of his imperial patron.[33]

---

[30] *Titus* 3; cf. *HN* pref. 5–6.

[31] Woodside (1942), 126.

[32] *Titus* 3; *Hist.* 2. 1 and 77 .

[33] For the concept of the *vir bonus* in Pliny's preface, see N. P. Howe, 'In Defense of the Encyclopedic Mode: On Pliny's Preface to the Natural History', *Latomus* 44 (1985), 561–76. For Cicero (106–43 BC), see **114–17** comm.

2.2. The Cultural Milieu

If the *HN* is in many respects a Flavian work, it cannot be divorced from its wider cultural context any more than the Flavians themselves can be considered wholly independently of their previous existence under Nero. Titus himself, for example, for all his fostering of his personal link with Britannicus (Suet. *Titus* 2), was in his education and talents in many respects an obvious product of the Neronian court. The sources also suggest a predilection for pleasure and luxury and even cruelty in the years before he became emperor.[34] Not all the artworks he acquired were on public display[35] and his private residence on the Palatine (Dio 65. 15. 4) may originally have been Neronian.[36]

The tendency to link Pliny with the high-minded, technically skilled but sometimes uninspiring epics of Valerius Flaccus and Silius Italicus ignores the fact that their work was probably Domitianic in date. Pliny's literary output prior to the *HN* would have been contemporaneous with the working lives of Lucan, Seneca, and Petronius, all of whom were prematurely cut down in the aftermath of the Pisonian conspiracy of 65. If Vespasian's cultural interests were limited,[37] the literary ambience of the 70s was by no means devoid of interest. Vespasian may have expelled philosophers (Suet. *Vesp.* 3) , but there was an important Hellenic input from figures connected with the first generation of the Greek cultural revival known as the Second Sophistic. The sophist and rhetor Dio Chrysostom was a friend of Titus and may have had other connections with the Flavians.[38] Pliny's self-consciously Roman tone and ambiguity towards Greeks[39] takes on extra significance when viewed in the context of a contemporary revival of Hellenic culture.

However, the ultimate inspiration for Pliny's literary endeavours may have come from an earlier source, the patron of his early years,

---

[34] *saevitia, luxuria, libido*: Suet. *Titus* 7. 1; Tac. *Hist.* 2. 2; Dio 65. 15. 4.

[35] Cf. Pliny, *HN* 34. 55, 37. 37; Josephus, *Ant.* 7. 162.

[36] Darwall-Smith (1996), 180–2; cf. 70–2 on the unclear fate of the Domus Aurea under the Flavians.

[37] Woodside (1942), 126. In common with many commanders, he did compose *commentarii* on his Judaean campaign, but these need not have been elaborate. See Josephus, *Vit.* 65.

[38] Though the account of Vespasian's meeting with Dio and other Greek intellectuals at Alexandria and other evidence comes from the notoriously unreliable Philostratus (*Vit. Apoll.* 5. 27).

[39] Beagon (1992), 18–20, 203 and nn. for bibliography; also below, 3.1.1 and n. 43.

P. Pomponius Secundus (suffect consul 44), under whom he had served in Germany. Pomponius was half-brother to Caesonia, wife of the emperor Gaius Caligula, and through him the young Pliny may have had contact with the imperial court which was later to be reflected in several vignettes in the *HN*.[40] It would also have been through Pomponius that Pliny got his information about the confinements of his patron's mother, which are detailed in 7. 39–40. He was a poet and playwright whose refined literary talent was rated by Tacitus above his winning of a triumph in Germany in 50 (*Ann.* 12. 28). Pliny, who was to write his biography (Pliny, *Ep.* 3. 5. 3), had seen ancient documents, dating back 250 years, in the handwriting of the Gracchi at his house. This suggests wider scholarly interests which may have struck a particular chord with his biographer; in particular, a Roman antiquarianism which, in addition to the documents, involved an interest in archaic language (Quintilian 8.3.31) and the writing of a *praetexta*, or serious drama on a Roman historical subject, the *Aeneas*. Here again was a man of versatile talents, who was, like Cicero and Titus, an embodiment of intellectual and political distinction: Pliny calls him 'consular poet' (7. 80) and 'poet and distinguished citizen' (13. 83). As with Titus, he does not distinguish the specifically military side of Pomponius' talent and once again, the comparison with Cicero, Pliny's preferred ideal Roman (*vir bonus*, literally 'good man'), is inescapable.

3. THE INTELLECTUAL BACKGROUND

3.1. Cultural Identity

3.1.1. *The Roman Moral Tradition*

In some respects the cultural antecedents of the *HN* were complex; in other respects it was clearly a work of its time. Its author is patently in sympathy with the moral ethos of Vespasian's court, which was to some extent a conscious policy to counter and override the perceived decadence of Nero's principate. The Flavian morality was itself nothing new, simply a revival of the ancient *mos maiorum* (literally, 'ancestral custom', traditional values), more recently associated with influxes of new blood into the Roman

---

[40] e.g. *HN* 9. 117 and possibly 10. 12, 14. 56.

governing class (Tacitus, *Ann.* 3. 55). This specifically Roman code of conduct was often expounded by Roman writers who enjoined a plain-living, hard-working, utilitarian ethos on their fellow-countrymen to ensure Rome's continued stability and success. This Roman ideal permeates the *HN*. There are basic utilitarian-humanitarian expressions of the book's purpose in pref. 16, where the useful book which performs a service is placed above that which merely provides entertainment. The famous statement of practical help as being the human ideal (2. 18)—for man to aid man, this is god—is then illustrated by its Flavian exemplars, Vespasian and Titus, ideal Roman rulers who through their restoration of the *Pax Romana* are re-establishing traditional values. Throughout the *HN*, much emphasis is placed on the usefulness of animals, plants, and other natural commodities and the human arts and skills associated with them. Luxury, decadence, and indolence are condemned.[41] Those practical physical labours, military and agricultural, so beloved of Roman moralists, were interlinked in the ideal of the Roman peasant soldiery, backbone of Rome's divinely approved success. In the *HN*, they are frequently presented as complementary skills, in the form of the farmer whose military care and precision elicit the greatest rewards from divine Nature.[42] The practical, dynamic nature of the Roman ideal was of course epitomized by the energetic lifestyle of Pliny himself, summed up by his remark in the preface that 'being alive is being awake', *vita vigilia est* (pref. 19), itself a military metaphor, since *vigilia* was the term used of the camp watch or guard.

The Roman perspective is just one of several strands which combine to form Pliny's approach to his subject (below, 3.1.2–3; 4.2), but it is vital to the conscious formation by the author of a cultural identity for his work. Rome was indebted to Greeks for her intellectual and cultural development. Pliny's indexes illustrate the inescapability of such dependence: Greek sources, though listed after Roman sources, outnumber the latter by two or three to one in most books. His acknowledgement of them in his text is often grudging and reluctant and his comments frequently reflect a general Roman prejudice, born partially of a cultural inferiority

---

[41] For the theme of *utilitas versus luxuria* in the *HN*, see S. Citroni Marchetti, *Plinio il Vecchio e la tradizione del moralismo Romano* (Pisa, 1991); but the distinction is not always simple: see Beagon (1992), 75–9, 190–4; and, generally, index s.v. 'luxury'.

[42] See Beagon (1992), 176–7.

complex, against the Greeks on the grounds of their flippancy, unreliability, and propensity to wordy theorizing.[43] In contrast to these Greek failings, Romans often claimed intellectual seriousness and an inherently practical attitude to knowledge (below, 3.1.2). The contrast was, of course, exaggerated, partly because of the very fact that the debt to Greek culture could never be shaken off altogether. Moreover, as we noted earlier (2.2), Pliny's era coincided with the early years of the Second Sophistic and the inextricable intertwining of the cultures was epitomized by some of the writers of the next two generations, most notably another scholar, Suetonius. Born nine years before Pliny's death and, like Pliny, indebted to the Greek traditions of scholarship, especially the compilatory and antiquarian studies of the Peripatetics and Hellenistic writers,[44] he went so far as to compose some of his works in Greek, whilst also producing Latin works the cultural tone of which was unambiguously Roman.[45] A century later, an Italian-born freedman, Claudius Aelianus, produced, among other writings, a work on animals which, in addition to being written in Greek, reflected in the treatment of its subject-matter a cultural ethos which was as Greek as Pliny's was Roman.[46]

However, Pliny's evident anxiety to establish a Roman identity for his work is in keeping with a more specifically Flavian interest in restoring and reviving the Roman historical and cultural tradition. Vespasian's eagerness to repair the damage done to the Capitol when it was burnt in AD 69 extended to the precious official records, which he tried to replace as far as possible.[47] His interest in Rome's heritage was complemented (and perhaps partially inspired) by his right-hand man, Licinius Mucianus (suffect consul in AD 64, 70, and 72). The latter's account of natural wonders observed whilst on official duties in the provinces was used by Pliny in the *HN* (below,

---

[43] For Pliny and Greek culture, see G. Serbat, 'Il y a Grecs et Grecs! Quel sens donner au prétendu antihéllénisme de Pline?', in Pigeaud and Oroz, *Pline l'Ancien*, 589–98; A. Wallace-Hadrill, 'Pliny the Elder and Man's Unnatural History', *G&R* NS 37 (1990), 80–96. See also above, 2.2, (Second Sophistic).

[44] See comm. **191–215. introd.** For Suetonius, A. Wallace-Hadrill, *Suetonius: The Scholar and his Caesars* (London, 1983), 44–5.

[45] e.g. his lost works on Rome's customs and traditions. See Wallace-Hadrill (1983), 132–3.

[46] Beagon, 'Plinio, la tradizione enciclopedica e i mirabilia', in *Storia della Scienza*, i: *La Scienza Antica* (Istituto della Enciclopedia Italiana, Rome, 2001), 735–45.

[47] Suet. *Vesp.* 8, cf. Tac. *Hist.* 4. 40.

3.3), but he was also responsible for eleven books, now lost, entitled *Libri Actorum* and three books of *Epistulae*, drawn from ancient documents and speeches (Tac. *Dial.* 37).

Finally, the frequently elaborate rhetorical style of Pliny's Latin is the product of an era which saw the appointment of Quintilian as Vespasian's professor of Latin literature. In his work on the teaching of rhetoric, Quintilian (book 1, especially ch. 10) espouses as an ideal the broadly based education with a practical emphasis. Such an ideal would have been immediately recognizable to the writer of the *HN*, whose encyclopaedic mentality was in many respects the quintessence of Roman practicality.

3.1.2. *The Encyclopaedic Mentality*

In discussing his subject-matter, Pliny declares that what the Greeks call *encyclios paideia* is particularly worthy of coverage (pref. 14). The phrase may originally have meant 'all aspects of a choric education', the training to make a man harmonious,[48] but by the first century BC, it had come to include all branches of learning. By Pliny's time, it denoted a general education, a practical basis for the well-rounded citizen which also prepared him for more specialized studies[49] and for life generally. But while the practicality of such broadly based education had been recognized in Greek culture by the Sophists and Aristotle,[50] the Greeks themselves, as Pliny points out in pref. 14, had never produced a compilation of such knowledge, preferring more specialized treatises of a less practical nature. It had been left to Roman writers to produce works which brought together the various components of *encyclios paideia*. The details of their and Pliny's treatment of their subject-matter will be discussed below (4.1). In general terms, they were producing a literature in which words were not divorced from actions. For Pliny, theory and practice were conjoined and knowledge was pursued not for its own sake, but for its role in modelling the Roman ideal, the cultivated man of action whose motto could be Pliny's own dynamic 'life is being awake'.

---

[48] e.g. L. M. de Rijk, '*enkuklios paideia*: A Study of its Original Meaning', *Vivarium*, 3 (1985), 24–93.

[49] Cf. Quintilian I. 10. 2; Vitruvius I. 1. 12; and, earlier, Cic. *De Orat.* I. 185–91.

[50] Beagon (1992), 12 for refs.

3.1.3. *The Philosophical Heritage*

This practical, non-specialist, non-theoretical attitude to knowledge was reflected in Pliny's own intellectual outlook. The study of nature in the ancient world was a branch of philosophy and in portraying nature in the *HN*, Pliny had been preceded by a vast heritage of cosmological and natural historical speculation from the Presocratics, Plato, and Aristotle to the Hellenistic philosophies of Epicurus and the Stoa. Pliny's nature was essentially the Stoic nature.[51] This was a pantheistic concept in which the natural world was imbued with divinity. It was also an anthropocentric one, in which the human race was the highest creation and, through the possession of reason (*ratio*), shared in the divinity of nature herself. As a result, man was, to a large extent, the very purpose of nature, since the rest of creation existed to serve his needs.

Pliny's Stoicism, however, was not the carefully worked-through theorizing of the specialist philosopher; it was the general background knowledge of a well-educated man,[52] a world-view in effect almost unconsciously absorbed and displayed. As such, it acts as a valuable indication of educated attitudes generally.

The increasing emphasis in later Stoicism on ethical ideals such as independence of mind and devotion to duty combined with an ascetic lifestyle, had coincided with the specifically Roman code of conduct embodied in *mos maiorum*. In Pliny's day, this coalescence produced extremists opposed to the Principate on the basis of what they perceived to be a challenge to the Roman principle of Liberty and a failure on the part of individual emperors to maintain Stoic ideals as a ruler. Pliny would almost certainly have had contact with members of the so-called 'Stoic Opposition', perhaps through his patron, Pomponius Secundus, whose literary connections with one of their number, Thrasea Paetus, have already been mentioned (above, Sect. 1). But since he came from Comum, he in any case shared a background with Thrasea, who came from Padua. The younger Pliny, too, knew and admired several members of the group, who were related by marriage.[53] The *HN*, however, is as

---

[51] Was the *HN*, with its 37 books, intended as a Stoic counterweight to the lost *On Nature* of Epicurus (frags. in G. Arrighetti, *Epicuro*² (Turin, 1973), 189–418; cf. *Vita Epicuri* 30; C. Bailey, *Epicurus: The Extant Remains* (Oxford, 1926), 161, 391–3), also in 37 books?

[52] Beagon (1992),12–15.

[53] Cf. *Ep.* 6. 29, 8. 22, 3. 16, 3. 11, 1. 14, 2. 18, 7. 19, 9. 13, 7. 30, 4. 21: see Sherwin-White (1966), ad loc.

far removed from the moral and political commitment of the 'Opposition' as it is from the intellectual commitment of a 'professional' philosopher like Seneca. What Pliny provides for us is interesting evidence of what must have been a more general trend: the adoption by the well-educated classes of a philosophical veneer, an intellectual wallpaper which never set them apart intellectually or politically, but remained in the background as an indefinable but permeating influence on their general outlook.

3.2. Equestrian Writing

The sense of moral purpose and the practical educational tone of the *HN* link it with another cultural phenomenon of the period. Senatorial writers had often devoted their literary talents to the writing of biographical, historical, and rhetorical works in their periods of leisure. By Pliny's time, however, there was an increasing output of scholarly and technical writing. Moreover, while some of this was still coming from the pens of senatorial writers such as Julius Frontinus, the bulk of it was written by 'new men' like Seneca, or members of the equestrian order, like Pliny himself. From the time of Augustus, the *equites* had been assigned an important role in the practical government of the empire as administrators and financial officials. Like the senatorial class of the late Republic, once their official duties (*negotium*, *officium*) had been fulfilled, they could employ their leisure time (*otium*) in literary pursuits worthy of and appropriate to their status. In general, the practicality of the public duties open to them both presupposed and encouraged[54] the practical interests which they wrote about. Numerous equestrian writers on geography, agriculture, architecture and other 'arts of life' are cited by Pliny in the *HN*'s indexes.[55] Moreover, the ideological and practical antithesis between *officium* and *otium*, which frequently surfaces in the writings of Cicero and his contemporaries, is much less obvious in the equestrian of the first century AD. The same may be said to a large degree of the first-century senator, given the disappearance of the political competition and senatorial activity of the Republic. Pliny's nephew describes summer and winter routines at his country villa, both of

---

[54] Beagon (1992), 6–8.
[55] Among the best known are the agriculturalist Columella and the geographer Pomponius Mela. For others, such as C. Julius Graecinus, Cornelius Valerianus, and Turranius Gracilis, see Syme (1969), 219–25.

which are dominated by literary pursuits; but the distinction between those connected with pleasure and those connected with his career at the bar is unclear (*Ep.* 9. 38; 9. 40). Intellectual activities were no longer to be pursued only when political activity was curtailed. If Pliny compliments his emperor by avowing that he devotes his days to official duties, leaving his studies to the night (pref. 18), the point is that they are both regarded as daily activities. Indeed, the hectic schedule portrayed by Pliny's nephew in *Ep.* 3. 5 suggests that a typical day was a complex combination of *officia* and *studia*;[56] the pragmatic realization of the moral, patriotic, and intellectual ideology espoused by the author in the *HN*.

3.3. Expanding Horizons

Another area of literary interest to the equestrian writers of Pliny's era at first sight bears little resemblance to the practical subjects mentioned in the previous section. Interest in the unusual and strange, particularly in the context of the natural world, had been reflected in classical literature as early as Homer and Herodotus. Increasing knowledge of the world around them as a result of geographical expansion, particularly in the wake of Alexander's conquests, served only to stimulate rather than modify such interest: the more extraordinary the actual discoveries, the greater the hope of things still more wondrous to come. Pliny, in *HN* 11. 6, sums up the mentality by commenting that the more he observes nature, the less inclined he is to consider any statement about her to be impossible. In Pliny's case, philosophical attitudes may also have come into play: the Stoics taught that the wise man was never shocked or discountenanced by the unexpected, but retained a calm and equable demeanour, whatever Fortune chose to throw at him (cf. Strabo 1. 3. 21, C61). But philosophical theory was in any case balanced by practical experience; the official duties of Pliny and his peers in Rome's provinces took them to many parts of the world where they observed strange phenomena and were doubtless told of many others. One noteworthy individual who made a point of recording such oddities encountered on his official tours of duty was Licinius Mucianus (above, 3.1.1), whose career included service under Domitius Corbulo and terms of duty in Lycia-Pamphilia and

---

[56] The younger Pliny's (*Ep.* 3. 5. 8) account in fact gives a less schematic impression, suggesting the blending of official and literary occupations throughout Pliny's waking hours; according to him, even the night might sometimes be taken up with imperial business.

Syria, in addition to his three consulships. His work on wonders, was, as mentioned earlier, cited by Pliny in the *HN*,[57] as were anecdotes by contemporary writers of his own class, which reflected similar interests. The wider historical context is relevant here. Just as Alexander's conquests had stimulated interest in the natural world generally and in *mirabilia* in particular, so too by the first century AD, Roman military and economic expansion exercised the curiosity of Pliny's contemporaries. In one notable passage (*HN* 5. 11–15), he mentions the pacification and organization of Mauretania under Claudius, and testifies to the eagerness for new knowledge and fresh discoveries displayed by senatorial commanders and equestrian officials. The stories they brought home, he implies, reflected enthusiasm above accuracy and a tendency to exaggerate or even invent to satisfy the growing demand for such tales.[58]

The sense of imminent and ever more exciting discoveries may have been increased by a feeling that Rome was on the verge of encompassing within her power the entire world and that with this would come the ability to encompass the totality of nature, intellectually as well as militarily and politically. Misconceptions of distances, a belief that the world was smaller than it really was, may have already prompted ambitious plans of conquest.[59]

Roughly contemporary with the expansionist visions of Alexander and, later, the Roman empire, was the flowering of a literature devoted exclusively to the cataloguing of *mirabilia* (wonders), mainly natural phenomena, the essential purpose of which was the entertainment of an audience hungry for such things. Paradox-

---

[57] Pliny used his work in the *HN* on numerous occasions, e.g. *HN* 3. 59, 4. 66, 5. 128, 7. 159, 12. 9, 13. 88.

[58] Beagon (1992), 6–7. For *mirabilia* as stories circulated at dinner, see Pliny, *Ep.* 9. 33. 1, cf. R. Saller, 'Anecdotes as Historical Evidence of the Principate', *G&R* 27 (1980), 70–1.

[59] P. Brunt, review of H. D. Meyer, *Die Aussenpolitik des Augustus*, *JRS* 53 (1963), 170–6 (= *Roman Imperial Themes* (Oxford, 1990), 96ff.); R Moynihan, 'Geographical Mythology and Roman Imperial Ideology', in R. Winkes (ed.), *The Age of Augustus* (Louvain, 1986), 148–57. On spatial awareness and conceptions of the world in this period, see C. Nicolet, *Space, Geography and Politics in the Early Roman Empire* (English trans., Ann Arbor, 1991), esp. 29–94; but also N. Purcell's review of Nicolet, *JRS* 80 (1990), 178–82. For a critique of the *HN* as a cataloguing summation of the world, see G. B. Conte, 'The Inventory of the World: Form of Nature and Encyclopaedic Project in the HN of Pliny the Elder', in *Genres and Readers*, trans. G. W. Most (Baltimore, 1994), 67–104, esp. 75, where, however, too much emphasis may be placed on the finality of Pliny's view; the mood of the *HN* suggests a feeling that reaching the world's limits was becoming a possibility rather than that this was a goal more or less already achieved. Pliny revels in the variety and multiplicity of his material: completeness is the impression given by, rather than a literal consequence of, the *HN*'s universality.

ography flourished from the third century BC to the second century AD, from the writings of the Hellenistic scholar Callimachus to the human oddities collected by Phlegon of Tralles, a freedman of the emperor Hadrian. Many such writers who wrote before or during Pliny's era are quoted in the *HN*, but especially in the index to book 7.[60] The essential vacuity of such works was later criticized by Aulus Gellius, just as Plutarch, in his treatise *On Curiosity*, was to attack the mentality of their potential readers, complaining that sensation-seeking curiosity was unhealthy and intellectually degrading. But curiosity was not necessarily a bad thing. Aristotle had recognized that it could stimulate inquiry, leading to knowledge through a desire to understand. In any case, such works cannot be separated from the more serious implications thrown up by the wider pre-occupation with *mirabilia* in the late Hellenistic and Roman periods generally and in the *HN* in particular. It is possible to draw analogies with the ambiguous position of wonders in late sixteenth- and seventeenth-century England, when wonder-books remained part of a common culture which linked the learned and popular traditions. The books were plundered for pleasure literature, and the tales also featured in compilations of popular learning which presented a culture of the educated layman as far removed from popular ignorance as it was from the studies of the professional scholar.[61] Inconsequential as the compilations condemned by Gellius may have been, the wider preoccupation with *mirabilia* in Pliny's era is in many ways fundamental to the understanding and appreciation of the spirit of the age. As we have seen, the predilection for the unusual encapsulated an expansionist and outward-looking mentality. Additionally, it was reflective of an historical consciousness which not only projected its horizons from the present to the future as a result of each 'new' discovery, but also contextualized the present through its conception of the past, as inspired by those discoveries which turned out to be relics of a bygone era (see **73** comm.). Far from being a compilation of

---

[60] Beagon (1992), 8.
[61] Gellius, *NA* 9. 1–12; Plutarch, *De Curiositate*, *Mor.* 517–21. For the implications of Aristotle, *Met.* 982^{b}11–983^{a}25 in the context of Pliny's *mirabilia*, see V. Naas, '*L'Histoire Naturelle* de Pline l'Ancien: est-elle une œuvre scientifique?', *Science antique, science médiévale (Actes du colloque international Mont-Saint-Michel, 4–7 Septembre, 1998* (Hildesheim and New York, 2000), 267. 16th-cent. wonder literature: K. Park and L. Daston, 'Unnatural Conceptions; the Study of Monsters in Sixteenth- and Seventeenth-Century France and England', *P&P* 92 (1981), 39.

wonder stories to titillate the palates of those hungry for superficial entertainment, Pliny's *mirabilia* are subordinate to an altogether more serious purpose. By calling his work *Historia Naturalis*, he has extended *historie*, the investigation usually centred on human activity, to the cosmology and natural science of the philosophers.[62] Against this all-embracing backdrop, the marvels of man and nature are no decontextualized tidbits, but essential articulators of a coherent cultural enterprise. It is to the nature of this enterprise that we shall now turn.

4. THE NATURE OF THE *NATURAL HISTORY*

4.1. The Literary Character and Structure of the *HN*

The cultural and political background of its author do much to explain the tone and character of the *HN*, but the work itself is more than the sum of its influences. Indeed, to the deceptively simple question, 'what is the *HN*?', there is no simple answer. As suggested in the previous section, the very connotations of the title, combining human 'history' with 'natural' science, imply that the *HN* has in some sense broken free of conventional boundaries. Pliny's comments on *encyclios paideia* (above, 3.1.2) of course suggest that we have in the *HN* an encyclopaedic work; the only ancient encyclopaedic work, in fact, extant in its entirety. As we saw, its sense of purpose is indeed encyclopaedic. Structurally, however, it matches no ancient encyclopaedia or other work that we know of. Other ancient encyclopaedias, for example those of Varro and Celsus, had divided knowledge up into neat compartments or subject divisions according to the *artes*, such as medicine or agriculture, which the work covered; divisions which were to develop into the *trivium* and *quadrivium* of the medieval liberal arts. Pliny, however, favours a single unified theme: 'my subject is nature, that is, life' (pref. 13), and takes as his framework the form of nature itself as represented by Aristotle in his *scala naturae*, the hierarchical classification of the parts of nature based on their degree of possession of specific

---

[62] For the novelty of the concept of *Historia Naturalis*, see e.g. P. Horden and N. Purcell, *The Corrupting Sea: A Study of Mediterranean History* (Oxford, 2000), 298–9: 'an intellectually ambitious amalgamation of interpretative traditions'. Cf also the comments in the Preface to the present volume.

powers.[63] Thus, after a description of the world as a whole (book 2), and its geographical divisions (books 3–6), Pliny proceeds down the scale, starting with the human race at the top (book 7) and continuing through the other animal species, birds, fish, insects, plants, and finally minerals. Yet, despite this evident debt to Aristotle, the *HN* owes little to the analytical approach to nature and its parts of the Aristotelian school. If classification was a main goal of Aristotle's study of nature, for Pliny it provides nothing more than a convenient backdrop for a very different enterprise.

4.2. 'My subject is nature, that is, life': Unity and Totality in Nature

In a few words (pref. 13), Pliny gives us a statement of intent, an indication of the vision of nature which is developed in the following 37 books. His nature is not a scientific entity, but the theatre of human life in which the focus is human interaction with nature, the 'natural history' of the title: thus, the *HN*'s books on plants are not merely classificatory lists of species, but are based primarily around the plants' usefulness to the human race in medicine, agriculture, and horticulture. The description of minerals is actually subsumed into a history of human art, since the bulk of human contact with them revolves around their use in painting, sculpture, and architecture. In the *HN*, nature meets culture and is indistinguishable from it. The philosophical and ideological aspects—Stoic, Roman, and practical—of Pliny's 'man in nature' theme, with its attendant anthropocentric view of nature, have already been discussed (3.1.1–3). The literary result is an all-inclusive, practical encyclopaedic guide to life.

In choosing nature and her parts as the framework for the *HN*, Pliny was, in effect, giving his work an unchallengeable inclusiveness and totality. What is outside the world (*mundus*), according to *HN* 2. 1, is not comprehendable by the human mind. His interest in

---

[63] See A. O. Lovejoy and G. Boas, *Primitivism and Related Ideas in Antiquity* (New York, 1935), 55–9; A. S. Pease (ed. and comm.), *De Natura Deorum* (Cambridge, Mass., 1955), on *ND* 2. 33–7. Yet the divisions are often blurred and suggestive of a gradually evolving totality (cf. A. O. Lovejoy, *The Great Chain of Being* (Harvard, 1932; repr. 1970), 55–9). For example, biological concepts of sex, parturition, and spontaneous growth were frequently applied to certain types of mineral by ancient writers, e.g. *HN* 36. 125: see J. André, R. Bloch, A. Rouveret, *Pline l'Ancien, Histoire Naturelle livre 36* (Paris, 1981), 212–13; and Healy (1999), 177–8.

cataloguing the totality of nature by enumerating his facts and sources (*HN* pref. 17), listing his authorities, and providing more internal referencing than any other ancient author resulted, according to one modern scholar,[64] in 'the most complete image of ancient common wisdom'.

The desire to categorize everything into a unifying totality reflects, on one level, an interest in compilation which went back to the Peripatetics and Hellenistic culture[65] and was a feature of the scholarly activities of Pliny's own era. Another facet of such contemporary activities, antiquarianism, is also clearly visible in the *HN*. While Pliny is anxious to include the latest information in his work, he is equally interested in preserving the legacy of past learning. Old and new learning together form an indivisible heritage, to be preserved, added to and handed on and he bemoans a contemporary slackness which has allowed much ancient wisdom to sink into oblivion (14. 3), thus greatly increasing his own research burden.

This interest in preserving past as well as present knowledge has the effect of giving the *HN* a temporal totality. Indeed, his reference to the 'storehouses' needed to contain the facts he has collected (pref. 16) has prompted parallels with the ancient concept of memory itself, according to which memories were often conceived as items to be retrieved from the storehouse of the mind. Significantly, for a work embracing 'nature, that is, life', Pliny calls memory 'the boon most necessary for life' (7. 88).[66] The preservation of the memory of ancient wisdom in a form which enables its retrieval by succeeding generations is a matter of some concern to the scholar Pliny, who, as we saw, berates those too lazy to research and preserve past wisdom (14. 3) and fulminates against the illiterate and secretive practitioners of herbal folk medicine, whose attitude hinders the preservation and dissemination of a knowledge potentially so beneficial to the human race (25. 1, 16). The fact that Pliny will record even ideas he does not agree with has been cited as another universalizing aspect of a work which seeks a notional audience as

---

[64] Conte (1994), 72.
[65] See below and comm. **191–215. introd.**
[66] *Rhetorica Ad Herennium* 2. 28, 3. 16; Quintilian 11. 2. 2; Augustine, *Conf.* 10. 8; M. Carruthers, *The Book of Memory: A Study of Memory in Medieval Culture* (Cambridge, 1990), 33–45. See further below, **88–90** comm.

comprehensive as the material it offers.[67] We should not, however, lose sight of the work's particular addressee, Titus. Blessed with a remarkable memory, according to Suetonius (*Titus* 3), he is an appropriate recipient for a work aiming at the preservation and transmission of the collective intellectual tradition. It may also be that Pliny has Titus in mind when he recounts at length in *HN* 8. 44 the story of Alexander the Great as cataloguer of the whole of nature, ordering information on every kind of animal to be sent to Aristotle.[68] Pliny (playing Aristotle to Titus' Alexander?) goes on to beg his readers' indulgence as he takes them on a journey through 'the whole of nature, the central interest of the most glorious of all rulers'.

Titus is also representative of totality on a spatial level; with his father, he controlled a world empire. The totality of the *HN*'s enterprise has an important spatial aspect, in that the work reflects a contemporary vision of Roman imperial expansion. Rome's control of the spatial and conceptual totality of empire was frequently expressed through the itemizing of its individual components in a collective format focused on the city itself.[69] Thus, obvious representations of the totality of empire, such as the map of Agrippa,[70] had counterparts in collections at Rome of items from all over the conquered territories. Augustus' temple of Mars had housed trophies and weapons from conquered peoples, while marble from various parts of the empire paved his forum.[71] Vespasian's temple of Peace had, according to Josephus, 'gathered in one place so many masterpieces which men had previously had to travel widely to see'.[72] So too the bringing of nature's *mirabilia* to Rome, where

[67] Conte (1994), 90 talks of the *HN*'s 'universal addressee' and stresses the importance of preserving even error in an inclusive project for the benefit of the human race.

[68] For Aristotle, see *OCD*³, 165–9. This particular story is probably apocryphal, though note R. French, *Ancient Natural History: Histories of Nature* (London, 1994), 105–7, who suggests that Alexander's lines of communication and administration were equal to the task and that Aristotle's information on elephants could plausibly have come, at Alexander's behest, from India. Alexander (*OCD*³, Alexander (3), 57–9), whose conquests brought him closer than any to being ruler of the natural world itself and a human wonder in his own right, features frequently in book 7's accounts of the extraordinary and the exceptional: *HN* 7. 11, 84, 95, 107, 125, 207.   [69] Nicolet (1991), esp. 73–4, 29–56, 95–122; Purcell (1990), 178–82.

[70] See *HN* 3.16–17: Agrippa intended 'to set the world before the eyes of the city of Rome': see Nicolet (1991), 110–11, comparing the opening formula of Augustus' *Res Gestae*.

[71] Zanker (1988), 214–15. Augustus was 'bringing the world into the city', as Ovid (*AA* 1. 171–4) remarked apropos of the grandiose naval spectacle put on by the emperor at the dedication of the temple in 2 BC.

[72] *BJ* 7. 159–60, discussed in Darwall-Smith (1996), 58–9 and 66–7.

they were frequently presented to the emperor and put on display in a public place,[73] emphasized his role as the controlling unifier and microcosm of nature herself.

Pliny's *HN*, with its storehouses of remarkable facts about nature in a self-consciously Roman setting, mirrors, on an intellectual level, Rome's totalizing and unificatory control of the world. The nature of Rome's dominance of the *oikumene*, the inhabited world, had been reflected to varying degrees in the thought of earlier scholars and intellectuals. The geographer Eratosthenes (285–194 BC) had viewed the world as a whole, while the Stoic Panaetius (185–109 BC) was formulating ideas about human kinship and the community of mankind in the wake of Rome's conquest of Carthage. The historian Polybius had noted the unifying effect both geographically and historically of Roman domination.[74] The thought of the Stoic philosopher and scholar Posidonius, a widely travelled investigator of all kinds of natural phenomena, was influenced by the effects of Roman imperialism on the world. Stoic philosophical theory and the actuality of the geographical and cultural unity brought about by Rome complemented, influenced, and strengthened each other and left their mark on Pliny: the totality of nature in the *HN* is both Stoic and Roman (below, 4.4).

4.3. Variety and Versatility

If there is unity, there is not uniformity in Pliny's nature. *Varietas naturae*, the variety of nature, is celebrated throughout the *HN*.[75] She is, in Stoic fashion, both rational and divine and, as Pliny explains in relation to the difference between humans and animals, the higher the rationality, the greater its versatility (*ingenii varietas*, 7. 52, comm. ad loc.). Nature's supreme power is proven through her supreme variety (7. 6–8, comm. ad loc.): even when working from a

---

[73] Suet. *Aug.* 43. 4; *HN* 7. 35, 74–6 with comm. ad loc.; 9. 92–3; 10. 5. See L. Friedländer, *Roman Life and Manners under the Early Empire*, iv (London, 1913), 6–10; R. Garland, *The Eye of the Beholder: Deformity and Disability in the Graeco-Roman World* (London, 1995), 49–50, 54–5; F. Millar, *The Emperor in the Roman World*[2] (London, 1992), 140; L. Casson, *Travel in the Ancient World* (London, 1974), 244–6. The practice of collection and display is also well attested in the late Republic, e.g. the statues of human *mirabilia* in Pompey's theatre complex (7. 34 and comm. ad loc.) and the show of marvels, including a sea-monster's skeleton, put on in 58 BC by the aedile M. Scaurus (*HN* 9. 11). For the interest in marvels and stories of marvels, see above, 3.3. For the spatial and temporal significance of their location and relocation, see Beagon 'Situating Nature's Wonders in Pliny's *Natural History*', forthcoming.

[74] See H. C. Baldry, *The Unity of Mankind in Greek Thought* (Cambridge, 1965), 135; Nicolet (1991), 30.   [75] See below, 5.2.2, and commentary on *HN* 7. 6–8.

limited palette, the ten basic features of a human face, she can produce a different, unique countenance every time, so superior to
human artistry is the divine artistry of nature. Indeed, she can
always produce something new to amaze the human race and
amuse herself: *mirabilia* such as the extraordinary races inhabiting
the ends of the earth, are 'ludibria sibi, nobis miracula' (*HN* 7. 32
and comm. ad loc., cf. 11. 102), a supreme manifestation of her
power. For man, intelligent as he is, they are surprises beyond even
his superior powers of imagination. Yet man's superior mental
powers are significant. As we saw (3.1.3), they mark him out as
superior to the rest of creation and bring him into a complex relationship with nature which is frequently close enough to merit his
portrayal as a microcosm, reflecting on a small scale the characteristics of nature herself. This, as we shall see (5.2.2), is a key theme of
book 7.

4.4. Rome in Nature, Roman Nature

Pliny's world-view is the result of his individual reaction to the
political and intellectual currents prevalent in the first century AD.
Its portrayal in the *HN* is thus at once reflective of its cultural roots
but at the same time unique. Its essence can best be appreciated by
consideration of a passage such as *HN* 27. 3, with its striking comparison of the Roman people to a second sun, in conjunction with
several other passages, where the cultural references and their
implications reveal the complexity of the writer's response to the
factors we have examined separately in 1–3 above.

In *HN* 27. 3, Pliny precedes an account of healing plants with a
paean of praise to nature for her providential kindness to the
human race. The plants are transported from every corner of the
world, even from the very edges, 'where nature herself is on the
wane'; all through the agency of 'the boundless majesty of the *Pax
Romana*, which displays in turn not only the human race divided
into its different countries and races, but also mountains with their
summits soaring into the clouds and their animals and plants. May
this gift of the gods be everlasting! So clearly do they seem to have
given the Romans, like a second sun, to humanity.'[76]

---

[76] . . . inmensa Romanae pacis maiestate non homines modo diversis inter se terris gen-
tibusque verum etiam montes et excedentia in nubes iuga partusque eorum et herbas
quoque invicem ostentante. aeternum quaeso, deorum sit munus istud! adeo Romanos velut
alteram lucem dedisse rebus humanis videntur.

Here, Pliny's Romanocentric outlook is combined with his Stoic-influenced humanitarianism. By protecting the distribution of the healing gifts of nature, the *Pax Romana*, Roman Peace, ensures *salus humana*, human welfare. The Stoic ideal of *commercium*, communication which links and unites through mutual aid the commonwealth of mankind,[77] is surely in Pliny's mind, giving a positive gloss to the world-wide trade in life-enhancing plants which flourishes under the security of the *Pax Romana*. The Roman people, controlling and guiding the commerce in nature's gifts, is itself equated with nature in terms of beneficence to the human race, but specifically in terms of its world-wide regulatory function. The sun was regarded as the particular embodiment of the divine rationality of the universe in Stoic thought[78] and is called 'the soul and mind of the world, the supreme ruling principle and divinity of nature' in *HN* 2. 13. By the first century AD, these Stoic cosmological ideas could add further resonances to a metaphor, originating in Greek political theory and developed under the influence of the Hellenistic philosophical tradition, which described the human ruler as the soul or mind of his people or empire, an embodiment of divine Reason or *Logos*.[79] The tradition was particularly clearly articulated in the Roman empire during the first and second centuries AD by writers such as the Stoic Seneca (n. 79 above) and the Platonist Plutarch (e.g. *Mor.* 779d–782e). Here, Pliny's comparison of the Roman people[80] to a 'second sun' develops the metaphor under broadly Stoic[81] influence and gives fresh impetus

[77] A concept which had been applied to the government of the Roman empire by Cicero in *De Officiis* and may have originated in Posidonius: see Griffin (1992), 238.

[78] Diogenes Laertius 7. 139; Cic., *Acad.* 1. 126, *Somn. Scip.* 4. 17, *ND* 2. 40ff. Beagon (1992), 31.

[79] See E. R. Goodenough, 'The Political Philosophy of Hellenistic Kingship', *YCS* 1 (1928), 55–102; G. F. Chesnut, 'The Ruler and the *Logos* in Neopythagorean, Middle Platonic and late Stoic Political Philosophy', *ANRW* 2. 16. 2 (1978), 1310–32. For 1st cent. AD examples, see Griffin (1984), 144, 205 n. 4, citing Seneca, *De Clem.* 1. 5. 1 (cf. 1. 3. 5–4. 1) and Marcus Aurelius, *Med.* 4. 40.

[80] The use of the metaphor collectively, of a ruling people in this instance, finds an echo in the late Republic: Cicero (*Cat.* 4. 11) referred to the city of Rome as *lux orbis terrarum* (light of the world).

[81] Analogy between the sun and the ruler was predominantly but not exclusively Stoic and was assimilated into an eclectic tradition: the possibly (see below, n. 83) Hellenistic treatise on kingship attributed to Ecphantus (Stobaeus 4. 7. 64: Wachsmuth and Hense 273. 1) had connected the ruler with light, variously interpreted as deriving from oriental/Egyptian sun symbolism (Goodenough (1928), 78–82) or from the Platonic light of the Good, compared to the sun in *Rep.* 7. 516b (for brief discussion, see Chesnut (1978), 1319). The writer of the treatise also makes an analogy between the true king's ability to withstand this light and the eagle's reputed ability to look straight at the sun. Plutarch drew an analogy between the

to the traditional justification of Roman imperialism as resting upon the beneficence of the Roman people. This metaphor, in which political theory is reinforced by philosophical, particularly Stoic, ideas, may be combined with another. Plutarch[82] and other writers in the same tradition[83] stressed the necessity of virtue in the ruler, who must be a moral exemplar and saviour to, as well as director of, his people. We have already seen (above, 2.1, 3.1.1) that the ideal Roman ruler could be portrayed as selfless in pursuit of his labours on behalf of his subjects. A philosophical model particularly favoured by Roman imperial writers was the ideal constructed around the hero Hercules by the Cynics and Stoics.[84] Augustus, whose victories rescued Rome physically and spiritually from the spiralling self-destruction of civil war and ensured her peace, had been associated with Hercules in contemporary poetry. As Vespasian, with his sons, 'comes to the rescue of an exhausted world' (*HN* 2. 18) in the wake of another civil war, Pliny's words clearly recall the achievements of the first emperor, on whom, as we saw, Vespasian in many respects modelled himself, and those of his heroic role-model. But the bringer of order and peace is equally an embodiment of the Stoic sun, which Pliny not only describes as regulating the world (2. 13) but even, in a striking metaphor, as 'calming the storm-clouds of the mind of man'. Seneca, in *De Clementia* 1. 7, came close to Pliny's parallels between imperial peace and the rule of the sun in the heavens when he compared the quiet, well-ordered *imperium* to a calm and shining sky and political disorder to a storm: in both cases, the implicit contrast is the presence or absence of the sun.

sun, 'the most exalted image of god', and the role of the ruler, embodying the divine Logos on earth (*To an Uneducated Ruler, Mor.* 781f–782a). For eastern ideas of the sun as regulator and king, see G.H. Halsberghe, *Sol Invictus* (Leiden, 1972), 37; and for general use of sun imagery in connection with Hellenistic rulers and ultimately the imperial cult, see S. Weinstock, *Divus Julius* (Oxford, 1971), 381–4.

[82] *To an Uneducated Ruler, Mor.* 780b; cf. 'Ecphantus' in Stobaeus 4. 7. 64 and 65 (Wachsmuth and Hense 274. 4, 278. 9).

[83] The dating of the so-called Neopythagorean treatises on kingship is disputed, but they may be as early as the 3rd cent. BC; see Chesnut (1978), 1315 for a summary of arguments and bibliography.

[84] G. K. Galinsky, *The Herakles Theme* (Oxford, 1972), 106, 126–49; Roman generals from Scipio onwards had associated themselves with the hero whose triumphs spanned the world. The selflessness of Hercules' labours, conquest on behalf of others for the sake of peace, was of importance in the Stoic interpretation of the hero; cf. Seneca, *Ben.* 1. 13. 3, who elsewhere condemns some of Rome's generals for being motivated by ambition: see Griffin (1992), 222–3, cf. 238.

When we consider Pliny's imagery against the broader contemporary political background, it is tempting to suggest that Vespasian's dedication to the sun god[85] of Zenodorus' colossal bronze statue of Nero, over one hundred feet high, which stood in front of the Domus Aurea,[86] was motivated by some consciousness of the philosophical and cosmological imagery which could be applied to the ruler or ruling people, and their empire. Later representations[87] show the sun-colossus with one hand on a rudder, symbol of cosmic governance as well as of political direction, in which context it was by now well established in both iconography and literary metaphor.[88] It thus proclaimed the approved ideology of a peaceful, well-regulated, world-wide *imperium* for the new dynasty and for Rome herself as mistress of empire. There were also, perhaps, more personal resonances for Vespasian. His cause had had its origins in the east. During the second battle of Cremona in 69, the soldiers of the Third legion, whose loyalty was regarded by Vespasian as crucial to his cause, and who had long been stationed in Syria before being transferred to Moesia, had saluted the rising sun in accordance with Syrian custom.[89] In addition, the dedication of his charioteering predecessor's statue to a god fre-

[85] The early 3rd-cent. BC Colossus of Rhodes was, of course, a statue of the sun god. Obelisks, symbols of the sun god in Egypt, had been sent to Rome by Augustus after Actium to be dedicated to Sol (*CIL* vi. 701, 702: Halsberghe (1972), 26). The one in the Campus Martius was used as a gnomon: see in general *HN* 36. 70–4.

[86] Pliny saw it under construction, *HN* 34. 45 (cf. Suet. *Vesp.* 8; Dio 65. 15. 1, Martial, *Spect.* 2. 1).

[87] The arguments concerning the nature and extent of possible alterations to the statue by Vespasian are summarized by K. Bradley, *Suetonius' Life of Nero* (Brussels, 1978), 175–7, whose own view, that Vespasian's dedication did not necessarily entail any alteration, despite later evidence for the statue's appearance, is probably too sceptical. Particularly intriguing is the question of whether there was any alteration to the facial attributes. Strabo (1. 1. 23, C13) says that the detailing on such statues was less important than the overall effect; yet the face seems to have provoked comment. Pliny (*HN* 34. 45) remarked on the original's likeness to Nero, whereas Dio (65. 15. 1), commenting on Vespasian's dedication, which he dates to AD 75, says that, while some thought it looked like Nero, others thought it looked like Titus. P. Howell, 'The Colossus of Nero', *Athenaeum*, 46 (1968), 295, suggests that the latter resemblance 'may not have been completely fortuitous'. For the recutting of marble statues of Nero to depict Vespasian, see J. Pollini, '*Damnatio memoriae* in Stone: Two Portraits of Nero Recut to Vespasian in American Museums', *AJA* 88 (1984), 547–55. See also below, n. 91.

[88] Cf. the metaphor of the ruler/statesman at the helm of the ship of state: Cicero, *Rab. Perd.* 26, *Sest.* 20, *Div.* 2. 3, *Rosc. Am.* 131, and esp. *Rep.* 2. 29, *rector et gubernator civitatis*, 'ruler and helmsman of the state'. For Seneca (*Hippol.* 903), the divine ruler of the cosmos is *poli gubernator*, 'helmsman of the heavens'.

[89] Tac. *Hist.* 3. 24; cf. 2. 74, 85. The eastern cult of Sol Invictus seems not to have become established at Rome before the 2nd cent. AD, but it appears that it was already entering Roman consciousness via the legions: see Halsberghe (1972), 37.

quently depicted in a *quadriga* (four-horse chariot) and linked to the games in the Circus Maximus[90]may have appealed to his sense of irony.[91] As a symbol of ordered cosmic government, the colossus would also have stood in implicit opposition to a growing tendency among Pliny's contemporaries to allow Fortuna, the epitome of the uncertain and irrational, to rule their lives. Pliny makes it abundantly clear that Fortune is a false god (*HN* 2. 22–5). True deity by contrast belongs to rulers who bring rational order and security to a troubled world. For Pliny, the Flavians epitomized the Stoic ideal of world-government.

Rome, regulator of the world and its diverse contents in *HN* 27. 3, is further assimilated to nature herself in 37. 201, where Italy is called 'ruler and second mother of the world'; the first mother being of course nature herself. That Rome was a microcosm of the world had become a commonplace in the early Empire,[92] but when Pliny, commenting on her wealth of fine buildings, calls Rome 'another world' (36. 101), he does so with an unexpected turn of phrase: if all Rome's buildings 'were piled up together and placed in one huge heap (*universitate . . . acervata et in quendam unum cumulum coiecta*), such grandeur would tower above us as to suggest that another world concentrated in one place was being described'. The image of piled-up buildings is not one which automatically fits the idea of nature as regulator and regulated; on the contrary, it is more akin to the chaos that preceded cosmogony.[93] One reason for the

---

[90] Tac. *Ann.* 15. 74; Tertullian, *Spect.* 8.

[91] There was more irony in the fact that Nero believed the all-seeing sun-god had saved him by revealing the Pisonian conspiracy of 65 (Tac. *Ann.* 15. 74). Neronian iconography yields other associations with Helios and it is possible that the Neronian colossus already possessed some attributions of the sun god: see Bradley (1978), 75–7, and, more recently, M. Bergmann, *Die Strahlen der Herrscher: Theomorphes Herrscherbild und politische Symbolik im Hellenismus und in der römischen Kaiserzeit* (Mainz, 1998), 189–201. Either way, as S. Carey, *Pliny's Catalogue of Culture; Art and Empire in the Natural History* (Oxford, 2003), 156–63, rightly argues, the rededication, rather than erasing memories of Nero, evoked negative memories of the previous regime which only served to heighten the contrast with the Vespasianic present.

[92] e.g. Ovid, *Fasti* 2.683; an idea which evolves out of increasing awareness of Rome's world domination, possibly from as early as the late 2nd cent. BC (Nicolet (1991), 30ff.). Cf. J. Romm, *The Edges of the Earth in Ancient Thought* (Princeton,1992), 121–3. The juxtaposition of *urbs* (city, referring to Rome) and *orbis* (world) to denote the cultural and political unity of a world controlled and embraced by Rome occurs frequently in literature from the late Republic to the Flavian era (see E. Breguet, '*Urbi et orbi*: un cliché et un thème', in J. Bibauw (ed.), *Hommages à Marcel Renard*, i (Brussels, 1969), 140–52). Stoic cosmopolitanism viewed the world as a cosmic city: Cicero, *Parad. Stoic.* 11. 18; Seneca, *Tranq. An.* 4.4.

[93] Ovid, *Met.* 1. 24 actually describes chaos as *caecus acervus*; though some piles are tidier than others: contrast Livy 5. 48. 3 with Cicero, *Tusc.* 5. 15.

unexpected simile is the fact that Pliny's city is a composite creation of time as well as space; all eight hundred years' worth of Rome's architecture, including, implicitly, that which has been destroyed or built over by Pliny's time, is under consideration. Comparisons have also been drawn with the imagery used by Josephus when describing the Jewish triumph of AD 71, where the assembled marvels are heaped up like a trophy, 'their collective exhibition on that day displaying the majesty of the Roman empire' (trans. H. St. J. Thackeray). Further on in the same passage, the spoils themselves are carried 'in promiscuous heaps'.[94] The 'towering grandeur' of Pliny's Rome also suggests that emphasis should be placed on the height of the pile, topped perhaps by the colossal sun-god, symbol of Rome herself, looking down, like his real-life counterpart, on the world he directs and controls.

4.5. The Composition of the *HN*: Sources, Methods, Chronology

4.5.1. *The Problem of the Sources*

The *HN*'s universality is chronological (above, 4.2) as well as ideological and geographical. It sums up knowledge to date in the same way that it amasses and displays the contents of Rome's and nature's empire. Pliny claimed to have consulted two thousand books by one hundred authors (pref. 17: in fact an underestimate), the latter, unusually in an ancient text, being arranged in lists together with a general subject index for each book. Pliny claims that this itemization is designed to save his imperial patron valuable time when consulting the *HN* on a specific subject. In fact, the indexes are too vague to be of much use. They and the lists of writers make perfect sense, however, in the context of the *HN*'s 'universal' enterprise.

In addition to his authorial lists, Pliny cites his sources in the body of his text comparatively frequently by ancient standards. This led to a scholarly trend in the later nineteenth and earlier twentieth centuries towards assigning the material in the *HN* to one

---

[94] *conveniat DCCCque annorum dociles scrutari vires*: see E. Gowers, 'The Anatomy of Rome, from Capitol to Cloaca', *JRS* 85 (1995), 23 on this 'fourth dimensional' aspect. On Josephus, *BJ* 7. 5. 132, see A. Rouveret, 'Toute la mémoire du monde: La notion de collection dans la *NH* de Pline', in J. Pigeaud and J. Oroz (eds.), *Pline l'Ancien: Témoin de son temps* (Salamanca, 1987), 442–3.

or other of the listed or cited authors, or even to one source above all others. Thus, in book 7, Münzer inclined to see Pliny as dependent above all on the late Republican scholar and antiquarian Varro,[95] in particular, his lost *Antiquitates Rerum Humanarum et Divinarum* or his *Admiranda*, also lost. Rabenhorst, however, favoured the *Rerum Memoria Dignarum Libri* of Verrius Flaccus, scholar and tutor of the emperor Augustus' grandsons. Since these works were themselves essentially encyclopaedic miscellanies, it would be possible to question whether many of the other sources Pliny lists had in fact been used at first hand at all. Yet the case for a predominant encyclopaedic source to which Pliny was indebted is itself unprovable. Other encyclopaedias and miscellanies, notably those by Valerius Maximus, who wrote in the reign of Tiberius, and Alexander Polyhistor, a Greek scholar of the first century BC, who originally came to Rome as a prisoner of war, are cited.[96] In any case, it was chronologically impossible for any of these writers to have been responsible for some of the material in book 7. There are citations by name in the text of later authors, such as Licinius Mucianus; and there are extracts from official records and imperial autobiographies, such as that of Agrippina, which are clearly later and which, in some cases, were most likely gathered by Pliny at first hand.[97] Overall, *Quellenkritik* of the *HN* raises some interesting questions but provides relatively few clear-cut answers. Moreover, by reducing Pliny's work to the status of an anonymous compilation, it can obscure understanding of the *HN* as the enterprise of an author whose ideas, influences, and conscious artistry[98] bring a distinctive coherence and unity to his work.

What is striking about the authorial lists is the variety of authorities cited. In the index to book 7 alone, we find, in addition to Verrius Flaccus and Valerius Maximus, antiquarians and biographers such as Varro, Alexander Polyhistor, and Cornelius Nepos.

---

[95] Münzer (1897). For Varro (116–27 BC), Rome's greatest scholar, and his vast and varied output, much of which is lost, see *OCD*[3], 1582.

[96] M. Rabenhorst, *Der ältere Plinius als Epitomator des Verrius Flaccus: Eine Quellenanalyse des siebenten Buches der Naturgeschichte* (Berlin, 1907). For Verrius Flaccus (*c*.55 BC–*c*.AD 20), see *OCD*[3], 1589. His major work, *De Verborum Significatu*, was lexicographical. For Alexander Polyhistor, see *OCD*[3], 60. Some thirty-five passages in *HN* 7 can be paralleled with passages in Valerius Maximus' *Memorable Deeds and Sayings*: a convenient table is provided in König and Winckler 247–8.

[97] e.g. *HN* 7. 46, Agrippina's memoirs; 162, Vespasian's census; and see P. G. Maxwell-Stuart, 'Dating by African Figs', *Mus. Helv.* 53 (1996=1996*b*), 256–8 for items postdating Verrius Flaccus.   [98] Beagon (1992), 21–4 and nn.

The listing of Herodotus, Thucydides, Xenophon, Aristotle, Cicero, Virgil, and Livy offers a cross-section of the foremost philosophers, poets, historians, and orators of both Greece and Rome. There are medical writings, imperial autobiographies, official records, and a host of Hellenistic works on topics ranging from *mirabilia* to magical apocrypha. We can probably never know for certain which were read at first hand and which were consulted indirectly through other writers. Whatever our conclusions, the significance of the lists lies at least as much in their contribution to the universalizing enterprise of the *HN* as in their contribution to the conjectural debate on the question of Pliny's indebtedness.

4.5.2. *Collecting Information: The Process of Research*

We may not now be able to match every fact in the *HN* to a particular source, but we do know something of Pliny's working methods in amassing so much information. His nephew describes his system of reading and excerpting, undertaken with the assistance of slave readers and shorthand secretaries,[99] which could be followed, with modifications, during meals, when travelling, and even at bathtime when he was not actually in the water. He had books read to him and indicated to his secretary the passages to be excerpted.[100] When travelling, a single secretary could perform the functions of both *lector* and *notarius*. The result was a huge collection of selected passages, the *commentarii*, written in a minute hand on both sides of the papyrus rolls, which Larcius Licinus, *iuridicus* of Hispania Tarraconensis, was so eager to buy from Pliny when he was procurator there in the early 70s.[101] The collection continued to grow; on Pliny's death in AD 79 it was left to his nephew, who tells us that it then numbered 160 rolls, considerably more than when Larcius Licinus had made his offer. The existence of a vast collection which was to grow considerably in the 70s leaves little doubt as to the provenance of the raw material for the *HN*. Its size at the time of the Larcius Licinus anecdote also suggests that it may well have been the repository drawn upon for Pliny's earlier works; the storehouse, in fact, of a lifetime's reading.

The fact that Licinus was willing to part with 400,000 sesterces,

---

[99] *Ep.* 3. 5. 11–12, 15; cf. 9. 20. 2 on the use of *lectores* and *notarii*.

[100] We can assume that he also read and took notes without assistance, as his nephew describes himself as doing at the time of the eruption of Vesuvius (*Ep.* 6. 20. 1–2, cf. 6. 18. 4).

[101] For the date, AD 72–4, see Syme (1969), 203–36, 755–6.

the minimum amount needed for membership of the equestrian order, suggests that the excerpts must have been organized and classified in such a way as to make them usable by, and comprehensible to, readers other than Pliny himself. Unfortunately, we are given no clear indication of how this might have been done. In addition to 'excerpting' (*excerpere*), Pliny's nephew talks of his uncle 'making notes on' (*adnotare*) what he read or had read to him and one modern scholar has suggested that this 'note-making' was some kind of retrieval or organizational aid for the excerpts; possibly marginal notes added to the *commentarii* or notes in the margins of the books being read.[102] However, it also seems likely that anything written during Pliny's hectic day would have been of an intermediate nature; the slave who assisted in his studies whilst travelling is specifically said to carry *pugillares*, normally wax-covered writing-tablets on which anything of an impermanent nature was inscribed.[103] All material may, then, have gone through an intermediate stage before being transcribed into a more permanent, systematically arranged collection.

4.5.3. *The composition of the* HN

The younger Pliny lists his uncle's works in order of composition. The *HN* is listed last, suggesting a compositional date in the 70s, which of course accords with the dedicatory date of 77 (above, Sect.

[102] See A. Locher, 'The Structure of the *Natural History*', in R. French and F. Greenaway, *Science in the Early Roman Empire: Pliny the Elder, his Sources and Influence* (London, 1986), 20–9. For detailed discussion of possible working practices, materials, and classificatory methods, see V. Naas, 'Réflexions sur la méthode de travail de Pline l'Ancien', *Rev. Phil.* 70.2 (1996), 305–32; and, on the compositional process generally, *Le Projet encyclopédique de Pline l'Ancien*, Coll. Ec. Fr. de Rome 303 (Rome, 2002), 171–234. J. P. Small (*Wax Tablets of the Mind: Cognitive Studies of Memory and Literacy in Classical Antiquity* (London, 1997), 169–201, esp. 188–9) warns against interpreting Pliny's working methods in terms of modern retrieval systems based on note-cards, emphasizing instead the importance of mnemotechnics in the compositional processes. Yet the storage of so much material must have involved some rationale for retrieval, as would have been the case in public and private archives (see M. Brosius, *Ancient Archives and Archival Traditions: Concepts of Record-Keeping in the Ancient World* (Oxford, 2003), 12–16; cf. C. Nicolet, 'A la recherche des archives oubliées: Une Contribution à l'histoire de la bureaucratie Romaine', in *La Mémoire perdue: A la recherche des archives oubliées, publiques et privées, de la Rome antique* (Paris, 1994), v–xvii). As well as using such archives in his literary researches, Pliny would also have become familiar with their organizational systems in the course of his official duties and may have assisted in their creation and maintenance. See Naas (2002), 194. Small also notes the difficulties of arranging the excerpts in an organized manner on the rolls; although here Licinus' interest surely indicates some degree of success.
[103] Pliny, *Ep.* 3. 5. 15. See C. H. Roberts and T. C. Skeat, *The Birth of the Codex* (Oxford, 1987), 11–14.

1) and with scattered references in the body of the text.[104] It has been suggested that composition on some sections may have begun even earlier, under Nero, and that this has complicated Pliny's notoriously vague use of temporal phrases such as *nuperrime* ('most recently'), *nostra aetas* ('our era') etc., if, as is likely, the *HN* was not subjected to detailed revision before publication. Certainly, much of the raw material of research may have pre-dated the final composition by many years.[105] The *commentarii* were both a long-term and ongoing project. As mentioned in the previous section, his nephew tells us that Pliny added considerably to his collection of excerpts during the 70s. Possibly some of these excerpts were destined for other projected works, never to be written due to Pliny's demise; just as a proportion of the notes amassed by the time of his procuratorship in Tarraconensis may, as suggested in the previous section, have been gathered primarily for works written before the *HN*. It seems likely, however, that the vast scope of the *HN* encouraged Pliny to draw on material both new and not so new, regardless of his original intentions (and we do not have to assume that he necessarily had any) for its use at the time of excerpting. The assimilation of such material into the *HN* in draft or final form over a period of time may well explain some of the temporal and other discrepancies to be found therein.

Despite these discrepancies, Pliny was largely successful in producing a coherent text; a considerable number of the numerous internal cross-references are accurate.[106] In addition, the *HN* was complex not only technically but also artistically. Some books, including book 7, are structured to form a self-contained unit. Others are part of larger units articulated by introductions and conclusions.[107] Elaborately crafted rhetorical passages occur throughout (3.1.1). All of which serves as a reminder that the *HN* was no mere compilation but a conscious creation reflective of its time.

---

[104] e.g. 19. 35, 32. 62; See B. Baldwin, 'The Composition of Pliny's *Natural History*', *Symbolae Osloenses*, 70 (1995=1995*a*), 72–81.

[105] Baldwin (1995*a*), 81, concludes that the *HN*, 'although written up in the 70s, was researched and drafted for many years before that'; cf. Syme (1969), 215; Maxwell-Stuart (1996*b*), 256–8.

[106] Baldwin (1995*a*), 74.

[107] For book 7's structure, see Commentary, *passim*. The structure of the *HN*, including the function of the index in book 1 and the rationale behind the use of introductions and conclusions, is treated at length in Naas (2002), 171–234.

4.6. The History of the *HN*

4.6.1. *Readership and Text*

The *HN*'s relationship to the scholarship of later centuries is as complex as its relationship to its own intellectual predecessors. Its scope and diversity ensured it played a role in the culture of later ages with a continuity and popularity unmatched by comparable ancient works, such as Varro's, which were lost in the Middle Ages, or by many later encyclopaedic works.[108] If its scope was an advantage, however, its size caused problems. While we can be sure that readers in the century or so after Pliny's death—his nephew, for example, and Suetonius and Aulus Gellius in the second century—knew the work in its complete form, its bulk led to abridgements and epitomes from an early date. After the third century, it is no longer clear whether a reader has access to an unabridged *HN* or is using an epitome. Shorter works heavily dependent on Pliny, such as the third-century *Collectanea Rerum Memorabilium* of Solinus, further complicate the picture. The famous 'ethnography' of book 7 was largely incorporated into Solinus' marvel-mongering anthology with the result that it is frequently impossible to deduce whether Pliny or Solinus is the source for those contributing to the flourishing tradition of the monstrous races, from the medieval period into the sixteenth century and later.[109] Yet Pliny's own work was still in circulation: towards the end of the fourth century, the orator Symmachus sent a copy to the Gallic-born poet Ausonius, whose famous poem on the Moselle bears possible traces of his Plinian reading.[110] St Augustine certainly possessed a copy of book 7,[111] even if other apparently Plinian passages in his writings come from Solinus. Bede's scientific interests led him to admire Pliny: he used book 2 extensively, and

---

[108] See above, 3.1.1. M. Chibnall, 'Pliny's *Natural History* and the Middle Ages', in T.A. Dorey (ed.), *Empire and Aftermath* (London, 1975), 57–78. For the reception of the *HN* by readers from antiquity to the 17th cent., see A. Borst, *Das Buch der Naturgeschichte: Plinius und seiner Leser im Zeitalter des Pergaments* (Heidelberg, 1994); more bibliography in Beagon (1992), 22–3.

[109] R. Wittcower, 'Marvels of the East: A Study in the History of Monsters', *JWCI* 5 (1942), 167; Chibnall (1975), 59.

[110] Symmachus, *Ep.* 1. 24. Cf. *Mos.* 303–4 with *HN* 7. 125, *Mos.* 311–17 with *HN* 34. 148, and *Mos.* 361–2 with *HN* 36. 159. *Mos.* 48–51's moralizing on human luxury as opposed to 'the work of nature' is Plinian in tone.

[111] H. Hagendahl, *Augustine and the Latin Classics* (Göteborg, 1967), 670–3; A. Roncoroni, 'Plinio Tardoantico', in *Plinio il Vecchio* (Como, 1982), 156.

probably up to half of the other books of the *HN*.[112] The *HN* is also attested in a number of libraries of the eighth and ninth centuries and in the tenth-century Bobbio list.[113]

Use of the *HN* continually adapted to the cultural requirements of the day. In the twelfth century it was important in the schools, often in an abridged form, excised in accordance with Christian doctrine; but it could also turn up in unexpected places, for example at Clairvaux, despite the tendency of the Cistercians to avoid the Pagan classics.[114] Later, it was plundered for the medieval encyclopaedias, thus continuing, in an indirect way and in another age, its original function in the tradition of *encyclios paideia*, as a handbook of general education.

With the advent of an age of scientific reason, the *HN* gradually fell out of favour as a repository of knowledge. In the twentieth century it has been subjected to criticism on the grounds of lack of originality and failure of critical judgement as to the veracity of its information. The latter complaint has proved to be almost as impervious to eradication as the Plinian 'errors' it has targeted. However, growing appreciation of the true nature of Pliny's enterprise, together with acknowledgement that he does not always vouch for the material in his inclusive work, seem finally to have laid this particular myth to rest. Yet a significant step in this direction had already been taken as early as the seventeenth century, by Sir Thomas Browne, who disposed of the charge in his *Pseudodoxa Epidemica* with typical elegance and precision. His words, unfortunately ignored by many later critics, deserve to be quoted in full:

Plinius Secundus of Verona, a man of great Eloquence and industry indefatigable, as may appear in his writings, especially those now extant, and which are never like to perish, but even with learning itself; that is, his Natural History. He was the greatest Collector, or Rhapsodist, of the Latines, and as Suetonius observeth, he collected this piece out of two thousand Latine and Greek Authors. Now what is very strange, there is scarce a popular error passant in our days, which is not either directly expressed, or diductively contained in this work; which being in the hands of most men, hath proved a powerful occasion of their propagation.

---

[112] M. L. W. Laistner, *The Intellectual Heritage of the Early Middle Ages* (Ithaca, 1957), 124–5, 128.

[113] Laistner (1957), 183. Well-known works of the period exhibiting Plinian undertones, direct or indirect, include the 8th-cent. *History of the Lombards* of Paul the Deacon: Pliny is specifically cited in 1. 2 and 1. 15 bears possible traces of *HN* 7. 33.

[114] See Chibnall (1975), 64.

Wherein notwithstanding the credulity of the reader is more condemnable than the curiosity of the Author: for commonly he nameth the Authors from whom he received those accounts, and writes but as he reads, as in his Preface to Vespasian he acknowledgeth. (Sir Thomas Browne, *Pseudodoxa Epidemica* i. 8. 5, from *The Works of Sir Thomas Browne, ed.* G. Keynes, vol. ii, 1928/64)

In recent years, the *HN* has finally started to regain some of its old reputation, as its historical value as a unique cultural record of the first century AD is finally recognized.[115]

4.6.2. *Manuscripts and Editions.*

The *HN* has a complex manuscript tradition; the large number of surviving manuscripts testifies to its continuous popularity. The size of the work, together with much unfamiliar and technical vocabulary, resulted in respectively manuscripts preserving only part of the complete work and numerous variations between manuscripts. The earliest date back to the eighth or ninth centuries.[116]

From the fourteenth century, attempts were made, by Petrarch among others, to purify the increasingly corrupt transmission of the *HN*'s text. The first printed edition, that of Spira, was published at Venice in 1469. It was one of the earliest books to be printed, the first of over 300 editions, partial editions, and criticisms to be published up to the present day. Later editions, criticisms, and commentaries of particular interest included Hermolaus Barbarus' *Castigationes Plinii* of 1492–3, the edition by the seventeenth-century Jesuit scholar P. Hardouin, and the Lemaire edition with commentary of 1827–32, in which the *libri de animalibus* (books 7–11), by Ajasson de Grandsagne, included Hardouin's text and annotations by the great French naturalist Georges Cuvier[117] among others. The first English translation was that of Philemon Holland, published in 1601.

Modern scholarship on the *HN* has its roots in nineteenth-century Germany which produced important editions by Sillig,

---

[115] See Beagon (1992), 23–4 and nn. See further below, 5.1. Most studies in the last fifteen years implicitly or explicitly recognize this, including: Citroni Marchetti (1991); Isager (1991); de Oliveira (1992); Healy (1999); Carey (2003).

[116] For a résumé of the tradition, see J. Ernout, *Pline l'Ancien Histoire Naturelle livre i* (Paris, 1950), 20–39.

[117] Letters indicate that his formative reading as a young man in the last decade of the 18th cent. included Pliny: see D. Outram, *Georges Cuvier* (Manchester, 1984), 33 and n. 24.

Jan, Detlefsen, and Mayhoff; the last two remaining the basis for later editions and translations. These include, in the last sixty years, the ten-volume Loeb text with English translation (1938–83) by H. Rackham and others, and the Budé edition (1947–) with text, French translation, and commentary by J. Beaujeu, J. André, A. Ernout, and others. Within the last thirty years, an upsurge of interest in the *Natural History* has been reflected in the increasing number of editions produced in Europe. In addition to the Budé series, a substantial contribution has been the Tusculum Bücherei edition (1973–94) by R. König, G. Winckler, and others, with text, German translation, and commentary. Smaller-scale complete editions include the five-volume Einaudi Italian text and commentary by G. Conte, A. Barchiesi, and C. Ranucci (Turin, 1982–8) and a Spanish edition (*Plinio el Viejo*, translation and commentary by G. Serbat, A. Fontán, and others, Madrid, Biblioteca Clásica Gredos, 1995–). The linguistic and practical challenges thrown up by Pliny's frequently technical subject-matter are being addressed by the interdisciplinary Pliny Translation Group of Germany. Within the last ten years a significant contribution to Plinian studies has been P. Rosumek and D. Najock's seven-volume Concordance to the *Natural History*.[118] The most significant editions with commentary of book 7 are those by R. König and G. Winckler (Munich, 1975) in the Tusculum series and by R. Schilling (1977) for the Budé edition, of which the latter is the more detailed. Published within two years of, and without reference to, each other, they both take Mayhoff's text as their starting-point, though with modifications. Except where specifically indicated in the commentary, the present translation is based upon the Budé text. Divergences between this and the Tusculum text do not, in most cases, substantially alter the general sense of what Pliny is saying. König and Winckler (249–5) provide useful tables comparing their own Tusculum text with other editions in passages where there are divergent readings.

---

[118] For an introduction to the Translation Group's work, see R. C. A. Rottländer, 'The Pliny Translation Group of Germany', in French and Greenaway (1986), 11–19. Concordance: *Concordantia in C. Plinii Secundi Naturalem Historiam*, 7 vols. (Hildesheim, Zurich, New York, 1996).

5. *H.N.* 7: THEMES AND APPROACHES

5.1. The Significance of HN 7

The *HN* has retained for the most part an enduring appeal over the two thousand years since it was written. During that period, the cultural and historical environment has undergone a series of transformations, producing successive world-views which have often had little in common with that of a first-century Roman. Yet, as we saw (4.6.2), the *HN* proved amenable to different usages and approaches, acquiring in time a kind of temporal universality to match its original breadth of scope and vision.

Today, the *HN* may be approached on more than one level. In some respects, it still retains its value as a storehouse of facts, providing the historian with a repository of information not found elsewhere. It can shed light on less familiar aspects of well-trodden topics and famous figures. The darker side of the Augustan success story receives its most detailed extant exposure; while an earlier example of physical toughness in the ancestry of the conspirator of 63 BC, L. Sergius Catilina, sheds unexpected new light on his family pride, documented in Cicero and Sallust. The breech birth of the emperor Nero offers a tantalizing glimpse of the lost autobiography of the emperor's redoubtable mother, Agrippina. Statistics on longevity are put together from records gathered in the Vespasianic census and otherwise unknown epigraphic material is incorporated into the chapters on Pompey's career.[119]

For the historian of science, the approach is more complex. Pliny's enterprise in writing about the natural world in the cultural atmosphere of the first century AD is in many respects very different from that of the modern scientist[120] yet there is still much to be gained from examination of the description of natural substances and the processes, such as mining, dyeing, and metallurgy, which harnessed them to human use.[121] For the art historian, the

---

[119] See comm. **147–50, 104–6, 46, 162–4, 95–9**. Apart from brief references, footnotes for Section 5 will be confined to material not covered in the Commentary on the passages cited.   [120] See French (1994); Naas (2000), 255–71.

[121] See Healy (1999). Careful re-examination of Pliny's text by those with scientific, rather than purely philological, expertise can elucidate difficult passages and enhance Pliny's standing as a scientific source. See e.g. E. Paparazzo, 'Pliny the Elder on the Melting and Corrosion of Silver with Tin in Solders: *prius liquescat argentum . . . ab eo erodi argentum (HN* 34.161)', *CQ* 53. 2 (2003), 523–9.

invaluable documentation by Pliny of otherwise lost or unknown works of art is enhanced by the evidence he offers of the aesthetic values and attitudes of his age.[122]

But perhaps the most significant change in modern approaches to the *HN*, from whatever angle, has been the increased tendency to value it as a work of its time; that is, to appreciate the cultural significance of the attitudes which determine the treatment of its material on art, or natural science, or political and social history. Of primary importance here is Pliny's Stoic-inspired vision of the centrality of human life in nature. This is coupled with his vision of an expanding Roman world, incorporating a fascination with the new and wondrous. Together, they characterize the whole of the *HN*. More specifically, they are epitomized in Pliny's portrait of the human race in book 7, which interweaves the various strands. It is by presenting man in book 7 as the ultimate marvel that Pliny asserts both the anthropocentricity and the Romanocentricity of his outlook, as we shall see (5.2–4), reinforcing his belief that 'nature is life' and that the natural world acts as a stage for the presentation of the human wonder in all its manifestations.

5.2. The Human Animal

5.2.1. *Book 7 in Relation to the Rest of the* HN

The overall coherence of the *HN* makes it impossible to consider any single book in total isolation from the rest of the work. However, it has long been recognized that book 7 is in many respects self-contained. It is sometimes referred to as Pliny's 'anthropology' or 'ethnography', isolating it both from the preceding geography and the four books on the rest of the animal kingdom which follow it. But, scrutinized in detail, only a small portion of book 7's content seems obviously ethnographic or anthropological in character and that material is confined mainly to chapters 1–33.[123] It is also possible to view books 7 to 11 as a unit, deriving from the Aristotelian treatment of man as part of the animal kingdom, but here, too, there are problems. If Pliny is Aristotelian in outline, which is a perfectly plausible construction (above, 4.1), he is less so in detail.

---

[122] See Isager (1991).
[123] F. Römer, 'Die Plinianische Anthropologie und der Aufbau de H.N.', *WS* NS 17 (1983), 104–8. On chs. 1–33, see M. Vegetti, 'Zoologia e antropologia in Plinio', in *Plinio il Vecchio; sotto il profilo storico e letterario* (Como, 1982), 117–31; and E. Bianchi, 'Teratologia e geografia', *Acme*, 34 (1981), 227–49.

Indeed, for the reader of Aristotle's works on animals who is also familiar with Pliny's expressions of admiration for and indebtedness to his great predecessor in books 7–11, the latter's treatment of man the animal is distinctly unexpected. There are nearly forty passages in *HN* 7 where some of the material relates to passages from Aristotle's *History of Animals*, *Generation of Animals*, or *Parts of Animals*. Yet, there are no systematic treatments of physiology, embryology, human growth and development. We look in vain for general rules and for the vital statistics of the average male and female. The most striking thing about book 7 is that it is not in fact a survey of Mr or Mrs Average at all, but a tale of the unexpected, a book of human records. Thus we find, for instance, not a description of average gestation and parturition, but a series of multiple, irregular-term, sexually ambiguous, monstrous, or otherwise unusual births (33–52). Discussion of the human lifespan (153 ff.) is in reality a collection of instances of exceptional longevity and the chapters on human stature (73 ff.) comprise a similar anthology of extremes in the form of giants and dwarves. Normality is sometimes described, but usually as a prelude to the extraordinary: for example, the actual discussion of the signs of approaching death is confined to two paragraphs (171–2); a further 17 deal with tales of bizarre and unusual deaths, and out-of-body and near-death episodes (173–90). The nature and frequency of *mirabilia* in book 7 does not have a parallel in the Aristotelian animal works and it may be significant that it is not until book 8 that Pliny acknowledges his debt to Aristotle (*HN* 8. 44–5). It is in books 8–11, rather than book 7, that we find material on the relative physiologies of the human race *as a whole* and that of animals; facts and figures about the average human occur most frequently not in the book dedicated to man but towards the end of the final two books dedicated to animals, 10 and 11. Thus *HN* 10. 171, for example, treats human reproduction in the context of animal reproduction generally and includes such general facts as the position of the human embryo (10. 183). Man's senses are compared to those of other animals and his sleeping habits discussed in connection with those of viviparous animals generally. The various parts of his anatomy are treated in conjunction with those of other animals (*HN* 11. 130–283). All of this is very much in the tradition of Aristotelian natural history, in particular of works like the *Parts of Animals* and *Generation of Animals*; though in these works too, of course, the essential primacy of man is not in question and Pliny's comments in books 10 (e.g. 171–2) and 11 can still put stress on man as the exception, most notably in the remarks on his unique personality and his ability to communicate his thoughts to others through speech.

However, books 8–11 are not lacking in wonder stories either, and it has been claimed[124] that it is precisely the *mirabilia* of books 7–11 which show the connection between man and the other animals: monstrous births link man with animal, whether through actual cross-species mating or in an animal-like product of human intercourse. Animals sometimes display human-like intelligence and other qualities.[125] The link is ambiguous: rather than portraying man as the highest creation, Pliny sometimes suggests that he is a substandard animal, as in the famous passage recounting the well-known theme of man's disadvantages at birth, courtesy of stepmother nature (*HN* 7. 3–7). He rises above animals only in his cruelty, which is refined by his power and intelligence. On this view, Pliny presents not an Aristotelian *scala naturae* but a natural arena of brutal combat for which he frequently uses imagery drawn from the ampitheatre and stage. It is undoubtedly true that combat and cruelty are features of the man–animal relationship in Pliny, as they are of relations between man and man and animal and animal. They mirror in a microcosmic manner the cruelty and showmanship which are features of nature herself in the *HN*.[126] But the idea of man's proximity to animal is less convincing. It is not the only interpretation which can be drawn from the evidence cited. Nor does it take account of all the evidence. Most notably, Pliny states unambiguously at the beginning of book 7 that the human race deserves pride of place in his scheme since nature revolves around its needs to a large extent; an idea in keeping with his largely Stoic-influenced philosophical stance (above, 3.1.3). The elaboration, in sections 2–5, of the stepmother theme can overshadow this declaration but should not be seen as invalidating it: man is indeed awarded first place in the *HN*, both in order of appearance and in the amount of space devoted to him.

But, given that man is at the top, where is he in relation to the next point on the scale? Is the descent to the next highest species of animal life a steep drop or a very gentle curve (above, 4.1)? Book 7

---

[124] Vegetti (1982), 117–31.
[125] 8. 1, 6, 15; 10. 82, 83, 85; 11. 7, 12: but see Beagon (1992), 139–43.
[126] Beagon (1992), 147–56.

offers more clues, even in the negative account of man's early days. Here, the assertion of his primacy is followed by a vivid description of his physical weakness; a weakness which is, moreover, unique to man. Thus in the opening chapters of book 7, Pliny has portrayed the human animal as a paradox, a unique paradox. Not only is it awarded first place in the animal kingdom but, crucially, it is also set apart. Its treatment separately in book 7 is a logical outcome of its uniqueness and the degree to which it is unique is explored through the proliferation of *mirabilia* associated with its natural history. In particular, three recurrent themes may be identified in book 7, which at once emphasize the uniqueness of man and the gulf existing between man and animal; variety, universality, and versatility. They are also representative of qualities inherent in nature herself: the human race, by exhibiting these qualities, becomes in effect a microcosm of nature.

5.2.2. *The Uniqueness of the Human Animal: Variety, Universality, Versatility*

The most fundamental of these themes is that of variety, which seems to lie at the heart of Pliny's discussion of man in book 7 and by implication, or, occasionally, by specific contrast, to separate him from the comparative uniformity of the other animal species. The huge variety of colours to be found among animals is compared to the countless different languages to be found within a single species, the human race; a diversity so marked that, to someone of another race, a foreigner scarcely counts as a human being (7). Still more striking is the uniqueness of every individual human countenance, despite the fact that each is comprised of only a dozen or so basic components (8: above, 4.3). The aim, moreover, is not merely to induce wonder. His examples of variety within the single species of humanity are designed, according to Pliny, to bring home in spectacular fashion the power and majesty of nature. Man the microcosm stands apart from the rest of creation, his variety epitomizing the unique variety of nature itself. The human species reveals within itself a huge variety of subdivisions, or races, and within that huge variety a uniqueness manifest in each individual, with infinite possibilities.

In addition to its variety, the human species possesses a universality of distribution which is not found in other animals. In fact, Pliny puts it down to the remarkable variety of nature, not that certain animals are absent from certain locations but that they actually die if they should be transported to them (*HN* 10.76). For species simply to be absent from an area is, he suggests, quite normal: eagles are absent from the island of Rhodes, storks from an area of lake Como. Similarly, in book 8. 225, he is surprised not so much at nature's assigning of different animals to different countries, but at their absence from some areas but not others within a single region: dormice are found only in one part of the Mesian forest in Etruria. Varieties of human, however, are to be found even beyond the main inhabited world, on the very fringes of the earth, in fact. Pliny tells us that his account of strange races will concentrate especially on people 'living more remote from the sea'; that is, from the inner seas of the inhabited world, as opposed to the Ocean flowing round the outer edge. These fringes were, of course, the traditional locations for such races and Pliny's account duly takes in northern regions beyond Scythia and the furthest reaches of India (*HN* 7. 9ff., 21 ff.). Yet even these 'fringe' races are not invariably confined to specific outlying locations: Pliny stresses that strange habits and customs are to be found much nearer home. The legendary Laestrygones and Cyclopes were said to have inhabited 'the central region of the world' (9); moreover, in recent historical times, just across the Alps, the Gauls had exhibited bizarre customs, including human sacrifice. Peoples with immunity to snake-bite are found not only in Africa (13) but actually within Italy: the Marsi were said to be descendants of Circe. To the Africans, Ethiopians, and Scythians said to possess the Evil Eye are added certain Roman women (17). The source is no Greek paradoxographer, but Marcus Tullius Cicero, who may also be responsible for the adjacent story of fire-walkers on Mount Soracte (19).

Unlike other animals, man is not subject to regional curbs, limitations, and restrictions. The species exhibits a universality in distribution and a variety within that distribution. Other natural limits observed by all animals except man are physiological: man alone can reproduce and give birth at any time of the year (38). Moreover, the period of human gestation varies from six to ten months or more (38); a possibility which gave rise to a judgement in favour of an heir allegedly born after thirteen months (40). Few animals except man have sex during pregnancy or provide examples of superfetation (48). Menstruation occurs only among women and evokes uniquely bizarre stories of its malign influence;

nothing, says Pliny, is more remarkable (63ff.). And yet here too variety is found, in the irregularities or total absence of menstruation in certain women.

The third theme is versatility, which gives rise to perhaps the most striking division between man and beast, when Pliny contrasts the versatility of the human mind with the sluggish uniformity of mental function in other animals (52: above, 4.3). He illustrates this by recounting a popular belief whose origins go back to Empedocles, that maternal impressions at the time of conception influence the physical appearance of the offspring. Moreover, he actually enhances this versatility by differing slightly from the mainstream view and suggesting that thoughts from either parent, not just the mother, may exert such an influence. The uniquely variable human face described in *HN* 7.8 is therefore at least partly the result of man's superior mind. Throughout the *HN*, of course, Pliny shows influence of popular philosophical, especially Stoic, thought (above, 3.1.3): he frequently suggests that man possesses unique powers of rational thought and with it a capacity for moral deliberation.[127] In general, this means that he can find within himself the power to imitate and enhance the variety that is a characteristic of nature itself, as happens in *HN* 7. 52. But he can go beyond or even overturn the normal limits, rules, and regulations of nature; all-year sexual activity, for instance, can lead to a unique insatiability (Claudius' consort Messalina is highlighted as the supreme example in book 10.171) and to immoral and deviant behaviour, crimes against nature, which once again separate man from animal.

Our other example of human mental versatility refers specifically to the problem posed at the beginning of this section: what sort of gap does Pliny envisage between man and the animals? At the end of his last book on animals, dealing with insects, Pliny makes some physiological comparisons between the species. In *HN* 11. 171, he discusses the characteristics of the human voice. Like the countenance, this has as many variations as there are people and it encapsulates a large part of the individual's personality. It is also the source of the linguistic differences between races. 'But above all, it is the source of the power of expressing the thoughts which has made us different from the beasts and has also caused another

---

[127] Beagon (1992), 63–79.

distinction between human beings themselves that is as wide as that which separates them from the beasts.' This is important on two counts. First, we are told that the gap between man and all the other animals is wide and that it is connected with the power of thought and the ability to communicate it to others. Secondly, Pliny uses the wide gap between man and animal to emphasize once again the theme with which we started; the enormous variety which exists within the human species alone. The image of the human species as the microcosm of nature is complete. To the variety and universality are added the versatility of mind, albeit with a twist; human powers of rational and moral deliberation allow for the possibility of perverting the natural law. There is, as Pliny states in *HN* 7. 18, no evil in nature which is not also present in man.

5.2.3. *Separation or Affinity? The Problem of Monsters*

Monstrous births might suggest an affinity rather than a separation between man and animal. There are several striking examples of such births in book 7 and it is worth considering whether they provide evidence of a physical contiguity between humans and animals. Two general points are worth making to start with. First, the fact that the Romans tended to regard such births as dire religious portents, usually requiring expiation and destruction ensured numerous references in annalistic history. One of many occurrences recorded by Livy (31. 12. 8) is specifically stated by the author to have caused horror because it seemed to cross an uncrossable border; nature confusing the species. Secondly, however, it is relatively rare to find such births attributed specifically to literal cross-species copulation, a phenomenon firmly rejected as impossible on grounds of gestatory periods by Aristotle (*GA* 4. 709[b] 13–25). An exception would seem to be the anecdote in Plutarch (*Mor.* 149c–e) about a hippocentaur born on the estate of the tyrant Periander of Corinth, the implied offspring of a mare and a man. The only such reference in Pliny is a story attributed to the paradoxographer Duris, and not confirmed by Pliny himself, that certain 'Indians' copulate with animals and produce animal hybrids (7. 30).

A decline in the interpretation of monstrous births and other wonders as religious portents in the late Republic and early Empire has often been noted (see **33** and **34** comm.). But what of biological attitudes? The Periander story in Plutarch, if, as Robert Garland suggested,[128] it reflects the intellectual climate of Plutarch's own time, has, in his words, merely replaced one form of superstition with another, biological, one. But the tone of that story may be slightly tongue-in-cheek; and the examples of animal-like births in Pliny other than the exotic anecdote from Duris do not suggest this or any other causatory theory. There are several in ch. 34, including two hippocentaurs, one recorded by Claudius as having been born in Thessaly and one actually sent to the emperor preserved in honey. In addition, there is an 'elephant' whose human mother featured in Pompey's public gallery of *mirabilia* and a snake born to a slave girl. These examples are elaborated only by two brief comments. Pliny remarks, apropos of the snake, that such births are definable as portents. The snake birth had occurred at the outbreak of the Social War (91–88 BC), which was in fact the last crisis in Roman history to produce a reasonable crop of reported omens. It may therefore tell us more about the attitudes of a bygone era than about those of the imperial age, in which records of human *monstra* are distinctly thin on the ground.[129] Pliny's own views are difficult to pin down; to judge from other evidence in the *HN*, he may have accepted omens, but on the basis of Sympathy in the universe,[130] as did some Stoics.

His other comment concerns the hippocentaurs; he has personally seen the one sent to Claudius. This, however, is no guarantee of his belief in its authenticity; it may have looked more convincing than the phoenix, also received by Claudius, which Pliny declares (*HN* 10.6) was a patent forgery, or it may have been too poorly preserved for a judgement to be passed either way.

There are, however, rather more serious grounds for doubting the existence in his thinking of a biological notion of human hybrids. Firstly, as we have seen (above, 5.2.2), he adopts the theory of maternal impressions, with which Aristotle (*GA* 4. 709^{b}13–25) specifically connects such births when rejecting literal hybrids on the grounds of differing gestatory periods. Secondly, seeing animal resemblance in such monsters is inevitable; what other point of reference could there be for a living creature which does not look human? We should be careful of reading too much into these refer-

---

[128] Garland (1995), 71–2.
[129] Tac. *Ann.* 15. 47 (reign of Nero); Phlegon fr. 36. 25 (Trajan).
[130] For refs. see Beagon (1992), 101.

ences and bear in mind Pliny's stress on human variety, a feature which in his view could, as we saw (5.2.2), lead to the tendency to regard even foreign speech as barely human. Such births might have struck him as unnerving examples of the infinite variety of nature encapsulated in man rather than evidence of human–animal contiguity.

Finally, it should be noted, briefly, that these animal-like monstrosities occur in the company of wholly human aberrations; hermaphrodites and examples of sex-change. The hermaphrodite's ominous status is specifically stated to be outmoded in favour of their entertainment value (34). They, too, are now examples of the variety of nature and her capacity to fascinate and entertain; just like the monstrous races who were described as nature's *ludibria* or playthings and instances of her marvellous variety (32: 4.3). There is no reason why we should not see the animal-like monstrous births, mentioned in the same section, in a similar light; dwindling in religious significance and lacking any further biological meaning or purpose beyond that of unusual variations on the normal human pattern. That pattern in Pliny's view had so great a potential for variation within itself that theories of cross-breeding with other species were redundant.

5.2.4. *The Human Race: A Species Set Apart*

That the human species was set apart from the other animals is in any case the most obvious conclusion to be drawn from Pliny's description of apparently human-like qualities exhibited by other animals. Three points are worth making briefly.[131] First, Pliny's attitude is similar to the Aristotelian view expressed in the *Historia Animalium* 588[a]; that animals possess to a small degree human emotions such as anger and timidity, but, in the case of human mental powers, animal attributes are analogous only, not identical. Secondly, his attribution of human-like qualities to animals is rarely unmodified; one anecdote, for instance, shows elephants exhibiting 'a sort of understanding of justice', just as they are 'thought' to respect religion or act 'as though' in supplication (*HN* 8. 15). Finally, stories which illustrate these achievements are actually unremarkable in terms of human attainment; the feats are

---

[131] This is a brief summary of arguments set out at greater length in Beagon (1992), 133–44, cf. 63–8.

mechanical and limited and involve lone individuals rather than the whole species: they are the exception rather than the norm for that species, wonders intended to surprise.

Elsewhere, scepticism at human resemblance stories soon creeps in. In *HN* 8. 48, lions alone among animals are said to show mercy. But Pliny is sceptical as to whether they really know what they are doing. Although his source, king Juba II of Mauretania,[132] thought they understood the meaning of entreaties, Pliny says merely that opinions on this point will vary. After a few more stories of apparent animal gratitude to benefactors, his terse comment on the feeding of Romulus and Remus by a she-wolf is that the episode says more about the ultimate destinies of the human twins than about the nature of wild animals (8. 61).

Romulus and Remus had, of course, transcended the law of nature outlined in the opening sections of book 7. Against the odds they survived unprotected the most vulnerable stage of human existence and contrary to expectation were nurtured by their natural predator: nature the stepmother in this instance turned out to be a mother after all. Overall, it seems that there is more evidence for stressing rather than underplaying the gap between man and other animals in the *HN*. Links there certainly are, but often tenuous and limited, as in the case of most anthropomorphic qualities observed in animals. The material in book 7 and the passages referring to man in the other books on animals all display his essential lack of uniformity and conformity. Whereas in the bulk of the animal material in books 8–11 Pliny refers generically to each species —the lion, the elephant, the ostrich, the whale, etc.—and to a general mode of existence common to all members of that species, this is not the case in the book dedicated to man. Certainly, there are examples of general features and statistics, for instance in the opening comments on pregnancy (*HN* 7. 41ff.), infant dentition (68), and human dimensions and weight (77). But they act as a background and benchmark for the tales of the unusual when these normal limits have been stretched or broken.

The material in book 7 is concerned with what makes man human rather than what makes him an animal. Links with books 8–11 are obvious, but the separate treatment of the human species is both logical and symbolic. As man is the *raison d'être* of nature,

---

[132] See *OCD³*, Juba (2) II, 799.

book 7 is pivotal, not just in relation to the following books on animals but to the *HN* as a whole.

5.3. Man the Roman

Over half of book 7, especially 81–130 and 131–90, consists of anecdotes and examples with a Roman background, many of which doubtless formed part of a stock of well-known stories, which Pliny took, directly or indirectly, from Varro, Livy, Valerius Maximus, Verrius Flaccus, and others (above, 4.5.1). The majority illustrate the positive side of the human paradox, by describing remarkable achievements. These are portrayed as worthy not only of note but also of emulation. Moreover, the models that they offer are Roman, with the result that human excellence is defined more specifically as Roman excellence. Cato in *HN*7. 110 is said to exemplify 'the three supreme human achievements; excelling alike as orator, general and senator'. A similar assessment is to be found in Valerius Maximus (*Mem.*8. 7. 1), but Pliny's citation is due to more than a probable predominance of Roman examples in his sources; he makes several statements asserting and promoting Roman domination of excellence and achievement (2.2; n.39). While he cannot disguise the predominance of Greek talent in literature and the arts (107–17), he nonetheless declares in 116 that 'there is a countless series of Roman examples, if one chose to pursue them, since a single race has produced more men of distinction in every field than all the other countries put together'. He skilfully manipulates his material to give Roman genius the edge: while Greek recognition of Greek genius is described first, he describes Roman leaders as having paid tribute 'even to foreigners' (7. 112). This forms an implicit contrast to the Greeks themselves who, as Pliny suggests elsewhere in the *HN* (3. 42), blow nobody's trumpet except their own. Romans, then, are more open-minded, more wide-ranging, more universal in their appreciation of talent, just as their own was shown to be uniquely varied and all-embracing compared to the rest of the world's.

The centrepiece in the collection of anecdotes detailing Roman appreciation of Greek learning is that of Pompey's visit to the philosopher and polymath Posidonius, where the general to whom east and west paid tribute, the epitome of the traditional Roman skills of government and warfare, pays tribute to the embodiment of learning (112). Not that the paths of culture and of the arts of government and warfare were necessarily separate. Posidonius' interests included political theory (112 comm.). In addition, when recounting the honours given to the scholar Varro (115), Pliny creates a complex interplay of the traditional Roman values he had attributed to Cato in 110 with intellectual achievement. Pollio, statesman and orator, honours Varro, an outstanding scholar. The leading general Pompey honours the same scholar for his bravery. Both honours, military and intellectual, are said to be of equal value; both are held by a Roman. Finally, the self-consciously rhetorical passage which forms an apt tribute to the genius of M. Cicero (7. 116–17) uses apostrophized paradox ('Hail, first recipient of a triumph in a toga', etc.) together with the notorious line from Cicero's poetry ('Let arms to the toga yield') to turn his lack of the military component of the Roman genius to his advantage. Here, however, Pliny ends by extolling Cicero's achievement as the father of Roman rhetoric above the laurels of any general. Paradoxically, he is quoting one of Rome's most gifted generals, Caesar. Even more paradoxically, it is questionable whether Cicero would have approved of this judgement in favour of his literary rather than political immortality. In part, it reflects, perhaps, Pliny's personal valuation of the literary creativity he himself pursued in addition to a political career whose scope was more limited than in Cicero's day.

The integration of literary with traditional political and military skills was, as we saw earlier (2.1), a characteristic of the *HN*'s dedicatee, Titus, which allowed Pliny an opportunity for a complimentary rhetorical conceit in the preface. More generally, the combination enhances the variety and scope of the whole Roman achievement. The Roman people thus encapsulate the achievement and wondrous versatility of the human paradox and Pliny completes his discussion of the various types of excellence with the statement that 'the one race of outstanding excellence (*virtus*) among all the races in the whole world is undoubtedly the Roman' (7. 129).

Overall, Pliny's comments on the Roman achievement epitomize the two basic characteristics of the human race as a whole, discussed earlier: variety and universality. Rome offers many examples of every kind of excellence and outstrips in her variety and comprehensiveness the whole of the rest of the world. The Roman race is a microcosm of the human race, a fact which justifies its predominance among the examples of book 7. We may compare briefly the passage discussed earlier (above, 4.4), *HN* 27. 3, in which Rome is described as a second sun, given by nature to the human race. By virtue of her fostering of global prosperity through the peace engendered by her military and imperial might she mimics the mind of the world and ruling principle of nature, to quote Pliny's own description of the sun in *HN* 2. 14. In her beneficence and power, she is, in effect, a microcosm of nature herself.

5.4. The Human Paradox

Throughout the *HN*, the themes of universality, versatility, and variety are used to enhance the overall uniqueness of the human animal. In a natural world which never ceases to excite wonderment, man is the ultimate natural wonder. The basic paradox is the discrepancy between man's apparent fragility and his actual potential, but even within each of these extremes, there is the potential for almost infinite variety and countless departures from the norm, as can be seen in the treatments of the physiological and emotional frailties of the human condition. In addition, the idea of paradox is expressed in the many different ways in which the individual examples of achievement break away from the norm to become exceptional. In both cases, the paradox offers an opportunity for literary embellishment in accordance with the rhetorical emphasis in the literature of Pliny's day.

Looking first at the general human condition, we find within the confines of human frailty an enormous potential for variety and the unusual. In addition to the famous paragraphs on the weakness of the human infant (7. 1–6), Pliny points to the finely balanced nature of human physiology in its prime; and then, finally, to the variety of ways in which death can strike. The emphasis is not on man's frailty and mortality as a sign of his affinity with the rest of the living organisms in nature. It is more on the exceptional contrast between his potential and his vulnerability; the human being is a construction whose finely tuned complexity renders it exceptionally sensitive. Thus, for example, Pliny decries the ease with which the human embryo can be spontaneously aborted (43) or the delicate human memory damaged by a comparatively minor accident (90). Old age appears to be as great a fiasco of nature as infancy, with the vital parts dying off in advance of the whole being (168). When it comes to diseases and modes of death, man is once more contrasted with the other animals in the variety of patterns (169–70) of disease which can strike him. The number and variety of such diseases is considered elsewhere in the *HN* (25. 29, 26. 3). For the human being, death does not even have to follow upon a set pattern of disease or physical disintegration: Pliny gives examples of the countless different ways in which death has struck a variety of individuals suddenly and for no obvious reason (180–6). These, he says, are among the most miraculous of natural occurrences (180). Most paradoxical of all are the cases suggesting the uncertainty of death even in so frail a creature. Sections 180–90 describe a variety of miraculous revivals of the apparently dead and near-death experiences.

The other basic paradox unique to human existence is that of quality of life. This, again, depends on an emotional capacity and an intellectual perception quantitatively and qualitatively greater than those of animals. The human being's excessive and potentially destructive emotions are listed in the stepmother passage (7. 5). Happiness is an elusive and subjective quality, according to Pliny in 7.130, and in the final analysis the very consciousness of human frailty and the possibility of fortune's mutability make total security and peace of mind impossible. In the following 22 sections, he explores the ups and downs of life. The more illustrious his individual example, the greater the paradox of success and setback. Unsurprisingly, the climax of this discussion is the Roman who was arguably the most powerful to date, the emperor Augustus (147–50).

If we move from the negative to the positive, we can return for a moment to the treatment of outstanding human intellects. The skill with which Pliny gives his discussion a Roman bias has already been noted (above, 5.3). Other aspects of his treatment in some ways reinforce the unique nature of the human intelligence. The achievement of the individual is not just important for the reputation of that individual but reflects the standards and aspirations of the rest of the human community, here represented by its most prestigious and powerful members: kings, emperors, and generals. The examples are not simply stated as self-evident but are accredited by external recognition. The supremacy of Homer, for example, is proclaimed by Alexander the Great (107–8), who also paid homage to Pindar and Aristotle. Lysander was reportedly inspired by a divine dream to allow the burial of Sophocles during the siege of Athens, Plato was honoured by Dionysius of Syracuse, and Menander by the kings of Egypt and Macedon (109–11). In the Roman sphere, the testimony of Pompey to the philosopher and scholar Posidonius has already been mentioned; while the younger Cato had a habit of collecting prize philosophers on his travels (113). Romans paid tribute to Romans: Scipio Africanus to Ennius, Augustus to Virgil, Pollio to Varro and the whole Roman people to Cicero. A similar pattern of high-profile or public recognition may be observed in the scientific and artistic examples of (123–7). The unique human powers of communication and memory described elsewhere by Pliny (*HN* 11. 271; 27. 7)[133] ensure recognition of one person's talents by another, leading to transmission, emulation, and the creation of a coherent tradition. Pliny is not talking here of some lone animal performing unusual tricks in isolation from its peers. The skill of such animals cannot be taught or passed on or even appreciated by other animals and has to be assessed in human terms of reference alien to its species. In addition, the examples of human genius are just the tip of the iceberg: the most distinguished exponents of their art attested by the most prestigious and authoritative of admirers. Together with the variety of the human genius stressed at the beginning of the passage (107), there is a universality, a common experience or standard from which outstanding examples are sprung and against which they can be measured.

Moving from the general human condition to the particular individual, the example of Pompey (95–9) incorporates the paradox idea on several levels. He broke with the normal constraints and conventions of the Roman political career, triumphing while still of equestrian rank and becoming an army commander despite never having served in the ranks (Pliny here ignores Pompey's service under his father in the Social War). The conquest of the world by a single man was also a paradox: while Pliny acknowledges that in this respect Pompey was outmatched by Caesar, whose iconography portrayed him with a globe, the former's triumphs over three continents were often portrayed as a world conquest and were represented as such in his triumph of 61 BC. The comparisons to legendary and historical world-conquerors which Pompey encouraged are articulated by Pliny (95–6), while the Pompeian conquests are portrayed as an ever-widening sweep, from Sicily and Africa to

---

[133] See Beagon (1992), 133–4.

the west, the seas, and finally the east. The overall impression is one of world-conquest, of the universality of Pompey's achievement and thus of Rome's. The language of Pliny's claim that Pompey 'found Asia on the fringes and left her at the heart of his country's empire' (99) conjures up an almost literal translocation, a modification of nature itself. This was, of course, the man whose displays of *mirabilia* as statues (34: and above, 4.2, n. 72) and as live exhibits (158) in his theatre are described elsewhere in book 7. They were symbolic of their extraordinary exhibitor whose triumphal procession in 61 included ebony trees, an implicit equation of his conquest of the world with that of nature itself. Another well-attested novelty, the elephants at the games of 55 BC, caused Pliny's younger contemporary, Seneca, to remark that Pompey was a man who thought he was above nature (*Brev. Vit.* 13. 7).

Our final example incorporates the extremes of the human paradox; the enhancement of the human capacity for achievement by the variety of circumstances which may curb or negate it any any time. What singles out Marcus Sergius Silus (104–6), great-grandfather of Cicero's opponent Catiline, is not his bravery as such: there were plenty of other examples of that in the annals of Roman history. It is his perseverance in the face of circumstances which would have deterred most others. The paradox of Marcus Sergius was multifaceted. He became a military hero although he lost the most basic physical attribute of a warrior, his right hand. He survived at the hands of Hannibal, Rome's deadliest enemy, not once but twice. More poignantly, he showed conspicuous bravery worthy of military decoration in campaigns which proved too calamitous to yield such rewards. Unfortunately, we do not know whether he won his final battle, with his fellow-praetors who sought to debar him from public sacrifice on the grounds of his disability. For Pliny, he is the greatest example of the supremacy of Roman *virtus* and of the triumph of the human spirit over fortune.

Sergius thus epitomizes the two strands of the human paradox. Man the animal defies his own human frailty by mental and emotional toughness and contradicts his natural condition. Man the Roman's moral and physical excellence, his *virtus*, conquers adversity. In Roman Stoic fashion, it even outweighs the absence of the normal external trappings of happiness; honours and the acclaim of his peers. Pompey had been acclaimed in three triumphs and had been heaped with wealth and honours; Cicero was accorded unparalleled honours as a civilian and won an accolade even from his enemy Caesar. Lack of conventional reward makes M. Sergius perhaps the most outstanding human paradox in book 7[134].

5.5. The Catalogue of Inventors, 7. 190–209

Pliny's emphasis on the close and complex interaction of man the wonder with nature also accounts for the extraordinary catalogue of human inventors and inventions in *HN* 7. 190–209. A detailed discussion of its literary and cultural antecedents is given in the commentary. At first sight, this list appears to have been added by way of an afterthought, after Pliny has concluded the final chapter in the natural history of man: a consideration of death and the fate of the soul. In fact, it is very much in keeping with the tone of the *HN* as a whole, in which so much of the natural world is described in relation to man's use and exploitation of it. We would expect, in a work where culture and nature are inextricably linked, to find a discussion of man's cultural as well as his natural history.

It is also the logical outcome of Pliny's historical instinct for such matters. The *HN* is dotted with small-scale cultural histories, three of which, on writing, hair-cutting, and time-keeping, follow the catalogue and close the book; the catalogue itself offers, in a book devoted to the human race, a kind of historical summary of the ultimate origins of every aspect of basic human culture. Additionally, it is, in a sense, a historicizing of the *mirabilia* mentality: contemporary discoveries point forward to future developments, but they are equally a reminder that everything was once new.

Finally, the catalogue form itself, with its hasty, truncated references to dozens of inventors and inventions, mirrors the catalogue of diverse human oddities invented by nature in 7. 9–33. Once again, in book 7, the spectrum of human genius is shown to rival the variety of nature itself.

The inclusion in book 7 of a catalogue of inventors further emphasizes its pivotal role as an epitome of the *HN* as a whole. This account of human interaction with and development in the natural world encapsulates on a small scale the macrocosmic sweep of the *HN* in its totality as a human history of the natural world. The enduring popularity of the *HN* has already been remarked upon,

---

[134] For a detailed discussion of Sergius, see Beagon, 'Beyond Comparison: M. Sergius, *Fortunae Victor*', in G. Clarke and T. Rajak (eds.), *Philosophy and Power in the Graeco-Roman World: Essays in Honour of Miriam Griffin* (Oxford, 2002), 111–32.

together with the changing approaches of successive generations to what it has to offer (4.6.1 and above, this section). In one sense, however, the appeal of the *HN* has been timeless and unchanging: human fascination with the human remains constant and will probably ensure the continuing survival of the *HN* as a whole, and of book 7 in particular.

TRANSLATION

(**1**) The world and its component lands, peoples, seas . . . islands and cities are as I have described above. The nature of its animals is as worthy of study as almost any other part thereof, if in fact the human mind is capable of exploring everything. The first place will rightly be assigned to man, for whose benefit great nature seems to have created everything else. However, for her considerable gifts she exacts a cruel fee; so that it is difficult to decide whether she is more of a kind parent or a harsh stepmother to man. (**2**) First and foremost, man alone of all her creatures nature dresses in borrowed clothes. To the others she assigns a variety of coverings: shells, bark, hides, spines, fur, bristles, hair, down, feathers, scales, fleeces. Even the tree trunks she protects from cold and heat by bark, sometimes in two layers. Man alone on his natal day she flings forth naked on the naked ground to erupt instantaneously into weeping and wailing. No other among so many animals is given to tears and these at the very beginning of life! In marked contrast, the well-known smile of infancy is, even in its earliest manifestation, given to no child before the fortieth day. (**3**) Chains of a kind experienced not even by domestic animals follow this introduction to the light of day and fetter all his limbs. Thus auspiciously delivered, the animal destined to rule all others lies bound hand and foot, weeping, and his life is initiated by punishment for one fault alone—the crime of being born. How misguided are those who believe that from these beginnings they were born to a position of pride!

(**4**) His initial promise of strength, his first taste of the gift of life, renders him similar to a four-footed beast. When can man walk? When can he speak? When is his mouth strong enough to chew food? For how long does his skull throb, marking him out as the weakest of all animals? Then there are diseases and all the cures contrived to counter illness, only to be themselves defeated in due course by new maladies. All other animals are instinctively aware of their own natures, one exercising fleetness of foot, another swiftness of flight, others their ability to swim. Man, however, can do nothing unless he is taught, neither speaking nor walking nor eating. In short, he can do nothing by natural instinct except weep! As a result, there have been many who have thought it best not to be born at all, or else to die as soon as possible.

(5) To man alone in the animal kingdom is granted the capacity for sorrow, for self-indulgence of every kind and in every part of his body, for ambition, avarice, unbounded appetite for life and superstition; for anxiety over burial and even over what will happen after he is dead. To no animal is assigned a more precarious life, more all-consuming passions, more disruptive fear, or more violent anger. Finally, the other animals coexist in a proper manner with their own kind. We see them flock together to make a common stand against animals different from themselves. Lions do not vent their ferocity against each other; snakes do not try to bite other snakes. Even the sea-monsters and fishes fight only against other species. But in man's case, by heaven, most dangers emanate from other men!

(6) The human race in general has for the most part been discussed in my account of the peoples of the world. Nor will I be dealing here with habits and customs, which are countless and almost on a par with the number of human communities. There is material, however, especially concerning those peoples furthest from the sea, which I do not think should be left out. It includes facts which will, I am sure, seem extraordinary and unbelievable to many readers. Who, after all, believed in the Ethiopians before actually seeing them? And what is not regarded as wondrous when it first gains public attention? How many things are judged impossible before they actually happen? (7) Indeed, the power and might of nature lacks credibility at every point unless we comprehend her as a whole rather than piecemeal. To say nothing of peacocks, the stippled coats of tigers and panthers, and the markings of so many animals, it is a small task to mention, but a boundless one to estimate, the great number of human languages, dialects, and modes of speech; so great, indeed, that to a man of another race a foreigner barely passes for a human being! (8) And again, although we possess few more than ten facial features, no two identical faces exist among so many thousands of human beings. This is something which no art could have succeeded in copying when using such a small number of components. Nonetheless, I shall not pledge my word as to the reliability of most of these facts, but shall ascribe them instead to the sources, who will be referred back to on all doubtful issues. We should certainly not disdain to follow the

Greek writers whose commitment goes further back in time and whose scholarship is correspondingly greater.

(9) I have mentioned that there are Scythian tribes, a good number in fact, which eat human flesh. This might well seem unbelievable were we not to bear in mind that in the centre of the world and in Sicily there once existed peoples equally bizarre, the Cyclopes and the Laestrygones; and that very recently, it was the custom of tribes beyond the Alps to practise human sacrifice, which is only one step removed from cannibalism.

(10) Next to those Scythians who face northwards and not far from the actual rising of the North Wind and the cave bearing his name, the place called the Entrance to Earth's Windpipe, are found the Arimaspi whom I spoke of earlier and who are distinguished by a single eye in the middle of their foreheads. Many writers, of whom the most distinguished are Herodotus and Aristeas of Proconnesus, tell us that these people are engaged in an ongoing battle over gold mines with the griffins, a type of winged animal according to popular tradition, which dig out the gold from their burrows. The beasts try to protect the gold while the Arimaspi try to steal it, both parties displaying amazing rapacity.

(11) Beyond other man-eating Scythian tribes, in a certain large valley on Mt. Imavus, is a region called Abarimon. Here live wild men of the woods whose feet are turned back to front. They run very fast and roam abroad with the wild beasts. These people cannot breathe in a foreign climate and for that reason cannot be brought to the neighbouring kings and had not been brought to Alexander the Great according to his route-surveyor, Baeton.

(12) According to Isigonus of Nicaea, the first-mentioned man-eating Scythians, who I said lived to the north ten days' journey beyond the river Borysthenes, drink out of human skulls, using the scalps, hair and all, like napkins to cover their chests. The same author says that in Albania there are born people with grey eyes who are white-haired from childhood and see better by night than by day. He also states that thirteen days' journey beyond the Borysthenes are the Sauromatae who eat every other day.

(13) According to Crates of Pergamum, there was a tribe near Parium in the Hellespont whom he calls the Ophiogenes. They used to cure snakebite by touch, drawing the poison out of the body by laying their hands on it. Varro says that there are still a few people there whose saliva is effective in the treatment of snakebites.

(**14**) There was a similar race in Africa called the Psylli, according to Agatharchides, named after king Psyllus who lies buried in the region of the Greater Syrtes. Their bodies contained a poison lethal to snakes and its smell was enough to render the creatures unconscious. It was this tribe's custom to expose their infants immediately after birth to the most savage snakes and by this method test the fidelity of their wives, since the snakes do not flee from those who are impure of blood. This people has itself been almost exterminated by the Nasamones who now occupy that area. But there are persons descended from those who had died or were absent at the time of the fighting who live on in a few places even today. (**15**) A similar race, the Marsi, survives in Italy. They are allegedly descended from Circe's son and consequently born naturally with this power. There is, however, a substance poisonous to snakes innate in every human being. For it is said that when snakes are touched with human saliva they flee as if scalded with boiling water; and if the saliva gets into their throat, they actually die, especially if it comes from the mouth of a fasting man.

Beyond the Nasamones are the Machlyae, their neighbours, who, according to Calliphanes, are hermaphrodites who possess the features of both sexes and cohabit with each in turn. Aristotle adds that their right breast is male and their left female. (**16**) According to Isigonus and Nymphodorus, there are in the same part of Africa certain families of sorcerers whose eulogies cause sheep to perish, trees to wither and babies to die. Isigonus adds that there are persons of the same sort among the Triballes [and the Illyrians] who bewitch with a mere glance and actually kill those whom they stare at for any length of time, especially if the stare is an angry one. Adults are more susceptible to their spell. A particularly remarkable feature is their double pupil in each eye.

(**17**) Apollonides says that there are women of this type in Scythia, called Bitiae. Phylarchus also reports the Thibii and many other tribes of the same kind in Pontus who he says are distinguished by a double pupil in one eye and the image of a horse in the other. He also claims that they cannot be drowned, even when weighted down with clothing. Damon records a similar tribe in Ethiopia, called the Pharmaces, whose sweat causes the bodies that it touches to waste away. (**18**) In addition, among our own Roman writers, Cicero tells us that all women everywhere with double pupils possess the Evil Eye. To such an extent did nature see fit, when she had planted in man the bestial habit of eating human flesh, to plant additional poisons in his whole body and even in the eyes of some people, so that no evil should exist which was not also present in man.

(**19**) In the territory of the Falisci, not far from Rome, are a few families called the Hirpi who walk across a heap of glowing charcoal at the annual festival of Apollo on Mt. Soracte without getting burnt. On account of this, they have been granted permanent exemption from military service and all other public duties by senatorial decree.

(**20**) Certain persons are born with bodily features exhibiting remarkable qualities in specific circumstances: the right toe of king Pyrrhus, for example, used to cure splenetic diseases at a touch. It is reported that this toe could not be cremated with the rest of his body and was stored in a casket inside a temple.

(**21**) India and the territory of the Ethiopians are particularly abundant in marvels. The largest animals are produced in India; her dogs, for example, are bigger than those found elsewhere. The trees, they say, grow so tall that it is impossible to shoot an arrow over them. So great is the fertility of the soil, the mildness of the climate and the supply of water that squadrons of cavalry are sheltered by a single fig tree, if you can believe it. The reeds are so tall that a section taken from between two nodules makes a boat for up to three people. (**22**) It is well known that many of the natives are over five cubits (2.2 m.) tall, do not spit and do not suffer any pains in the head, teeth or eyes and rarely in any other part of the body, so toughened are they by the moderate heat of the sun. Their philosophers, whom they call Gymnosophists, stare steadfastly at the sun from dawn to dusk with unflinching eyes, standing for the whole day first on one foot then on the other in the burning sand.

On a mountain called Nulus, according to Megasthenes, there are people with feet turned backwards and eight toes on each; (**23**) while on many mountains there is a race of dog-headed men who dress in animal skins, bark rather than talk and live on animals and birds which they hunt armed only with their nails. He says there were more than 150, 000 of them at the time he was writing.

Ctesias also writes that in a certain Indian tribe the women give birth once in a lifetime and the hair of their children starts turning grey from the moment of birth. He also says that there is a race of men called the Monocoli ('One-legged men') by virtue of their single leg which enables them to jump with amazing agility. They are also called Sciapodae ('Shady-feet') because when it gets too hot they lie down on their backs on the ground and protect themselves with the shadow of their foot. Ctesias says they live not far away from the Trogodytae ('Cavemen') and that to the west of the latter live men without necks who have eyes in their shoulders.

(24) There are also satyrs in the east Indian mountains (the region of the Catarcludi); the satyr is an exceptionally fleet-footed creature with a human appearance which runs sometimes on all four legs and sometimes upright. Because of its swiftness only old or sick specimens are captured. Tauron mentions a forest tribe called the Choromandae who do not talk but emit harsh shrieks. They have hairy bodies, grey eyes, and the fangs of a dog. According to Eudoxus, there are men in southern India with feet a cubit (.444 m.) long, and women with feet so small they are called Struthopodes ('Sparrowfeet').

(25) Megasthenes describes a tribe of nomadic Indians called the Sciratae who only have holes where their nostrils should be and snake-like strap feet. At the easternmost borders of India near the source of the Ganges he places the Astomi, a people with no mouths. They have hair all over their bodies and dress in cotton-wool. They live only on the air they breathe and the odours they inhale through their nostrils. They have no food or drink but only the smells from the roots, flowers, and crab-apples which they take with them on long journeys so as never to lack a scent supply. A slightly stronger smell than usual can easily kill them.

(26) Beyond them, in the remotest region of the mountains are reputed to live the Trispithami ('Three-span men') and the Pygmies. They are never more than three spans in height, that is, twenty-seven inches (.666 m.). Protected by the mountains from the North Wind, the climate is healthy and perpetually spring-like. Homer has also recorded that this tribe is plagued by cranes. The story goes that in springtime the whole company goes down to the sea, mounted on the backs of rams and nanny-goats and armed with arrows, to eat the cranes' eggs and chicks. The expedition is over in three months and without it, the Pygmies would be overcome by the growing flocks of cranes. Their houses are made of mud, feathers and eggshell. (27) Aristotle, however, says they live in caves, although in other respects his account accords with the rest. Isigonus says that the Indian tribe called the Cyrni live for 140

years, as do the long-lived Ethiopians, the Seres, and the inhabitants of Mount Athos, the latter because they live on snake-meat and their hair and clothes are therefore not infested with parasites. (28) Onesicritus says that in the parts of India where no shadows fall, men grow to be five cubits and two spans tall, live for 130 years, and do not grow old but die middle-aged. Crates of Pergamum mentions Indians who live more than a hundred years. He calls them Gymnetae, though many people call them the Macrobii or Long-livers. Ctesias says that one of their tribes in the mountain valleys, the Pandae, live for two hundred years and are white-haired in youth but grow black-haired in old age. (29) Others, however, neighbours of the Macrobii, live no longer than forty years. Their women give birth just once in a lifetime. The same story is told by Agatharchides, who adds that they live on locusts and are fleet-footed. Clitarchus calls them the Mandi and Megasthenes attributes three hundred villages to them. He also says that the women bear children at 7 and that old age starts at 40.

(30) Artemidorus says that on the island of Ceylon, the people live very long lives without the onset of bodily infirmity. Duris claims that some Indians copulate with animals and the offspring are human–animal hybrids; and that among the Calingae who live in the same part of India, the women conceive at 5 years old and do not live longer than 8 years, and in another part of India he says that men with hairy tails are born who can run very fast; others are entirely enveloped by their ears.

The Oritae are separated from the Indians by the river Arabis. The only food they know is fish, which they tear apart with their nails and roast in the sun. In this way they make bread from them, according to Clitarchus. (31) Crates of Pergamum says that beyond the Ethiopians are Trogodytae who are swifter than horses. He also says there are Ethiopians more than twelve cubits high: they are called Syrbotae. The tribe of nomad Indians called the Menismini along the river Astragus to the north is twenty days' journey from the sea. It lives on the milk of the animals we call Cynocephali, herds of which it pastures, killing the male animals except when needed for breeding purposes.

(32) In the African deserts human phantoms suddenly appear before your eyes and then vanish away in a moment.

Nature has cleverly contrived these and similar species of the human race to amuse herself and to amaze us. As for the individual creations she produces every day, and almost every hour, who could possibly reckon them up? Let it be a sufficient revelation of her power to have placed entire races among her miracles. From these, we turn to acknowledged facts concerning the individual man.

(33) The birth of triplets is a phenomenon well attested by the cases of the Horatii and the Curiatii. Higher multiple births are to be ranked as portentous except in Egypt, where drinking the waters of the Nile enhances fertility. Near the time of the divine Augustus' funeral, a plebeian woman called Fausta gave birth at Ostia to two boys and two girls, clearly predicting the famine which followed. We also find a case in the Peloponnese of a woman who gave birth four times to quintuplets and the majority of infants from each of the births survived. In Egypt, Trogus reports a case of septuplets.

(34) People are also born participating in both sexes at once. We call them hermaphrodites, and, though they were once called *androgyni* and regarded as portents, they are now regarded as pets. Pompey the Great placed among the decorations of his theatre the statues of renowned marvels, sculpted for this purpose with particular attention by the virtuosity of leading artists. Among them can be read the name of Eutychis, who was carried to her funeral pyre in Tralles by twenty children, having given birth thirty times; and of Alcippe, who gave birth to an elephant. This, however, should be classed as a portent, for a slave girl also gave birth to a snake at the beginning of the Marsic war and all sorts of monstrous births are recorded as prodigies. (35) Claudius Caesar writes that a hippocentaur was born in Thessaly and died on the same day; and in his principate I actually saw one which had been brought to him from Egypt preserved in honey. Amongst other examples is the case of an infant from Saguntum who went straight back into the womb in the year the city was destroyed by Hannibal.

(36) Women changing into men is no fantasy. We find in the Annals that during the consulship of P. Licinius Crassus and C. Cassius Longinus a girl living with her parents in Casinum changed into a boy and was transported to a barren island at the command of the soothsayers. Licinius Mucianus has recorded that he actually saw at Argos a man called Arescon who had been given the name Arescusa at birth and had even married a husband, but then grew a beard, developed male attributes, and took a wife. He also records seeing a boy at Smyrna who had experienced the same

sex change. I myself saw in Africa one L. Consitius, a citizen of Thysdrus who had turned into a man on his wedding day [and who was still alive at the time of writing].

(37) . . . when twins are born, it is rare for the mother or more than one baby to live. If there is one baby of each sex, the survival of both children is even less common. Girls are born more quickly than boys, just as they grow old more quickly. Boys move more often in the womb and are generally carried on the right side, while girls are carried on the left.

(38) Other animals have a fixed season for parturition and gestation. The human animal, however, gives birth at any time of the year and the human period of gestation is variable, some women giving birth in the seventh month, others in the eighth and even as late as the beginning of the eleventh month. A baby born before the seventh month is never viable. Only children conceived on the day before or after a full moon or at the time of no moon are born in the seventh month. (39) In Egypt, it is quite normal to give birth in the eighth month and even in Italy such births are viable, despite the view to the contrary held by our ancestors. All such matters exhibit considerable variations. Vistilia, the wife of Glitius and later of Pomponius Secundus and then Orfitus, all most distinguished citizens, had by these husbands four children, all of whom were born in the seventh month. But she then produced Suillius Rufus in the eleventh month and Corbulo in the seventh, both of whom became consuls. After them came Caesonia, later wife of the emperor Gaius Caligula, born in the eighth month.

(40) For infants born in the eighth month, the period of greatest risk is that prior to the fortieth day after birth. For their mothers, it is the fourth and eighth month of pregnancy: miscarriages in these periods are fatal.

Masurius tells us that when an heir in the second degree went to court for the possession of an estate, the praetor, L. Papirius, found against him since, although the first heir's mother declared he had been born in the thirteenth month, no fixed period of gestation seemed to have been laid down.

(41) Ten days from conception, headaches, dizziness, fainting, distaste for food and vomiting are signs that an embryo is being formed. Women carrying a boy have a better colour and an easier delivery and feel movement in the womb on the fortieth day. With a girl, all the signs are the opposite; the burden is difficult to carry,

there is slight swelling of the legs and groin and the first movement is felt on the ninetieth day.

(42) But in the case of both sexes, the greatest tiredness is felt when the foetus is growing hair and at the time of the full moon, a period which is also especially dangerous to all new-born babies. Her gait and just about every other aspect of her life is so important in the pregnant woman, that those who eat over-salted food bear babies lacking nails and those who do not hold their breath give birth with greater difficulty. Indeed, yawning in childbirth can be fatal, just as sneezing after intercourse causes abortion.

(43) If we consider the precarious origins of the proudest of animals, we are filled with pity and shame. The very smell from lamps being put out is often enough to cause abortion. Yet it is from such beginnings as these that tyrants and murderers are born! You who trust in your physical strength, (44) you who embrace the gifts of fortune and consider yourself not merely her foundling but her true-born child, you who aspire to rule all and, when swollen with some success or other, think that you are god himself: could you be annihilated in so trifling a manner? In fact, you can today be obliterated by a smaller mishap still, as tiny as the tooth of the snake that bites you, or the morsel of raisin which choked the poet Anacreon, or the single hair in a drink of milk which choked the praetor, Fabius Senator. In order, then, to achieve a balanced view of life, it is necessary to be ever mindful of human frailty.

(45) It is unnatural to be born feet first. For this reason, those who are born in this manner are called 'Agrippa', meaning 'born with difficulty'. It is said that Marcus Agrippa was one such person and his was almost the only instance of a fortunate destiny among all those born in this way. Yet even he is thought to have suffered the misfortune predicted by his unnatural birth, since he was plagued by lameness, had a miserable childhood, passed his adult life amidst strife and death and left a legacy of destruction, since his progeny all brought misfortune on the world; in particular, the two Agrippinas, mother and daughter, who gave birth respectively to the emperors Gaius and Domitius Nero, both of them destructive firebrands of the human race. In addition, his life was cut short (46) and he was snatched away in his fifty-first year, tormented by the adulteries of his wife and oppressed by his subjection to his father-in-law. Nero, too, who was until recently emperor and whose reign proved him to be an enemy of the human race, is said

by his mother Agrippina in her memoirs to have been born feet first. It is the law of nature for a human being to be born head first and it is the custom for him to be carried to his grave feet first.

(47) Those delivered when their mother has been cut open are born under better auspices. The elder Scipio Africanus was one such, as was the first of the Caesars, who owed his name to the surgery performed on his mother, the same operation which gave rise to the family name Caeso. Manilius, who entered Carthage with an army, was born in a similar fashion.

The surname Vopiscus was given to a twin child retained in the womb and carried to term after the other had perished through premature delivery. For it is a fact that there are rare but remarkable cases of survival in such circumstances.

(48) Few animals apart from humans have sexual intercourse while pregnant and in only one or two at most does superfetation occur. We find in the medical archives and in the records of those interested in researching such phenomena that, in one instance, twelve foetuses were expelled in a single abortion. But when only a short space of time has elapsed between two conceptions, both may be carried to full term; (49) as is shown by the case of Hercules and his brother Iphicles, and also by the case of a woman who gave birth to twins, one of whom resembled her husband and the other her lover. Similarly, a slave girl from Proconnesus gave birth to twins, one of whom resembled her master and the other his steward, having originally had intercourse with both men on the same day. Another woman gave birth in a single confinement to a five-month foetus and a full-term baby. Yet another case was that of a woman who gave birth to a seven months' child and was then delivered of twins in the following months.

(50) The following facts are well known: sound parents may produce deformed children and deformed parents may produce sound children or children with the same deformity as themselves. Birthmarks, moles, and even scars can reappear in descendants, a tattoo sometimes recurring up to the fourth generation among the Dacians.

(51) In the family of the Lepidi, we are told that three children were born, though not in successive generations, with an eye covered by a membrane.

Other children, again, may resemble their grandfather, and, in the case of twins, one may resemble the father, the other the mother. A child born a year later may resemble an elder sibling as if they were twins. Some women always bear children like themselves, others bear children like their husbands, and others again bear children with no resemblance to either parent. Some women bear girls resembling the father and boys resembling the mother herself. Incontrovertible evidence is offered by the case of the famous boxer Nicaeus who was born in Byzantium. His mother was the offspring of an adulterous relationship with an Ethiopian. Yet although her skin pigmentation was no different from that of the rest of the family, her son was the image of his Ethiopian grandfather.

(52) Resemblances offer considerable food for thought. They are believed to be influenced by many chance occurrences, including sight, hearing, memory, and images absorbed at the very moment of conception. Even a chance thought which briefly crosses the mind of one or other parent may form or confuse the resemblance. This is the reason why there are more variations within the human race than there are among all the other animals: the swiftness of man's thoughts, his mental agility and the versatility of his intelligence produce a wide variety of features; whereas the minds of other creatures are sluggish and exhibit a uniformity in keeping with their particular species.

(53) A low-born man called Artemo bore such a striking resemblance to king Antiochus of Syria that his queen, Laodice, having murdered her husband, successfully used the lookalike to stage a play aimed at effecting her commendation and succession to the throne. A plebeian called Vibius and a mere freedman, Publicius, so closely resembled Pompey the Great that they were almost indistinguishable from him. Both mirrored that honourable countenance and the nobility of that distinguished brow.

(54) A similar coincidence encumbered Pompey's father with the surname Menogenes, the name of his cook, when he already had the surname Strabo because of an eye defect, a fault also replicated in his slave. The lowly slave of a pig dealer gave the name Serapio to a Scipio. In a later generation, the actor Salvitto gave his name to a Scipio of the same family branch. Similarly, Spinther and Pamphilus, who acted second and third roles respectively, gave their names to the consular colleagues Lentulus and Metellus; a fluke which resulted in an extremely unfortunate coincidence when spitting images of both consuls appeared simultaneously on stage.

(55) Conversely, the orator L. Plancus gave a surname to the actor Rubrius and on the other hand, Burbuleius and Menogenes, both actors, gave their names respectively to the elder Curio and the former censor, Messalla. A fisherman in Sicily reproduced not only the physical appearance of the proconsul Sura but even the way he opened his mouth when talking, his drawling tone, and his confused speech. The famous orator Cassius Severus was taunted for his resemblance to the gladiator Armentarius.

[Recently, in Annaeus' house it was difficult to distinguish Gallio from the freedman Castellanus or the senator Agrippinus from the actor Sannius, whose surname was Paris.]

(56) The slave-dealer Toranius sold to Mark Antony after he became triumvir two exceedingly handsome boys, one of whom had been born in Asia and the other north of the Alps. Yet they were so alike that he marketed them as twins. Later on, when the boys' speech had eventually given his game away, he was up-braided by a furious Antony, who complained especially about the enormous price he had had to pay (two hundred thousand sesterces in fact). The cunning dealer replied that he had charged such a large sum precisely because, although there was nothing remark-able about resemblances between a pair of true twins, the discovery of such a degree of similarity between two children of different nationalities was of inestimable value. And so successfully did he instil a suitable sense of amazement in Antony, that the mind behind the proscriptions, which a moment earlier had been seething with insults, now became convinced that no other posses-sion was more appropriate to his status.

(57) Some people are physically incompatible: couples who are infertile may produce children when they take different partners, as was the case with Augustus and Livia. Similarly, there are some men and women whose offspring are exclusively male or female, though for the most part the sexes are produced alternately, as was the case with the mother of the Gracchi on twelve occasions and Germanicus' wife Agrippina on nine. Some are sterile when young, others produce a child just once in a lifetime. (58) Some women do not carry their children to term, but if this problem is overcome by medical care, they normally produce a girl.

Among other unusual circumstances connected with the deified Augustus is the fact that he lived to see his great-great-grandchild: M. Silanus, the grandson of his granddaughter, was born in the year of the emperor's death. While he was governor of Asia, after his consulship, he was poisoned by Nero when the latter became emperor. (**59**) Q. Metellus Macedonicus, who left six children, also left eleven grandchildren and, including his daughters and sons-in-law, a total of twenty-seven people in all who addressed him as 'father'. (**60**) In the public records dating from the time of the deified Augustus, when he was consul for the twelfth time with L. Sulla as colleague, it is stated that, on 9 April, C. Crispinus Hilarus, a freeborn man of plebeian status from Faesulae, offered a sacrifice on the Capitol accompanied by his eight children, including two daughters, together with twenty-seven grandsons, eighteen great-grandsons, and eight granddaughters, in a procession which outshone all others.

(**61**) A woman does not give birth after she is 50 and for the majority, menstruation ceases at 40. With regard to men, however, it is well known that king Masinissa had turned 86 when he fathered a son whom he called Methimannus; and Cato the Censor was past 80 when he had a son by the daughter of his client Salonius. (**62**) This is why the descendants of his other children are surnamed Licinianus, but this branch of the family, from which Cato of Utica was descended, is called the Salonian. It is common knowledge that L. Volusius Saturninus, who died recently during his city prefecture, fathered a son, Volusius Saturninus who became consul, by Cornelia of the Scipio family, when he was 62 years old. Among the lower classes, the fathering of children commonly continues right up to the age of 75.

(**63**) Woman is the only creature to have monthly periods and as a result she alone has what are termed moles in her womb. This mole is a shapeless and lifeless mass of flesh, which is resistant to cutting with a sharp knife. It is mobile and blocks the monthly flow as does the foetus. In some women it proves fatal, while with others, it grows old as they do. Sometimes it slips out when the flow is heavier than usual. Something similar, called a tumour, can occur in the stomach of men, as happened in the case of Oppius Capito, a man of praetorian rank.

(**64**) But it would be difficult to find anything more bizarre than a woman's menstrual flow. Proximity to it turns new wine sour; crops tainted with it are barren, grafts die, garden seedlings shrivel, fruit falls from the tree on which it is growing, mirrors are clouded by its very reflection, knife blades are blunted, the gleam of ivory

dulled, hives of bees die, even bronze and iron are instantly corroded by rust and a dreadful smell contaminates bronze. Dogs go
mad when they have tasted it and their bite is imbued with a dead-
ly poison. (65) Moreover, bitumen, normally a sticky and viscous
substance which at a certain time of the year floats on the surface of
the Judaean lake called Asphaltites cannot, since it sticks to everything with which it comes into contact, be separated except by a
hair which this poison has tainted. Even the tiniest of creatures, the
ant, can, so they say, sense its presence; it drops the grain it has been
carrying and doesn't come back for it afterwards.

(66) This amazingly virulent scourge occurs on average every
month, and more copiously every three months, although in some
women it occurs more frequently, just as in others it never occurs at
all. Such women, however, do not bear children, since this substance is also the human generative material: the male semen acts
as a binding agent and forms a mass which is then in due course
endowed with life and body. Hence, when this bleeding occurs in
pregnant women, the children are, according to Nigidius, weak or
still-born or covered in blood. (67) The same author says that a
nursing mother's milk will not go bad if she becomes pregnant
again by the same man. The easiest conceptions are said to take
place when menstruation is starting or finishing. I have read that it
is a sure sign of fertility in women if traces of an ointment used to
treat her eyes turn up in her saliva.

(68) It is well established that children cut their first teeth at six
months; those in the upper jaw generally appearing first. Once they
are 6 years old, these teeth fall out and are replaced by others.
Some people are actually born with teeth; they include well-known
individuals such as Manius Curius who was for this reason surnamed Dentatus, and Cnaeus Papirius Carbo. Such an occurrence
in a woman was regarded as a bad omen in the regal period.
(69) When Valeria was born with teeth the *haruspices* were consulted and replied that she would bring ruin upon any city to which
she was taken. She was sent to Suessa Pometia, a thriving city at
that time, and the prophesied disaster duly followed. [When
females are born with the sexual organs closed it is a bad omen, as
the case of Cornelia, mother of the Gracchi, proves.] Some people
are born with a solid ridge of bone in place of teeth. King Prusias of
Bithynia's son's upper jaw was of this formation.

(70) The teeth are so indestructible by fire that they do not burn

when the rest of the body is cremated; but although they are impervious to flame, they are rotted by diseased phlegm. A certain drug will whiten them. They are worn down by use but in some cases they fall out well before this happens. Not only are they necessary for chewing food: the front teeth also regulate the voice and speech. The tongue's impact on them enunciates a blend of sounds and, in accordance with the regularity of their structure and their size, they can clip, modulate and soften speech. Once they fall out, clarity of diction is impossible.

(71) This part of the body is also believed to furnish auguries. Apart from the Turduli tribe, men have 32 teeth. Some have been born with more, and this is believed to presage unusual longevity. Women have fewer; those who have a pair of dog teeth on the right-hand side of the upper jaw, as was the case with Agrippina, Nero's mother, are assured of fortune's favour. On the left-hand side, the omens are the opposite. (72) [Among all nations, it is customary not to cremate a person who dies before his teeth come through.] I shall have more to say on the subject of teeth in my systematic review of the parts of the human body (book 11. 160ff.).

Only one person, Zoroaster, is recorded as having laughed on the same day as he was born. So strong was the throbbing of the same child's brain that it dislodged a hand placed on his head and presaged his future wisdom.

(73) It is an established fact that a person has grown to half of his future stature by the age of three years. But it is noticeable that, in general, the human race as a whole is getting smaller as time goes by, and that few individuals grow taller than their fathers. This is because the fertility of the semen is being dried up by the conflagration into whose era the cycle of ages is now declining. In Crete, after an earthquake split open a mountain, a body was found measuring forty-six cubits (approx. 20.5 m.). Some said it was Orion, others Otus.

(74) The body of Orestes, exhumed on the orders of an oracle, was seven cubits (approx. 3.1 m.) tall if the records are to be believed. And indeed, nearly a thousand years ago, the great poet Homer never ceased to bemoan the small stature of his contemporaries compared to the men of old. The records do not tell us how tall Naevius Pollio was, but he was clearly thought to be a prodigy since he was almost crushed to death by crowds of sightseers. The tallest man of our era was brought from Arabia in the reign of the

deified Claudius. He was called Gabbara and he measured nine feet and nine inches (2.88 m.) in height. (75) In the reign of the deified Augustus, there was a couple called Pusio and Secundilla who were half a foot taller (approx. 3 m.) and their bodies were preserved as curiosities in the Sallustian gardens.

In the reign of the same emperor, the smallest man was a dwarf called Conopas, who was two feet and a palm (.666 m.) in height. He was the pet of the emperor's granddaughter Julia and he had a wife called Andromeda, a freedwoman of Julia Augusta. Marcus Varro tells us that the Roman knights Manius Maximus and Marcus Tullius were just two cubits (.888 m.) tall and I have actually seen their bodies preserved in coffins. Everyone knows that there are infants born measuring eighteen inches or more (.444 m.), whose life's span is complete by the age of 3.

(76) We find in our sources that in Salamis the son of Euthymenes grew to be three cubits tall (1.33 m.) in three years. His gait was slow and his senses dull. He had actually reached puberty and his voice had broken before he died suddenly of a seizure at the age of three. Not long ago, I myself saw almost all of these characteristics except puberty in the son of Cornelius Tacitus, a Roman knight who was financial procurator in Gallia Belgica. The Greeks call such people *ektrapeloi*, deviants, but there is no corresponding term for them in Latin.

(77) It has been observed that a man's height from head to toe is the same as the distance from tip to tip of his longest fingers when his arms are fully stretched out. on either side. It has also been observed that the right side of the body is the stronger, but sometimes both sides are equally strong and in some people the left hand predominates, although this is never the case with women. Men are heavier than women and the bodies of all creatures are heavier when they are dead than when they are alive and when they are asleep than when they are awake. Male corpses float on their backs but female corpses float on their faces as though nature were preserving their modesty even in death.

(78) I have read that there are people who have solid bones without any marrow in them. They can be recognized by the fact that they do not experience thirst and they do not perspire. We know, however, that thirst can actually be overcome by will-power. A Roman knight called Julius Viator from the tribe of the Vocontii, one of our allies, had developed dropsy in his youth and was

forbidden liquids by his doctors. This regime became second nature to him and he progressed to old age without drinking a drop. There are many similar examples of such self-control.

(**79**) We are told that Crassus, whose grandson of the same name was killed fighting the Parthians, never laughed and was called Agelastus, Mirthless, as a result. There have been many examples of people who did not weep. The famous philosopher Socrates always wore the same expression on his face, never happier or sadder. However, this equability of temperament sometimes turns into a sort of rigidity of character and a hard inflexible severity lacking the normal human emotions. The Greeks call such persons *apatheis* or emotionless and offer many examples; (**80**) in particular, strangely enough, among their philosophers: Diogenes the Cynic, Pyrrho, Heraclitus, and Timon. The last mentioned was actually carried to the extreme of hating the whole human race.

But minor peculiarities of nature take many forms and are very common. Drusus' wife, Antonia, for example, did not spit and the poet and one-time consul, Pomponius, never belched.

'Horny'-boned is the term used to describe those whose bones are naturally solid; quite a rare phenomenon.

(**81**) In his account of marvellous examples of strength, Varro tells us that Tritanus, who was a famous gladiatorial fighter in Samnite armour, was slightly built but possessed outstanding strength. His son, a soldier under Pompey the Great, had a network of sinews in a criss-cross pattern all over his body, even on his arms and hands. He defeated with his bare hands an enemy whom he had challenged to a duel, finally picking the man up with one finger and carrying him off to the camp.

(**82**) Vinnius Valens, a centurion in the emperor Augustus' Praetorian Guard, used to lift up carts loaded with wineskins until they had been emptied. He would take hold of wagons with one hand and immobilize them, defeating the efforts of the draught animals trying to pull them. There were also other marvellous exploits of his which can be seen carved upon his tombstone.

(**83**) Varro also tells us the following story: Rusticelius, nicknamed Hercules, used to lift up his mule; Fufius Salvius used to climb steps with two one-hundred-pound (32.745 kg.) weights on his feet, two more in his hands and two two-hundred-pound (65.49 kg.) weights on his shoulders. I myself have seen a man called Athanatus who could perform a marvellous exploit: he walked across a stage wearing a five-hundred-pound (163.725 kg.) leaden breastplate with boots on his feet of the same weight. When the athlete Milon of Croton stood firm, no one could dislodge him and when he held an apple no one could straighten a single one of his fingers.

(84) Philippides' 1,140-stade (approx. 211 km.) run from Athens to Sparta in two days was a great achievement, until the Spartan runner Anystis and Alexander the Great's courier Philonides ran from Sicyon to Elis in a day—a distance of 1,305 stades (approx. 241.4 km.).

Nowadays, we are well aware that there are runners who can manage 160 miles (approx. 236 km.) in the Circus and recently, when Fonteius and Vipstanus were consuls, a boy of 8 ran 75 miles (approx. 111 km.) between midday and evening. The real wonder of this achievement only sinks in when we bear in mind that the longest 24-hour journey by carriage ever recorded was made by Tiberius Nero as he hurried to his brother Drusus who had fallen ill in Germany. The distance covered then was 200 miles (approx. 296 km.).

(85) Perhaps the most incredible stories are those involving keen eyesight. According to Cicero, Homer's *Iliad* was copied on to a scrap of parchment which could fit into a nutshell. He also claims that there was a man who could see clearly from a distance of 135 Roman miles (approx. 200 km.) and Varro actually gives his name: Strabo. He says that, in the Punic war, he used actually to count, from the promontory of Lilybaeum in Sicily, the number of ships in a fleet sailing out of the harbour at Carthage. Callicrates used to carve ivory ants and other creatures so tiny that no one else could make out the details. A certain Myrmecides became famous through the same sort of artistic achievement, when he made a four-horse chariot, also from ivory, which a fly could cover with its wings, and a ship which could be hidden under the wings of a tiny bee.

(86) There is one amazing story connected with hearing: the battle which destroyed Sybaris was heard of on the same day at Olympia. However, the tidings of the victory over the Cimbri and the Castores who announced the victory over Perseus at Rome on the day it happened were visions and premonitions of divine origin.

(87) Of physical endurance, thanks to the frequency with which disaster is man's lot in life, there are countless instances. Among

women, the most famous is that of the prostitute Leaena who under torture refused to reveal the names of the tyrannicides Harmodius and Aristogiton. Among men it is Anaxarchus who, when tortured for a similar reason, bit off his tongue and spat the one hope of betrayal into the tyrant's face.

(**88**) Of good memory, the most indispensable of life's advantages, it is difficult to name an outstanding example, since so many people have attained distinction in this field. King Cyrus knew the name of every soldier in his army. Lucius Scipio knew that of every Roman citizen and Cineas, king Pyrrhus' ambassador, knew that of every member of the senatorial and equestrian orders at Rome the day after his arrival. Mithridates, who ruled over twenty-two peoples, dispensed justice in as many languages, making speeches to each race without the aid of an interpreter. (**89**) A certain Charmades of Greece would recite by heart on demand any book in a library, as though he were reading it. Memory finally became an art form, invented by Simonides the lyric poet and perfected by Metrodorus of Scepsis. It facilitated word-perfect repetition of anything heard. (**90**) No other human faculty is so fragile; it is adversely affected by damage from illness and accident and even fear, sometimes in specific areas and sometimes completely. After being hit by a stone, a man forgot only letters. A man who fell from a very high roof forgot his mother and all his friends and relations, another also forgot his slaves, and the orator Messala Corvinus actually forgot his own name. Indeed, memory is often on the brink of slipping away even from a calm and healthy person. It is cut off so effectively by the insidious onset of sleep that the bereft mind wonders where it is.

(**91**) In my opinion, the most outstanding example of mental vigour was the dictator Caesar. By vigour I do not mean moral excellence or resolution, nor the intellectual capacity which embraces everything under the sun. I mean an innate mental agility, with the penetrating speed and rapidity of fire. We are told that Caesar used to read or write, while at the same time dictating and listening. Indeed, he used to dictate his letters, which were on matters of the highest importance, four at a time [to his secretaries; and if he was not doing anything else, seven at a time]. (**92**) He also fought 50 pitched battles and was alone in breaking the record of M. Marcellus, who fought 39. The number of those killed in his battles, if we exclude the civil wars, amounted to 1,192,000, but

such a crime against humanity cannot, in my opinion, add anything to his glorious reputation, even if we allow that it was forced
upon him. Indeed, he himself implicitly admitted as much by not
publicizing the extent of the civil war carnage at all.

(93) There would be more justice in assigning to the credit of
Pompey the Great the 846 ships which he captured from the
pirates. To Caesar there may be credited, in addition to those qualities already mentioned, the peculiar distinction of his clemency in
which he surpassed all others, ultimately to his own detriment. He
provides an example of magnanimity to which no other can compare. (94) If I were to list in this context all the shows that he gave,
the largesse he distributed and the splendour of his public buildings, I would be condoning luxury. But he displayed the genuine,
unrivalled loftiness of an invincible spirit when the private papers of
Pompey the Great at Pharsalus and later those of Scipio at Thapsus
fell into his hands and he made it a point of honour to burn them
without reading them.

(95) But to enumerate at this point all the records of Pompey the
Great's victories and all his triumphs redounds not just to the glory
of one man but to that of the Roman empire itself; rivalling in
splendour as they do not only the deeds of Alexander the Great but
almost even of Hercules and Bacchus.

(96) After he had recovered Sicily, which heralded his debut as
his country's champion in the service of Sulla, and had subjected
and brought under Roman domination all Africa, carrying away
as a trophy the title of 'the Great', he rode back in a triumphal
chariot though only of equestrian rank, which was unprecedented.
Immediately afterwards, he departed for the west, set up trophies in
the Pyrenees and added to the tally of his glorious career a total of
876 towns brought under Roman rule, from the Alps to the frontiers of Further Spain; refraining, with considerable magnanimity,
from mentioning Sertorius' name. After crushing the civil war
which was throwing our foreign affairs into confusion, he brought
into the city his triumphal chariots for the second time as a Roman
knight who had also been a general twice, without ever having
served in the ranks.

(97) Afterwards he was sent out to all the seas, and then to the
east, returning with countless titles for his country, like the winners
of the sacred contests who are not themselves crowned but crown
their country. These honours, then, he bestowed upon the city in

the temple of Minerva which he was dedicating from the spoils of war: 'General Gnaeus Pompeius Magnus having ended a thirty years' war and having routed, scattered, killed or received the surrender of 12,183,000 people; having sunk or captured 846 ships; having received the submission of 1,538 towns and fortresses; and having subjugated the lands stretching from the Maiotians to the Red Sea, makes his offering duly vowed to Minerva.'

(98) This is a summary of his eastern exploits. As for his triumphal procession on 28 September in the consulship of M. Piso and M. Messala, the official announcement was as follows: 'After ridding the sea-coast of pirates and restoring domination of the seas to the Roman people, he triumphed over Asia, Pontus, Armenia, Paphlagonia, Cappadocia, Cilicia, Syria, the Scythians, Jews, and Albanians, Iberia, the island of Crete, the Basternae and, in addition to these, king Mithridates and Tigranes.'

(99) The crowning glory of his renown was, as he himself claimed when recounting his achievements in a public meeting, to have found the province of Asia lying on the fringes and to have restored it to his country at the heart of the empire. If on the other hand anyone wishes to review in a similar way the achievements of Caesar, who proved himself greater than Pompey, then he must surely reckon up the whole world; which, it will be agreed, is a boundless endeavour.

(100) Passing on to other types of virtue, there are many individuals who have been outstanding in a variety of ways. The first of the Porcian family to bear the name Cato was considered to be outstanding in three of the most prestigious fields of human endeavour, since he was a brilliant orator, general, and senator. In all of these fields, however, I am of the opinion that Scipio Aemilianus played a more distinguished, if later, role than Cato, and without the unpopularity which plagued the latter. Thus we may more appropriately assign to Cato the distinction of forty-four lawsuits; no one has been accused so often and acquitted on each occasion.

(101) The most outstanding example of bravery is a matter of endless speculation, especially if the legends of the poets are taken into consideration. Q. Ennius particularly admired T. Caecilius Teucer and his brother, adding a sixteenth book to his *Annals* in their honour. L. Siccius Dentatus, who was tribune of the plebs in the consulship of Spurius Tarpeius and A. Aternius, not long after the expulsion of the kings, receives possibly the greatest number of

votes as a result of his 120 battles, his 8 victories won in single combat and the distinction of having 45 scars all on the front of his body and none on his back. (102) He captured 34 trophies, was awarded 18 ceremonial spears, 25 bosses, 83 necklets, 160 bracelets, 26 crowns (of which 14 were civic, 8 were gold, 3 were mural, and one the siege-hero's crown), a chest of bronze and 10 prisoners of war together with 20 oxen. He escorted 9 generals in triumphs of which he was the main architect and furthermore—his greatest achievement in my opinion—he secured the conviction of one of his commanders, T. Romilius, on the termination of the latter's consulship: he was tried before the people on a charge of military misconduct.

(103) The military glory of Capitolinus would be equally great had he not erased it by the manner of his career's conclusion. Before he was 17, he had already taken spoils from the enemy on two occasions. He was the first knight to receive the mural crown, as well as 6 civic crowns and 37 decorations. He received 23 wounds on the front of his body and saved the life of P. Servilius, the Master of Horse, although he himself was wounded in the shoulder and thigh. Above all, he alone saved the Capitol and thereby a critical situation from the Gauls; if only he had not saved it to make himself king.

(104) In these cases it is clear that courage played a great part, but fortune played one greater still. In my opinion at least, no one could justly rate any man higher than Marcus Sergius, even though his great-grandson Catiline detracts from the honour of his name. In his second campaign he lost his right hand; in the course of two campaigns he was wounded twenty-three times with the result that he was partially disabled in both hands and both feet, his spirit alone remaining undiminished. Though a disabled soldier, he fought on through many subsequent campaigns. Twice he was captured by Hannibal (for it was with no ordinary enemy that he was engaged), twice he escaped from captivity, although he was kept shackled hand or foot every day for twenty months. He fought four times with his left hand alone, and two horses he was riding were killed under him. (105) He had a right hand made for himself out of iron and, fighting with it tied on, he raised the siege of Cremona, defended Placentia, and captured twenty enemy camps in Gaul. All these incidents appear in the speech he made during his praetorship when his colleagues were trying to debar him from the sacrifices because of his infirmity. What piles of decorations would

he have accumulated with a different enemy; (**106**) for it makes the greatest of differences in what historical circumstances each man's heroism occurs. What civic crowns did Trebia, Ticinus, or Trasimenus bestow? What crown was won at Cannae where flight was the summit of courage? Others certainly have conquered men but Sergius conquered fortune also.

(**107**) Who could possibly compile a list of outstanding geniuses, when the field comprises so many different areas of study and such a variety of subjects and writings—unless, perhaps, it can be agreed that there was none more inspired than the Greek poet Homer, whether he is judged by the success or by the content of his work. (**108**) A comment of Alexander the Great's is relevant here (for it is most appropriate and least invidious if such presumptuous assessments are made by the most distinguished of judges). After a golden casket of perfumes richly encrusted with pearls and precious stones had been captured in the booty won from Darius king of Persia, Alexander's friends were pointing out various uses for it, but the king, a battle-soiled soldier who had no time for perfumes, replied 'No! Let it be used instead to hold texts of Homer', so that the most precious product of the human mind might be preserved in the richest possible product of human craftmanship. (**109**) Alexander also ordered that the home and household of the poet Pindar be spared during the sack of Thebes. He restored the birthplace of Aristotle, combining with his outstandingly famous exploits equally outstanding evidence of his kindness.

Apollo exposed the killers of the poet Archilochus at Delphi. When the leading tragic poet Sophocles died during the Spartan siege of Athens, Father Liber ordered his burial, frequently warning the Spartan king Lysander in dreams to permit the burial of the god's favourite. Lysander asked who had died in Athens. He had no difficulty working out which of those named the god meant and duly ordered a truce for the funeral.

(**110**) The tyrant Dionysius, who was normally cruel and proud, sent a ship bedecked with garlands to meet Plato, the high priest of wisdom; and, riding in a chariot drawn by four white horses, met him in person when he disembarked. Isocrates sold a single speech for twenty talents. The leading Athenian orator Aeschines read the speech he had made as prosecutor to the Rhodians but then went on to read them Demosthenes' defence speech which had driven him into exile. When they admired it, he told them that they would have admired it even more had they heard it from the orator himself. As a result of his own misfortune he had thus become a weighty witness to his enemy's case.

(111) As a general, Thucydides was exiled by the Athenians, but as an historian he was recalled; his compatriots admiring the eloquence of the man whose military skills they had condemned. Weighty evidence was also offered of Menander's standing as a comic poet when the kings of Egypt and Macedon sent a fleet and ambassadors to bring him to them; but even weightier evidence was offered by his own preference of literary merit to royal fortune.

(112) Leading citizens of Rome, too, have borne witness even to foreigners. When Gnaeus Pompeius, at the end of the Mithridatic war, was about to enter the house of the eminent professor of philosophy, Posidonius, he forbade his *lictor* to knock in the usual manner and he to whom East and West bowed in submission, bowed the *fasces* to the door of learning. When the distinguished embassy of three leading Athenian philosophers visited Rome, Cato the Censor, after listening to Carneades, advised that the ambassadors be sent on their way as quickly as possible because, when Carneades was expounding an argument, it was difficult to tell where truth lay. (113) How customs change! Whereas this Cato had on other occasions recommended the wholesale expulsion of Greeks from Italy, his great-grandson, Cato of Utica, brought one philosopher home with him after a spell abroad as military tribune, and another after he had been on an embassy to Cyprus. Thus of the two Catos, the elder is remembered for having driven out and the younger for having introduced the same language.

(114) But let us also review the renown of our fellow-Romans. The elder Scipio Africanus ordered that a statue of Ennius be placed in his own tomb and that the famous surname or rather, trophy, which he derived from a third of the world, be read together with the poet's epitaph over his mortal remains. The deified Augustus overrode the modesty of Virgil's will and forbade the burning of his works, thus providing a more convincing testimonial to his poetic genius than would have been achieved by authorial commendation.

(115) In the library established by Asinius Pollio, the first in the world to be endowed from the spoils of war, the only statue of a living person to be set up was that of Marcus Varro. This crowning honour, awarded by a leading orator and citizen to Varro alone out

of the numerous distinguished intellectuals living at the time was no less glorious in my opinion than the actual naval crown awarded to him by Pompey for his part in the war against the pirates.

(**116**) In fact, for those interested in following them up, there are countless examples of Roman pre-eminence, since that race alone has produced more outstanding individuals in every field of excellence than all other countries put together. But how could I justify not singling you out for mention, Marcus Tullius? By which outstanding characteristic can I most aptly highlight your pre-eminence? What could be more appropriate than the unanimous decree of the most illustrious people in the world, selecting out of your entire life the achievements of your consulship alone? (**117**) As a result of your speech, the tribes rejected the agrarian law, that is, their very livelihood. As a result of your advice, they forgave Roscius, the proposer of the theatre law, and accepted with good grace the inferiority implied by the allocation of seating. As a result of your eloquence, the sons of the proscribed were ashamed to seek public office. It was your brilliance which put Catiline to flight; it was you who proscribed Mark Antony. Hail, first citizen to receive the title father of his country, first civilian to win a triumph and a laurel wreath for eloquence, father of oratory and Latin literature; winner indeed, in the words of your former enemy the dictator Caesar, of laurels greater than those of any triumph, inasmuch as it is greater to have advanced so far the frontiers of Rome's genius than those of her empire.

(**118**) Moving on to the remaining qualities of mind, there are those who have distinguished themselves above all others by their wisdom; among the Romans, those who have acquired surnames such as Catus and Corculus, (**119**) and among the Greeks, Socrates, who was placed before all men in this respect by the oracle of Pythian Apollo. It was men, on the other hand who placed Chilo of Sparta on a footing with the oracles, by consecrating in letters of gold at Delphi his three famous precepts. These are as follows: 'Know thyself'; 'Nothing in excess'; and 'The companion of debt and litigation is misery'. The whole of Greece, moreover, followed in his funeral procession, after he died of joy on the occasion of his son's Olympic victory.

The most renowned instances of the gift of divination and a sort of communion with the celestial gods were the Sibyl among women and among men the Greek Melampus and the Roman Marcius.

(**120**) Only once since the foundation of Rome has the title 'most excellent of men' been awarded by the senate on oath—to Scipio Nasica, who was nonetheless stigmatized by the populace who rejected him on two occasions when he stood for election. At the end of his life, he was not allowed to die in his native land; no more, indeed, than Socrates, although judged the wisest of men by Apollo, was allowed to die unfettered by chains. Sulpicia, daughter of Paterculus and wife of Fulvius Flaccus, was on one occasion declared 'purest of women' by a consensus of the Roman matrons. She was elected from a short-list of one hundred women to dedicate the statue of Venus in accordance with the Sibylline books. On another occasion, Claudia was so designated by means of a religious test, when the Mother of the Gods was brought to Rome.

(**121**) There have been countless examples of conspicuous devotion throughout the world but Rome offers one which stands out from all the others. A plebeian woman, whose name is not recorded because she was of humble origin, had recently given birth. She obtained permission to visit her mother, who was in prison as a punishment. She was always searched beforehand by the jailer to prevent her bringing in food, but she was caught feeding her parent with her own breast milk. As a result of this marvel, the daughter's devotion was rewarded with the mother's freedom and both were given maintenance for life. The place where the marvel occurred was consecrated to *Pietas* (Duty) and a temple to that goddess was built on the very site of the prison in the consulship of C. Quinctius and M'. Acilius, where the theatre of Marcellus now stands.

(**122**) When two snakes were caught in his house, the father of the Gracchi was told by the oracle that he himself would live, provided that he killed the snake of the opposite sex. He, however, replied, 'No: kill my snake instead. Cornelia is young and still able to bear children.' This effectively saved his wife's life and served the interests of his country. He died soon afterwards. M. Lepidus died for love of his wife Appuleia after divorcing her. P. Rutilius, while suffering from a mild illness, heard that his brother had been defeated in the election for the consulship and died on the spot. P. Catienus Philotimus was so attached to his patron that he threw himself on the dead man's funeral pyre, even though he had been made heir to the whole of his property.

(**123**) The individuals who have excelled in the various arts and sciences are beyond counting; yet they must be touched on in our anthology of human achievement. Outstanding in astrology, then, was Berosus, to whom, on account of his inspired predictions, the Athenians at public expense erected a statue with a gilded tongue in the gymnasium. Outstanding in philology was Apollodorus, whom the Amphictyons of Greece honoured. In medicine, Hippocrates excelled. He predicted a plague that was coming from Illyria and sent his pupils out to the various cities to give assistance; for which service the Greeks voted him the same honours which they had given Hercules. The same profession, in the person of Cleombrotus of Ceos, received a reward of one hundred talents at the Megalensian festival from king Ptolemy for saving the life of king Antiochus. (124) Critobulus, too, won great renown for removing an arrow from king Philip's eye and treating his loss of the eye without disfiguring his face. But the greatest renown of all goes to Asclepiades of Prusa. He founded a new sect, spurned the envoys and promises of Mithridates, devised a method of treating the sick with wine, and retrieved a man from his funeral pyre and restored him to life. Above all, he made a pact with fortune that he would lose his credibility as a doctor should he himself ever fall ill in any way. And he actually won his bet, because he died as a result of falling down stairs when a very old man.

(125) Outstanding tribute was paid by M. Marcellus to Archimedes' genius in geometry and technology when, at the capture of Syracuse, he ordered that he alone should be spared; an order that was, however, to no avail, owing to a soldier's ignorance. Honour was also accorded to Chersiphron of Cnossos for building the wonderful temple of Diana at Ephesus; to Philo for constructing a dockyard for four hundred ships at Athens; to Ctesibius who discovered the principle of the pneumatic pump and hydraulic engines; and to Dinochares who was surveyor to Alexander when he founded Alexandria in Egypt. It was Alexander who decreed that Apelles alone should paint his portrait, Pyrgoteles alone sculpt his statue and Lysippos alone cast his effigy in bronze. There are many outstanding examples of all these arts.

(126) King Attalus bid one hundred talents for a single picture by the Theban artist Aristides. The dictator Caesar paid eighty talents for a pair of paintings by Timomachus, a Medea and an Ajax, to dedicate in his temple of Venus Genetrix. King Candaules paid its weight in gold for a painting of considerable size by Bularchus which depicted the destruction of the Magnesians. King

Demetrius, nicknamed the Besieger, did not fire Rhodes in case he burnt a picture by Protogenes which was stored in that part of the fortifications. (**127**) Praxiteles was renowned for his marble statues, especially that of Venus at Cnidos which was notorious for the insane passion it inspired in a certain young man and for the value set on it by king Nicomedes, who tried to take it in payment for a large debt owed him by the Cnideans. Jupiter at Olympus bears daily testimony to the genius of Phidias as do Capitoline Jupiter and Ephesian Diana to that of Mentor who engraved the vessels consecrated to them.

(**128**) The highest price to date for a man born into slavery has been, to the best of my knowledge, the sum paid for Daphnis, a skilled grammarian, who was sold at auction by Attius of Pisaurum to Marcus Scaurus, the leading statesman, for 700,000 sesterces. This sum has been exceeded quite considerably in our own day by actors, but these men were purchasing their own freedom: (**129**) the actor Roscius, it should be recalled, was already in the time of our ancestors reputed to be earning 500,000 sesterces a year. At this point, someone might perhaps expect me to mention the paymaster of the recent Armenian war fought on account of Tiridates: Nero manumitted him for the sum of 13,000,000 sesterces. This price, however, reflected the value of the war rather than that of the slave himself; as surely as it was the lust of the buyer rather than the inherent beauty of the slave which caused Clutorius Priscus to buy Paezon, one of Sejanus' eunuchs, for 50,000,000 sesterces. He was able to pull off this scandalous deal at a time of national mourning, when nobody had the chance to expose him.

(**130**) Of all the peoples in the whole world it is the Roman race which is outstanding in terms of virtue. As far as happiness is concerned, no one can say who has excelled, since each person defines happiness in his own way in accordance with his own disposition. In fact, if we want to reach an accurate verdict and exclude all the flatteries of fortune when making our decision, no human being is happy. When fortune deals generously and kindly with him, a man can justly be called not unhappy. Even supposing that other misfortunes are lacking, there is always the fear that fortune might grow weary and once that fear is entertained, happiness has no firm foundation. (**131**) What of the saying that no man is wise all the time? If only as many people as possible would regard it as untrue and not as an oracular utterance! Delusory and ingenious in their self-deception, mortal men make their calculations in the manner of the Thracian tribe which puts into a pot stone counters of different colours, corresponding to each day's experience, and on the last day counts out the separate colours and thus makes its judgement on each individual. (**132**) But supposing that this man traced the seeds of his misfortune to the very day praised as happy by a gleaming white stone? How many people have been prostrated by the acquisition of power? How many have been destroyed and plunged into direst suffering by their goods; if 'goods' they can be called for yielding for the time being a fleeting hour's pleasure? And so it goes on: one day passes judgement on another, but only the last day passes judgement on them all and for that reason we should not put our trust in any one day. What of the fact that good things are not equal to bad, even when they are of equal number, and that no joy can compensate for the smallest grief? Alas, what pointless and ignorant precision! We are counting the days when it is their weight that we are seeking!

(**133**) Only one woman in the whole of history can be found who was daughter, wife, and mother of kings. She was the Spartan Lampido. Only one, Berenice, was daughter, sister, and mother of Olympic victors. Only one family, the Curiones, produced three orators in successive generations and only one, the Fabii, produced three successive leaders of the senate: M. Fabius Ambustus, his son Fabius Rullianus, and his grandson Q. Fabius Gurges.

(**134**) Otherwise, there are countless examples of the vicissitudes of fortune. For what great joys does she produce except following disasters and what overwhelming disasters except following enormous joys? She protected a senator, Marcus Fidustius, for thirty-six years after he was proscribed by Sulla, only to proscribe him a second time. He survived Sulla but lived until the time of Antony, who notoriously proscribed him for no other reason than that he had been proscribed before. (**135**) It was fortune's will that only Publius Ventidius should celebrate a triumph over the Parthians, but, when he was a boy, she led him in the triumph of Gnaeus Pompeius after Asculum. Masurius, however, says he was led twice in triumphal processions, Cicero says that he was a mule driver for an army bakery, and many writers say that in his poverty-stricken youth he made a living as a foot soldier.

(**136**) Cornelius Balbus the elder became consul, but was accused and handed over to a judicial council to decide if he was legally liable to flogging; for he was the first foreigner, indeed the first native of the Outer Ocean to have held an honour refused by our ancestors even to Latium. Among other notable examples is Lucius Fulvius, consul of the Tusculani when they were in revolt against Rome and who, on changing sides, was immediately invested with the same honour by the Roman people. He is unique in having celebrated a triumph at Rome in the same year that he had been Rome's enemy, over a people whose consul he had been.

(**137**) Lucius Sulla is the only man to date who has assumed the surname *Felix* (Fortunate); a title obviously derived from slaughtering his fellow citizens and attacking his country! By what proofs of his good fortune was he persuaded? The fact that he was able to proscribe and murder so many thousands of citizens? What a perverted interpretation of good fortune, so unfortunate for the future! Were not those who perished at the time more fortunate than he? Today, they are pitied, while Sulla is abhorred by all. (**138**) Again, surely his own death was crueller than the fate of all those he proscribed, when his body ate itself away and bred its own tortures? Although, on the grounds that he disguised his suffering and on the basis of that final dream in which, so to speak, he died, we may believe that in his case alone hatred had been overcome by glory; yet he nonetheless admitted that one thing was lacking to that good fortune of his, namely, that he had not dedicated the Capitol.

(**139**) Quintus Metellus gave a funeral oration in honour of his father, Lucius Metellus, who was priest, twice consul, dictator, Master of Horse, member of the Board of Fifteen for land distribution, and the first man to lead elephants which had been captured in the first Punic war in his triumphal procession. In this speech, he left it in writing that his father had achieved the ten greatest and best objectives in pursuit of which wise men spend their lives. (**140**) That is to say, he had aimed to be a first-rate warrior, a most accomplished orator, and the bravest of generals; to have control of affairs of the utmost importance, to enjoy the greatest honour, to possess supreme wisdom and to be acknowledged as the foremost senator; to make a large fortune in an honourable fashion, to leave behind him many children, and to be the most distinguished individual in the country. According to the son, all these things had been achieved by his father and by no one else since the foundation of Rome. (**141**) It would take a long time to refute these claims and it would in any case be pointless since a single mishap will more than suffice as a contradiction: this Metellus lived out his old age in blindness, having lost his sight in a fire when he snatched the Palladium to safety from the temple of Vesta; a motive worthy of renown but unfortunate in outcome. Although he ought not to be termed unhappy as a result of his accident, yet he cannot be called happy either. The Roman people paid him a tribute which has been offered to no other man since the beginning of time: whenever he attended a meeting of the senate, a chariot conveyed him to the senate house. It was a great and noble reward, but given in return for his sight.

(**142**) The son of this Quintus Metellus who wrote those facts about his father is himself cited among the rare examples of human happiness. For in addition to the greatest honours and the surname Macedonicus, he was carried to his funeral pyre by four sons, one of whom was of praetorian rank, while three had been consuls. Two of the consulars had celebrated triumphs and one was an ex-censor. Each circumstance on its own was an honour granted to few men. (**143**) Yet, at the very peak of his pre-eminence, while returning from the Campus Martius at midday when the Forum and Capitol were deserted, he was snatched away by C. Atinius Labeo, surnamed Macerio, a tribune thrown out of the senate by Metellus when he was censor. Macerio intended to throw him from the Tarpeian rock. Although that large cohort of sons rushed to his aid, it was inevitable that in a sudden crisis such as this they arrived late; so late as to be almost in time for his funeral, since, as it was unlawful for him to oppose and repel the sacrosanct tribune, he was about to die for his honourable conduct as censor. With difficulty, however, a tribune was found to veto proceedings and recall him from the very threshold of death. (**144**) Yet afterwards he lived on the charity of others, since his property had also been consecrated by the man he had condemned; as though the tribune's vengeance had not been satisfied when a rope was tied around his victim's neck and the blood forced through his ears! Personally, I should also count among his misfortunes the enmity of the younger Africanus, on the evidence of Macedonicus himself who said 'Go, my sons, and celebrate his last rites; you will not see the funeral of a greater citizen'. This was said by the man who already held the title Macedonicus, to sons who already held the titles of Baliaricus and Diadematus.

(**145**) But taking into account this one injury alone, who could justly call Macedonicus happy when he was in peril of perishing at the pleasure of an enemy and one, moreover, who was not even an Africanus? Besides, what honours and chariots did Fortune not drive back by her violence in dragging a censor through the centre of the city (this humiliation was the only reason for delaying his death), dragging him to the very Capitol to which, as a general arrayed in the insignia of the god, he had not dragged even his captives in such a manner? (146) This crime was rendered even greater by the happiness which followed, since Macedonicus was in danger of losing that glorious funeral in which he was borne to the pyre by sons who had celebrated triumphs, as though his funeral procession, too, was triumphal. Clearly, then, there is no firm foundation to a happiness which is shattered by an insult to a man's career, let alone by one as great as this. In conclusion, I am not sure whether to attribute it to the glory of their traditions or to the pain of their resentment that, despite such a multitude of Metelli, this wicked crime of Atinius' remained forever unavenged.

(147) In the case of the deified Augustus, too, whom men unanimously include in their list of happy individuals, a careful investigator of all the facts would find great changes of human fortune. There was his failure to obtain the office of Master of Horse from his uncle, when Lepidus' candidacy was preferred to his; the hatred he incurred as a result of the proscriptions; and his association in the triumvirate with the worst citizens without even an equal share in power, but with Antony predominant. (148) Then there was his illness at the battle of Philippi, followed by his flight and concealment for three days in a marsh while swollen with dropsy, according to Agrippa and Maecenas. His shipwreck in Sicily was followed by another period of hiding, this time in a cave. He entreated Proculeius to kill him when they were hard pressed by a detachment of the enemy in a naval rout. There were the pressures of the Perusine war, the anxieties of Actium, and his fall from a tower in the Pannonian wars. (149) There were all the mutinies in his armies and all his critical illnesses. There were his suspicions of Marcellus' vows, the shameful banishment of Agrippa, and the many conspiracies against his life. There were the accusations of involvement in his children's deaths and the sorrows that were not due solely to his bereavement: his daughter's adultery and the discovery of her plot to kill her father; the insolent retirement of his stepson, Nero; and another adultery, this time his granddaughter's.

Then in addition there was a long series of other misfortunes: shortage of money for the army, the revolt in Illyricum, the enlisting of slaves, the shortage of manpower, plague at Rome, famine in Italy, his determination to kill himself and the four days' fast which brought him to within an inch of death. (**150**) On top of this was the disaster of Varus and the disgraceful affront to his dignity; and the disowning of Agrippa Postumus after his adoption, followed by a sense of loss after his banishment. Then there were the suspicions with regard to Fabius and the betrayal of secrets, followed by the intrigues of his wife and Tiberius which were plaguing him at the end of his life. In the end, this god (whether deified by machination or merit I cannot tell) died leaving his enemy's son as his heir.

(**151**) While we are on this subject, there come to mind the Delphic oracles sent forth by the god seemingly for the purpose of chastising human vanity. Here are two of them: 'Happiest of men is Pedius, who recently fell fighting for his country'; and secondly, in answer to Gyges, the greatest king of his time, 'Aglaus of Psophis is happier'. This was an old man who, in a very confined corner of Arcadia, worked a farm which was small but amply sufficient for his annual subsistence. He had never left it and, as his way of life showed, he had few desires and so experienced few misfortunes in life.

(**152**) On the order of the same oracle and with the agreement of Jupiter the supreme deity, the boxer Euthymus who always won at Olympia, suffering only one defeat, was to his own knowledge deified while still a living man. He came from Locri in Italy. I see that Callimachus regarded it as an unparalleled marvel that a statue of him in Locri and another at Olympia were both struck by lightning on the same day and the god ordered sacrifice to be offered, which was done frequently both during his life and after his death; but there is nothing surprising about this, except that the gods decreed it.

(**153**) Human longevity is an uncertain matter, being affected by place, time, and the personal destiny allotted to each individual at birth. Hesiod, who was the first to record some thoughts (fantastical in my opinion) on this matter, made the human lifespan the point of reference for many others, assigning nine of our lifespans to the crow, four of the crow's to the stag, and three of the stag's to the raven. Other calculations of his with regard to the phoenix and the nymphs were even more fantastic. (**154**) The poet Anacreon says that Arganthonius, king of the Tartessians, lived for 150 years, Cinyras king of Cyprus for 10 years longer, and Aegimius for 200 years; while Theopompus assigns 157 years to Epimenides of Cnossus. Hellanicus claims that some members of the tribe of the Epii in Aetolia reach an age of 200 years; a figure supported by Damastes, who records that Pictoreus, one of the most remarkable of them by reason of his physical strength, actually lived 300 years. (155) Ephorus records Arcadian kings living for 300 years, while Alexander Cornelius claims a lifespan of 500 years for a man called Dando from Illyria. In his *Periplus*, Xenophon claims that a king of the island of the Lutmii lived to be 600 and, as if that lie wasn't big enough, he claims that his son lived to be 800. All such stories are due to inadequate knowledge of chronology. Some commentators counted the summer period as one year and the winter as a second. Others counted each quarter of our year as one year, for example the Arcadians whose years were three months long. Others again counted each waning of the moon, as the Egyptians do, the result being that among them individuals are actually recorded as having lived 1,000 years.

(156) But turning to established facts, Arganthonius of Gades in all probability reigned for 80 years; he is thought to have started his reign at the age of 40. There is no doubt that Masinissa reigned for 60 years and Gorgias of Sicily lived to the age of 108. Q. Fabius Maximus was augur for 63 years. M. Perperna and, most recently, L. Volusius Saturninus, outlived all those senators whose opinions they had sought in debate when consul. Perperna left behind only seven of those whom he had enrolled in the senate as censor. He lived to be 98. (157) While on this subject, I should add that there has been only one five-year period during which no senator has died: from the time when the censors Flaccus and Albinus made the lustral sacrifice in 175 BC to the next pair of censors. M. Valerius Corvinus reached the age of 100; the period between his first and sixth consulships was 46 years. He occupied a curule chair 21 times, a record matched by no other person, though the priest Metellus equalled his lifespan.

(158) Examples of female longevity include Livia, wife of Rutilius, who lived over 97 years, Statilia, a woman of noble family in the reign of Claudius, who lived beyond 98, Terentia, Cicero's wife, who lived beyond 103, and Clodia, Ofilius' wife, who lived beyond 115 and also bore 15 children. Lucceia, the actress of

mimes, appeared on stage over a period of 100 years. Galeria Copiola, an actress of interludes, was brought back onto the stage at the age of 104, in the consulship of C. Poppaeus and Q. Sulpicius, on the occasion of the votive games celebrated for the wellbeing of the emperor Augustus. She had been engaged for her debut performance by the aedile M. Pomponius in the consulship of C. Marius and Cn. Carbo ninety-one years earlier and brought back, when an old woman, as a marvel by Pompey the Great, at the dedication of his great theatre. (**159**) According to Pedianus Asconius, Samulla also lived to be 110.

I am less surprised that Stephanion, who introduced Roman dancing, danced at both sets of secular games, those of Augustus and those held by Claudius Caesar in his fourth consulship, since the intervening gap was no more than 63 years. All the same, he lived for a long time after that. Life expectancy on the summit of Mount Tmolus, called Tempsis, is 150 years according to Mucianus. The same age was declared by Titus Fullonius of Bononia in the census held by Claudius. The emperor was interested in verifying his claim and, when compared with returns he had made in previous censuses and the evidence provided by his life, it was found to tally.

(**160**) This subject calls for the opinions of those who have studied the stars. Epigenes said that no one could live for 112 years while Berosus said it was impossible to live beyond the age of 116. Petosiris and Nechepsos' theory, called the theory of 'quadrants' because it divided the zodiac into four groups of three signs, has lasted until today. It established the possibility of living to the age of 124 on Italian soil. They said that no one could live beyond an ascending measure of 90 degrees, which they call an anaphore, and that these anaphores are cut short when their paths are crossed by ill-omened stars or even by their rays and those of the sun. Again, the school of Asclepius, which says that length of life is dictated by the stars, does not give a precise maximum age (**161**) but says that longer lifespans are rare because at certain critical points in the lunar days, such as the seventh and fifteenth hour, counting by day and night, large numbers of people are born who are destined to die in accordance with the established scale of years called climacterics. Those born in such circumstances do not normally live longer than 54 years.

(**162**) To start with, then, the lack of unanimity among

astrologers illustrates what an uncertain subject longevity actually is. We also have the results of the most recent census, taken within the last four years by the emperors Vespasian Caesar, father and son, in their capacity as censors. There is no need to raid all the archives; we will restrict ourselves to examples from the area midway between the Apennines and the river Po. (**163**) At Parma, three people gave their age as 120, as did one at Brixillum. Two in Parma said they were 125, while a man at Placentia and a woman at Faventia declared an age of 130. 135 was the age given by L. Terentius son of Marcus at Bononia and at Ariminium 140 was given by M. Aponius and 137 by Tertulla. In the hills, before you reach Placentia, is the town of Veleia, where six people gave their age as 110, four as 120, and one, M. Mucius Felix, son of Marcus, of the Galerian tribe, as 140. (**164**) Finally, lest we linger over too many examples from well-established facts, in the eighth region of Italy, fifty-four men were recorded as being 100 years old, fourteen as 110, two as 125, four as 130, another four as 135 or 137, and three as 140.

(**165**) Here are some other examples of the uncertainties of human destiny. Homer tells us that Hector and Polydamus, heroes whose destinies were so different, were actually born on the same night. M. Caelius Rufus and C. Licinius Calvus were born on the same day, 28 May, in the third consulship of C. Marius and Cn. Carbo. They were both orators, but their careers took very different paths. With regard to identical birth-times, then, the facts of the matter are that masters and slaves, princes and paupers, are produced simultaneously, world-wide and on a daily basis.

(**166**) P. Cornelius Rufus, who was consul with M'. Curius, went blind in his sleep, while dreaming that this was happening to him. Conversely, Jason of Pherae, who was despaired of by his doctors when he was ill with a tumour, sought death in battle but was cured by the enemy who wounded him in the chest. While fighting the Allobroges and Arverni near the river Isarus on 8 August, a battle in which 130,000 of the enemy were killed, the consul Q. Fabius Maximus was cured of a quartan fever.

(**167**) In life, nature has given us a gift which is too precarious and fragile, whatever our lot; one, indeed, which is niggardly and short even for the most bountifully endowed, particularly if we are considering the eternity of time. Furthermore, if we take into account the amount of time spent asleep at night, does not each of us live for only one half of his life, the other half being spent in a state similar to death, or to torture if we are unable to sleep? And this is not counting the years of our infancy when the senses are lacking, or those of old age, when life is torment, or all the accidents, illnesses, fears and worries or the pleas for death so frequently uttered that this is the commonest of all prayers. (**168**) The truth is that nature has given man no better gift than shortness of life. The senses grow dull, the limbs become sluggish, sight, hearing, mobility, even the teeth and digestive organs die prematurely and yet this period still counts as life. The case of the musician Xenophiles who lived to 105 without any bodily infirmity is therefore to be regarded as miraculous and unique. (**169**) The rest of mankind, unlike all other animals, is, alas, subject to a pestilential heat or chill which returns to various parts of the body at particular hours; and not only at particular hours but also on particular days and nights in the case of tertian and quartan fevers, or even at intervals of a whole year. In addition, septenary death is a kind of disease. (**170**) For nature has also imposed laws upon diseases: a quartan fever never begins at the winter solstice or during the winter months. Some illnesses do not attack those over 60, while others stop at puberty, especially in the case of women. Old men are least susceptible to plague. In fact, illnesses can attack both the population as a whole and also particular sections of society, sometimes the slaves, at other times the aristocracy, and so through other classes. On this subject it has been observed that epidemics always travel from southern areas westward and rarely otherwise. They do not occur in winter and do not last longer than three months.

(**171**) I turn now to signs of approaching death, which include: in cases of dementia, laughter, but in cases of delirium, plucking at the fringes and making folds in the bedclothes; the patient's lack of response to those trying to rouse him from sleep; urinary incontinence. The most unmistakable signs are the appearance of the eyes and nostrils; lying constantly on the back; the irregular or fluttering pulse; and all the other signs which have been noted by Hippocrates, the leading authority on medicine.

There are countless signs portending death but none which portend health and safety, a point summed up by Cato the Censor's virtually oracular statement to his son concerning healthy people too: 'a senile youth is a sign of premature death'.

(**172**) There is an infinite variety of diseases. Pherecydes the

Syrian died when a swarm of maggots burst out of his body. Some people suffer from a perpetual fever, as did C. Maecenas, who did not sleep a wink during the last three years of his life. Every year, the poet Antipater of Sidon was smitten with a fever on one day alone, his birthday. It was on that day, after a reasonably long old age, that he died.

(173) The ex-consul, Aviola, came to life again on his funeral pyre, but because no one could come to his aid due to the fierceness of the flames, he was cremated alive. A similar death is recorded for L. Lamia, a man of praetorian rank, while C. Aelius Tubero, a former praetor, is said by Messala Rufus and most other authorities, to have been recovered from his pyre. Such is the human condition! We are born exposed to these and similar accidents of fortune to the extent that no confidence should be placed in matters pertaining to man; not even in his death!

(174) Among other examples, we find that the soul of Hermotimus of Clazomenae used to leave his body and roam abroad. In its wanderings it would send back information from far away which only an eyewitness could have known. During such periods, his body would remain in a comatose state, until one day, enemies of his called the Cantharidae burnt it, thus depriving his soul on its return of what could be called its sheath. The soul of Aristeas in Proconnesus was actually seen flying out of his mouth in the form of a raven; as tall a tale as that which follows. (175) I for my part view with similar scepticism the story of Epimenides of Cnossus who, as a young boy, tired by the heat of his journey, is supposed to have slept in a cave for 57 years. Upon waking as though it was the next morning, he was amazed at how things had changed. After this he aged rapidly over a period of days equal in number to the years he had slept, yet he lived to the age of 157. The female sex seems especially susceptible to this kind of disorder. It is caused by a turning of the womb, but, if this is corrected, breathing is re-established. A relevant study, well-known in Greece, is that of Heraclides concerning a woman ostensibly dead for seven days who was restored to life.

(176) Varro for his part records that when he was a member of the Board of Twenty for land distribution at Capua, a man who was being carried to his grave returned from the forum to his home, on foot; and that there was a similar incident at Aquinum. He also says that Corfidius, his maternal aunt's husband, returned to life

after his funeral had been arranged and himself took part in the funeral of the man who had previously arranged his. (**177**) He adds some extraordinary happenings which it would be appropriate to set out in full. There were two brothers of equestrian rank called the Corfidii. It happened that the elder of the two apparently died. The will was opened and the younger brother, who had been named as heir, began to make the funeral arrangements. Meanwhile, the brother who had apparently died summoned his slaves by clapping his hands and told them he had come from his brother, who had entrusted his daughter to his care and had furthermore shown him where he had secretly buried some treasure. He had also asked that the funeral rites which he had prepared be used for himself. While he was telling them this, his brother's slaves came rushing in with the news that their master had died and the gold was found in the place he had indicated.

(**178**) Life is in fact full of such prophecies but they are not worth collecting as they are for the most part false, as I shall show with a striking example. During the Sicilian war, Gabienus, the bravest fighter in Octavian's fleet, was captured by Sextus Pompey, who ordered his throat to be cut. He lay on the shore all day with his throat almost severed. Then, as evening approached and his moans and pleas had attracted a crowd of people, he begged that Pompey should come to him or send one of his closest friends, as he had returned from the land of the dead with a message for him. (**179**) Pompey sent a number of his friends and Gabienus told them that the gods of the underworld approved Pompey's cause and his followers who had right on their side; that future events would turn out as he wished; and that he had been ordered to deliver this message, the truth of which would be proven by his death immediately on completion of his mission. This occurred exactly as predicted.

There are also instances of people being seen after burial, but I am investigating natural rather than supernatural phenomena.

(**180**) Among the most marvellous and frequent occurrences, which I shall show are natural, are sudden deaths, life's greatest happiness. Verrius has recorded scores of examples, but I shall limit myself to a selection. People who died of joy include, besides Chilo of whom I spoke earlier, Sophocles and Dionysius the tyrant of Sicily, in both cases after hearing news of their tragedy's victory in a dramatic contest; and the mother who saw her son return unharmed from the battle of Cannae, contrary to a false report.

Diodorus the professor of logic died of shame when he was unable to solve immediately a problem put to him as a joke by Stilpo.

(181) Deaths from no obvious cause include those of two Caesars, who died while putting on their sandals in the morning. One, a praetor, died at Rome, the other, an ex-praetor and father of the dictator, at Pisa. Q. Fabius Maximus died in similar circumstances during his consulship, on the day before the first of January, which led to C. Rebilus standing for a consulship of just a few hours to replace him. The senator C. Volcatius Gurges also died in this manner. All these men were so fit and well that they were thinking of going out. Q. Aemilius Lepidus died in the act of going out, when he stubbed his toe on the threshold of his bedroom, while C. Aufustius had gone out and was on his way to the senate house when he tripped in the Comitium. (182) An ambassador, who had pleaded the cause of the Rhodians before the senate to great acclaim, died suddenly as he made to cross the threshold of the Curia. Cn. Baebius Tamphilus, another ex-praetor, died while asking his slave the time, Aulus Pompeius on the Capitol after honouring the gods, the consul Manius Iuventius Thalna whilst sacrificing, and C. Servilius Pansa while standing in the Forum near a shop, leaning on his brother Publius, at the second hour of the day. The judge Baebius died while ordering a court appearance to be postponed, M. Terentius Corax while writing on tablets in the Forum. (183) Only last year, a Roman knight died while whispering in the ear of an ex-consul, in front of the ivory statue of Apollo which stands in the Forum of Augustus. Strangest of all, the doctor C. Julius died after accidentally passing a probe through his eye while applying ointment, the ex-consul A. Manlius Torquatus while reaching for a cake at dinner, L. Tuccius Valla, a doctor, while having a drink of mead, and Appius Saufeius when he had drunk some mead and was eating an egg after returning from the baths. P. Quintius Scapula died while dining with Aquilius Gallus, the scribe Decimus Saufeius while breakfasting at home. (184) The ex-praetor Cornelius Gallus died while making love, as did T. Hetereius, a Roman knight. So did two members of the equestrian order, who caused a recent scandal when they each died while in bed with the same pantomime artiste, Mysticus, the handsomist youth of his day.

A most artistically contrived tableau of serenity in death, involving M. Ofilius Hilarus, is recorded by the ancient sources.

(**185**) This comic actor, who had always enjoyed popular success, held a banquet on his birthday. When the meal had been served, he called for a hot drink and, gazing at the mask he had been wearing that day, transferred to it the wreath on his head. In this attitude he grew stiff without anyone noticing, until the diner next to him warned him that his drink was getting cold.

(**186**) These are happy deaths, but there are countless instances of unhappy ones. L. Domitius, a member of an illustrious family, was defeated at Massilia and captured at Corfinium, in both instances by Julius Caesar. Weary of life, he took poison, but, after he had drunk it, tried desperately to save himself. It is stated in the public records that, at the funeral of Felix, a charioteer of the Reds, one of his fans threw himself on the funeral pyre, but in a ludicrous attempt to prevent the incident redounding to the glory of the deceased artiste, rival fans claimed the man was overcome by the abundant funerary perfumes. Not long before, M. Lepidus, a man of the noblest lineage, whom we earlier mentioned as having died of grief after his divorce (above, (**122**)), was thrown from his funeral pyre by the fierceness of the flames. Since the heat prevented replacement of the body, it was burnt next to the pyre, naked, on a makeshift pile of brushwood.

(**187**) Cremation is not a long-established practice among the Romans: originally, they buried their dead. However, cremation was introduced after it became known that the bodies of those who had fallen while fighting in far-off lands were disinterred. Even so, many families have preserved the old practices: for instance, no one in the Cornelian family was cremated before Sulla, who feared retaliation for his disinterment of the body of C. Marius. [Sepulture is a term used of any sort of funerary disposal, but inhumation refers specifically to burial in earth.]

(**188**) Following burial, we find a variety of vague theories about spirits of the dead. After our last day, we are all in the same state as we were before our first; body and soul have no more sensation after death than they had before birth. It is human vanity, once again, which prolongs itself even into the future and falsely fabricates life even in death, attributing to the soul sometimes immortality and sometimes transformation; or else endowing the dead with sensation, worshipping their spirits and making a god out of what has ceased even to be a man. As though man's mode of breathing were any different from the rest of the animals and there were not many creatures to be found with longer life-spans, for whom, however, a similar immortality has not been posited! (**189**) Taken on its own, what is the substance of the soul? What is it made of? Where is its power of thought? How does it see, hear, or touch? What use can it get from these senses or what good can it experience if it lacks them? Finally, where is the abode and, after so many centuries, how great is the number of these spirits or shades? These are the fabrications of childish fancy and of mortality greedy for immortality. The same vanity lies behind the preservation of corpses and their resurrection as promised by Democritus, a man who did not come back to life again himself. (**190**) Scoundrel! What is this mad idea that life is renewed in death? What peace will the generations ever find if consciousness is retained by their souls in the upper world and their shades in the underworld? Such seductive delusions in reality destroy nature's supreme gift, death, and double the sorrow of those who are going to die by the prediction of sorrow to come. Moreover, if life is sweet, who can find the end of life sweet? But how much simpler and surer it would be were we each to trust in ourselves and derive from our prenatal experience the model for our future serenity!

(**191**) Before we leave the subject of man's nature, it seems appropriate to append a list of inventions and inventors. Mercury started the practice of buying and selling, Father Liber the harvesting of the vintage. The latter was also responsible for the introduction of the royal emblem of the diadem and the triumph. Ceres introduced corn (men had previously lived on acorns) and the art of grinding it into flour in Attica, or, according to other sources, in Sicily. Because of this, she was regarded as a goddess. She or, as others think, Rhadamanthus, was the first to give laws.

(**192**) In my opinion, the Assyrians have always had writing, but some authorities, such as Gellius, prefer to see it as instituted by Mercury in Egypt, while others again assign its origins to Syria. Both schools of thought agree that Cadmus brought sixteen letters to Greece from Phoenicia, to which Palamedes added four at the beginning of the Trojan war. These were H, Y, Φ, and X. After him, Simonides the lyric poet added another four, Ψ, Ξ, Ω, and Θ, the sounds of which are recognized in our own alphabet. Aristotle prefers an original total of eighteen letters, with the two letters Φ and X added by Epicharmus rather than Palamedes. (**193**) Anticleides says that writing was invented in Egypt by a man called

Menon, 15,000 years before Phoroneus, the most ancient of the Greek kings, and he attempts to prove this by reference to records. On the other hand, Epigenes, a first-rate authority, tells us that the Babylonians had astronomical observations inscribed on baked bricks going back 720,000 years, while Berosus and Critodemus, who quote the shortest length of time, make it 490,000 years. This suggests that writing has always been in use. It was brought to Latium by the Pelasgians.

(**194**) The Athenian brothers Euryalus and Hyperbius were the first to introduce brick-kilns and houses. Before that, men had lived in caves. According to Gellius, Toxius son of Caelus invented building with clay, taking swallows' nests as his model. Cecrops gave his name to the first town, Cecropia, which is now the Acropolis of Athens. Some authorities place the foundation of Argos by king Phoroneus earlier and certain others that of Sicyon also; while the Egyptians date their own town of Diospolis much earlier.

(**195**) Cinyra son of Agriopas invented tiles and the mining of metals, both in Cyprus. He also invented tongs, hammer, crowbar, and anvil. Wells were invented by Danaus after he sailed from Egypt to the part of Greece known as 'Dry'Argos; quarries by Cadmus at Thebes or, according to Theophrastus, in Phoenicia; walls by Thrason; towers by the Cyclopes according to Aristotle, or the Tirynthians according to Theophrastus. (**196**) Woven fabrics were invented by the Egyptians, wool-dyeing by the Lydians in Sardis, the spindle for wool-working by Closter son of Arachne, thread and nets by Arachne herself, the art of fulling by Nicias of Megara, and the art of shoemaking by Tychius of Boeotia.

The Egyptians claim to have discovered medicine themselves, but others attribute it to Arabus, the son of Babylon and Apollo. Botany and pharmacy were discovered by Chiron, son of Saturn and Philyra.

(**197**) Aristotle thinks that the melting and working of copper was first demonstrated by Scythes the Lydian, while Theophrastus attributes it to the Phrygian Delas. Some authorities attribute the working of bronze to the Chalybes, others to the Cyclopes. According to Hesiod, iron was discovered by the people called the Idaean Dactyli in Crete. Erichthonius of Athens or, according to others, Aeacus discovered silver. Mining and melting gold was discovered by Cadmus the Phoenician near Mount Pangaeus or, according to other accounts, by Thoas or Aeacus in Panchaia, or, again, by Sol son of Oceanus to whom Gellius also attributes the discovery of the medicinal uses of metals. Tin was first imported from the island of Cassiterris by Midacritus. (**198**) Iron-working was invented by the Cyclopes, pottery by Coroebus of Athens, the potter's wheel by Anacharsis the Scythian or, according to others, Hyperbius the Corinthian. Daedalus is credited with woodwork, together with the saw, axe, plumb-line, auger, glue, and isinglass; while Theodorus the Samian is credited with the square, level, lathe, and key and Phaedon of Argos or, according to Gellius, Palamedes with measures and weights.

The art of striking fire from flint was discovered by Pyrodes son of Cilix and the art of keeping the flame in a fennel-stalk by Prometheus. (**199**) The Phrygians invented the four-wheeled vehicle, the Carthaginians invented commerce, Eumolpus of Athens viticulture and arboriculture, Staphylus son of Silenus the mixing of wine with water, Aristaeus of Athens oil and oil-presses. He also discovered honey. The ox and the plough were introduced by Buzyges the Athenian or, according to others, Triptolemus.

(**200**) The Egyptians invented monarchy and the Athenians democracy, after Theseus. The first tyrant was Phalaris of Agrigentum. The Spartans invented slavery. The first capital trial took place before the Areopagus.

The Africans first fought a battle with staffs, called *phalangae*, against the Egyptians. Proetus and Acrisius invented shields when making war on each other; or else it was Chalcus, son of Athamas. Midias the Messenian invented the breastplate, while the Spartans invented the helmet, sword, and spear and the Carians the greaves and helmet plumes. (**201**) Scythes son of Jupiter invented the bow and arrow, though others say that arrows were the invention of Perses son of Perseus. Light spears were invented by the Aetolians, the spear thrown with a thong by Aetolus son of Mars, the skirmishing spear by Tyrrenus, the javelin by the Amazon Penthesilea, the axe by Pisaeus, hunting spears and the scorpion, one of the missile engines, by the Cretans, the catapult by the Syrians, the ballista and sling by the Phoenicians, the bronze trumpet by Pisaeus son of Tyrrenus, the tortoise by Artemon of Clazomenae, (**202**) the horse, a siege-machine now called the ram, by Epius at Troy. Horse-riding was invented by Bellerophon, reins and saddles by Pelethronius, fighting on horseback by the Thessalians called Centaurs who lived on Mount Pelion. The Phrygian people first harnessed pairs of horses, Erichthonius a team of four. Army formation, the giving of signals, watchwords, and sentries were inventions of Palamedes during the Trojan war, the campaign in which Sinon instituted signalling from watch-towers. Lycaon introduced truces, Theseus treaties.

(203) Auguries from birds were introduced by Car, from whom Caria got its name. Orpheus developed the same art using other animals, Delphus divination from the entrails of victims, Amphiaraus pyromancy, the Theban Tiresias divination from the entrails of birds, and Amphictyon the interpretation of prodigies and dreams. Astronomy was discovered by Atlas son of Libya, but others attributed it to the Egyptians and others again to the Assyrians. Anaximander of Miletus discovered the celestial sphere and Aeolus son of Hellen the principle of the winds. (204) Amphion invented music, Pan son of Mercury the pan-pipe and the single oboe. Midas in Phrygia invented the transverse flute, while in the same country Marsyas invented the double oboe. Amphion invented the Lydian mode, the Thracian Thamyras the Dorian mode, the Phrygian Marsyas the Phrygian mode. The lyre was invented by Amphion, though others say Orpheus and others again Linus. Terpander was the first to play a seven-stringed lyre, having added three strings to the original four. Simonides added an eighth, Timotheus a ninth. Thamyris was the first to play the lyre without vocal accompaniment while Amphion or, according to others, Linus, was the first to combine the lyre with singing. Terpander composed songs for lyre and voice. Ardalus of Troezen introduced singing to a flute accompaniment. The Curetes taught dancing in armour, Pyrrhus the Pyrrhic dance, both in Crete.

(205) We owe epic verse to the Pythian oracle. The origin of poetry is a matter of considerable debate; its existence is attested before the Trojan war. The first prose writer was Pherecydes of Syros in the reign of king Cyrus, and the first historian was Cadmus of Miletus.

Lycaon instituted gymnastic games in Arcadia, Acastus funeral games in Iolcus, and after him Theseus at the Isthmus and Hercules at Olympia. Athletic contests were instituted by the Pythian god, the ball game by Gyges of Lydia.

The Egyptians introduced painting. In Greece, Aristotle attributed its introduction to Euchir, a relative of Daedalus, and Theophrastus to Polygnotus of Athens.

(**206**) Danaus was the first to journey by boat, from Egypt to Greece. Before that, rafts had been invented by king Erythras, for sailing between the islands in the Red Sea. There are those who think that the Mysians and Trojans had invented them earlier in the Hellespont, when they crossed to make war on the Thracians. Even today, on the British Ocean, there are coracles made from osier lined with leather, while on the Nile there are vessels made from papyrus, rushes, and reeds. (**207**) According to Philostephanus, Jason was the first to sail in a long warship, but Hegesias says it was Parhalus, Ctesias Samiramis, and Archemachus Aegaeon. According to Damastes, the bireme was invented by the Erythraeans. Thucydides attributes the trireme to Ameinocles of Corinth, (**208**) Aristotle the quadrireme to the Carthaginians, and Mnesigiton the quinquereme to the Salaminians. According to Xenagoras, the Syracusans introduced vessels with six rows, while Mnesigiton says Alexander the Great increased this to ten and Philostephanus that Ptolemy Soter further increased this to twelve, Demetrius son of Antigonus to fifteen, Ptolemy Philadelphus to thirty, and Ptolemy Philopater, surnamed Tryphon, to forty. Hippus of Tyre invented the freight carrier, the Cyrenaeans the cutter, the Phoenicians the skiff, the Rhodians the yacht, and the Cypriots the yawl.

(**209**) The Phoenicians invented navigation through observation of the stars, the town of Copae invented the oar, and the Plataeans its blade, Icarus invented sails, Daedalus the mast and sail-yard. The Samians, or Pericles of Athens, invented the horse-carrier, the Thasians the warship with decks; previously fighting had taken place only at the prow and stern. Pisaeus son of Tyrrenus added beaks, Eupalamus the anchor, Anacharsis the two-pronged anchor, the Athenian Pericles grappling irons and claws, and Tiphys the tiller. Minos was the first to fight a naval battle. [Hyperbius son of Mars was the first to kill an animal, Prometheus an ox.]

(**210**) The first tacit agreement among all nations was the decision to use Ionian letters. That ancient Greek letters were almost the same as today's Latin ones can be confirmed by the ancient Delphic bronze dedication which may be seen today on the Palatine, through the generosity of the emperors, in the library. It is dedicated to Minerva and bears the following inscription: 'Nausicrates dedicated to the daughter of Zeus the tithe . . .'.

(**211**) The second agreement of the nations concerned the employment of barbers, but the Romans adopted this practice later than the rest. Barbers were first brought to Rome from Sicily in 300 BC by P. Titinius Mena, according to Varro. Before that date, long hair and beards were the norm. The younger Africanus was the first Roman to introduce daily shaving, a practice conscientiously adopted by the deified Augustus.

(**212**) The third agreement concerned time-keeping, and was on this occasion in keeping with scientific theory. I have already indicated in book 2 when and by whom this was invented in Greece (2. 187). This practice, too, reached Rome later. In the Twelve Tables, only sunrise and sunset are recorded. Some years later, midday was added and announced by the consuls' attendant when from the senate house he saw the sun between the Rostra and the Graecostasis. When the sun was declining from the Maenian column to the prison, he announced the last hour, but only on clear days and until the first Punic war.

(**213**) According to Fabius Vestalis, the first sundial was erected eleven years before the war with Pyrrhus by L. Papirius Cursor, in front of the temple of Quirinus which he was dedicating in fulfilment of his father's vow. However, Fabius indicates neither the principle of the sundial's construction, nor its maker or provenance, nor his source. (**214**) Marcus Varro records that the first sundial in a public place was set up by the consul M'. Valerius Messalla, on a pillar beside the Rostra, after the capture of Catania in Sicily during the first Punic war; and that it was imported from Sicily thirty years after the traditional date of Papirius' sundial, in 263 BC. The lines of this sundial did not agree with the hours, but they were followed for 99 years, until Q. Marcius Philippus, who was censor with L. Paulus, placed a more precisely constructed one next to it; a gift which was the most appreciated action of his censorship. (**215**) Even then, however, the hours remained uncertain on cloudy days until the next *lustrum*. Then, Scipio Nasica, the colleague of Laenas, was the first to use a water-clock to mark the equal hourly divisions of night as well as day. He dedicated this clock, which was installed under cover, in 159 BC. For so long had the Roman people been without a means of dividing their day!

Now we shall turn our attention to the rest of the animals, starting with those that live on land.

COMMENTARY

1–5. *The human animal: pinnacle or misfit of creation?*
The paradox of the human race, given its most explicit treatment
in these paras., recurs throughout *HN* 7 in various guises: see
Introd. 5. 4. For the ambiguity of human status in relation to the
rest of the animal kingdom, see 5. 2. 1 and 5. 2. 3.

1. The world The nature and constitution of the earth and
heavens are discussed in book 2.

lands . . . cities These were described in the geographical books
3–6.

peoples . . . cities That man and his works were part of the cosmos is in the ancient cosmographical tradition, cf. [Aristotle] *De
Mundo* 2. 391^{b}9–10; 3. 392^{b}19–20. The idea received various philosophical treatments, reinforcing arguments for an intelligent universe (Cicero, *ND* 2. 88) or for a divide between the terrestrial world
and the divine (Seneca, *Ad Marc.* 18. 2ff.). P.'s cosmology is remarkable for its stress on the human element for its own sake. Man is
often nature's partner, e.g. *HN* 36. 101, Roman public buildings
create 'another world' (cf. Cicero, *ND* 2. 152: a Stoic idea). See
Introd. 4. 4.

seas . . . Corrupt. Many MSS have *insignia*, 'notable' following
'seas', but the subject is missing. Emendations include ⟨flumina
insignia⟩, 'notable rivers' (Mayhoff), 'rivers and bays' (Sillig); and,
taking *insignia* substantively, 'ornaments' (cf. Cicero, *ND* 1. 100;
Schilling 125: but the 'ornaments' are specified there, whereas P.'s
remain vague).

if in fact . . . everything. I translate here Schilling's *si quidem
omnia exsequi humanus animus queat*. Alternatively, read *etsi ne hic quidem
omnia . . .*, 'albeit here too the human mind is not capable . . .', etc.
(Mayhoff). In either case the point seems to be that the size and
scope of this area of nature are almost inconceivable, cf. **7–8** below
and books 8–11 on the enormous variety exhibited within the
animal kingdom and its remarkable nature. The human mind is

dazzled by nature's variety (*varietas*) and bemused by her wonders (*mirabilia*). See Introd. 5. 2. 1–2.

The first place . . . created everything else. P.'s clearest statement in the *HN* of the teleological view rooted in earliest Greek thought, which made man the focal point of the universe and which he generally upholds. Later it was fundamental to Stoic cosmology according to which man was unique as a result of his possession of reason. See Introd. 5. 2. 2. Man was thus not only at the top of the scale of living things (cf. Plato, *Timaeus* 77); he was also fundamentally different from the rest of creation (R. Renehan, 'The Greek Anthropocentric View of Nature', *HSCP* 85 (1981), 247–50). Pliny's enthusiasm for the rest of the animal kingdom (books 8–11) at no time amounts to a denial of man's essential superiority (Beagon (1992), 133–44). Nor does his pungent account of man's weaknesses: see below, **2–5** and comm.

gifts There were problems with the Stoic-influenced view of nature's providence and kindness towards the human race. Elsewhere in the *HN* P. tries to circumvent them, e.g. 21. 77–8 (apparent 'evils' are in fact beneficial to man); 34. 138 (it is only man's misuse which makes substances like iron evil). In the end, he has to accommodate exceptions to his general rule: the bad things in nature are far outweighed by good ones (18. 5). See below, **parent . . . stepmother.**

parent . . . stepmother Cf. Cicero, *Rep.* 3. 1 = Augustine, *Contra Iulianum Pelag.* 4. 12. 60. See above, **gifts**, on nature's ambiguity. P. now examines the attributes given to man and concentrates on man's physical weakness in comparison to other animals. He follows a tradition of writing on the differences between man and animal (Cicero, *Rep.* 3. 1, Philo, *Post. Caini* 160–2, Seneca, *Ep.* 124; Plutarch, *Mor.* 98c–e; and, earlier, Plato, *Protag.* 321 ff.). Trends in philosophy towards moral questions and consequent stress on the mind's superiority to the body had led to man's mind ultimately giving him the edge in such comparisons. P.'s stress here on the physical weaknesses, combined with his comments on animal intelligence (*HN* books 7–9) has sometimes been interpreted as a denial of man's natural supremacy. But see Beagon (1992), ch. 4 and note that superiority is assumed in **1** ('The first place will *rightly* be assigned') and below in **3** ('the animal destined to rule all others').

Man's superiority is not at issue for P.; the complacancy and arrogance it inspires is. See below, **3. born to a position of pride.**
This is typical Plinian moralizing; a traditional topos is incorporated and the rhetorical possibilities of the paradox of man the weakling/ ruler are exploited (see below, **3. destined to rule**, and Introd. 5. 4).

2. variety of coverings   Cf. Cicero, *ND* 2. 121; Plato, *Protag.* 321a; Lucretius 4. 935–6.

Man alone . . . wailing.   Note the close resemblance to Lucretius 5. 222–7. Echoes of Lucretian pessimism are found elsewhere in the *HN* (see below, **5**) although Pliny's overall tone is one of optimism.

given to tears   Early editors, adding *pronius*, amended to 'more prone to tears' but some commentators objected on the grounds that animals did not shed tears, cf. Ajasson de Grandsagne (1827), i. 6.

smile   Cf. Aristotle, *HA* 7. 16, 587[b]; *GA* 5. 1, 779[a]. His statement that very young babies also cry only in their sleep is perhaps explained by his belief that they were in a state of sleep for most of the time. Solinus' (I. 72) and Augustine's (Introd. 4. 6. 1) later comment that an infant's first reaction to the light of day is to cry rather than laugh may derive directly from *HN* 7. For exceptional precocity, see **72. Zoroaster**.

3. chains . . . limbs.   The fetters and chains which shackle the human infant from birth are in part a metaphor for his physical helplessness but also refer to the literal restraints provided by the custom of swaddling; cf. the early 2nd-cent. AD physician, Soranus 2. 14 (83), describing a method which, despite his rejection of actually binding the infant into a kind of wooden strait-jacket, is nonetheless comprehensively incapacitating.

auspiciously   P. uses *feliciter*—'happily', 'favourably', 'successfully'—ironically, in alliterative contrast with *flens*, 'weeping'. The mechanics of the birth may have been successful but the infant's immediate prospects look anything but favourable. Its present misery in turn contrasts with its long-term destiny (see below, **destined to rule**).

destined to rule   This rhetorical paradox, that the future ruler starts out in fetters like a prisoner or slave, gives extra point to P.'s vivid portrayal (above, **chains . . . limbs**) of the infant's immobility.

the crime of being born.   Related to the commonplace that it would be better for man not to be born at all (e.g. Theognis 1. 425, Sophocles, *Oed. Col.* 1388–9; cf. Epicurus, *Ep. ad Men.* 126; Clement, *Strom.* 3. 14. 2) since life is so wretched (Empedocles B. 124 (Diels); [Plato] *Axioch.* 366d). Here, it is adapted specifically to P.'s 'prisoner' metaphor.

those who believe . . . born to a position of pride.   Literally 'born to pride'(*superbia*). The alliteration of the translation is designed to convey the rhetorical flourish of the final *sententia*. For man's tendency to get carried away by self-importance, see **43–4** below. Note P.'s language makes a careful distinction between man's natural destiny: 'born to rule' and the destiny some men misguidedly claim. To be proud and overbearing is to rule badly or cruelly, cf. **43. such beginnings . . . tyrants and murderers**, below. The moralizing approach to man's activity here and elsewhere (e.g. below, **131–2**) stems from Aristotle, *NE* 1111^{b}4ff., 1144^{b}24ff.: man, the possessor of reason, alone has the power of moral deliberation, cf. the later Stoic equation of *ratio*, reason, with *virtus*, moral excellence.

4. initial promise . . . gift of life   P.'s train of thought in this and the following sentences revolves around the cruel ambiguity of nature towards man. The 'promise' and 'gift' are illusory (cf. **1. parent . . . stepmother** above); the early 'animal' characteristics of the gait and voice being in fact signs of a weakness and slowness of development, which actually differentiate man from most quadrupeds. The toothless mouth and throbbing skull then emphasize a clear physical inferiority to animals.

walk   Man's upright stance was the most naturally perfect (*HA* 494^{a}30) according to Aristotle. It was also closest to the divine (Aristotle, *PA* 656^{a}5–10), a theme which developed into a commonplace (cf. Xenophon, *Mem.* 1. 4. 11; Cicero, *Leg.* 1. 26, *ND* 2. 140, Manilius 4. 903ff.; Seneca, *Ep.* 65. 20). Physically, upright growth followed the greater heat rising from the uniquely copious blood around the human heart (Aristotle, *PA* 653^{a}31). Young children cannot walk because the top half of the body is disproportionately large ('imperfect and dwarfish', Aristotle, *PA* 710^{b}13–15; cf. *HA* 501^{a}2), although in time the lower part will develop faster, enabling them to walk.

speak   Another power peculiar to man (Aristotle, *HA* 536^{b}1), and see below, **speaking**. Aristotle says it is only gradually attained by children, in whom the tongue is imperfect and does not develop complete mobility for a while *(PA* 660^{a}25). The absence of teeth also contributes; the nature of man's teeth (see below, **mouth . . . food**), especially the front teeth *(PA* 661^{b}15), is partially determined by speech: see below, **70. the front teeth . . . soften speech**. P. says *(HN* 11. 270) that the infant speaks when a year old: precocity can be a bad omen, as in the case of king Croesus of Lydia.

mouth . . . food   Other animals are more perfect at birth and therefore, unlike man, possess teeth *(*Aristotle, *GA* 745^{b}10*)*. However, Aristotle singles out man's teeth as being singularly well suited to their task of processing food *(PA* 661^{b}6).

skull throb   In *HN* 11. 135, P. says the brain throbs until the child first begins to talk. He refers to the anterior fontanelle, which closes about 18 months after birth. Aristotle calls it *bregma (HA* 491^{a}31) and regards it as a separate bone *(HA* 495^{a}10) 'the weakest in the head'. He explains that man's brain is larger than other animals' and generates more coldness and moisture to counterbalance the excessive heat around his heart (see above, **walk**). Continuous evaporation through the *bregma* above the brain causes this part of the skull to be the last to solidify *(PA* 653^{a}35–6). For excessive throbbing as a sign of precocity, see below, **72. Zoroaster**.

diseases . . . maladies.   We can look beyond this present passage, with its air of the rhetorical set-piece, to discover a genuine and uncharacteristic streak of pessimism in Pliny on this subject. He reflects bitterly on the large number of diseases *(HN* 25. 23) and expresses horror at the appearance of new ones *(HN* 26. 9). See Beagon (1992), 238; below, **not to be born at all**; and again in **167–9**, where the theme of the physical shortcomings of the human existence is reprised. Increasing ease of communication in the Roman empire may have helped to spread known diseases further afield, and introduce new ones. In *HN* 26. 1–4, P. describes a skin disease newly introduced from Asia Minor and discusses the habits

of new diseases generally; cf. frequent records of epidemics, e.g.
Dio 72. 14. 3–4 (brought back from Mesopotamia by Lucius Verus'
army in AD 189); Suet. *Nero* 39. 41; and earlier, Livy 39. 41; 40. 19, 36;
41, 21: see below **167. old age . . . torment, accidents . . .
worries** and **168. illnesses . . . classes**.

aware of their own natures   A. S. Pease (*M. Tulli Ciceronis De
Natura Deorum*, Cambridge, Mass., 1955) on Cicero, *ND* 2. 124 lists
numerous passages dealing with this primary law of nature. Cicero
(*ND* 121–30) treats the Stoic idea of nature's providence and
animals' instinctive knowledge of self-preservation and may be P.'s
source here: see above, **2. variety of coverings**.

taught . . . natural instinct   See above, **1. parent . . . stepmother**. Cicero (*Rep.* 3. 1–7) portrayed the exercising of man's
mental power as his triumph over initial physical weakness to attain
his supreme place in creation; cf. Lactantius, *Op. Dei* 3. 16–19, an
attitude in tune with P.'s premiss above, **1. The first place . . .
else**, and overall attitude in the *HN*. Here, however, he portrays
the need to acquire knowledge as another obstacle put in man's
way by stepmother nature; at least when it must be exercised to
acquire even the most basic skills of life given automatically to other
animals. The tone is not that of culture's triumph (cf. Plato *Protag.*
320c–322d; Euripides, *Suppl.* 201–15; Sophocles, *Ant.* 332–75; or
even the more ambiguous Lucretius 5. 1011–1457), but its uphill
struggle against an indifferent or hostile nature (cf. Virgil, *G.* I.
121–46) at its earliest and most fundamental stage.

speaking   Most ancient sources regarded speech primarily as an
acquired art, the most complex explanation coming from Epicurus
(*Ep. ad Herod.* 75–6), who saw it as the consequent refinement by
man of the basic sounds with which Nature had endowed him (see
C. Bailey (*Titi Lucreti Cari De Rerum Natura*, Oxford, 1947, iii) on
Lucretius, *RN* 5. 1486–90, for this and other ancient theories). That
communication with his own kind is effectively an acquired skill
rather than a natural gift is suggestive of nature's malevolence.

walking . . . eating   The human infant learns something of
these motions by imitation, but in turning from the role played by
slow physical development (above, **4. walk, mouth . . . food**) to a
need for learning in walking and eating P overstates the case. He
does, of course, exaggerate even the physical contrast with animals:

witness the early suckling of mammals and the flightlessness of fledgelings.

weep See above, 2. **given to tears.** Juvenal (15. 131ff.) remarked on the contradiction between man's unique refinement in sensitivity and his equally unique refinement in aggression (below, 5. **other species . . . man's case**).

not to be born at all This commonplace originated in the satyr Silenus' reply when captured and asked what was best for men, cf. Sophocles, *Oed. Col.* 1224–7; Theognis 425–8; Plutarch, *Mor.* 115b–e. Cicero, *Tusc.* 1. 113–15 quotes the Silenus and other stories to show that death is a blessing. P. states this at *HN* 2. 27 and elsewhere, especially in the context of the suffering caused by disease (above, 4. **diseases . . . maladies**): see below, **168. The truth . . . life**; and in *HN* 4. 89, 20. 199, 25. 24, and 28. 9 where ironically, it becomes nature's greatest gift to man. See Beagon (1992), 238–9.

5. P.'s picture of the ambiguity inherent in man increases in complexity as he moves from the physical weakness which may be set against his mental strength to the various emotions which undermine the mind itself.

To man alone Stoics tended to see emotions as the malfunctionings of a disturbed soul. Since animals lacked soul or reason (*logos, ratio*) they could not experience emotions.

sorrow . . . superstition Stoics divided emotions into four classes: pain, fear, desire and pleasure (Diogenes Laertius 7. 110, cf. Cicero, *Fin.* 3. 35). They were based on mistaken beliefs about good and evil, disturbing the harmony of the soul and the individual's chance of a good and therefore happy life. See *SVF* iii. 378 etc.; M. R. Wright, *Cosmology in Antiquity* (London, 1995), 145–8; A. A. Long and D. Sedley, *The Hellenistic Philosophers* (Cambridge, 1987), vol. i, sect. 65, 410–23; I. G. Kidd, 'Stoic Intermediates and the End for Man', in A. A. Long (ed.), *Problems in Roman Stoicism* (London, 1971), 200–15; B. Inwood, *Ethics and Human Action in Early Stoicism* (Oxford, 1985), ch. 5; J. M. Rist, *Stoic Philosophy* (Berkeley and London, 1978), 22–36. For excessive emotional repression amongst philosophers, see below, **79. However . . . philosophers**.

sorrow The logical emotion to start with, in view of the pessimistic view of life described here.

self-indulgence . . . body *Luxuria* (here translated as self-indulgence) is a key theme in Pliny's account of man in nature. Traditionally, it was an element in the perceived decline of Roman civilization from the simple morality of old—*mos maiorum*, 'ancestral custom'—a theme which became a commonplace in Roman writers (Sallust, *Jug.* I. 7; *Cat.* 11. 5; 12. 2; 13. 1–5; Livy 1, pref. 11–12). P.'s interest is partly due to his traditionalism but it also forms an integral part of his personal philosophy (see Introd. 3. 1. 1). He condoned the comfortable trappings of civilization, so long as their dispensability was recognized (see also below, **ambition, avarice**). But the disproportionate value man too often attached to them, and the ingenuity he could use in contriving them was a misuse of his mind, producing a passive decadence (*HN* 14. 1–6, cf. *Jug.* 1–3) and sometimes an arrogant perversion of nature itself (*HN* 9. 139; 22. 118); the opposite of life based in and according to nature (Beagon (1992), 17–18, 75–9, 190–4).

ambition, avarice The vices most famously paired in Sallust's depiction of the decline of the Roman republic (*Cat.* 10. 3–6; 11–12) and not as prominent as *luxuria* in the *HN*. However, examples such as *HN* 2. 118, where the eager trader's avarice blinds him to the danger of the sea, illustrate well the distorting effect of such emotions on the mind. P. follows the Stoic principle that the good things of life are to be preferred but not sought after to an unreasonable degree: *SVF* iii. 128; 124; Beagon (1992), 70, 75–7, 182.

unbounded appetite for life P. uses *cupido*, a desire taken to inordinate lengths: i.e. particularly irrational in view of his opinion that death is life's greatest blessing (above, **4. not to be born at all**, and below, **168. The truth . . . life**). Further scorn is poured on the irrationality of belief in an afterlife in **189–90**, especially **189. mortality . . . immortality**.

superstition Pliny was unusually sceptical by Roman standards, pouring scorn not only on all forms of popular religion, magic, and astrology but even on the traditional Olympian religion, most notably in *HN* 2. 14–27, and asserting a pantheistic belief in the divinity of nature. Cf. *HN* 30. 1 ff., 13, 19; 7. 179; 28. 29; 29. 76; books 20–32 *passim*; Beagon (1992), ch. 3.

burial . . . dead See below, **189–90**, where P. demolishes the idea of an afterlife, specifically linking it to another of the human follies mentioned here, greed for life (**189. mortality . . . immortality**). Burial was necessary to gain access to the underworld and avoid polluting the celestial gods (Homer, *Il.* 23, 71 ff.; Sophocles, *Aj.* 589; *Ant.* 1016 ff.; Virgil, *Aen.* 11. 51): hence the religiously sceptical Pliny's dismissive tone. Belief in an afterlife was by no means a clearly defined Roman attitude, however; for many, *memoria*, remembrance among the living, would have been the primary concern, and would be enhanced by a suitably dignified funeral. But this preoccupation, too, was illogical for one about to be consigned to blissful oblivion, although of considerable importance to survivors concerned for the family's prestige (see below, **139. funeral oration**).

To no animal . . . anger   These four categories of emotion are similar to those attributed to Stoic theory, above, **sorrow . . . superstition**.

precarious   Pliny's word, *fragilitas*, is twice used by Seneca, *Ad Marc.* 11. 3, to describe man's frailty. Physical injury and ageing can affect the mind as well as the body: see below, **90. No . . . fear** and **167–9.**

all-consuming . . . disruptive . . . violent   The adjectives vividly illustrate the threat posed by the emotions to fragile man. There is perhaps a hint of the greater compassion towards the human predicament to be found in later Stoicism (Beagon (1992), 71).

fear   The fundamental element of most emotional disturbance, according to Seneca (*Ad Marc.* 7. 4). Epictetus considered it a threat to Stoic freedom (4. 3. 7). The Epicurean Lucretius aimed to free man from fear of death by materialistic explanation of nature. For P., too, rational explanation of natural phenomena such as eclipses is helpful in combatting superstitious fear and ensuring the harmony of man's mind with nature (2. 31, 53–4; Beagon (1992), 72–4).

the other animals   A commonplace sentiment on animal superiority, cf. Horace *Epod.* 7. 11–12; Juvenal 15, 159–66, but not entirely borne out by statements in P. himself. He knows that some spiders may eat each other (*HN* 10. 198), cf. 10. 25 (mistaken beliefs about the cuckoo). Aristotle knew that hunger might occasionally drive animals to attack others of the same species (*HA* 8, 608^{b}19–26) and there might be fights for other reasons (610^{a}15, elephants).

other species . . . man's case   Fighting between different species fulfilled the need for natural balance (cf. *HN* 8. 91) and survival, though P. sometimes suggests that gratuitous violence was inherent in nature (*HN* 9. 13, 18. 34, Beagon (1992), 152). But his humanitarian ideal (*HN* 2. 14, for man to aid man is godlike), inspired by late Stoicism, made man's misuse of his own species the least acceptable of his perversions of nature.

6–8. *The diversity of the human race*

On human diversity as a major theme in *HN* 7, see Introd. 5. 2. 2 and 4. 3.

6. human race . . . discussed   Some ethnographical detail was included in the geographical books, 3–6.

habits and customs   P. does not intend to produce ethnographical and anthropological details of the kind collected by Herodotus and many historians after him. Book 7 concentrates on man the animal and the wonders of his body and mind, but see below, **countless.**

countless   This is why P. does in fact include an excursus (**9–32**) on strange races and their habits. One of the main themes in the *HN* is the variety of nature (e.g. *HN* 9. 102; 11. 123; 21. 1). In book 7 her variety is encapsulated in the human race (below, **7–8, 52**; Beagon (1992), 75): man is, in effect, a microcosm of nature, a status which emphasizes his supremacy within the natural order. See Introd. 4. 3, 5. 2. 2.

peoples furthest from the sea   By 'sea', P. means the Mediterranean and the other inner seas, as opposed to the ocean which encircled the earth and thus lay beyond the remotest outposts of land (*HN* 2. 173). Such peoples were mysterious and exotic because remote and therefore almost unknown. Areas nearest to the sea were the best known. Italy, according to Pliny (*HN* 3. 41), ran into the sea, positively seeking commerce and ensuring her position as centre of the world, 'uniting scattered empires'. Seafaring was the primary and easiest means of communication in the ancient world, whereas inland exploration could be hampered by impenetrable terrain: cf. Herodotus 4. 24–5. Gazetteers, such as Pliny's in books 3–6, tended to follow the primarily coastline descriptions (*periploi*) of military and mercantile seafarers (*HN* 2. 167–70), the seas defining the land masses (*HN* 3. 3–5) and the known interior being described in relation to the coast (*HN* 3. 46).

Ethiopians The epitome of the exotic and far-flung people, placed by Homer in the east and west extremities of the world (*Od.* 1. 23–4), by the shore of the Outer Ocean itself (*Il.* 23. 205) and frequently designated 'the furthest of men'. They were often endowed with a utopian longevity (Herodotus 3. 23), stature, beauty (Herodotus 3. 20), and virtue (Homer, *Il.* 4. 423; Nicolaus Dam. fr. 12). Although by P.'s time the name denoted an actual people south of Egypt (*HN* 5. 48; 6. 177–97, cf. Herodotus 3. 97), the term had often been used loosely, as Strabo points out when discussing the problem of the Homeric east–west division (1. 2. 24–8, C30–5), to describe all lands to the far south, from Mauretania in the west to Egypt and sometimes as far as India (below, **21**) in the east (J. Y. Nadeau, 'Ethiopians', *CQ* NS 20 (1970), 339–49; J. Ramin, *Mythologie et géographie* (Paris, 1979), 73–80). P.'s Ethiopians do not seem to extend further east than the Nile (*HN* 5. 47–8, 53; 6. 177; J. Desanges, *Histoire Naturelle V.1–46* (Paris 1980), 483–4), with a possible east–west division somewhere in Africa (*HN* 5. 43, cf. Desanges (1980), 445–6): his description of the Ethiopia south of Egypt (*HN* 6. 177–97) eventually ranges back to African tribes south of Mauretania and the Sahara, already described in book 5 (5, 10, 11–16, 17. 30, 34, 43, 44), some even bordering the Outer Ocean. But the stress here is on the resonance of the name, rather than geographical exactitude. Besides the more familiar tribes, P.'s Ethiopians included tribes to the west described as 'fabulous' (*HN* 6. 195) and ones in the southern extremities beyond Egypt, where the heat caused unusually large numbers of mutations and monstrosities (*HN* 6. 187: and below, **21. so great . . . water**); cf. the unspecified areas of Ethiopia rich in *mirabilia*, below, **21. India . . . Ethiopians**. For the mythical tradition, see A. Lesky, 'Aithiopika', *Hermes*, 87 (1957), 27–38; F. Snowden, *Before Color Prejudice: The Ancient View of Blacks* (London and Harvard, 1983), 3–17, 46–59; Romm (1992), 45–60.

what is not regarded as wondrous . . . attention? Truth is stranger than fiction; an attitude probably encouraged rather than dampened by the contemporary expansion of geographical knowledge (see Introd. 3. 3), when strange discoveries heightened expectation of what was to come. Relevant to his mention of Ethiopians is contemporary interest in Suetonius Paulinus' exploits in Africa (AD 42, *HN* 5. 11–15) a little known country (*HN* 22. 143) whose ability to produce new surprises was legendary (*HN* 8. 42). Cf. also the Augustan and Neronian expeditions into Ethiopia beyond Egypt (*HN* 6. 181). Yet despite eagerness for the new, P. is quite cautious over accepting *mirabilia:* see below, **8. I shall not pledge . . . issues**.

7. the power . . . piecemeal. P. suggests that individual wonders may seem unbelievable if examined in isolation: the extraordinary power of nature must, however, be accepted if the combined sum of all reputed wonders is taken into account. The infinite variety of nature is proof of her supremacy.

peacocks . . . tigers   Cf. *HN* 10. 43–5; 8. 6, 62–4.

markings   Nature's variety was found also in sea-shells (*HN* 9. 102), animal horns (*HN* 11. 123–4), and flowers (*HN* 21. 1), where P. depicts her as revelling in her virtuosity; as well as in protective coverings and means of locomotion (cf. above, **2. variety of coverings** and **4. aware of their own natures**).

boundless . . . human being   The various inflections of the human voice create differences among not only languages and dialects but even among individual human beings 'as great as that between them and the animals' (*HN* 11. 271, cf. Aristotle, *HA* 4. 536^{b}1–23). P. picks out aspects of the human voice and physiognomy (below) which set the scene for book 7's celebration of the ultimate superiority of humanity in two ways: first, by emphasizing the man–beast divide (cf. *HN* 11. 271, the human being's unique ability to voice thoughts); and secondly, by stressing the infinite variety of nature to be found in humanity as a race and even as individuals, in contrast to the uniformity of animals (see below, **52. This is the reason . . . particular species**): man is a microcosm of nature (see below, **18. Nature . . . present in man**). See Introd. 4. 3; 5. 2. 1–2.

8. few more than ten facial features   Only the human being has a face (*HN* 11. 138). P. describes various features in 11. 136–59 (ear, brow, eyes, eyelids, eyelashes, cheeks, nose, lips, mouth, chin, cf. Aristotle, *HA* 1. 491^{b}9–493^{a}4; *PA* 2. 657^{a}25–8; 662^{b}23). Some, such as cheeks (11. 157) and chin (11. 159), are unique to humans; others, such as eyelashes (11. 154) and a projecting nose (11. 158), are almost unique.

no two identical . . . components. Like the voice, eyes in particular display variations between man and man (*HN* 11. 141), both physical (shape, slant, etc.) and psychological (mirroring the thoughts and emotions of a unique mind, *HN* 11. 145–6). Subtle variations are possible, allowing nature to produce a variety beyond human art, working from an apparently small palette. Here and elsewhere (e.g. *HN* 11. 1–4, virtuosity on a minute scale in insects), P. reflects the Stoic concept of nature as supreme artist (Beagon (1992), 31–2, 65–6, 84–6, 130–1, 141). Despite noting the eyes as window of the soul in 11. 145–6, he dismisses as naive and inexact the human art of physiognomy, which attempts to divine an individual's psychology from facial features alone (11. 273–4; Beagon (1992), 113–19).

I shall not pledge . . . the sources . . . doubtful issues. See Introd. 5.5, for sources, and commentary ad loc. for individual authors. In **9–32** P. clearly takes a non-committal stance (see below, **9–32. introd.**), referring back continually to various Greek paradoxographical writers (see Introd. 3. 3). Several of the names coincide with those condemned in Aulus Gellius' (2nd cent. AD) attack on wonder literature (*NA* 9. 4. 3–4). His mention of Pliny's use of such stories (*NA* 9. 4. 7) clearly refers to *HN* 7. 9–32 and ignores his disclaimers here. However, P.'s eyewitness account of a sex-change is quoted at length (*NA* 9. 4. 13–16, cf. below, **34. hermaphrodites** and **36. I myself . . . in Africa**) and apparently prevents Gellius from condemning him outright.

Greek writers . . . greater. Normally, Pliny is prejudiced against Greek writers, due to his consciousness that Latin learning is being established in the shadow of the Greek achievement (see Introd. 2. 2, 3. 1. 1). He likes to suggest that Greek character failings such as levity, unreliability, and downright mendacity adversely affected their writings (*HN* 3. 48, 152; 25. 24; 28. 5–6; 29. 17; and see especially *HN* 37. 31–41 on the provenance of amber: Beagon (1992), 15–20). Here, however, such feelings are apparently submerged by his feeling for tradition and the authority of his predecessors (cf. *HN* 2. 54, 62; 14. 1). Additionally, P. might include stories for the sake of completeness, even if he thought them unreliable (cf. *HN* 29. 98), which could be a motive in this account of the human race. However, despite his justification (above, **6. what is not regarded as wondrous . . . attention?**), the virulent attacks on Greek mendacity elsewhere as well as the suspension of an authorial guarantee here, should raise some doubts as to the depth of his commitment to such stories.

9–32. introd. *Diverse strange and exotic races*

Although the exotic monstrosities described in sections **9–32** also appear scattered through the pages of many Greek and, later, Roman authors, it was P.'s assembly of so many all together in these chapters which helped to make him the *locus classicus* for later references: see J. B. Friedman, *The Monstrous Races in Medieval Art and Thought* (Harvard, 1981), 5–25; J. Céard, *La Nature et les prodiges: L'Insolite au 16e siècle en France* (Geneva, 1977), esp. pp. 12–21. For the wonder tradition generally, see Introd. 3. 3; Romm (1992); W. Hansen (trans. and comm.), *Phlegon of Tralles' Book of Wonders* (Exeter, 1996); J. D. P. Bolton, *Aristeas of Proconnesus* (Oxford, 1962); J. Hartog, *The Mirror of Herodotus* (Berkeley, 1988); E. Gabba, 'True History and False History in Classical Antiquity', *JRS* 71 (1981), 50–62; Wittcower (1942), 159–97 and bibliography under **21. India . . . Ethiopians**. The tradition was pre-eminently Graeco-Roman (Friedman (1981), 87) and was associated above all with the remotest regions of the world (see above, **6. peoples furthest from the sea**; and below, **21. India . . . Ethiopians**), in accordance with the tendency to marginalize culturally and spatially aspects of the abnormal, including the magical (R. Gordon, 'Aelian's Peony: The Location of Magic in the Graeco-Roman Tradition', *Comparative Criticism*, 9 (1987), 59–95, esp. 71–3) and paranormal (S. Johnston, *Restless Dead* (California, 1999), 59, 116, 170–2) as well as the exotic.

P., however, points out that monstrous races had once inhabited Italy and Sicily, the centre of the world (below, **9. Cyclopes, and Laestrygonians**) and that even today, races with strange and wondrous powers inhabit the heart of the Roman empire (below, **9. centre of the world . . . Sicily, 15. Marsi, 19. Hirpi** and cf. **9. very recently . . . human sacrifice**). Their inclusion in a catalogue of human *mirabilia* drawn predominantly from the far north or south serves to enhance P.'s idea of the pervasiveness of nature's power, the ubiquity of her variety (above, **7**; cf. *HN* 2. 208; 11. 4 etc.: see Introd. 3. 3; 5. 2. 2). Less consciously, perhaps, it is indicative of the change of attitude from fear to fascination in respect of many aspects of the unusual, as implied by Pliny's comment on inter-sexuals (below, **34. once . . . pets**). See Beagon, 'Situating Nature's Wonders in Pliny's *Natural History*', forthcoming.

For the most part, however, the stress is on the edges of the world. The geographical details given rarely offer the possibility of identification with any known locality, but serve instead to enhance the exoticism of the material. The descriptions frequently highlight extremity (boundaries, borders, river sources) and inaccessibility (mountains, mountain valleys, forests, deserts). Points for wonder among the races described include, besides the obvious physical anomalies (single feet, eyes in shoulders, etc.) which are preserved in the teratological tradition of the Middle Ages and later (Wittcower, (1942), 159 ff.), the bending or breaking by nature of her own rules of normality. P. includes transgressions of the natural law with regard to human longevity and the ageing process (**27–30**), nourishment (**9, 12, 25, 30**), and sexual maturity and proclivity (**15, 23, 29, 30**). The boundary between man and animal is sometimes blurred (dog-headed men) and even specifically crossed (man–animal hybrids).

Numerous sources are cited, including paradoxographers like Isigonus and Agatharchides but also many of the Alexander historians and other writers on India whose writings evidently contained much that was fantastic, as Aulus Gellius (9. 4. 4) confirms for Ctesias and Onesicritus. Traditions concerning the remote north derive primarily from Herodotus and probably (though not directly) the lost poem attributed to Aristeas of Proconnesus (see below, **10. Aristeas of Proconnesus**). It is unlikely that P. read them all at first hand; epitomes of wonder-writing, like that posited for the 2nd-cent. Greek scholar Agatharchides of Cnidos (below, **14. Agatharchides**) and extant in the case of another 2nd-cent. writer, Apollonius (*OCD*[3], Apollonius (5), 127), may have been useful. The Greek origins of these tales are reflected in the names given to the monstrous races: Monocoli, Sciapodae, Trogodytae, Cynocephali (see below, comm. ad loc.). It should be noted that all the material, with the possible exception of sections **31–2**, is clearly attributed to other authors without personal corroboration from

Pliny. This is not always clear in translation but it was often ignored even by those reading the original, with the result that this passage played a major role in the creation of the well-worn myth of the 'credulous Pliny' (e.g. Wittcower (1942), 166–7; cf. Beagon (1992), 11; Introd. 4. 6. 1). Pliny's own attitude was rather more sophisticated than straightforward credulity or scepticism. The catalogue format (compare the catalogue of inventions, Intro. 5. 5 and **191– 215. introd.**), by which both wonders and authorities are listed in quick succession, is a feature of paradoxological works and is evident in P.'s treatment, particularly from **21** onwards. It has been seen as both encouraging belief by the factual tone, while at the same time absolving the author from personal responsibility by frequent citation of sources (see Romm (1992), 92ff.): *caveat lector*, but without assuming gullibility on the part of the author. The catalogue format has two further effects; one, obviously, is the imparting of authorial *auctoritas* through the citation of such a plethora of sources. The second is the reinforcement by so many natural wonders of P.'s *leitmotif* in book 7 and elsewhere in the *HN*: the variety of nature (see above, **6–8**, Introd. 4. 3, and cf. Beagon (1992), Romm (1992), 104–7). These are nature's sports, displayed in a lighthearted if virtuoso performance: see below, **32. cleverly contrived . . . amaze.**

9–12. *Strange peoples of the far north*

9. I have mentioned   *HN* 4. 88; 6. 50, 53.

Scythian   A group of mainly nomadic and pastoral tribes in central Asia: *OCD*[3], Scythia, 1374–5; J. Matthews, *The Roman Empire of Ammianus* (London, 1989), 332–42; R. Rolle, *The World of the Scythians* (London, 1989); A. I. Melyukova, 'The Scythians and Sarmatians', in D. Sinor (ed.), *The Cambridge History of Early Inner Asia* (Cambridge, 1990), 97–117. The area known to Herodotus as Scythia (book 4) was between the Carpathian mountains and the river Don, but P.'s Scythia is a vaguer and wider entity embracing the whole of north Asia from the sea of Azov to China in the east, and India in the south. His imprecise geography is made more perplexing by the mistaken belief in a northern outlet of the Caspian Sea into a Northern or Scythian Ocean, whence the coast gradually bent eastwards to a seaboard beyond China (see J. André and J.

Filliozat, *Pline l'Ancien Histoire Naturelle livre 6* (Paris, 1980), on *HN* 6. 53 ff.). His image of the unknown northern extremities of the Asiatic land-mass is thus somewhat truncated.

a good number P.'s wider definition of 'Scythian' explains his divergence on this point from Herodotus (*Hist.* 4. 18), who stresses that the far northern man-eaters are not really Scythians at all. Strabo (4. 5. 4, 201C) plays down the extent of Scythian cannibalism.

eat human flesh P. distinguishes two groups of cannibals; one to the far north (**10**: near the North Wind, **12**: ten days' journey beyond the Borysthenes [the Dneiper]) and 'others' to the north of the Himalayas (see below, this note). The former description fits in with *HN* 4. 88, where Scythian cannibals are placed to the north beyond the sea of Azov, and *HN* 6. 53–4, where man-eaters are placed on the coast of the Northern Sea (see above, **Scythian**), to the east of an uninhabitable area of snow. While cannibalism was occasionally attributed to southern peoples (*HN* 6. 195; Solinus 30. 7; Philostratus, *Vit. Apoll.* 6. 25), it was overwhelmingly a character-istic associated with the north and, in particular, with the Scythians (Herodotus 4. 100, 106; Aristotle, *NE* 7. 5, 1148[b]; Strabo 4. 5. 4, C201; cf. also below, **12. drink out of human skulls, 23. dog-headed men**). The tradition had a long life, with northern Anthropophagi featuring in later wonder literature and appearing on maps, e.g. the 14th-cent. Hereford Mappa Mundi. Certainly, P.'s stress is on the remote north, just as his Ethiopians and Indians (**6** and **21–31**) epitomize the exotic south, cf. Herodotus' Maneaters (4. 18), well to the north of his Scythia and bordering on 'utterly lifeless desert'. The vague reference to 'other' cannibals (below, **11. other man-eating tribes**) may reflect confusing information about the fluctuating nomadic tribes (*HN* 6. 50) or splits in migrating groups (cf. W. W. How and J. Wells, *A Commentary on Herodotus with Introduction and Appendixes* (Oxford, 1912), on Herodotus' 'separate' Scyths, 4. 22); and P. did know of man-eaters as far south as India 'towards Scythia' (*HN* 6. 55, the Cassiri; cf. Herodotus 3. 38, 3. 99, and, north of India, the Massagetae and Issedones, 4. 25, 1. 216: see Bolton (1962), 104–18). In any case, actual geographical location is secondary to the imagery by which severe cultural anomalies such as cannibalism tended to place their practitioners on the very edges of the world, even when, as was the case with the Scythians, they were not as remote as some of the purely mythical peoples (see Hartog (1988), 12–14). In general, cannibalism enhanced the picture of remote peoples as savages, marginal, inhuman and even bestial (cf. below, **18. bestial habit**), in opposition to the civilized norm of the Mediterranean centre (M. Détienne, *Dionysus mis à mort* (Paris, 1977), 142–5; D. Hughes, *Human Sacrifice in Ancient Greece* (London, 1991), 188–9); though, conversely, remote peoples could be idealized and used to comment on the centre's decadence, a theme familiar from Hellenistic philosophy and later, though also present earlier (see Romm (1992), 45–9). Hence an alternative picture of Scythians as milk-drinking paragons of justice, cf. Strabo 7. 3. 9, C302. However, P.'s stress on the ubiquity of nature's variety to some extent weakens the fringe–centre antithesis in his writing: he points out that her wonders are not entirely confined to her extremities (see above, **9–32. introd.**) with refs. and below, **centre of the world**).

centre of the world . . . Sicily   The words 'and Italy' are omitted, since they are probably a gloss (Hardouin 15). By 'centre of the world', Pliny in fact means Italy (cf. *HN* 37. 201); whereas Sicily is a separate geographical entity (*HN* 2. 204). For the fringe–centre antithesis and P.'s modification of it in keeping with his natural variety theme, see above, **9–32. introd.**, and **eat human flesh**. Thus, wondrous peoples had not always been confined to the edges of the world and cannibals (see below, **Cyclopes** and **Laestrygones**) had once inhabited the heartlands of Rome's empire, while human sacrifice was until recently practised on her doorstep. See also below, **15. Marsi** and **19. Hirpi**, for Italian peoples with bizarre powers.

Cyclopes   One-eyed giants who, according to one tradition (Hesiod, *Theog.* 149), were divine craftsmen, often associated with Hephaestus and his volcanic forges, most famously Mt. Etna in Sicily (Virgil, *Aen.* 8. 440). See below, **195. towers . . . Cyclopes . . . Theophrastus, 197. Cyclopes** and **Hesiod . . . Dactyli . . . Crete; 198. Iron-working . . . Cyclopes**. But uppermost in P.'s mind here is the Homeric tradition of savage cannibals (*Od.* 9. 106 ff.), later associated with Sicily. See *OCD*[3], 417.

Laestrygones   Fabulous cannibalistic giants who featured in

Homer's *Odyssey* (10. 86–132) and were later located either in Sicily (Thucydides 6. 2. 1) or in Italy at Formiae (Cic. *Att.* 2. 13. 2) as does P. in 3. 49 (although *HN* 3. 89 preserves the Sicilian tradition). Homer's (*Od.* 10. 82 f.) reference to short nights suggests the original story in fact assigned them to the mythical fringes of the world. See above, **6. peoples furthest from the sea, 9. centre of the world**; and *OCD*3, 811–12.

very recently . . . human sacrifice   P. refers to the sacrifices of the Celtic Druids (Caesar, *BG* 6. 16; Cicero, *Font.* 31, Strabo 4. 4. 5, C198; Diodorus Siculus 5. 31. 3–4, cf. Cicero, *Rep.* 3. 13–15; Minucius Felix, *Oct.* 30. 4; also Strabo 7. 2. 3, C294 (the Cimbri)). Like cannibalism, human sacrifice was a potent marker of other-ness, alien to Graeco-Roman civilization. See J. Rives, 'Human Sacrifice among Pagans and Christians', *JRS* 85 (1995), 65–84. P. expresses this sense of alienation especially strongly in *HN* 30. 13. In the case of the Gauls, while founded apparently in fact, the practice offered the Romans above all an excuse to suppress the Druids, a caste whose learning and authority made it the focus and instigator of nationalist resistance to Rome. P. attributes the suppression to Tiberius (*HN* 30. 13) possibly after the Gallic nationalist uprising of Julius Sacrovir (AD 21). Druidic secrecy and inaccessibility may explain why more than one suppression is mentioned in our sources, ranging from the time of Caesar or Augustus (Strabo 4. 4. 5, C198) to Claudius (Suet. *Claud.* 25); and why there were still Druids at large in AD 71 to prophesy Rome's destruction (Tac. *Hist.* 4. 54. 2). However, the foundation of Augustodunum at Bibracte, site of an important Druidic school, may have precipitated an inex-orable decline in their influence as significant as any active sup-pression. Rome's abhorrence of the sacrificial rites may be slightly exaggerated: in times of crisis she had buried alive couples from peoples with whom she was at war (or who were regarded as arche-typal enemies of Rome: A. M. Eckstein, 'Human Sacrifice and Fear of Military Disaster in Republican Rome', *AJAH* 7 (1982), 69–95), e.g. in 228 BC (Orosius 4. 13. 3), after Cannae in 216 BC (Livy 22. 57), and in 114 BC (Livy, *Per.* 63, cf. Plutarch, *RQ* 284c); and P. says the practice was banned as late as 97 BC (*HN* 30. 13). He even suggests an isolated revival at Rome in his own time—*nostra aetas vidit*, 'our age has seen' (*HN* 28. 12)—possibly to be attributed to Claudius (but see below on P.'s temporal phrases), who was known for his superstition as well as his antiquarianism, cf. his execution of a knight from the Gallic Vocontii for using Druidic magic in a court-case (*HN* 29. 54) and his attempts at extirpating the caste mentioned by Suetonius (*Claud.* 25). See R. Syme, *Tacitus*, i (Oxford, 1958), 456–9; H. D. Rankin, *Celts and the Classical World*[2] (London, 1996) 285–94.

That the Druidic suppression was 'very recent' has led to suggestions (Schilling xv, 128) that P took the passage from the Tiberian writer Verrius Flaccus (Introd. 4. 5. 1), but P.'s temporal adjectives are often loosely used: see Introd. 4. 5. 3. In addition, as we saw, Tiberius' suppression need not necessarily have been the latest. P. may in any case have had personal knowledge (see Introd. 1) of Gaul and her customs.

one step removed   For the Greeks, eating the sacrificial meat was normally an integral part of the sacrificial ceremony. Hence, alien sacrificial rites, too, might be closely associated with alien alimentary custom; see Hughes (1991), 188–9.

10. Scythians who face northwards   See above, **Scythians**.

the North Wind . . . Earth's Windpipe   Boreas' northern kingdom was a well-established tradition in classical literature. His cave (Sophocles, *Ant.* 981; Silius Italicus 8. 514) was seven-chambered (Callimachus, *Hymn. Del.* 62 ff.) and its northerly situation sometimes described as Thracian or Scythian (Lucan, *Phars.* 5. 603) or situated in the mythical northern Rhipaean mountains (Strabo 7. 3. 1, C295), as in *HN* 4. 88. See Wernicke, *RE* 3. 1, Boreas (2), 722–3; *OCD*[3], 253. For a belief prevalent in central Asia and Siberia that winds lived in caves in the mountains and for travellers' records of winds sweeping violently through narrow mountain defiles, in particular the Dzungarian gate, in the region of the Altaic steppe, see Bolton (1962), 94–6, who suggests the translation given here of the Greek name *Ges Cleithron* as the most appropriate (45). *Cleithron* is normally rendered 'door-bar' (cf. Rackham, 191), but is used to mean the epiglottis or 'entrance to the windpipe' in the Hippocratic corpus (*De Morbis* 2. 28. 2, 11, 7. 46 L). For anatomical metaphor in describing geographical locations, see Bolton, loc. cit. The application of such metaphors to the earth in particular was encouraged by the Stoic idea of the world as a living organism: cf. Seneca, *NQ* 3. 15. 1 on earth's veins and arteries, Pliny *HN* 33. 1–2, on her *viscera*, 'entrails'.

Arimaspi See *OCD*³, 157. In *HN* 6. 50, P. places these just to the south of the mythical northern Rhipaean mountains (see below, **gold mines**) and, in *HN* 4. 88, to the far north of the Maeotae who live on the coast of the Sea of Azov. According to Herodotus (4. 130), evidence for their existence was mere hearsay, tales told of 'the distant north' by the Issedones, who were themselves on the margins of the known northern lands (Herod. 4. 24–6), perhaps to the north-east of the Caspian Sea, or even as far east as Central Asia, according to Ptolemy, towards the borders of China. The location of these numerous and nomadic northern tribes was a vexed question even in antiquity, cf. P.'s comment in *HN* 6. 51. The geographical theories of modern commentators are examined by Bolton (1962), 104–18, who places the Issedones between the Irtysh and the Syr, and the Arimaspians (in his view 'not entirely creatures of the imagination', 74–85) around the upper Irtysh. The name 'Arimaspi' meant 'one-eyed' in Scythian, according to Herodotus (4. 27). Yet, despite alternative modern derivations, or attempts to rationalize the 'one eye', or to identify them with actual peoples, such as ancestors of the Huns and Turks, and assign them to a specific territory (see André and Filliozat (1980), 69, on *HN* 6. 50; Wernicke, *RE* 2. 1, Arimaspoi, 826–7), they are essentially mythical savages like the one-eyed Cyclopes (see above, **9. Cyclopes**). P.'s point is, once again, the human *mirabilia* of these mysterious marginal areas of the world.

Herodotus The 5th-cent. BC Greek historian from Halicarnassus, whose excursuses on peoples and customs both historical and fabulous were of central importance in the development of the ancient geographical, ethnographical, and paradoxographical traditions (see Introd. 3. 3). See *OCD*³, 696–8.

Aristeas of Proconnesus Knowledge of this semi-legendary poet and servant of Apollo (probably of the first half of the 7th cent., Herod. 4. 15) comes mainly from Herodotus 4. 13–16. See *OCD*³, Aristeas (1), 159–60; Bethe, *RE* 2. 1, Aristeas, 876–8; How and Wells (1912), i. 306–7; Bolton (1962), *passim*. His poem, the *Arimaspea* seems to have been lost sometime in antiquity, though its stories survived indirectly in other writings, including, perhaps, paradoxographical compilations which P. might have used: see Bolton, 20–38. It described a journey he claimed to have made while possessed by Apollo to the Issedones (above, **Arimaspi**), and included their tales of the peoples living beyond them; see Bolton (1962), 119–41; Romm (1992), 71–4. The miraculous feats of Aristeas himself, connected with the cult of Apollo (Herod. 4. 14–15) were as strange as anything in his poem and elicit scepticism from P. See further below, **174–5. among other examples**, and **174. Aristeas . . . raven**.

gold mines   Central Asia was rich in metals, including gold. P.'s mention of the mythical Rhipaean mountains beyond the Arimaspi in *HN* 4. 88 could suggest the gold-bearing Urals, but more likely they are the Altai further east, where there is clear evidence of early gold-mining (Rolle (1989), 52–3) and ancient trade routes from China to the West. The sand in the foothills of the Altai also yielded particles of placer gold: see A. Mayor, *The First Fossil Hunters* (Princeton, 2000), 37. Herodotus' description of the region (4. 17 ff.), starting from Greek Olbia on the north coast of the Black Sea, through Scythia to the Arimaspi, griffins, etc., follows an ancient trade route. See also Bolton (1962), 104–18; cf. above, **Arimaspi**, who favoured the Tarbagatai mountains with their gold-bearing streams.

griffins   Griffins were mythical animals found in both Greek and Oriental culture and popular in art. They were also found in the animal-style art of the Scythians (E. D. Phillips, *The Royal Hordes: Nomad Peoples of the Steppes* (London, 1965), 55–63), which was influenced by various cultures including Anatolia, the Near East, and Greece. The Chaldaean griffin was a winged lion, while the Egyptian and Greek type had the body of a lion with the head and wings of an eagle, often with ears (see Pliny, *HN* 10. 136). Gold-digging monsters existed in central Asian myth, though they may not originally have had the griffin shape: see Bolton (1962), 85–93; Ziegler, *RE* 7. 2, Gryps, 1902–9. Adrienne Mayor (2000), 15–53 has ingeniously argued that inspiration for the eagle-headed griffin came from the numerous well-preserved skeletons of the Cretaceous dinosaurs Protoceratops and Psittacosaurus, often found partially or wholly exposed in the Gobi desert, the foothills of the Altai and Tien Shan, and westwards into Uzbekistan. She notes their birdlike beak and hip structures and suggests that gold particles scattered over the fossil beds of dinosaur skeletons and nests by rains and sand storms 'might well have sparked the ancient idea that griffins had gathered the gold' (45). In her view, the main inspiration for the Graeco-Roman griffin originated in Scythian lore, inevitably elaborated as it travelled west.

burrows This translation of *cuniculis* (burrows, holes, tunnels) offers the most plausible form of mining for an animal and offers a parallel with the gold-digging ants of India (below, **The beasts . . . steal**), both animals being classed by P. in *HN* 33. 66 as providing one of four possible ways in which to dig for gold. Although he does use *cunicula* to denote underground tunnels in mines (*HN* 33. 71), it is in the context of the deep *arrugiae*, which he classes as the most difficult and dangerous type of mine. The notion that the griffins throw up gold from burrows may in fact be a reference to its nesting activities, cf. Aelian's later description, in which he says that the griffins dig up gold and weave it into their nests. He also dismisses the idea (below, **The beasts . . . steal**, and **amazing rapacity**) that they are guarding the gold; rather, they fear for their chicks when they see gold prospectors approaching (*NA* 4. 27).

The beasts . . . steal For Aelian's scepticism as to the griffins' intentions, see above, previous note. The story is found in Herodotus (3. 116, 4. 13, 4. 27) and Aeschylus *(PV* 802–4) and became popular in Greek art from the 5th cent. BC. Some see the story as a mythologizing of the difficulties of getting a rare and precious commodity from the very edges of the world where, according to Herodotus (3. 116), such things were so often situated. The griffins were analogous to the gold-digging ants Herodotus (3. 102 ff.) placed in north India and sometimes interchangeable with them, to judge from Ctesias, who places griffins in north India (Ctesias, *Ind.* 26; cf. Aelian, *HA* 4. 27: see How and Wells (1912), i. 307 and Bolton (1962), 64–7).

amazing rapacity P. moralizes on the well-worn topic of human greed for gold in *HN* 33. 1–57 and sees it as the root cause of many of the vices attendant upon civilization. The greed is compounded by the unnatural act of mining, which involves forcing from an unwilling earth unnecessary or even harmful commodities which she has deliberately hidden (*HN* 33. 2–3), cf. Horace, *Od.* 3. 3. 49; Seneca, *Ep.* 94. 56–7. He is surprised to find such covetousness so far from the central areas of civilization, among savage men and wild beasts who are beyond the reach of the less salutary effects of the *Pax Romana* as described in *HN* 14. 2–6. His comment undermines the idealization of such primitive struggles (see Romm (1992), 69–70; *cf.* above, **9. eat human flesh**) as epitomizing qualities of hardy resourcefulness in the struggle against untamed nature, long lost to *polis* culture. Indeed, he is no more enamoured of unnecessary primitivism than he is of unnecessary luxury: see Beagon (1992), 75–9.

11. other man-eating Scythian tribes See above, **9. eat human flesh.**

Mt. Imavus Imavus, Imaus, Imaos, and Hemodus are variants on the same name: see André and Filliozat (1980), 980 on *HN* 6. 60, where P. derives the name from 'snowy'. The Himalayas are probably meant, although P.'s distinction in *HN* 6. 60 and 6. 64 between Hemodus and Imaus might suggest he is referring to different parts of the huge ranges to the north of India. Imaus in *HN* 6. 64 is a 'projection' of the Hemodi mountains, which could make it more specifically the Karakoram range or even the Tien Shan to the north. For various interpretations, see Hermann and Wecker, *RE* 9, Imaon, Imaos, 2541–3; E. H. Bunbury, *A History of Ancient Geography* (London, 1879), ii. 286, 417; H. F. Tozer, *A History of Ancient Geography*[2] (Cambridge, 1935), 149; André and Filliozat (1980), 980; Schilling (1977), 129.

wild men . . . back to front Cf. Gellius, *NA* 9. 4. 6; Augustine, *CD* 16. 8. The legend was long-lived; a reverse-footed man appeared in Ulisse Aldrovandi's *Monstrorum Historia* of 1642. For the breathing problems and the swiftness, compare the Astomi (below, **25**) and the Indian 'monkey' tribe (below, **30**) respectively and cf. the wild men of Strabo 15. 1. 57, C711. Poisinet (Ajasson de Grandsagne 1827: 17) commented on a visual illusion which makes runners viewed from afar appear to have reversed feet. The creature is in some ways an ancient counterpart of the modern Himalayan myth, the Yeti, whom Bolton (1962: 186, n.90) noted had acquired backward feet, a characteristic of supernatural beings in the east, in some modern reports.

brought to the neighbouring kings The tradition of presenting to kings and emperors rare and strange items symbolized the ruler's status: the most recondite and exotic objects from within his realm or even from the furthest corners of the world were nonetheless placed within his power. Garland (1995), 45 notes that monsters were in some sense analogous to the ruler's 'constitutional, social and amoral uniqueness'. See also Millar (1992), 139–40. P. has many wonder stories involving Alexander (*HN* 8. 149–50) and Roman emperors (e.g. *HN* 9. 9–10, 10. 5). See below, **34, 56, 74, 75,** and Introd. That the wild men cannot be brought to kings, etc. is an insurance against proven deception which at the same time enhances, through its unobtainability, the prestige of this particular wonder.

Baeton See K. Müller, *The Fragments of the Lost Historians of Alexander the Great* (Paris, 1846; repr. Chicago, 1979), 134–5; Schwartz, *RE* 2. 2, Baiton 2779. Together with Diognetus, another bematist, he is used by P. for his itinerary of India (*HN* 6. 61–3, 69). Knowledge of the man and his work on Alexander's journeys is derived from these references and Athenaeus 10. 442b.

12. Isigonus of Nicaea A paradoxographer of uncertain date (1st cent. BC/AD: Gossen, *RE* 9. 2, Isigonos, 2082), he is cited by P. in **16** and **27** (below) and in the index to books 11, 12, and 13 (Giannini fr. 146–8, pp. 15–20), cf. Gellius, *NA* 9. 4. His subject-matter included waters (cf. Paradoxographus Florentinus, Giannini 315–29) and peoples, as here. See *OCD*³, 768.

first-mentioned . . . Scythians See above, **9. eat human flesh.**

Borysthenes The Dnieper.

drink out of human skulls Herodotus said that the Scyths collected scalps and gilded the skulls of enemies to use as drinking cups (4. 65–6, cf. Plato, *Euthydemus* 299, Strabo 7. 3. 7, C300); possibly partly in order to absorb the enemy's power (Rolle (1989), 82 and cf. also their custom of drinking the blood of the first enemy slain, Herodotus 4. 64 and below, **23. dog-headed men**). Like cannibalism (above, **9. eat human flesh**), this was a savage custom particularly associated in ancient thought with northerners, including Germanic and Celtic tribes. In 216 BC, the victorious Boii converted a Roman commander's skull into a sacred vessel (Livy 23. 24). In AD 566, the skull of Cunimund, king of the Gepidae, was similarly converted by the Lombard king Alboin, according to Paul the Deacon (*History of the Lombards* i. 27), who claimed to have seen the cup 200 years later (ii. 28).

Albania   A country on the west coast of the Caspian Sea, with fertile flat-lands watered by the river Cyrus (Pliny, *HN* 6. 29, 38–9; Strabo 11. 4. 1–8, C491). See *OCD*³, 50.

white-haired . . . see better by night   These are not mentioned in Strabo's account (11. 4. 1–8, C491). The white hair and poor daylight vision (cf. Apollonius, *Parod.* fr. 24, Giannini) fit the condition of albinism, in which the pigment which colours the hair, skin, and eyes is lacking, and photophobia and other visual problems occur. The irises look transparent at birth, but can darken slightly with age: hence, perhaps, P.'s reference to their 'blue/grey' colour (*caesus*), which in *HN* 11. 142 is also said to be the colour most suitable for night-vision. Although it is rare, and occurs among all races, it is also genetic and more prevalent in some races than in others. However, Pliny's association of the condition with a country is likely to derive from the association of the country's name with *albus*, white.

The Sauromatae   The Sauromatae or Sarmatae (Pliny uses both names, cf. *HN* 4. 88) were a nomadic people living east of the Don in Herodotus' day (Herodotus 4. 116) but gradually migrating westwards towards the Danube from 250 BC (*OCD*³, Sarmatae, 1367; Phillips (1965), 92ff.; Melyukova (1990), 110–17). Pliny mentions the two main tribes, the Iazages and Rhoxolani, as being north of the Danube (*HN* 4. 80–1) but his references reflect the people's numerous subdivisions, intermingling with the Scythians they had displaced and covering a wide area around the north coast of the Black Sea, and as far as the mouth of the Don and the north-western Caucasus (*HN* 4. 88, 6. 17, 19, 30–1, 38–40). The Sarmatians mentioned here are possibly east of the northern man-eaters (cf. *HN* 4. 88).

eat every other day   In *HN* 25. 82, Scythians are said to ward off hunger and thirst by placing in their mouths a plant, Scythice, which grows around the Sea of Azov. These comments on Sarmatian alimentary customs may reflect their harsh, nomadic lifestyle and the severity of the climate in these regions (Strabo 7. 3. 18, C307). Strabo also suggests that some northern nomads 'beyond the Chersonese' relied almost solely on their horses for survival, living largely on mare's milk and cheese and horse meat (7. 4. 6, C311). In dire need, Scythians bled their horses and survived on the blood (Rolle (1989), 82).

13–20. introd. *People with uncanny powers*

P. offers a survey of peoples who possess magical and mysterious powers. Most are situated in the northern (Scythia, Pontus) or southern (Africa) fringes, but one, the Marsi, hails from Italy itself (see above, **9–32. introd.**; and Beagon, 'Situating Nature's Wonders', forthcoming). Their powers are often manifest in particular parts of the body: the gaze of the eye (**16, 17**), the sound of the voice (**16**), the touch of hand or foot (**13, 19, 20**), or the application of body fluids (**13, 14, 15, 17**), cf. **18. Nature . . . present in man**. It is to be noted that the features given most emphasis here—snake-charming, saliva, and the Evil Eye—are closely interconnected in magical lore. The snake was an ambiguous, marginal creature, a land animal without legs, associated with the underworld (see G. E. R. Lloyd, *Science, Folklore and Ideology* (Cambridge, 1983), 10–11). According to Pliny *HN* 29. 71, the malignancy of snake's venom was in some way triggered by the moon, a heavenly body closely connected with magic, witchcraft, and demonic powers and, by virtue of its humidity, possessing a rapport with various terrestrial humours, including saliva, and their medico-magical potency. On these and other lunar qualities, see below, **38. only children conceived . . . no moon**, **42. full moon . . . babies**, and **66. This amazingly . . . occurs at all**. Snakes' eyes were strange: their poor sight (*HN* 8. 87) could be medicinally enhanced (*HN* 8. 99), and they could even be regrown if one was lost (*HN* 11. 153). They could fascinate their prey and the legendary basilisk's glance could kill a man (*HN* 8. 78, 29. 66). The strange facial decoration donned by the younger Pliny's colleague in the lawcourts, M. Aquilius Regulus, whose *cognomen* was a Latin translation of the Greek *basiliskos*, may have been intended as a likeness of that snake. Perhaps he wished to intimidate opponents by threatening them with fascination (J. Heurgon, 'Les Sortilèges d'un avocat sous Trajan', *Scripta Varia* (Brussels 1986), 99–104), although J.-B. Clerc, pointing to the homoeopathic use of the snake, like the eye, as an amulet against fascination, suggests his intention might have been defensive (J. -B. Clerc, *Homines Magici* (Bern, 1995), 100–1). Spitting was an apotropaic action against the Evil Eye common in folklore (Thompson, D 2071. 1. 1 and below, **15. snakes . . . saliva**; cf. Pliny, *HN* 28. 36, 39) and was also effective against snakes. The envious possessor of the Evil Eye was frequently compared to a poisonous snake, covertly building up its poison: see K. M. D. Dunbabin and M. W. Dickie, '*Invida rumpantur pectora*: The Iconography of *phthonos/invidia* in Graeco-Roman Art', *Jahrbuch für antike und Christentum*, 26 (1983), 7–27. Such an individual could be throttled or even burst by envy (Martial 8. 61, Virgil, *Ecl.* 7. 25); just as the snake could be choked or burst if spat upon, especially if the saliva entered its throat (below, **15. throat . . . fasting man**). Incantations could similarly 'blast' and 'burst' snakes (Lucil. fr. 605; Virgil, *Ecl.* 8. 71; Ovid, *Met.* 7. 203, *Am.* 2. 1. 26, *Med. Fac.* 39; cf. *HN* 22. 106, 28. 19), an image surely to be explained by this connection between snakes and the Evil Eye, rather than by the poetic/superstitious exaggeration suggested by A.-M. Tupet (*La Magie dans la poèsie Latine* (Paris, 1976), 194; ead., 'Rites magiques dans l'antiquité romaine', *ANRW* 2. 16. 3 (Berlin and New York, 1986), 2624–5). Snakes and other poisonous creatures and the Evil Eye could be grouped together when general apotropaic measures were taken (*PGM* P3). In Pliny's account of remedies from the human body in *HN* 28, his comments on snake-charmers (28. 30) are preceded by a reference to the Evil Eye and followed by an account of the curative powers of saliva (below, **15. snakes . . . saliva**). A connection between vital body fluids and the Evil Eye in folklore has been highlighted by A. Dundes ('Wet and Dry, the Evil Eye, an essay in Indo-European and Semitic Worldviews', in A. Dundes (ed.), *Interpreting Folklore* (Indiana UP, 1980), 93–133): the Evil Eye frequently dries up sap, semen, breast milk, etc., causing infertility and death. Apotropaic gestures (e.g. spitting) or amulets (e.g. phallic symbols) may signify production of such liquids to prove that the victim's life-force is undiminished. This may well be relevant to ancient attitudes, although, in cases where the moon is seen as an 'evil eye' in Graeco-Roman thought (see below, **42. full moon . . . babies**), its danger lies in its tendency to over-irrigate rather than desiccate its victims. In addition, however, there was an actual physiological connection between the eye and various body fluids in ancient thought (see below, **16. bewitch**); a idea which may, of course, have acted as a prompt to the desiccation theory. While Dundes suggests that, in certain folktales, snakes too, by suckling breasts and drinking milk from vessels, drain vital fluids, the prevalent link here is surely the opposition to one potent body fluid (snake venom) presented by another (human saliva or even sweat): see below, **14. poison . . . smell, throat . . . fasting man**.

13. Crates of Pergamum Crates of Mallos, a Stoic philosopher, scholar and first head of the library at Pergamum, visited Rome around 168 BC (Suet. *Gramm.* 2). See *OCD*³, Crates (3), 406.

Ophiogenes From the Greek meaning 'offspring of serpents'. They are attested at Parium by Strabo 13. 1. 14, C588. Pliny also has Ophiogenes in Cyprus, one of whose envoys passed a snake-repelling test at Rome (*HN* 28. 30). For ancient snake-charmers and repellers, and the similar methods employed by their modern counterparts in Egypt, Africa, and Turkey, see Tupet (1976), 187–95 and (1986), 2617–25.

laying their hands on Cf. *HN* 28. 30. It is possible that P. may mean that physical pressure was applied to squeeze out poison (Tupet (1976), 191). This would be similar in effect to sucking the bite (cf. *HN* 28. 30; Lucan 9. 922–37; Plutarch, *Cat. Min.* 56); a perfectly rational medical solution, the employment of which was, according to Celsus (5. 27. 3), the explanation behind the apparently magical powers of the Psylli, cf. Dio 51. 14. It is more likely, however, that he refers to the practice of transference: Strabo 13. 1. 14, C588 says the Ophiogenes transferred the inflammation to themselves, which accords with Pliny's idea that the Psylli and other peoples described below possessed an innate personal antidote/poison (below, **14. poison ... smell**, cf. **18. Nature ... present in man**). In *HN* 28. 30 'mere touch' (*tactu ipso*) is given as the alternative to suction as a means of poison removal. Transference of disease was a medico-magical procedure attested elsewhere in the *HN*; e.g. 28. 86, 155; 30. 64: Beagon (1992), 110 n.; Tupet (1976), 173. For its relative ease, cf. *HN* 28. 28, on the accidental transference of the powers of medicines, if they are set down on a table before they have been administered to the patient. A simple example, whereby sufferers from jaundice can transfer their affliction to the 'jaundice bird' by looking at it (*HN* 30. 94), is used by Plutarch (*Mor.* 681c) as an analogy to the working of the Evil Eye, another of the mysterious powers treated in **13–20**; see below, **16. bewitch**.

Varro Cited by Priscian (10. 32, p. 524H) on the Ophiogenes and Psylli.

saliva ... snakebites See below, **15. snakes ... saliva**.

14. Africa ... Psylli For the same story, cf. Lucan, *Phars.* 9. 893–900, who places them in a coastal area of eastern Cyrenaica,

HN 28. 30 and Strabo 17. 1. 44, C814. For the name used of modern Egyptian snake-charmers, see Tupet (1976), 190. It is hardly surprising to find such a people in Africa, home to numerous venomous snakes, as it was to strange, exotic, and dangerous species generally: see below, **16. same part of Africa**. According to legend, the snakes were engendered from drops of blood which fell on Libyan soil from the severed gorgon's head as Perseus flew over the country (Lucan, *Phars.* 9. 696–732). See M. Leigh, 'Lucan and the Libyan Tale', *JRS* 90 (2000), 95–109.

Agatharchides A Peripatetic from Cnidos and tutor at the Ptolemaic court in Alexandria, *c.*116 BC. His work included geographical and wonder literature. (Giannini pp. 144–5 and fr. 1; *OCD*³, 36).

The Greater Syrtes The Gulf of Sidra on the coast of North Africa.

poison . . . smell Cf. *HN* 8. 93, where P. mentions a people on the Nile whose scent repels crocodiles (at 28. 30, the snakes are said to flee at the mere sound of their voices). The poison could manifest itself in bodily secretions (see below, **15. snakes . . . saliva** and **16. bewitch**): thus, the Ophiogenes of Cyprus smelled bad in Spring, according to Pliny, and their sweat, as well as their saliva, had curative properties. Indeed, the powers of such peoples generally were so strong that their presence alone could have a repellent effect (*HN* 28. 30).

custom to expose their infants . . . blood Blood from outside the tribe would vitiate the power, cf. Lucan, *Phars.* 9. 900 and Gellius 16. 11. 2 on the Marsi. Pliny uses *adulterinus* in the sense of 'adulterated', i.e. not possessing pure tribal blood, rather than 'adulterous', which might, of course, include offspring fathered by fellow-tribesmen: note, however, *HN* 8. 86, where the snake's sole virtue is said to be its outstanding conjugal fidelity (cf. below, **122. two snakes . . . Gracchi**).

Nasamones Cf. Herodotus 4. 172 ff., where, however, the Psylli are said to have been obliterated as a result of a bizarre natural disaster. cf. also Gellius 16. 11. 3–8.

15. Marsi A people of central Italy near the Fucine lake. Their descent and snake-charming powers were well known according to

Pliny, *HN* 25. 11, cf. 21. 78; 28. 19, 30; Cicero, *Div.* 1. 131, 2. 70; Virgil, *Aen.* 7. 750–60; Juvenal 3. 169, 14. 180; and Gellius, *NA* 16. 11. 2. See Tupet (1976), 195–8; *OCD*[3], Marsi, 929–30. That this slightly sinister aspect of Marsic culture should have figured so prominently in the Roman consciousness may be a relic of an earlier period when they and other peoples of the central Apennines were regarded as marginal peoples and dangerous enemies of Rome. See E. Dench, *From Barbarians to New Men* (Oxford, 1995), 154–74, who discusses the other magical practices associated with these peoples; M. W. Dickie, *Magic and Magicians in the Graeco-Roman World* (London, 2001), 134–5; G. Piccaluga, 'I Marsi e gli Herpi', in P. Xella (ed.), *Magia: Studi in memorie R. Garosi* (Rome, 1976), 207–31; Beagon 'Situating Nature's Wonders', forthcoming; and cf. the magical genealogy mentioned below, **Circe's son**.

Circes' son Homer's (*Od.* 10) powerful witch-goddess lived on the fabulous island, Aeaea, later identified as the promontory of Circeii in Latium (*HN* 25. 11). Her son, by Odysseus, was Telegonus (cf. the lost *Telegonia*), though Hesiod named two, Agrius and Latinus (*Theog.* 1011 ff.). Cf. Solinus 11. 27–9; Gellius 16. 11. See *OCD*[3], Circe, 332.

snakes . . . saliva Human saliva was an antidote to most snakebites according to Aristotle (*HA* 8. 29, 607ᵃ). That it does not possess this power, nor those attributed to it here by Pliny (Tupet (1976), 192) is hardly to the point. Saliva was a potent and versatile prophylactic substance in popular medicine and magic (F. W. Nicholson, 'The Saliva Superstition in Classical Literature', *HSCP* 8 (1891), 23–40); cf. *HN* 24. 172, 25. 167, 26. 93 and esp. 28. 35–9 where, in addition to snake-bite, it cures sores and growths (28. 37) and guards against the Evil Eye (28. 36, 38–9; see below, **16. bewitch** and **67. it is a sure sign . . . saliva** and cf. Euripides, *Hec.* 1275 ff.; Theocritus 6. 39, 7. 127). It does in fact have undoubted antiseptic qualities. Lucan's description (*Phars.* 9. 923–37) of the Psylli's treatment of snake-bites included 'marking the wound with saliva' which, even if it did not, as alleged, confine the poison to the wound, would have helped limit secondary infection.

throat . . . fasting man Cf. *HN* 25. 36 and 28. 38, where, like the toad, the snake is said to burst if a man, especially a fasting man, spits in its open mouth; a fact P. attributes to Ofilius, who is probably Opilius, a 1st-cent. BC freedman and source of Varro and Verrius Flaccus (see Introd. 4. 5. 1), cf. Lucan, *Phars.* 6. 491. For the gesture, see above, **13–20. Introd.** Fasting, for reasons that are unclear (Nicholson (1891), 28: but see below, **16. bewitch**), made saliva more potent (*HN* 28. 35), e.g. as a cure for eye diseases (*HN* 28. 76: for a possible rationale, see below, **67. it is a sure sign . . . saliva**), incipient boils and skin complaints (*HN* 28. 36–7). This belief in the efficacy of 'fasting saliva', especially on swellings and boils of all kinds continued to flourish in later eras (see J. Brand, *Observations on Popular Antiquities* (London, 1842), iii. 140–1) and persisted into the 20th cent., cf. P. Saintyves, *Le Guérison des verrues* (Paris, 1913), 43–4). Fasting also played a part in other magical rituals, e.g. *HN* 26. 91; see below, **16. bewitch**.

Machlyae Probably the 'Machroae' of *HN* 5. 28 at the western end of the Greater Syrtes. Herodotus had placed them further west, perhaps on the shore of the Lesser Syrtes (4. 178, 180) but made no mention of their sexual anomalies. Thus some translate 'next to the Nasamones and their neighbours, the Machlyae, are Hermaphrodites'. See How and Wells (1912), i. 359–60; J. Desanges, *Histoire Naturelle V.1–46* (1980), comm. on *HN* 5. 28, Schwabe, *RE* 14. I, Machlyes 157–8.

Calliphanes Otherwise unknown.

hermaphrodites See below, **same part of Africa** and **34.**

Aristotle Rose 8. fr. 563, p. 1570.

16. Isigonus See above, **12.**

Nymphodorus A wonder-writer from Syracuse, fl. *c.*335 BC. See Giannini pp. 112–15 and fr. 8; *OCD*³, 1055–6.

same part of Africa Africa's abundance of exotic species (see below, **21. India . . . Ethiopians**), included freaks, like the hermaphroditic Machlyae just mentioned, and magicians (e.g. Herodotus 2. 33. 2, 4. 105. 2), as here. Pliny, *HN* 8. 106 on the sex-changing, magical hyena, combines the two characteristics. Even the paranormal flourished there (cf. below, **32. African . . . phantoms** on mirages in the deserts and the Libyan provenance and parentage of the demon Lamia, who may also have had hermaphroditic qualities: see Johnston (1999), 182–3).

eulogies Pliny uses *laudationes*, which at first sight might seem odd; but excessive praise could have a deleterious effect, as Gellius explains in his exposition of this passage (*NA* 9. 4. 7–8). For superstitious fear of excessive praise or prosperity, see Virgil, *Ecl.* 7. 27, Catullus 5. 10–13, Theocritus 6. 39–40. It was associated with belief in the Evil Eye (below, **bewitch**, etc. and cf. *Schol in Juv. Sat.* 7. 112, *fascinum verborum*), since prosperity might invite, and praise be partially motivated by, envy. See E. S. McCartney, 'Praise and Dispraise in Folklore', in Dundes (1980), 9–38; Clerc (1995), 90–1, 93, 101–8. In a number of cultures, including the Judaic tradition, praising a baby, as well as looking at it (*HN* 28. 39), might be cause for alarm and possible evil effects, which could be nullified by spitting on the child; a belief still present today in various countries, including Italy and India (L. W. Moss and S. C. Cappannari, '*Mal'occhio, Ayin ha ra, Oculus fascinus, Judenblick*: The Evil Eye Hovers Above', in C. Maloney (ed.), *The Evil Eye* (Columbia, 1976), 7; C. Maloney, 'Don't say "Pretty baby" lest you Zap it with your Eye: The Evil Eye in South Asia', ibid. 121; W. B. McDaniel, *Conception, Birth and Infancy in Ancient Rome and Modern Italy* (Florida, 1948 = 1948*a*), 42–4). 'It is by no means allowable to praise a horse or any other animal, unless you say "God save him" or spit upon him' (Brand (1842), iii. 151, quoting Camden, *Ancient and Modern Manners of the Irish*). For the withering and dessicating effects of *fascinum*, see above, **13–20. introd.**

the Triballes [and the Illyrians] Isigonus fr. 19 Giannini. They were Thracians from Lower Moesia, only later identified with the Illyrians. This suggests that Isigonus mentioned only the Triballes and that the presence of 'Illyrians' in Pliny is a gloss. See Schilling 131. Gellius replaces the 'Triballes' with 'people among the Illyrians' (9. 4. 8),

bewitch The Evil Eye was the most ancient, widespread, and deep-seated belief in the Mediterranean basin: see Tupet's discussion of this passage (Tupet (1976), 178, 390ff., cf. (1986), 2606–10). The Mediterranean, Near East, and southern Asia remain at the centre of the distribution of the belief today according to modern anthropological studies. The idea may have spread from the Near East with the development of complex peasant-urban cultures associated with dairying and agriculture: see Maloney (1976), xi–xvi. Charms to ward off the Evil Eye proliferated in the Graeco-

Roman world (Dunbabin and Dickie (1983), 7–27). Although it might be inherent in those with ocular peculiarities, e.g. a double pupil (below, **17. double pupil**), which might be hereditary (cf. Pliny's tribes here), its influence was also connected with the emotions of imagination and envy (Tupet (1976), 178–81, cf. **eulogies** above) and the hereditary and emotional causes were frequently confused (see M. Dickie, 'Talos bewitched', *Papers of the Leeds International Latin Seminar*, 6 (1990), 267–96, esp. 271–2). Plutarch (*Mor.* 680b–682b) offers the most detailed account and attempts an explanation, based on the idea that the eye of the possessor sent malign shafts to the victim. The theory seems to go back to Democritus, who said that the damage was done by particles of hatred and malice which emanated from the eyes of the caster (Democritus v. 5. 68 A 77 Diels). Emanations, in the form of streams of atomic particles, could issue from the body in other forms, e.g. voice, odour, and breathing. The breath and speech of the possessor of the Evil Eye were also infectious (cf. Heliodorus, *Aeth.* 4. 5. 5; and see above, **eulogies**), although vision, being the swiftest and connected with the life-force *pneuma*, was the most powerful of these emanations, according to Plutarch (*Mor.* 680f–681a). Emotion increased its effect (see below, **especially . . . angry one**). Its power may also have been enhanced by the fact that the eye was believed to be physiologically connected to various bodily fluids, including saliva, which themselves possessed medicomagical powers: see above, **15. snakes . . . saliva**, below, **42. full moon . . . babies** and especially **67. it is a sure sign . . . saliva**. Just as saliva was believed to be more potent from a fasting individual (above, **15. throat . . . fasting man**), so, too, the idea that the gaze of a possessor of the Evil Eye is particularly destructive before he has breakfasted is found in English folklore (Thompson, D 2071; Brand (1842), iii. 24). Possibly food and drink were thought to dilute the body fluids and associated bodily emanations. Certainly, in the case of emanations, certain conditions in the body, e.g. heat, and in the external atmosphere, e.g. still air, ensured greater effectiveness (Plutarch, *Mor.* 682c–f).

See generally Kuhnert, *RE* 6. 2, Fascinum, 2009–14; G. Lafaye in DS 2. 2, 'Fascinum', 983–7, F.T. Elworthy, *The Evil Eye* (London, 1895); Hastings, v. 608–15, W. Deonna, *Le Symbolisme de l'œil* (Berne, 1965), Tupet (1976), 178–81, P. Walcot, *Envy and the Greeks: A Study of Human Behaviour* (Warminster, 1978), 77–90, Dunbabin and Dickie

(1983), **13–18. introd.**, V. Limberis, 'The Eyes Infected by Evil: Basil of Caesarea's Homily, *On Envy*', *H. Th. R.* 84. 2 (1991), 163–84; Clerc (1995), 85–152. Maloney (1976) offers some modern anthropological studies. On *fascinum* and associated vocabulary, see C. Guzmán Arias, 'Nota a Plinio *Naturalis Historia* VII.2. 16–8', *Faventia*, 12–13 (1990–1), 437–42. For an extensive bibliography, see Dundes (1980), 265–76. See further below, **especially . . . angry one**.

especially . . . angry one. Possessors of the Evil Eye did not necessarily use it intentionally (cf. above, **16. bewitch**), although Plutarch, *Mor.* 682c–f suggests that, even if deliberate and specifically aimed envy was not involved in such cases, the power was possessed only by those with a disposition to envy. However, the emotions increased the violence of the body's emanations (see above, **16. bewitch**), so that a malicious glance is more destructive than a non-malicious one, just as a dog-bite is more severe when the dog is angry (681a–682a; cf. Heliodorus, *Aeth.* 3. 7). Modern anthropological studies suggest that envy is involved in some functioning of the belief everywhere but the possibility of involuntary action on the part of the caster is also admitted: see Maloney (1976), vii.

Adults An unusual feature: children were generally more susceptible to the Evil Eye, as they were to other forms of magic (below, **42. full moon . . . babies**): cf. Plutarch, *Mor.* 680b on the Thibii of Pontus (below, **17. Thibii . . . horse**) who can harm adults as well as children.

double pupil Possession of a physical anomaly such as a cast or squint or a single eye could increase the likelihood of the eye's magical power (Tupet (1976), 178, 390–4; (1986), 2606–10; cf. above **16. bewitch**). The doubling of the pupil would double the number of openings from which the eye emitted its shafts (cf. Plutarch, *Mor.* 680f–681a), thus doubling the possessor's magical powers (see W. B. McDaniel, 'The *pupula duplex* and Other Tokens of an Evil Eye in the Light of Ophthalmology', *CPh.* 13 (1918), 335–46, esp. 341; K. F. Smith, 'Pupula duplex', in *Studies in Honour of Basil L. Gildersleeve* (Baltimore, 1902), 287–310). The potency of the double pupil is mentioned by Ovid (*Am.* 1. 8. 15), while an eye with several pupils appears in Irish folklore (Thompson F 541. 3). Doubling or further multiplication of various organs was often associated with malign beings in later folklore (Deonna (1965), 32 n. 8). Thus, the psychological rationale for the belief seems clear, irrespective of the fact that there is no such anatomical condition. However, modern scholars have suggested more literal physical or linguistic explanations (see Smith (1902), McDaniel (1918), Tupet (1976), loc. cit. above). The eye abnormality known as bridge coloboma, a type of coloboma in which a ring-shaped cleft in the iris creates the appearance of a second pupil (McDaniel, 345–6, cf. B. McDonald, 'The Special Senses: The Eyes', in J. W. Keeling (ed.), *Foetal and Neonatal Pathology*² (London, 1992), 673–4, and below, **51. eye covered by a membrane**) could conceivably precipitate exaggerated descriptions of a 'double' pupil in popular superstition. So, too, could certain drug-induced conditions (see Tupet (1976), 393, and below, **17. Scythia . . . Bitiae**).

17. Apollonides   A geographer of the 1st cent. BC. Berger, *RE* 2. 1, Apollonides (28), 120.

Scythia . . . Bitiae   Cf. Gellius 9. 4; Solinus 1. 1. Other magical powers were attributed to Scythian women (Ovid, *Met.* 15. 359 ff.). For Scythian use of hallucinogenic plants, see Herodotus 4. 75. The Black Sea area had other links with magic: Colchis was Medea's legendary home and near Pontus were the Thibii (see above, **16. adults** and **double pupil**; and below, **Thibii . . . horse**).

Phylarchus   See also Plutarch, *Mor.* 680d = *FGH* 81 F 79a. He was an Athenian historian of the 3rd cent. BC, whose writings included *mirabilia*, cf. Apollonius fr. 14 and 18 (Giannini). On the question of Phylarchus as source, see M. W. Dickie, 'Heliodorus and Plutarch on the Evil Eye', *CPh.* 86 (1991), 18–20.

Thibii . . . horse   On the Thibii, see above, **adults**. Confusion with the name of an eye condition called *hippos* ('horse') by ancient medical writers (e.g. Galen 16. 611 K) is often cited to explain this bizarre statement (Tupet (1976), 391). However, this condition, known today as *nystagmus*, is not a physical abnormality of the eye, but a kind of involuntary eye-movement which, moreover, nearly always occurs in both eyes, not just one. McDaniel (1918), 343–5 argued for an imagined horse shape in the eye, citing ancient physiognomical writers' fascination with variations of pigmentation in the iris (R. Förster (ed.), *Scriptores Physiognomici Graeci et Latini*

(Lipsiae, 1893), ii. 118, 124, 126) and the later medieval notion of 'witch signs' in the eyes, cf. Thompson F 541. 2. He suggested two possible medical conditions which might have produced the 'image'. One was persistent pupillary membrane, in which remnants of a foetal membrane lie across the eye and which may, unlike *nystagmus*, affect only one eye. See McDonald (1992), 669–70 and fig. 28. 2, and below, **51. eye covered by a membrane**. The other was a coloboma of the iris, in which the fissure in the iris gives the impression of an irregular shape to the pupil (see also above, **16. double pupil**). This condition can occur in conjunction with persistent pupillary membrane (see McDonald (1992), 673–4), thus adding to the unusual appearance and allowing more scope for a particular image to be imagined. However, there are other possibilities. Holmes–Adie syndrome, for example, in which the pupil, usually in one eye only, is abnormally dilated and sometimes irregular in shape, could produce a similar impression. This condition is interesting in that it is almost entirely restricted to women.

This idea of an actual image in the eye is probably to be connected with the notion that the pupil of the eye held an image of the individual's soul, and possibly evolved from a primitive interpretation of the actual reflection of a person observed in the gazer's eye (Deonna (1965), 30–2). It should also be noted that Plutarch, in his explanation of the Evil Eye (see above, **16. bewitch**), slightly modified the Democritean theory by playing down the notion that the possessor of the Evil Eye actually sent some sort of image or phantom (*eidolon*) to the victim (*Mor.* 682f–683a). Unusual images were indicative of special powers (cf. the snake image in the Nordic hero Sigurd's eye: Deonna (1965), 31); above all, of malign powers. In such cases, the image was very frequently found in just one eye, the left (for the unfavourable associations of the left, see below, **37. right side . . . left**). Why the alleged image should be that of a horse is unclear. However, later 'witch signs' could include, besides the double pupil, the image of a toad or a horse (Deonna (1965), 32 nn. 4–5), indicating, perhaps, an ability to change into the creature of the image. Among its many associations in antiquity, the horse was connected with supernatural monsters (Mormo, Theocritus 15. 40) and demons of the night which could take the shape of a horse: see J. Fontenrose, *Python* (Berkeley, 1959), 345 n.38. It was of course strongly associated with Poseidon who, with his hippomorphic consorts Erinys and Medusa, had some sinister aspects (Johnston

(1999), 180–1); as it was with other chthonic deities, Demeter and Hecate (E. Bevan, *Representations of Animals in Sanctuaries of Artemis and other Olympian Deities*, BAR ser. 315 (i) (Oxford, 1986), 194–200). Rohde (E. Rohde, *Psyche*, trans. W. B. Hillis (London and New York, 1925), 200–1 and n. 105) noted that Greek sculptural reliefs of banquets of the dead often featured a horse or horse's head and posited an equine connection with the spirit world and the chthonic powers (cf. O. Keller, *Die Antike Tierwelt* (Hildesheim, 1963), i. 252–3; Bevan (1986), 194–7; E. Mitropolou, *Horses' Heads and Snakes in Banquet Reliefs and their Meaning* (Athens, 1976), 68 and plates). Later, witches and devils who take horse form, ride horses, or turn their victims into horses are common in various folk traditions: see Thompson G 211. 1. 1ff. and G 303. 3. 3. 1. 3; G. L. Kittredge, *Witchcraft in Old and New England* (New York, 1958), 218–20; and M. O. Howey, *The Horse in Magic and Myth* (London, 1923), 35–50, 152–5, 172–9, who noted (154) in Spain a modern charm against the Evil Eye of stag's horn on a cord of hair from a black mare's tail. Less probably, perhaps, we should look to the provenance of these Pontic tribes of evil-eyed sorcerers. From the same region came another possessor of the evil eye, the witch Medea. Her eyes had a golden gleam (Apollonius Rhodius, *Arg.* 4. 683f.; 725–9), the inheritance of the descendants of Helios, to whom horses were sacrificed at Rhodes and Taygetos (Pindar, *Ol.* 7. 126, Pausanius 3. 20. 4: see L. R. Farnell, *Cults of the Greek States*, vol. v (Oxford, 1909), 419, 451).

cannot be drowned The magician was commonly perceived as going against nature (Ovid, *Met.* 7. 199, reversing rivers, moving mountains; Ps.-Quintilian 10. 15: Beagon (1992), 100) and this would be an obvious breach of natural law. The medieval ordeal by water to detect thieves (the guilty would float) was used by the late 16th cent. to detect witches (K. Thomas, *Religion and the Decline of Magic* (London, 1971), 259–60; 658 and n.); but with a Christian rather than a *contra naturam* rationale (baptismal waters would reject the satanist).

Damon *FGH* 666, fr.*4. A Hellenistic historian from Byzantium mentioned by Athenaeus 10. 442c. see Schwartz, *RE* 4. 2, Damon (16), 2072.

Pharmaces Unattested elsewhere. The name is probably

derived from the Greek for magician, *pharmakeus*. For Ethiopia as the epitome of the exotic and therefore wonder-producing land, see above, **6. Ethiopians**, and below, **21. India . . . Ethiopians.**

waste away Some MSS and edd. read *efferat*, i.e. 'relieves wasting disease', rather than *afferat*, as translated here. Certainly, the sweat of the Psylli is said, in *HN* 28. 31, to have healing powers, but the context here is evil powers, as the end of **18. Nature . . . present in man** (below) makes clear; cf. Strabo 15. 1. 37, C703, reporting Megasthenes' description of flying snakes on the eastern edges of the world whose urine or sweat causes the skin of those it touches to rot away. For the medico-magical powers of body fluids, see below, **64. It . . . menstrual flow** and **67. it is a sure sign . . . saliva**.

18. Cicero The only citation of this passage, which probably comes from the great Republican orator and politician's lost *Admiranda*, a wonder-work cited by P. on remarkable waters and soils in *HN* 31. 12 and 51. See also below, **74. Naevius Pollio**; Introd. 5. 2. 2.

women . . . Evil Eye See above, **16. bewitch**, and **double pupil**.

nature . . . present in man Ancient ideas which stressed man's centrality and primacy in the natural world were reinforced by the idea of man as microcosm of nature. Here, P. shows that nature has made man into a true microcosm which reflects her darker as well as her more positive aspects. See Introd. 5. 2. 2, Beagon (1992), 36–42, 49–50, and below, **52. This is the reason . . . particular species.**

bestial habit See above, **9. eat human flesh.**

19. Falisci A people living between Monte Cimino and the Tiber north of Veii, who were related to the Latins but influenced by the Etruscans: *OCD*[3], 585–6.

Hirpi Varro had called them Hirpini, according to Servius (*In Aen.* 11. 785), the name being the Sabine word for wolf (cf. Festus p. 93, 25L): having chased wolves who stole the entrails from their sacrifice, the people had encountered a pestilence at the wolves' cave (chasing wolves was unlucky: see R. Coleman (ed. and comm.), *Virgil: Eclogues* (Cambridge, 1977), on *Ecl.* 9. 54) and had expiated it by 'becoming wolves' (see below, **Apollo**). See Piccaluga (1976), 207–31.

walk across . . . burnt　Virgil (*Aen.* 11. 787) attributed the feat to the favour of Apollo, Strabo (5. 2. 9, C226) to the local deity Feronia. Varro, however, said they had treated their feet with a herbal preparation (Servius, *In Aen.* 11. 787), and modern experiment suggests that damage does not occur because the heat is not as great as it might appear. The fire's ritual role in this case may have been enhanced by its wolf-repellant function. Some form of initiation may also be involved: see below, **Apollo**.

Apollo　On the cult, see J. Gagé, *Apollon romain* (Paris, 1955), 82–8. Servius says the sacrifice was to a god of the underworld, Dis Pater, also called Soranus; hence the full name of the people, Hirpini Sorani (*In Aen.* 11. 785). Virgil, like P., identified the god with Apollo of Soracte, cf. Silius Italicus 5. 175 ff. Soranus was perhaps originally a pastoral deity protecting flocks from wolves (Gagé (1955), 84; Marbach, *RE* 3 A 1, Soranus (1), 1130–33). For Apollo's connections with wolves, see Wernicke, *RE* 2. 1, Apollon, 1–111; Keller (1909/1963), i. 87; Fontenrose (1959), 421–2 and nn.; and K. Kerenyi, *Apollon; und Niobe* (München, 1980), 40, 351, 355. Servius, *In Aen.* 4. 377 says he could take wolf form and, as a pastoral god, kill wolves. Mephitic, 'plague-bearing', caves offered an underworld aspect and hence a link with Dis Pater. According to Gagé (1955: 87), assimilation with Apollo, too, may have been encouraged by the infernal aspect of that god, who could cause as well as avert plague. He was also connected with initiation (for refs., see *OCD*[3], Apollo, 122–3), a possible function of the ritual fire-walking.

Soracte　A mountain 26 miles north of Rome. Wild and remote locations suited myths and rituals connected with wolves, creatures 'outside civilization' in Graeco-Roman thought: see R. Buxton, 'Wolves and Werewolves in Greek Thought', in J. Bremmer (ed.), *Interpretations of Greek Mythology* (London, 1987), 60–79, on the associations of Mt. Lykaion in Arcadia. The Neuri, who according to Herodotus (4. 105) became werewolves once a year, were placed by him in the remote north, next to the Scythians and the 'man-eaters', which accords well with Pliny's association of uncanny and bizarre powers with the peoples of the earth's extremities in **9–32**. See also Beagon, forthcoming.

20. King Pyrrhus King of Epirus, 319–272 BC. See *OCD*³, 1282.

right toe . . . temple Cf. Plutarch, *Pyrrhus* 3. 4–5, Valerius Maximus 5. 1., ext. 4. The temple was at Dodona (Januarius Nepotianus, *Epit. Libr. Val. Max.* 9. 24), a shrine connected with Pyrrhus' mythical ancestors, Achilles and his son Neoptolemus/ Pyrrhus. The healing ritual included the killing of a white cock (Plutarch, *Pyrrhus* 3. 6–9) and the placing of the foot on the affected part. J. Gagé ('Pyrrhus et l'influence religieuse de Dodone dans l'Italie primitive', *RHR* 164 (1954), 137–65, esp. 144–9) adduced parallels with other sanctuaries in which healing was effected, including the Serapeion at Alexandria, where, in AD 70, the foot of another ruler, Vespasian, apparently acquired healing powers, albeit temporarily. The rationale is unclear: Gagé (1954: 147), citing the unshod, unwashed feet of the priestly Selloi of Dodona, suggested that the foot was believed to pick up special powers from its contact with the earth. But possibly a two-stage transference of the disease from the patient (see above, **13. laying their hands on**) in the opposite direction was visualized, the disease being passed first to the foot, then to the trodden earth: some remedies were believed to lose their efficacy to the earth if they touched it (e.g. *HN* 28. 34, 42, cf. 28. 28, above **13. laying their hands on**). In the case of Pyrrhus, our information is more specific: his powers were apparently centred on his big toe, which could cure inflammation of the spleen. Tying the big toe to the next is mentioned in *HN* 28. 42 as a cure for groin swelling. The miraculous toe may be also connected with another physical anomaly: his upper jaw had solid bone in place of teeth (Plut. *Pyrrhus* 3. 6–9; cf. **69. Some people . . . teeth**, below) and his unusual dentition may have had something to do with his ability specifically to cure splenetic complaints. Splenetic disease was normally characterized in ancient medical writings as resulting from an excess of moisture, in particular of black bile (Celsus 2. 7. 21). This bile was a residue left over from the formation of blood in the liver, which, in a healthy body, passed to the spleen and from there to the stomach which evacuated it. When the process went wrong, the residue could build up, causing the spleen to swell, but also ascending to the head and mouth, precipitating diseased gums, bleeding, and a foul taste. Possibly, the bony and unusual appearance of Pyrrhus' teeth was associated with a particularly hot, dry, bile-free constitution (for the connection between solidity of bone and lack of moisture, cf. below, **22. pains . . . toughened**, and **78. I have read . . . perspire**), and his healing touch was believed to have much the same effect as the warm and diuretic poultices recommended by physicians (e.g. Celsus 3. 21. 14; 4. 16. 1–4). That it should later survive cremation was in keeping with exceptional hardness and dryness of his teeth, since even ordinary teeth were believed to survive burning (see below, **70. indestructible . . . cremated**). Pyrrhus appears to be the only known example of a royal thaumaturge from classical antiquity (if we exclude the imperial episode of AD 70, on which see G. Anderson, *Sage, Saint and Sophist: Holy Men and their Associates* (London, 1994), 152–3): see P. Lévêque, *Pyrrhos* (Paris, 1957), 217–18, 627 n. 3).

21. India . . . Ethiopians Sections **21–32** assemble a definitive selection of human *mirabilia* from the eastern and southern extremities of the world (see above, **9–32. introd.**), where the warm climate (below, **so great . . . water**; also **33. portentous . . . fertility** and **39. In Egypt . . . eighth month**) encouraged a natural fertility so exuberant and multifarious that monstrosities and oddities unparalleled elsewhere proliferated, prompting the saying quoted by both Aristotle and P. that Africa was always producing something new (Aristotle, *GA* 746^{b}7–13; *HA* 606^{b}17; Pliny, *HN* 8. 42). The southern/eastern extremities were often conceived of as a single, ill-defined entity: the vagueness of 'Ethiopia' as a concept (see above, **6. Ethiopians**) sometimes led to the idea that India and Africa were actually joined together, cf. Polybius 3. 338. 1 and that their major rivers were interconnected or even to be identified with each other; crocodiles were noted on the Indus as well as the Nile and the idea that the Nile might actually flow into Ethiopia was current at the start of Alexander's Indian expedition (Arrian, *Anab.* 6. 1. 2; cf. J. O. Thomson, *History of Ancient Geography* (Cambridge, 1948), 82, 361–2). The sense of distance and of the unknown enhanced the exotic aura of the east: the assumed Oceanic eastern boundary of India had not been reached even by Alexander, whose march to the Hyphasis became a wonder legend in its own right (see Romm (1992), 83ff., 94–120). For the classical tradition on and actual knowledge of India, see J. W. Sedlar, *India* *and the Greek World: A Study in the Transmission of Culture* (New Jersey, 1980), 8–13.

largest animals Cf. Herodotus 3. 106. For individual species, see *HN* 8. 32 (the Indian elephant supposedly bigger than the African); Aelian, *NA* 16. 11, 12; 17. 26. For size as a major ingredient of eastern *mirabilia*, see Strabo 15. 1. 37, C703 (quoting Megasthenes): everything there is reported to be bigger and more freakish.

dogs P. says they were often sired by tigers (*HN* 8. 148, cf. Aristotle, *HA* 746ᵇ5–7). Ctesias (Photius, *Biblio.* 45b 13–14) claimed they could tackle lions, cf. Strabo 15. 1. 37, C703 (quoting Megasthenes); Aelian, *NA* 4. 19. Perhaps the lion- and elephant-baiting dog given by the king of Albania to Alexander on his way to India was itself Indian (*HN* 8. 149–50).

trees . . . fig tree Since timber and fruit were two of the most basic natural commodities (Pliny, *HN* 12. 3–5), new species aroused particular interest and many were naturalized in Italy for their wood, shade, fruit, or ornamental beauty (e.g. *HN* 12. 6–12, 14–16) or their products imported (e.g. ebony, first seen at Rome in Pompey's eastern triumph, *HN* 12. 17–20 and below, **99. whole world**; it was later supplied primarily by India). See R. Meiggs, *Trees and Timber in the Ancient Mediterranean World* (Oxford, 1982), esp. 270–99. Nero's expedition to Ethiopia (*HN* 12. 19) specifically reported on the type and density of the trees found. The huge trees of India made a considerable impression on Alexander's expedition, cf. *HN* 12. 22; Diodorus 17. 90. 5; Arrian, *Indica* 11. 7 (quoting Nearchos); Q. Curtius 9. 1. 10. For the arrow story, see Virgil, *G.* 2. 122–5. For the large numbers afforded shelter by a single tree, see e.g. Arrian, *loc. cit.* P. uses the same means of expressing size in *HN* 16. 6 (cf. 4. 90), where the heights attained by the arching roots of the oaks in the famous Hercynian forest are measured by their capacity to accommodate squadrons of cavalry. A number of these descriptions, including Strabo 15. 1. 21, C 694, seem to be of the Indian fig, or banyan, whose huge size and artistically vaulted dome of pendulous branches is described in *HN* 12. 22–3. See Beagon (1992), 85. Especially large trees, or, at any rate, logs from them, could be exhibited at Rome: *HN* 16. 200–2.

So great . . . water   The importance of heat and moisture for biological growth had been recognized from earliest times. The interplay of heat and cold, dryness and moisture was at the heart of the cosmological theories of the Presocratic philosophers, one of whom, Anaximander, made the earliest extant attempt to explain the origin of animal life by positing spontaneous generation of organisms from slime heated by the sun (KRS fr. 133, 135, 136), an idea which became standard. P. suggests that part of India, at least, has an ideal combination of the two elements (cf. Strabo 15. 1. 20, C693; 15. 1. 28, C698, 15. 1. 32, C700), as did another southern region closer to the Mediterranean centre, Egypt (below, **33. portentous . . . fertility**; **33. In Egypt . . . septuplets**; **39. In Egypt . . . eighth month**). Such superabundance could produce a paradisical idyll, cf. Ctesias in Photius, *Biblio.* 46b 35–7 and 40–1 on the fertility of the sheep and the rivers flowing with honey. However, extreme fertility brought its own problems: where multiple pregnancies occurred, insufficient space might be available in the mother's uterus for the proper development of all the foetuses, leading to an increased likelihood of abnormalities, a phenomenon Aristotle attributes to Egypt in particular (*GA* 770ᵃ35–6): see below, **33. In Egypt . . . septuplets**. More generally, the mobility of the elements fire and water also made them liable to excessive, uncontrolled fertility which encouraged the breeding of hybrids and monstrosities. The variety and diversity of nature is pushed to extremes at the world's edges. However, this was not always, as here, the effect of the two elements in a balanced combination; more frequently, the margins of the world are portrayed as suffering from climatic extremes in the sense that one of these unstable elements predominates. Thus, the excessive heat of the Ethiopian desert (*HN* 6. 187) can produce animal and human monstrosities, 'moulded by the mobile element of fire', cf. Diodorus Siculus 2. 51. 2–4, where the strength of life-giving heat in equatorial lands is responsible for the myriad forms of their wildlife. An excess of water had a similar effect—hence the proliferation of monsters in Ocean's depths (*HN* 9. 1–2; though for a different theory, see *HN* 2. 13: celestial 'seeds', debris from the zodiac, falling in greater numbers on the sea than elsewhere, were responsible for its generation of monsters). This view of the teratogenous powers of the elements is very different from Aristotle's rationalizing of African hybrids as being the result of different species being thrown together by the scarcity of watering holes in a very hot country (*GA* 346ᵇ7–13); a theory repeated by Pliny in *HN* 8. 44, a more sober, Aristotelian-influenced survey of Africa's animal species. See also Beagon, forthcoming.

reeds . . . people Cf. Herodotus 3. 98, Ctesias fr. 57. 6, 63. For the type of reed, see How and Wells (1912), i. 288: Pliny says they were the size of trees (*HN* 16. 162).

22. five cubits 7. 5 Roman feet. Varro considered 7 feet to be the maximum attainable height (Aulus Gellius, *NA* 3. 10. 11; below, **74. The body of Orestes**).

do not spit Probably regarded as a result of the desiccating effect of the heat (see below, **pains . . . toughened**) and nothing to do with any medical disorder or behavioural quirk (see below, **80. Drusus' wife, Antonia**).

pains . . . toughened Cf. Herodotus 3. 11 on the tough, thick skulls of Egyptians who expose shaven heads to the sun, and below, **78. I have read . . . perspire**, for a connection between solidity of bone and lack of moisture. Theories of health and disease based on the Four Humours (blood, phlegm, yellow and black biles), on the opposites of Dry and Wet, Warm and Cold, and on climatic conditions were long-lived in ancient medicine. Heat could produce tougher bodies (Hipp. *Airs, Waters, Places* 20, 2. 72–4 L) and cold could induce excess phlegm which caused head and chest disease (Hipp. *Regimen for Health* II. 62, 6. 576 L, III.70, 6. 608 L).

Gymnosophists The holy men of India were noted generally by the classical sources for their asceticism and, as here, for their nakedness and meditative poses; though the writers do not distinguish between brahmins and Buddhists or Jains. Greek interpretations of 'gymnosophists' may owe much to Cynic influence: see Sedlar (1980), 68–74. The best-known descriptions occur in passages dealing with Alexander's contacts with holy men. When Onesicritus was sent to bring some of them to the king, he found them meditating in various positions which they held until evening (Strabo 15. 1. 63–8, C715–18; cf. Plutarch, *Alex.* 64–5; Arrian, *Ind.* 11. 1–7; Diodorus Siculus 11. 35–42; Megasthenes *FGH* 715, fr. 28).

Mount Nulus Mythical; Megasthenes 715, fr. 28; Stein, *RE* 17. 1, Nulo, 1242.

Megasthenes   An Ionian Greek (*c*.350–290 BC) who was the main source for most later writers on India, including Arrian and Strabo. He gained personal knowledge of the country through visits (302–291 BC) as an envoy of Seleucus I, and his four-volume *Indica*, if often uncritical, was more detailed than the works produced on Alexander's expedition which had fuelled western interest in India. *OCD*[3], 952; *FGH* 715.

feet turned backwards   See above, **11. wild men . . . back to front.** Megasthenes *FGH* 715, fr. 28.

23. dog-headed men   These had appeared in literature as early as the Hesiodic *Periodos Ges*, fr. 150 Merkelbach–West, cf. Ctesias in Photius 20, 22–3 and Megasthenes according to Solinus 52. 57, Gellius 9. 4. 9, Aelian, *HA* 4. 46, and Augustine, *CD* 16. 8. 135. Like the reverse-footed men and the Monopods (below, **Monocoli . . . Sciapodae**), they became an enduring monstrous 'type' (cf. Wittcower (1942), 160, 163; pls. 42a–c, 43d–f, 44b and f, 48c), possibly deriving from Sanscrit literature (Romm (1992), 87). The wonder element in this species was above all its taxonomic ambiguity (Romm 79), a creature between man and animal, having a share of the features of both. This ambiguity was largely responsible for the evolution of a complex tradition of thought. Ctesias, while stressing their dog-like characteristics, had also described them as just and the most long-lived of men. P.'s Dog-heads are human in their use of clothing, but animal in their lack of speech. Cynocephalus was also the name given to the unambiguously non-human baboon, a fierce biting creature, according to Pliny, *HN* 8. 216 and Solinus 2. 58 (p. 143 Münzer): and cf. **31** below, where P. gives a wholly animal definition of the term. P.'s description here in **23** is neutral in tone, but, in later sources, their animal ferocity was frequently highlighted, partly encouraged by Christian use of the Cynocephalus to symbolize the unconverted and the infidel (Friedman (1981), 61–71). As geographical knowledge grew, their location also shifted, from the East to the far north, which was less known (Friedman (1981), 1), cf. the 14th-cent. Hereford Mappa Mundi, which depicts them in Scandinavia. However, the classical tradition adds extra texture to this later image of ferocious monsters of the frozen north. The Cynocephali might have become fire-breathing monsters in later recensions of the Alexander Romance, but even in the earliest parts of that tradition, from around the 3rd cent. AD, they were aggressive (*Ep. Alex. ad Arist.*, p. 33). More significantly, their northern location may have been reinforced by ancient medical theory and actual knowledge of the northern tribes. A connection between climate and temperament which went back to the Hippocratic writings (see above, **22. pains . . . toughened**) and continued in Galen (4. 767–81 K) and later, presupposed harsh and savage inhabitants in harsh and savage environments; similar ideas were fostered by Stoics such as Posidonius, and were reflected in literature of the late Republic and early Empire; e.g. Cicero, *ND* 2. 42 and Vitruvius 6. 1. 3–4, 10, who explains that the cold and moisture of far northern climes gave their inhabitants thicker blood, making them warlike and rash. Such theories were to some extent borne out by what became known of the historical Scythians and Celts (cf. above, **9. eat human flesh** and **12. drink out of human skulls**) and later the Alans and Huns (and cf. also Matthews (1989), 348, citing Ammianus 31. 16. 6 on another nomadic people, but in this case eastern, the Saracens). It is instructive to compare a Roman at the turn of the 1st cent. AD talking about a German tribe, with two 8th-cent. sources discussing Cynocephali and the descendants of the same German tribe. Tacitus (*Germ.* 40) said of the Langobardi that their ferocious fighting spirit compensated for their lack of numbers. Earlier, Velleius (2. 106) had said of the same people that their spirit was 'more fierce than ordinary German savagery'. In the 8th cent., the *Cosmographia* of Vergil of Salzburg located the Cynocephali near the Germans, commented on their paucity of numbers and described them as truculent (16, 2–5). Another 8th-cent. source, Paul the Deacon, brought together Cynocephali and the Langobardi. Recounting the early migration from Scandinavia to Germany of the Lombards' ancestors, he described how they compensated for the inferior size of their army by terrifying the opposition with rumours that their forces included Cynocephali who drank human blood (*Hist. Lombard.* 1. 11, cf. Gibbon, ch. XLII). The inhuman savagery of the image is echoed in a medieval illustration of a dog-headed man apparently gnawing on a human leg (Sion College Bestiary in Friedman (1981), 11). Eating human flesh (above, **9. eat human flesh**) and drinking human blood were well-known attributes of the people of the northern fringes (though in the case of the blood-drinking, cf. also the Saracens, Matthews loc. cit. above, this note), in particular the Scythians, whose conversion of their enemies' skulls also found later Germanic and Lombard parallels: see above, **12. drink out of human skulls**.

Ctesias *FGH* 3.C, 688, fr. 45. A 5th-cent. Greek doctor at the Persian court, he wrote on geography and (unreliably) on history and produced the first separate work on India. See *OCD*[3], 411–12.

the women . . . moment of birth For eastern *mirabilia* which stretch or transgress the biological norm, see above, **9–32. introd.**

Monocoli . . . Sciapodae They had been called Sciapodae by Scylax (Tzetzes, *Chil.* 7. 629), Ctesias (*FGH* 3.C, 688, fr. 60), and by Hecataeus of Miletus (*FGH* 1, fr. 327) who placed them in Ethiopia (see above, **21. India . . . Ethiopians**). Cf. also Gellius, *NA* 9. 4. 9; Solinus 52. 29. See L. Pearson, *The Early Ionian Historians* (Oxford, 1939; repr. Connecticut, 1979), 95–6; Romm (1992), 85–6. Like other monstrosities in this section of book 7, they appealed to later cartographers. For 15th- and 16th-cent. pictorial representations, see Wittcower, pls. 42c, 44c, 46a–h; and for later literature, Friedman (1981), index. Modern rationalizations have included 'observation of Hindus in a yoga position' (Garland (1995), 161).

Trogodytae This tribe or tribes inhabited Ethiopia (see above, **6. Ethiopians**) which in effect meant that Trogodytae could be situated anywhere from North Africa to the east coast of the Red Sea or to the south of Egypt, or occasionally even India. The form *troglodytae* which implies they were cave-dwellers does not fit all the people included under the title (see *OCD*[3], Trogodytae, 1555, where they are tentatively identified with the modern Beja; Jahn, *RE* 7 A 2, Trogodytae, 2497–2500), though some of the North African Trogodytae (*HN* 5. 44–5, below) may have been cave-dwellers like the Troglodytes north of the Caucasus. Ethiopian Trogodytae were renowned for their swiftness (see below, **31**), and squeaked rather than spoke, according to Herodotus (4. 153). By the time of Strabo (16. 4. 17, C775–6) and Diodorus (3. 31. 4–33. 7), they are very much part of the *mirabilia* tradition, a people of the southern extremities (Diod. 3. 31. 4) living among exotic animals (sphinxes, cynocephali, huge serpents: Strabo 16. 4. 17, C775): cf. *HN* 5. 44–5, where the North African Trogodytae are cave-dwellers living in the vicinity of sub-human, semi-human, and monstrous tribes.

men . . . who have eyes in their shoulders Mentioned in Gellius, *NA* 9. 4. 9 and similar to the Blemmyae who had faces in their chest (*HN* 5. 46, cf. Herodotus 4. 191), another enduring monstrous type (Wittcower, pls. 44d–e, 45, 46h). For possible explanations, including tribes who painted faces on their chests or wore masks, see Garland (1995), 161.

24. satyrs in the east Indian mountains . . . human appearance These, like the dog-headed men (above, **23** and below **31**) may have been monkeys and are in fact designated as such in *HN* 8. 215–16. The satyr of classical myth embodied the wilder side of nature, and although artistic representations made them progressively more human, they also possessed horse and, later, goat attributes: see Kuhnert, 'Satyros', in Roscher *Lexikon*, 444–531 and *OCD*³, satyrs, 1361. This ambiguity is captured by P.'s remark in *HN* 5. 46: apart from their shape, there is nothing human about them. For their swiftness, Aelian, *NA* 16. 21. For the mountainous location, see **9–32. introd.**

Catarcludi Aelian, *NA* 16. 21 mentions a region called Kolunda. Tomaschek suggested P. misread Ctesias' *kata kolundon* (*RE* 3. 2, 1285).

Tauron Known only from P.'s reference here and in the index for book 7. Cf. *FGH* 710, fr. 1.

Choromandae . . . fangs of a dog They are not named elsewhere but the description in Solinus 57. 32 fits. Confusion with the swift-footed Persian Choramnaioi (Ctesias, *FGH* 3.C, 688, fr. 12) is unlikely (Schilling 135). As with the satyrs above, the story may be based on monkeys.

Eudoxus A mathematician of the first half of the 4th cent. BC who came from Cnidos and was also an important astronomer and geographer. His *ges periodos* (fr. 340, Lasserre) is referred to here. See *OCD*³, Eudoxus (1), 565–6.

25. Megasthenes See above, **22.** His tales of 'men without nostrils' and 'men without mouths' (see below, **Astomi . . . no mouths**) are among the examples given by Strabo in his scathing condemnation of Megasthenes, Onesicritus, Nearchos, and other writers on India as liars (2. 1. 9).

Sciratae   Megasthenes, *FGH* 3.C, 715, fr. 29. See Aelian, *NA* 16.
22.

snake-like strap feet   Rackham associates 'snake-like' with the
lack of nostrils and translates *loripes* as 'bandy-legged'. The precise
nature of the foot-deformity implied by *loripes* is uncertain but it is
usually rendered 'strap-footed' (cf. *lorum*, a leather strap). See *OLD*,
s.v. *loripes*, 1044; *Thes. Ling. Lat.* 1679–80. ln *HN* 5. 46, it is attributed
to an Ethiopian tribe called the Himantopodes, who are said to
crawl or glide, thus suggesting a connection between the deformity
and the movement of a snake and hence the translation given here.
There may well be a link between Pliny's monsters and the iconography associated with the giants or titans, who were sometimes portrayed as being anguipede, and appear as such on Roman coins,
e.g. M. Crawford, *Roman Republican Coinage* (London, 1974), ii, nos.
310.1 and 374.4. For the existence of congenital racial foot deformities (though not obviously related to this description) see Garland
(1995), 5, 166.

easternmost . . . source of the Ganges   See above, **21. India
. . . Ethiopians.** According to P., in *HN* 6. 64–5, the source of the
Ganges was thought by many to be as mysterious as that of the Nile,
though he also mentions a theory that it rises in the Scythian mountains. Similarities between the Nile and the rivers of central India
were often noted and literal connections were even conjectured;
see above, **21. India . . . Ethiopians**.

Astomi . . . no mouths   Their name derived from the Greek
astomos, which meant 'mouthless'. Megasthenes, *FGH* 3.C, 715, fr.
27, 30; Solinus 52. 30. See above, **25. Megasthenes**.

cotton-wool   Literally 'down of leaves'. Rackham (523) translated 'cotton-wool', suggesting that the substance 'combed from
leaves' by the Chinese in *HN* 6. 54 was cotton rather than silk
(which P. correctly attributes to the silk-worm chrysalis in *HN* 11.
76); cf. *HN* 5. 14, a 'silk-like substance drawn from the down of
leaves'. Pomponius Mela mentioned 'wool' growing on Indian
trees due to the heat and fertility of climate (3. 7,62). Aulus Gellius,
NA 9. 4. 10 has these people dressed in feathers.

live only on the air   See above, **9–32. introd.**

26. remotest region of the mountains   See above, **9–32. introd.**

Trispithami   See Strabo 15. 1. 57, C711, citing Megasthenes. These and the Pygmies seem often to have been regarded as one and the same, cf. Strabo 2. 1. 9, C70 ('Pygmies . . . a race only three spans high'); cf. Ctesias fr. 57. 11 (p. 81 Dindorf), where the average height of a pygmy is said to be 1. 5 cubits, i.e. roughly three spans.

Pygmies . . . cranes   The story of a dwarf-like tribe which fought with cranes goes back to Homer, *Il.* 3. 6. See Wust, *RE* 23. 2, Pygmaioi, 2064–7; *OCD*[3], pygmies, 1281. Interest was increased in the wake of Alexander's expeditions and the story was elaborated by later writers. Like the Trogodytae (above, **23**), they are normally a people of the southern extremities, to be found in Ethiopia (above, **6. Ethiopians**), particularly in Africa (Aristotle, *HA* 8. 12, 597ᵃ), Southern Egypt (Hecataeus, *FGH* 1.A, 1, fr. 328b, cf. *HN* 6. 188), and India (Megasthenes, *FGH* 3.C, 715, fr. 29); though also in Scythia and Thrace (see below, this note). Pygmies may have a factual basis in the dwarf people of central Africa, but they became a type of the exotic: cf. P.'s locating them in the 'remotest regions of the mountains', beyond a race he has already placed at the easternmost edges of India. While P. seems to accept them as human, their status in other accounts was, like that of some other exotic races, ambiguous: they were primitive and earth-born (Hesiod fr. 150 17–18) and P. quotes Aristotle (below, **27**) for their dwelling in caves like the speechless Troglodytes of Herodotus 4. 183. See V. Dasen, *Dwarfs in Ancient Egypt and Greece* (Oxford, 1993), 175–88. Their opponents, the cranes, were themselves extraordinary; Aristotle said they travelled exceptional distances when migrating. Starting from the Scythian plains in the far north (hence perhaps references to northern Pygmies in Juvenal 5. 167 and Pliny *HN* 4. 44) and finishing in the marshes above the Nile (*HA* 597ᵃ), or, according to Homer, at the southern stream of Ocean (*Il.* 3. 6), they traversed the known world from northern to southern extremity.

Protected . . . from the north wind . . . springlike   The climate is like that of the fabulous Hyperboreans, *HN* 4. 33, whose name means 'beyond the north wind'.

27. Aristotle   *HA* 8. 12, 597ᵃ. See above, **26. Pygmies.**

Isigonus   See above, **12**. See Giannini XI, fr. 20.

Cyrni   Schilling identifies these people with the Cyrnii whose longevity Athenaeus attributes to honey (2, 47a).

140 years   See **9–32. introd.**

long-lived Ethiopians   See Herodotus 3. 23–5; and for their location and characteristics, Romm (1992), 49–60, 73–8. See above, **6. Ethiopians**.

Seres   The Chinese (see *OCD*³, Seres, 1392–3), who were on the easternmost frontiers of Roman knowledge. By Augustus' time, they were famous for producing silk (cf. *HN* 6. 64, 11. 76, and above, **25. cotton-wool**) and by Nero's they were known for other products (*HN* 34. 145). Although by the middle of the 1st cent. AD their general geographical position beyond India was better known, they still epitomized remoteness in the manner of the Scythians, Indians, and Ethiopians (above, **9–32. introd.**). When Pomponius Mela wrote during the time of Gaius or Claudius, he described the most remote areas of Asia as being inhabited by the Indians, the Seres, and the Scythians (3. 7. 59–61). For their longevity, see Strabo 15. 1. 37, C702.

the inhabitants of Mount Athos . . . live on snake meat . . . parasites   The inhabitants of Mt. Athos were a byword for longevity. Aelian records an anecdote about Plato who, when advised by his doctor to move from the unhealthy site of the Academy to the Lyceum, replied that he would not even move to the summit of Mt. Athos in order to enjoy longer life (Aelian, *VH* 9. 10). They lived up to 130 years according to Lucian (*Macrob.* 5). Pomponius Mela specified their town as Acrothoon on the summit (2. 2. 32), whereas Pliny calls it Apollonia (*HN* 4. 37). Longevity was also associated with the summit of another mountain, Mt. Tmolus in Lydia (below, **159. Mount Tmolus**). Associations between mountains and longevity may have been encouraged by the rarefied atmosphere and the immortals of Mount Olympus, and high ground generally was known to be healthier than low-lying areas: see below, **169. The rest of mankind . . . quartan fevers**. Lucian mentioned diet as an important factor in longevity, but did not specify snake-eating. Dioscurides, however, does (2. 16. 1); and note also *HN* 29. 120–1. Here, a mixture of burnt viper and salt is recommended in small doses as a general tonic, while snake broth is said to remove lice from the body. Perhaps the eater was believed to be imbued with just enough poison to kill the vermin (cf. above, **14. Africa . . . Psylli**), severe infestations of which were believed to be life-threatening: see below, on Sulla and Pherecydes (**138. his own death . . . tortures** and **172. Pherecydes . . . body**). Possibly, it was a matter of like killing like: in **172** Pliny calls the creatures infesting Pherecydes *serpentes*. (On the imprecision of ancient descriptions of such infestations, see **138. his own death . . . tortures**). For 20th-cent. travellers' observations of snake-eating in Turkey and Egypt, believed to confer some kind of immunity to snake poison, see Tupet (1986), 2617–25.

28. Onesicritus A Cynic philosopher who was a sailor on Alexander's expedition and produced a romanticized history of the latter (*OCD*³, 1068; cf. *FGH* 2.B, 134, fr. 11).

live for 130 years . . . die middle-aged See above, **9–32. introd.**

Crates of Pergamum Fr. 13, Mette. See above, **13.**

Gymnetae The name means 'the naked' and similar names occur for other southern tribes, e.g. the Gymnetes somewhere east of the Nile (6. 190) and cf. the Indian Gymnosophistae, above, **22.**

Ctesias *FGH* 3.C, 688, fr. 52. See above, **23.**

Pandae . . . two hundred years . . . forty years . . . give birth just once An Indian tribe called Pandae is mentioned in *HN* 6. 76, hence the emendation (Hardouin; see Schilling 137) of Pandes here. Valerius Maximus 8. 13, ext. 5 quotes Ctesias as saying they lived for 120 years. For abnormal lifespans, ageing processes, and fertility among marginal peoples, see **9–32. introd.**

Agatharchides *FGH* 2.A, 86, fr. 22, see above, **14.**

Clitarchus *FGH* 2.B, 137, fr. 22. He came from Alexandria and sometime after 280 BC wrote a popular but unreliable history of Alexander. See L. Pearson, *The Lost Historians of Alexander the Great* (New York, 1960), ch. 8; Müller (1979), 74–6. See Jacoby, *RE* 11. 1, Clitarchus (2), 622–54.

Megasthenes *FGH* 3.C, 715, fr. 13d. See above, **22.**

Ceylon . . . bodily infirmity Taprobane (*OCD*³, 1473) or Ceylon had been described by Onesicritus and Megasthenes and others. Trade links were established by the 1st cent. BC and featured in the *Periplus of the Erythraean Sea* (61. 20), where its products are said to include pearls, precious stones, and tortoiseshell. But in *HN* 6. 79–91 Pliny reports an account of the island given by a Sinhalese embassy to Claudius. They claim that 100 years is a moderate lifespan, though they make no mention of the lack of senile infirmity among their people. Despite the fact that the speaker is a native Sihhalese, the tone of Pliny's account is that of a slightly idealized fantasy land on the borders of Roman knowledge. E. H. Warmington, *The Commerce between the Roman Empire and India*² (London, 1974), 117 ff. mentions Dionysius Periegetes' statement that there were sea-monsters round the island and comments that old fables were not dispelled because the island was not being regularly visited. In the post-Roman period, however, it seems to have played a central role in the eastern trade network of the Sassanians. See J. Carswell, 'The Port of Mantai, Sri Lanka', in V. Begley and D. de Puma (eds.), *Rome and India; The Ancient Sea Trade* (Wisconsin and London, 1981), 197–203.

Duris *FGH* 2.A, 76, fr. 48. A tyrant of Samos who lived around 340–260 BC and wrote anecdotal historical and other works. See *OCD*³, 498–9.

copulate . . . hybrids See above, **9–32. introd.** A habit generally attributed to remote peoples, though Theopompus claimed it for the Etruscans (fr. 222). This and other, less drastic, forms of deviation from the perceived sexual norm were a sign of otherness. Herodotus had already stated that Indians copulated in the open, i.e. like animals, 3. 101, as did a tribe in the Caucasus (1. 203, cf. Xenophon on the Mossynoeci south-east of the Caspian, *An.* 5. 4. 33). Monstrous births, when they were characteristic of a whole tribe or people in a faraway and exotic location, were in a sense normalized in that particular context and could be treated with more detachment than the isolated monstrosities occasionally thrown up in Roman society which marked an alarming deviation from the norm (see below, **33. portentous . . . fertility, 34. once . . . pets**), but for which there were other explanations (below, **52. They are believed . . . confuse the resemblance**), though bestiality was cited by some; see Garland (1995), 71 on the well-known story about the creature born to the tyrant Periander's mare (Plutarch, *Mor.* 149e). See further, Introd. 5. 2. 3.

Calingae For the name, cf. *HN* 6. 64.

conceive . . . 8 years See **9–32. introd.**

hairy tails . . . run very fast The description strongly suggests apes or monkeys. See above, **24. satyrs** and **Choromandae.**

enveloped by their ears These monsters were first mentioned by the early 5th-cent. writer Scylax of Caryanda and became another of the types favoured in medieval and later teratologies. For illustrations, see Wittcower (1942), pl. 43 a–c.

Oritae See *HN* 6. 96, where besides the separation from Indians by the river, they are said to have a non-Indian language.

separated . . . Arabis For this river as the border between the Oritae and the Indian Arabaeans, see Arrian, *Ind.* 21. 8, 22. 8. It is possibly the Purali (Curtius 9. 10. 6). See Tomaschek, *RE* 2. 1, Arabis (1), 363–4.

Clitarchus *FGH* 2.B, 137, fr. 27. See above, **29.**

31. Crates of Pergamum Fr. 14 Mette. See above, **13.** Pliny now turns from Indian *mirabilia* back to Ethiopia and Africa **32.**

Trogodytae See above, **23.**

Syrbotae Cf. *HN* 6. 190.

Menismini In *HN* 6. 190, identical characteristics are attributed to the Alabi 'next to' the Medimni and Schwabe identifies the Menismini with the latter: Schwabe, *RE* 15. 1, Menismini, 895.

Cynocephali See above, **23. dog-headed men.** But the creatures here are unambiguously called animals and are kept as herds by a human tribe. For Augustine (*CD* 16. 8. 135), their dog-heads and lack of human speech allowed their categorization as animal rather than human.

32. African . . . phantoms Probably a description of the mirage phenomenon. For genuine ghosts and revenants, of which P. is largely sceptical, see below, **179. supernatural . . . phenomena.**

cleverly contrived . . . to amuse . . . amaze   Nature's cleverness, often remarked on by P. , is here ingenuity (*ingeniosa natura*)
rather than artistry (*natura artifex, HN* 11. 1–4). As often in book 7, it
is displayed in the amazing variety of her creations (see Introd. 4. 3,
5. 2. 2). The human *mirabilia* just discussed are deliberately contrived and are not mistakes or imperfections on her part, a notion
in keeping with P.'s broadly Stoic stress on her providence. Nature
does nothing in vain: but it is hard to assign a purpose to these
exotic people. P. suggests that such *mirabilia* exist solely as manifestations of the ultimate power of a nature who creates purely for her
own amusement (**amuse herself**) and as a statement to others of
her virtuosity (**amaze us**). The theme of nature at play appears
elsewhere in P. in connection with her capacity for variety (*HN* 9.
102, 11. 123, 21. 1, Beagon (1992), 49, 81) and is often redolent of the
capricious power of the Olympian gods. Later, Christian writers,
too, were keen to stress that monstrosities were deliberate manifestations of a power beyond human comprehension and not mistakes
on the part of the divine creator. For Augustine (*CD* 16. 8), God
alone has the wisdom to see how diversities such as these contribute
to the pattern that makes up the overall design of creation.

individual creations . . . miracles   P. is referring in particular
to individual creations which differ from the norm; these are too
numerous to count but this does not matter since the wondrous
races already described offer sufficient evidence of nature's power.
The passage suggests that individual monstrosities, too, are perhaps no more than examples of nature's inscrutable variety and not
the terrifying portents of discord and disaster they were once
thought to be. See below, **34. Once . . . pets**, **pets**, and **Alcippe
. . . elephant**. See also Introd. 5. 2. 2 and 5. 2. 3. Augustine later
stressed that monstrous individuals, like monstrous races, were part
of the divine plan (*CD* 16. 4): they are indeed miracles, illustrating
the supreme power of god (*CD* 21. 8).

33–215. *Acknowledged facts concerning the individual human being*

33–72. introd. *Birth, pregnancy, and early development*

For the rest of book 7, P. deals with universal facts concerning the
individual human being, starting with reproduction. Sections

33–72 deal with the beginning of the human lifespan: birth, pregnancy, and early characteristics as follows:

33. Exceptional multiple births

34–6. Portentous and monstrous births; sex changes

37. [*lacuna*] Twins

38–40. Conception and gestation; variations (**40.** A lawsuit hinging upon lack of uniformity in the gestatory period).

41–56. Pregnancy and delivery; embryology; transmission of characteristics

41–2. Symptoms of pregnancy

43–4. Various causes of miscarriage

45–6. Unusual full-term deliveries

47. Trauma/Death in childbirth (Caesareans; sole surviving twins)

48–9. Superfetation and superfecundation

50–6. Transmission of characteristics: deformity not necessarily genetic; unusual cases of resemblance; maternal/paternal impressions at time of conception affect the appearance of the unborn; strange coincidences of likenesses between non-related persons

57–67. Fertility: exceptionally large families; period of fertility; instances of exceptional age; menstruation

68–72. Early infant development: dentition and precocity. (Abnormal instances of those born with teeth; Zoroaster's unique precocity.)

As with book 7 in general, the stress is on variety rather than uniformity and even on the exceptional rather than the norm. See Introd. 5. 2. 1 and 5. 2. 2. Thus, we start with multiple and monstrous births (**33–7**) and, even on the general topic of gestation, Pliny's first comment is that it admits of much variety (below, **38. Other animals . . . varies**), though he may also have taken his cue here from his main source for **37–50**, Aristotle, *HA* 7 584^{a}ff., who is at pains to stress variety in human as opposed to animal reproduction. But it is noticeable, for example, that P, unlike Aristotle does not specifically state the average length of human gestation. (On the extent of P.'s debt to Aristotle, see Introd. 5. 2. 1, cf. 4. 1 and 4. 2).Variations even within the birth patterns of individual women are given prominence (below, **39. Vistilia**). Despite the previous comments on the *mirabilia* of the earth's extremities, the numerous Roman *exempla* in book 7 drawn mainly from authors such as Varro, Verrius Flaccus, and Valerius Maximus (see Introd. 4. 5. 1) suggest that it is Rome above all which epitomizes the unique variety of humanity (see Beagon, forthcoming).

Pliny's references to women thoughout the *HN*, including those relating to the reproductive processes, are collated and discussed by J. Vons, *L'Image de la femme dans l'oeuvre de Pline l'Ancien*, Coll. Lat. 256 (Brussels, 2000), esp. 157–210.

33. Horatii and the Curiatii   Cf. Livy 1. 24. 1. They lived in the time of king Tullus Hostilius (673–642 BC), according to popular tradition, and, during his campaign against Alba Longa, fought each other in combat on behalf of the Roman and the Alban armies respectively. One of the Horatii was the only survivor. According to Dionysius of Halicarnassus (3. 13–14), the two sets of triplets were cousins, their mothers being twins. See *OCD*[3], Horatii, 727; R. M. Ogilvie, *Commentary on Livy books 1–5* (Oxford, 1965), 109 ff.

portentous . . . fertility   To be classed as portentous, a phenomenon must be against the general run of nature. Although Julius Obsequens (*Lib. Prod.* 14) included in his list of prodigies the birth of triplets in 163 BC, the story of the Horatii may have ensured that, normally, triplets were a cause for celebration rather than alarm, cf. Dion. Hal. 3. 22. 10. Gaius (*Digest* 34. 5. 7), commenting on a woman from Alexandria (cf. Julianus, *Dig.* 46. 3. 36; Phlegon, *Mir.* 29: see also below, **49. seven-months' child . . . following months**) who gave birth to quins in Hadrian's reign, echoes Pliny's statement that *more* than three births at one time may be considered portentous (34. 5. 7). See M. Delcourt, *Stérilités mystérieuses et naissances maléfiques dans l'antiquité Classique* (Liège and Paris, 1938), 103–5. However, P. suggests that what is portentous in some circumstances will not be so in others. The Nile was frequently mentioned for its fertility-enhancing qualities, cf. Athenaeus 2. 15, quoting Theophrastus, although other springs and rivers were noted for similar qualities (*HN* 31. 8, 10). See further, below, **In Egypt . . . septuplets**, **39. In Egypt . . . eighth month**, and above, **21. so great . . . water.** Note also the optimistic picture of Umbria in Ps.-Aristotle, *Mir. Ausc.* 80, where it is said to be the norm for women to bear twins and triplets.

Fausta . . . two boys and two girls   See also Solinus 1. 51. For the birth of quintuplets in the Laurentine region of Italy in

Augustus' reign, see Aulus Gellius, *NA* 10. 2, and cf. below, **82. seen . . . tombstone**.

Ostia   Rome's main port, and vital for grain imports to the capital. See *OCD*³, 1081–2.

clearly predicting the famine which followed   The corn supply was a matter of continuous concern for Augustus and by AD 14, he had appointed a prefect to take charge of it. According to Velleius 2. 94, Tiberius, as Quaestor Ostiensis, had played an important role in alleviating the effects of the 22 BC grain shortage, but no famine is reported in the sources between AD 9 (Dio 56. 12. 1) and AD 19 (Tacitus, *Ann.* 2. 87. 1: see P. A. Garnsey, *Famine and Food Supply in the Graeco-Roman World: Responses to Risk and Crisis* (Cambridge, 1988), 219–22). However, as Tiberius reminded the senate *(Ann.* 3. 54. 6), Italy was dependent on external supplies and that always held an element of risk. The famine mentioned here may have been a minor or localized crisis. Despite Pliny's comment on the portentous nature of the birth and the similar comment of Gaius under Hadrian (above, **portentous . . . fertility**), it is unclear to what extent multiple births were taken seriously as portents by the time of Augustus. The woman mentioned by Gellius (for refs., above, **Fausta . . . two boys and two girls**) was apparently commemorated by the emperor as a celebrity, without sinister overtones. It was probably the combination of factors: a grain shortage, a rare multiple birth in the town at the centre of grain distribution, and the death of the restorer of Italy's peace and prosperity which gave rise to the anecdote as P. reports it. (For omens at the time of Augustus' death, see Dio 56. 29.) The arrival of an unusually large number of extra dependants at a time when the food supply was under strain presumably enhanced the birth's portentous significance. See also Introd. 5. 2. 2; **34. Once . . . pets**, **pets**, and **Alcippe . . . elephant**.

Peloponnese . . . survived   Aristotle (*HA* 7. 4, 584ᵇ) mentions the same story without giving a location.

In Egypt . . . septuplets   Trogus fr. 3 (Seel). Aristotle says (*HA* 7. 4, 584ᵇ) that the biggest ever multiple birth was of quintuplets (the maximum number modern medicine considers can be carried to term). Aulus Gellius, *NA* 10. 2 says Aristotle placed this occurrence in Egypt, although Aristotle's language could refer to any of the places to which he attributes a higher fertility rate: Strabo says Aristotle thought India was even more fertile than Egypt (15. 1. 22–3, C695); cf. above, **21. So great . . . water**. He also says Aristotle mentioned a case of septuplets, but the passage is not extant. Multiple pregnancies increased the likelihood of birth abnormalities, which was probably one reason why areas of high fertility were also believed to be rich in monstrosities: see above, **21. So great . . . water**. The boy with an extra set of eyes in the back of his head which Pliny reports as being successfully reared in Egypt (*HN* 11. 272) cf. below, **39. in Egypt . . . eighth month**) may have been an example of Siamese twins. For other multiple pregnancies, see above, **Fausta . . . two boys and two girls** and **portentous . . . fertility**; and below, **48–9** and **82. seen . . . tombstone**. For iconography and attitudes to multiple births in antiquity, see V. Dasen, 'Multiple Births in Graeco-Roman Antiquity', *OJA* 16. 1 (1997), 49–63.

Trogus   Pompeius Trogus was an Augustan historian and naturalist from Gallia Narbonensis, who wrote a 44–book history as well as works on botany and zoology which were used by Pliny. See *OCD*[3], 1217; A. Momigliano, 'Livio, Plutarco e Giustino su virtù e fortuna dei Romani: Contributo alla ricostruzione della fonte di Trogo Pompeo', *Athenaeum*, NS 12 (1934), 45–56.

34. hermaphrodites   Aulus Gellius cites this passage, *NA* 9. 4. 16: see above, **8. I shall not pledge . . . doubtful issues**. The name is derived from the Greek bisexual god who was possibly a rationalization of bisexual elements in ancient ritual; and was later explained in mythical terms as a child of Hermes and Aphrodite who exhibited the sexual characeristics of both parents. But Ovid (*Met.* 4. 285–388) makes him the son of the two gods, feminized by fusion with the nymph Salmacis. See M. Delcourt, *Hermaphrodite: Mythes et rites de la bisexualité dans l'antiquité classique* (Liège and Paris, 1958), 65–103.

once . . . pets   Hermaphrodites were 'a symbol of considerable potential' (P. M. C. Forbes-Irving, *Metamorphosis in Greek Myth* (Oxford, 1990), 151), since they confused the most basic of natural categories, the sexes. One of Phlegon of Tralles' (see Introd. 3. 3) most striking wonder stories involved a hermaphroditic child and a revenant, another transgressor of a basic natural boundary, that between life and death (*Wonders* 2). P. suggests that the name *androgyni* coincided with an earlier attitude of fear and superstition at Rome, cf. *androgyni* in Livy, Obsequens, and Orosius as portents in the late 3rd and early 2nd cents. BC (J. Briscoe, *A Commentary on Livy Books xxi–xxxiii* (1973), 89). In Livy's descriptions of contemporary reactions, the words 'disgusting', 'obscene', 'deformed', and 'accursed' recur (e.g. 27. 11, 37; and 31. 12). 'Hermaphrodite' by contrast, belongs to a more recent era in which the fear has subsided. The Greeks were less alarmed by human *terata* generally, helped in the case of intersexuals by the existence of the cult of Hermaphroditus (above, **hermaphrodites**): see Garland (1995), 3, 65–70. At Rome, however, gross bodily deformities had been regarded as indicative of divine anger and of 'disorder in the body politic' (Garland (1995), 69), cf. Cicero, *Div.* 1. 121. See also Beagon (2002), 118–19. Most of the documented instances (Livy, Orosius, Diodorus Siculus) come from times of political upheaval: the second Punic war and the period from the Gracchi (133 BC) to the Social War (90 BC). The reason for the change of attitude which P. notes is not clear. A hundred years earlier, Diodorus Siculus had insisted that hermaphrodites were not monsters (32. 10. 2: see below, **36. barren desert island . . . soothsayers**). Greater confidence in Rome's political survival may have helped precipitate a change in religious attitude: far fewer portents of all kinds were recorded and no more intersexual portents are found in Livy after 92 BC: see Garland (1995), 70–2 and Introd. 5. 2. 3. Rome's destruction of hermaphrodites ironically coincided with their popularity in Hellenistic art, cf. the famous sleeping hermaphrodite of the 2nd cent. BC and the statue described as 'noble' in *HN* 34. 80 (Delcourt (1958), 83, 89, 97; H. le Bonniec, *Pline l'Ancien Histoire Naturelle livre 34* (Paris, 1953), 260: that the two are identical is not certain). By the 1st cent. AD they were popular as artistic subjects at Rome (Delcourt (1958), 97 on Pompeii paintings), but this is likely to have been a symptom rather than a cause of changing attitudes on a wider scale. The expansion of geographical knowledge in P.'s era aroused curiosity at all levels of society (Beagon (1992), 8–10; above, **6. what is not regarded as wondrous . . . attention?** and Introd. 3. 3; see below, **35. I actually saw**) and indicated the existence of creatures far more extraordinary than hermaphrodites (Wittcower (1942); E. Bianchi, 'Teratologia e geografia', *Acme*, 34

(1981), 227–49). Gellius cites this passage in the context of *mirabilia*. The hermaphrodite, like many other oddities of nature, is becoming a curiosity, though the more superstitious and less artistically influenced lower classes may have preserved older attitudes to some extent: Livy says that *androgyni* is a term 'used by the *common people (vulgus)*' (27. 11). Three centuries later, Augustine gives both terms equal weight as names for the same phenomenon (*CD* 6. 8). Certainly, any change was not a clean break with past attitudes: Phlegon (*Wonders* 25) has a case, albeit isolated, of the destruction by priests of another once-feared monstrosity, Siamese twins, as late as AD 112, while earlier, a similar monstrosity had apparently been exhibited to Nero as a curiosity (Phlegon, *Wonders* 20). Nor was there always a distinction in attitude to be made in terms of class; when a sex-changer was exhibited to him, the superstitious Claudius 'had an altar built to Jupiter Averter of Evil because of the portent' (Phlegon, *Wonders* 6). Many centuries later, in the Christian era, attitudes could oscillate between fear and curiosity: in 10th-cent. Byzantium, Siamese twins who, when one of them died, were to be subjected to the first and only recorded attempt at surgical separation before the late 17th cent., were initially admired as a curiosity, but then banished as a bad omen before returning to the city again (Theophanes continuatus, *CSHB* 33: 433, see G. E. Pentoglos and J. C. Lascaratos, 'A Surgical Operation Performed on Siamese Twins during the Tenth Century', *BHM* 58. 1 (1984), 433). See also below, **36. barren island . . . soothsayers**. A shift in attitude in some ways analogous to that implied by Pliny took place in post-Reformation Europe, with monsters increasingly regarded as entertaining natural wonders rather than religious prodigies. Here, too, however, the social history of the change was complex: see Park and Daston (1981), 20–54.

androgyni   A fusion of the Greek words for 'man' (*aner, andros*) and 'woman' (*gune*) (Livy 27. 11. 4). Augustine (*CD* 16. 8) says that both names are regarded as masculine, their bearers being assigned the 'better sex'. But note that P. can talk of 'hermaphrodite mares' owned by Nero in *HN* 11. 262, see below, **36. women . . . men**.

pets   Human oddities such as dwarves also occur as pets of the rich, as do cretins and hunchbacks cf. below, **75. Conopas**. Here and in **75**, P. uses the term *deliciae*, 'pet', which often had sexual overtones: deformity had erotic appeal, as P.'s story of the rich Gegania and her humpback slave Clesippus (*HN* 34. 11) amply illustrates (for other examples, see Garland (1995), 52–4) and the hermaphrodite's attraction in this respect was obvious (cf. Garland (1995), 119). Augustus, however, abhorred such 'sports of nature and omens of evil' (Suet. *Aug.* 83. 2), though he was not averse either to exhibiting freaks, including dwarves, publicly (Suet. *Aug.* 43. 3) or to amassing a personal collection of other types of *mirabilia* (Suet. *Aug.* 72. 3). Augustus' may have been a personal dislike. Dwarves were not normally regarded as ominous and in any case attitudes towards *terata* were evidently changing (see previous note), with increasing perception of nature's 'sports' as examples of her virtuosity rather than of divine wrath, even in the case of individual monstrosities. Pliny had of course portrayed nature as deliberately creating the monstrous *races* of men as 'sports' for herself (above, **32. cleverly contrived to amuse . . . amaze**), but these could hardly be mistakes or departures from the 'norm': cf. the definition of *teras*, a monstrosity, as a creature different from its parents, Aristotle, *GA* 4. 3, 767[b]; Aeschines, *Ktes.* iii. Cf. *HN* 11. 6, 'The more I observe Nature, the less prone I am to consider any statement about her to be impossible'; and contrast the horrified Romans (of 200 BC) in Livy 31. 12, for whom deformed animals and humans were a result of nature mixing up the species, a serious malfunction signifying divine displeasure (cf. R. Bloch, *Les Prodiges dans l'antiquité classique* (Paris, 1963), 118–19). See Introd. 5. 2. 3.

Pompey the Great 106–47BC. Caesar's son-in-law and eventual adversary. See below, **95–9**.

theatre The first permanent theatre at Rome, dedicated in 55BC (Asconius, *In Pis.* 1) in the Campus Martius. It probably held about 10,000 spectators rather than Pliny's 40,000 (36. 115), and, after several restorations, was still regarded as a building of distinction in the 4th cent. AD (Ammianus Marcellinus 16. 10. 14: S. B. Platner and T. Ashby, *A Topographical Dictionary of Ancient Rome* (London and Oxford, 1929), 515–17; C. Nash, *Pictorial Dictionary of Ancient Rome*[2] (New York, 1981), ii. 1216–23; M. Bieber, *The History of the Greek and Roman Theater* (Princeton, 1961), 184; L. Richardson, *A New Topographical Dictionary of Ancient Rome* (Johns Hopkins, 1992), 383–5; J. Leach, *Pompey the Great* (London, 1977), 134; P. Greenhalgh, *Pompey the Republican Prince* (London, 1981), 54–7).

statues ... artists   Perhaps part of the collection organized by Cicero's friend Atticus for Pompey (Cic. *Att.* 4. 9. 1). Besides the *mirabilia* mentioned here, there were also representations of the fourteen nations Pompey had conquered (*HN* 36. 41; Suet. *Nero* 46), the first examples of what became a popular Roman genre (K. Jex-Blake and E. Sellers, *The Elder Pliny's Chapters on the History of Art* (London and New York, 1896), 212–13). Statues extant include Pans, the Dioscuri, and a bronze Hercules (Bieber (1961), 184; J. van Ooteghem, *Pompée le Grand, bâtisseur d'Empire* (Namur, 1954), 404–8; F. Coarelli, 'Il Complesso Pompeiano del Campo Marzio e la sua decorazione scultorea', *Rend. Pont.* (1971–2), 99). It is unclear where the statues stood; slight differences in Pliny's phrasing might suggest that, whereas the *mirabilia* were within the theatre proper, the fourteen nations were in the porticus to the south-east, where there were also paintings by Greek old masters (*HN* 35. 59, 114, 126, 132). The statues of the nations were by a Roman artist, Coponius, but if Atticus was involved, a Greek provenance for at least some of the others, including the *mirabilia* (the two specified have Greek subjects) seems very likely.

Eutychis   Solinus 1. 52 misreads Pliny and has Pompey exhibit the actual woman. She came from Caria.

Alcippe ... elephant ... portent   Tatian, *Ad Graecos* 34. 26–35. 3 (Schwartz) mentions statues of various women who experienced unusual births, including a 'Glaucippe' sculpted in bronze by the Athenian Niceratus. Livy 27. 11 records an elephant-headed child, perhaps significantly during the Punic wars, amongst the portents at Sinuessa in 209 BC (F. B. Krauss, *An Interpretation of the Omens, Portents and Prodigies recorded by Livy, Tacitus and Suetonius* (Pennsylvania, 1930), 129; and cf. Valerius Maximus 1. 6. 5). Men with elephant heads were described and illustrated in later teratologies. See Ajasson de Grandsagne 45 for Hardouin's examples and Cuvier's suggested biological malformations behind the 'elephant-head' stories. Cranio-facial tumours and clefts and other congenital conditions such as herniation of brain and meninges through a skull defect cause severe and bizarre deformity (see D. J. David, D. C. Hemming, R. D. Cooter, *Craniofacial Deformities* (New York, 1990). The 'Elephant' Man's most striking deformity was his head, massively misshapen by bone and soft-tissue tumours (see L. Fiedler, *Freaks: Myths and Images of the Secret Self* (London and New

York, 1978), 170–7). P.'s classing of this as a portent, due to similarities with lists from the outbreak of the Social War, is something of an afterthought. He sometimes echoes the Stoics' assimilation of portents (Cic. *Div.* 1. 3. 6) to the principle of cosmic sympathy (e.g. *HN* 2. 97, Beagon (1992), 101) but more often records omens without committing himself to a personal opinion. The overriding theme here (see **32. individual creations . . . miracles** above) and in the *HN* generally is that, even when they are called omens or prodigies by P., the oddities listed are marvels of nature; manifestations of her infinite *varietas* rather than signs of divine disfavour. See Introd. 5. 2. 3.

snake   Cf. Obsequens 57 (83 BC).

Marsic war   The Social War of 91 BC.

all sorts . . . prodigies   On war crises and prodigies, see Bloch (1963), 129–30. P. may be drawing on lost books of Livy. Sisenna also collected the portents for this period (Cic. *Div.* 1. 99).

35. Claudius Caesar   The emperor Claudius (AD 41–54: *OCD*[3], Claudius (Tiberius Claudius Nero Germanicus), 337–8; see Introd. 2. 1) had scholarly and antiquarian interests. See Suet. *Claud.* 41–2 for his writings, which included a Roman history, an Etruscan and a Carthaginian history (both in Greek), an autobiography, a defence of Cicero, and a work on the alphabet. Of the eight fragments thought to come from the histories (Peter ii. 92–4), six are found in Pliny (*HN* 5. 63, 6. 27, 6. 31, 6. 128, 7. 35, 12. 78). Münzer (1897: 390 ff.) suspected there were others. Possibilities are *HN* 5. 58, 8. 37, and 10. 5, all *mirabilia* of Claudian date. For emperors as patrons and even as embodiments of the extraordinary, see Millar (1992), 140, and Garland, (1995), 48–52 (and below, **75. Conopas**).

hippocentaur   The centaur was a mythical human–equine hybrid. See Pease on Cic. *ND* 1. 105 and idem (*M. Tulli Ciceronis de Divinatione libri duo*, Darmstadt, 1973) on *Div.* 2. 49. Hippocentaur means 'horse-centaur', and Pease (loc. cit.) notes that this compound name, rather than the simple 'centaur', was sometimes used to distinguish the man-horse from other similar combinations, such as the onocentaur (man-donkey). Diodorus Siculus, however, thought that the original centaurs were men, whose mating with mares produced the hippocentaurs (4. 69. 5–70. 1). Ancient writers rationalized them in various ways, from cloud-pictures (in myth, the original centaur was fathered on a cloud-image) to misinterpretation of cavalry by horseless nations (below, **202. fighting . . . Pelion** and cf. **196. Chiron**). They became a type of the nonexistent creature for philosophers and jurists, cf. Cic. *Tusc.* 1. 90, but this did not halt so-called personal sightings such as this one.

I actually saw For autopsy in Pliny, see below, **36. I myself... in Africa**. Items of interest were frequently displayed at the games, at an imperial residence (if a gift to the emperor), or in any convenient place at Rome: Suet. *Aug.* 43. 4; and below. See Introd. 4. 2; Beagon, forthcoming; and below, **74–5**. The unusual exhibits might be genuine (cf. *HN* 8. 65, 68, 69, 70, 96) or the product of wishful thinking on the part of the procurer and the viewers as here, though some fakes were obvious (*HN* 10. 5, Claudius' phoenix). Emperors were bombarded with wondrous items of all types, from bumper ears of corn (*HN* 18. 94–5) to outright monstrosities (Strabo 15. 1. 73, C719; Dio 54. 9. 8; Phlegon 20, cf. Suet. *Tib.* 60 and Juvenal, *Sat.* 4 on giant fish). For monstrosities, Plutarch, condemning unhealthy curiosity, suggests there existed a permanent display area-cum-market (*Mor.* 520c).

Egypt Cf. Phlegon, *Wonders* 34: it was originally sent to Egypt from Arabia, but did not survive the journey, so it was enbalmed by the prefect of Egypt before being sent on to Rome. (For Egypt's outlandish fertility, see above, **33. portentous . . . fertility**.)

honey Elsewhere, P. says that honey was a preservative, even of bodies (*HN* 22. 108; cf. Xenophon, *Hell.* 5. 3. 19; Diodorus 15. 93; Josephus, *Ant.* 14. 7. 4; cf. Lucretius, *RN* 3. 889; also *HN* 15. 65, quinces and *HN* 30. 115, earthworms, for medicinal purposes). See Beagon, forthcoming. Experiment (G. Majno, *The Healing Hand* (Cambridge, Mass., 1975), 139) suggests that only small bodies or parts of bodies could be preserved for any length of time. Soothing and antibacterial, it had a variety of uses in Indian and Egyptian, as well as Greek medicine (Majno, index s.v. 'honey'), and there is a revival of interest in its uses in the treatments of wounds today.

Saguntum 16 miles north of Valencia in Spain. Saguntum was an ally of Rome, when it was besieged and captured by Hannibal in 219–218 BC. This was regarded as one of the immediate causes of the second Punic war. See Livy 21. 6–15.

36. Women changing into men . . . at the time of writing
This passage is reproduced in Aulus Gellius, *NA* 9. 4. 15.

Women . . . men True hermaphrodites, possessing both testicular and ovarian tissue, are very rare (W. A. van Niekirk, *True Hermaphroditism: Clinical, Morphological and Cytogenetic Aspects* (New York and London, 1974), 83). Chromosomal and hormonal abnormalities more often produce individuals with ambiguous external sex organs. The metamorphoses in Pliny and other ancient writers tend to be from female to male. This 'one-way' tendency could be justified by physiological theory: Galen famously depicted the female genitalia as inverted and internalized male genitalia which might be extruded if the body's heat was significantly increased (see below, **developed male attributes**). However, it is likely that a cultural bias, reflected in philosophical and medical theories of female inferiority, which saw the female state as 'less stable' (R. Flemming, *Medicine and the Making of Roman Women* (Oxford, 2000), 152), was also at work. Nature tended to move towards the more perfect, in this case, the male condition, an attitude still being voiced in the 17th cent. (see T. Laqueur, *Making Sex: Body and Gender from the Greeks to Freud* (Harvard, 1990), 127–8). In the 16th-cent. surgeon Ambroise Paré's words, 'nous ne trouvons jamais en histoire veritable que l'homme aucun soit devenu femme, pour-ce que nature tend tousjours à ce qui est la plus parfaict, et non au contraire faire ce qui est parfaict devienne imparfaict' (*Des monstres et prodiges*, ed. J. Céard (Geneva, 1973), vii. 53–5, p. 30). Actual observation of the rare but well-documented 'crowing hen' phenomenon (e.g. Aristotle, *HA* 631^{b}7–12) may have encouraged this conviction. A hen or other female bird gradually takes on masculine characteristics in appearance and behaviour, a transformation now known to be due to the reproductive system becoming diseased or atrophied by age: see T. R. Forbes, *The Midwife and the Witch* (Yale, 1966), 1–22. But, in the case of humans, external transformation is in any case most likely to be observed in 'females' who are in fact male pseudo-hermaphrodites possessing external ambiguities. Many ancient sex-changes could have resulted from hormonal changes at puberty precipitating greater external masculinization, such as those associated with the rare genetic disorder 5–alpha reductase deficiency syndrome, found today in certain parts of the world including the Dominican Republic and among the Sambia of Papua New Guinea: see G. Herdt, 'Mistaken Sex: Culture, Biology and the Third Sex in New Guinea', in G. Herdt (ed.), *Third Sex, Third Gender: Beyond Sexual Dimorphism in Culture and History* (New York, 1994), 419–45, who compares the mistaken female gender assignment found in the ancient 'sex-changers' to the situation of these modern examples. There are also physical similarities. Genetically XY males born with 5–alpha reductase deficiency resemble females at birth and during childhood, but, as they approach puberty, gradually become more masculine. The subjects of the Greek and Roman anecdotes are young (e.g. Pliny's first and second examples) and are often said specifically to change sex around the time of their marriage (which for girls in Graeco-Roman society normally coincided with puberty); whether just before (Phlegon, *Wonders* 7), on the day itself (Pliny's African, Phlegon's (*Wonders* 6) 13-year-old), or a short time after (Pliny's Arescon/Arescusa, Phlegon, *Wonders* 9, and two detailed stories in Diodorus 32. 10–12). These stories diverge from the modern phenomenon only in the emphasis on the suddenness of the change, but this may have been enhanced in retelling for dramatic effect (Hansen (1996), 125). See generally Delcourt (1958); Fiedler (1978), ch. 7.

In *HN* 11. 262, Pliny suggests that the description 'hermaphroditic' can be used of any external anomaly in the sexual organs of an individual who is otherwise recognizably male or female: 'a few women possess a startling resemblance (to the male genitalia), as do hermaphrodites of either sex . . .', in which context he mentions Nero's mares, *hermaphroditae . . . equae*.

no fantasy   There were various well-known sex-change stories in Greek myth, including Teiresias who changed from a man to a woman and back to a man again and Kainis who changed to a man (Kaineus). See Forbes Irving (1990), 149–70.

Annals   The *Annales Maximi* were a yearly chronicle of events, including prodigies, compiled until the late 2nd cent. BC by the Pontifex Maximus and collected into 80 volumes. See *OCD*[3], 98.

Crassus . . . Longinus   Consuls in 171 BC, cf. Livy 42. 28. 5.

Casinum   On the Via Latina in the far south of Latium. (Gellius' 'of C. Licinius' instead of the place-name is unlikely; P. gives place-names in all the other examples.)

barren island . . . soothsayers A woman who turned into a
man at the beginning of the Social War was burnt alive on the
orders of the soothsayers (Diodorus Siculus fr. 32. 10–12, cf.
Obsequens 25). This was followed by a similar case at Athens.
Soothsayers' advice in the case of the hermaphrodites in Livy 27. 37
and 31. 12 led to their drowning, cf. Obsequens 22, 27, 34, 36, 47, 50;
and Orosius 5. 4 for later, Christian, disapproval. Sometimes this
was the fate of other kinds of major monstrosity, cf. Phlegon 25
(Siamese twins), and Seneca, *Dial.* 3. 15. 2 (deformed children
generally), but it was above all sexual monstrosities that were ruth-
lessly eliminated (Krauss (1930), 130–2; cf. B. MacBain, *Prodigy and
Expiation: A Study in Religion and Politics in Republican Rome*, Coll. Lat.
177 (Brussels, 1982), 126–35). Their abnormal fertility was prevented, living or dead, from polluting the fertile earth by destruction in fire or water, cf. Livy 27. 37, 'removed from contact with the
earth'. The girl's deportation looks less drastic but the result may
have been death by starvation. Barren areas were chosen for
deportations imposed as judicial punishments (*Digest* 48. 22. 7); but
this island may have been completely barren, thus ensuring once
again that earth's fertility was free from pollution. Strangely, no
action was taken with regard to the other examples of sex-change
given by Pliny, perhaps because they were so much later (cf. above,
34. once . . . pets). But Krauss points to Livy 24. 10 where as early
as 214 BC no action is reported in a sex-change case, cf. MacBain
(1982), 127 n. 238. Possibly, definite changes from one sex to the
other were not always as alarming as the ambivalent hermaphrodites. See above, **34. once . . . pets**.

Licinius Mucianus See Introd. 3. 1. 1, 3. 3, 4. 5. 1.

developed male attributes Diodorus Siculus fr. 32. 10–12
gives sensational details of male genitals bursting out of tumours on
feverish patients. The apparently bizarre nature of the transformation was readily explicable in terms of ancient theories of sexual
differentiation which persisted for centuries. Galen had described
female genitalia as morphologically identical to the male, but
inverted and internalized; whether they protrude from the body to
create a male depends upon sufficient heat being present (*De Usu
Part.* 11. 297, 299 K; cf. also Ps.-Galen 14. 719 K, Rufus, *Onom.*
193–8). Some fifteen hundred years later, Sir Thomas Browne
spoke of man's 'androgynal condition' (*Pseudodoxia Epidemica*, 1646).

The greater heat of the superior male was a fundamental difference between him and the inferior female in Aristotelian biology (below, **37**). For post-Aristotelian views of men and women as variants on a single sexual model, see Laqueur (1990), esp. 4–7, 25–35, 63–4, 127–30, 141–2; Flemming (2000), 119–22. The generation of extra heat was necessary for transformation according to this theory. The heat of the male might be expected to increase at puberty— hence the fever of the patients described in the ancient case studies of Diodorus, whose descriptions of masculinization in these cases as a process initiated by feverish heat which ultimately leads to the externalization of the genitalia is eminently rational according to the ancient pattern of thought as described by Galen. The cases described by Ambroise Paré in his study of monstrosities were pre-cipitated by extra heat generated at puberty and/or physical or sexual exertion (1973: viii, pp. 29–30). Paré claimed that heat pro-duced the transformation, causing internalized genitalia to extrude (1973: vii. 43–5, p. 30). Members which projected outwards could never turn inwards, thus, in Laqueur's words, obeying the laws of thermodynamics (141–2) and offering an explanation as to why such changes always seemed to be from the female to the male state (see above, **Women . . . men**). Diodorus indeed claims that he is trying to promote rationality about such phenomena to counter the superstition that had led to the burning of hermaphrodites (32. 12. 1); but his details, whether deliberately or not, may have appealed to the sensationalism deplored by Plutarch (*Mor.* 517f–518c) for whom even doctors, 'in whom curiosity is a salutary thing', are expected not to pry unasked into others' infirmities (518d).

I myself . . . in Africa   Pliny declares autopsy here, in **34** above (**I actually saw**), and in **83** below (**I myself . . . Athanatus**). He also implies it in **82** (**seen . . . tombstone**). These personal guar-antees give authority to tales which might otherwise be dismissed as exaggerations or fabrications: compare the hippocentaur 'seen' by P. (**34**) with the phoenix dismissed by him as a forgery in *HN* 10. 5. The purpose in the present instance may be to give authority to a story from an area notorious for inspiring speculative fantasies: see below, **Africa**. In **82** and **83** his intention may be not just to enhance the veracity of the other, second-hand, tales of super-human strength recounted there, but also to assert his own author-ity in the company of their main source, the formidable Roman scholar, Varro. Autopsy can also help to reconstruct P.'s career (Syme (1969), 201–36 and (1991), 496–511, modifying Münzer 1897). P.'s stay in Africa is comparatively well attested by this and two other reports (*HN* 17. 41, 25. 123) and by at least four other accurately detailed and enthusiastic descriptions (95. 41, 13. 104ff., 18. 188, and 35. 169), but its date remains uncertain: see Introd. 1.

Africa A country among the least familiar to the Greeks and Romans, and thus the home of many *mirabilia*. See above, **9–32. introd.** Elsewhere, P. quotes the well-worn Greek saying that Africa 'is always producing some novelty' (*HN* 8. 42). Contemporary new inroads following the quelling of the Mauretanian revolt in the early years of Claudius raised speculations in this area, producing wild stories (*HN* 5. 11–12, cf. 5. 1–4): see Introd. 3. 3; Beagon (1992), 6–7. These P. puts down with a firmness made more explicable if he had had personal experience of the province himself (see above, **I myself**).

Thysdrus Modern El Jem in Tunisia.

and who ... writing Missing in P.'s text but present in Gellius, who has to this point given a word-for-word rendition of the passage.

37. ... when twins are born ... less common There is a lacuna in P.'s text, but the sense may be gathered from his source, Aristotle, *HA* 584^{b}35: '*In the case of man*, few twins survive if one is a boy and one a girl ... ', cf. *GA* 775^{a}5–27, where Aristotle explains that the male embryo is hotter than the female: they are therefore bound to develop at different rates and not mature at the same time (cf. also *PA* 648^a, where he discusses the differing views among the Presocratics on the hot/cold issue, and *PA* 670^{b}17–33). These and the following comments on male and female in **37**, which P. bases on Aristotle, rest on the latter's premiss that the female is colder and weaker, and, in a sense, a deformity of the male ideal (*GA* 775^{a}15). Modern studies confirm that maternal and foetal complications and perinatal mortality are indeed higher in the case of twins than in singleton pregnancies, whatever the sex of the babies. Ancient observation of this higher mortality rate was no doubt combined with the preconceptions concerning the developmental differences of the sexes.

Girls are born . . . grow old more quickly   According to
Aristotle, *HA* 584ª26, the male is born more quickly because he is
stronger and fights to get out of the womb harder. Some (e.g.
Hardouin, cf. Schilling 140) have suggested replacing P.'s 'are
born' with 'develop' or something similar, thus equating his statement with that in *GA* 775ª14ff. and *HA* 583ᵇ24, where Aristotle says
that although the female takes longer to develop in the womb, once
born she reaches maturity and old age more quickly (cf. Hipp. *Oct.*
9. 6 7. 450 L; Galen 17. 1. 445 K). This is due to her natural inferiority, the female being wetter, weaker and, above all, colder than
the male. Warmth and humidity were the basis of life (Hipp. *De
Vict. Rat.* 1. 3. 2, 6. 472 L). However, although moisture contributes
to longevity (Arist. *De Long. et Brev. Vitae* 5. 466ᵇ), it is made clear that
heat is the decisive factor (ibid. 466ᵇ, 467ª). The female's ageing
tendency is sometimes exacerbated by the ageing effect of childbearing (*HA* 582ª22–5, cf. 583ᵇ29); a phenomenon which Pliny
reports in both the animal (*HN* 9. 89) and vegetable (*HN* 16. 118)
kingdoms. The slower development of the female in the womb is
said in *GA* 775ª25–7 to be unique to the human species; elsewhere,
the faster ageing of the female after birth is said to be the rule
throughout the animal kingdom (Arist. *De Long. et Brev. Vit.* 5.
466ᵇ–6. 467ª). See also below, **71. Women . . . fewer**.

Boys move more often   See Aristotle, *HA* 584ª26ff. This is
attributed to the male's greater heat in *GA* 775ª5ff. (see above,
when twins . . .), when Aristotle says that this restlessness made
the male foetus more prone to damage than the passive female. As
a result, more males than females are born deformed.

right side . . . left   The association between the male and the
right and the female and the left corresponds to traditional socio-
religious belief in the right as the superior, dominant, and auspicious side and the left as inferior and inauspicious. See G. E. R.
Lloyd, 'Right and Left in Greek Philosophy', *JHS* 82 (1962), 56–66;
also P. Lévêque and P. Vidal-Naquet, 'Épaminondas Pythagoricien: Ou le problème tactique de la droite et de la gauche', *Historia*,
9 (1960), 294–308; R. Hertz, 'La Prééminence de la main droite,
étude sur la polarité', in *Death and The Right Hand* (Oxford, 1960). In
ancient medical theory, the idea was applied in various ways and
'considering its total lack of foundation, had a very long lease of life
. . .' (J. Needham, *A History of Embryology*² (Cambridge, 1959), 31,

referring to its inclusion in 18th-cent. editions of the *Callipaedia* of Claude Quillet). According to Aristotle (*Met.* 986ᵃ23–ᵇ5), the Pythagoreans associated the female with the left and the bad, the male with the right and the good. Some works in the Hippocratic corpus (e.g. *Aph.* 5. 48, 4. 550 L), Parmenides (DK 17; A. H. Coxon, *The Fragments of Parmenides* (Assen and New Hampshire, 1986), fr. 18 and pp. 252–3 for testimonia), and Anaxagoras (DK 59a 42. 12) suggested that the male originated on the right of the womb, females on the left, but Aristotle (*GA* 764ᵃ33, 765ᵃ5 ff.) argued at length against this and against the theory that males are generated by semen from the right testis and females by semen from the left. In *HA* 583ᵇ4, however, he says males generally move on the right after 40 days and females on the left after 90 days (see below, **41. women carrying a boy . . . ninetieth day**), but he stresses that this is not a hard and fast rule. See Coxon on Parmenides fr. 18 ad loc., 253–4.

38. Other animals . . . variable For the stress on human variety in book 7 generally, see **33–72. introd**. and Introd. 5. 2. 1, and for the breaking of physiological limits observed by other animals, see 5. 2. 2. In *HN* 10. 171–2 man alone of animals is said to indulge in unlimited sexual intercourse at any time of the year, cf. above, **5**, where P. moralizes on man's uncontrolled passions. Ancient medical opinion, however (cf. Hipp. *Mul.* 1. 2, 8. 16, 1–2 L; Soranus, *Gyn.* 1. 31), advocated regular sexual intercourse for women to ensure easy and wholesale evacuation of regular menses. For the uniqueness of human menstruation, see below, **63. women . . . periods**.

seventh month . . . beginning of the eleventh month Cf. Aristotle, *GA* 772ᵇ7–11: children are born at seven months and at ten months and at times in between. This was the normally quoted range in antiquity and is found as early as Empedocles (DK 31A 75). In *HA* 584ᵃ35 ff., ten months is said to be the norm. The problem was that ancient methods of calculation varied. Pregnancy was usually measured in months, both in medical texts and in general parlance: see O. Montevecchi, 'Poson menon estin', *ZPE* 34 (1979), 113–17. The 'month' in question would normally be the lunar month of 29. 5 days, which also corresponded to the average female menstrual cycle. Some sources round this up to thirty days. Thus, the Hippocratic treatise *On Fleshes* 8. 613 L states that a full-term baby is born after 'nine months and ten days', a length of time divisible into seven-day periods (for the significance of the latter, see below, **39. In Italy**), making 280 days in total, the figure which is considered to be the normal period of gestation today. Calculation by months was usually inclusive, and such a child would be called a tenth-month child. *On Nutriment* 42, 9. 113–15 L, however, gives a figure of 270 days for a full-term pregnancy, i.e. just nine months of thirty days, but adds that there is an upper limit of 300 days, or ten months of thirty days. As the writer admits of 'a few days more or less', we reach here Pliny's upper limit of 'the beginning of the eleventh month'. The main cause of discrepancies, however, was ascertaining the starting point of pregnancy: see A. E. Hanson, 'The Eighth Month Child: Obsit Omen', *BHM* 61 (1987), 589–91. For example, Aristotle's belief that conception normally took place after menstruation, which happened at the waning of the moon, implicitly places conception around new moon and the first half of the month (*HA* 582^{b}12). However, the author of the Hippocratic treatise *On the Eighth-Month Child* (13, 7. 458–60 L) believed that conception did not take place before the middle of the lunar month, once menstruation, which, he implies, started with the new moon, but varied in length, was over. See below, **66. This amazingly . . . occurs at all** and **67. easiest . . . finishing**, cf. below, **Only children conceived . . . no moon**. Even then, other factors might delay conception (13, 7. 458 L). His 'first' month was therefore no more than 15 days (cf. 1, 7. 436 L) and often less, meaning that, for example, a term baby of 280 days might be born in either the 'tenth' or the 'eleventh' month; while a seventh-month baby might have been in the womb for little more than five lunar months plus a few days of a 'first' and 'seventh' month at either end. Inaccuracy was inherent in some methods, since they relied on the mistaken idea that a woman somehow sensed after intercourse whether she had conceived. See also below, **38. Only children . . . no moon, 39. In Egypt . . . eighth month** and **In Italy . . . our ancestors**.

A baby . . . never viable   Aristotle, *HA* 584^{b}2. See above, **seventh month**.

Only children conceived . . . no moon   The moon was associated with the feminine and with the softness and moisture attributed to the female in Greek biological and medical thought (cf. e.g. below, **67. it is a sure sign . . . her saliva**); just as the sun was associated with the male, heat, and dryness. See Pliny, *HN* 2. 221–3. The moon's effect on terrestrial phenomena had been noticed in the case of tides early on (cf. Herodotus 2. 2) and accurate observations had been recorded in the 2nd cent. BC by Seleucus (Strabo 3. 5. 9, C174). This interaction, together with the monthly lunar cycle of growth and decrescence, offered further scope for sympathetic links with the biological cycles of man, animals, and plants (cf. e.g. Manilius, *Astr.* 2. 87–104; Apuleius, *Met.* 11. 1; Basil, *Hex.* 6. 10). The earliest observation of a moon rhythm in a living organism was made by Aristotle, who noticed that the ovaries of sea-urchins in some areas swelled up at the time of full moon (*HA* 544^{a}18–20; *PA* 630^{a}33). Oysters and other shellfish, too, were known to increase and decrease in size in accordance with the phases of the moon (Pliny *HN* 2. 109, 9. 96; Plutarch, *Mor.* 658a–59; Gellius, *NA* 20. 8; Macr. *Sat.* 7. 16. 15–34; Manilius and Basil as above); the Stoics cited this and other examples of lunar rhythms as evidence of the sympathetic force which binds the universe together (Cic. *Div.* 2. 33–4). Human menstrual, fertility, and parturition patterns were all thought to be linked to lunar rhythms. Some writers believed that menstruation tended to start when the moon waned (Aristotle, *HA* 582^{a}34ff.; *GA* 767^{a}1ff.) and that the likelihood of conception waxed and waned with the moon (*CMG* 1. 2. 1 88ff.; *HA* 582^{b}2ff.). See Lloyd (1983), 170ff.; C. Préaux, *La Lune dans la pensée Grecque* (Brussels, 1973), 88ff.: for the Greeks the new moon was therefore a propitious time for weddings; S. Lunais, *Recherches sur la lune* i: *Les Auteurs Latins de la fin des guerres Puniques à la fin du règne des Antonins* (Leiden, 1979), 68–77. See above, **seventh . . . eleventh month** and below, **66. This amazingly . . . occurs at all**.

The period of 'no' moon, called by Pliny *interlunium*, was, strictly speaking, the very beginning of the new lunar cycle, when the moon was normally invisible for at least one, and usually two or three, days. Varro called the *interlunium* an 'intermediate' day between the old month and the new moon, on which, theoretically, both old and new moon could be seen (*LL* 6. 10; cf. *RR* 1. 37. 1, where it is called *intermenstruum* or 'time between two months'). It was also known as the day of the moon's silence (*luna silens, HN* 16. 190). In *HN* 28. 77, Pliny suggests that the *interlunium* was not in certain circumstances a favourable time for matters connected with conception, but the dangers mentioned do not pertain to the child: see below, **64. It . . . menstrual flow; 66. This amazingly . . .**

occurs at all. Later folk beliefs regarded *births* during the *interlunium* as difficult and likely to result in stillbirth or sickly infants (P. Saintyves, *L'Astrologie populaire: Étudiée spécialement dans les doctrines et les traditions relatives à l'influence de la lune* (Paris, 1937), 218–19, on Cornwall and parts of France); a supposition possibly derived from the ancient belief that births were easiest around full moon, when the celestial body's emollient and loosening effects on the female humours were at their greatest (e.g. Plutarch, *Mor.* 658e). However, it is possible that the name *interlunium* derived from an old belief that the day of 'no moon' actually represented a gap between lunar cycles (see Lunais (1979), 336), and that, in some cases, her generative influence was thought to be at its lowest in her 'absence'. Such a belief is perhaps reflected in *HN* 16. 190, where the *interlunium* is said to be the best day for cutting timber, a job normally done when the moon and its generative powers were waning (see below, same note); and in the emperor Tiberius' hair-cutting custom (*HN* 16. 194, below, **42. full moon . . . babies**). Overall, however, the period from new to full moon was regarded by Aristotle as that of optimum fertility, and in general it was regarded as the time of growth: see below, this note. Pliny's *interlunium* denotes the very beginning of this period, just as his dates before and after the full moon fall at its end. Children conceived during this time had a head start developmentally, since conception had occurred in the first half of their 'first' month (see above, **38. seventh month . . . eleventh month**), and therefore they were best equipped to be born at the earliest possible viable time, 'in the seventh month'. However, we still need to consider why Pliny apparently narrows down the possibility of seven-months' birth to those conceived *only* in the days marking the beginning / end and mid-point of the lunar month, and why the day of the full moon itself is excluded. The answer to the first problem may lie in the importance of seven-day periods and their multiples in biological rhythms, including that of human gestation (see below, **39. In Italy**), the existence of which is to an extent borne out by modern studies. Chronobiology examines all the rhythms, including lunar rhythms, which may be discerned in the time structure of living organisms, and has identified a semi-lunar, or syzygian, lunar pattern of 14. 75 days, to which the dates assigned to seven-months' conceptions roughly adhere. In human beings, a circaseptan or weekly rhythm has also been found to be behind some health patterns, e.g. the development and reduction of sprains and swellings and the dynamics of fever patterns in certain illnesses. Thus, dates which are multiples of seven are significant in health matters, as indeed they have been since antiquity, when the Hippocratics and Galen frequently described case histories in which critical days were grouped around whole-number multiples of seven. Celsus offers a convenient summary: the 'critical' days are: 3, 5, 7, 9, 11, 14, and 21. Of these the most important are: 7, 14, and 21 in that order (3. 4. 11). See also below, **160. lunar days** and **seventh and fifteenth**. See K. P. Endres and W. Schad, *Moon Rhythms in Nature: How Lunar Cycles affect Living Organisms*, trans. C. Von Arnim (Edinburgh, 2002), 137 and fig. 36. That hebdomadal patterns should be involved in the conception of seven months' children is, of course, particularly appropriate (below, **39. In Italy**).

Finally, there remains the question of why Pliny avoids the actual day of the full moon, preferring the day before or after. The connections of the full moon with witchcraft and other evil influences harmful to the newborn and to the unborn and their mothers, are probably behind this: see below, **42. full moon . . . babies**. A foetus which, in addition to being blighted at conception, was then born prematurely, might not be expected to survive. Yet seven-months' children were regarded as survivors (below, **39. in Italy**). It may therefore have been assumed that the child who survived at seven months could have been conceived close to, but not actually on, such a risky day.

That the cycles of many living organisms are related to lunar rhythms has been corroborated by modern studies. 19th-cent. observations of lunar rhythms in the behaviour of the Samoan Palolo worm raised awareness of the phenomenon. The observations of Aristotle and others on the sea-urchin were followed up in the 1920s and shown to fit the behaviour of sea-urchins near Suez, although the rhythms of those in the Mediterranean were different (H. Munro Fox, 'Lunar Periodicity in Reproduction', *Proc. Roy. Soc. B* 95 (1924), 523–50).

In addition, popular belief from ancient times has linked the new moon with frenetic change and vigorous growth in living organisms above the earth, and the old moon with more stable activity, such as the rooting of crops below the earth, setting and fruiting, and the preservation of dead organisms such as felled wood, peat (Brand (1842), iii. 77, on the Isle of Skye), and meat. The Roman agricultural writings, including sections of the *Natural History*, are a rich source of such beliefs. Pliny (*HN* 18. 314, 321, 322) says that all storage, all trimming, gathering and cutting of trees and gelding of animals should be done when the moon is waning (cf. Columella 6. 26. 2, 12. 55. 3). The Roman farming treatises emphasize the importance of putting hens to sit during the waxing of the moon, timing the operation so as to ensure that hatching also occurs in the first half of the lunar cycle (Varro, *RR* 3. 9; Columella 8. 5. 9). A belief that some fruit and vegetables experience a growth spurt and seeds germinate better around full moon persists in parts of rural Italy today, and experiments in the 1920s showed that a number of crops did germinate better, grow larger, and produce better harvests if sown two days before full moon, rather than two days before new moon (Endres and Schad (2002), 110). Other crops displayed different lunar patterns, however, cf. *HN* 18. 322 on sowing certain crops around new moon, at least upon wet land; though this may have been a special arrangement to avoid the even greater humidity engendered by a fuller moon; cf. the sowing of moisture-hating vetch towards the end of the lunar cycle (*HN* 18. 228, cf. Columella 2. 10. 30). In general, the ancient agriculturalists follow the general rule that processes involving growth require a waxing rather than waning moon.

Overexposure to the moon's rays could 'turn' food (see below, **42. full moon . . . babies**; **66. This amazingly . . . occurs at all**) and the supposed enhancement of the ripening and subsequent flavour of fruits picked by moonlight has been the subject of media reports in recent years (e.g. *Daily Telegraph*, 17 July 2000).

Other studies have found links between the lunar cycle, particularly the full moon, and increased psychiatric problems, psychotic crime, and accidents, although these are controversial (G. G. Luce, *Body Time* (London, 1972), 239–40; but see Endres and Schad (2002), 218). As far as the human reproductive cycle is concerned, sporadic studies over the last eighty years have in some circumstances found links between the lunar and menstrual cycles (for ancient ideas, see below, **66. This amazingly . . . occurs at all**). Studies into lunar birth patterns have produced inconclusive results: geographical and social contexts play important roles here. However, the persistent belief that more boys are born with the waxing moon and more girls with the waning (another reason why the first half of the lunar cycle was seen as 'best' for conception : J.

Gélis, *History of Childbirth: Fertility, Pregnancy and Birth in Early Modern Europe*, trans. R. Morris (Cambridge, 1991), 39) has been borne out in one study. See Endres and Schad (2002), 126–31; 129–30; 216; Luce (1972), 239; *Daily Telegraph*, 17 May 2000. As for Aristotle's idea that animals tended to be born on the rising tide and die on the outgoing tide (cf. *HN* 2. 220), it can at least be shown that lunar rhythms of birth and death run in opposition to each other (Endres and Schad (2002), 127, fig. 34). In the case of some of the human phenomena, it has been suggested that the moon's gravitational pull affects fluid in the hypothalamus which regulates various aspects of body behaviour and diurnal pattern. For other aspects of lunar influence, see below, **42. full moon . . . babies.**

39. In Egypt . . . eighth month   Aristotle (*HA* 584ᵇ6 ff.) says that eighth-month babies are viable in places such as Egypt where fertility is high and the birthrate prolific. See above, **33. portentous . . . fertility** and **In Egypt . . . septuplets**; for the problem of the viability of the eighth-month child, see below, **In Italy**. The warmth of the climate may have enhanced the fertile power of the waters of the Nile, as in India (above, **21. so great . . . water**); the extreme fertility of these countries arises out of the combination of climatic heat and moisture, to the extent that normally non-viable life-forms, including the monstrous, are not only produced but are produced in quantities and flourish. Aristotle loc. cit. says that infants in Egypt can live *even if deformed*, and P. (*HN* 11. 272) reports the rearing in Egypt of a boy with eyes at the back of the head (cf. above, **33. In Egypt . . . septuplets**. For the effects of heat and moisture, together and separately, see above, **21. So great . . . water**.

in Italy . . . our ancestors   Aulus Gellius, *NA* 3. 16. 7–9, tells us that Varro said the opposite: namely that early Romans, unlike the Hippocratic writers (cf. on the *Eighth-Month Child* 3, 7. 438 L, *On Fleshes*, 8. 612 L), who thought all eighth-month babies died, did not consider this an unnatural rarity, even though they considered that nine or ten months was the normal gestation period. Aristotle (*HA* 584ᵇ10) said that few such children survived around Greece, as opposed to Egypt (see above, **In Egypt . . . eighth month**). In the eighth month, the foetus began to descend in the uterus and was in danger of exposure to various diseases which, together with the birth trauma itself, might prove fatal (*On the Eighth-Month Child* 3, 7.

438–40 L; 5, 7. 444 L): see L. Dean-Jones, *Women's Bodies in Classical Greek Science* (Oxford, 1994), 210. At seven months, the child was believed to be fully-formed and to have acquired enough strength in some cases to break through the membranes. The chances of survival were greater now than in the following month, since the dangers of the latter had been pre-empted. These dangers were such that even a child born in the earlier part of the ninth month was in some jeopardy, since it had had insufficient time to recover from them before coming to birth and facing the new set of risks posed by the first forty days after birth (*On the Eighth-Month Child*, 1, 7. 436 L; 2, 7. 438 L; 6, 7. 444 L). A further gloss on this idea was provided some fifteen hundred years after Pliny by Ambroise Paré: the child who tried but failed to emerge from the womb at seven months needed to remain there in order to regain its strength after such a struggle. Expulsion in the dangerous eighth month would be premature and fatal for such a child (quoted and discussed in Gélis (1991), 64–5).

But the durability of the popular belief that the eighth-month child could *never* survive, whereas the seventh-month child could, owes much to numerological superstition, especially concerning the number 7, which had positive connotations, whereas the number 8 did not, a vital difference summed up by Ps.-Galen 19. 454 K. In general, odd numbers, especially prime numbers like 7, had fortunate connotations (cf. Virgil, *Ecl.* 8. 75 and Servius comm. ad loc.; Pliny, *HN* 28. 23, 'In all matters, odd numbers are more powerful . . .'). Aristotle said that the fourth and the eighth months of pregnancy were the most difficult and risky for the mother as well as the foetus (*HA* 584$^{\rm b}$15; see below, **40. For their mothers . . . fatal**). For the significance of seven-day periods in ancient medical thought, see also above, **38. Only children . . . no moon**, and below, **160. lunar days**; and for other numerological superstitions connected with pregnancy and birth, below **40. For infants . . . birth**. Thus, the Hippocratic treatise *On Fleshes* 8. 613 L states that the seventh-month child lives because of the qualities and properties of the number 7: it is born at 210 days, after thirty periods of seven days. Similarly, a child born at term is in the womb for 280 days, 'and this too has seven-day periods'. Cf. *On the Eighth-Month Child* (7, 7. 446; 10, 7. 452; 13, 7. 458 L), where the best survival rate is said to be among those born after 'seven periods of forty days'.

In Hanson's (1987: 589–602) view, ancient calculations of gestation (see above, **38. seventh . . . eleventh month**) could not provide the precision needed to separate a seven months' from an eight months' gestation so markedly and to claim that the premature baby that died was an eighth-month child may have offered the bereaved parents the 'psychological comfort that there was nothing anyone could have done' (1987: 596). This supposition is certainly in line with the psychology suggested in Aristotle, *HA* 584ᵇ12–15, where he comments that, if an eighth-month child does survive, the women simply assume that they made a mistake in their calculations.

All such matters . . . variations. For P.'s stress on variety, see above, **33–72. introd**.

Vistilia She may have been a daughter or possibly sister to the praetorian Sex. Vistilius, former friend of the elder Drusus, brother of the emperor Tiberius, who was forced to commit suicide by the latter at an advanced age in AD 32 (Tac. *Ann.* 6. 9). The Vistilia who, although of praetorian family, prostituted herself and was banished in AD 19 (*Ann.* 2. 35) may also have been a relative of the seven children mentioned. The last, Milonia Caesonia, was already the mother of three daughters and regarded as relatively mature at the time of her marriage to the emperor Gaius in AD 39 (Suet. *Gaius* 25. 3). She may have been born as early as AD 5 (Barratt (1989), 95) and surely before *c.* AD 15. Thus, Vistilia's earlier confinements are likely to have taken place by the end of the first decade AD. See R. Syme, 'Domitius Corbulo', *JRS* 60 (1970), 27–39 = *Papers*, ii (1979), 811–12; C. Cichorius, *Römische Studien, Historisches, Epigraphisches, Literargeschichtliches* (Leipzig, 1922), 429–32.

Glitius Possibly father of P. Glitius Gallus, exiled for his part in the Pisonian conspiracy of AD 65 (Tac. *Ann.* 15. 56 and 71; cf. Schilling 141).

Pomponius Secundus Probably the father of Q. Pomponius Secundus, suffect consul in AD 41 and of P.'s friend P. Pomponius Secundus, suff. AD 44 (see Introd. 2. 2). See Syme, *Papers*, ii. 811–12. The latter gave a banquet for Gaius Caligula in AD 39 (*HN* 14. 56; cf. Cichorius (1922), 431), perhaps in honour of the emperor's marriage to the brothers' half-sister, Caesonia (below; and above, **Vistilia**). He may also have been the source for P.'s detailed knowledge of his mother's confinements.

Orfitus   Perhaps the father of the consul of AD 51, Ser. Cornelius Salvidienus Orfitus (Cichorius (1922), 431).

four children   Probably two by Pomponius (above) and one each by Glitius and Orfitus.

Suillius Rufus   The notorious prosecutor P. Suillius Rufus (*OCD*³, Suillius Rufus, 1454), suffect consul in the early 40s AD (Syme (1970), 30–1); or one of his sons (Tac. *Ann.* 1. 2), P. Suillius Rufus, consul before AD 50 (Cichorius (1922), 431, cf. *CIL* vi. 24729 and Schilling 142).

Corbulo   Cn. Domitius Corbulo, suffect consul *c*.AD 39, served under Claudius and Nero (the latter forcing him to suicide in AD 66) and was the greatest general of his era. See *OCD*³, Domitius Corbulo, 492.

Caesonia   See above, **Vistilia**.

40. For infants born . . . fortieth day after birth   The 3rd-cent. grammarian Censorinus remarks on the significance given by the Greeks to forty-day periods in pregnancy and birth, cf. especially the Hippocratic treatise *On the Eighth-Month Child* 9, 7. 447–51 L. Both mother and baby are at risk before the fortieth day after birth (cf. *Eighth-Month Child* 9, 7. 451 L) and therefore that day is celebrated as a festival (Censorinus, *DN* 11. 7–8). The infant does not smile before the fortieth day (Censorinus, *DN* 11. 7, cf. *Eighth-Month Child* loc. cit., Aristotle, *HA* 587ᵇ and above **2. smile**). The period is risky to all new mothers and neonates, but the vulnerable eighth-month child (above, **39. in Italy . . . our ancestors**) is in particular danger, as the Hippocratic *Eighth-Month Child* makes clear. This treatise also defines as a forty-day period the time, starting 'towards the eighth month' of pregnancy, during which the foetus is at risk from disease and, if born prematurely as an eighth-month child, will die (9, 7. 451 L; 10, 7. 453 L; see above, **39. in Italy**). More positively, the ideal full-term pregnancy was sometimes expressed as seven periods of 40 days (*Eighth-Month Child* 10, 7. 453 L), but the favourable number seven made all the difference: an eight-month pregnancy involved the inauspicious number eight: see above, **38. seventh month . . . eleventh month**. Besides the Greek medical tradition of forty-day periods, which also applied to the first forty days of pregnancy during which miscarriage was a constant danger and the last, fortieth, day of which marked the full articulation of the male foetus and the beginning of its movement (*Eighth-Month Child* 9, 7. 448–50 L; Aristotle, *HA* 583ᵇ3–7), there were also 40-day pre- and post-natal religious prohibitions; see R. Parker, *Miasma: Pollution and Purification in Early Greek Religion* (Oxford, 1983), 48–51 and app. 2; G. Rocca-Serra, *Censorinus, Le Jour Natal; traduction annotée* (Paris, 1980), 52.

For their mothers . . . fatal. Cf. Aristotle, *HA* 584ᵇ15. The numbers 4 and 8 fit in with the patterns of 8 and 40 already established in connection with the eighth-month child, besides marking the half- and full-term points of such pregnancies. The disease risk for the foetus in the eighth month (see above, **39. in Italy**) presented risks for the mother as well: cf. Hipp. *Eighth-Month Child* 3, 7. 438–40 L; and also *Epid.* 2. 3, 5. 118 L on the pains in the womb at this time.

Masurius Masurius Sabinus (*OCD*³, 985–6; Steinwenter, *RE* I A 2, Sabinus (29), 1600–1; fr. 24 Huschke), a jurist of the first half of the 1st cent. AD and thus a contemporary of P.'s, wrote a standard work in three books on civil law, as well as a number of other works, and gave his name to one of the two main schools followed by jurists up to the mid-2nd cent. AD.

an heir in the second degree This heir would inherit if anything happened to the primary heir, who was evidently the son of the deceased. He seems to have challenged the primary heir's claim to the property on the grounds that he was illegitimate, having been born too long after his alleged father's death.

L. Papirius Probably L. Papirius Maso, urban praetor 176 BC (Livy 41. 14. 5 and 15. 5); cf. Hanslik, *RE* 18. 3, Papirius (62), 1064.

found against him . . . laid down Aulus Gellius (*NA* 3. 16. 23) has P.'s story and earlier gives a similar story about an eleventh-month child whose legitimacy was questioned in the courts. In the case of the eleventh-month child, Gellius says the accusation was based on the statement in the Twelve Tables that a child is born in the tenth month (iv. 4 Scholl, cf. Ulpian, *Dig.* 38. 16. 3. 11), but that it was dismissed by the emperor Hadrian after he had consulted philosophical and medical writings on the subject. In P.'s story, the legal basis of the accusation and decision are not entirely clear.

Schilling (143) assumes the accusation was based on the Twelve Tables and when Papirius decided that 'no fixed period seemed to have been laid down' he was referring to the terms of the deceased's will; Varro (quoted by Gellius 3. 16. 18) shows that wills could include clauses giving upper limits for the gestatory period of children to be accepted as legitimate heirs. However, 'seemed to have been laid down' may have a more generalized meaning, referring to the praetor's own conclusion, similar to Hadrian's, that despite the Twelve Tables, there was no upper limit on human gestation. Significantly, Gellius writes in his version: *ei videretur*, 'it seemed *to him*'. Some Hippocratic writers had suggested that pregnancies of eleven months or more were due to miscalculation of the time of conception: see Dean-Jones (1994), 209; and see above, **38. seventh month . . . eleventh month**.

41. Ten days . . . formed Aristotle, *HA* 584^{a}5 says that some women get these signs at ten days and some later; cf. Solinus 1. 62.

Women carrying a boy . . . ninetieth day Cf. Aristotle, *HA* 484^{a}10ff., 583^{b}12–21. For the length of time before boys move, see *HA* 583^b and above, **40. for infants born . . . fortieth day after birth**. The inferior, colder female foetus developed more slowly, not moving until the ninetieth day and often causing longer, more problematic pregnancies: see above, **37. when twins are born . . . less common** and **Girls are born . . . quickly**. Soranus concurred (1. 45) and said that women carrying girls were more prone to nausea. That women carrying a girl have a more difficult pregnancy was a long-lived belief which has lasted into the present day. Possibly, the different hormones produced by the male or female foetus, testosterone and oestrogen respectively, did in fact affect some mothers' constitutions. Even in the last fifty years, cravings were believed to be stronger and the birthmarks arising from unsatisfied cravings were thought to be more frequent when the foetus was female rather than male (Gélis (1991), 89–90; Y. Verdier, *Façons de dire, façons de faire* (Paris, 1979), 49–53). One recent study is reported to have given some backing to the ancient idea that women suffering severe nausea during pregnancy were more likely to be carrying girls (*Daily Telegraph*, 3 Sept. 2002).

42. greatest tiredness . . . growing hair Cf. Aristotle, *HA* 584^{a}23. Aristotle said that hair grew when moisture from the body

seeped through the skin and left a residue behind (*GA* 728ᵇ19–23).
For the foetus, formation of such material, in addition to the overall growth of its body, involved gaining extra nourishment from its
mother, thereby, perhaps, increasing the drain on her resources
and consequent fatigue: see Dean-Jones (1994), 84, 208 and further,
below, **full moon . . . babies**. Galen's theory of hair-growth was
in many respects similar to Aristotle's: the humour from which the
sediment derived determined the hair colour, while the consistency
of the sediment or the nature of the pore from which it issued determined whether it was straight or curly (*Mixtures* 2, 1. 614–17 K).

full moon . . . babies   For the moon's connection with pregnancy and childbirth, see above, **38. only children conceived
. . . no moon**. The moon's fertility derived from the absorption of
water from, and subsequent dissemination of the moisture onto,
the earth (cf. *SVF* iv. 675, 680). The resulting warm humidity of its
rays could 'turn' food (see above, **38. Only children . . . no moon**
and below, **66. This amazingly . . . occurs at all**), sometimes
with positive results, e.g. ripening fruit or encouraging the leaven-
ing of bread (Plutarch, *Mor.* 659a), but also in a negative sense,
causing curdling and the putrefaction of meat (Plutarch, *Mor.*
658a–659e; Galen 9. 903–6 K; Macr. *Sat.* 7. 16. 15–34; Basil, *Hex.* 6.
10; a belief recorded as late as the 19th cent.: Verdier (1979), 73).
The balance of moisture in the human body could also be unbal-
anced by too much exposure to moonlight. The effects of moonlight on the head, with its high concentration of moisture in the
brain (Aristotle, *GA* 743ᵇ27–31; and for similar beliefs in later eras,
Saintyves (1937), 181–91), included headache, epilepsy, and madness ('lunacy'): Aelian, *NA* 14. 27; Lucian, *Philopseud.* 16; Galen 9.
903–5 K; Alexander of Tralles, *Med.* 1. 15. The moon could also
have a deleterious effect on another moist organ (Aristotle, *GA*
747ᵃ15), the eye, precipitating cataracts (perceived as congealed
moisture) and other complaints: Aelian, *NA* 14. 27, cf. Pliny, *HN* 2.
110, some eye diseases of cattle increase and decrease with the
moon; Saintyves (1937), 178. The constitution of the pregnant
woman and the newborn child was especially moist and additional
moisture from the moon could overload the system. If anyone slept
under a full (and therefore especially strong and humid) moon, they
would wake lethargic, due to over-absorption of moisture; but the
rays could increase the already abundant moisture in infants to

dangerous levels, causing convulsions (Plutarch, *Mor.* 658a–9e). The child was already at risk while still in the womb. According to the Hippocratic treatise *On the Sacred Disease* (8–10, 6. 374–80 L), the origins of epilepsy lay in the failure of an intrauterine purging process which should rid the developing foetal brain of excessive moisture. According to later Icelandic tradition, if a pregnant woman looked at the moon, her child would be born a lunatic (Saintyves (1937), 216). It is therefore not surprising that the moisture-laden pregnant woman herself was also at particular risk from the effects of the full moon. According to a modern Greek superstition, exposure to any of the nocturnal heavenly bodies particularly endangers the newly-delivered mother and her baby for up to forty days after birth, as well as spoiling leaveners and preservatives (J. C. Lawson, *Modern Greek Folklore and Ancient Greek Religion* (New York, 1964), 10–12). The foetal hair-growing process just described would be especially risky at this time, since all hair growth (above, **greatest tiredness**) coincided with the waxing moon and was exacerbated by its moisturizing and regenerative powers (above, **38. Only children . . . no moon**), reaching a climax at full moon. Later, popular belief insisted that hair and nails should be cut only from the full moon onwards, once the growth spurt was over, ensuring that they grew back more slowly. See Gélis (1991), 39. Ancient commentators advocated the same practice to minimize the risk of hair-loss and headaches. Pliny reports that Varro (cf. *RR* 1. 37. 2) advised cutting hair just after the full moon to avoid hair-loss, and that the emperor Tiberius only had his cut at the *interlunium* (see above, **38. Only children . . . no moon**). He also reports a Roman custom (*HN* 28. 28) of cutting hair on the seventeenth and twenty-ninth days of the month, to prevent hair loss and headaches. Finally, a bizarre modern report (*Daily Telegraph*, 17 July 2000): a German hairdresser was prosecuted for trading after the 9 p.m. limit, having offered hair-cuts at full moon, when, it was alleged, germs collected at the hair tips. This last idea is in general accordance with the Aristotelian theory of hair generation as a sediment left by moisture (above, **42. greatest tiredness . . . growing hair**), enhanced by the cumulative effect of lunar generation and humidity.

When Aristotle (*HA* 588ª10) says that the generative powers of the full moon aggravate infant illnesses, he could be referring to the risk of convulsions mentioned by Plutarch. He could also be thinking of the notion that even diseases might be fed by these powers. In this context, L. Gil (*Therapeia* (Madrid, 1969), 412–13) notes that the noxious as well as the healing powers of plants are of course increased at this time; the *Homeric Hymn to Demeter* 227–30 implies possible attacks on an infant by the 'plant-cutter'. A study in the early 1980s found that plant extracts which increased heart-rate differed in their efficacy depending on the stage of the lunar cycle in which they were gathered (Endres and Schad (2002), 111).

Diseases thought to involve excess moisture, including fluid retention, consumption, asthma, skin swellings, humour-filled pustules, warts, ulcerous and haemorrhaging wounds, as well as the above-mentioned mental disturbances and eye fluxes attributed to excessive humours in the already moist brain and eyes, were long considered to wax and wane with the moon, climaxing at full moon. Fevers were similarly affected, since they were believed to be caused by excess humour causing the body to overheat (cf. Ps.-Aristotle, *Prob.* 1. 8. 860ª5: fevers and eye problems both due to excess humour; *HN* 2. 221: blood in the body increases and diminishes with the moon's light). See below **169. The rest . . . quartan fevers** and **170. puberty . . . women**. Internal complaints, such as parasitic worms in children, also observed a lunar cycle. See Luce (1972), 239–40; Gélis (1991), 39; Saintyves (1913), 13–16; id. (1937), 176–81; Préaux (1973), 91–4; Verdier (1979), 62–3; Lunais (1979), 74–8; Endres and Schad (2002), 217–18; cf. below, **66. This amazingly . . . occurs at all**. Astrology connected all these complaints with unfavourable aspects of the moon: e.g. Firmicius Maternus, *Math.* 4. 4. 1, 5. 6, 9. 9, 8. 3, 11. 7, 12. 9, 13. 6, 14. 3, 15. 1. Any or all of these maladies might have triggered Aristotle's warning and Pliny's later comments here.

Finally, young children and women carrying unborn children, were particularly susceptible to witchcraft (see above, **16. adults**), which in turn had associations with the moon, especially when full, cf. remarks on noxious plants, above. The common connection once again seems to be moisture and growth. It was because children's constitutions were exceptionally moist that they were especially vulnerable to change and therefore to the effects of the Evil Eye (Ps.-Alexander, *Problema Physica, PMG Minores* II. 2. 53 Ideler), which have been connected with the production/destruction of moisture (above, **13–20. introd.**) and which Pliny connects with sorcery (above, **16. bewitch**). As already mentioned, the eye was a particularly moist area, prone to damage from lunar rays. It was believed to be physiologically connected with body fluids, some of which, such as saliva, themselves had medico-magical properties (below, **67. it is a sure sign . . . saliva**, and above, **15. snakes . . . saliva, 16. bewitch**). It was also connected with the moon itself, which was, like the sun, regarded as an eye of the heavens, specifically the left eye in some medico-magical texts (Préaux (1973), 1122–4, 307). Drawing the moon down from the sky (Préaux (1973), 122 and 127 n. for refs.) and obtaining from it a mysteriously noxious foam or milky deposit which enhanced the deadliness of their spells was a traditional witches' activity, but one in which the charmer, significantly, risked losing a child or an eye (schol. on Zenobius, *Epitome* 401: see D. E. Hill, 'The Thessalian Trick', *RM* 116 (1973), 221–8, esp. 222; cf. also Valerius Flaccus, *Arg*. 6. 445 f.; Statius, *Theb*. 11. 284 f.; Ovid, *Met*. 7. 268; Lucan, *Phars*. 6. 669; P. J. Bicknell, 'The Dark Side of the Moon', in A. Moffatt (ed.), *Maistor: Classical, Byzantine and Renaissance Studies for Robert Browning* (Canberra, 1984), 67–75, Tupet (1976), 92–103). Other well-documented supernatural threats to pregnant women and infants were the malignant female ghosts and demons, normally characterized by untimely deaths (hence possessing a vengeful desire to inflict a like fate and in its most extreme form by targeting those at the very beginning of life) and sometimes personalized (Lamia, Gello, Mormo): see Johnston (1999), 161–99, esp. 164–5. Restless ghosts and other spirits, being of intermediate status between man and god, were frequently associated with the ambiguous, shifting moon (F. E. Brenk, 'In the Light of the Moon: Demonology in the Early Imperial Period', *ANRW* 2. 16. 3 (1986), 2008–2145, esp. 2089–90, 2096 and nn.): possibly their powers, too, were regarded as waxing and waning with the moon, and the banquets to Hecate set out at the time of the new moon, the *noumenia* (cf. Athenaeus, *Deipn*. 7. 126, 325a), may have marked the beginning of a cycle of activity which culminated at full moon. According to Préaux (1973), 123, the sacrifice to the underworld deity marked the 'death' of the moon on this moonless day, before the dedication of the following day, the first of the new month, to Apollo god of light, while Johnston ('Crossroads', *ZPE* 88 (1991), 220) considers that the offerings to Hecate at this 'disquieting' time marked her function as a goddess of transitions. However, these theories are not mutually exclusive. The possibility that more sacrifices were offered on the 16th around the time of full moon (cf. J. Mikalson, *The Sacred and Civil Calendar of the Athenian State* (Princeton, 1975), 14) could mark the propitiation of Hecate's dangerous associates as well as another important lunar transition.

Her gait . . . woman Cf. Soranus 1. 46–56 for detailed instructions on exercise and diet at the various stages of pregnancy.

over-salted food . . . lacking nails Cf. Aristotle, *HA* 585ª25. As with hair, the growth of nails involved the foetus obtaining extra moisture from the mother in order to form its own residues (see above, **greatest tiredness**). Possibly this moisture was in some sense diverted away or spoiled by the salt. This belief survived into the early modern period, when such infants were believed to be destined to die early (Gélis (1991), 82).

do not hold their breath . . . difficulty See Aristotle, *GA* 775ª32–3, Soranus 2. 70b, 4. 59. Holding the breath was also believed to be a way of preventing conception in the first place (Soranus 1. 61).

yawning . . . sneezing Quoted by Aulus Gellius, 3. 16. 24. Yawning was thought to draw up the uterus, making the birth more difficult (Aristotle, *GA* 719ª19–21). Sneezing after intercourse could expel the semen (Hipp. *Eighth-Month Child* 5, 7. 476 17–19 L; Soranus 1. 46) and was sometimes recommended to facilitate delivery of baby or afterbirth (Hipp. 4. 550 3–4 L).

43. If we consider . . . pity and shame The trivial causes of miscarriages and still births just mentioned lead P. to moralize on the presumption of the human animal whose very existence is anything but a foregone conclusion. The train of thought is very similar to **2–5** above, especially **3. those who believe . . . born to a position of pride;** and cf. **130–2** below, where fortune's mutability severely limits any notion of true human security and happiness. See Introd. 5. 2. 1 and 5. 4.

smell . . . abortion Aristotle, *HA* 604ᵇ29–605ª1 says this applies to mares but also happens to some women. This is probably to be connected with the general idea that miscarriage could be caused by pungent substances and sternutatives (Soranus 1. 46). The womb itself was thought by the Hippocratics to be repelled by some smells and attracted by others (e.g. *Mul.* 3. 14, 7. 332, 6–7 L): on their rationale, the smell might have repelled the womb to the lower part of the body to an excessive degree, inducing it to shed its load (cf. below, **63. It is mobile** and **175. female sex . . . turning of the womb**). However, Soranus (3. 29) is sceptical of the womb's being attracted and repelled in this way. The effect of this particular smell would also have been inspired by popular analogy; the notion of the extinguished light leading to that of the extinguished life.

such beginnings . . . tyrants and murderers The weak and uncertain beginning of human life is contrasted with the arrogance of those who assail the lives of others. Cf. again, above, **3. those who believe . . . born to a position of pride.**

44. embrace the gifts of fortune . . . true-born child Fortune here is closely linked with the ambiguous stepmother nature of **1**. P. criticizes those who assume that they are fortune's true-born rather than foster-child, just as in **1** he questioned uncritical acceptance of nature as mother rather than stepmother.

aspire to rule all Cf .above, **3. those who believe . . . born to a position of pride** and below, **132. How many . . . power . . . pleasure!**, where P. states that power may lead to a downfall.

think that you are god To this extent, they are ironically children of blind fortune, who is herself, according to P. (*HN* 2. 22), elevated to divine status by the foolish.

Anacreon A 6th-cent. lyric poet from Teos (*OCD*[3], 79–80), who worked in a number of Greek cities including Samos and Athens. The manner of his death is recorded by Valerius Maximus (9. 12, ext.6).

Fabius Senator Otherwise unknown; Groag, *RE* 6. 2, 'Fabius' (144), 1868.

to achieve a balanced view of life . . . frailty P. ends his rhetorical moralizing with an appropriate apophthegm: man's judgement of his quality of life is often one-sided and shallow, cf. **132. counting . . . weight** below, where he criticizes simplistic assessments of human happiness.

45. It is unnatural . . . feet first. Aristotle, *HA* 586[b]5ff. says that the human foetus is 'bent up' with its head resting on the knees. Like all animal foetuses, it is initially positioned in the womb with the head towards the mother's head, but, in common with them, turns as it moves towards the birth outlet, so that birth is 'head-first'. Some, however, 'are born bent up and feet-first contrary to nature'. For the negative connotations of breech birth, see below, **46. It is the law of nature . . . feet first.**

'Agrippa' . . . 'born with difficulty'. P. here derives the name Agrippa from *aegre partus*, 'born with difficulty'; cf. Solinus 1. 65. Aulus Gellius (16. 16. 1), however, derives it from *aegritudo*, 'difficulty' and *pedes*, 'feet'; cf. Servius, *In Aen.* 8. 682; Quintilian, *Inst. Orat.* 1. 4. 25; Nonius 556, 31 M. It is possible that the true etymology might have been purely descriptive (*agri-ped-, 'feet first'), rather than unfavourable, as in these authors. See J. Vendryes, 'Agrippa et Vopiscus', *Miscelânea Scientifica e Literaria dedicado ao Doutor J. Leite de Vasconcelos*, i (Salamanca, 1934), 428–33.

Marcus Agrippa Born in 64 or 63 of obscure family, M. Vipsanius Agrippa remained the emperor Augustus' right-hand man until his death in 12 BC. He served as general, statesman, and, eventually, son-in-law and father of Augustus' intended heirs when, in 21 BC, he married the emperor's only child, Julia. His geographical commentary was used by P. The glittering career and the wealth which accompanied it might make him appear the supreme example of Fortune's favour, but P. queries this as he later queries the true happiness of the emperor he served (below, **147–50**). See R. Syme, *The Roman Revolution* (Oxford, 1939), 129; *OCD*[3], 1601–2; and, on Pliny's treatment of Agrippa, J.-M. Roddaz, *Marcus Agrippa*, BEFAR 252 (Paris, 1984), 512–18.

strife and death After Caesar's death, Agrippa helped Octavian to raise an army, took a prominent role in the Perusine war and saw action while governor of Gaul in 39 BC. He played a vital role in the wars against Sextus Pompeius and Mark Antony and was responsible for the victories at Hylae, Naulochus, and Actium. He also spent two periods in the eastern empire (23–21 BC and 17/16–13 BC) and quelled trouble in Gaul, Spain, and Pannonia (20, 19, and 12 BC).

legacy of destruction . . . the two Agrippinas The fateful progeny were Gaius and Lucius Caesar, Agrippa Postumus, Julia, and Agrippina. The first two brought misfortune on their grandfather's dynastic plans by their tragically early deaths, which led to the succession of Tiberius and, ultimately, of Gaius and Nero (see below). Agrippa Postumus was disinherited by Augustus, apparently because of his depraved character (Tac. *Ann.* 1. 3). Julia, like her mother (below), was banished for adultery in AD 8 (Tac. *Ann.* 4. 71; 3. 24; Suet. *Aug.* 19. 1) and her husband, L. Aemilius Paulus, executed for conspiracy. Agrippina married Tiberius' brother Drusus' son, Germanicus. Of their nine children, one was the future emperor Gaius Caligula. Another was the younger Agrippina, who married Cn. Domitius Ahenobarbus and was the mother of Nero. See Syme (1939), index and *OCD*[3], Iulius Caesar, Agrippa, 779–80; Vipsania Agrippina (1) and (2), 1601; Iulius Caesar (2), Gaius, 782–3; Iulius Caesar (4), Lucius, 784; Iulia (4), 777.

Gaius and Domitius Nero . . . firebrands   In the cases of both emperors, P. had personally witnessed the gradual corruption by power of their inadequate characters. Gaius, nicknamed Caligula, succeeded Tiberius in AD 37. His increasingly cruel and autocratic behaviour, which led to his murder in AD 41, suggested a basic instability, possibly exacerbated into madness by a serious illness in AD 37. P. provides some vignettes of his extravagent court (*HN* 9. 117, 12. 10, 14. 56). See J. P. V. D. Balsdon, *The Emperor Gaius* (Oxford, 1934) and 'The Principates of Tiberius and Gaius', *ANRW* 2. 2 (1975), 86–94; A. A. Barratt, *Caligula: The Corruption of Power* (London, 1989); *OCD*[3], Gaius (1), 619–20. Nero was adopted by Claudius as the guardian of his son, Britannicus, due to the machinations of his new wife, Nero's mother and Claudius' own niece, Agrippina. He succeeded Claudius in 54, and Britannicus was soon murdered, as was the domineering Agrippina. Obsessed by his artistic talents, Nero became, like Gaius, corrupted by power, persecuting and murdering any he perceived to be a threat to that power, before revolts of the provincial armies ultimately forced him to suicide. P. had lived through the terror and reserved particular hatred for its perpetrator (see below, **Nero . . . enemy of the human race** and Introd. 2. 1). Describing Nero as a firebrand had an appropriate resonance in view of the rumour that he had been responsible for the great fire of AD 64.

46. tormented . . . wife   Julia's adulteries did not apparently become known to Augustus until 2 BC, when she was banished, but the list of adulterers and the spectacular fall have suggested political undercurrents (Syme (1939), 426–7). Tac. *Ann.* 1. 53, however, suggests that a liaison with Ti. Sempronius Gracchus went back to the period of her marriage with Agrippa.

oppressed . . . subjection to his father-in-law Velleius (2. 79. 1) hints at his ambition and propensity to chafe at the bit, cf. Suet. *Aug.* 66; Syme (1939), 343–4. In particular, rivalry between Agrippa and Augustus' nephew, Marcellus, may have caused particular tension in the obscure court politics of 23 BC (Suet. *Aug.* 66; Syme (1939), 341–3) and the former's mission to the east in that year may be significant; P. calls it a 'banishment' (see below, **149. Marcellus' vows . . . Agrippa**).

Nero . . . enemy of the human race It is not clear whether P. held any public posts under Nero after his third spell of military service in Germany in AD 57–8 or whether he lived in retirement for the duration of the reign. See Introd. 1 and Beagon (1992), 3 and nn. In either case, his experiences, coupled with a natural inclination in favour of the aims and ethos of the succeeding Flavian dynasty, only partially explain his intense animosity towards Nero in the *HN*. In fact, the emperor was the antithesis of many of the moral ideals expressed in the *HN* (see Beagon (1992), 117–18; Introd. 2. 2). Here, as 'enemy of the human race', he is the negation of P.'s humanitarianism and his feet-first birth is symbolic of his unnatural character (but on this interpretation of the birth, see below, **Agrippina**).

Agrippina . . . memoirs Cf. Peter, *HRR* ii. 94, fr.2. The memoirs of the younger Agrippina were also cited by Tacitus (*Ann.* 4. 53). For another possible use of this work, see below, **71**. Her literary talent was encouraged by Augustus (Suet. *Aug.* 83). The memoirs may have been written in the late part of Claudius' reign to promote her family (cf. Tacitus loc. cit.) and facilitate her plans for Nero's succession (Griffin (1984), 23); in which case she presumably gave a positive interpretation to the breech birth, as being a family trait associating her son with his distinguished grandfather in particular. Although breaking the laws of nature could mark out an individual as a positive as well as a negative exception (see below, **68. Some . . . teeth**), P.'s generalization about the unlucky nature of such births—Agrippa is mentioned as the exception which proves the rule—is likely to have been the prevalent opinion (see below, **It is the law of nature**). However, hindsight would have played a part: Nero's breech birth probably encouraged negative interpretations in later writers, especially when the murder of Agrippina herself by her own son gave an additional ironic twist to the knowledge that his mode of delivery had been a difficult and dangerous one for his mother. The Neronian connection, derived from Pliny or an excerptor, probably influenced the attribution of such a birth, with its negative connotations, to a later villain, Shakespeare's Richard III (*Henry VI*, pt. 3, v. 6. 69–73): see R. Scarcia, 'Fragmentum Agrippinae: Ipotesi di un ricupero (e un riscontro Shakespeariano)', *GIF* 43 (1991), 243–63 and cf. Beagon (2002), 131–2.

It is the law of nature . . . feet first   The belief that bodies should be disposed differently at birth and at death had a long history in European thought. The dead were carried feet first over the threshold, while children crossed the threshold of life head first. As Sir Thomas Browne later wrote, 'That they [the ancients] carried [their dead] out of the world with their feet forward [is] not inconsonant unto reason, as contrary unto the native posture of man and his production first into it' (*Hydriotaphia*, ch. iv). The formal 'lying in state', or *collocatio*, which formed part of Roman funerary custom, involved laying out the dead on a special couch in the *atrium* with the feet towards the main door. According to later superstition, placing a newborn infant with its feet towards the door of the house was to risk its premature death: see N. Belmont, *Les Signes de la naissance: Étude de representations symboliques associées aux naissances singulières* (Paris, 1971), 136–45. Standing between the feet of the dying and the door interrupted the alignment of death and made the process more painful and prolonged (ibid. 136), just as crossing the legs or otherwise engaging in an act of 'binding' could stall the process of giving birth; cf. *HN* 28. 59; Thompson T 582. 3, and the famous story of Hera's attempt to block the birth of Heracles. By extension, a network of European beliefs linked shoes and death. The dead might be shod in new shoes prior to burial, to protect them on the long journey to the next world. The shoe thus became a symbol of death (Belmont (1971), 142). In antiquity, having one foot shod and the other unshod could sometimes be a ritual act associated with funerary and infernal rites (W. Deonna, '*Monokrepides*', *RHR* 12 (1935), 55). The participant effectively had a foot in both worlds.

That death was a rite of passage to be made feet first is a practice attested as early as Homer (*Il.* 19. 212). Cf. also Seneca, *Ep.* 12. 3, Persius 3. 104 ff. For the possibility that this was originally a precaution to stop the dead person's spirit walking back into and haunting the house, see Rohde (1925), 47 n. 26; cf. the belief that closing the eyes of the dead prevented them seeing and haunting anyone in future (Cic. *Verr.* 5. 118). With such precautions compare practices surviving in the 18th and 19th cents. (Brand (1841), ii. 144, Orkney) and even into the modern era (e.g. in rural France, Verdier (1979), 101, 139), where all the windows were shut in the house of the dead and reflective surfaces, such as mirrors, covered to prevent the image of the dead being trapped in them forever. Those falsely believed dead could not reverse their final journey by recrossing the threshold and had to be returned to their home through the roof or, in Greece, by a more specific rebirthing ceremony: see below, **173–8. introd.**

The child who entered the world 'against nature', feet first, would have an unlucky, even sinister, destiny. Connections with the world of the dead and with magic were to be feared. A midwife in the Friuli, denounced to the religious authorities in 1587, claimed that it was customary to place infants born feet first on a spit and turn them three times over a fire to prevent them falling into witchcraft (quoted in C. Ginzburg, *The Night Battles* (Baltimore, 1983), 73–4). Passing them over a flame or carrying a flame around them was a protection against evil spirits practised on newborns generally, for example in 18th-cent. Scotland: Brand (1841), ii. 48–9. But already, in the 1st cent. AD, Pliny himself had noted Nero's attempts at necromancy (*HN* 30. 14–17). That they were unsuccessful did not diminish the significance of the emperor's aspirations to the ultimate crime against nature. The connotations of breech birth are almost uniformly negative, although, in later folklore, individuals born in this manner were sometimes credited with curative powers. These usually involved curing with the feet, by trampling on the affected part, or curing afflictions of the feet, such as sprains (Belmont (1971), 134).

47. Those delivered . . . cut open The manuscripts read *enecta* (or *enecata*) *parente* 'when the mother has died', 'through the death of the mother', although Rackham (p. 536) made it conjunct (*e necata*). Although a case can be made for leaving the text as it is, there are also good reasons for emending it slightly to read *esecta parente*, 'when the mother has been cut open', a suggestion I owe to Prof. David Langslow. It is true that *neco*/*eneco* were often used of deaths by suffocation, stifling, etc. (J. N. Adams, 'The Uses of *neco*' I, *Glotta*, 68 (1990), 230–55), which might be appropriate to the lingering process of death in childbirth and could echo some of the popular interpretations of childbirth difficulty as being caused by the unborn child remaining high up and stifling the mother. It might be possible to extend its attested use for the death of the unborn child (Adams loc. cit.) to that of the mother. It was certainly employed of plants which killed other plants (Adams, 'The uses of *neco* II', *Glotta*, 69 (1991), 94–123), a situation similar to the one under discussion, since the birth of the child and death of the mother could be causally connected. However, there are important arguments in favour of *esecta* being read in place of *enecta*. First, and most compellingly, there is the context of Pliny's remarks. *Secto*, which is used of surgical incisions, ensures a smooth transition into the etymological explanations which follow. His example of such a birth, that of the 'first of the Caesars', and the specific derivation of the name 'Caesar' from the operation performed on his mother, makes it quite clear that the maternal deaths in question are those connected with the operation now known as Caesarean section. The more general *enecta parente* would have allowed of other possibilities besides Caesarean section; for example, occasional instances of spontaneous delivery of a dead mother's unborn child have been recorded (D. Trolle, *The History of Caesarian Section* (Copenhagen, 1982), 15–16; Gélis (1991), 235): the otherwise unknown Gorgias of Epirus was born on his mother's bier according to one tradition (Valerius Maximus 1. 8, ext. 5), and the motif appears in Irish legend (Thompson T 584. 2. 1, cf. 584. 2). This rare and striking mode of entry into the world is not, however, considered by Pliny in this passage. Secondly, phrases similar to Pliny's but employing *secto* and *esecto* rather than *neco*/*eneco* are favoured by other authors describing the same phenomenon; thus Virgil *Aen.* 10. 316 and Servius ad loc. (*secto matris ventre*; *exsecto matris ventre*); Virgil, *Aen.* 7. 761 (*exsecto ventre*); Festus, *Verb. Sign.* 50 (*Caesares . . . ex utero matris exsecti . . .*); Emporius 568 Halm (*qui matrum uteris exsecantur . . .*). Finally, an early manuscript 's' might be mistaken for an 'n'.

The surgical removal of an unborn child from the mother's womb was known from very early times: a cuneiform tablet of the

second millennium BC mentions a child 'pulled out' of the womb (L.
A. Oppenheim, 'A Caesarian Section in the Second Millennium
BC', *JHM* 15 (1960), 292–4) and at Rome the pre-Republican *leges
regiae* included an injunction to cut out an unborn child from a dead
mother, to avoid the destruction of a potentially living being, *spem
animantis* (*Digest* 11. 8. 2). References also occur in Judaic and Indian
tradition.

Even if Pliny's text doesn't specifically mention the 'death' of the
mother, it may well be implied: early Caesareans were very likely
performed *post mortem*. The first really reliable medical records of
Caesareans on living women appear in the later 16th cent. Even
then the mortality rate was over 70% and risk for both mother and
child remained extremely high: up to the end of the 18th cent.,
nineteen operations were recorded in Britain 'from which just two
mothers and seven children survived' (J. H. Young, *Caesarian
Section: The History and Development of the Operation from Earliest Times*
(London, 1944), 63). Improvement came only with the introduction
of the closure of the uterine wound and antiseptics (from the late
18th cent.), anaesthesia (mid-19th cent.), and (towards the end of
the 19th cent.) asepsis (Trolle (1982), 82–3).

Caesarean section on a live woman in earlier times is not impossible (though an apparent reference in the Jewish Mishna (3rd cent.
BC–3rd cent. AD) may be purely hypothetical: see R. Blumenfeld-
Kosinski, *Not of Woman Born* (Cornell, 1990), 23): some successful
'live' Caesareans have been recorded among primitive peoples in
the 19th and 20th cents. (J. Pundel, *L'Histoire de l'opération Césarienne*
(Brussels, 1969), 28). Also, P. here records live births as a result of
the operation, a rare occurrence, even in modern times, if the operation is done *post mortem* (see Trolle (1982), 83), though one that
figures in a number of folklore traditions (Thompson T 584. 2).
However, the tradition which interpreted Pliny's discussion here as
including a reference to the birth of Julius Caesar, whose mother
lived to see her son's adulthood, is mistaken, as discussed below,
the first of the Caesars.

Finally, a major difficulty in assessing P.'s comments is the
dearth of references to Caesarean operations in Greek and Latin
literature outside myth and poetry (cf. Virgil, *Aen.* 10. 315 on Lichas
and below, **under better auspices**). Among the medical writers,
the Hippocratics (refs. in Lloyd (1983), 82 n.87) and Soranus (*Gyn.* 4.
9–13) refer only to embryotomy, the cutting up for extraction of a

foetus where normal delivery is impossible. Trolle (1982: 170) suggests lack of ancient medical interest is connected to the possibility that the operation was a purely *post mortem* procedure and the cutting up of dead bodies was relegated to lowlier individuals than doctors. Post-classical references to the operation are largely lacking but from the 12th cent. in Europe, religious emphasis on the importance of baptism led to a revival of the principle of the *Lex Regia* and references to the operation in legal and medical texts (Pundel (1969), 79–103).

under better auspices That is, Caesarean births are more auspicious than breech births. In a number of cultures, Caesarean birth was regarded as an exceptional mode of entry into the world, and was therefore attributed to exceptional individuals, often gods and heroes. Asclepius (Ovid, *Met.* 2. 680ff., Servius, *In Aen.* 7. 761, 10. 315–18) and Dionysus (Ovid, *Met.* 3. 310–12) were both taken from the womb of a dead mother. Legend also attributed Caesarean birth to Persian Rustam, Icelandic Volsung, Germanic Tristan, and Buddha (Pundel (1969), 23–7; Blumenfeld-Kosinski (1990), 160 n. 7).

The Christian tradition incorporated the motif into the *Vitae* of saints and great churchmen. An 11th-cent. abbot of Saint-Gall was cut from his dead mother and nicknamed *Ingenitus*, while the early 13th-cent. Spanish San Ramon, similarly delivered, was called *Nonnato* and became an intercessor for women in childbirth (Gélis (1991), 237). That such a child was somehow 'unborn' and lucky was a notion that persisted (cf. Macduff in Shakespeare's *Macbeth*, who was the subject of the prophecy that 'none of woman born | Shall harm Macbeth' (act iv, sc. 1), fulfilled when he informs Macbeth that 'Macduff was from his mother's womb | Untimely ripp'd') and was still current as late as the 18th cent. Nordic superstition held that such 'unborn' persons had special abilities, including the securing of wandering ghosts in their graves (Trolle (1982), 24). Perhaps only the unborn could deal with the undead? If we substitute 'untimely born/dead' for 'unborn', 'undead', the link becomes clearer. Wandering ghosts were often those whose normal lifespan had been prematurely cut off. Women who died before completion of their 'natural' female cycle of marriage and childbirth were particularly prone to be both restless and vengeful (see Johnston (1999), 164–5). The countering by the untimely born of their own parturient mothers' ghosts seems particularly appropriate. If we accept that most Caesarean births were in effect births from a dead, rather than a living, woman, such children already had a closer than normal association with the other world. The only negative tradition about Caesarean birth seems to be the Germanic legend that the Antichrist would be so born. This element of the Antichrist's *Vita* does not appear until the second half of the 15th cent. and appears to be the end result of a complex accretion of ideas. These included the association of the Antichrist with the viper, whose abdomen bursts in order to bring the young to birth; and with Roman emperors, especially Nero, often represented in medieval iconography as cutting open his own mother. The Roman link would also have brought to mind the legend, by now well-entrenched, of Julius Caesar's birth (see below, **the first of the Caesars**). See Blumenfeld-Kosinski (1990), 125–42. The stress is evidently on the perceived unnaturalness of this mode of delivery, cf. P. above (**45. It is unnatural** and **46. Agrippina . . . memoirs**) on the breech birth of Nero.

47. The elder Scipio P. Scipio Africanus the Elder, victor of Zama (*OCD*[3], 398). His mother, Pomponia's, death *in childbirth* is recorded by Silius Italicus (13. 615–46), who does not, however, indicate that Scipio's birth was necessarily by Caesarean section.

the first of the Caesars P.'s list of examples of Caesarean births has been misconstrued and misinterpreted over the centuries. Solinus (1. 68) interprets Pliny as saying that Scipio was 'the first of the Caesars', writing that Scipio, having been cut from the womb, was the first to bear the *cognomen* Caesar; an identification repeated by a number of modern commentators on the origins of Caesarean section (refs. in Pundel (1969), 19). But Solinus was not the most reliable reader of Pliny and it seems more natural to take 'Scipio' (who is not otherwise known to have used the name Caesar) and 'the first of the Caesars' as two separate examples in a list of four. However, the most contentious of these misinterpretations has been the citation of this passage as the origin of the widespread and long-lasting tradition (see Pundel (1969), 15–20; Trolle (1982), 25–8) that 'the first of the Caesars' cut from his mother was the dictator, Julius Caesar, precursor of the Roman emperors who used the name Caesar. It is highly unlikely, for a number of reasons, that P. means Julius Caesar. First, although he occasionally uses the term *Caesares*, Caesars, to describe the emperor Vespasian and his son and partner in government, Titus (see Introd. 2. 1 and below, **162. most recent census . . . father and son**), the context here of the phrase *primus Caesarum* is that of family names: it is immediately followed by remarks about the meaning of other family names, the Caesones and the Vopisci. The natural interpretation of the phrase is therefore 'the first person to bear the surname Caesar', i.e. not Julius Caesar but one of his ancestors.

   Secondly, according to Suet. *Caes.* 26, cf. 13, Caesar's mother Aurelia was still alive well into her son's fifth decade, dying in 54 BC. Suetonius' account of Julius Caesar's birth and childhood is unfortunately lost; but if he had recorded a Caesarean birth involving survival of both mother and child in those lost chapters he would have been presenting a not impossible, but very unlikely, scenario (see above, **Those delivered . . . cut open**).

   Thirdly, a later exploration of the popular etymology behind the name Caesar (*SHA*, Aelius Spartianus, *Aelius* 2–3) gives several possible derivations for the name of 'the first Caesar'. According to one of these, he killed an elephant (Punic *caesai*) in battle, an exploit perhaps to be associated with Sextus Julius Caesar, praetor in the second Punic war and apparently commemorated by the dictator Caesar on a denarius of *c.*49–48 BC showing an elephant crushing a serpent (Crawford (1974), i. 89; ii, pl. lii, no. 443; D. R. Sear, *The History and Coinage of the Roman Imperators* (London, 1998), no. 9, pp. 8–9). According to another, he was cut (*caeso*) from his mother (cf. Nonius Marcellus 984 L). The other suggested possibilities are that he was born with a shock of hair (*caesaries*), or with grey-blue eyes (*caesiis*). In all cases, the 'first Caesar' more naturally refers to the first holder of the *cognomen* rather than the proto-emperor.

   Fourthly, the texts which could be taken to imply that the Caesar in question was the dictator are considerably later than Pliny. The 4th-cent. Virgilian commentator Servius (*In Aen.* 1. 286) mentions the birth etymology in the context of a discussion of the dictator. Isidore of Seville in the 6th cent. AD cites both the 'Caesarean birth' and the 'shock of hair' derivations for the name of Caesar, 'after whom the emperors who followed were called Caesars'. This may have encouraged the misinterpretation of earlier references such as Pliny's. Blumenfeld-Kosinski (1990), app. 3, 143–53, shows how the idea then entered the Arabic and especially the European medieval tradition which saw Caesar as a popular hero and was thus predisposed to attribute to him a marvellous birth. Unreliable compilations from the Roman historians, such as the *Faits des Romains*, coupled with an interest in 'elaborate and far-fetched etymological speculations', fuelled the growth and elaboration of the myth: see also Pundel (1969), 32–43.

Caeso Unlike P., Festus ((43) 57. 13 Mueller) derived only the name Caeso from the idea of cutting (*caeso*), citing the 'shock of hair' explanation for the name Caesar. The name Caeso is found in the *gens Fabia* (Stein, *RE* 6. 2, Fabius (18), (19), (159), 1745–6, 1783) and among the Quinctii (Hanslik, *RE* 24, Quinctius (8), 1000–1).

Manilius A M'. Manilius was consul in 149 BC, the first year of the Punic war which ended in 146 with the destruction of Carthage (Munzer, *RE* 14. 1, Manilius (12), 1135–40.

Vopiscus Nonius Marcellus (894 L) has a similar definition. Vopiscus was used as a *cognomen*, e.g. of the Manlii (Fluss, *RE* 14. 1, Manlius (29), (30), (31), 1142–4). The original derivation of the name is uncertain. Vendryes (1934: 428–33) suggested that the word came into Latin from a Celtic or Ligurian dialect, and that it derived from *uo-pit-sko or *uo-peit-sko, meaning 'one born with two souls', the 'second soul' being that of the twin who died.

48. few animals . . . pregnant Aristotle, *HA* 585^{a}3 names only the mare apart from man. Nearly the whole of **48** is paraphrased from *HA* 585^a.

in only one or two . . . superfetation occur Superfetation, the result of conceptions in different menstrual cycles leading to the development of foetuses of different gestational ages in the uterus, is a rare and possibly hereditary phenomenon in humans (E. M. Bryan, *Twins and Higher Multiple Pregnancies: A Guide to their Nature and Nurture* (London, 1992), 18–19). Its occurrence in man was acknowledged in the Hippocratic corpus (*On Superfetation* 1, 8. 476 L). Aristotle (*HA* 585^a) says it occurs in the hare but not in the mare, although Littré, commenting on the Hippocratic treatise, offered several early 19th-cent. examples which included a mare, as well as a goat and a woman. In the past, the weight discrepancies, which are now known to occur between normal twins for a variety of reasons, may have caused the incidence of apparent superfetation in

humans to be overestimated. In addition, foetuses of multiple pregnancies which died in mid- or late gestation and were expelled
together with a full-term live birth, might also have led to incorrect
assumptions of superfetation.

We find . . . twelve foetuses were expelled The story is
found in Aristotle, *HA* 585ª10ff.

when only a short space of time . . . full term P. refers to the
phenomenon known as superfecundation, the conception of twins
through separate acts of sexual intercourse in one menstrual cycle.
This can result in twins of different paternities, as has been proven
in modern medicine by blood-tests and other methods.
Interestingly, the theory of maternal impressions (see below, **52**)
was sometimes cited as late as the 17th and 18th cents. (e.g. F.
Mauriceau, *Traité des maladies des femmes grosses et accouchées* (Paris,
1681), quoted by Bryan (1992), 18) to explain twins of markedly
different appearances, possibly to avoid the adulterous implications of dual paternities. See Bryan (1992), 18–19; G. A. Machin,
'The Pathology of Twinning', in J. W. Keeling (ed.), *Foetal and Neo-
natal Pathology*[2] (London, 1992), 223.

Hercules . . . Iphicles Cf. Aristotle, *HA* 585a. Alcmene conceived the hero Heracles by Zeus and on the next night conceived
Iphicles by her husband Amphitryon. Cf. Hesiod, *Theog.* 5. 46ff.

woman . . . lover Cf. Aristotle, *HA* 585ª15ff.

a slave girl from Proconnesus An example not found in
Aristotle. Proconnesus is modern Marmora.

Another . . . full-term baby Aristotle, *HA* 585ª17ff. records the
case of a woman who bore full-term twins together with a five
months' foetus.

seven months' child . . . following months Cf. Aristotle, *HA*
585ª21ff. An interval between multiple births is possible; twins, for
example, are usually born just 30 minutes apart, but, in some cases,
the gap can be as much as ten days. A gap of 28 days was reported
in the national press a few years ago (*Daily Telegraph*, 13 June 2000),
between an infant born 14 weeks prematurely and its twin, delivered four weeks later by Caesarean; but in Pliny's time, this would
no doubt have been an example of the phenomenon described in

47. Vopiscus above, whereby a twin born prematurely dies, but the other infant is retained in the womb and safely delivered at the normal time. According to Ulpian (*Dig.* 5. 4. 3), an Alexandrian woman in the reign of Hadrian bore quadruplets, followed by a fifth child forty days later; though other sources (e.g. Gaius, *Dig.* 5. 4. 3; above **33. portentous . . . fertility**) suggest all five were born at the same time: see Friedländer (1913), iv. 9 for refs.

50. sound parents . . . as themselves Aristotle, *HA* 585^{b}29 mentions defective children of defective parents, but goes on to say that it is not the norm; such children are usually sound (585^{b}35–586^{a}3). The theme of **50–1** is the variety displayed in the transmission of characteristics from one generation to another. Both the nature of the transmitted characteristic (e.g. scars) and the manner of its transmission (e.g. skipping generations) provide unexpected departures from the norm as the specific examples of the Dacians and the Lepidi illustrate. The passage as a whole is a rather hastily compressed version of *HA* 585^{b}35–586^{a}15. There is no specific statement of the principle of skipping generations. Instead, this has to be inferred from the slightly ambiguous 'not in succession' (below, **51**) in the example of the Lepidi. The example of the Dacians replaces Aristotle's individual with a tattoo. The Lepidi are a Plinian addition, in keeping with his preference for providing Roman examples where possible.

even scars Hippocratic writings (*Airs* 14, 2. 60 L; *Genit.* 11, 7. 484 L) suggest that it is possible to inherit even post-natally acquired characteristics, in accordance with the theory of pangenesis, by which the male and female generative material is drawn from every part of the body; the Hippocratics, but not Aristotle, believed that women as well as men produced 'seed' (below, **66. This substance**). See Dean-Jones (1994), 162–6, cf. 78–80. The various features of the individual child were determined by which parent had provided the most seed for that part. Although Aristotle did not accept this theory, he does, albeit cautiously, endorse the possibility of passing on even post-natally acquired features (*GA* 721^{b}30ff.; *HA* 585^{b}30–5), see also above, **50. sound parents**). In *GA* 721^{b}30f., he describes a 'confused and indistinct' brand mark inherited from his father by a man from Chalcedon. The version of the story in *HA* 585^{b}34 has the mark skipping a generation, to reappear in the grandson. For the vexed question of Aristotle's own theory of resemblance, as outlined mainly in the *GA*, see Dean-Jones (1994), 193–9. Like the theory of maternal impressions (below, **52**), the inheritance of acquired characteristics continues to resurface today in popular anecdote (cf. *Daily Telegraph*, 29 October 2002).

tattoo . . . Dacians Attempts have been made to emend P.'s *Dacorum*, 'Dacians' to e.g. *aliquorum*, 'some people', but Schilling, app. crit., p. 55, rightly cites *HN* 22. 2, where P. ascribes to the Dacians and Sarmatians a practice which is in all likelihood that of tattooing. Pliny's *nota* ('mark'), then, may be specifically a tattoo, and is thus translated here. For the inheritance of non-congenital characteristics, cf. above, **even scars**, on an inherited brand-mark in Arist. *HA* 585^{a}34 and *GA* 721^{b}29 ff. On the association of decorative tattooing with barbarian races, especially the Thracians (e.g. Herod. 5. 6. 2), see C. P. Jones, 'Stigma: Tatooing and Branding in Graeco-Roman Antiquity', *JRS* 77 (1987), 139–55. Other peoples with the same custom included the Illyrians, the Iapodes in the eastern Alps, the Mossynoikoi on the Pontic coast, and the Britons (Strabo 7. 5. 4, C315; Xenophon, *An.* 5. 4. 32; Herodian 3. 14. 7).

51. the family of the Lepidi The Lepidi were a branch of the Aemilii, a leading patrician clan of the Republic and early Empire. Prominent members included M. Aemilius Lepidus, cos. 187 and 175, Pontifex Maximus from 180 and Princeps Senatus from 179 BC; M. Aemilius Lepidus, the Triumvir with Octavian and Mark Antony; and M. Aemilius Lepidus, cos. AD 6, capable of attaining the Principate, but disdaining it, according to Augustus (Tac. *Ann.* 1. 13. 2). The last of the line, M. Aemilus Lepidus, married Caius Caligula's sister Drusilla and was named by the emperor as his heir-apparent before being executed by him in AD 39. See *OCD*³, 20–1; Klebs and Rohden, *RE* 1. 1, Aemilius (60)–(84), esp. (68), (73), (75), and (76), 550–64. This anecdote is not recorded elsewhere and there is no indication as to which members of the family were thus affected.

not in successive generations Probably the most likely meaning of P.'s *intermisso ordine*, 'not in succession': the inspiration is Aristotle, *HA* 586^a (cf. 585^{b}34), where cases of family resemblances skipping a generation or two before reappearing are mentioned; cf. **incontrovertible evidence** below. For Aristotle's explanation of this recessive phenomenon by means of the theory of 'relapse', see

Dean-Jones (1994), 197–8. Plutarch, too, discusses inherited characteristics which skip one or more generations (*Mor.* 563a).

eye covered by a membrane Latin *membrana* is used to describe a thin skin-like covering, for example of the internal organs of the body (*Thes. Ling. Lat.* s.v. 'membrana', 629–30). It could refer to the natural membranes protecting the eyes (Cic. *ND* 2. 142) or to their changed appearance when diseased (Vegetius, *Mulo.* 2. 17. 1). It could also refer to the foetal membranes (Jerome, *Virg. Mar.* 18, Macr. *Somn.* 1. 66. 3). Pliny could mean that the infants suffered from congenital cataract, a symptom of some rare genetic diseases. Another possibility is that he is refering to a persistent pupillary membrane, where strands of a foetal membrane of the eye which normally disappears at birth remain visible, lying across the eye: see above, **17. Thibii . . . horse**. This condition, too, is frequently hereditary. However, the remains tend to be fairly vestigial, consisting of tiny strands rather than a complete covering of the eye. Alternatively, this may be the earliest reference in classical literature to an obstetrical phenomenon which was the object of considerable superstition even into the 20th cent. An infant may occasionally be born with a fragment of the amniotic membrane, or caul, adhering to all or part of its head. According to Aelius Lampridius (*Diad.* 4), midwives used to sell the caul to advocates as it was believed to assist pleaders (cf. another birth anomaly, the 'wind egg', allegedly produced by snakes, a specimen of which was brought into court by a Gaul to give him victory in court, according to Pliny, *HN* 29. 54). The connotations of the caul were generally positive. Its quality over the centuries has been protective, guarding those who possessed it from being wounded, and also from drowning, the latter attribute underlying a brisk trade aimed at seafarers in 18th- and 19th-cent. England; though many believed its efficacy extended only to one born with it and his or her immediate family. Its courtroom function seems to have been an extension of this protective aspect; a 12th-cent. canonical source reports that it acted as a charm against any who spoke against its possessor (Migne, *PG* 137: 722–3). Aelius Lampridius (loc. cit. above) reports that great things were expected of the emperor Diadumenianus or Diadematus (AD 217–18), born with the caul rolled into a sinewy diadem around his head, a destiny belied by his premature murder.

A belief common to several European and non-European cultures saw the caul as the residence of the child's guardian spirit, or even as a sort of outer soul, a link between the world of the living and that of the dead. The child had brought with it something from the other world whence it had come. Thence, a whole complex of beliefs connected the caul with the supernatural; those born with it might see and consort with the dead and be involved with witchcraft and magic. The Italian Benandanti, in the 16th and 17th cents., were a ritual association of those born with the caul who, on the nights of Ember days, would apparently leave their bodies behind (see below, **174–5. amongst other examples** and commentary on **174** *passim*) and fight to protect crops against witches or associate with the dead.

See generally T. R. Forbes, 'The Social History of the Caul', *Yale Journal of Biology and Medicine*, 25 (1953), 495–508; id. (1966), 94–111; Belmont (1971), 19–129, esp. 19–51; Hastings iii. 639–63; vol. viii. 44–5. On the Benandanti, see Ginzburg (1983).

In a sense, then, being born with a caul is analogous to breech and Caesarean births, each of which is, in its own way, so paradoxical as to share features in common with death as well as birth and has its own links with the supernatural. See above, **46** and **47**.

Other children . . . mother herself The remark about children resembling grandfathers ties in with the idea of characteristics skipping generations (above, **not in successive generations**). The rest of the passage derives more specifically from Aristotle's discussion of the permutations to be found in hereditary similarity between mother and child, which are based on variations in the predominance of the father's form and the mother's matter. Unlike P., Aristotle states a general rule (girls usually resemble their mothers and boys their fathers), before listing the variations and exceptions (*HA* 506[a]5–6). For a variation on the general theory, see Censorinus, *ND* 6. 6–9.

Incontrovertible evidence That is, of the fact that the next generation need not necessarily reproduce the features of its parents and, more specifically, that resemblances may actually skip a generation.

Nicaeus . . . grandfather For Nicaeus, see also Solinus 1. 79; Snowden (1983), 52 n. 87. The mixed alliance which produces a white child in the second generation and a black in the third is rare but genetically possible. A similar phenomenon, the case of black parents who produced one black child followed by two white ones, was reported some years ago in the press (e.g. *Daily Telegraph*, 10 Apr. 1998); the father had had a white grandmother. Aristotle has an identical story concerning the descendants of a Sicilian woman (*HA* 7. 6. 586ᵃ) and of a woman from Elis (*GA* 1. 18. 722). Some editors have replaced 'Sicily' with 'Elis' in the *HA* passage, since 'Elis' is the reading in identical stories in the paradoxographer Antigonus of Carystus (112b Giannini) and Aristophanes of Byzantium (*Nat. An. Epit.* II, 272). Elis had had links with Egypt (Herod. 2. 160, Diodorus 1. 95) and continued contact might explain the provenance of a black father. In all versions, the woman had a white child by a black man, with a black child appearing in the third generation (see also above, **not in successive genera-tions**). Such occurrences laid the mother open to charges of adultery, cf. Plutarch, *Mor.* 563a and Jerome (*Quaest. in Gen.* 30, 32. 33), who says that Quintilian exonerated a white woman who gave birth to a black child by referring to the theory of maternal impressions (see below, **52. They are believed . . . confuse the resemblance**; cf. Snowden (1983), 95–6.

the rest of the family P.'s actual phrase is vaguer; 'no different from others', but a reference to the child's similarity to Nicaeus' mother's white blood relatives, as opposed to the black members of her father's family, seems the most plausible interpretation.

52. They are believed . . . confuse the resemblance. P. turns from the idea of heredity to other causes of resemblance. Outside circumstances at the moment of conception were believed to play a crucial part in foetal development. These ranged from the superstitious (Hesiod warns against intercourse after a funeral, *WD* 1. 735f.) to the physical (parents too young, Aristotle, *Pol.* 7. 1335ᵃ11–17, *GA* 4. 766ᵇ29–31; semen too hot or too cold *GA* 2. 743ᵃ27–30) and the environmental (Celsus 2. 1. 14 on weather factors). P.'s reference here is to a popular idea derived from sympathetic magic, that sensory impressions and mental images at the time of conception will affect the child's physical appearance: see Empedocles DK 31A 81. 20–2. Garland (1995), 151, quotes Soranus, *Gyn.* 1. 39, on women whose impressions of beautiful statues and paintings at the moment of conception led to their producing

beautiful children, cf. Heliodorus' (*Aeth.* 4. 8) black queen who produced a beautiful—but white—daughter after looking at a picture
of a white Andromeda. Bizarre images led to bizarre-looking
offspring. For the motif, see Thompson, T 550. 4, cf. T 562. Note
that P., in contrast to other ancient sources, suggests that mental
images in the mind of either parent, not just the mother, at the time
of conception, have this effect (see below, **This is the reason . . .
particular species**); a notion later repeated in the 16th cent. by
Ambroise Paré (1973), ch. ix. 5, p. 35. The imagination of the
mother could still be a threat in the early weeks, before the foetus
was fully articulated (ibid., ix. 26–30, p. 37 Céard). The belief in the
sensory/mental impression effect lasted, with modifications, at
least until the 18th cent. (see M. Reeve, 'Conceptions', *PCPS* 215
(1989), 81–112). It proved tenacious even among the educated: see
P.-G. Boucé ('Imagination, Pregnant Women and Monsters in
Eighteenth-Century England and France', in G. S. Rousseau and
R. Porter (eds.), *Sexual Underworlds of the Enlightenment* (Manchester,
1987), 86–100) on the controversy between the 18th-cent. English
doctors Turner, who supported the theory, and Blondel, who was
sceptical. Although both theses found support, Turner's was being
upheld as late as 1788 in a scholarly dissertation. Popular belief was
even longer lived: the 'Elephant Man' claimed that his condition
was due to his pregnant mother having been knocked down by a
circus elephant (Fiedler (1978), 168). According to Boucé (1987), 99
n. 8), visual impression in the tradition of Heliodorus (see above,
this note) was at least aired, if not necessarily believed, as an explanation for the colour of children illegitimately fathered in Normandy
by black American servicemen in 1945. Not all cases were as
dramatic as these: often, the result was in the form of a significantly
shaped birthmark, situated at a place corresponding to the position
of the mother's hand when she suffered the visual or mental upset.
Even an unsatisfied maternal craving might translate itself into an
aptly shaped birthmark on her child (Gélis (1991), 56; McDaniel
(1948a), 11, commenting respectively on 16th-cent. France and
20th-cent. Italy). A celebrated alleged instance of the phenomenon
from the early 19th cent. could be reported as a quaint historical
curiosity in a medical journal of the 1970s (T.E.C. Jr., 'The power of
maternal impression causes the alleged father's name to appear in
legible letters in his infant son's right eye (1817)', *Pediatrics*, 58 (1976),
901), but the general idea still thrives in popular folklore today: wit-

ness the anecdotes gathered from readers in a national newpaper
(*Daily Telegraph*, 13 Aug. 2002; 3 Sept. 2002; 10 Sept. 2002; 1 Oct.
2002).

This is the reason . . . particular species P. now uses this
theory, with stress on the mental rather than sensory aspect, to
emphasize his belief in the infinite variety of the human race and its
superiority in respect to the rest of the animal kingdom (see Introd.
5. 2. 2). He maximizes the extent of this variety by allowing mental
impressions to come from either parent. This is significant. Other
sources mention only the woman's role as shaper of her future
offspring in this manner. Given the fact that the mother-to-be had,
in addition to the moment of conception, nine months of intimate
contact with the developing foetus, this might not be so surprising.
Thus, Aristotle (*Pol.* 7. 18, 1335^b) comments that the foetus derives
its nature from its mother as plants do from earth. It is to the
woman only, even at intercourse, that Soranus addresses a warning
against drunkenness: not only does she risk producing a child misshapen by her drunken fantasies, but also one whose soul replicates
her deranged and unstable mind (*Gyn.* 1. 39. 1–2). By including both
parents, and effectively doubling the possible permutations, Pliny
gives maximum emphasis to his explanation for this phenomenon:
the innate superiority of man's mind over the minds of other
animals. For Aristotle, man's mind had qualities such as wisdom
and understanding which could not be equated with the qualities
exhibited by animals (*HA* 8. 1. 588^{a}28–31) and the power of moral
deliberation was uniquely human (*NE* 1111^{b}4ff., 1144^{b}24ff.). The
quality of deliberative rational thinking (*ratio*) was unique to man in
P.'s view (Beagon (1992), 133–7), not only in terms of a moral
dimension (cf. the Stoic equation of moral excellence, *virtus*, with
ratio), but also in terms of pure brain power (see below, **91. mental
vigour . . . the sun**), hence the stress here on **swiftness . . .
agility . . . versatility**. This mental superiority was pivotal to P.'s
concept of human primacy in the natural world and it is not surprising to find it cited as the key to human variety. Influence from
purely sensory impressions, however, was sometimes attributed to
animals (Oppian *Cyneg.* 1. 3. 28–67, cf. Reeve (1989), 85–7 on the
biblical story of Jacob's sheep).

53. Artemo . . . Antiochus . . . Laodice The series of striking
physical resemblances between unrelated individuals is drawn for

the most part from Valerius Maximus 9. 14. Antiochus II (*c.*287–246 BC) of Syria repudiated his wife and cousin Laodice and her children in favour of Berenice, daughter of Ptolemy II of Egypt. The war of succession following Antiochus' death went ultimately in Laodice's favour. The anecdote here describes an early attempt to stake her claim, though the detail that she actually murdered Antiochus is generally discounted. Valerius Maximus 9. 14, ext. I makes Artemo a royal relative. P.'s version, 'a low-born man' appropriately provides a more unexpected and striking case of resemblance. See *OCD*[3], Antiochus (2) II, 108; and Laodice (2), 814.

Vibius . . . Publicius . . . Pompey   Cf. Valerius Maximus 9. 14. 1.

honourable countenance . . . distinguished brow Pompey's look of noble integrity is referred to again in *HN* 37. 14, where P. remarks on the irony of its rendition in pearls, the epitome of luxurious decadence, in a portrait carried at his triumph of 62 BC. For Sallust (Suet. *Gramm.* 15), Pompey's integrity (*probitas*) was no more than skin deep, but Cicero's final verdict on Pompey was more generous: '[a man of] good character, clean life and serious principle' (*Att.* 11. 6. 4, trans. Shackleton-Bailey).

54. Pompey's father . . . slave Pompey's father was Cn. Pompeius Strabo, cos. 89 BC. Cf. Valerius Maximus 9. 14. 2.

Serapio . . . Scipio Valerius Maximus 9. 14. 3 makes Serapio a *victimarius*, slaughterer at public sacrifices rather than a pig-dealer. According to Livy, *Per.* 55, the name was applied to Publius Cornelius Scipio Nasica, cos. 138 BC, by a tribune, Curiatius. P.'s reference in *HN* 21. 10 may be a confusion with his son, cos. 111 BC, who bore the same name (J. André, *Histoire Naturelle livre 21* (Paris, 1969), 97; Münzer, *RE* 4. I, Cornelius (355), 1504–5).

Salvitto . . . Scipio Cornelius Scipio Pomponianus Salvitto, who was with Caesar in Africa in 47 BC, was a nonentity who acquired the actor's name as some sort of criticism of his lifestyle (Suet. *Jul.* 59, cf. Plutarch, *Caes.* 51. 3, Dio 42. 58). See Münzer, *RE* 4. I, Cornelius (357), 1505–6.

Spinther . . . second and third roles i.e. actors who took secondary roles in plays, see Valerius Maximus 9. 14. 4.

Lentulus P. Cornelius Lentulus Spinther, friend of Cicero and consul in 57 BC. He fought for Pompey and was executed after Pharsalus: see *OCD*³, Cornelius Lentulus Spinther, Publius, 396; Münzer, *RE* 3. 2, Cornelius (238), 1392–8.

Metellus Q. Metellus Nepos, who, as tribune in 62 BC, had attacked Cicero over his handling of the Catilinarian affair. *OCD*³, Caecilius Metellus Nepos, Quintus, 269; Münzer, *RE* 3. 1, Caecilius (96), 1216–18.

55. The orator L. Plancus L. Munatius Plancus served under Caesar in Gaul. Later he fought for Antony, but ultimately went over to Octavian, for whom he proposed the name Augustus in 27 BC (Suet. *Aug.* 7). Cicero commented on his eloquence (*Fam.* 10. 3. 3), cf. Pliny, *HN* pref. 31.

the elder Curio C. Scribonius Curio, cos. 76 BC was nicknamed after the comic actor Burbuleius due to his bodily gestures (Valerius Maximus 9. 14. 5) which, according to Cicero (*Brut.* 216), excited ridicule when he was declaiming. *OCD*³ Scribonius Curio (1), Gaius, 1370; Münzer, *RE* 11 A 1 Scribonius (10), 862–7.

the former censor, Messalla M. Valerius Messalla Niger, cos. 61 BC and censor in 55 BC. A barrister and friend of Cicero, he bore a facial resemblance to the actor Menogenes (Valerius Maximus 9. 14. 5). *OCD*³, Valerius Messalla, Marcus, 1579; Münzer, *RE* 8 A, Valerius (266), 162–5.

Sura P. Cornelius Lentulus Sura (cos. 71 BC) had perhaps been in Sicily in 74 BC (Münzer, *RE* Cornelius (240), 1400; *Beiträge* (1897), 111–12; cf. Valerius Maximus 9. 14, ext. 3) as propraetor rather than proconsul. Languid and disjointed delivery is hinted at by Cicero (*Brut.* 235), who says that, while the sound of his voice was strong and pleasant, his thoughts and speech were slow. His expulsion from the senate (70 BC) and subsequent attempts to regain his political status led to involvement with Catiline and execution in his second praetorship in 63 BC. See *OCD*³, Cornelius Lentulus Sura, 396; Münzer, *RE* 4 A 2, Sura (5), 962–3; *RE* 4. 2 Cornelius (240), 1399–1402.

Cassius Severus An impressive but savage orator (Tac. *Dial.* 19, 26) who was too sharp for his own good (Quintilian 10. 1. 117) and was exiled in AD 8 by Augustus (Tac. *Ann.* 1. 72; 4. 21). *OCD*³,

Cassius Severus, 301; Brzoska, *RE* 3. 2, Cassius Severus (89), 1744–9.

the gladiator Armentarius P. says he was a *murmillo*, or heavy-armed gladiator.

[Recently . . . Paris] This passage, found in the margin of a single manuscript, may be an interpolation: see Schilling 151.

56. slave-dealer Toranius Toranius Flaccus was a dealer whose wares included girls (Suet. *Aug.* 69. 2) and musicians; cf. Macrobius (*Sat.* 2. 4. 28), who supplies the *cognomen* and suggests that he was a man of wealth and good connections, thus probably specializing in the luxury end of the market, as P. implies: see W. V. Harris, 'Towards a Study of the Roman Slave Trade', *MAAR* 36 (1980), 129.

Antony after he became triumvir M. Antonius, a friend of Caesar, with whom he held the consulship in 44 BC, was a distinguished general. After Caesar's murder, he eventually joined Lepidus and Octavian, later the emperor Augustus, in the second triumvirate (effectively a triple dictatorship: for the so-called 'first triumvirate', a purely unofficial alliance, see below, **93**), by the pact of Bononia in Sept. 43. *OCD*[3], Antonius (2), Marcus, 115–16.

two hundred thousand sesterces Solinus 1. 84–6 repeats P.'s story but says the sum was 300,000, It is difficult to gauge an 'average' slave price, partly because it is difficult to define an 'average' slave and partly because so many variables, including political and economic circumstances, would have affected prices. See J. Schmidt, *Vie et mort des esclaves* (Paris, 1973), 40–2, who quotes a figure of 150–300 denarii (600–1,200 sesterces) at the end of the second Punic war, a price which may have remained relatively stable into the imperial period. A legionary's annual pay under Augustus was 225 denarii. Allowing for the exaggeration of a moral tirade, an idea of comparative values, but also of the way in which the market could be skewed by luxury tastes, may be gleaned from *HN* 9. 67. Once, says Pliny, people complained that a cook cost more than a horse. Now, however, a cook is the price of three horses, while exotic fish for the table cost as much as three cooks. The ancient sources tend to mention only those slaves whose qualities raised them above the ordinary. In *HN* 10. 84, P. suggests that prices at the top end of the market could go a lot higher even than that quoted for the so-called twins: 'nightingales fetch prices that are given for slaves', he says, quoting a price tag of 600,000 sesterces on an especially rare white bird to be given to Agrippina. For more slave price records, see below, **128–9**. Such prices may well reflect the growing taste for the exotic and unusual (see Introd. 3. 3), which could lead to bizarre or even deformed slaves fetching higher prices than normal ones (Quintilian *Inst.* 2. 5. 11). Martial depicts an irate customer in the same situation as Antony; demanding his money back when his 'idiot' slave, purchased for 20,000 sesterces, turns out to be of normal intelligence. Faking was evidently not unique (cf. Martial 14. 21) and reflects the buoyancy of the market in *mirabilia*.

nothing remarkable . . . inestimable value The dealer's original plot suggests that identical twins would themselves have had a rarity value but he clearly plays upon his client's desire for exclusivity, at the same time reflecting the contemporary interest in *mirabilia* (cf. Agrippina's nightingale, above, **two hundred thousand**). Antony, he suggests, has gained the ultimate paradox of nature: twins who are not twins rank far more highly as *mirabilia* than the real thing. See below, **no other . . . status**.

the mind behind the proscriptions Despite Dio (47. 7) and later apologists for Octavian (Syme (1939), 191), P. is not necessarily placing responsibility for the proscriptions which followed the formation of the second triumvirate primarily with Antony: **147** below suggests that some responsibility at least was thought to rest with Octavian, whom Suetonius (*Aug.* 27. 3) portrayed as ultimately more cruel than his colleagues, despite his initial reluctance; cf. his earlier behaviour after Philippi (*Aug.* 12) and later after Perusia (*Aug.* 15). But Cicero's death, at least, is implicitly ascribed to Antony, **117** below.

no other . . . status Rare and unusual items were sought after by the elite, emperors in particular acquiring *mirabilia* by gift or purchase (Garland (1995), 45–50). Such items at once reflected and enhanced the extraordinary position in society of their possessor. See Introd. 3. 3.

57. Some . . . partners Cf. Aristotle, *HA* 585b. The background information may come from a Greek source but the examples are Roman (Schilling, 152).

Augustus and Livia As a couple, they were childless, apart from a miscarried infant (Suet. *Aug.* 63), but Augustus had Julia by his first wife, Scribonia, and Livia had two sons, Drusus and the future emperor Tiberius, by her first husband, Tiberius Claudius Nero. See *OCD*[3], Augustus, 216–18; Livia Drusilla, 876.

Similarly . . . alternately Aristotle, *HA* 585[b]9–11. Aristotle does not mention that alternation is the general rule, but he does say that some women when young produce only females and when older produce only males, and vice versa (585[b]15). For P.'s meaning, see below, **Germanicus.**

mother of the Gracchi Cornelia, who married Ti. Sempronius Gracchus, *c.*175–165 BC; cf. **122** (below). Of the twelve children, only three, the future tribunes Tiberius and Gaius, nine years apart (Plutarch, *C. Gr.* 1. 2, *Ti. Gr.* 3), and their older sister Sempronia (Plutarch, *Ti. Gr.* 4. 4), survived. There is no evidence on the other children to clarify P.'s remarks about alternation see below, **Germanicus' wife Agrippina . . . nine.** It was only the later deaths of the two famous brothers which was of public interest, as Seneca makes clear: 'The rest whom the state never knew as either born or lost, matter little' *(Ad Marc.* 16. 3, cf. *Ad Helv.* 16. 6). See *OCD*[3], Cornelia (1), 392; Münzer, *RE* 4. 1, Cornelia (407), 1592–5. For Cornelia, see also below **69. [When females . . . proves.].**

Germanicus' wife Agrippina . . . nine Germanicus, eldest son of the emperor Tiberius' brother Drusus and the younger Antonia, married Agrippina the elder, daughter of Marcus Agrippa and Augustus' daughter Julia, in AD 4. See *OCD*[3], Vipsania Agrippina (2), 1601; Julius Caesar, Germanicus, 783. On the problem of the children's birthdates and order, see T. Mommsen, 'Die Familie des Germanicus', *Hermes*, 13 (1878), 245–65; J. Humphrey, 'The Three Daughters of Agrippina Maior', *AJAH* 4 (1979), 128–43, H. Lindsay, *Suetonius Life of Caligula* (Bristol, 1992), 61–3, D. W. Hurley, *An Historical and Historiographical Commentary on Suetonius' Life of Caligula* (Atlanta, 1993), 16–18. Recent sequences such as Lindsay's (summarized below) modify Mommsen's slightly: (1) Nero, AD 5 (possibly AD 6), cf . Tac. *Ann.* 3. 29. 1; (2) Drusus, AD 7–8, cf. Tac. *Ann.* 4. 4. l; (3) infant, AD 8–10, either Tiberius (*CIL* vi. 888) or unknown male (*CIL* vi. 890); (4) Gaius, AD 11 (died in childhood, Suet. *Calig.* 8. 2: born a year belore Caligula); (5) Caligula, AD

12, cf. Suet. *Calig.* 8. 1; (6) infant, either Tiberius (*CIL* vi. 888) or unknown male (*CIL* vi. 890), cf. Tac. *Ann.* 1. 44. 2, on Agrippina's pregnancy; (7) Agrippina, Nov. AD 15, cf. *Fasti Arvales* I. 2. 249; (8) Drusilla, late AD 16–17; (9) Livilla, early AD 18, cf. Tac. *Ann.* 2. 54. 2. The problem with P.'s statement is that, since all three early deaths, according to the scheme outlined above, were male (making the total number of births 6 males and 3 females), it is impossible to get a strict alternation between male and female children, even without the constraints of the known or likely dates for the six surviving children. Furthermore, Suet. *Calig.*7 says that the three girls were born in a three-year period (*continuo triennio anno*), a statement which Hurley (17) suggests was a deliberate rebuttal of Pliny's claim about alternating births. Yet Pliny would surely have known about the girls' birth dates and even about the dates and sex of the dead infants: he was well informed, having written his *Bellum Germaniae*, which was probably the main source on Germanicus and his family for Suetonius and Tacitus, and we know he consulted the *Acta diurna* with its birth records (below, **60. In the public records**), and the younger Agrippina's memoirs (above, **46. Agrippina . . . memoirs**). It is possible that he does not mean to imply a strictly regular alternating pattern; simply that she produced both boys and girls. It is also possible that in 'alternating', he includes giving birth first to one sex and then to the other, taking his cue from Aristotle, *HA* 585^b (see above, **Similarly . . . alternately**) where some women are said to bear girls only in youth and boys only later on, and vice versa, which fits Agrippina's pattern. His use of the numerical adverbs *noviens* (nine times) and *duodeciens* (twelve times) could not in that case be taken literally in conjunction with 'alternating', but only as an indication of the total number of births, perhaps translating 'who gave birth nine times . . . twelve times.'

Some are sterile . . . produce a girl Cf. Aristotle, *HA* 585^{b}18–20.

58. medical care Apart from obvious precautions such as rest, there were few medical options for the prevention of miscarriage. Then, as now, many herbal and other medicines were known to have the opposite effect. In the *HN*, for instance, there are frequent warnings that miscarriage is a side-effect of some remedies (e.g. *HN* 26. 153; 27. 80, 110). For other causes of involuntary miscarriage, see above **43. smell . . . abortion**. Similar in their effect would have been the numerous recipes for removing a dead foetus, or promoting ease of delivery and ejection of the afterbirth (e.g. *HN* 26. 152–4, 159, 161; 27. 30, 135; 28. 251–2). It is probably no coincidence that the majority of aids to the retention of the foetus in the womb are listed among the dubious claims of the Magi in book 30 (123–8). They include a drink containing cremated porcupine, a body rub made from hedgehog ash, and an amulet made from worms. In fact, amulets seem to have been the main standby, cf. *HN* 28. 247, *HN* 36. 153, and, above all, 30. 130 and 36. 149–51, on the eagle stone (*aetites*). This was a hollow stone containing a detached kernel, and thus suggestive of the state of pregnancy (cf. *HN* 10. 12, 'pregnant with another stone inside'). Its reputation outlasted antiquity and continued into the modern era (Gélis (1991), 68, 99–110, cf. 115–16: still in use in Europe in the 19th cent.).

M. Silanus . . . death   Cf. Tac. *Ann.* 13. 1: M. Junius Silanus, son of M. Junius Silanus and Aemilia Lepida, daughter of Augustus' granddaughter, the younger Julia. See *OCD*³, Junius Silanus (3), Marcus, 790; Hohl, *RE* 10. 1, Junius (176), 1099–1100. The year was AD 14.

While . . . consulship   There was a gap of several years between his consulship (AD 46) and his proconsulship in Asia (AD 54).

poisoned by Nero . . . emperor   Tac. *Ann.* 13. 1 says Agrippina got rid of this potential rival to her son without the latter's knowledge soon after Nero's accession in AD 54; but Pliny as usual does not give Nero the benefit of the doubt. See Introd. 2. 1.

59. Metellus Macedonicus   For his career, see below, **142.** **greatest . . . Macedonicus**. He had seven children, not six, four boys and three girls (Cic. *Fin.* 5. 82, Valerius Maximus 7. 1. 1).

60. In the public records   The *Acta diurna* (sometimes called *Acta publica*, Suet. *Tib.* 5, *diurna populi Romani*, Tac. *Ann.* 16. 22. 3, or simply *acta*, as here) were records of events in the city exhibited for public perusal and stored in the state archives. For their origin and development, see below, **186. public records**. By P.'s day, they included judicial and assembly proceedings and possibly material which overlapped with the *acta senatus*, the senate proceedings (B. Baldwin, 'The *Acta Diurna*', *Chiron*, 9 (1979), 189–203). There was also more general news, including imperial court affairs and records of births and marriages (Juvenal 2. 136, 9. 84) and anything strange or startling, as here and below, **186**; also *HN* 10. 2 (fake phoenix sent to Claudius) and possibly the portents of *HN* 2. 147, see Baldwin, op. cit.

Augustus . . . L. Sulla In 5 BC.

C. Crispinus Hilarus . . . outshone all others This exceptional procession and its patriarch are not mentioned elsewhere.

A woman . . . 40 Aristotle, *HA* 545^{b}26–31 puts the average age for menopause at 45–50 years. *HA* 585^b sets the norm at around 40, but allows for the possibility of menstruation and even parturition at 50.

With regard to men P.'s examples are of the exceptional. For the average limits, see Aristotle, *HA* 545^b, who says that men normally cease fathering children around 65 to 70 years. *HA* 585^b sets the normal limit at 60, while those who exceed this limit may go on to 70 and a few actually procreate at the age of 90. For ancient views on the differing reproductive lifespans of men and women, see Dean-Jones (1994), 103–9.

king Masinissa . . . Methimannus Born *c*.238 BC and an ally of Rome during the second and third Punic wars, Masinissa of Numidia lived to be 90: see below, **156. Masinissa**. For the son of his old age, see also Polybius 36. 16, Valerius Maximus 8. 12., ext.1 and Solinus 1. 59, who, however, makes the king only 72 at the time. See *OCD*³, 934.

Cato the Censor The Roman statesman (234–148 BC) famous for his traditionalist moral and political outlook. His literary output included letters, speeches, historical and agricultural works which were consulted by Pliny. See *OCD*³, Porcius Cato (1), Marcus, 1224–5; Helm, *RE* 22. 1, Cato (9), 108–65. see below, **100** and Introd. 2. 1.

past 80 . . . Salonius Cf. Plutarch, *Cat. Mai.* 24; Aulus Gellius, *NA* 13. 20.

62. Licinianus . . . Salonian The younger son was called Cato Salonianus after his maternal grandfather (Gross, *RE* 22. 1 Cato (15), 168); he died in his praetorship (*Cat. Mai.* 27. 5). The elder was called after the family of his mother, Cato's first wife Licinia (Gross, *RE* 22. 1, Cato (14), 167–8); he died when praetor elect (Aulus Gellius, *NA* 13. 20. 8, cf. *Cat. Mai.* 24).

Cato of Utica Born in 95 BC and so called because in 46 BC, he committed suicide at Utica in North Africa rather than submit to Julius Caesar during the civil war of 49–45 BC. His republican principles were strengthened by his devotion to Stoicism and he became an icon for later upholders of similar ideas. See *OCD*[3], Porcius Cato (2), Marcus, 1225–6; Helm, *RE* 22. 1, Cato (16), 168–21.

L. Volusius Saturninus A nonagenarian like Masinissa (above, **61**), he died in AD 56 aged 93 (Tac. *Ann.* 13. 30; *HN* 11. 223). Cf. also below, **156**. His younger son by Cornelia, Q. Volusius Saturninus, was consul in the year of his father's death (Tac. *Ann.* 13. 25). See Hanslik, *RE* suppl. 9, Volusius (17) and (20), 1861–2 and 1863–4.

Among the lower classes . . . 75. The implication seems to be that paternity at an advanced age is more common among the lower classes than among the elite. This may be a reflection of a tendency on the part of the elite to limit procreation in the interests of long-term family status. More children would involve greater subdivision of the family wealth and the possibility that no one son would be sufficiently wealthy to uphold the position in society enjoyed by his father. In addition, the Roman elite tended to marry earlier, a practice actively promoted among the senatorial class by the Augustan marriage laws: see R. P. Saller, *Patriarchy, Property and Death in the Roman Family* (Cambridge, 1994), 38.

63. Woman . . . periods Aristotle, confusing menstrual with oestrous cycles (see below, **67. easiest . . . finishing**), said that all vivipara had an external discharge (*GA* 727ᵃ20ff., cf. *HA* 527ᵃ30–573ᵇ30); women simply had more than the others. Solinus (1. 54) cites Democritus as authority for P.'s assertion of uniqueness.

mole *Myle* (Hipp. *Mul.* 8. 148. 24–150. 22 L; Aristotle, *GA* 775ᵇ25), or *mylos* (Soranus 3. 9. 36), literally 'millstone', was a term used of a fleshy mass formed in the uterus, in particular the various types of what are still termed 'molar' pregnancies today. A tumour forms on the uterine wall as the result of a pregnancy which has failed to develop normally: see A. E. Szulman, 'Trophoblastic Disease: Pathology of Complete and Partial Moles', in G. B. Reed, A. E. Claireaux, and F. Cockburn (eds.), *Diseases of the Fetus and Newborn*[2] (London, 1995), 187–99. This hydatidiform mole is benign, but occasionally a malignant choriocarcinoma develops from it. Another type of mole, the carneous mole, is formed from the tissue of a missed abortion, which, if retained for longer than a few weeks, loses moisture and shrinks into a compacted mass: see I. E. Moore, 'Macerated Stillbirth', in J. W. Keeling (ed.), *Foetal and Neo-natal Pathology*[2] (London, 1992), 185 and fig. 9. 3, and Machin (1992), 227, and below, **resistant . . . knife**. In practice, it cannot always have been easy or possible for the ancient doctor to distinguish between the mole and other hard tumours in the uterus. In theory, however, a number of different types of similar internal uterine growths were identified by the ancient medical writers, including the *scleroma* (Galen 19. 429–30 K), which was slightly less hard and resistant than the *scirrhus* (below, **Something . . . men**), and possibly included such growths as fibroids.

shapeless and lifeless Galen (10. 987 K) said *myle* was the name for unformed flesh (cf. 2. 304 K, inactive, unformed flesh). Galen explained the mole as a pregnancy which had gone wrong. The Hippocratic treatise *On Women's Diseases* blamed the malformation on weak, sickly semen (whether male or female 'seed' (see above, **50. even scars**) is unclear) (8. 148 L). Aristotle's explanations suggest that the male's contribution to conception in such cases was insufficient or invalidated, resulting in something analogous to the infertile wind egg (*HA* 638[a]22). Intercourse (*GA* 775[b]25) occurred, but the formation of a foetus was hindered because it was insufficiently 'concocted' by the male's semen, like meat that had been undercooked; hence its hardness. The problem lay in an excess of menstrual blood (*GA* 776[a]10 ff.) and in this respect the mole was an extreme form of the monstrosities produced by insufficient mastery by the male semen over the female's generative material, which Aristotle describes in *GA* 769[b]11 ff. Pliny himself (*HN* 10. 184) rules out male involvement altogether: the mole is the result of a woman 'conceiving of herself alone'. Given the insufficiency or lack of the male input, the mole was not *zoon*, animal, but not *apsychon*, soulless, either (*HA* 638[a]24), since the female material possessed the nutritive soul which causes growth but not the sensitive soul necessary for animal life (*GA* 741^{a}18f.; 757^{b}16; cf. *HN* 10. 184). Later ages distinguished between the mole that was begotten by the woman alone (a 'false' mole), and that which had had an input of male semen which was, however, too weak or overpowered by menstrual blood (the 'true' mole): see P. Crawford, 'Attitudes to Menstruation in Seventeenth-Century England', *P&P* 91 (1981), 64 n. 103. Crawford also cites a tendency in this period to blame moles on intercourse during menstruation, regarded then as a taboo practice, whose negative consequences in the ensuing child were believed to range from freckles and birthmarks to leprosy and out-right monstrosity (Gélis (1991), 14–15, 58, 264: see below, **64. It . . . flow** and **66. Hence . . . blood**). Even in this later superstition there remains a trace of Aristotle's conjectures about the ill-effects of excess menstrual blood; its direct inspiration, however, may have come from the Judaic tradition in 2 Esdras 5: 8: 'menstruous women shall bear monsters'; a text popularly quoted at the time in the context of prodigies (see Park and Daston (1981), 25). According to another later folk-belief, recorded in parts of Europe (Saintyves (1937), 196–7), women could conceive by the moon and the result was the mole, which was also known in English as a 'moon-calf' (Brand (1842), iii. 73; the name appears in e.g. the late 17th-cent. midwifery manual by John Pechey: see Boucé (1987), 92). While this idea is not recorded in antiquity, it is in keeping with ancient beliefs about the moon's fertility (see above, **38. Only children . . . no moon**; **42. full moon . . . babies**). As time went on, moles became objects of superstition and bizarre beliefs, products of witchcraft which could run, fly, or attempt to re-enter the womb (Gélis (1991), 258–9).

resistant . . . knife   Cf. *GA* 775^{b}35. See above, **mole**, and **shapeless and lifeless.** The tumour is 'hard and stonelike' (Soranus 3. 9. 36, cf. Aristotle *GA* 775^{b}35, 776^{a}8). See above, **mole** and cf. the *lithopedion*, below, **In some . . . they do.**

It is mobile   Soranus suggests the name 'millstone' was given partly on account of its immobility and heaviness (3. 9. 36). A mole would be attached to some degree to the wall of the uterus, but the notion of mobility may simply refer to the fact that all or part of it could in some cases be spontaneously ejected from the womb (see below, **slips out . . . heavier than usual**). The idea that it could move may also have been encouraged by the ancient idea that the

womb itself was mobile and wandered about the body (Hipp. *Mul.*
8. 266. 11, 272. 9, 310. 6–7 L: see Dean-Jones (1994), 69–77; below,
175. female sex . . . turning of the womb; and cf. above, **43.
smell . . . abortion**); or, in cases where the growth was not in fact
a mole but fibroids, by the later growth of more, giving the impression that an earlier one had moved. One type of malignant invasive
mole (choriocarcinoma) can spread outside the uterus. The mole
was also immobile in the sense that it could not move about spontaneously, unlike a genuine foetus; a characteristic which might
lead to the molar pregnancy being distinguished from a true pregnancy after a few months (cf. e.g. the comments made in a 17th-
cent. midwives' manual by Marguerite De La Marche discussed in
Boucé (1987), 86).

blocks the monthly flow . . . foetus   See above, **shapeless
and lifeless.** With hydatidiform/carneous moles, all the physical
features of pregnancy occurred: cessation of menses, swelling of
abdomen and breasts, sickness and later stabbing pains (Soranus 3.
9. 36, cf. Aristotle, *GA* 775^{b}25–30, *HA* 638^{a}10–17) but no birth.

In some . . . they do.   Aristotle (*HA* 638^{a}35; *GA* 775^{b}34) suggests
the condition is chronic and can last until death, rather than
actually causing death, cf. Soranus 3. 9. 39. The distinction is probably between the malignant tumours which kill, and benign forms
of tumour. Since Pliny goes on to mention tumours of the stomach
in men which are analogous to moles in women, he or his source
may also have been aware of rare cases where an extrauterine pregnancy is discovered after death to have been retained in the
abdominal cavity for many years to form a *lithopedion* or calcified
foetus. See A. Mattieu, 'Lithopedion developed from Extrauterine
Gestation in Intrauterine and Extrauterine Pregnancy', *Am. J.
Obstet. Gyn.* 37 (1939), 297–302; I. E. Moore (1992), 185; and cf.
Ambroise Paré's *enfant pétrifié*, discovered in the body of a 68-year-
old woman from Sens (Paré 91973), xi. 8–15, pp. 42–3).

slips out . . . heavier than usual   Aristotle (*GA* 775^{b}31, *HA*
638^{a}15 ff.) relates a case-history of a woman who, after being 'pregnant' for three or four years, had a bad attack of dysentery and gave
birth to a mole. Soranus (3. 9. 39), perhaps describing the evacuation of the dead or diseased tissue of a missed abortion, says treatment can result in a sudden discharge of a large amount of clotted
and blackened blood which removes the disease.

Something . . . men   The *scirrhus* was a hard, normally painless tumour (*Thes. Ling. Graec.* s.v. *skiros*, 401–2) and the word is still used today to describe a hard, stone-like growth. Ps.-Galen (*Med. Def.* 19. 442 K, cf. 10. 962 K) describes it as hard, heavy, and with a low degree of mobility and sensibility. Pliny is clearly right to draw analogies with the mole on these grounds. Just as the mole arose from a misconcoction of the generative fluids in the womb, the *scirrhus* and the similar *scleroma* (see above, **mole**) arose from corrupted humours: black bile in the case of the *scirrhus*, which occurred particularly in the liver and spleen, organs associated with such bile, and diseased phlegm in the case of the uterine *scleroma*. However, the *scirrhus* was not simply the male's equivalent of a mole: it could sometimes affect women as well, being found, like the mole, in the womb (*Med. Def.* 19. 430 K), as well as in the spleen and liver (*Med. Def.* 19. 430 K): see above, **mole**. It is true that some cancers of the abdominal cavity, such as stomach cancer, are more prevalent in men than in women.

Oppius Capito   He may have been the propraetor in charge of Antony's fleet in 37–35 BC; Münzer, *RE* 18. 1, Oppius (24), (25), 742–7.

64. It . . . bizarre . . . menstrual flow   In **64–6** and again in *HN* 28. 77–86, P. provides the earliest and fullest account in ancient literature of the extraordinary and dangerous powers attributed to menstrual fluid. Like his description of the peoples at the edges of the earth (above, **9–32**), it became a *locus classicus* for later writers. H. Von Staden ('Women and Dirt', *Helios*, 19 (1992), 7–30) has argued that Hippocratic references to women are suggestive of a particular need to purify them. Yet, rather strikingly, there seems to be comparatively little evidence in classical sources pre-dating Pliny of the tensions concerning menstruation which are common to many other ages and cultures. In particular, there are few indications of the widespread taboo against sexual intercourse during menstruation. Rather, some references in the Hippocratic medical texts and Aristotle seem to advocate coitus during menstruation as being conducive to conception (see below, **67. easiest . . . finishing**). See Parker (1983), 102–3; Dean-Jones (1994), 225–53, esp. 234–6. Even Pliny repeats one Greek author's opinion that intercourse with a menstruating woman was a cure for quartan fever

(*HN* 28. 83: see below, **170. puberty ... women**). And although there were similarities between the symptoms attributed by Pliny and his sources to children born of mothers who continue to menstruate during pregnancy and those which, in later times, were attributed to children allegedly conceived during menstruation, these were purely physical. There is no hint in the former of the negative ideology intrinsic to the latter: see below, **66. Hence ... blood**. He does at one point specifically condemn intercourse during menstruation as being dangerous to the male partner, but only at certain times in the lunar cycle (28. 77, see below **66. This amazingly ... occurs at all**).

However, Pliny's overall tone is one of alarm and anxiety about menstruation generally and he stresses its power—*vis*—throughout the passage. It has been suggested that Pliny's comments here reflect the beginnings of a cultural concern, a growing reaction to the increasing autonomy of women from the Hellenistic period onwards (Dean-Jones (1994), 248–50). Certainly, surviving textual parallels to Pliny's comments in **64–6** and in 28. 77–86 are no earlier than Ps.-Aristotle (see below, **mirrors ... reflection**) and tend to be contemporary with or later than Pliny himself (see e.g. below, **crops ... shrivel**). We cannot, however, rule out the possibility of an earlier, lost, literature on the subject. In the parallel discussion to the one under consideration, *HN* 28. 77–84, a number of Greek sources are named. Unfortunately, only one, Metrodorus of Scepsis, is datable, and he takes us back no further than the 1st cent. BC. It is possible that Pliny was tapping in to the medico-magical subculture of folk beliefs which he describes so vividly in book 25 and which, he complains, is for the most part without a literature. The obscurity of the writers might be symptomatic of this neglect, and the fact that they include several women, including one, Sotira, specifically identified as a midwife, might suggest individuals motivated by first-hand experience at a basic level in society. At the very least, we cannot say for certain that the notion of menstrual blood as dangerous was relatively new.

Given his comparative lack of antecedents, Pliny's sensational tone is all the more striking. He uses the epithet *monstrificum*, 'bizarre', of menstrual fluid **64**, and this is elaborated in **65** (*virus*, 'poison') and **66** (*malum*, 'evil'); and again in *HN* 28. 77 (*dira ac foedera*, 'terrible and unspeakable'). The vehemence with which his sentiments are expressed raises the question of (i) the possible reasons for believing the substance was so potent and (linked to this) (ii) the nature or the manifestations of that potency.

(i) Menstrual blood may have been particularly alarming for a number of reasons:

(*a*) Bleeding of any sort was alarming but especially involuntary bleeding with no external cause (W. B. McDaniel, 'The Medical and Magical Significance in Ancient Medicine of Things Connected with Reproduction and its Organs', *JHM* iii (1948 = 1948*b*), 525–46, esp. 531).

(*b*) It was linked to the womb, itself, according to an old belief (Plato *Tim.* 91c: see above, **63. It is mobile**), inclined to wander around the body, beyond the woman's own control. This lack of control on two counts suggested a mysterious super-human potency which made the idea of its manipulation and control attractive to magicians; much magic was connected with the uterus and its effluent (J.-J. Aubert, 'Threatened Wombs: Aspects of Ancient Uterine Magic', *GRBS* 30. 3 (1989), 423–5).

(*c*) Its potency was enhanced because it was believed to be the material from which a new human being was formed (see below, **66. this substance**). However, its life-giving potential had been thwarted. Plutarch (*Mor.* 651c–e) described it as corrupt, diseased, and cold, which may explain why its potency was now directed towards the termination rather than the enhancement of life (see below, (ii) and **crops . . . shrivel**).

(*d*) As purged matter, it was regarded as impure (Parker (1983), 101–3; von Staden (1992), 14 ff.) and polluted or polluting matter often had powerful magical attributes.

(ii) The alarming and polluting nature of the fluid ensured that its effects were primarily negative. It was a destructive force, killing living things, corroding and clouding inanimate material, and causing madness and corruption; examples occur in other sources, e.g. Ps.-Aristotle, *On Dreams* 459[b]–460[a]; Columella, *RR* 10. 357–63; Plutarch, *Mor.* 700e and the 10th-cent. AD *Geoponica*, besides P. However, like other pollutants, it can also be beneficial. It can, for example, cure by a process of homoeopathy (Gil (1969), 84: it causes and cures hydrophobia). It can also cure by a process of transference (Gils, 83, 84, 167: drawing fevers out of the sufferer, cf. Priscianus p. 251. 1–5 Rose). The fact that it was avoided in the normal course of events was enough to endow it with considerable potency in special situations, whether ritual or medical. Parker (1983: 233) quotes Theodorus Priscianus (*Physica* p. 151. 2–5), who says that Democritus explicitly calls for a pollutant, such as menstrual blood, to treat fever. Appropriately, it drew off warts, boils, gout, eye-fluxes, and, once again, fevers (*HN* 28. 82–4), humour-induced complaints which, like itself, exhibited a lunar periodicity (see above, **42. full moon . . . babies** and below, **66. This amazingly . . . occurs at all**). By drawing other pollutants to itself, the pollutant acts as a cleanser: see below, **65. since it sticks . . . tainted**. It therefore possesses a power that is transferable in a bad sense (*contagio*) but also in a good sense (*contactus*); cf. H. Wagenwoort, *Roman Dynamism* (Oxford, 1947), Gil (1969), 153 f.

Boosted by the menstrual taboos in the Judaic tradition (cf. Thompson C 140–6. 1), belief in the powers of menstrual fluid continued through the Christian era: the 15th-cent. *Malleus Maleficarum*, which set out procedures for identifying witches, repeated Pliny's claims about the powers of menstruating women. Some medieval churchmen refused communion to a menstruant. Even into the 20th cent., menstrual blood was believed to madden and kill animals and, in order to prevent the corruption of food and wine, menstruating women would refrain from salting meat or butter or entering the larder or cellar, as they had refrained for centuries previously. Ancient belief in the power of menstruation to calm storms (*HN* 28. 77; Plutarch, *Mor.* 700f: cf. below, **66. This amazingly . . . occurs at all**) has persisted into recent times; as has its alleged ability to affect the hair (treatments, such as perms, have been avoided). See Crawford (1981), esp. 61; Gélis (1991), 13; Thomas (1971), 43, Verdier (1979), 19–23, 27, 36–7, 64. Because of its connection with fertility, menstrual blood was also popular in recipes for contraceptives and aphrodisiacs (McDaniel (1948*b*), 534–5, on modern Italy). For the many remedies in the *HN* aimed at the control of menstruation and treatment of its irregularities, see Vons (2000), 147–52.

turns new wine sour   See above, **It . . . bizarre . . . menstrual flow** (ii).

crops . . . grafts . . . shrivel   Menstrual effluent was itself a blighted life-force, deprived of its creative potential (above, **64. It . . . flow** (i)(*c*): a touch from a menstruating woman would kill rue and a mere glance shrivel young plants (Columella 11. 3. 38, 3. 50; cf. *HN* 28. 79). But its propensity to kill could also work to the farmer's advantage; it was an effective insecticide against dangerous cantharid beetle or Spanish Fly and much else (*HN* 28. 78; cf. Columella 7. 5. 17, 10. 357–68; Aelian, *NA* 6. 36).

fruit falls . . . growing There were spells to counter the problem of premature fruit fall, cf. Aubert (1989), 438, quoting from the *Geoponica*. The effect of the menstrual blood here is analogous to its attested reputation as an abortifacient (e.g. *HN* 28. 80–1).

mirrors . . . reflection The idea that the glance of a menstruating woman will cloud the mirror into which she gazes is found in Ps.-Aristotle, *On Dreams* 459^b–460^a, probably a Hellenistic gloss on Aristotle's text (for arguments, see Dean-Jones (1994), 229–30), and is repeated in *HN* 28. 82. Menstrual blood reached the eyes through the interconnecting passageways of the female body, on which theory see below, **67. it is a sure sign . . . saliva.** That menstrual blood reached the head through this internal network may offer an analogy as to why diseased effluent from teeth had a similar effect on a mirror: see below, **71. This . . . auguries.** According to *HN* 28. 82, brightness can be restored if the woman looks at the back of the mirror, an idea attributed by Pliny to the otherwise unknown Bithus of Dyrrhachium. See also below, **smell . . . bronze.**

knife blades blunted Cf. *HN* 28. 79.

hives of bees die In *HN* 28. 79 they are said merely to fly away if their hives are touched, but cf. the lethal effect on insects, above, **crops . . . shrivel.**

bronze and iron . . . corroded Cf. *HN* 28. 79 and see below, **smell . . . bronze.**

smell . . . bronze The reading *aes*, 'bronze' is preferable here to *aera*, 'air', given P.'s reference to bronze acquiring an unpleasant smell from contact with menstrual blood in *HN* 28. 79. The particular sensitivity to the presence of menstrual blood which Pliny attributes to both metals and mirrors may be connected to the common observation that many metals appeared to react in the presence of various kinds of moisture. The rusting mentioned by Pliny in the previous sentence is the most commonplace instance of such reaction to moisture. Mirrors were made of bronze or, more frequently in Pliny's time, of silver, according to his own assertion in *HN* 33. 129–30. These were the metals frequently employed in the manufacture of tableware (*HN* 34. 7, 14), the 'dishes' Pliny mentions as leaving smudges on sideboards (themselves often inlaid with bronze or silver: *HN* 33. 139–40; 145–6) in the humid conditions which preceded a storm (*HN* 18. 365), a phenomenon also noted in later eras: Brand (1842), iii. 88. Human breath and urine, as well as mineral spring water and salt sea breezes tarnished silver (*HN* 33. 137; 158). In *HN* 34. 146, Pliny mentions that human blood makes iron more prone than usual to rust. No doubt such an effect would be magnified in the case of potent menstrual fluid, effluent of the moisture-laden female body. A later, 16th-cent., source makes a further connection between metallic reaction and the fertility of the humid female: a needle placed in a bowl of a woman's urine overnight would be marked by reddish spots next morning if she were pregnant (Forbes (1966), 42). Probably as a result of their observable reactions to moisture, many metals and their by-products were regarded medicinally as astringents, used to draw out moisture in wounds, ulcers, and skin eruptions, to stem haemorrhaging and cure all kinds of eye fluxes (*HN* 25. 42; 33. 84, 92, 102, 105, 109, 127, 163; 34. 105, 118, 122, 126, 169–72). All these complaints were among those exacerbated by the moisture-bearing moon (see above, **42. full moon . . . babies**), as were intestinal worms, which could be killed by one of these metallic remedies (*HN* 34. 126). It is as an antidote to one of the effects of lunar humidity, the putrefaction of meat (see above, **42. full moon . . . babies**) that Plutarch advocates driving a bronze nail into the joint (*Mor.* 659c–d), citing the astringent properties of bronze and copper. He surmises that the nail draws the moisture to itself, citing the staining found in its immediate vicinity. The same line of reasoning could have been used to explain tarnishing and rusting generally. However, it is particularly apt in the case of the mirror clouded by the menstruant's gaze, since, like moonlight, menstrual blood was believed to curdle and putrefy food: see above, **64. It . . . menstrual flow** (ii).

Dogs go mad . . . poison Those bitten can be cured homeopathically by the same substance, through 'Sympathy' (*HN* 28. 84, cf. 82). See above, **64. It . . . bizarre . . . menstrual flow** (ii).

65. bitumen See below, **since it sticks . . . tainted.** For the natural phenomenon and the alleged effect of menstrual blood, see Tac. *Hist.* 5. 6. 9, cf. *HN* 28. 80.

Judaean lake called Asphaltites   The 'lake of bitumen' or the Dead Sea.

since it sticks . . . tainted.   Von Staden (1992: 18 and nn.), commenting on the use of polluting/dangerous substances in the medicinal or ritual purification of other polluting/dangerous substances, cites references in the Hippocratic Corpus to the use of bitumen as a medicinal purifier for women, although it smells bad and is dangerous. The case of the cantharid beetle is analogous; the latter is killed by menstrual fluid (above, **crops . . . grafts . . . shrivel**) but can also be used as a purifying pessary (von Staden 9–10).

66. This amazingly . . . occurs at all.   That menstruation occurred at monthly intervals was commonly accepted in antiquity, cf. Aristotle, *GA* 777^{b}17–30; Soranus 1. 21 ('It occurs monthly, not with precision in all cases, but broadly speaking, for sometimes it is advanced or retarded a few days' (trans. Temkin).

Many writers believed that the female cycle was synchronized with and controlled by the lunar cycle. Aristotle and others thought that menstruation coincided with the waning of the moon, the coldest part of the month, an idea widespread enough to cause Aristotle to quote a popular saying that the moon was female because its waning and women's menstruation occurred together (*HA* 582^{a}35–^{b}2; and note an Indian belief that the waning moon was undergoing a menstrual period, Thompson A 755. 7). However, Soranus (1. 21) rejected this and not all the Hippocratic writers appear to accept it: the author of *On the Eighth-Month Child* implies that menstruation began at the new moon (13, 7. 458–60 L: see above, **38. seventh . . . eleventh month**). A tendency to synchronicity in menstruation among women living sequestered lives at close quarters, as might have happened in some Greek households, may have encouraged such views: see Dean-Jones (1994), 97–9. Modern surveys do suggest that some correlations with the lunar cycle can occur (for references, see above, **38. Only children conceived . . . no moon**). Pliny does not connect menstruation with a particular phase of the moon, but claims that the effluent is more powerful and dangerous if it takes place either when there is no moon, or when there is an eclipse (*HN* 28. 77). This serves to emphasize the close connection between lunar and menstrual cycles, to the point of suggesting that there is something unnatural and therefore dangerous about a flow which occurs even when the regulatory moon is hidden. It is also significant that this is the only passage in the *HN* where intercourse at the time of menstruation is viewed negatively: see above, **64. It . . . menstrual flow**. It is the coincidence of menstruation with these particular lunar phases and not menstruation on its own (see above, **64. It . . . menstrual flow** (ii)), which constitutes a danger of 'disease and death towards the man', when he attempts intercourse.

A general link between the lunar and menstrual cycles can be discerned in other ancient beliefs about the powers of menstrual blood and those of the moon. Changes in the lunar cycle were associated with weather changes, and exposure of a menstruating woman to the unruly elements was supposed to calm the storm (*HN* 28. 77; see above, **64. It . . . menstrual flow**). Skin problems, fevers, and gout, complaints which were believed to exhibit some lunar periodicity in their development, crises, and subsidence (above, **42. full moon . . . babies**), were all treatable with menstrual blood (*HN* 28. 82–3, cf. above, **64. It . . . menstrual flow**). See Saintyves (1913), 13–16; and, on modern studies suggesting a lunar rhythm in malarial attacks, Endres and Schad (2002), 217. For intercourse with a menstruant as a fever cure (*HN* 28. 84) see above, **64. It . . . menstrual flow**: cf. below, **170. puberty . . . women**; **169. The rest . . . quartan fevers**. Just as menstrual blood can sometimes kill shoots and wither blossom and fruit, so too can the dews cast to earth by the moon at certain times of the year when she is particularly cold (full moon in summer, no moon in winter: *HN* 18. 275–7; 278–9). Compare modern beliefs e.g. in some parts of rural France, where the lunar cycle of late April to May is particularly feared for this reason and even marriages are avoided in case they, too, produce the blighted fruit associated with unions during menstruation: see Verdier (1979), 63–73. Lunais suggests that belief in 'la lune rousse' was prevalent in Roman times, citing *HN* 18. 286, on the dangers of a full moon between 25 and 28 April, and the concentration of agricultural festivals to counteract dangers to the crops in the second half of April (Lunais (1979), 65–7). The Romans, too, avoided May for weddings (Ovid, *Fasti* 5. 487–90; Plutarch, *RQ* 86), but there is no indication that this was due to a lunar/climatic threat to fertility.

P.'s statement that the flow is more copious every three months may be connected with the puzzling sentence in an early Aristotelian work (*HA* 582ᵇ3–4) where the majority of women are said to menstruate 'every third month': see Dean-Jones (1994), 96 n. for a discussion of this phrase.

this substance . . . binding agent   That the menstrual fluid played a vital role in reproduction was a general belief in ancient medical writings. Some, like Aristotle, saw it as the matter to which the male semen brought form, producing a foetus. This was then nourished by the rest of the menses, which was less pure than the menses 'set' by the semen (*GA* 728ᵃ26–31) cf. *GA* 729ᵃ; 739ᵇ25; 776ᵃ25–31: the semen acts like rennet on the menstrual fluid. See Needham (1959) 42–3; the semen-blood theory continued in the Hellenistic writers and Galen (Needham (1959), 73), the rennet analogy being repeated by e.g. Clement of Alexandria, and was in circulation as late as the 17th and 18th cents. (Needham (1959), 150, 170). This seems to be the theory P. adopts here. Others, however, including Empedocles, Anaxagoras, and some of the Hippocratic writers, believed that both men and women produced seed to create a foetus, and the menstrual fluid provided only the means of nourishment for its development. See Dean-Jones (1994), 148–53, 184–93, 206–8.

mass . . . life and body.   Theories about the development of the human embryo and the question of prenatal life occupied philosophy from the Presocratics onwards. Some considered that the embryo was fully formed in miniature from the start. Others, including Aristotle, argued that different parts grew at different stages (*GA* 734ᵃ⁻ᵇ), with varying estimates of the time of full articulation (e.g. 30 days for a male and 42 for a female: Hipp. *Nat. Puer* 18, 7. 500. 1–2 L), or 40 and 90 days respectively (Aristotle, *HA* 583ᵇ3–7): for the sex differentiation, see above, **41. Women carrying a boy . . . ninetieth day**. Whether the foetus was in any sense and at any stage alive before birth was also a matter of controversy. There are hints of conflicting theories in the Presocratics (Needham (1959), 27–31). Aristotle believed that a development in the nature and sophistication of the foetus' soul mirrored its bodily formation, nutritive ('plant') soul existing even in the unfertilized material of the embryo, with sensitive ('animal') soul developing as the body was articulated (*GA* 736ᵃ33–736ᵇ); a similar position being adopted later by Galen (*On the Formation of the Foetus*, 4. 543 and 667 K; cf. 15. 403 and 19. 329 K). Others considered it to be inanimate or, as did the Stoics, in possession of only a nutritive soul before birth, becoming animate only when it started to breathe (*SVF* ii. 756, cf. 757, 804–8). P.'s wording here is vague but suggests an Aristotelian source cf. above, **this substance . . . binding agent**. Moral, social, and, in the Christian era, religious considerations further complicated the issue. In Roman law, the foetus was not an animate entity independent of the mother, though an unborn child had to be removed from a dead mother (see above, **47. Those delivered when their mother has been cut open**) and the foetus' *potential* for life is recognizable in the phrase *spes animantis*, which may have fostered some doubts about abortion, though these were mainly influenced by social and moral considerations (parental rights, general propriety), rather than by the question of foetal life (for refs., see Beagon (1992), 217–18 on *HN* 25. 24). It was the Christian emphasis on the soul which brought about a prohibition on abortion on the grounds of foetal life, though estimates as to when soul was attained varied: from conception according to Tertullian, but in the second month according to Augustine, and, following him, Canon law, which forbade abortion after 40 days. See Needham (1959), 27–76; *OCD*[3], abortion (1); embryology (552–3).

Hence . . . blood P.'s 'hence' (*ergo*) suggests this is a result of the menstrual fluid's expulsion as a corrupt effluent rather than being retained to perform its proper function in pregnancy of forming and nourishing the unborn child (see above, **this substance**). Aristotle, *HA* 582[b] says such children will be inferior and sickly but does not add Nigidius' (see below) *saniosus*, 'full of/covered with bloody matter' (fr. 110, Swoboda). The latter characteristic was presumably due to contact with this effluent. In the 17th cent., some children's disorders were attributed to contact with corrupt menstrual blood while in the womb (Crawford (1981), 52 and n.). There are superficial similarities here with the afflictions attributed in later ages to children conceived during menstruation, the unfortunate products of 'unions in blood', who, as well as being small and sickly, might incur skin complaints, disease, monstrosity (see above, **63. shapeless and lifeless**), and even a figurative 'bloodiness', red hair: see Gélis (1991), 14–15; Verdier (1979), 46–9; Boucé (1987),

92–3. However, the rationale is very different. Although both sets of disadvantages are to some degree the result of physical contact between unborn child and menstrual blood, the weaknesses attributed by ancient writers to the children of mothers who continue to menstruate in pregnancy are a result of the physical hitch in the natural process of gestation, not punishment for the breaking of a moral prohibition: see above, **64. It . . . bizarre . . . menstrual flow** (ii). The connection between bleeding in pregnancy and sickly or stillborn offspring may also have been encouraged by observation of the effects of antepartum haemorrhage, in which bleeding occurs after the twenty-eighth week of pregnancy, normally because of a problem with the placenta. The unborn child is at risk from lack of oxygen or from prematurity if the bleeding triggers labour.

Nigidius   P. Nigidius Figulus (d. 45 BC) was a friend of Cicero and supporter of Pompey. His rather obscure scholarly interests included Pythagoreanism, magic, and natural science. He occurs frequently in the *HN* indices (fr. 110–11 Swoboda). See *OCD*[3], Nigidius, 735; Kroll, *RE* 17. 1, Nigidius (3), 200–12; E. Rawson, *Intellectual Life in the Late Roman Republic* (London, 1985), 291–2 and index; A. Momigliano, *On Pagans, Jews and Christians* (Connecticut, 1987), 60–1; M. Dickie, 'The Learned Magician', in D. R. Jordan, H. Montgomery, and E. Thomassen (eds.), *The World of Ancient Magic* (Bergen, 1999), 168–72. See also below, **178. Sextus Pompey**.

67. The same author . . . man   Fr. 111 Swoboda. Some editors place this sentence in parentheses, but there is more connection between this remark and the previous statements on menstrual bleeding than is immediately apparent. Aristotle (*GA* 739ᵇ25) said that milk and menstrual blood were essentially the same secretion, used first as blood to fashion the embryo (cf. above, **66. this substance**) and then concocted into the form of milk to feed the infant (*GA* 776ᵃ15–777ᵃ22). The belief seems to have become fairly common: a speech of Favorinus of Arles (2nd cent. AD), reported by Aulus Gellius (*NA* 12. 1. 13), appears to accept it. Hence there is no menstruation while breast-feeding and if the woman does conceive, the milk dries up, because nature can't produce enough secretion to supply both the formative needs of the foetus and the nutritive ones of the newly born infant (*GA* 777ᵃ15–20). It is in fact

true that women occasionally become pregnant again while nursing; it is also true that the restarting of menstruation can lead to less-
ening of the milk supply. It may therefore be that the incorrect
statement in the ancient sources that the milk dries up when the
woman becomes pregnant again is a confusion derived from these
two observations. Galen (*San. Tu.* 1. 9, 6. 54 K), believed that intercourse stimulated the restarting of the menses which soured the
milk; cf. *HN* 28. 123: conception while nursing turns the milk thick
like cheese (but the text is confused, cf. C. P. E. Jones in the Loeb
edn., vol. 8, pp. 86–7; J. Ernout, *Pline L'Ancien Histoire Naturelle livre
28* (Paris 1962), 63). Nigidius' idea that pregnancy *by the same man as
before* will somehow not affect the milk in fact goes some way
towards the truth that renewed pregnancy will not affect the milk
supply, and may ultimately have derived from actual observations
in the case of married couples.

easiest . . . finishing Aristotle (*GA* 739ᵃ26) says that the menstrual fluid must be present (cf. its role in forming the foetus, above,
66. this substance . . . binding agent). This did not in itself indicate a particular point in the cycle since he believed that the blood
flowed into the uterus throughout the month. However, he also
says that what was left after menstruation was the right amount for
the foetus to start its formation (*GA* 727ᵇ12–18). The Hippocratic
writers, who thought that menstrual blood played no part in conception, also advocated intercourse just after menstruation, when
the womb and the passages of the body through which the female
seed (above, **50. even scars**, **66. this substance . . . binding
agent**) must travel, were empty of blood: see Dean-Jones (1994),
62–4. In *HA* 582ᵇ11 ff., Aristotle says that normally conception took
place after the period had ended, although some might conceive
during the evacuation, providing that the flow was not so strong as
to wash the semen away (cf. *GA* 727ᵇ). Ovulation is in fact most
likely to occur a few days after menstruation. Conception while still
menstruating may be a possibility encouraged in part by Aristotle's
confusion of the human menstrual cycle with the oestrous cycle of
other mammals (Aristotle, *HA* 572ᵇ31–3), where a female 'on heat'
bleeds: see Dean-Jones, 186–7 and above, **63. Woman . . .
periods**.

it is a sure sign . . . saliva Cf. Aristotle, *GA* 747ᵃ. This test is
based on two important assumptions in ancient medical theory: the

significance of the condition of body fluids; and the belief that the female body housed an interconnecting network of passages through which they travelled. The importance attached in ancient medical theory to a connection between bodily fluids and the condition of the various parts of the body goes back to the Hippocratic writings, e.g. *On the Nature of Man*, where health depended on the relative balance of the four humours, black bile, yellow bile, blood, and phlegm. Many types of bodily secretion were believed to offer clues as to the body's physical health: the colour of urine, for example, reflected morbid conditions in various other parts of the body (*HN* 28. 68–9). The bodily fluids of women were particularly significant, since the Hippocratics had regarded the female body as softer, more porous, and moister than the male, with a more complex network of channels through which the body fluids flowed and which were progressively opened through menstruation and childbirth (*Diseases of Women* 1. 1, 8. 10–12 L; *Glands* 16, 8. 572 L). Menstrual blood was supposed to be unused nourishment which was soaked up from the stomach and passed on to the womb. The Hippocratic writers imply that a passage, or interconnecting passages, linked the mouth and nose, and according to some the eyes and ears as well, to the vagina, so that the smell of a pessary inserted into the vagina would be smelt on the breath, provided that the passageways were not blocked (e.g. 7. 412–14; 8. 322, 424, 488–90 L). The test is also found in Egyptian sources as early as 2000 BC (Forbes (1966), 43). If the required result is not forthcoming, the passages have become blocked and the woman will not be able to conceive. See Dean-Jones (1994), 72–3; ead., 'The Cultural Construct of the Female Body in Classical Greek Science', in S. B. Pomeroy (ed.), *Women's History and Ancient History* (Chapel Hill, NC, 1991), 124–5; A. E. Hanson, 'Continuity and Change: Three Studies in Hippocratic Gynecological Therapy and Theory', in Pomeroy (1991), 85–6; ead., 'Conception, Gestation and the Origin of Female Nature in the *Corpus Hippocraticum*', *Helios*, 19 (1992), 39–40; H. King, 'The Daughter of Leonides: Reading the Hippocratic Corpus', in A. Cameron (ed.), *History as Text* (London, 1989), 22–4; ead., 'Once upon a Text: Hysteria from Hippocrates', in S. L. Gilman, H. King, R. Porter, G. S. Rousseau, E. Showalter, *Hysteria beyond Freud* (California, 1993), 3–90. This use of pessaries later surfaces in English, German, and Italian texts of the 15th and 16th cents. (Forbes (1966), 44). Sometimes, it serves as a pregnancy test, since blockage of the pessary's smell could be caused by a foetus in the womb (see Gélis (1991), 47 on the use of garlic in 17th-cent. France). Fumigation via the vagina could aid conception, according to 15th-cent. Irish sources drawing on Dioscurides (Forbes (1966), 44–5), presumably by opening up the passageways. The same principle of a passageway linking the organs of the head to the womb and vagina seems to have been behind the practice recorded during the 14th to 16th cents., of holding open the mother's mouth and cervix while performing a Caesarean, so as to allow air to reach the foetus (Blumenfeld-Kosinski (1990), 26, 33). Holding open the mouth may even have been thought at one time to provide an alternative exit for the child; the maidservant who foiled Hera's plan to seal Alcmene's womb and prevent the birth of Heracles was transformed into a weasel—doomed to give birth through the mouth: see Belmont (1971), 24–6.

Pliny's fertility test on the eyes relies upon a similar notion of the female body as a network of interconnecting passageways and is mentioned in both the Hippocratic Corpus and Aristotle (GA 747^{a}10–15; cf. Hipp. $Nat. Mul.$ 99, 7. 416, 1–3 L). The transferral to the saliva of a substance placed in the eyes indicated that the passages were open and the male seed and female generative material could reach the womb and intermingle. That such a test should be centred on the head might seem surprising, but Aristotle explains that the seminal secretion from which, in women, the menstrual discharge was formed, was particularly attracted to the head, since the natures of the secretion and the brain were similar. According to him, the eyes were the most 'seminal' part of the head, as was shown by the fact that sexual intercourse affected their appearance (GA 747^{a}15–20). The Hippocratic Corpus mentions a changed appearance in the eyes of a pregnant woman, which appear sunken, with the whites discoloured ($Steril.$ 215, 8. 416. 8–11 L), a symptom which recurred in later eras, when signs of pregnancy were sought in the changed appearance of the eyes (Gélis (1991), 47). The sunkenness attributed to the the sexually over-indulgent and the pregnant would probably be due to the seminal/generative material being drawn away from the eyes towards the womb by the sexual act or by the foetus in need of nourishment respectively.

Besides the interconnection of the internal network through which the female humours flowed, the natures and qualities of the body fluids themselves were, to a certain degree, interchangeable.

Thus, menstrual fluid and milk were essentially the same secretion in Aristotle's physiology (above, **67. The same author . . . man**), milk being a further decoction of menstrual blood which was superfluous to the formation of the foetus (*GA* 777^{a}5–20).

Finally, specific connections between the eyes and various body fluids appear frequently in medical remedies: milk and saliva in particular were believed to be effective in the treatment of eye diseases (*HN* 28. 65–6, 72–6, 78, 82) as, indeed, was menstrual blood, *HN* 28. 82. Moreover, saliva, like menstrual blood (*HN* 28. 68–9), had potent medico-magical powers (*HN* 28. 35–9, 43, 65–9, 72–5, 77–86, cf. above, **15. snakes . . . saliva**), a potency no doubt enhanced when connected with the eyes, a powerful means of projecting magical influences, such as the Evil Eye (see above, **16. bewitch** and cf. **42. full moon . . . babies**). Ps.-Aristotle (*On Dreams* 459^b–460^a) combines magical with physiological ideas when he explains that a menstruating woman's glance clouds a mirror because the menstrual blood reaches the eyes and other parts of the body through the blood vessels (see above, **64. mirrors . . . reflection**). The Evil Eye, when emanating from a menstruating woman, was regarded as particularly dangerous in some cultures (cf. Dundes (1980), 120).

68. six months . . . others   Literally 'in the seventh month', 'in the seventh year', cf. Aristotle, *HA* 587^{b}15; Aulus Gellius, *NA* 3. 10. 12, citing Varro, and Censorinus *ND* 7. 4. The chronology is accurate, though Aristotle (and Pliny, *HN* 11. 166) wrongly suggest that man is unique in being born without teeth.

Some . . . teeth   According to Aristotle, this was 'against nature' because they had come before they were necessary for eating (*GA* 788^{b}10 ff.). Pliny's remarks suggest that, while unlucky in the case of a woman, it was not necessarily so for a man: for a possible rationale behind this, see below, **Such . . . period**. In any case, breaking the laws of nature can mark out a positively (e.g. lucky, good, heroic) as well as a negatively (unlucky, bad, villainous; cf. above **45. It is unnatural . . . feet first**), exceptional individual as the account of Caesarean births (above, **47. under better auspices**) suggests. Infants born with teeth appear later in popular history and folklore, e.g. Shakespeare's Richard III (*Henry VI*, pt. 3, v. 6. 43 ff., 74–7: negative); and a child of heroic size born in Dublin in 1488 (J. O'Donovan, *Annals of the Kingdom of Ireland*, iv (Dublin,

1856), 1163; cf. Thompson T 585. 5: positive/negative significance unclear). In modern Italy an infant, of either sex apparently, born with teeth was considered unlucky (McDaniel (1948*a*), 47–8), while more recent occurrences have been reported in the press (e.g. *Daily Telegraph*, 29 Dec. 1997: believed to be 'lucky', although the infant was female).

Dentatus M'. Curius Dentatus, cos. 290, 284 (suff.) 275 and 274 BC was a military hero of humble origins, whose bravery (Cic. *Rep.* 3. 6), incorruptibility and frugality (Valerius Maximus 4. 3. 5) became legendary. See *OCD*[3], Curius Dentatus, Manius, 414.

Cn. Papirius Carbo Tribune in 92 BC and colleague of Cinna (85 and 84 BC) and the younger Marius (82 BC) in the consulship, his campaign against Sulla ended with his capture and execution in Sicily by Pompey in 81 BC. See *OCD*[3], Papirius Carbo, Gnaeus, 1108.

68–9. Such . . . period For the ominous qualities of teeth, see below, **71. This . . . auguries**). Livy 41. 21. 12 records that a girl born with teeth at Auximum in 174 BC, at a time of plague, was regarded as an omen on a par with two male *monstra*, respectively two-headed and one-handed. Such precocity in a woman may have been seen as unnatural in a sinister sense (*a*) because of the belief (below, **71. women . . . fewer**) that women had fewer teeth than men anyway and (*b*) (probably linked to this), a feeling that it was dangerously unnatural for a woman rather than a man to be precociously armed with what were, in many animals (Aristotle, *HA* 538[b]), regarded as one of nature's weapons and which were normally present in the female of a species in less robust form, if they were present at all (*HN* 11. 162, 168).

69. Valeria . . . followed This strange story is found only in Pliny. The Valerian *gens* figured prominently in the semi-legendary history of the later regal period and the founding of the Republic, partly, though not entirely, owing to the efforts of their fellow clansman, the historian Valerius Antias. Recent scholarship argues that Münzer's claims (*De Gente Valeria*, diss., Opole, 1891) of exaggeration remain uncorroborated: other sources (Cic. *Pro Flacco* 25) suggest that the clan's reputation was established well before Antias wrote (S. Oakley, *Commentary on Livy VI–X* (Oxford, 1997), 91, 98–9; T. J. Cornell, 'The Formation of the Historical Tradition of Early

Rome', in I. S. Moxon, J. D. Smart, A. J. Woodman (eds.), *Past Perspectives* (Cambridge 1986), 77–8). Pliny's Valeria is beyond more specific identification, although both a sister and a daughter of the famous P. Valerius Poplicola (*OCD*[3], 1580), traditionally prominent in the downfall of the monarchy and the birth of the Republic, feature in other accounts of the period (Dion. Hal. 8. 39; Plutarch, *Coriol.* 33; *Popl.* 19, cf. *HN* 34. 29). As with other figures highlighted in the tradition of early Rome, the historicity of Poplicola and his relatives has been questioned. For E. Pais (*Ancient Legends of Roman History*, trans. M. E. Cosenza (London, 1906), 164), Pliny's Valeria and the sister and daughter of Poplicola all originated from an early female gentilician divinity. However, the historical narrative about the Valerii has a certain consistency, in that they share in common active roles in some versions of the struggles with Rome's rivals, in particular the Volsci (cf. Plutarch *Coriol.* 33). Coarelli connects Pliny's story with another tale strangely inserted into the Coriolanus episode, in which Valeria the daughter of Poplicola founds the temple of Fortuna Muliebris at the place on the Via Latina where Coriolanus, leading the Volsci against Rome, met his mother (Dion. Hal. 8. 39. 2; 55. 4). He also notes the sources' frequent naming of Valerii commanding armies against the Volsci in the 5th and 4th cents. BC, suggesting that the clan might have controlled lands bordering on the Pontine territory of the Volsci (F. Coarelli, 'Roma, i Volsci e il Lazio Antico', in *Crise et transformation des sociétés archaïques de l'Italie antique au V* siècle av. J.-C.*, Coll. Ec. Franc. Rome, 137 (Rome, 1990), 149–53). The link between the Valerii and this area, and the integration of Pliny's story into the Valerian tradition, are enhanced if, as many historians now believe, Suessa Pometia is to be identified with Satricum (see C. M. Stibbe, 'Satricum e Pometia: Due nomi per la stessa città?', *Mededelingen van het Nederlands Instituut te Rome*, 47 (1988), 7–16). Pometia, the town to which Valeria was dispatched, disappears from the historical record around the time that Satricum is first mentioned. Both were located north of the Pomptine marshes, their possession disputed between the Latins and Volsci. Pometia was sacked and destroyed in 495 BC by Rome (Livy 2. 25. 4), while Satricum was taken by the Volsci under Coriolanus in 488 BC (Livy 2. 39. 3). Archaeological evidence from Satricum suggests a large and prosperous place in the 7th and 6th cent., before its name is mentioned in the sources and the historical tradition concerning Pometia appears to match this evidence: see Stibbe (1988), 7–16. If the identification is accepted, then the *Lapis Satricanus*, an inscription probably of the late 6th cent., is significant for the historical contextualizing of Valeria and her *gens*. This dedication to a Poplios Valesios by his *sodales* could represent the commemoration by his companions of a powerful warlord; possibly even the famous Publius Valerius himself. (See H. S. Versnel, 'Historical Implications', in C. M. Stibbe, G. Colonna, C. de Simone and H. S. Versnel (eds.), *Lapis Satricanus; Archaeological, epigraphical, linguistic and historical aspects of the new inscription from Satricum* (Rome 1980), 95–150; T. J. Cornell, *The Beginnings of Rome* (London, 1995), 144–5; for other interpretations, e.g. J. A. K. E. de Waele, 'The Lapis Satricanus and the Chronology of the Temples of Mater Matuta at Satricum', *Ostraka*, 5 (1996), 231–42, contra, Versnel, 'IUN]IEI, A New Conjecture in the Satricum Inscription', *Mededelingen van het Nederlands Instituut te Rome*, 56 (1997), 177–200.) There can be no certainty, but the combination of a Valeria involved in the fall of Pometia, a Valerius commemorated in a disputed border town, and a tradition in which members of the clan struggle with the Volsci does suggest a basic historical coherence. There can be no certainty, either, concerning the disaster which followed Valeria's dispatch in Pliny's story. Pliny calls the town Pometia and may not have realized that it was the later Satricum: he puts both names in a list of vanished towns (*HN* 3. 68). A sack attributed to 'Pometia' should therefore be sought. Although Pometia was ravaged in 495 BC, Pliny's comment that the town was extremely prosperous might suggest that he was thinking of the earlier and more famous sack by Tarquin the Proud (Livy 1. 53. 1–3), when the rich spoils enabled the king to found the Capitoline temple (cf. also Tac. *Hist.* 3. 72). Pliny specifically states that the anecdote dated to the time of the kings, so it is not inconceivable that the removal of Valeria to Pometia was connected to the king's machinations against the city. The use of subterfuge appears in other stories about Tarquin and about the Capitoline temple. Sending false gifts or infiltrators to bring about the fall of an enemy city was a motif which went back to the tale of the Trojan horse. It was present in other tales of early Rome, including the siege of Veii (Livy 5. 15, 21. 8), but, in particular, the infiltration of Gabii by Tarquin through his son Sextus (itself modelled on earlier Greek stories from Herodotus, see Ogilvie on Livy 1. 53. 4–54. 10). The religious aspect of the story, whereby the dangerous prodigy is not only removed but transferred to an enemy, is reminiscent of another early story in Pliny and others (*HN* 28. 15–16) regarding the foundation of the Capitoline temple, in which an attempt was made to transfer a favourable sign from Rome to Etruria by trickery.

We do not know where Pliny found the Valeria story. It does not feature in the work of another member of the family, Valerius Maximus, whom P. may have used for several stories in book 7 (e.g. 7. 90; and cf. the naming of Valerius Maximus in the index to book 7); its provenance is probably in a source common to both writers, Varro (who may himself have got it from Antias, cf. Ogilvie (1965), 12–16, Münzer (1897), 114, 292 n. 2); or P. may have found it in M. Valerius Messala Rufus' work on families, which is also mentioned in his index for book 7. It could also have featured among the wonders collected by Licinius Mucianus (above Introd. 3. 1. 1, 3. 3, 4. 5. 1), which had included the Pomptine marsh with its twenty-four lost cities (*HN* 3. 59).

haruspices A group of Etruscan diviners who were called upon by Rome to interpret and propose remedies in connection with strange events, thunderbolts, and entrails. See *OCD*[3], 668. Mac-Bain (1982) has analysed patterns of haruspical activity: disposing of various types of *monstrum* is the most typical expiation recommended by these seers. Valeria is one of only two recorded disposals by deportation, both of which are ascribed to the *haruspices*.

[When females . . . proves.] The sudden break in the account of teeth has suggested that this passage has been displaced. However, as a dangerous female augury, it fits in with the Valeria story above. An imperforate vagina (cf. A. E. Garden, *Paediatric and Adolescent Gynaecology* (London, 1998), 52–4) is mentioned by Aristotle (*GA* 773[a]16, cf. *HA* 636[b], Celsus 7. 28) as a minor sexual deformity, remedied in some cases by spontaneous bursting of the membrane at first menstruation or by surgical intervention. It would obscure the woman's natural, childbearing, status, just as precocious teeth obscured her non-aggressive status. For Cornelia and her children, see above, **57. mother of the Gracchi**. The omen was fulfilled by the violent deaths of the Gracchi brothers according to Solinus 1. 67, two of only three surviving children out of twelve births; the other, Sempronia, was later suspected of poisoning the husband who opposed her brothers (Livy, *Per.* 59).

Some people . . . teeth A similar deformity was seen on a skull, one of several anomalous skeletons, from Plataea (Herod. 9. 83); and attributed to Pyrrhus of Epirus (Plutarch, *Pyrr.* 3. 4; Festus 148 M s.v. *monodos*: see **20. right toe . . . temple**, above). Pollux, *Onom.* 2. 94 and Tzetzes, *Chil.* 3. 956–67 offer other examples. This could be a reference to an hereditary condition, *amelogenesis imperfecta*, in which enamel formation is disturbed, giving the teeth an unusual surface (J. H. Scott and N. B. B. Symons, *Introduction to Dental Anatomy*[5] (Edinburgh and London, 1967), 171); a 'bone-like' appearance is emphasized by the ancient sources. However, Pliny's *continuus*, 'unbroken', is problematic. It is clear from the other references to Prusias' son's condition (see below, **Prusias of Bithynia**), and in particular from Plutarch's description of the identical condition of Pyrrhus (*Pyrr.* 3. 4), that the 'bone' was a single unbroken strip in which the separate teeth were not articulated; his jaw was 'one continuous bone on which the intervals between the teeth were indicated by a slight depression'. In *amelogenesis imperfecta*, the teeth normally remain differentiated. However, teeth can appear as double or connated teeth, joined together by their crowns and/or roots (J. V. Soames and J. C. Southam, *Oral Pathology*[3] (Oxford, 1998), 6–7). Abnormal masses of calcified dental tissue, which can result in grossly deformed teeth, are another possibility; though Valerius Maximus (1. 8, ext. 12) implies that Prusias' son's deformity (see below, **Prusias of Bithynia**) was not unsightly. For which reason, a hare-lip (König and Winkler, 182) is also highly unlikely. Plutarch's description of Pyrrhus' appearance is more ambiguous: he had the terror, rather than the majesty of kingship (Pyrr. 3. 6). For Pyrrhus' unusual powers and their possible link with this condition, see above **20. right toe . . . temple**.

Prusias of Bithynia The son (Habicht, *RE* 33. 1, Prusias (3), 1127) of Prusias II Cynegus (182–149 BC: *OCD*[3], Prusias (2), 1268), called Pausanias by Valerius Maximus (1. 8., ext. 12). For his deformity, see Livy, *Per.* 50; Festus 148 M s.v. *monodos*; Arrian *FGH* 156 F 29; Valerius Maximus 1. 8., ext. 12; and Solinus 1. 70.

70. indestructible . . . cremated. In fact, they simply take longer to burn than the other bones. Sir Thomas Browne in his *Hydriotaphia* (ch. III) later recalled ancient ideas concerning the accumulation of moisture in the head: 'the metropolis of humidity seems least disposed unto (fire), which might render the skulls of these urns less burned than other bones'; cf. above, **42. full moon . . . babies**; **67. It is a sure sign . . . saliva**. But he did not single out teeth as being particularly incombustible.

rotted by diseased phlegm   This seems to refer, not to external attack from oral fluid, but to the ancient humoral theory according to which the teeth were attacked from within by disease in one of the four bodily humours: cf. Hippocratic corpus, *Affections* (4, 6. 212. 18–24 L), where pain is caused by phlegm getting into the roots of the teeth. Galen posited an abnormal condition of the blood in which acrid corrosive humours attacked the tooth's internal structure. Thus, teeth were harmed from within, by a systemic malfunction of the body; an idea which continued into the 18th cent., as did another ancient and popular 'internal' theory, attack by worms. See A. W. Lufkin, *A History of Dentistry*[2] (London, 1948), 214, 221. However, a connection with external effects from food was suggested as early as the Hippocratic corpus. This was the closest ancient ideas got to the modern explanation of local external attack, first on the enamel and later on the dentine, by the acid from bacterial breakdown of sugars.

A certain drug . . . them   Elsewhere, Pliny is more specific. He (*HN* 28. 178–82, 29. 46, 30. 22) and other authorities such as Dioscurides (*MM* 2. 4, 2. 21, 5. 131, 166) and Marcellus (*De Med.* 13 Niederman) offer numerous preparations, mainly powders and pastes made with burnt and ground shell, bone, pumice, marble, and other minerals mixed with spices and honey for general cleaning, conditioning, and, in some cases, specifically 'whitening' the teeth (Marc. *De Med.* 13. 8, 10, 13, 20 Niederman), a process assisted by regular cleaning (Marc. *De Med.* 13. 8; cf. Ovid, *AA* 3. 216).

They are worn . . . happens.   Archaeological studies of skeletons have suggested that caries was less common than now, due to a lower amount of sucrose in a diet devoid of sugar and less abundant in sweet foods (K. Manchester and C. Roberts, *The Archaeology of Disease*[2] (Stroud, 1997), 48–50). However, a coarser diet, especially at poorer levels of society, would increase the incidence of severe wear (ibid. 52–4).

the front teeth . . . soften speech.   Cf. Arist. *PA* 661[b]13–15, and see above, **4. speak**.

71. This ... auguries. Besides this simple prognostic function, teeth, like other bodily excrescences (hair, nails), fluids, and waste products, had magical significance. Both animal and human teeth featured in popular medicine, but often as amulets rather than in drugs (*HN* 28. 41, 45, 258, 30. 21, 32. 137) Human teeth were particularly effective if the donor were a pre-pubertal child or died violently, a common stipulation in magical uses of other body parts (*HN* 28. 41, 42, 45), perhaps because the life-force left in them by one who died prematurely was more vital. They also contained 'a sort of poison' (*HN* 11. 170) which could kill young pigeons and cloud mirrors. Possibly this was simply an aspect of their magicality, but hair and nails, unlike some body fluids, are not mentioned as being inherently poisonous, so it was more probably a result of the theory that teeth could be attacked from within by diseased bodily humours (above, **70. rotted by diseased phlegm**). Body fluids generally had potent magical qualities. One of them, saliva (see above, **15. snakes . . . saliva**), was in constant external contact with the teeth, but the wording of 11. 170 suggests that the poison is more likely to be within the tooth, caused by diseased humour travelling through the body's internal passageways. Another notoriously powerful fluid, menstrual blood, could travel up to a woman's eyes and have precisely the same effect on a mirror when she looked at it (above, **64. mirrors . . . reflection**), and may provide an analogy for the effect of the diseased humours on the teeth. It is therefore unsurprising that the human bite was particularly dangerous (*HN* 28. 40) but could be cured by another body effluent (for the significance of these, see above, **67. it is a sure sign . . . her saliva**), earwax.

Turduli A tribe from Lusitania in southern Spain, cf. *HN* 3. 8, Varro 2. 10. 4, Livy 28. 39. 8. Racial differences in tooth formation and number can happen, especially in isolated, inbreeding communities (Scott and Symons (1967), 28).

Some . . . longevity Cf. *HN* 11. 274; Hipp. *Epid.* 2. 6. 1, 5. 132 L. According to Aristotle (*HA* 501^{b}22), men live longer than women as a result of their having more teeth (see below, **Women . . . fewer**). P., citing Mucianus, claims that the exceptionally old might grow a new set of teeth (*HN* 11. 167): as happened to a Samothracian aged 140. In fact, a new tooth may occasionally be grown quite late in life; cf. press reports (*Daily Telegraph*, 14 July 2000) of this occurring to a man in his 60s, and, in more recent correspondence on the same theme (ibid. 11 Nov. 2003), to a 98-year-old woman, this last being mentioned in conjunction with an 18th-cent. claim to a third set of teeth grown by a 107-year-old woman.

Women . . . fewer Falsely asserted by Aristotle, who connects this with a shorter female lifespan (see previous note); cf. *PA* 661^{b}34–6, where women are said to be less endowed with the parts needed for eating. Both deficiencies illustrate his theory of female inferiority: see above, **37. Girls . . . more quickly**. Arguments of natural necessity are also relevant, cf. *GA* 662^b on the discrepancies between male and female animals whose teeth are weapons: the human female's physique was smaller, both in terms of size of jaw and of food consumption. Empirical evidence might have appeared to back Aristotle's theory; see Dean-Jones (1994), 82 n. 136, (cf. 1991: 126–7 n. 76), suggesting more frequent female dental loss due to inferior diet and calcium deficiency in pregnancy. That he might have been comparing young wives whose wisdom teeth had not yet appeared with their older husbands (Dean-Jones 1994) seems unlikely: he is clearly aware of the delayed emergence of wisdom teeth, since in the same passage, *HA* 501^{b}25, he cites examples of their appearance even in extreme old age, which Pliny repeats in *HN* 11. 166.

those who have . . . opposite The information on the younger Agrippina may have come from her memoirs (above, **46. Agrippina . . . memoirs**), where its positive significance was presumably used to support her dynastic ambitions. The canines or eye teeth are normally four in number and are situated third from the middle on either side in both the upper and lower jaw. Although the upper incisor area is a common site for supernumerary teeth, duplication of the canines is rarer (Scott and Symons (1967), 11, 362). Canines may have had extra superstitious significance due to their intermediate position as boundary markers between the front biting teeth and the back grinding teeth (Arist. *HA* 501^{b}16ff.) and their possession of the characteristics of both these types (*PA* 661^{b}10f.). They are sometimes specified as amulets (*HN* 11. 166; 28. 45) or remedies (*HN* 30. 21).

72. [Among . . . through.] This sentence was thought by

Mayhoff to have been displaced from the end of secton **69**. Juvenal (*Sat.* 14. 140) speaks of an infant 'too small for the funeral pyre'. Cremation of infants in classical antiquity seems to have been very rare: see R. Garland, *The Greek Way of Death*[2] (Bristol, 2001), 78–80. If it was thought that teeth alone did not burn (above, **70. indestructible . . . cremated**), avoidance of infant cremation may possibly have stemmed from a belief that too little would be recovered for a proper interment of the ashes: see J.-P. Néraudau, 'La Loi, la coutume et le chagrin: Réflexions sur la mort des enfants', in F. Hinard (ed.), *La Mort, les morts et l'au-delà* (Caen, 1987), 196. More generally, possession of teeth in a child may have been seen as marking its progress towards a fuller place in society. The younger the child, the less elaborate was the ritual surrounding its death, since 'it did not involve disposal of an acknowledged social personality' (H. Lindsay, 'Death, Pollution and Funerals in Rome', in V. M. Hope and E. Marshall (eds.), *Death and Disease in the Ancient City* (London, 2000), 155). Never having joined the society of the living fully, the infant's soul, unentangled in earthly matters, can return swiftly and immediately to its proper abode (Plutarch, *Mor.* 611e–612a, cf. Seneca, *Ad Marc.* 23. 1). Another source (Servius, *In Aen.* 3. 68) tells us that cremation was intended to speed up the process whereby the soul separated from the body. Taken with Plutarch's comments, this suggests that cremation was quite unnecessary for a young child. Similar restrictions with regard to teeth exist in other societies where the child is not regarded as a full member of society. Hertz (1960), 151 n. 328 quoted Pliny's comments in connection with the Indian Laws of Manu, which prescribed that a child under 2 was not to be cremated (*Laws of Manu* 4. 69, cf. 3. 245); cf. also J. Duff's note on Juvenal, *Sat.* 14. 140 (*Juvenal Satires* (London, 1898: repr. 1975), 446), drawing attention to Hindu practice. The Laws of Manu also prescribed much simpler and briefer funerary practices for infants (4. 68, 70, 78). In other societies, simpler rites were performed for those under 7 (Hertz (1960), 84): the age at which social progression was marked by the shedding of the milk teeth? For adult cremation, see below, **187**.

I shall . . . body Cf. *HN* 11. 160 ff.

Zoroaster The 7th/6th-cent. reformer of Persian religion was known to the Greeks by the 5th-cent. BC and, by the Hellenistic period, the basic details of his philosophy were known, together with a plethora of other details of variable reliability. P. names the 4th-cent. mathematician and scholar Eudoxus of Cnidos as a source of information (*HN* 30. 4) and in *HN* 11. 242, refers to the story of the prophet's stay in the desert, where he is said to have survived on goat's cheese. A vast body of writings was ascribed to him, often spuriously; they are mentioned in *HN* 30. 4. See *OCD*³, 1639–40; J. Bidez and F. Cumont, *Les Mages Hellénisés: Zoroastre, Ostanes et Hystaspe d'après la tradition greque*, i (Paris, 1938; repr. 1973), 7–263; J. Duchesne-Gillemin, *The Western Response to Zoroaster* (Oxford, 1958), ch. 4.

laughed . . . born. See above, **2. smile.**

So strong . . . wisdom See above, **4. skull throb**, where the normal throbbing of the fontanelle is less optimistically interpreted as a symbol of human physical weakness.

73–130. introd. *Human maturity: Statistics and achievements*

P. moves from his discussion of pregnancy, birth, fertility, and early infant development (**41–72**) to a consideration of the statistics and achievements of human maturity. The first part of the discussion (**73–99**) focuses largely on physical statistics and records. Sections **88–99** form a gradual transition from physical to intellectual and moral qualities. In all cases, P.'s emphasis is once more on the exceptional: see Introd. 5. 2. 1. The specific citation of Varro's (Introd. 4. 5. 1) 'account of marvellous examples of strength' for the stories in **81–3**, with other citations in **75** and **85**, suggests that much of the material on these human records may have come from him; his lost *De Admirandis* is a likely source, though another possibility is the lost *Antiquitates*, to which some passages have traditionally been assigned.

A general structure for the first part of the discussion may be discerned as follows:

73. Stature: degeneration of the human race
74–5. Giants and Dwarves
76. Precocious physical development
77–80. Other statistics of human maturity, including:
    77. Facts about size and weight

78–80. Peculiarities of physiology (e.g. lack of need to drink) and temperament (unemotional, misanthropic characters)

81–130. Exceptional instances of physical and mental achievements, including:

81–4. Strength

85–6. Sight

87. Endurance

88–90. Memory and its fragility

91–9. The exceptional achievements of Caesar and Pompey, which introduce

100–29. examples of various kinds of *virtus*.

73. It . . . three years. Aristotle, *GA* 725^{b}23f. says this takes about five years.

But it is noticeable . . . fathers This passage is cited by Augustine (*CD* 15. 90) in support of his theory that the stature of the human race was greater before the flood. The degeneration of the human race physically as well as morally derives from the description of the successive inferiority of the five races of man (Gold, Silver, Bronze, Heroes, Iron) in Hesiod, *WD* 110–201, which may have derived ultimately from an oriental, possibly Mesopotamian, source: Babylonian, Judaic, Indian, and Zoroastrian versions exist. See M. L. West (ed. and comm.), *Hesiod: Works and Days* (Oxford, 1978), 173–7 with bibliography. Hesiod's Heroes, a temporary improvement in an otherwise degenerative sequence, were probably an interpolation into the metallic pattern to accommodate the Greeks' views of their early history, cf. **74. nearly a thousand years** (below). Although Hesiod does not specifically mention decreasing stature, this featured in his other myths of earlier eras (e.g. the Gigantes, *Theog.* 50, 185, cf. **Orion . . . Otus** below) and is frequently suggested of the Greek and Trojan heroes in Homer (below, **74. nearly a thousand years**) and Virgil (e.g. *Aen.* 12. 899–900). Biologically, as Mayor (2000: 201) notes, very large species do tend to become unviable and diminish in size over time. Although Hesiod is seen as the source for all later classical versions of the ages, including the Greek philosophers' and the Roman adaptation of the Golden race into the Golden Age (West 177), it is possible that P. had also read of a similar theory connected with Zoroaster (see above, **72. Zoroaster**). There might then be some semi-conscious thought-process behind the juxtapositioning of his apparently isolated remarks on Zoroaster just prior to this passage. For the combining of the idea of physical human degeneration with the physical/cosmological ideas of the philosophers, see following note.

This is because . . . declining. Pliny here combines the Hesiodic theory of human degeneration with the Stoic theory that the world is periodically consumed by fire (*ekpyrosis*, *SVF* ii. 596–632) and then renewed. In certain respects, his image of the desiccating effects of the approaching fire on human fertility resembles Diodorus Siculus' Epicurean description of the earth's early loss of her ability to produce animals spontaneously because of the desiccating effect of sun and winds (1. 7. 6). The decline of nature is more marked in Epicurean writings, where the emphasis is on the growth and decay of innumerable finite worlds in an unceasing pattern of change (cf. Lucretius 2. 1105–74, 5. 821–36), than it is in Stoic thought, where eternity through continual rebirth is stressed. According to Lucretius (*RN* 5. 827), the earth was running out of generative material like an old woman moving towards infertile old age, resulting in progressively shorter stature for successive generations. This Epicurean image, in which Hesiodic decline merged with cosmological theory, was frequently echoed in a more general way: human stature diminishes as the cosmos grows older: e.g. Aulus Gellius, *NA* 3. 10; Phlegon, *Mir.* 15. 2 (in the context of discoveries of giant bones: see below, **In Crete . . . found**).

In Crete . . . found   Solinus (1. 91) and Philodemus (*Methods of Inference* 3, col. ii. 11–15 de Lacy) give slightly different measurements (33 and 48 cubits respectively) and Solinus assigns the incident to a flood during the war of 68–67 BC which gained the Roman general who measured the skeleton, Q. Caecilius Metellus, the *cognomen* Creticus. Discoveries of giant skeletons in antiquity, even when given an anthropomorphic interpretation, can normally be attributed to the uncovering of prehistoric animal bones. Those apparently found in coffins (cf. Phlegon *Mir.* 17 and 18) may have been discovered and given 'heroic' reburial in earlier centuries before being disinterred a second time: see G. Huxley, 'Bones for Orestes', *GRBS* 20. 2 (1979), 145–8; Mayor (2000), 111–13; and below, **74. The body of Orestes . . . believed**. Giant proportions might be suggested by the huge size of individual pre-

historic bones, especially scapulas and femurs, 'enormous counterparts of our own ancestry' (Mayor (2000), 77), or by the arrangement of jumbled bone deposits into approximately humanoid
shape by their discoverers (see below, **74. nine feet and nine
inches**). The tendency to interpret such remains as human may be
due to the predominantly anthropocentric view of nature in the
ancient world; although in fact the decline theory could envisage
giant animals as well as humans in the remote past (cf. Aulus
Gellius, *NA* 3. 10; the legend of the Samian Neades in Plutarch,
Mor. 303d–e, Euagon *FGH* 535 F 1 and Heraclides Ponticus, *Pol.* 10,
Müller, *FHG* ii. 215; and Suet. *Aug.* 72, where the phrase 'bones of
heroes' is acknowledged as a purely figurative expression). By
Pliny's time, such skeletons might be put on display as *mirabilia* (see
Introd. 3. 3, 4. 2; above, **34. pets** and **35. I actually saw**; and
below, **74** and **75**, also Beagon forthcoming). The recording of
their prodigious dimensions had originally perhaps been stimulated by the predisposition to theories of decline from former glories
(cf. Phlegon, *Mir.* 15 and Augustine, *CD* 15. 9 on such bones as proof
of the decline theory), but was now encouraged afresh by a spirit
which positively embraced whatever was bigger, stronger, and
more spectacular (cf. the care devoted to figures in the recording of
ever more elaborate and exotic displays in the Roman arena in
Pliny and elsewhere: e.g. *HN* 8. 64–5; Augustus, *RG* 22–3; Suet.
Titus 7. 3; Dio 66. 25, 68. 15. 1). The wonder, however, was not
superficial sensationalism. The clear interest in such relics as evidence of the past indicates a collective historical consciousness (cf.
S. C. Humphreys, 'Fragments, Fetishes and Philosophies: Towards
a History of Greek Historiography after Thucydides', in G. W.
Most (ed.), *Collecting Fragments: Fragmente Sammeln* (Göttingen, 1997),
216–20). There may also have been an awareness of such an interest as an indication of developed civilization: Phlegon implicitly
contrasts the careful measuring and display of Greek and Roman
bone discoveries with the behaviour of the barbarians of the
Bosporus, who threw the remains they had found into the sea
(*Mir.* 19).

On the Cretan discoveries, Mayor (2000: 127–8 and nn.) suggests
that these huge ancient finds may confirm that large ancestors of
the modern elephant did once exist on the island, despite modern
views that the prehistoric species there were smaller.

earthquake   Earthquakes, volcanic activity, changes in sea-level, landslides, and flooding were regular manifestations of the geographical instability of the Mediterranean area: see Horden and Purcell (2000), 305–8. These natural disturbances of the earth frequently precipitated discoveries of prehistoric bones in antiquity. A number of finds occurred in the aftermath of the earthquakes which affected Asia Minor, Pontus, and Sicily in Tiberius' reign (Phlegon, *Mir.* 13–14; cf. Tac. *Ann.* 2. 47. 1; *HN* 2. 200). Skeletons also appeared in the Bosporus (Phlegon, *Mir.* 19) and Lydia (Philostratus, *On Heroes* 8. 8) after earthquakes. For P.'s interest in seismicity as a natural phenomenon, see B. Bousquet, 'Pline et la Sismicité en Mediterranée', in J. Pigeaud and J. Oroz (eds.) Pline *l'Ancien; témoins de son temps*, Conventus Pliniani Internationalis, Nantes, 22–26 Octobre 1985 (Salamanca and Nantes, 1987), 267–75. For ancient explanations of earthquakes, see *OCD*³, earthquakes, 501.

Orion ... Otus   Orion, the legendary hunter identified with the constellation (Homer *Il.* 18. 486, *Od.* 5. 121, 11. 572–5) and Otus (*Od.* 11. 305–20), who, with his brother Ephialtes tried to attack Olympus by piling Mount Pelion on Ossa and Ossa on Olympus, were giants struck down by the gods. See *OCD*³, Orion, 1077; Scherling, *RE* 18. 2, Otos, 1879–81.

74. The body of Orestes ... believed.   Herodotus 1. 68 says the body of the mythological hero who killed his mother Clytaemnestra and her lover in revenge for their murder of his father Agamemnon was discovered in Tegea and taken to Sparta on the instructions of the Delphic oracle. The relics of heroes came to be highly sought after in Archaic Greece. From the late 8th cent. to the 5th cent. BC, they conferred considerable political and religious prestige on the emerging city-states who laid claim to them. Authenticated by oracles (H. W. Parke and D. E. W. Wormell, *The Delphic Oracle*² (Oxford, 1956), i. 96), they 'helped first to define the *polis* and then reflect its nature as it developed' (D. Boedeker, 'Hero Cult and Politics in Herodotus: The Bones of Orestes', in C. Dougherty and L. Kurke (eds.), *Cultural Poetics in Archaic Greece* (Cambridge, 1993), 164–77; cf. C. M. Antonaccio, *An Archaeology of Ancestors: Tomb Cult and Hero Cult in Early Greece* (Maryland and London, 1995), 205–6). Huxley (above, **In Crete ... found**) suggests the bones of 'Orestes' were those of prehistoric animals from the Megalopolis basin, rich in Pleistocene remains, originally discovered and given a hero's burial in the late 8th cent., only to be rediscovered and appropriated by Sparta in the mid-6th cent. Other high-profile recoveries of heroes included Cimon's removal of Theseus' bones to Athens. The height of seven cubits was dismissed by Aulus Gellius in favour of seven feet, that being the maximum height attained by man, according to Varro (above, **22. five cubits**): but see above, **In Crete . . . found**.

nearly a thousand years . . . of old e.g. Homer, *Il.* 5. 304, 12. 383, 447–9, cf. Virgil, *Aen.* 12. 899–900, Juvenal 15. 69–70. Other Latin writers of the late Republic and early Empire assign a similar rough date to Homer (e.g. Aulus Gellius, *NA* 17. 21. 3, citing Cornelius Nepos; Velleius 1. 5. 3). For declining stature, see above, **73. But it is noticeable . . . fathers, This is because . . . declining**, and **In Crete . . . found**.

Naevius Pollio A Roman citizen who was 'a foot taller than the tallest of other men' (Columella 3. 8. 2). Columella cites Cicero, perhaps from his *De Admirandis*, the lost wonder-work mentioned elsewhere by P. (*HN* 31. 12, 51; cf. above, **18. Cicero**).

The tallest . . . height Cf. Solinus 1. 89. This may be the man 'of Jewish race' Columella records in a recent procession at the Games (3. 8. 2). See Schilling 160, for the likely Aramaic provenance of the name (signifying strength and domination) and the man himself. According to Josephus (*Ant.* 18. 4. 5), a tall Jew had also been sent to Tiberius. Giants, like dwarves and other anomalies, could be kept as 'pets' in high-status households (e.g. the slaves Polyphemus and Scylla in Martial 8. 13, who, however, puts more stress on their ugliness than their height). See below, **75. Conopas.**

nine feet and nine inches For Varro's upper limit of seven feet, see above, **The body of Orestes . . . believed**. In the modern era a number of individuals have been recorded as being over 2.2 m. tall. The 18th-cent. Irish giant O'Brien's skeleton was 2.49 m., while another, at Trinity College, was 2.59m tall: see L. H. Behrens and D. P. Barr, 'Hyperpituitarism Beginning in Infancy: The Alton Giant', *Endocrinology*, 16 (1932), 120–8.

75. Pusio . . . Secundilla Cf. Solinus 1. 88. The names, 'little boy' and a diminutive form of Secunda, are obviously inverse witticisms about their size. If Pliny is right, they were over 3 m. tall.

Mayor (2000: 144) suggests that, if the remains were skeletal, they could have been faked composites of human and animal bones. If they were mummified bodies, however, faking might have been more difficult, though not impossible. Faked monsters were a familiar hazard of the craze for *mirabilia*: see Beagon forthcoming and below, **Conopas . . . Julia.**

preserved as curiosities For the fascination with and display of curiosities of all kinds, see above, Introd. 3. 3 and 4. 2, **34. pets** and **35. I actually saw**, as well as notes to **74** above.

Sallustian gardens These pleasure gardens, stretching from the Quirinal in the south to the line of the later Aurelian wall to the north, passed from the historian Sallust to his great-nephew, C. Sallustius Crispus. See Platner–Ashby (1929), 271–2; P. Grimal, *Les Jardins Romains*² (Paris, 1969), 135–8; Nash (1981), i. 491; Richardson (1992), 202–3. Crispus was probably responsible for their luxurious trappings, among which prominent *mirabilia* would be appropriate. They then passed to the emperor, probably on Crispus' death, in AD 20, and by P.'s day were a favourite venue for Vespasian to receive visitors (Dio 65. 10. 4); so P. probably saw the exhibits for himself (see below, **I have actually seen**).

Conopas . . . Julia Dwarves can be as little as 70 cm. tall, although most are between 1 m. and 1.4 m. Conopas (perhaps 'gnat' from Greek *konops*) was unusually small, though not without parallel: see Dasen (1993), 7 on Tom Thumb's reported height of just 63. 5 cm. Julia, daughter of Agrippa and Augustus' daughter Julia, was exiled for adultery in AD 8 (above, **45. legacy of destruction . . . the two Agrippinas**). Describing the dwarf as her 'pet', *deliciae*, may have sexual connotations: see above, **34. pets** and the story of the hunchback 'admitted to his mistress's bed and then into her will', *HN* 34. 11. The deformed and the very powerful are both social anomalies; hence the former's prominence in imperial and royal households: see Garland (1995), 48–52 and above, **35. Claudius Caesar**. In addition, dwarves and hunchbacks were believed to have apotropaic qualities, which may have increased their appeal (Garland 104, 109; D. Levi, 'The Evil Eye and the Lucky Hunchback', in *Antioch-on-the-Orontes*, iii: *The Excavations of 1937–9* (Princeton, 1941), 220–32). Evidence for earlier domestic roles of dwarves in Egypt and Archaic and Classical

Greece is collected in Dasen 200–4, 244. Philodemus (*Methods of Inference* 3, col. II. 15–18 de Lacy) mentions 'pygmies' shown at Acoris in Egypt, 'like those recently brought back from Syria by Antony' (on whose interest in collecting human *mirabilia* see above, **56**). The half-cubit-high dwarf with a huge head, 'exhibited by the embalmers' (3, col. II. 4–9) was evidently a fake.

Julia Augusta   By the terms of his will, Augustus' wife Livia was adopted into the Julian family, acquiring this name (Tac. *Ann.* 1. 8).

Marcus Varro   See above, **73–130. introd.**

Manius Maximus . . . two cubits tall   Like Pusio and Secundilla above, the *cognomen* Maximus ('largest', 'greatest') is humorously ironic. For Manius as a family rather than a first name, see Münzer, *RE* 14. 1, Manius (1), 1147, cf. Schilling 161.

I have actually seen   They may have been another exhibit in the Sallustian gardens or a similar venue.

infants . . . three   P. follows this statement with two examples of abnormally precocious growth, the first of which also exhibited signs of precocious sexual development. Both conditions, together with abnormal length at birth, are documented in modern medicine and can result from disorders of the pituitary gland which controls the production of growth and sex hormones: see C. Smith, 'Clinical Features of Growth Hormone Deficiency', in P. E. Belchetz (ed.), *The Management of Pituitary Disease* (London, 1984), 467–70. The confident statement that such children do not live longer than three years is explained by Seneca's comment (*Ad Marc.* 23. 5) on an earlier example of precocious growth recorded by Papirius Fabianus: the child's early demise was generally expected as untimely death is the natural concomitant of untimely maturity (cf. also below, **171. Cato . . . oracular . . . death**, which probably refers to mental attitudes rather than to literal signs of ageing).

76. in Salamis . . . three.   Cf. Solinus 1. 92. For the medical condition, see above, **75. infants . . . three**.

I myself . . . Cornelius Tacitus . . . Belgica.   This was most probably the father of the historian, providing evidence of the latter's origins (Syme (1958), ii. 613–14). Syme notes the historian's detailed information on the Rhineland, especially for the years AD

55–8, and posits this period for his father's post. P. could then have had contact with him during his final spell of military duty on the Rhine in the mid/late 50s (Syme (1991), 499–501, 507, 511); the procurator of Belgica was paymaster to the Rhine legions.

The Greeks . . . Latin.   Greek *Ektrapelos* means 'turning from the common course', 'deviant' and so strange, monstrous. It lacks the admonitory, portentous sense of *teras*, 'marvel', 'monstrosity', cf. *Thes. Ling. Graec.* s.v. *teras*, 2021, and may have a more active meaning (*Thes. Ling. Graec.* s.v. *ektrapelos*, 6045), which would suit cases of excessive growth. But Pliny's comment is more indicative of the greater flexibility and variety of the Greek language than of any clearly defined classification of deformities: Latin *monstrum* would cover all types.

77. It has been observed . . . never the case with women. These two statements on the symmetries of the human body are paralleled in Solinus (1. 93–4) but with interesting amplifications, suggesting he used another source besides Pliny, perhaps the same one that P. himself used; possibly Varro (see above, **73–130. introd.** and below, **81. Tritanus . . . His son**) or Verrius Flaccus (see Introd. 4. 5. 1).

a man's height . . . either side   The circle-forming radii of the spreadeagled human body from the navel to the tips of the extremities of the limbs was most famously described by Vitruvius (3. 1. 3), who saw in the symmetries and proportions of the human form nature's blueprint for the architect's canon. The idea provoked much debate in later centuries (see P. Gros (ed. and comm.), *Vitruve De l'Architecture 3*, Coll. Univ. France (Paris, 1990), 67–70, who reproduces Leonardo da Vinci's famous drawing). The Vitruvius passage suggests macro/microcosmic ideas and Solinus is specific: the symmetry prompted philosophers to see man as the microcosm of the [spherical/circular] world, an idea which went back to Plato (*Tim.* 44d), at least with regard to the sphericity of man's brain and head. Cf. also Zeno in Plutarch, *Epit.* 4. 21, Diels, *Doxogr.* p. 411; Synesius, *De Prov.* 1; more general connections, Seneca, *NQ* 3. 15. 2; Ambrose, *Hex.* 6. 9. 55: see G. P. Conger, *Theories of Macrocosms and Microcosms in the History of Philosophy* (New York, 1922), 13–14; R. Allers, 'Macrocosmos: From Anaximandros to Paracelsus', *Traditio*, 2 (1944), 319–407.

It has also . . . predominates   P.'s second observation, that the right-hand side of the body is generally stronger than the left becomes in Solinus a differentiation between right and left sides on the basis of *types* of strength, the right being better for movement, the left for stability. This may again be linked with his macro/microcosmic ideas: some philosophers thought that the world had a left (western) and right (eastern) side, the latter initiating its movement (Stobaeus, *Ecl.* I. 15. 6). P.'s statement is in fact a more detailed account of the mobility/dexterity later simply attributed by Solinus to the right side of the human body. His observation that this quality does not always predominate on the right suggests that he is thinking of handedness; some are ambidextrous, others, as he states specifically, actually left-handed.

although . . . women.   At first, the assertion is surprising, given the associations in Aristotelian biology and elsewhere of the female and the left (see above, **37. right side . . . left**). But a more limited capacity for versatility and mobility would also fit in with the notion of female passivity and inferiority. In addition, empirical observation would be likely to occur more often among men, handling tools and weapons.

Men are heavier . . . even in death.   Of these statements, the first is obviously true as a general rule. The second is likely to have been prompted by the greater difficulty of moving the 'dead weight' of an unconscious person or a corpse. The third derives from moralizing fiction rather than biological fact.

78–9.   A pattern may be discerned behind the apparently inconsequential sequence of the remarks in these two sections. Following his remarks on the body's symmetry of structure, Pliny comments on a rare anomaly he has read about in the structure of certain individuals whose bones are 'solid' and who are recognized by a lack of need to drink. This prompts him to an example of non-drinking caused not by solid bones but by deliberate choice. He proceeds to other examples of self-repression, both emotional (Crassus, the philosophers) and physical (Antonia, Pomponius). He ends with another comment on the solid-boned individuals; they are called 'horny'-boned. As well as a physical parallel (fishes' bodies are 'horny', *HN* 31. 102), Schilling (163) gives a moral parallel to this phrase which may be more significant than he implies: Persius (*Sat.*

1. 47) talks of being not so 'horny-hearted' (*cornea fibra*) as to be entirely proof against desire for praise. In other words, he is not totally impervious to emotions. It may well have been P.'s digression on to examples of lack of emotion, *apatheia* (below), which leads him to this displaced remark on the topic with which he began.

78. I have read . . . perspire   Possibly in a source also used by Solinus, who (1. 74) gives an example not in P. of a solid-boned Syracusan athlete. Varro (see above, **73–130. introd.**, and below, **81. Tritanus . . . His son**) is likely; or possibly Verrius Flaccus (Introd. 4. 5. 1). Certain medical conditions which lead to abnormal bone density can be recognized today under X-ray, e.g. osteosclerosis and the congenital condition osteopetrosis, but the ancients' connection between solid bones and lack of moisture is probably derived from a belief that the latter condition would make the bones harder and drier in texture, like horn: see above, **78–9**; also **20. right toe . . . temple** and **22. pains . . . toughened**.

We know . . . doctors.   An identification with a Ti. Julius Viator, a freedman's son and cavalry commander known from an inscription from Aquileia (*ILS* 1. 2703, Stein, *RE* 10. 1, Iulius (531), 872) is possible. His name may date his youth to the reign of Tiberius. P. may have known him personally through his own military career. The Vocontii were situated among the western foothills of the Alps and were 'allied' in the sense that they were a *civitas foederata*.

79. Crassus . . . Agelastus   The triumvir M. Licinius Crassus died fighting the Parthians at Carrhae in 53 BC. His grandfather was praetor in 127 BC (Münzer, *RE* 13. 1, Licinius (57), 269–70), a contemporary of the satirist Lucilius who is quoted as source for this story by Cicero (*Fin.* 5. 92, *Tusc.* 3. 31), according to whom Lucilius claimed that Crassus laughed just once. According to Diogenes Laertius (8. 20), Pythagoras never laughed, a characteristic in keeping with the ascetic's high level of bodily control. See further below, **However . . . philosophers**.

Socrates   The Athenian philosopher's (469–399 BC; *OCD*³, 1419–20) calm serenity was famous: cf. *Tusc.* 3. 31 (contrasted with Crassus' dour look), *De Off.* 1. 90, Aelian, *VH* 9. 7. Pliny contrasts it with the excessive rigidity of some other philosophers (below).

However . . . *apatheis* . . . philosophers It was not so strange that philosophers should furnish the majority of examples of excessive emotional suppression (see refs. above, **Crassus . . . Agelastus**); the Stoics in particular argued that the wise man should not be unduly swayed by his emotions: cf. above 5. **sorrow . . . superstition.** Cicero devotes books 3 and 4 of the *Tusculan Disputations* to a discussion of the extent to which this could, or should, be the case. The term *apatheis* derives from the Greek term used by the Stoics, *apatheia*, 'freedom from emotion'. Later, Aulus Gellius used a Latinized form of the word, recording Herodes Atticus' objections that complete *apatheia* was unnatural and that *sectatores apathiae* ('followers of *apatheia*'), rather than being brave, calm, and steady, were reduced to a mental torpor due to lack of emotional stimuli (*NA* 19. 12. 1–10). This fits Pliny's strictures here about abnormal rigidity. Pliny interprets *apatheia* in a general sense without limiting himself to specifically Stoic doctrines, as the following examples show.

Diogenes the Cynic Diogenes of Sinope (*c*.400–325 BC), founder of the Cynic sect which taught that happiness was a state of self-sufficiency and shamelessness achieved by living only on basic necessities and doing what is natural rather than what is merely conventional. *Apatheia* perhaps arose through the extreme measures he took to inure himself to hardship, according to Diogenes Laertius (6. 23), and his contempt for his contemporaries (6. 24). See generally Diogenes Laertius 6. 20–81; *OCD*³, Diogenes (2), 473–4.

Pyrrho (*c*.365/60–275/70 BC) of Elis, founder of Greek scepticism which taught that positive knowledge was impossible and that the suspension of judgement would lead to a state of calm, *ataraxia* ('freedom from disturbance'), although some said it would lead to *apatheia* (Diogenes Laertius 6. 108). See Diogenes Laertius 6. 61–108; *OCD*³, 1283.

Heraclitus (*c*.540–480 BC) An early natural philosopher from Ephesus whose cosmology was based on a ceaseless conflict of opposites governed by an unchanging principle, *Logos*. The biographical tradition used by Diogenes Laertius describes him as misanthropic and arrogant (9. 1–17). See G. S. Kirk, *Heraclitus: The Cosmic Fragments* (Cambridge, 1954), 3–5; *OCD*³, 687.

Timon . . . race   The Athenian misanthrope seems to have been a real contemporary of Aristophanes (*Birds* 1547, *Lys.* 805) or possibly a proverbial type (N. Dunbar (ed. and comm.), *Birds* (Oxford, 1995), 708–9). For his nickname, *misanthropos*, cf. Cic. *Tusc.* 4. 25. Whether Pliny is correct to class him as a philosopher is questionable. He may have confused him with Pyrrho's (above) follower of the same name, cf. Diogenes Laertius 9. 112–13, who says that the latter kept himself to himself. See *OCD*³, Timon (1) and (2), 1529; Lenschau, *RE* 6 A 2, Timon (12), 1300. Strictly speaking, as Cicero pointed out, Timon was not passionless but driven into an extreme state of passion; an example not of settled calm but of chronic disorder (*Tusc.* 4. 23–7).

Drusus' wife, Antonia   The younger daughter of Mark Antony and Octavian's (later Augustus) sister Octavia, the younger Antonia (36 BC–AD 37) married the future emperor Tiberius' brother Drusus in 16 BC and was mother to another emperor, Claudius. See *OCD*³, Antonia (3), 113.

Pomponius   P. Pomponius Secundus, who was suffect consul in AD 44 and died probably in the mid-50s AD, was a friend and patron of P.'s. See Introd, 1, 2. 2, and Syme (1991), 496–500.

'Horny' See above, **78–9**.

81. Tritanus . . . His son   Varro, *Ant. Rer. Hum.* 1, fr. 7 (Mirsch): see above, **73–130. introd.** The son could have been known to Varro (d. 27 BC) but attempts to identify the father with the Tritannus in Lucilius (ii. 19 Charpin, ii. 88–94 M) are problematic because Lucilius calls him a centurion. F. Charpin (ed. and comm.), *Lucilius: Satires*, vol. ii (Paris 1978), 223, quoting Manilius 4. 225, suggests a career change to the arena by a soldier ill-adapted to civilian life; or perhaps it was the grandfather of P.'s soldier who was a gladiator, father and son both being soldiers. The name is uncommon: see Münzer, *RE* 7 A 1, Tritanus, 241.

Samnite armour   The Samnites were defeated by Rome and her Campanian allies in 309 BC. According to Livy (9. 40. 1–17), the Campanians used some of the captured enemy weapons, which were of new and splendid design, to equip gladiators. After 264 BC, the 'Samnite' became the prototype of the Roman gladiator, later being joined by three other types, the *murmillo* (above, **55. the**

gladiator **Armentarius**), the *retiarius*, and the Thracian: see
*OCD*³, 637–8; M. Grant, *Gladiators: The Bloody Truth* (1967, rev. edn.
Harmondsworth, 1971), 55–9.

82. Vinnius Valens See Hanslik, *RE* 9A 1, Vinnius Valens (2),
151.

centurion . . . Praetorian Guard Established by Augustus as
a permanent bodyguard to the emperor, this elite force consisted of
nine cohorts of 500 or 1,000 men stationed at Rome and nearby
towns: see *OCD*³, praetorians, 1241. Centurions were found in the
Praetorian Guard and in the auxiliaries, as well as in the regular
legions (*OCD*³, centurio, 311).

wineskins The *culleus* was in fact a measure of capacity; 20
amphorae. The basic measure, the *sextarius* (0.546 l.) was 1/48 of an
amphora.

seen . . . tombstone Valens' deeds were apparently sculpted on
his tombstone and seen by P. at first hand. Was Augustus involved
in this commemoration of his praetorian centurion's exploits? For
a similar commemoration of personal *mirabilia*, as distinct from
more conventional achievements, on an individual's tombstone by
order of the emperor himself, see Aulus Gellius on a mother who
died after giving birth to quintuplets (*NA* 10. 2, cf. **33. Fausta . . .
two boys and two girls**). A similar insertion by P. of first-hand
evidence into an account derived mainly from other writers occurs
below, **83. I myself . . . Athanatus**; and cf. above, **36. I myself
. . . in Africa**.

83. Rusticelius . . . Fufius . . . shoulders. Varro, *Ant. Rer.
Hum.* 1, fr. 8 Mirsch (see above, **73–130. introd.**). These individuals are not attested elsewhere, though Schilling (164) noted that
the unusual names appear in Cic. *Brutus* 169 and Horace, *Sat.* 2. 3.
60 respectively. For Rusticelius' nickname, note a similar story in
Aelian, *VH* 12. 22 (cf. 14. 47b). The cowherd Titormus was given the
same name by Milon of Croton, who observed him preventing two
bulls from running in opposite directions by holding one with each
hand; a feat with similarities both to Rusticelius' here and to
Vinnius Valens' exploits with the loaded carts, above. The popularity of freaks and oddities (cf. the crowds around the giant,
Naevius Pollio, above, **74**) evidently extended to the sorts of

displays given by these individuals and by Athanatus (below, **I myself . . . Athanatus**) and some may have formed part of the entertainment at the games, cf. Suet. *Aug.* (43. 3) on the dwarf Lycius with the stentorian voice, or at less formal venues. These feats of strength were evidently among the more edifying acts, at least in comparison to that of the compulsive eater, to whom, it was alleged, Nero wished to feed living men (Suet. *Nero* 37, cf. *Vit. Aurel.* 50). See Introd. 3. 3, 4. 2.

I myself . . . Athanatus Again, not attested elsewhere. The name means 'immortal' in Greek. For the insertion of first-hand evidence into a second-hand narrative, see above, **82. seen . . . tombstone** and **36. I myself . . . in Africa**.

Milon of Croton An athlete of the late 6th cent. BC, he is attested in many sources, having gained six victories in both the Olympic and Pythian games. There are many tales of his amazing strength. P. (*HN* 37. 144, cf. Solinus 1. 77) says he made himself invincible by using *alectoriae*, stones found in cocks' gizzards. (The same qualities were attributed to an agate by the Magi, *HN* 37. 142.) Quintilian, *Inst.* 1. 9. 5 suggests the real secret was more prosaic— training. See *OCD*³, 981; Modrze, *RE* 15. 2, Milon (2), 1672–6.

apple . . . fingers Cf. Aelian, *HA* 6. 55; Pausanias 6. 13. 6. The exception, with regard to the apple, was his girlfriend, according to Aelian (*VH* 2. 24).

84. Philippides Philippides or Phidippides (for the confusion over the name, see *OCD*³, Phidippides, 1158; F. J. Frost and E. Badian, 'The Dubious Origins of the "Marathon"', *AJAH* 4 (1979), 159–66; Miller, *RE* 19. 2; Pheidippides, 1936) was sent by Athens to Sparta for help when the Persians landed at Marathon in 490 BC: see Herod. 6. 105–6, Cornelius Nepos, *Miltiades* 4. 3; Pausanias 1. 28. 4.

1,140–stade run Other sources give slightly different figures (1,200 stades in Isocrates, *Panath.* 24; 1,240 in Solinus 1. 98). Herodotus says Philippides reached his destination on the day after he set out and all the sources agree that the journey was completed within 48 hours and possibly in little more than 24 (cf. P.'s 'the next day'). It would be possible, even allowing for the mountainous terrain, for a trained runner today to complete this distance within 24 hours; even so, Philippides' achievement was outstanding; see D. E. Martin, H. W. Benario, R. W. H. Glyn, 'Development of the Marathon from Pheidippides to the Present, with Statistics of Significant Races', in 'The Marathon: Physiological, Medical, Epidemiological and Psychological Studies', *Ann. N.Y. Ac. Sci.* 301 (1977), 821–52. For the probable feasibility of other long-distance runs recorded in antiquity (e.g. Plutarch. *Arist.* 20), see V. J. Matthews, 'The *Hemerodromoi*: Ultra Long-Distance Running in Antiquity', *Classical World*, 68 (1974), 161–9. Martin *et al.* note that the American record of 13 hrs 33. 06 min. for a 100–mile run may be compared with some of the statistics for these runners, e.g. 1,000 stades (115 miles) in 15 hours.

Anystis . . . Philonides Philonides is also mentioned in *HN* 2. 181, where the distance is given as 1,200 stades. The Greeks developed a courier service using runners, *hemerodromoi* (i.e., trained to run for a day or more). For Roman *cursores*, see Varro, *LL* 5. 11, cf. Strabo 5. 4. 13; W. A. Krenkel, 'Cursores Maiores Minoresque', *Classical World*, 70 (1976), 373–4. Philippides (see above), too, was a *hemerodromos*. The distance and timing as given here are certainly feasible (see above, **1,140–stade run**) though the suggestion in *HN* 2. 181 that the outward journey was completed in roughly nine hours is impossible (cf. Matthews (1974), 166). Pausanias mentions a statue of Philonides at Olympia (6. 16. 5), while an inscription found there describes him as *hemerodromos* and *bematistes* (route-measurer) of Alexander (*SIG³*, 303).

160 miles Phidippides' run had been 142. 5 miles. Such runners would complete 320 laps if, as is likely, the Circus Maximus' course was four stades long: cf. Matthews (1974), 167, who claims that this is a feasible record for a 'non-stop' run, in which the aim is to cover as much distance as possible without stopping, rather than a fixed distance.

the Circus P. probably refers to the earliest and most famous of the Roman circuses, primarily enclosures for chariot-racing. This was the Circus Maximus, which lay between the Palatine and Aventine hills, and was rebuilt by Julius Caesar (*HN* 36. 102). Others were the Circus Flaminius, dating from 221 BC and the Circus Vaticanus (*HN* 16. 201, 36. 74), built by Gaius and Nero. This last named is another possibility as the venue for the boy's feat (see below, **Fonteius**). Circuses were also built throughout Italy and the provinces. See *OCD*³, Circus, 332–3; Nash (1981), i. 234ff. They were used for foot-racing in Italy (cf. Cic. *Tusc.* 2. 56, Suet. *Aug.* 43. 2) because of a lack of stadia for athletics, a Greek sport: the first permanent one, built by Nero, had been burned down in 62 (Tac. *Ann.* 14. 47).

Fonteius and Vipstanus　C. Fonteius Capito and C. Vipstanus Apronianus were consuls in AD 59. The occasion of the feat described may have been one of the public entertainments of 59 put on by Nero, who personally participated in the chariot-racing in the Vatican circus that year. See Tac. *Ann.* 14. 14–15; Dio 52. 17–20; Suet. *Nero* 34.

75 miles　In the ideal running conditions of the Circus, this record would be achievable by trained adult runners (see above, **Anystis . . . Philonides**), provided that we allow P.'s vague 'midday to evening' to be stretched to 9 hours, but is highly unlikely for a child (Matthews (1974), 168).

Tiberius . . . Germany　Cf. Val. Max. 5. 5. 2; Dio 55. 1–2. 3. Drusus fell mortally ill in 9 BC as a result of a fall from his horse while campaigning in Germany. Tiberius travelled from Ticinum in northern Italy to Drusus' summer quarters and reached him before he died.

85. According to Cicero　Possibly more citations from Cicero's lost work on wonders (above, **18. Cicero**, **74. Naevius Pollio**, and Introd. 5. 2. 2). For the possibility of such a feat, provided that the parchment (probably chosen in preference to papyrus because it could be made extremely thin) was a roll, see Roberts and Skeat (1987), 13–14. For miniaturist works generally see **Callicrates** below.

He also claims　The Sicilian is mentioned in *Acad. Prior.* 2. 81.

Strabo.　See Münzer, *RE* 4A, Strabon (2), 76. P. stresses the name (cf. Varro, *Ant. Rer. Hum.* 1, fr. 9 Mirsch) for the sake of irony, since it means 'cross-eyed', 'squinting'. It may be a nickname: joking, if implying a defect, descriptive if referring to a contorted, peering visage. Besides the Cicero references above, the story is also found in Val. Max. 1. 8., ext. 14; Aelian, *VH* 11. 13; Strabo 6. 2. 1, C267; and Plutarch, *Mor.* 1083d.

Punic war The first Punic war (264–241 BC), when much of the struggle focused on control of Sicily and the challenging of Carthaginian sea-power, is probably meant.

from . . . Lilybaeum . . . Carthage Lilybaeum was a Punic stronghold which fell to Rome in 341 BC. It was on the westernmost tip of Sicily and was the closest part of the island to Africa. Pliny's estimate of 135 miles works out at roughly 200 km., as does Cicero's 1,080 stades. Carthage was about 215 km. distant. For the impossibility of such a feat, see D. Wardle (ed. and trans.), *Valerius Maximus' Memorable Deeds and Sayings* (Oxford, 1998), 282 and the calculation in Healy (1999), 150–2, according to which Strabo would have had to be standing on top of Mt. Etna, in order to allow for the curvature of the earth. For a similarly over-optimistic estimate of visual capacity, see Strabo 12. 2, 7, C538, who suggested that it was possible to see both the Pontic and the Issian seas from the top of Mt. Argaeus in Cappadocia.

Callicrates . . . Myrmecides Cf. *HN* 36. 43, where they are less plausibly assigned marble as the material for their miniatures (gold (as suggested by jewellery finds), or perhaps bronze are more plausible suggestions: Jex-Blake and Sellers (1896), 88–90). Callicrates came from Sparta (Solinus 1. 100) and Myrmecides was born in Miletus and worked in Athens (Varro, *LL* 7. 1; 9. 108; Cicero, *Acad. Prior.* 3. 120), but their dates are uncertain. Myrmecides' name is perhaps a nickname derived from the Greek *myrmex*, an ant, tiny models of which he (rather than, as here, Callicrates) also made (Cicero, loc. cit.). They are mentioned together in Aelian, *VH* 1. 17; Athenaeus 11. 782b; and in Plutarch, *Mor.* 1083d where they are also accredited with inscribing two verses of Homer on a sesame seed, cf. P.'s nutshell story, above. The same passage also mentions the Lilybaeum story (above) and Münzer (1897), 172–4 suggested all three came from Cicero's *Admiranda* (above, **18. Cicero, 74. Naevius Pollio, 85. According to Cicero**: see Introd. 5. 2. 2) through Varro. For interest in miniaturist works and other types of artistic *mirabilia* cf. *HN* 34. 83 and 34. 77, and Sellers loc. cit.

86. Sybaris . . . Cimbri . . . Perseus Two of the three stories feature among stories of divine intervention in human affairs in Cicero, *ND* 2. 6. See in general Pease's extensive notes, *ND* 2. 6 (1955), ii. 552–60.

Sybaris   Sybaris, a wealthy city on the gulf of Tarentum, was destroyed by Croton in 510 BC. Pliny has confused the two cities; in the late 6th cent. a battle look place between the Locrians and the Crotoniates, resulting in a decisive defeat for the latter at the Sagra, where two giant youths, identified by some sources as the Dioscuri, were seen fighting on the Locrian side, cf. Justin 20. 2. 9–20. 3. 9, Strabo 6. 1. 10, C261; Plutarch, *Aem. Paul.* 25. 1 (for others, see Pease comm., *ND* 2. 6 (1955), ii. 559). All stress that the news of the victory was somehow relayed to the Greek mainland on the very same day. There was a Graeco-Roman tradition of important events miraculously made known on the days of their occurrence: see Pease 557–8. P. seems to want to make a distinction between the Sagra episode and cases where the clairvoyance was in fact due to a divine messenger-service. It is true that no divine messengers are specifically mentioned in the other versions of the Sagra story e.g. Cicero, *ND* 2. 6, and in Plutarch, *Aem. Paul.* 25–6, a number of such incidents are described simply as mysteriously early rumours. But Justin and Strabo (loc. cit.) note the intervention in the actual battle by the Dioscuri (cf. their representation on the pediment of an Ionian temple at Locri, refs. in Pease 559), who are often mentioned as bearing miraculously swift tidings in similar stories. See below, **Castores**.

tidings   A lacuna in the text has been variously filled by different editors. Some, e.g. Schilling (166–7) prefer *nuntii* (Jan), 'messengers', as a parallel with the Castores (Dioscuri). However, the vaguer *fama*, 'tidings' (Mayhoff), would suit the story P. has already told in *HN* 2. 148 about the Cimbri. See below, **Cimbri**.

Cimbri   The Cimbri, a Germanic tribe who were migrating and threatening northern Italy, were eventually defeated by Marius in 101 BC. In *HN* 2. 148, P. says that during the Cimbric wars 'the sound of arms clashing and trumpets blaring' was heard coming from the sky; an omen (and therefore a type of divine announcement) similar to those attested in Livy 24. 44. 8 (213 BC), Plut. *Sulla* 7. 3–4 and Caesar, *BC* 3. 105 (sounds of armies and trumpets heard simultaneously in Antioch, Ptolemais, and Pergamum on the same day as the battle of Pharsalus). See F. B. Krauss, *An Interpretation of the Omens, Portents, and Prodigies recorded by Livy, Tacitus, and Suetonius* (Pennsylvania, 1930), 163–4. Florus 1. 38. 20–1 attributes a same-day announcement once again to the Dioscuri.

Castores The Dioscuri, twin sons of Zeus, were often known as the Castores at Rome, the name of one twin signifying the pair, cf. Suet. *Jul.* 10. 1 (Bibulus, overshadowed by Caesar in their joint aedileship of 65 BC, said he was Pollux to Caesar's Castor). Their temple in the Forum was often referred to as the temple of Castor. They frequently appeared as twin warriors on horseback, giving aid to mortals in danger in battle or at sea. See *OCD*[3], Castor and Pollux, 301–2. For references, see Pease comm. *ND* 2. 6 (1955), ii. 553–4, 555–6. They also often carried miraculously swift news of the action, including the battles at the Sagra (above), Sybaris, lake Regillus, and Pydna (see below, **Perseus**): Cic. *Tusc.* 1. 28, cf. *ND* 2. 6; Plutarch, *Marius* 26; Valerius Maximus 1. 8; Florus 1. 28. 14–15, Ammianus Marcellinus 28. 4. 11; Lactantius, *Inst.* 2. 7. 10.

Perseus Perseus, king of Macedon, was defeated at Pydna *c.*168 BC by L. Aemilius Paulus. See *OCD*[3], Perseus (2), 1143–4. For the Dioscuri's announcement, see Cic. *ND* 2. 6, Dion. Hal. 6. 13, Valerius Maximus 1. 8. 1, Florus 1. 28, Lactantius 2. 1. 10, etc. cf. Pease, comm. *ND* 2. 6 (1955), ii. 556.

87. Leaena . . . Aristogiton Cf., at greater length, *HN* 34. 72. Laeana was mistress of either Harmodius or Aristogiton, members of an ancient Athenian family who attempted to kill the Athenian tyrant Hippias but instead killed his brother at the Panatheneia of 514 BC. Harmodius was killed on the spot, Aristogiton after torture. After the expulsion of Hippias in 510 BC, they were honoured by the Athenians as liberators. The story of Laeana, who died rather than reveal any information about the plot, seems to be later; it is not in Herodotus or Thucydides. Pausanias 1. 23 claims to be the first to have written it down. The name means lioness, a popular name for prostitutes, and the legend may have grown up around the statue of a tongueless lioness attributed to Amphicrates (*HN* 34. 72), cf. Athenaeus 13, 596 f.; Plutarch, *Mor.* 505d–e, Polyainos, *Strategem.* 8. 45; Jex-Blake and Sellers (1896), lxxvi, n. 3, 59; Geyer, *RE* 12. 1, Laeana (3), 1045–6; *OCD*[3], Aristogiton, 162–2.

Anaxarchus A 4th-cent. BC philosopher of Abdera, disciple of Democritus and teacher of Pyrrhon the Sceptic. A friend of Alexander the Great, he was later cruelly killed by Nicocreon tyrant of Cyprus, because of an alleged insult, but defied him in the way described by P. See Diogenes Laertius 9. 58–60; Plutarch, *Mor.*

449e; Valerius Maximus 3. 3, ext. 4; Cic. *Tusc.* 2. 52; Kaerst, *RE* 1. 2, Anaxarchos (10), 2080, *OCD*³, Anaxarchus, 86.

88. memory . . . advantages   P. turns from the powers of the human body to the powers of the human mind as manifest in memory and the intellectual gymnastics of Julius Caesar (**91**). Memory is an appropriate quality with which to signal the change of direction, since the memory process was conceived of as, to some extent, a physical process involving physical sense-organs (M. Carruthers, *The Book of Memory* (Cambridge, 1990), 48–9). The well-developed human memory was integral to the superior quality of the human mind. P. implies (*HN* 27. 7; Beagon (1992), 133–4) that animal memory is inferior or non-existent. Seneca (*Ep.* 99. 24) said that it was short and did not develop with age (*Ep.* 121). See below, **90. No . . . fear**. Collective memory was of course fundamental to the development of human culture and tradition, but P.'s interest here is directed at the mental faculty itself and at feats of artificial memory, the cultivation of which was of considerable importance in the ancient world, partly because less information was stored in a written medium, but also because it was an essential cultural tool in education and rhetoric. For the difference between natural and artificial memory, see [Cicero], *Rhet. Her.* 3. 28. In general, see F. Yates, *The Art of Memory* (London, 1966), 1–49; H. Caplan, *Of Eloquence: Studies in Ancient and Medieval Rhetoric* (Ithaca and London, 1970), 196–246; J. Bonner, *Education in Ancient Rome* (London, 1977); N. Horsfall, 'Statistics or States of Mind?', in *Literacy in the Ancient World, JRA* suppl. ser. vol. 3 (1991), 61–4; Carruthers (1990), esp. chs. 1–3; J. P. Small and J. Tatum, 'Memory and the Study of Classical Antiquity', *Helios*, 22 (1995), 149–77; J. P. Small, *Wax Tablets of the Mind: Cognitive Studies of Memory and Literacy in Classical Antiquity* (London, 1997); and below, **Simonides**. See also Introd. 4. 2.

King Cyrus . . . reading it.   Other ancient sources offered similar examples of prodigious feats of memory: for a detailed list, which includes those Pliny mentions here, see Caplan (1970), 216–19. Quintilian (11. 2. 51) implied they were apocryphal and, earlier, Cicero (*Tusc.* 59) had emphasized that examples such as Cyrus and the rest were exceptional and not representative of the average memory. Some modern critics have suggested exaggeration (W. V. Harris, *Ancient Literacy* (Cambridge, Mass., 1989), 30–3), but cf. Horsfall (1991), 61; Small (1997), 128). The point remains that the potential strength of a trained memory in antiquity was impressive.

Cyrus Founder of the Achaemenid Persian dynasty (*c*.557–530 BC): *OCD*[3], Cyrus (1), 423. According to Xenophon, *Cyr*. 5. 3. 46, it was the names of the officers he knew. Cf. Valerius Maximus 8. 7, ext. 16; Solinus 1. 108.

Lucius Scipio L. Cornelius Scipio Asiagenes, cos. 190 BC and younger brother of P. Scipio Africanus (*OCD*[3], Cornelius Scipio Asiagenes, 398–9; Münzer, *RE* 4. 1, Cornelius (337), 1471–83) is mentioned several times in the *HN*: pref. 10; 33. 138, 148; 35. 22; 37. 12. See Urlichs 54. But the *praenomen* is common in the Scipio family. The quaestor L. Scipio, son of Asiagenes (Henze, *RE* 4. 1, Cornelius (324), 1431), assigned to king Prusias of Bithynia as a guide around the city of Rome in 167 BC (Livy 45. 44. 7) would also be a plausible candidate for such encyclopaedic knowledge. The political advantages had long been evident: Plutarch mentions that Themistocles bolstered his popularity by his knowledge of every citizen's name (*Them*. 5. 4).

Cineas The Thessalian ambassador of Pyrrhus of Epirus (120–63 BC) came to Rome after the city's defeat at Heraclea (280 BC) but was unsuccessful in negotiating peace, though he was remembered as an admirer of Rome; cf. Cicero *Tusc*. 1. 59, *OCD*[3], Cineas, 332.

Mithridates Mithridates VI Eupator Dionysus, king of Pontus 120–63 BC, whose expansionist policies led to war with Rome and his eventual defeat by Pompey, followed by suicide after a reign of 56 years. *OCD*[3], Mithridates, 990–1. For his linguistic memory, see also Quintilian 11. 50, Aulus Gellius, *NA* 11. 17. In *HN* 25. 5–7, he is described as a polymath with a practical interest in medicine and antidotes to poison; cf. also *HN* 29. 24–5.

Charmadas An Academic philosopher, pupil of Carneades, active in 109 BC when the orator Antonius met him in Athens (Cic. *De Orat*. 2. 360). His memory is also mentioned in Cic. *Tusc*. 1. 59. For his method, see below, **Simonides**.

Simonides A Greek elegiac poet from Ceos (*c*.556–46 BC). (see also below, **192. Simonides . . . poet, 204. Simonides . . .**

eighth, and *OCD*[3], Simonides, 1409). Cic. *De Orat.* 2. 351–7 cites him as the inventor of a mnemonic system, where it is stressed that arrangement is the key to successful memorizing. The numerous systems were developed in the Roman rhetorical tradition including the sequencing of material in places (*loci*) in an architectural or other physical setting (Cic. *De Orat.* 2. 351–60; *Rhet. Her.* 3. 29; Seneca, *Controv.* 1, pref. 2–3; Quintilian 11. 2. 1–51). For bibliography, see above, **memory . . . advantages** and Introd. 4. 2. According to Cicero (*De Orat.* 2. 360), Charmadas (above) and Metrodorus of Scepsis (below) perfected a system whereby they wrote down things they wished to remember 'in certain *loci*, by means of images, as though inscribing letters on wax . . . ', an image elaborated in *Rhet. Her.* 3. 17 and which lasted into the Renaissance.

Metrodorus of Scepsis . . . heard   A writer and scholar, probably also the Metrodorus nicknamed 'Rome-hater' (cf. *HN* 34. 34) as well as being renowned for his memory (Cic. *Tusc.* 1. 59, *De Orat.* 2. 360 (see above, **Simonides**); Quintilian 11. 2. 26). A friend and ambassador of Mithridates (see above), he fell out of favour and was killed: Plutarch, *Luc.* 22. *OCD*[3], Metrodorus (4), 977.

90. No . . . fear   See above, **1–5** and **43–4** on man's paradoxical weakness, especially **4. skull throb**, where the fragility of the head is epitomized by the throbbing fontanelle of the human infant. The two accidents Pliny goes on to describe imply, but do not specify, head injury and it is clear that ancient ideas of the physiology of memory did not necessarily connect it with the function of the brain. In the *Timaeus*, Plato made the head, and in particular the brain (39d), the seat of the intelligence, but only because he regarded it as the most 'divine' part of man (44 d–e), and not because of medical deduction. Aristotle had suggested that the heart played an important role (*HA* 666[a]10–15; *GA* 781[a]21–3) and it was left to the Alexandrian doctors Herophilus and Erasistratus to attribute neurological functioning to the brain (C. Singer and R. A. Underwood, *A Short History of Medicine* (New York and Oxford 1962). Ancient Greek sources often associated memory with *psyche*, 'soul' or 'spirit' (cf. Aristotle, *De Memoria* 449[b]30–450[a]22), while a number of Latin ones, including Pliny himself (below, **bereft mind**) mention *mens*, 'mind', as well as soul, without necessarily implying a particular physical process or location. In *HN* 11. 251, Pliny does suggest that the physical seat of memory is in the ear

lobe, which is touched when calling a person to witness. The association with *psyche* may have encouraged expressions of memory in
connection with the breath, lungs, and lips (Small (1997), 131–7), but
it is unclear how far such expressions were anything more than
figurative. Certainly, Pliny's reference to the ear lobe in *HN* 11. 251
is one of a number made there to parts of the body which have a
kind of religious significance (*quaedam religio*) and are touched in
certain symbolic gestures, e.g. the chin, touched in supplication by
the Greeks, and the 'seat of Nemesis', behind the right ear, which is
touched after the mouth when something has been said which
might incur divine wrath. Its association with mind, however,
might also explain Pliny's physical location of memory in proximity to the eyes and the brain. The latter are connected, both
anatomically (by a vein, *HN* 11. 149), and functionally, since the
eyes transmit images to the mind (*HN* 11. 146–7), and deep thought
is said to blind the eyes by 'withdrawing the vision within', to the
mind. The physical quality of memory was expressly denied by
Cicero (*Tusc.* 60–1): it is not a quality of heart, blood, brain, or
bone, but, like the soul, of divine origin. The notion that, 'like wax,
the soul (*animus*) has marks impressed upon it and that memory
consists of the traces of things impressed upon the mind (*mens*)' is
rejected.

a man . . . letters   According to Valerius Maximus 1. 8, ext. 2,
the man was a scholar who, by a cruel twist of fate, lost only that
portion of memory most important to his learning. See Wardle
(1998), 271. This and the following examples of partial memory loss
fit patterns found in cases of brain damage today.

Messala Corvinus   M. Valerius Messala Corvinus (*c.*64 BC–AD
8), cos. 31 BC, had a distinguished public career under Augustus. He
was also an orator and literary patron to a number of poets, including Tibullus. According to Jerome (*Chron. ad Olymp.* 198, 12 AD,
Migne, *PL* 27. 442), he could barely speak for two years and when
his condition was exacerbated by an ulcer, he starved himself to
death; cf. Sol. 1. 110. See *OCD*[3], Valerius Messala Corvinus,
Marcus, 1580; Hanslik, *RE* 8 A 1, Valerius (261), 131–58.

bereft mind   The notion that memory is associated with or
actully situated within, the mind, is found in Cic. *Tusc.* 1. 61; Varro,
LL 6. 44; Serv. *In Aen.* 2. 224 and 2. 736. See above, **No . . . fear**.

Indeed . . . wonders where it is.   P.'s vivid language here portrays memory as an elusive and delicate creature. It is continually
looking for chances to escape its prison in the human mind and is
susceptible to ambush by the stealthy predator, sleep. The frequent
ancient imagery which associated thoughts and memories with
birds and other winged creatures (Carruthers (1990), 35–7) may be
the inspiration for his metaphor.

91. the dictator Caesar   C. Julius Caesar (100–44 BC) held a
series of temporary dictatorships from 49 to 45 BC, followed by a
permanent dictatorship granted between late Jan. and mid-Feb. 44
BC. Refs. in Broughton, *MRR* ii. 256, 272, 286, 294–5, 305, 317–18.

vigour . . . moral excellence . . . the sun   Caesar's all-round
genius (Cic., *Phil.* 2. 116) and his general energy and dynamism
were legendary. Here P. refers to his mental energy, using a phrase
also found in Velleius 2. 41. 2. Biographical collections such as those
of Atticus or Nepos may have enshrined the basic points of later
descriptions (M. Gelzer, *Caesar: Politician and Statesman* (Oxford,
1968), 272 and n.). P. tries to make the concept of mental vigour
more specific by explaining what he is not describing, namely
Caesar's moral and intellectual dynamism. 'Moral excellence'
(*virtus*), a term in the Roman value system denoting a man of worth
in the broad sphere of Roman public life, including war and politics, required moral, physical, and mental effort, as Cicero (*Pro Mur.*
15–17) stressed in the face of aristocratic complacency which viewed
it as a primarily hereditary endowment. So, more obviously, did
constantia, 'resolution', 'determination'. See D. Earl, *The Moral and
Political Tradition of Republican Rome* (Ithaca, 1967, repr. 1984), especially chs. 1–2. Despite Caesar's evident political and military success, doubts were expressed as to whether his achievements were in
the true moral spirit of the code. See below, **92. Indeed . . . at all**
and Cic. *Att.* 7. 11. 1 with P. A. Brunt, 'Cicero's *Officium* in the Civil
War', *JRS* 76 (1986), 12–32, esp. 15 and nn. Commenting on
Caesar's claim to be protecting his *dignitas* ('prestige', 'standing') in
the civil war of 49 BC, Cicero asked: 'Where is *dignitas* without
honestas ("honour")?' For other Roman aristocratic/political values, see below, **100. Cato** and **139. ten greatest and best
objectives**.

'Intellectual capacity' etc. essentially denotes depth and subtlety
of understanding. (The idea of embracing 'everything under the

sun' may be a deliberate pun; Schilling (170) compares the words P. uses to describe Caesar's new calendar, which 'brought the years back into line with the course of the sun' (*HN* 18. 221).) In contrast, the 'mental vigour' of Caesar does not imply either moral attainment or intellectual understanding. It is a more superficial virtuosity, a mental agility.

We are told . . . seven at a time] Cf. Solinus 1. 107. The last part of the sentence may be an interpolation. This sort of virtuosity would have had a particular appeal to P., who went to great lengths to read and write while engaged in other (albeit non-intellectual) pursuits. See Introd. 4. 5. 2. Small (1997: 172–3) compares the similar skills in simultaneous dictation of Galba in Cicero, *Brutus* 23. 87, and, later, of St Thomas Aquinas. For the speed and ease with which Caesar himself wrote, see Hirtius in *BG* 8, pref. 6.

92. 50 pitched battles Cf. Solinus 1. 106, who has 52, leading some scholars to emend Pliny's text. Velleius (2. 47, 'many') and Plutarch (*Caes.* 15, 'more than anyone else') do not commit themselves to figures. Whether or not P.'s figures for the battles and the casualties (below) are correct, such statistics could have featured in Caesar's triumphal announcements and in other official documents and inscriptions, cf. below, **97.** and **98. official announcement**.

M. Marcellus M. Claudius Marcellus, five times consul, was a vigorous and successful general in the first Punic war (264–241 BC), defeating the Insubrian Gauls, campaigning against Hannibal in Italy, and then serving in Sicily, where he took Syracuse in 211 BC. Nicknamed the Sword of Rome, his military exploits became legendary. *OCD*[3], Claudius Marcellus (1), 340–1.

The number . . . forced upon him Velleius (2. 47) gives 400,000 for the Gallic wars, Plutarch (*Caes.* 15) one million (cf. *Pomp.* 67). P. is alone in criticizing this particular record on humanitarian grounds, a moral/philosophical attitude based on the idea that mass slaughter was a symptom of man's moral decline (see Lucretius *RN* 5. 999–1000 with Bailey (1947), iii. 1480) or, at least, the general ambiguity of his progress. See L. Edelstein, *The Idea of Progress in Classical Antiquity* (Baltimore, 1967), 50.

Indeed . . . at all Reticence over the civil war casualties does not, of course, suggest that Caesar took P.'s view that *all* casualty figures were an embarrassment. Casualty figures for some of the major battles in the civil war did appear in Caesar's commentaries, e.g. 15,000 for Pharsalus (*BC* 3. 99. 4) but it was Asinius Pollio who stated specifically that 6,000 of these were Roman citizens (Plutarch, *Pomp.* 72. 4, *Caes.* 46. 3; Appian, *BC* 2. 345–6). The commentaries on the African and Spanish wars also contain some figures (*Bell. Afr.* 86. 1, but cf. Plutarch, *Caes.* 53. 2; *Bell. Hisp.* 31. 9, cf. Plutarch, *Caes.* 56. 3), but their Caesarean authorship is doubtful. However, P. is probably referring to the practice of flaunting such figures officially, e.g. in triumphs (below, **95. records**, **97**, **98**), which, in the case of the civil war casualties, Caesar did not do. The sources show that he recognized that 'Roman' victories were a sensitive issue and modified direct references to them in the triumphs of 46 BC (Dio 43. 19; Plutarch, *Caes.* 55, Appian, *BC* 2. 101–2; Suet. *Jul.* 37). But he did not go far enough: in the African triumph, ostensibly over king Juba, names and numbers were absent, but there were clearly recognizable images of Cato, Scipio, and Petreius (Plutarch, *Caes.* 55. 1; Appian 2. 101). The Spanish triumph of 45 BC, being almost impossible to disguise as a foreign victory, gave even more offence (Dio 43. 42, Plutarch, *Caes.* 56. 4). But however reticent Caesar was about the civil losses, their magnitude was obvious from mere observation of the remaining population, as well as from the censuses conducted by Caesar himself, according to Dio (43. 25. 2).

93. Pompey the Great Caesar's one-time colleague, with M. Crassus, in the 'first triumvirate' (see above, **56. Antony after he became triumvir**), then his rival and finally his opponent in the civil war of 49–45 BC. See *OCD*³, Pompeius Magnus (1), 1215–16; above, **34. Pompey the Great**, below, **94. Pompey at Pharsalus**, and **95–9.**

846 . . . pirates See below, **97. sent out to all the seas** and **846 ships**.

clemency . . . detriment See e.g. Cic. *Att.* 14. 22; Suet. *Jul.* 73–5; Velleius 2. 56. 3. Caesar had stated his policy of clemency in a letter of March 49 BC quoted by Cicero (*Att.* 9. 7c). The term *clementia* was Cicero's, Caesar favouring *lenitas* ('mildness') and *misericordia* ('mercy'), perhaps to emphasize that the policy arose from personal disposition, rather than pragmatism: see M. T. Griffin, 'Clementia after Caesar: From Politics to Philosophy', in F. Cairns and E. Fantham (eds.), *Caesar against Liberty? Perspectives on his Autocracy*, Papers of the Langford Latin Seminar, vol. 11 (Cambridge, 2003), 157–63. His comment that, with the exception of Sulla, previous victors who had shown cruelty had not in fact been able to maintain their victories for long, suggests that the policy was in reality primarily tactical ('artful clemency', Cic. *Att.* 8. 16) rather than due to his natural disposition, although in public speeches Cicero was more flattering (*Lig.* 38, cf. 6, 10, 15, 19, 29, 300). In 44 BC a temple was decreed to his Clemency as a thank-offering (Plutarch, *Caes.* 57. 3; Appian, *BC* 2. 16. 106; Dio 44. 6, cf. E. A. Sydenham, *The Coinage of the Roman Republic* (London, 1952), 1076; Crawford (1974), ii, no. 480.21; Richardson (1992), 88). Ultimately, the policy failed: his murderers included ostensibly conciliated Pompeians such as M. Brutus, whom he had gone out of his way to favour. Disaffected senators perhaps saw in such a policy the self-confidence of a tyrant secure enough in his supremacy to be indulgent (cf. Earl (1967/84), 59–61). Gelzer (1968: 331 n.1) quotes Dio's account (75. 8. 1) of a speech by Septimius Severus in AD 197 in which he stated that Pompey and Caesar ultimately met their downfall through clemency, whereas for Marius, Sulla, and Augustus, cruelty had been the key to success.

magnanimity Taking his cue from Caesar's clemency, P. now identifies more moral aspects of his character which were specifically excluded from the initial discussion of mental agility (above, **91. vigour . . . the sun**).

94. If I were to list . . . luxury For Caesar's handouts, games, and public buildings, see Suet. *Jul.* 38, 39, 44; Dio 43. 49. 3, 43. 21. 3–24; Appian, *BC* 2. 102; *HN* 8. 21–2, 53, 69, 182, 36. 102, 103. Such lavish public benefactions could be regarded as an aspect of the generosity of spirit displayed in his *clementia*, cf. Sallust, *Cat.* 54. 2: see M. T. Griffin '*Clementia* after Caesar: From Politics to Philosophy', in F. Cairns and E. Fantham (eds.), *Caesar against Liberty? Perspectives on his Autocracy*, Papers of the Langford Latin Seminar 11, ARCA 43 (Cambridge, 2003), 179; M. B. Roller, *Constructing Autocracy: Aristocrats and Emperors in Julio-Claudian Rome* (Princeton, 2001), 173–93. However, P. has a less materialistic manifestation in mind. The reference to luxury may reflect not only P.'s personal crusade against it in the *HN* but also contemporary criticism of Caesar for the vast amounts he spent on his triumphs and their associated games and celebrations in 46–45 BC (Dio 43. 18. 2, 24. 1–2).

genuine . . . invincible spirit i.e. an altruistic generosity of spirit, to be contrasted with the materialistic benefactions which enhanced his popularity and enshrined his unique position of power. He could have gained personal advantage from the papers but refused to do so.

Pompey at Pharsalus Pompey was defeated at Pharsalus in Thessaly (P. calls it 'Pharsalia') in Aug. 43 BC. He fled as his camp was captured (Caesar, *BC* 3. 96–7) and was later murdered in Egypt (Plutarch, *Caes.* 45–6). For the papers, see also Dio 41. 63. 5; Seneca, *De Ira* 2. 23. 4.

Scipio at Thapsus For the papers, see Dio 43. 13. 2. Q. Caecilius Metellus Pius Scipio Nasica (cos. 52 BC with his son-in-law, Pompey) took control of the Pompeian army after Pharsalus, when it regrouped in Africa. His army was put to flight and his camp captured near Thapsus in April 46 BC. He died while escaping to Spain. See Dio 43. 9; Plut. *Caes.* 53; [Caesar], *Bell. Afr.* 80–5: *OCD*3, Caecilius Metellus Pius Scipio, Quintus, 270.

95. records P. drew directly on official records (*acta*; for public records generally, see below, **186. public records**) of Pompey's triumphs (*HN* 37. 13). *Tituli* (as here) can refer to inscriptions and monuments (below, **97, 98. official announcement**) and also to placards carried in the triumph, describing spoils, prisoners and representations of conquered peoples and places, cf. *HN* 5. 37 (Balbus' triumph).

one man . . . empire An echo of the Livian–Augustan image of Pompey as champion of the republic and Caesar as self-seeking military despot (Syme (1939), 317 ff.). For a recent reassessment, see M. Toher, 'Julius Caesar and Octavian in Nicolaus', in F. Cairns and E. Fantham (eds.), *Caesar against Liberty? Perspectives on his Autocracy* (Cambridge, 2003), esp. 133–6, with bibliography of past and present scholarship on this issue (nn. 4–5).

Alexander the Great Pompey consciously modelled himself

on Alexander (Plutarch, *Pomp.* 2; Sallust, *Hist.* 3. 88); quite literally so in his portraits (P. Zanker, *The Power of Images in the Age of Augustus* (Ann Arbor, 1988), 9–11). Others took up the comparison (Cicero, *Arch.* 24; Livy 9. 17. 6), some going too far (Plutarch, *Pomp.* 46, cf. Appian, *B.Mith.* 12. 117 on Pompey wearing a chlamys said to have been Alexander's). See J. C. Richard, 'Alexandre et Pompée: À propos de Tite-Live IX.16. 19–19. 7', in *Mélanges de philosophie, de littérature et d'histoire ancienne offerts à Pierre Boyancé*, Coll. Ec. France de Rome, 22 (Rome, 1974), 653 ff. and below, **96. triumphed . . . for the second time.**

Hercules . . . Bacchus Associated with world conquest (J. Noiville, 'Les Indes de Bacchus et d'Heraclès', *Rev. Phil.* 55 (1929), 245–69; Richard (1974), 662–3). Both figures were also 'ancestors' of Alexander and consciously emulated by him (A. B. Bosworth, *Conquest and Empire: the Reign of Alexander the Great* (Cambridge, 1988), 278–90) and thus also by Pompey. Stories of their travels pre-dated Alexander but were elaborated in the wake of his exploits (G. W. Bowersock, *Hellenism in Late Antiquity* (Michigan, 1990), 47–9, and 'Dionysus as Epic Hero', in N. Hopkinson (ed.), *Studies in the Dionysiaca of Nonnos* (Cambridge, 1994 = 1994*a*), 156–64). The comparison was a metaphor for Pompey's victories, from the Pillars of Hercules in the west to Asia in the east. For Hercules, see below, **96. Alps . . . Further Spain**; For Bacchus, *HN* 8. 4 and below, **96. triumphal chariot.** The idea of Pompey as champion of his country (above, **95. one man . . . empire**) may also be reflected in the comparison with Hercules, who by P.'s time was a model of selfless labour on behalf of others: see Introd. 4. 4.

96. recovered Sicily . . . in the service of Sulla From the Marians under Cn. Carbo whom he killed (82 BC: Appian, *BC* 1. 96. 449; Livy, *Per.* 89; Plutarch, *Pomp.* 10). That P. skips Pompey's significant (Cicero, *Leg. Man.* 30) part in the initial Sullan struggle in 83 BC when, aged 23, he raised an army and marched to join Sulla (*Leg. Man.* 61; Appian, *BC* 1. 80. 336; Plutarch, *Pomp.* 6–8), may be because Sicily was his first independent command (Schilling 172); but also because P. is concerned with the geographical spread of Pompey's achievements. He is also sensitive about victories over fellow-Romans (above, **92. Indeed . . . at all** and below, **96. triumphal chariot** and **refraining . . . Sertorius' name**).

Africa   In 81 BC Pompey defeated the Marian Domitius Ahenobarbus and his ally king Iarbas of Numidia (Appian, *BC* I. 80. 368;
Sallust *Hist.* I. 53; Livy, *Per.* 89; Velleius 2. 30. 2; Plutarch, *Pomp.* 12).

'the Great'   Pliny like Plutarch dates the title to this period rather
than 61 BC (Appian, *BC* 2. 86. 363, 91. 384; Livy, *Per.* 103): see also
Plutarch, *Pomp.* 13. 7, cf. 23. 2 and Cicero, *Leg. Man.* 67. The two
versions of the acclamation recorded in Plutarch, attributing it
(*a*) to Sulla and (*b*) to the African army, but later confirmed by Sulla
are glossed over by P.; as is the assertion that Pompey only started
to use the title himself when he was out in Spain from 77 BC
(Plutarch, *Pomp.* 13. 7). For the choice of name, see above, **95.
Alexander the Great**. For its use on his coinage, see A. Bruhl, 'Le
Souvenir d'Alexandre le Grand et les Romains', *MEFRA* 47 (1930),
206; Sydenham (1952), no. 1028; Crawford (1974), i. 83, 412–13; ii.
pl. 50. 6, no. 402; Richard (1974), 662–3.

triumphal chariot   The date was 12 March (Licinianus 31). The
year is disputed; probably 81 BC (E. Badian, 'The Date of Pompey's
First Triumph', *Hermes* 83 (1955), 107–18). Roman sensibilities were
observed by celebrating it over Iarbas (Appian, *BC* I. 80. 368; Livy,
Per. 89; Licinianus 31, Eutropius 5. 9. 1) rather than fellow-Romans
(contrast Caesar's Spanish triumph, Plutarch, *Caes.* 56; cf. the tact-
less African triumph, Appian, *BC* 2. 101. 420). The abortive attempt
(*HN* 8. 4, Plutarch, *Pomp.* 14; Licinianus 31) to use captured African
elephants to draw the *triumphator's* chariot symbolized not only his
conquest of Africa (cf. Sydenham and Crawford, above, previous
note) but also his emulation of Alexander (Bosworth (1988), 129–30
on coins of Alexander's victory over Porus' elephants; cf. 180) and
also of Bacchus (*HN* 8. 4).

equestrian rank   Technically, triumphs were given only to
magistrates holding *imperium* (Plut. *Pomp.* 14). Pompey had another
prerequisite, victory in a foreign war, but was not even a senator
and held command through an extraordinary senatorial grant of
propraetorian *imperium*.

unprecedented   Cicero, *Leg. Man.* 61; Appian, *BC* I. 80. 368;
Livy *Per.* 89; Licinianus 31. Pompey persisted where others didn't
think of trying, cf. the elder Africanus, victorious in Spain in 210 BC
as *privatus* with special proconsular *imperium* (Plut. *Pomp.* 14). Pompey
wallowed in the *paradox* of his position as knight-*triumphator*, a point

picked up by P. below, **civil war ... ranks**: see Introd. 5. 4. However, the story of his participation in an equestrian discharge parade after his second triumph (Plut. *Pomp.* 22) seems to be apocryphal and anachronistic: see M. I. Henderson, 'The Origins of the *equester ordo*', *JRS* 53 (1963), 62.

the West In 78 BC (P.'s 'immediately' is loose), Pompey was sent with (probably) propraetorian *imperium* against the Marian Sertorius in Spain (Plut. *Pomp.* 17; Florus 2. 10. 6).

trophies in the Pyrenees Sallust, *Hist.* 3. 89; Strabo 3. 4. 1, 7, 9; 4. 13, C156–63; Dio 41. 24. 3. The 'trophies' were incorporated into a monumental structure: *HN* 37. 15–16 (Pompey's statue crowned it), and *HN* 3. 17 (where P. gives the number of towns as 366). See Goessler, *RE* 21. 2, 2045ff.; G.-C. Picard, *Les Trophées Romains: Contribution à l'histoire de la religion et de l'art* (Paris, 1957) 181–90. Permanent monuments of military victories date back to the 4th cent. BC, often becoming more personal symbols of the general's achievement from Sulla onwards; thus, Pompey's marks territory conquered rather than a particular battle site. Now lost, the monument was still visible as a ruin in the early Middle Ages. It perhaps resembled the later extant trophies at La Turbie (Augustus, *HN* 3. 136) and Adamklissi (Trajan, *OCD*3, 11).

Alps ... Further Spain Cf. Sallust, *Hist.* 2. 98. 4. The monument thus stood in the middle of the conquered territory as well as on the provincial boundary (cf. Cicero, *Inv.* 2. 69; *Prov. Cons.* 4) between Gaul and Spain. Pompey's route from Spain to Italy recalled Hercules' travels and may suggest a 70 BC date for his dedication or restoration of a temple to Hercules (*HN* 34. 57; Vitruvius 3. 5; B. A. Marshall, 'Pompey's Temple of Hercules', *Antichthon*, 8 (1974), 83; Richardson (1992), 187–8; cf. Crawford (1974), ii, no. 426.4a–b). Cf. also Augustus' western exploits, Horace, *Od.* 3. 14. 1.

refraining ... Sertorius' name For sensitivity over Roman adversaries, see above, **96. triumphal chariot**. The monument still caused resentment (Dio 41. 24. 3).

magnanimity The mark of true greatness in P.'s opinion. He does not mention but may also have in mind here Pompey's destruction of Sertorius' papers (Plutarch *Sert.* 27, *Mor.* 204a; Cicero, *Verr.* 5. 152ff.). See above, **93–4**, where he enthuses about

Caesar's magnanimity in destroying Pompey's and Scipio's papers after their defeats.

crushing the civil war   Sertorius was murdered by his lieutenant Perperna who was himself finally defeated by Pompey in 72 BC. The triumph was of course *ex Hispaniis* (above, **refraining . . . Sertorius' name**) (Velleius 2. 30; Florus 2. 10. 9).

civil war . . . ranks   P. brings out the paradoxes in Pompey's career (see above, **unprecedented**; Introd 5. 4): a civil war which was also a foreign one; twice *triumphator* yet only a knight; and twice a commander but never a subordinate (ignoring Pompey's service in 89 under his father in the Social War).

triumphal . . . for the second time   On the last day of 71, the day before taking up the consulship of 70 BC, Pompey having earlier been involved in the crushing of Spartacus: Cicero, *Leg. Man.* 62, *Pis.* 58, *Div.* 2. 22; Velleius 2. 30; Plutarch, *Pomp.* 22; Appian, *BC* 1. 121. 561; Lucan 7. 14 ff.

97. sent out to all the seas   In 67 BC a wide-ranging *imperium*, covering the whole Mediterranean area and extending up to fifty miles inland from its coasts, was granted to Pompey by the *Lex Gabinia* to deal with piracy (Appian, *B. Mith.* 12. 94, 97; Velleius 2. 31. 2; Dio 36. 37. 1–2; Plutarch, *Pomp.* 25–6). Whether this *imperium* was *maius* or *aequum* (Velleius, cf. *Laud. Agrippae* 11–12 with E. W. Gray, 'The *Imperium* of M. Agrippa', *ZPE* 6 (1970), 227–38; R. K. Sherk, *The Roman Empire: Augustus to Hadrian* (Cambridge, 1988), no. 12 n. 5) is uncertain, but his allocation of troops and money was large and the propraetorian *imperium* of his legates unprecedented.

the east   The command against Mithridates, granted to Pompey by the *Lex Manilia* in 66 BC which extended the powers granted by the *Lex Gabinia* (above, **sent out to all the seas** and Dio 42. 4).

countless titles   A network of new provinces and client-kingdoms produced vast new power and wealth for Rome and for Pompey personally (Appian, *B. Mith.* 12. 114; Plutarch, *Pomp.* 45. 3), but the honours granted to him were unprecedented: *ILS* 8776, 9459, *SIG³* 338, 749a; see M. H. Crawford, 'Hamlet without the Prince', review of E. S. Gruen, *The Last Generation of the Roman Republic, JRS* 66 (1976), 216.

winners . . . crown their country   Cf. the Olympic, Pythian,

Nemean, and Isthmian games in Greece. In *HN* 16. 10, P. states even more clearly that there was no actual crowning of the victors in his day. This was not the case in the classical period (H. A. Harris, *Greek Athletes and Athletics* (London, 1964), 36, 169) and, close to Pliny's period, Nero, at least, personally received and kept his crowns (Suet. *Nero* 25). That the *honour* of the victory belonged as much to the city as to the victor himself was of course well established (Pindar, *Nem.* 10. 1–3, 5. 8; *Isth.* 1. 66–7; *Ol.* 3. 2, 4. 2, 8. 15–16; Harris (1964), 37), and P. may be interpreting over-literally figurative declarations such as Nero's in Dio 63. 14. 4, that 'Nero Caesar wins this contest and *crowns* the Roman people and his own universe'; cf. Pindar, *Pyth.* 2. 6, 9. 4. For the patriotic connotation of Pompey's personal achievements, see also above, **95. one man . . . empire**.

spoils of war *Manubiae*: that part of the booty expropriated by the general for himself and often used to finance public building (I. Shatzman, 'The Roman General's Authority over Booty', *Historia*, 21 (1972), 204). J. Bradford Churchill ('*Ex qua quod vellet facerent*; Roman Magistrates' Authority over *praedia* and *manubiae*', *TAPA* 129 (1999), 85–116) argues that, strictly speaking, *manubiae* remained in public ownership, to be put to use in the public interest. Because few temples in the Republic are specifically said to have been constructed with *manubiae*, E. Orlin (*Temples, Religion and Politics in the Roman Republic* (Leiden, 1997), 132–5) thinks Pliny is wrong to interpret the inscription as a reference to the dedication of the temple from *manubiae* and that it simply refers to an offering dedicated from the spoils and left in the temple. Apparent rarity, however, is not a compelling reason to reject Pliny's claim. On this, again, Churchill, *Bryn Mawr Classical Review* (1999. 07. 02).

temple of Minerva Known only from P. See Richardson (1992), 88. Minerva was chosen perhaps for her military connections, cf. Athene Nike (Altheim, *RE* 15. 2, 1791). But Minerva's role as patron of Hercules may have appealed to his emulator.

thirty years' war Initial action against Mithridates was taken by Sulla as propraetor of Cilicia in 92 BC (Plutarch, *Sull.* 5. 3).

12,183,000 Lack of condemnation by P, (above **92. The number . . . forced upon him**) suggests these were mainly captives rather than fatalities.

846 ships   Appian, *B. Mith.* 12. 117 has 800, from a placard in the triumph, cf. Plutarch, *Pomp.* 45. 2, who says they were piratical.

Maiotians   Sarmatians on the eastern bank of Lake Maiotis (the sea of Azov). Mithridates was eventually killed in the area (Plutarch, *Pomp.* 35; Appian, *B. Mith.* 12. 107–11).

the Red Sea   On the problems of this term in ancient literature, see F. R. D. Goodyear, *The Annals of Tacitus books 1–6* (Cambridge, 1981), 387–93; R. Syme, 'Tacitus: Some Sources of his Information', *JRS* 72 (1982), 70–1. That this reference is specifically to what we call the Red Sea (cf. *HN* 6. 103) and not the Persian Gulf (contra Schilling 173–4) seems clear from Pompey's march as described in Plutarch, *Pomp.* 38–41, cf. Appian 12. 106. But his desire to reach the Red Sea 'so as to extend his conquests to the Outer Ocean' (ibid. 38) also suggests he perceived the sea in its wider aspect, the Indian Ocean, of which the Red Sea and the Persian Gulf are inlets (cf. *OCD*[3], Red Sea, 1296–7). By reaching the outer circle of Ocean which surrounded the world (*HN* 2. 166, 171, 173), he enhanced his image as an extender of the empire to encompass world conquest (Cicero, *Sest.* 67). Cf., again, the Alexander echoes, and below, **99. whole world**.

98. triumphal procession   His third, in 61 BC, for the pirates and the Eastern campaigns. Cf. Plutarch, *Pomp.* 45; Appian, *B. Mith.* 12. 116–17; Dio 37. 21. 2; Diodorus Siculus 40. 4; *Inscr. It.* xiii. 1, 84–5, 566. See Broughton, *MRR* ii. 181. For its distinctive honours, see S. Weinstock, *Divus Julius* (Oxford, 1971), 38–9.

28 September   It lasted two days, 28–29 Sept.: Plutarch, *Pomp.* 45. 1; Appian, *B. Mith.* 12. 116; *HN* 37. 13: 29 Sept. was also Pompey's birthday, *Inscr. It.* xiii. 1, 566.

official announcement.   Presumably taken from the *acta* mentioned in *HN* 37. 13 (above **95. records**). More details were displayed on the placards in the procession (Plutarch, *Pomp.* 45. 2; Appian, *B. Mith.* 12. 117). Countries and peoples from 'Asia' to 'Albania' correspond exactly with *Inscr. It.* xiii. 1, 566; both are similar to the more detailed inscription (Diodorus 40. 4) possibly from the temple of Venus Vitrix, in the complex which included Pompey's theatre and statues of the conquered nations (above, **34. theatre; statues . . . artists**). Cf. M. Gelzer, *Pompeius* (Munich, 1949), 32–3.

For details of the individual campaigns, see Appian, *B. Mith.* 12. 97ff.; Plutarch, *Pomp.* 25–42; Dio 36. 20–37. 21; Velleius 2. 37, 40. 1–3. Captives from each graced the procession in national costume (Appian 12. 117) as did their rulers, either in person or as effigies (Appian, *B. Mith.* 12. 116–17). Unusually few were later killed: the Jewish king Antiochus, who had revolted, and the son of Tigranes (below).

Crete A contentious claim: Pompey and Metellus Creticus both claimed the submission of Crete and, though Metellus triumphed in 62, Pompey snatched his most important captives (Dio 36. 17, 18, 19. 3; Florus 2. 13. 9).

king Mithridates Rome's adversary of thirty years was dead but images were displayed in various tableaux. Five sons and two daughters were present in person (Appian, *B. Mith.* 12. 117).

Tigranes Pardoned and restored as king of Armenia and remained loyal until his death in 56 BC; but his son plotted with the Parthians and was paraded as a captive, then killed (Appian, *B. Mith.* 12. 117).

99. public meeting Cf. Livy, *Per.* 103 for acclamation of Pompey at a public meeting after the 61 triumph.

Asia . . . empire Cf. Cicero, *Prov. Cons.* 31; Florus 1. 40. 31. Asia was now flanked by the provinces of Pontus, Bithynia, Cilicia, and Syria. Further protection was provided by client kingdoms. P.'s language suggests almost a literal rearrangement of Asia within the expanded empire. See Introd. 5. 4.

Caesar . . . greater A play on 'Magnus' and fleeting recognition by P. of Caesar's greater ultimate success (below, **whole world**) despite earlier reservations **92. The number . . . forced upon him, 95. one man . . . empire**.

whole world By virtue of his civil war victories, Caesar held all Pompey's conquests, as well as new territory for Rome in Gaul (59–50 BC) and had plans for Parthia. For the iconography of Caesar as world-conqueror (the individual replacing the corporate dominance of Rome, see above, **95. one man . . . empire**), with a globe or a personification of *Oikumene* (P. Arnaud, 'L'Image du globe dans le monde romain: Science, iconographie, symbolique',

MEFRA 96. 1 (1984), 53–116) in submission to him, see Weinstock (1971), 47–52, who contrasts this direct personal association with Pompey's less focused claims and quotes P.'s assertion here. Pompey had, however, shown a representation of the world in his 61 triumph (Dio 37. 21. 2, cf. Diodorus Siculus 40. 4) and a globe, probably symbolizing totality, appeared on a coin of *c.*56 BC (Sydenham (1952), 882; Crawford (1974), i. 449–51; ii. no. 426.3–4). Domination of the seas (Cicero, *Prov. Cons.* 31; see above, **97. Red Sea**) and exhibition of ebony trees in the triumphal procession (*HN* 12. 20), like Caesar's captive Ocean and Gallic rivers (Florus 2. 13. 88), suggested conquest of nature herself, cf. Seneca, *Brev. Vit.* 13. 7. His three triumphs over three continents could be portrayed as world conquest (e.g. Plutarch, *Pomp.* 45; Velleius 2. 40. 4; Cicero, *Balb.* 9; M. E. Deutsch, 'Pompey's Three Triumphs', *CPh.* 19 (1924), 277–9); as could the extent of his exploits in east and west (**112** below; cf. Lucan, *Phars.* 2. 483).

100–29. introd. *Examples of various kinds of virtus*

The exceptional achievements of Caesar and Pompey in the previous sections (**91–9**) prompt an examination of pre-eminent examples of *virtus*, excellence, which often has moral connotations and can take different forms in different contexts. See below, **104. courage . . . fortune**, **106. men . . . fortune**, and **130. virtue**. P. (**100**) starts with Cato the Censor, renowned for his pre-eminence in rhetoric, generalship, and statesmanship, the three main areas of activity in Roman public life. He then (**101–6**) looks at another Roman speciality, *virtus* specifically in the military context, as *fortitudo*, culminating in the example of M. Sergius. The discussion then moves on to intellectual genius (**107–17**) and then (**118–29**) the remaining gifts of the mind. The sequence can be summarized as follows:

100. Cato the Censor
101–6. Examples of *virtus as fortitudo*
107–17. Intellectual genius:
    107. The variety of achievement in the various disciplines
    108–12. Greek literary genius (**110**—recognized by kings and statesmen)
    112–13. Roman leaders and Greek genius

114–17. Roman intellectual eminence (Scipio and Ennius; Augustus and Virgil; Pollio's library; Pompey and Varro; Cicero)

118–30. The remaining gifts of the mind:

118–19. Other intellectuals, Greek and Roman: philosophers and prophets

120. Moral excellence

121–2. *Pietas*

123–5. Scientists

126–7. Artists

128–9. Postscript: Valuable slaves, linked by their talents to the overall theme of human excellence.

A sentence on the *virtus* of the Roman people as a whole at the beginning of (**130**) concludes this section and starts a qualitative assessment of human life which precedes Pliny's discussion of its limits (longevity) and its final end, death (**130–90**).

100. Cato M. Porcius Cato the Censor (234–149 BC) was, according to Plutarch (*Cat. Mai.* 1), originally surnamed Priscus, but was later called Cato from *catus* meaning 'wise, prudent'. See *OCD³*, Porcius Cato (1), 1224–5; A. E. Astin, *Cato the Censor* (Oxford, 1978).

outstanding . . . senator He excelled in the three main areas of Roman public life, although Valerius Maximus 8. 7. 1 adds a fourth, knowledge of civil law, an ability proven early on in his career (Plutarch, *Cat. Mai.* 3. 3); see also below, **139. ten greatest and best objectives** and, for a similar analysis, Livy 39. 40. He was a pithy orator: Cicero knew over 150 speeches and fragments from eighty are extant. His military distinction was shown in his governorship of Spain in 194 BC for which he gained a triumph (Plut. *Cat. Mai.* 11. 3). As senator, he was famous for his robust advocacy of traditional values, most notably during his censorship of 184 BC.

Scipio Aemilianus Scipio Aemilianus Africanus Numantinus (185/4–129 BC) was the son of L. Aemilius Paullus and was adopted by P. Scipio, son of Scipio Africanus. His military success in the third Punic war led to his election to the consulship by special dispensation in 147 BC, although he had not held the praetorship. His policy resulted in the eventual fall of Carthage in 146 BC, for which he celebrated a triumph. He was later chosen consul for a second time to undertake the problematic war against Numantia, which he destroyed in 133 BC. He opposed Tiberius Gracchus' legislation but died at the height of the ensuing controversy. Besides this military and political pre-eminence, he was a man of culture and a fine speaker. Cicero made him his ideal statesman in his *Republic*. See *OCD*[3], Cornelius Scipio Aemilianus Africanus, 397–8.

forty-four . . . each occasion Plutarch says he was prosecuted 'nearly thirty' times (*Cat. Mai.* 15. 3–4), attacks evidently encouraged not only by his opposition to the Scipios and by his sumptuary legislation (18), but also by his addiction to prosecuting others (15. 1). His last case as defendant was at the age of 86 and, as prosecutor, 90 (15. 4, cf. Valerius Maximus 8. 7. 1).

101. Q. Ennius . . . honour Q. Ennius (239–169 BC) was an early Latin poet from Calabria. The most original and important of his works was the *Annales*, the first Latin hexameter verse epic. It was an account of Roman history, originally in 15 books of which only fragments survive. Almost nothing is known of a further 3 books added later, except that they covered the Istrian war of 178–177 BC and events thereafter. The exploits of the two Caecilii, otherwise unknown, were presumably in the context of that war. See *OCD*[3], Ennius, 525–6; Münzer, *RE* 3. 1, Caecilius (122), 1233.

L. Siccius Dentatus . . . votes A primitive and essentially legendary hero and champion of the plebs, 'the Roman Achilles' (Aulus Gellius, *NA* 2. 11) was later associated with the period of the patrician Decemvirs (451–449 BC). Ogilvie (1965: 476) suggests that the pairing of Dentatus with the historical M. Sergius Silus, as here in Pliny (see below, **104–6**) was well known. (Valerius Maximus 3. 2. 24 derives the story from Varro among others.) The fullest extant account of his exploits is in Dionysius of Halicarnassus 10. 36–52. His plebeian sympathies led the consul of 455 BC, Titus Romilius, to try to get rid of him by sending him on a perilous mission during the war against the Aequi, from which he was able to extricate himself. He was elected tribune in 454 BC (Dion. Hal. 10. 47) and later successfully prosecuted his old commander for crimes against the state and the murder plot against him (Dion. Hal. 10. 48–90). He was treacherously murdered by the Decemvirs (Dion. Hal. 11. 26) in 449 BC (the only part of the story which appears in Livy (3. 43)). See *OCD*[3], 1401.

120 battles . . . architect This catalogue of military achievement and awards appears also in Gellius 2. 11, Dion. Hal. 10. 37, and Valerius Maximus 3. 2. 24, with one or two minor variations. Given the semi-legendary status of Dentatus, these award details, like the account of his career generally, are of dubious historical value and are probably anachronistic: it is doubtful, for example, whether specific crowns for saving the lives of Roman citizens and scaling the enemy's walls had developed as early as this. See V. A. Maxfield, *The Military Decorations of the Roman Army* (Berkeley, 1981), 42–5.

102. 34 trophies 36 in Valerius Maximus 3. 2. 24. *Spolia* were the arms and armour from a defeated enemy.

18 ceremonial spears . . . siege-hero's crown A variety of decorations—*dona militaria*—were awarded for military bravery. In the Republic, different awards were given for different types of deeds; appropriation according to rank did not become established until the 1st cent. AD. See Maxfield (1981), 42–5.

ceremonial spears The *hasta pura* was awarded to a soldier who voluntarily engaged and killed an enemy (Polyb. 6. 39. 3–4). Its exact nature is disputed. Defined as a spear 'without iron' (*sine ferro*) by Varro (Servius, *In Aen.* 6. 760), the evidence does not support the view that it was 'headless'; cf. Maxfield (1981), 55–6, who suggests that *pura* meant ritual purity—a ceremonial spear never used to kill. But what of *sine ferro*? Two imperial references suggest that they may have been tipped with precious metals (Josephus, *BJ* 7. 15, *CIL* xi. 7264 = *ILS* 9194). Certainly, the ambiguity of iron, at once the material of the implements of peaceful agriculture and the weapons of murderous war, was not lost on ancient writers. Pliny's own stress on this latter usage as a corruption of iron is particularly relevant (*HN* 34. 135–41).

bosses Bosses (*phalerae*) are not attested for specific exploits. They may originally have been awarded to cavalrymen (Maxfield (1981), 92) and were given in conjunction with other awards.

necklets . . . bracelets Necklets (*torques*) and bracelets (*armillae*) would originally have derived from the spoils taken from barbarian enemies such as the Gauls. There are no indications of specific conditions for their award.

crowns   See also *HN* 16. 14. Crowns (*coronae*) included the highest and, according to Pliny (*HN* 22. 6), the oldest award, the siege-hero's crown (*corona obsidionalis*). It was made of grass (hence the alternative name, *corona graminea*) and awarded to the saviour of a besieged city or army. There were only eight recipients down to and including Augustus, acccording to Pliny (*HN* 22. 9–13). The civic crown (*corona civica*) of oak leaves was the next most prestigious and was awarded for saving the life of a Roman citizen who must have acknowledged the fact (Aulus Gellius *NA* 5. 6. 13–14; Pliny, *HN* 16. 12–13). The mural crown (*corona muralis*) went to the first soldier over the wall of an enemy town or city. The golden crown *(corona aurea)* was for bravery not covered by the more specific awards. See *HN* 16. 7–14, 22. 6–13; Aulus Gellius, *NA* 5. 6; Maxfield (1981), ch.4; *OCD*[3], crowns and wreaths, 411.

chest of bronze ... 20 oxen   Not specifically mentioned by the other sources. The 'bronze' would have been *aes rude*, uncoined bronze, at this early period. Coins were not minted by Rome before the late 4th cent. BC. See *OCD*[3], coinage, Roman, 358–61.

9 . . . architect   An implausibly large number for the period attributed to Siccius. See Schilling 177.

T. Romilius   See above, **101. L. Siccius Dentatus . . . votes**. P. admires Dentatus' victory of right over wrong more than his military ones; cf. his closing remarks on M. Sergius Silus (below, **106. men . . . fortune**).

103. Capitolinus   M. Manlius, cos. 392 BC, defeated the Aequi and repulsed a night attack by Gauls on the Capitol in 390 BC after being warned by the cackling from the geese kept there. Hence, according to the story, the surname Capitolinus, although in fact (Ogilvie (1965), 694) the name probably derived from the area in which a particular branch of the Manlius family lived. See *OCD*[3], 918.

career's conclusion   After the Gallic crisis, Manlius, a patri-cian, became a champion of the plebs, but was suspected of fomenting revolution to make himself king and was executed in 384 BC. See Livy 6. 15–20.

Before ... crowns   Later, at the time of the treason trial, Livy (6. 20. 7–8) has Manlius claiming the spoils of thirty enemies, two mural and eight civic crowns. For the significance of the various awards, see above, **101. ceremonial spears,** etc. Livy includes the crowns in the total number of decorations, which he places around 40, and leaves unspecified the number of his scars.

37 . . . decorations Various other awards might be made by a successful general to his soldiers, including money, brooches, and oxen (cf. above, **102. chest of bronze**). See Maxfield (1981), 99.

P. Servilius In Livy 6. 2. 6 his name is given as C. Servilius Ahala. He was appointed Master of Horse by the dictator M. Furius Camillus in 389 BC during the Volscian wars (cf. Diodorus Siculus 14. 117. 1). The connection with Manlius, perhaps part of the later embellishment of the Capitolinus legend, is also mentioned in Livy (6. 20. 8), without the detail of the latter's wounds. See Münzer, *RE* 2A 2, Servilius (34), 1772.

Capitol . . . king See above, **Capitolinus**, and **career's conclusion.**

104. courage . . . fortune *Virtus*, 'excellence' (see above, **100–29. introd.**), is in this military context translated as 'courage'. *Virtus* and *fortuna* could be either complementary or contrasting qualities (below, **130. virtue**). P.'s examples of *virtus* in **101** ff. are exclusively military and so a more specialized meaning of *fortuna*, as a synonym for the *felicitas* or good luck of a Roman general, may also be relevant (cf. W. D. Erkell, *Augustus, Felicitas, Fortuna: Lateinische Wortstudien* (Göteborg, 1952), 43–59). Unlike *virtus*, however, *felicitas* was felt to be outside the individual's control (E. Wistrand, *Felicitas Imperatoria* (Göteborg, 1987), 10–11; though for a moral aspect, cf. below, **130. virtue** and **137. Lucius Sulla . . . Felix**), and it was the personal qualities of *virtus* which attracted admiration. Indeed, Pliny's treatment of Sergius ultimately highlights a moral-philosophical antithesis, increasingly popular in Roman writers, between *virtus* and *fortuna*, virtue and chance (see below, **130. virtue**; Beagon (2002), 111–32). This emphasis marks out the Sergius *exemplum* from the previous examples of bravery rewarded, although the structure is the same: in place of the enumeration of military decorations, Pliny lists the material honours Sergius did *not* win. For Sergius as the ultimate human paradox in *HN* 7, see Introd. 5. 4.

Marcus Sergius   M. Sergius Silus, praetor 197 BC (Livy 32. 27. 7;
31. 6; 33. 21. 9, 24. 4; Broughton, *MRR* i. 333; Münzer, *RE* 2A 2,
Sergius (40)). Like that of Siccius Dentatus (above, **101. L. Siccius
Dentatus . . . votes**), an *exemplum* probably derived from Varro,
cf. Valerius Maximus 3. 2. 24. Maximus, however, attributes the
Siccius story to 'others' besides Varro, suggesting such *exempla*
were standard. Later, Solinus 1. 104–5 does little more than paraphrase **104–6**. For his posthumous reputation, see below, **great-
grandson Catiline**. Identification of the statue mentioned in
Suet. *Nero* 41. 3 as a representation of Sergius (G.-C. Picard, 'Le
Monument qui réconforta Neron', *CRAI* (Jan.–Mar. 1990),
659–66) is unconvincing.

great-grandson Catiline   The conspirator of 63 BC: see *OCD*[3],
Sergius Catilina, Lucius, 1393. The relatively large generation-gaps
involved were probably the result of late remarriages to younger
women, cf. Pliny's examples of paternity in old age, **61–2** above. P.
is alone in giving this genealogy. Catiline's attested hardiness
(Sallust, *Cat.* 5. 1–4), stubbornness, and ultimate bravery (cf. Sallust,
Cat. 61. 4) befit his lineage: although comparatively obscure, the
Sergii were patrician and claimed a mythical ancestor (T. P.
Wiseman, 'Legendary Genealogies in Late Republican Rome',
G&R 21 (1974), 154). Although his family pride (Sallust, *Cat.* 31. 7)
was not specifically connected with this ancestor, that of another
great-grandson was, cf. Crawford (1974), i. 302; ii. pl. 39. 24, no. 286
on the denarius of quaestor M. Sergius Silus, dated to *c.*116–115 BC,
though others have placed it slightly later, to *c.*109 BC. This depicts
his great-grandfather on horseback with his sword and the severed
head of a Celt in his *left* hand; the Gallic rather than Punic enemy
perhaps being a more tactful subject for commemoration (cf.
below, **105–6. decorations . . . fortune**) and possibly more topical if, as is likely, the coin dates to the final years of the 2nd cent. BC,
which saw the build-up of barbarian threats from Thracian and
migrating Germanic tribes and the beginning of a decade in which
the latter defeated Roman armies on three occasions. Note also
that at about the same time (113–112 BC), another legendary Gallic
victory, that of Manlius Torquatus in single combat against a giant
Gaul, had been commemorated by a torque encircling the head of
Roma on the obverse of a coin minted by one of his descendants
(Crawford 295, pl. 40, 13). Later, it was perhaps not entirely fortui-

tous that P. Fonteius Capito in the mid-50s BC and A. Licinius
Nerva in the early 40s BC also produced coins apparently bearing
images of barbarian-slaying ancestors in a period when Gallic
wars—Caesar's—were of renewed topical interest (Crawford ii, pl.
52.4, no. 429.1, ?55 BC; pl. 53.24–5, no. 454.1–2, early 40s).

second campaign   During the second Punic war. All military
events narrated preceded 197 BC when Sergius as praetor made the
speech on which P. is drawing (see below, **105. speech**). For the
chronology of events, see below, **105. Cremona ... Placentia ...
Gaul.**

lost his right hand   See below, **105. right hand.**

captured by Hannibal   One of these two periods of captivity
may have been after Cannae, when, according to Livy 27. 19. 18
there were 1,500 equestrian prisoners.

105. right hand   There is literary evidence for wooden legs and
feet from Graeco-Roman antiquity (e.g. Herod. 9. 37) and even
some physical survivals, but this is the only reference to an artificial
hand and to an iron prosthetic of any type. See L. J. Bliquez,
'Greek, Etruscan and Roman Prosthetics', *ANRW* 37. 3 (Berlin and
New York, 1996), 2640–76; Garland (1995), 126. In certain extreme
medical situations, e.g. advanced gangrene, surgical amputations
might be performed, according to Celsus (5. 34 D; 7. 33), who
describes smoothing the cut end of the bone and covering it as far
as possible with skin, a technique still in use nearly two millennia
later, in the First World War. Archaeology corroborates this textual evidence, with finds of appropriate instruments and, recently,
by the reported discovery of a thigh bone bearing surgical saw
marks in a tomb at Isola Sacra. Wear on the cut end suggests use of
a prosthetic limb. It is unclear from Pliny's text whether Sergius'
disability was the result of traumatic amputation during the battle
itself, or a surgical amputation performed later. The former may
have been a rare, but not impossible, occurrence if inflicted by an
ancient sword, according to C. Salazar, citing just Livy 4. 28. 7;
battle-axes may have been more dangerous in this respect (C.
Salazar, *The Treatment of War-Wounds in Graeco-Roman Antiquity* (Brill,
2000), 13).

Cremona ... Placentia ... Gaul   Both founded as buttresses against the Boii and Insubres in 213 BC (Polybius 3. 39). Identification of Sergius' campaigns is problematic. Schilling (178) places them in 218–217 BC in the context of clashes (Livy 21. 57) following the Roman army's withdrawal to these colonies after the Trebia defeat (Livy 21. 56. 8), cf. also Münzer, *RE* 2 A 2, Sergius (40). But (1) a praetor of 197 would have been very young in 218 (though not impossibly so; and cf. Capitolinus (**103**), albeit for an earlier period) and fitting in the two earlier campaigns is difficult. (2) Livy does not suggest the major action implied by Pliny, nor does he mention Cremona and Placentia as its focus. (3) There is no obvious context for the capture of the Gallic camps which Pliny implies was part of this episode. Slightly earlier action in 213 when the Boii overran the Cremona–Placentia region before Hannibal's arrival is plausible for all three spheres of action but the chronological problem is even greater.

The best solution is probably to be based on Urlichs's (1857) suggestion that campaigns against Mago in 205–203 may be meant. (1) Action in all three areas—against Placentia and Cremona and in the territory of the Insubrian Gauls is attested (Livy 28. 11. 10). (2) Pliny's narrative now follows the order of events: (i) early campaigns in which he lost a hand; (ii) 2 captures by Hannibal; (iii) the Po campaigns. (3) P. implies that S. was in a position of some authority in these campaigns which makes better sense in 205–203 than in 218–7. (4) Comparatively recent exploits would be more useful to Sergius' case in 197 BC as they would be fresher in the minds of his listeners.

Another possibility is the Gallic campaign of 200–199 BC in which the Gauls burnt Placentia and Cremona was eventually liberated (Livy 31. 10–11; 31. 21); but the burning of Placentia would probably preclude its 'saving' by Sergius, and Livy does not list Sergius as a subordinate commander in this campaign (31. 21: I owe this point to Dr John Briscoe).

speech   Pliny alone provides evidence: *ORF²*, 97.

praetorship   See above, **Marcus Sergius.**

infirmity   Rules for *secular* office were not hard and fast, cf. T. Mommsen *Romisches Staatsrecht³*, i (Leipzig, 1887), 494. S was not debarred from a magistracy (cf. Cic. *Att.* 1. 16, lame tribune), even a potentially military one. For a later period, contrast Dio 54. 26. 9, Augustus avoids disabled senators, though this seems to be a concession rather than a penalty; cf. Theodosius (Ulpian) 3. 1. 1. 5, referring to blindness (see below, **141. blindness . . . Vesta**) and for an earlier one, Dionysius of Halicarnassus 5. 25. For *religious* office the ban was more rigid, cf. Dion. Hal. 2. 21; Aulus Gellius, *NA* 1. 12. 4 (Vestals); and Seneca the Elder (*Contr.* 4. 2: a priest of unsound body should be avoided: see below, **141. blindness . . . Vesta**). Seneca, however, makes the subject a matter of debate, and avoidance is not as strong as prohibition. In any case, there is no evidence that Sergius was a priest: the most natural interpretation of Pliny's words is that Sergius was participating in sacrifice in his capacity as praetor. In that case, there may have been some flexibility, especially as Sergius' previous exploits suggested that he would not be a practical liability in the sacrificial process. However, the fact that he now had to use his left hand, with its inauspicious connotations (cf. Lloyd (1962), 56–66) may have raised some doubts. Sympathy with Sergius' case is to be expected from Pliny, who saw excessive dependence on ritual and superstition as detrimental to man's liberty and rationality (Beagon (1992), 97–9, cf. 99). We do not know the outcome of the plea. See, in more detail, Beagon (2002), 113–20.

105–6. decorations . . . fortune If Sergius had participated in military successes rather than in the spectacular defeats P. lists here (see below, **Trebia . . . Cannae**), he would have been decorated many times over. As it was, rewards were not forthcoming for the brave individual involved in a general débâcle. However, they may not have been entirely absent, cf. *HN* 16. 14, where P. says that Scipio Africanus refused a wreath for rescuing his father at Trebia (Ticinus, according to Livy 21. 46. 7–10 and Polybius 10. 3. 2: see F. W. Walbank, *An Historical Commentary on Polybius* (Oxford, 1957–79), ii. 198–9 for other refs.). His refusal was, presumably, on the grounds that his action did not go beyond the normal call of filial duty; but a distaste for personal honours in the midst of general defeat need not be ruled out. P.'s point is that Sergius won an exceptional moral victory over those very circumstances which precluded official recognition of his valour. See below, **men . . . fortune**. Solinus (1. 105) oddly interprets P. to mean that Sergius alone received decorations for these campaigns.

Trebia A Hannibalic victory in 218 BC, the first year of the second Punic war: see *OCD*[3], 1548.

Ticinus Hannibal defeated the Romans at the confluence of the Ticinus and the Padus, later the site of Ticinum, in 218 BC: see *OCD*³, Ticinum, 1525.

Trasimenus The lake in Etruria where Hannibal destroyed the consul Flaminius in 217 BC: see *OCD*³, Trasimene, 1547.

Cannae On the banks of the Aufidius in Apulia, where Hannibal defeated the armies of C. Terentius Varro and L. Aemilius Lepidus in 216 BC: see *OCD*³, 286.

flight . . . summit of courage Cf. Livy on the Roman survivors' break through the victorious enemy to the safety of Canusium (Livy 22. 50).

men . . . fortune See above, **104. courage . . . fortune** for military links between *virtus* and *fortuna*. Here, though, *virtus* is in conflict with, and ultimately conquers, fortune. The concept here is that of the superiority of the human spirit to fortune, where fortune is pure chance (Cic. *Tusc.* 2. 30, 3. 36, 5. 2, 17); or where, as later in Seneca, she has acquired the fickle/malicious attributes of Fortuna-Tyche (Seneca, *Ep.* 98. 2, *Prov.* 4. 12, *Vit. Beat.* 4. 2). See Introd. 5. 4, below, **130. virtue**; and Beagon, (2002), 120–6. This latter fits in well with P.'s discussion in **130–50** on the nature of human happiness and the effect of fortune's mutability. The general idea stems from Hellenistic philosophy, especially Stoicism, cf. *SVF* iii. 567–81. It became popular at Rome due to the importance of *virtus* in Roman ideology. See I. Kajanto, 'Fortuna', *ANRW* 11. 17. 1 (Berlin and New York, 1981), 502–58.

107–27. *Outstanding achievements of the human mind*

P.'s treatment falls into three sections. First, **107–17** give examples of intellectual genius; poets, philosophers and orators. These are predominantly Greek, but Pliny manages to increase the Roman emphasis in a number of ways (see Introd. 5. 3) and the climax of the list is the rhetorical paean to Cicero which ends the section (**116–17**). In the second section (**118–22**), Roman examples predominate. It deals with moral rather than intellectual qualities of mind: *sapientia* (wisdom), *pudicitia* (chastity), and *pietas* (devotion), all of which are central to the Roman moral tradition (see Earl 1968/

repr.1984). Finally, **123–7**, P. deals with the various arts and sciences (*artes*), gifts of the mind with a practical application, including medicine, engineering, painting and sculpture. All these qualities can loosely be grouped under the general heading of *virtus* (see above, **100–29 introd.**).

107. geniuses Pliny here discusses *ingenium*, the basic meaning of which was 'innate quality, character'. Pliny is, however, using it in the narrower, intellectual, sense of 'genius', 'talent'.

Homer Above, **74, 85**. For his status, cf. *HN* 2. 13 (*princeps litterarum*) though note *HN* 35. 96 where Pliny says Apelles' portrait of Artemis surpasses her portrayal in *Od.* 6. 102.

108. Alexander 'The Great' of Macedon, 356–323 BC. See Introd. 3. 3, 4. 2 and *OCD*[3], Alexander (3), 57–9.

casket . . . craftsmanship. P. attributes the introduction of perfume to the Graeco-Roman world to this incident (*HN* 13. 2). The anecdote was well documented according to Plutarch (*Alex.* 26). He says (*Alex.* 8) that Alexander regarded the *Iliad* as a handbook on the art of war: a copy known as the 'casket copy', annotated by Aristotle, accompanied him on campaign.

booty . . . Darius Darius III, king of Persia (336–330 BC) was defeated by Alexander at the battle of Issus in 333 BC. See *OCD*[3], 430.

109. Pindar Pindar (*OCD*[3], 1183–4) came from Boeotia whose leading city, Thebes, rebelled against Alexander the Great and was sacked in 335 BC. Schilling (179) cites Pindar's friendship with Alexander I (498–454 BC) for this favour (cf. Pindar fr. 120), but P.'s point is that it derived from Alexander the Great's appreciation of the poet's genius for its own sake; cf. Arrian, *Alex. Anab.* 1. 9. 10; *Suda* s.v. Pindar; the same story had also been told about Pindar and the Spartan general Pausanias: see M. Lefkowitz, *The Lives of the Greek Poets* (London, 1981), 60, with refs. to the biographical tradition.

restored . . . Aristotle Aristotle (*OCD*[3], 165–9) was born in Stagira (or Stagirus) in Chalcidice which most sources agree was destroyed by Philip II of Macedon, Alexander's father, in 349 BC (Diodorus Siculus 16. 52. 9). It is less clear whether it was Philip or Alexander who restored it at Aristotle's request, perhaps, as

Plutarch's version (*Alex.* 7) ascribing it to Philip shows, because it was connected with Aristotle's tutorship of Alexander. Cf. Aelian, *VH* 3. 17; and Valerius Maximus 5. 6, ext. 5 (who attributes both destruction and restoration to Alexander). Mayhoff emended to 'Alexander regarded Aristotle's birthplace as his own'.

Apollo ... Archilochus   Tradition said that the killer ('killers' in Pliny alone, cf. Solinus 1. 117) of the early 7th-cent. BC lyric poet Archilochus (*OCD³*, 145–6) of Paros was accused and ordered away by the Delphic oracle while trying to consult it (Galen, *Protr.* 9, 1. 22 K; cf. Eusebius, *Praec. Ev.* 32, *Suda* s.v. Archilochus; Heraclides Ponticus, *Pol.* 8: see H. D. Rankin, *Archilochus of Paros* (Parke Ridge, NJ, 1977), 16–17).

Sophocles ... Father Liber ... Lysander   Cf. *Life of Sophocles* 15. The tragedian (*OCD³*, Sophocles (1), 1422–5), born in the 490s BC, died in late 406/early 405 (Aristophanes, *Frogs* 82) after a long career in which he won more victories in the dramatic contests than either of the other great 5th-cent. playwrights, Euripides and Aeschylus; hence 'favourite of Father Liber', i.e. Dionysus, god of the theatre (see above, **95, 102, 109,** and below, **191**). Like much of the biographical material on the poets (cf. Lefkowitz (1981), viii), this story would seem to be apocryphal: Athens was not besieged by Sparta until after the battle of Aegospotami in late summer 405 BC. Lysander was admiral of the Spartan fleet, not king.

110. Dionysius ... Plato   Dionysius II, tyrant of Syracuse (367–357 BC: *OCD³*, 477) invited the Athenian philosopher Plato (*c*.429–347 BC: *OCD³* Plato (1), 1190–3), founder of the Academy, to visit him on two occasions, the first of which, *c*.336 BC, is referred to here (cf. Westermann VII, 1. 1–3, 382–97; Plutarch, *Dio* 13; Plato, *Ep.* 7).

cruel and proud   A complex of factors has coloured the sources (see A. S. Riginos, *Platonica* (Leiden, 1976), 70–92). Dionysius' passion for philosophy caused political tensions which led ultimately to a split with Plato. His character defects were later exaggerated by the Academic tradition, as were those of his father Dionysius I to whom Plato may earlier have paid a visit. See B. Caven, *Dionysius I: Warlord of Sicily* (London and Yale, 1990), 167–9, 213–17, 226–7; *OCD³*, Dionysius I and Dionysius (2) II, 477.

Isocrates Athenian orator (436–338 BC) whose written speeches reflected, and to an extent influenced, the central political issues of his era and whose rhetorical theory and teaching were highly influential. The speech in question was addressed to Nicocles, son of Evagoras, ruler of Cyprus, *c.*435–374/3 BC (Plutarch, *Vit. Orat.* 838a). See *OCD*³, Evagoras, 578, Isocrates, 769–71.

Aeschines . . . Demosthenes . . . himself Cf. also Cicero, *De Orat.* 3. 56. 213 and Valerius Maximus 8. 10, ext. 1. The Athenian orators Aeschines (*c.*397–322 BC: *OCD*³, Aeschines (1), 25–6) and Demosthenes (384–322 BC: *OCD*³, Demosthenes (2), 456–8) disagreed over the stance Athens should take with regard to Macedon in the 340s and 330s BC. In 330 Aeschines prosecuted Ctesiphon, who had proposed in 336 that Demosthenes should be crowned at the Dionysia for his services to his country. Demosthenes replied with his greatest speech, the *De Corona*. Aeschines was defeated and, having been penalized for failing to secure one-fifth of the jury's vote, retired to Rhodes, the setting for this anecdote.

As a result . . . case. P. points up the paradox of a testimonial from a rival and enemy by extending the imagery of their legal battle: Aeschines, his courtroom adversary, becomes prime witness in the case for Demosthenes' genius.

111. Thucydides . . . condemned As one of the ten Athenian generals in 424 BC, the historian Thucydides (*c.*460–400 BC; *OCD*³, Thucydides (2), 1516–21) failed to save Amphipolis from the Spartan Brasidas during the Peloponnesian war, and was exiled, returning 20 years later (Thucydides 5. 26) as a result of a vote in the popular assembly (Pausanias 1. 23. 9). P.'s attributing this recall to Thucydides' 'eloquence' as a historian need not be taken literally to suggest public familiarity with any part of the *Histories* (contra Schilling 182); almost nothing is known about their publication other than the story that book 8 was prepared for publication by Thucydides' daughter (*Life of Thuc.* 43), and the question of composition is itself complex and much debated. See *OCD*³, Thucydides (2), 1518–20; A. W. Gomme, A. Andrewes, K. J. Dover, *A Historical Commentary on Thucydides v: Book 8* (Oxford, 1981), app. 1 and 2; S. Hornblower, *Thucydides* (London, 1987), 136–54.

Menander's . . . Egypt . . . Macedon Menander (*c.*344/3–292/1 BC: *OCD*³, Menander (1), 956–7) was the leading exponent of New Comedy. There is no other evidence of these offers of royal patronage, although tradition recorded a correspondence between the playwright and Ptolemy I Soter (367–283 BC) (*Suda* s.v. Menander; Westermann IV, 179). The king of Macedon was Demetrius Poliorcetes (336–283 BC), but popular tradition (e.g. Phaedrus, *Fab.* 5. 1) linked M. with the man Demetrius ousted as regent of Athens in 307, Demetrius of Phaleron (317–307 BC).

112. Gnaeus Pompeius . . . Mithridatic war. See above, **93. Pompey the Great**, **97. the east**, and **95–9**. *passim.*

Posidonius   Influential Stoic philosopher (*c*.135–*c*.51 BC), and polymath from Apamea on the Orontes whose school at Rhodes became a focal point of the intellectual world, visited by scholars and leading statesmen (*OCD*³, Posidonius (2), 131–3; Introd. 4. 2). P. refers to the second (in 62 BC) of two visits by Pompey, who may, in keeping with his conscious emulation of Alexander the Great, (above, **95**), have seen Posidonius as his modern Aristotle (Rawson (1985), 106). Relations were close enough for Posidonius to receive him despite being ill (Cic. *Tusc.* 2. 61, claiming Pompey as source) and to write an account of Pompey's wars (Strabo 11. 1. 6, C492); and possibly for Pompey to be influenced by Posidonius' teachings when negotiating a humane settlement for the defeated pirates (H. Strasburger, 'Poseidonius on the Problems of the Roman Empire', *JRS* 55 (1965), 40–53, but cf. Rawson, 'Roman Rulers and the Philosophic Advisor', in M. T. Griffin and J. Barnes (eds.), *Philosophia Togata: Essays on Philosophy and Roman Society* (Oxford, 1989), 240–1), as well as laying aside the symbols of his *imperium* in the present anecdote in deference to his intellectual superior. For the anecdote, see above, Introd. 5. 3.

lictor   Lictors were attendants who carried the *fasces* (see below) for a magistrate with *imperium*, announcing his approach and implementing his powers of arrest. Promagistrates in the Republic had 12 (*OCD*³, *lictores*, 860; N. Purcell, 'The *Apparitores*; a Study in Social Mobility', *PBSR* 51, NS 38 (1983), 125–73.

fasces   Bundles of wooden rods and an axe carried by lictors as a symbol of magisterial authority and power (*OCD*³, *fasces*, 587–8).

embassy . . . Rome   See Plutarch, *Cat. Mai.* 22. 1–7; Aulus Gellius, *NA* 6. 14. 8–10. In 155 BC an Athenian embassy consisting of the Stoic Diogenes, the Peripatetic Critolaus, and the Academic

Carneades went to Rome to plead against a fine imposed on
the city. Carneades' dialectical skills caused a sensation (below,
Carneades).

Cato the Censor See above, **100**. Despite his public opposition
to Greek culture as a threat to Roman tradition and morality,
memorably expressed in a work addressed to his son and quoted by
Pliny in *HN* 29. 13–14, he was in fact well versed in Greek language
and literature; see below, **113. Thus . . . language**.

Carneades (214/13–129/8 BC) Proponent of scepticism and
founder of the New Academy, who came from Cyrene. He criticized dogmatic philosophies by arguing both for and against a particular proposal. On the occasion of the embassy, he argued for and
against justice on consecutive days, to great acclaim, arousing
Cato's concern that such techniques could subvert moral certainties. See M. T. Griffin, 'Philosophy, Politics and Politicians at
Rome', in *Philosophia Togata* (Oxford, 1989), 3; *OCD* ³, Carneades,
293.

113. expulsion of Greeks Occasional expulsions of aliens
from Rome were ordered, in connection with external hostilities or
internal political struggles over Roman citizenship in the Republic.
Religious (e.g. Jews) and intellectual (e.g. astrologers and philosophers) subversives might also be banned. It was the Greek
intellectual threat (see above, **Carneades**) which Cato feared;
philosophers had in fact been banned twice not many years before
the 155 embassy, in 173 and 161 BC (Athenaeus 12. 547a; Suetonius,
Rhet. 1; Aulus Gellius 15. 11. 1). See J. P. V. D. Balsdon, *Romans and
Aliens* (London, 1979), 98–102; 106–8.

Cato of Utica See above, **62**.

one philosopher . . . tribune While serving as military tribune
in Macedonia in 67 BC, Cato visited Pergamum and persuaded the
Stoic Athenodorus Cordylion to return with him (Plutarch, *Cat.
Min.* 10; cf. Solinus 1. 122).

another . . . Cyprus Cf. Solinus 1. 122. Cato was sent to annex
Cyprus in 58 BC. The philosopher's name is unknown; possibly
Philostratus, an Academic whom he knew in Sicily in 49 BC
(Plutarch, *Cat. Min.* 57. 5); or one of the two little-known philoso-
phers who were with him at the end of his life (*Cat. Min.* 65. 11, cf.

De Off. 2. 86). An actual person (Urlichs (1857), 65), rather than the statue mentioned in *HN* 34. 92, may be implied, although a humorous reference to the latter is a possibility.

Thus . . . language   The elder Cato's attitude was less clear-cut than P. implies. He knew Greek himself, read Greek literature (Valerius Maximus 8. 7. 2), and one source suggests he was responsible for bringing the poet Ennius, skilled in Greek, Latin, and Oscan, to Rome in 198 BC (Nepos, *Cato* 1. 4; cf. *De Vir. Illustr.* 47. 1: but see N. Horsfall, *Cornelius Nepos: A Selection, including the Lives of Cato and Atticus* (Oxford, 1989), 50).

114. The elder Scipio . . . Ennius   Ennius (see above, **101**) was friendly with the family of Publius Cornelius Scipio Africanus the Elder (236–184 BC: cf. **47. the elder Scipio**) and seems to have written a play, *Scipio*, as well as recording Africanus' victories against Hannibal in his *Annales* and composing an epitaph for him. For the statue, cf. Livy 38. 56. 4, Cic. *Pro Arch.* 22, but apparently placed with those of Publius and Lucius Scipio outside the Scipionic tomb on the Appian Way and not on the actual grave of Africanus at Liternum or at the latter's request as P. implies, cf. Valerius Maximus 8. 14. 1. See O. Skutsch (ed., introd. comm.), *The Annals of Quintus Ennius* (Oxford, 1985), 2 on the confusion.

surname . . . world   i.e. the *cognomen* Africanus which he received after he defeated Hannibal at Zama in 202 BC. A tripartite division of the world into three continents, Europe, Asia, and Africa, is used by Pliny in *HN* 3. 3 and goes back to the earlier Greek geographical tradition; see e.g. Pindar, *Pyth.* 9. 8. Strictly speaking, these three continents together represented in Pliny's day the known, inhabited world, the *oikumene* or *orbis terrarum*. However, from the time of Aristotle, there had been speculation, later encouraged by the development of methods of earth measurement, about further 'worlds' in the southern hemisphere and even a further pair of worlds in the western hemisphere. See Romm (1992), 124–40. For a similar description of a general's honorific *cognomen* as part of his war spoils, see above, **96. 'the Great'**.

Virgil's will   See *Vit. Don.* 37–41. V. had intended to spend three years on the finishing touches to the poem. After his death, it was edited by L. Varius Rufus and Plotius Tucca and published on Augustus' orders.

115. Asinius Pollio C. Asinius Pollio (76 BC–AD 4, see *OCD*[3], Asinius Pollio, 192), a skilful and independently-minded politician, historian, orator, and man of letters (J. André, *La Vie et l'œuvre d'Asinius Pollion* (Paris, 1949); Syme (1939), 5–7 and *passim*), supported Mark Antony and maintained a dignified retirement under Augustus.

the first . . . war Julius Caesar had planned a public library at Rome which was never built (Suet. *Caes.* 44; see below, **only statue . . . at that time**). Public libraries already existed in the east (e.g. Alexandria and Pergamum), endowed by Hellenistic monarchs. By the late Republic, private libraries were becoming popular with the Roman nobility, and individual generals had secured notable foreign collections as a result of war (e.g. Aristotle's collection, taken by Sulla at the sack of Athens, 86 BC), see Rawson (1985), 39–42. Pollio's library, in the Atrium Libertatis near the Forum (Suet. *Aug.* 29. 5; Richardson (1992), 41, cf. 59) was the first public one in Rome (cf. *HN.* 35. 10), financed from the booty (*manubiae*, see above, **97. spoils of war**) won in his victory against the Parthini in 39 BC, for which he received a triumph (*CIL*[2], p.50, Dio 48. 41. 7: Syme (1939), 222–3).

only statue . . . Varro . . . at the time For Varro, see Introd. 4. 5. 1, 5. 3. Libraries would have a statue of their patron, but there were also likenesses of the authors represented in the collection, attested by Pliny (*HN* 35. 9–10) for Pollio's library and probably already present in the great Hellenistic libraries. *HN* 35. 9–10 shows that the portraits were often imaginary ones of famous authors long dead, such as Homer, though by the 5th cent. AD, Sidonius Apollonaris can boast that his statue is on show in the library of Trajan (*Epist.* 9. 16, Friedländer (1909–13), iii. 38) and contemporary busts may have been common much earlier in private collections (Horace, *Sat.* 1. 4. 21). Varro's unique honour is not surprising. Immensely learned, with a vast range and output, he was rightly regarded as Rome's greatest scholar during his long lifetime (e.g. Cic. *Fam.* 13. 9, 13. 25) and after (Aulus Gellius, *NA* 4. 16. 1, Augustine, *CD* 6. 2): Caesar had selected him as the organizer of his earlier projected library (above, **the first . . . war**), and Pollio, an intellectual in his own right, was also an exacting critic of the talents of others (refs. Syme (1939), 482–6). Pliny, *HN* 35. 10–11, suggests the honour was fitting for another reason: Varro had 'bestowed immortality' on no less than 700 other famous people by publishing their portraits in his volumes of *Imagines*.

naval crown   For crowns generally, see above, **102. crowns**. The *corona navalis* (also called *classica* or *rostrata* because it was decorated with images of ships' prows) was originally awarded to the first soldier to board an enemy ship (Festus p. 156 16 L) and later to the winner of an outstanding naval victory. P. mentions only one other recipient, M. Agrippa (above, **45. Marcus Agrippa**), awarded the crown by Augustus after the victory at Naulochus against Sextus Pompey in 36 BC.

Pompey ... pirates   In 67 BC Varro was Pompey's quaestor and had command of a fleet in the Ionian sea (Broughton, *MRR* ii. 145; Varro, *RR* 2, pref. 6) in the war against the pirates (above, **97. sent out to all the seas**). He took part in other Pompeian campaigns and fought on his side in the civil war. See Dahlmann, *RE* suppl. 6, Terentius (84), 1172–1277.

116. In fact . . . put together   So far, P. has listed twelve outstanding Greek intellects and just two Roman. Rather than evoking invidious comparisons by struggling to equal or surpass the Greek figures or ending lamely with this vague generalization (for which, however, see below, **130. of all . . . Roman race**), he chooses to close this section with an emphatically Roman flourish, a personal encomium of the famous orator, M. Tullius Cicero (106–43 BC: *OCD*³; Tullius Cicero, Marcus (1), 1558–64). For Cicero, statesman and intellectual, as Pliny's ideal, see Introd. 2. 1, 5. 3.

But how could I . . . those of her empire?   P.'s personal tribute to Cicero is couched in appropriately rhetorical language which acts both as a compliment to the subject and a means of achieving emphasis by varying the tone and texture of his own prose narrative. Besides the rhetorical questions and apostrophes, the rhythmical balance of the sentence construction, with its careful repetition of particular words and phrases, and use of alliteration, is characteristic of Cicero's own rhetorical style. See e.g. L. Laurand, *Études sur le style des discours de Cicéron*³ (Paris, 1926), ii. 117–40. Pliny's assessment may well be based on his own reading of Cicero's writings, but he follows the general lines of other 1st-cent. encomia of Cicero (e.g. Velleius 2. 66. 4–5; Valerius Maximus 2. 2. 3, 5. 3–4) in singling out the struggles with Catiline and Antony, in addition to the intellectual achievement. On Cicero in Pliny, see R. E. Wolverton, 'The Encomium of Cicero in Pliny the Elder', in C. Henderson (ed.), *Classical, Medieval and Renaissance Studies in Honor of B. L. Ullman*, vol. i (Rome, 1964), 159–64; A. Darab, 'Cicero bei Plinius dem Älteren', *ACD* 31 (1995), 33–41.

which . . . characteristic . . . pre-eminence? As well as oratory, Cicero's varied intellectual pursuits included philosophy, encompassing rhetorical and political theory, and poetry.

What . . . consulship alone? Cicero's rhetorical skills had facilitated his rise to political pre-eminence and in particular to the consulship in 63 BC, a prize which hitherto had rarely fallen to a man of non-senatorial birth and never to one in the earliest year of eligibility. His pride in this achievement was continually reflected in his writings and led him to overestimate the real worth of his consular activities: 'Happy Rome, born when I was consul!' (*De Consulatu Suo*, Ps.-Sallust, *In Cic.* 3. 5, W. W. Ewbank, *The Poems of Cicero* (London, 1933; repr. Bristol, 1977), 77). P.'s choice thus aptly reflects Cicero's own estimation of his achievement and the manner in which the intellectual element was inextricably intertwined with the political.

unanimous . . . world In *Leg. Ag.* 2. 3. 7, Cicero uses very similar language to describe his election.

117. As a result of your speech This and the following 'consular' speeches are listed in Cic. *Att.* 2. 1. 3.

the tribes rejected the agrarian law At the beginning of 63, the tribune P. Servilius Rullus brought forward a wide-ranging bill for distribution of public land to veterans and the needy. Cicero, taking the usual senatorial stance on such bills, while claiming that it was against Pompey's interests (Crassus and Caesar apparently were backing it) opposed it successfully in the speeches *De Lege Agraria*, first in the senate on 1 Jan. and then before the people (*Att.* 2. 1. 3).

Roscius . . . seating L. Roscius Otho had as tribune in 67 BC passed a law allocating specially reserved seats in the theatre for the equestrian order. In 63, Roscius, now praetor, was hissed in the theatre by the populace but Cicero calmed them into aquiescence (Cic. *Att.* 2. 1. 3; Plut. *Cic.* 13).

the sons of the proscribed . . . public office   The dictator Sulla had debarred from public life the sons and grandsons of enemies he had proscribed (82–81 BC) after the civil war with Marius and Cinna. Cicero successfully opposed a tribunician attempt to restore these rights (*In Pisonem* 2–4, cf. *Att.* 2. 1. 3).

put Catiline to flight   L. Sergius Catilina (above, **104. great-grandson Catiline**), a patrician, repeatedly failed to be elected consul and, after the elections of 63, plotted to gain power by force, gaining supporters through revolutionary plans for debt abolition. To Cicero as consul fell the task of exposing and containing the threat. Although lacking conclusive evidence of Catiline's intentions, Cicero boldly challenged him on 8 Nov. at a senate meeting in the first and most famous of the four Catilinarian speeches and succeeded in driving him out of Rome, diminishing the immediate danger (Cic. *Cat.* 1; *Att.* 2. 1. 3; Sallust, *Cat.* 31).

you . . . proscribed Mark Antony   P. here deviates from the consular speeches. The duel between Cicero and Antony was a set-piece in the rhetorical exercises of the 1st cent. AD, cf. Seneca the Elder, *Contr.* 7. 2 and *Suas.* 6–7; Quintilian 3. 8. 46. Soon after the murder of Caesar in 44, Cicero was complaining that the dictator's friend and consular colleague Antony should have been killed as well. In his view, Antony embodied the worst aspects of the dead dictator and was the Republic's main enemy. Between Sept. 44 and Apr. 43, he made fourteen speeches against him, the *Philippics*, which contained some of his most brilliant and virulent rhetoric and finally persuaded the senate to declare Antony a public enemy. But the subsequent alliance of Antony with Octavian and the formation of the second triumvirate led to Antony's revenge by the proscription and murder of Cicero on 7 Dec. 43. P. plays on the verb *proscribo*, 'write in front of', 'publish by writing', which was used in particular of outlawing individuals by publishing a written list. Cicero's condemnation and ultimate outlawing of Antony as a public enemy was immortalized in fourteen published speeches; a character assassination far more effective and enduring than Antony's murderous revenge.

first citizen . . . father of his country   Cf. *Phil.* 2. 12. He was acclaimed by the crowds after the execution of the Catilinarian conspirators in 63 (Plutarch, *Cic.* 22) and then by Cato in a speech

(Plutarch, *Cic.* 23. 6). In Juvenal, *Sat.* 8. 236–44, the acclamation of
Cicero, civilian in a free country, is contrasted with the grant of the
title 'father of his country' in 2 BC to Augustus, *de facto* military
dictator. Livy mentions an earlier, unofficial, acclamation (of
Camillus, 5. 49. 7) in a military context.

civilian . . . triumph . . . eloquence   Strongly reminiscent of a
notorious line from *De Consulatu Suo*, 'Cedant arma togae, concedat
laurea laudi' (or 'linguae', a variant even closer to P.'s wording, but
not in the best manuscript tradition, see Ewbank (1933/77), 77,
123–4); 'Let arms yield to the toga, the laurel to achievement (or "to
the tongue")'. Cicero made favourable comparisons between the
military triumphs and spoil won by military leaders in foreign wars
and his own role, though only a civilian, in saving the homeland
itself: see *In Cat.* 4. 21–2, and *De Off.* 77–8, where he defends this
quotation from his poem and specifically ranks his achievement
above any triumph. (In his account of the aftermath of the Catilinarian executions (*Cic.* 22. 5), Plutarch actually put this comparison
into the mouths of the military leaders themselves, Cicero's fellow-
senators! Perhaps he took his cue from the praise of Cicero attributed to Pompey in *De Off.* (1. 78), who allegedly claimed that his
foreign victories would have been worthless, had not Cicero preserved the homeland in which he could celebrate them.) In *In Cat.*
4. 23, Cicero specifically claims he has rejected the chance of a triumph and military honour (he had given up the province allotted
to him for 62 earlier in the year, *Fam.* 5. 2. 3, *Att.* 2. 1. 3) in favour of
his domestic role as civilian saviour of his country. He later altered
the oath customary on leaving office to a declaration that he had
saved his country (*Fam.* 5. 27, *In Pis.* 6, *Pro Sulla* 34). All this did not
stop him from making strenuous efforts to win a military triumph
for his campaigns as governor of Cilicia in 52 BC (e.g. *Att.* 5. 20, *Fam.*
15. 4, 5, 6, 13). On 'laurel wreath', see further below, **father of
oratory**.

father of oratory . . . those of her empire   P.'s concluding
words show that he is taking the figurative 'triumph and laurels'
beyond the sphere of Cicero's achievements in domestic politics
and applying them to his intellectual achievements as orator and
writer. The laurel wreath was not only the emblem of the victorious
general but also of Apollo, a god connected with peace and the arts
of poetry and music cf. *HN* 15. 133–8. Caesar was Cicero's 'enemy'

because, despite his political overtures, Cicero always considered his aims and methods fundamentally opposed to the senatorial tradition of republican government and rebuffed him. They shared common ground in their literary interests, however, and Caesar's words look like a rather pointed adaptation to literary achievement of the very phrase Cicero notoriously used to promote his political stature.

118–22. *Remaining qualities of mind*

See above, **107–27**.

118. wisdom *Sapientia* had moral and practical as well as intellectual and literary applications and thus translates as 'wisdom': hence the examples of Socrates (who left no writings) and Chilo with his gnomic sayings. Hence also the implication that large numbers of Romans laid claim to it (below, **surnames**): according to the Roman traditional code of values, it was an important attribute of any participant in public life (U. Klima, *Untersuchungen zu dem Begriff Sapientia von der republikanischen Zeit bis Tacitus* (Bonn, 1971), 56–60): cf. below, **139. ten greatest and best objectives**, **140. supreme wisdom**, though the more overtly practical *prudentia* is more frequently mentioned (e.g. Cicero, *De Orat.* 1. 197). The meaning of *sapientia* developed over time. Initially, it had predominantly practical connotations, at first, perhaps, in the military sphere (see E. L. Wheeler, '*Sapiens* and Stratagems: The Neglected Meaning of a *cognomen*', *Historia*, 37 (1988), 166–95), and then, more generally, in the political and legal spheres. Connotations of philosophical learning are later, and may be associated with Scipio Aemilianus in the late 2nd cent., although Wheeler thinks that this usage really began with Cicero. But all we can say for certain is that Cicero in the 1st cent. BC knew of several different reasons for calling a man *sapiens*. Three are mentioned in *De Amic.* 6–7: skill in civil law, general political shrewdness, and scholarship. These he applied respectively to L. Acilius (the 'Atilius' of Livy 32. 37. 7, praetor in 197 BC? See Badian, loc. cit. next note, 12), Cato the Censor in his old age (died 146 BC), and C. Laelius (consul 140 BC), friend and associate of Scipio Aemilianus. He attributes *sapientia* as a general to Q. Fabius Maximus, hero of the second Punic war in the late 3rd cent. BC (*Verr.* 2. 5. 25), but also to L. Lucullus, in the context of his command against Mithridates in the early 60s BC (*De Imp. Cn. Pomp.* 20). In the same speech, it should be noted that *consilium* ('good judgement', 'understanding'), which closely partners *sapientia* in the governance of state affairs (*De Orat.* 1. 8), is also a quality of the 1st-cent. general (*De Imp. Cn. Pomp.* 29: *consilium in providendo*, 'good judgement in strategy').

surnames . . . Catus and Corculum   Surnames (*cognomina*) were originally unofficial names applied to individuals but many gradually became hereditary, some families ending up with more than one. Confined, until the end of the Republic, to the aristocracy, they were derived from many sources, including physical and, as here, mental attributes. See *OCD*[3], names, 1024–6; I. Kajanto, *The Latin Cognomina* (Helsinki, 1965), 62–9; E. Badian, 'The Clever and the Wise: two Roman *cognomina* in Context', in N. Horsfall (ed.), *Vir Bonus Discendi Peritus: Studies in celebration of Otto Skutsch's Eightieth Birthday*, BICS suppl. 51 (London, 1988), 6–12. Cic. *Tusc.* 1. 9. 18, derives Corculum (Kajanto 226) from *cor*, heart, sometimes said to be the seat of the intellect. He mentions P. Scipio Nasica Corculum (cos. 162, 155 BC, cf. *OCD*[3], 399), son of Africanus, famed for his rhetorical and legal expertise, and quotes Ennius (*bene cordatus*, 'a very wise man', *Ann.* 184) for Sextus Aelius Paetus (cos. 198 BC), nicknamed Catus ('sharp', so 'clever', cf. Varro, *LL* 7. 46: Cato also derives from it), a shrewd statesman and legal expert (Cicero, *Brut.* 78; *OCD*[3], 19; Kajanto 249–50). Wheeler (1988: 189) notes that both Catus and Corculus were very rare in the late Republic and may have been archaic.

119. Socrates . . . Apollo   Socrates (469–399 BC: *OCD*[3], 1419–20) was the Athenian thinker whose ideas and personality were immortalized in the writings of his followers, especially Plato. For the oracle, cf. Plato, *Apol.* 5; Valerius Maximus 3. 4, ext.1.

Chilo of Sparta   Ephor *c.*560 BC (Diogenes Laertius 1. 68) and one of the Seven Wise Men (Plato, *Protag.* 343a). See *OCD*[3], 322. For his precepts, see respectively Diogenes Laertius 1. 40; Clement, *Strom.* 1. 14, p.300; Diodorus Siculus 9. 9 and Diogenes Laertius 1. 73 (the more literal version of the last, usually quoted, 'a pledge and ruin is near'). For his death, Diogenes Laertius 1. 72, Pliny, **180**.

Sibyl   Originally referring to a single seer, the name became a generic one for prophetess. P. probably refers to the Cumaean

Sibyl, from whom, according to legend (Dionysius of Halicarnassus, *Ant. Rom.* 6. 17), Tarquinius Priscus obtained three books of prophecies which were to form the core of a state collection for consultation by the senate. See *OCD*³, 1400–1; H. W. Parke, *Sibyls and Sibylline Prophecy in Classical Antiquity*, ed. B. C. McGing (London, 1988), 75–9, and *passim*, cf. Pliny, *HN* 13. 88, 18. 286, 34. 22, 29.

Melampus Mythical Greek seer with the gift of understanding the language of birds and even woodworms (Homer, *Od.* 11. 281–97; 15. 231–6; Apollodorus, *Bibl.* 1. 9. 11; Pliny, *HN* 10. 137, 25. 47). A family of seers, the Melampodids, claimed descent from him (*OCD*³, 952; Pley, *RE* 15. 1, Melampus, 392–9).

Marcius Alleged author of Latin prophecies which in 213 BC predicted the disaster of Cannae and ordered the institution of games to Apollo to get rid of Hannibal (Livy 25. 12. 3–12). Later authors mention him as a famous prophet (or prophets, cf. 'brothers Marcii' , Cic. *Div.* 1. 89, 115), and Servius (*Aen.* 6. 72) associates him with the Sibyl. See *OCD*³, 922; Parke (1988), 199–200.

120. 'most excellent of men' Literally, 'best of men', which, in Roman society, was often synonymous with its elite: the nobly-born, well-educated, and rich (cf. Sallust, *Cat.* 34. 2). It could also refer to moral character, as it evidently does here, in the case of Scipio and, as such, it is closely linked with the moral connotations of *virtus*, as the translation implies. Nobility of birth and nobility of character were, however, frequently linked in the Roman mind and it is likely that Scipio's aristocratic lineage contributed to his acclamation. Indeed, Pliny implies that his rejection at elections was a slur on his *dignitas*, the standing in society which was achieved through a combination of birth, ability, achievement, and character; and that this to some extent undermined the title he had been awarded.

Scipio Nasica P. Cornelius Scipio Nasica, cos. 191 BC and father of Corculum (above, **118. surnames . . . Corculum**), was thus acclaimed and chosen to receive the statue of the Magna Mater (below, **Claudia**) when it arrived in Italy in 204 BC (Livy 29. 14. 8–11; cf. Ovid, *Fasti* 4. 347; [Aurelius Victor] *De Vir. Ill.* 46. 1–2). He was in fact 'rejected' three times at elections: once for the 192 BC consulship (Livy 35. 10. 2–9) and twice for the censorship (189 and 184, Livy 37. 57. 10 and 39. 40. 2). And it was not he, but his grandson, P. Cornelius Scipio Nasica Serapio, who died abroad at Pergamum, where the task of annexing Asia removed him from the backlash following his part in the death of Ti. Gracchus (133 BC), cf. Valerius Maximus 5. 3. 2, 7. 5. 2; *OCD³*, 399.

Socrates . . . unfettered See above, **119**. **Socrates . . . Apollo.** Convicted of impiety and corrupting the young, he was executed in prison in 399 BC. He was not, however, literally in chains at the time of his death, cf. Plato, *Phaedo* 59a.

Sulpicia . . . Venus Cf. Valerius Maximus 8. 15. 12; Ovid, *Fasti* 4. 133–62; Solinus 1. 126; R. Schilling, *La Religion romaine de Vénus depuis les origines jusqu'au temps d'Auguste* (Paris, 1954; repr. 1982), 390–4. Chosen to dedicate a statue of Venus Verticordia, 'changer of hearts', erected in an attempt to promote female morality. Her father was Servius Sulpicius Paterculus (Münzer, *RE* 4A 1, Sulpicius (82), 817), brother of the consul of 258 BC and her husband the famous Q. Fulvius Flaccus (Münzer, *RE* 6. 1, Fulvius (59), 243–6), four times consul (237, 224, 212, and 209 BC). Since the statue antedates the temple of Venus Verticordia founded in 114 BC to atone for the unchastity of some Vestal Virgins (Obsequens 37; Orosius 5. 15. 21–2; Ovid, *Fasti* 4. 157–60) by about a century, it may have been placed in the temple of Venus Ericina or Venus Obsequens (Richardson (1992), 411).

Claudia When the boat carrying the Magna Mater (above, **Scipio Nasica**) ran aground, Claudia Quinta, granddaughter (probably) of Appius Claudius Caecus, miraculously freed it, thus disproving rumours of her unchastity (Livy 29. 14. 12; Ovid, *Fasti* 4. 305 ff.; Cicero, *Cael.* 34). See Münzer, *RE* 4. 1, Claudia (435), 2899.

121. devotion The latin *pietas* means loyalty, a sense of duty, especially towards parent, deity, country, etc., the quintessentially Roman characteristic, cf. Cicero, *ND* 1. 116, *Inv. Rhet.* 2. 66. Virgil's hero Aeneas epitomized every Roman's duty towards his country and its gods, his family and his comrades. Some noble families adopted Pius as a *cognomen* and the emperor's *pietas* was important in Augustan iconography, being a key element in his programme of moral and political renewal (Zanker (1988), 92–7, 102–4). Pliny, however, chooses an *exemplum* of *pietas* from the lowest class, perhaps to reinforce the idea that the virtue permeated the whole of Roman society and was not confined to an aristocratic code of conduct.

plebeian woman   Cf. Valerius Maximus 5. 4. 7, Festus p. 228, 28 L. The theme, of a woman giving her milk to an aged parent (male or female) appears in both Greek and Latin variants: see Solinus 1. 24; Valerius Maximus 5. 4, ext. 1; Hyginus, *Fab.* 254. 3. It is not clear how a version of the myth became attached to the temple of *Pietas*, which was vowed by M'. Acilius Glabrio in 191 BC after he had defeated Antiochus III at Thermopylae: Livy 40. 34. 4, and dedicated ten years later by his son (Livy 40. 34. 4, Valerius Maximus 2. 5. 1, Festus 228, 28 L: Richardson (1992), 290). *Pietas* was not an obvious deity to thank for success in battle and we are not told Glabrio's reason for his choice, though some have suggested an act of devotion between father and son in battle (G. Wissowa, *Religion und Kultus der Römer* (Munich, 1902), 275). See Orlin (1997), 48. This obscurity in itself may have triggered a later search for alternative aetiologies. The Columna Lactaria in the Forum Holitorium where poor infants were given milk (Paulus, *Ex Fest.* 105 L = Mueller (88), p.118) must have been near the temple of *Pietas*, and may account for the association. It is also possible that there had been a prison on or near the site of the temple. See below, **prison . . . punishment**. The animal equivalent of the motif is the stork who supports its parent (cf. e.g. Aristotle, *HA* 615^{b}23; Plutarch, *Mor.* 962e; Aelian, *NA* 3. 23) and often appears as a symbol of piety beside representations of *Pietas* personified. The history and elements of the myth are discussed by P. Pavón, 'La Pietas e il carcere del Foro Olitorio: Plinio *NH* 7. 121', *MEFRA* 109. 2 (1997), 633–57.

prison . . . punishment   Imprisonment as such was not normally a penalty for the free-born; the public prison was primarily for the holding of those awaiting execution or the restraint of those who defied a magistrate. But P.'s *supplicii causa* could mean 'awaiting execution' as *supplicium* often meant the death penalty and capital punishment is specifically mentioned in Valerius Maximus' version (5. 4. 7) of the story. See R. A. Bauman, *Crime and Punishment in Ancient Rome* (London, 1996), *OCD*³, 1248. Pavón (1997) argues that there is no reason to doubt the existence of a prison on this site at some stage during the Republican period, despite lack of confirmatory evidence.

temple . . . Acilius . . . Marcellus   Glabrio's temple was in the Forum Holitorium, but, despite the views of some earlier scholars (e.g. H. L. Axtell, *Deification of Abstract Ideas in Roman Literature and Inscriptions* (New Rochelle and New York, 1907, repr. 1987), 28), it is very probably identical with the one struck by lightning 'in the Circus Flaminius' in 94 BC (Cic. *Div.* 1. 98, Obsequens 54). It was destroyed in 44 BC to make way for Caesar's planned theatre, later the theatre of Marcellus (Dio 43. 49. 3; Nash (1981), 241 ff., Platner–Ashby (1929), 513 ff.). Caesar may simply have moved it (Richardson (1992), 290), or it may have been rebuilt in the imperial era (Pavón (1997), 643), since the anniversary of the temple 'in the Circus Flaminius' was still being observed well into the imperial period. The consuls T. (not C.) Quinctius Flamininus and M'. Acilius Balbus were consuls in 150 BC, whereas the temple was dedicated in 181 BC (above, **plebeian woman**). The appearance in both contexts of the name M'. Acilius (Schilling 189) may have contributed to the confusion. How much of this was due to Pliny himself and how much to a copyist's error is unclear.

122. two snakes ... Gracchi   T. Sempronius Gracchus, consul in 177 and 163 BC (see *OCD*[3], Sempronius Gracchus (2), Tiberius, 1384), in which year he married Cornelia (above, **57. mother of the Gracchi** and **69. [When females ... proves]**), thirty years his junior. The story of the snakes was publicized by his son Gaius (above, **57**, **69**, cf. Cicero, *Div.* 1. 36, 2. 62; Valerius Maximus 4. 6. 1). Pliny's emphasis on the killing of one or other of the snakes may be a slight change of slant on the original prophecy: Cicero's version, which he claims to be derived from the letter of Gaius Gracchus, puts the emphasis on releasing a snake. In both versions, however, the outcome seems to be that one snake will be released, while the other will be killed. Cornelia will die if the male snake is released, Tiberius if the female is released; in which case, asks Cicero, taking a sceptical stance, why on earth did Tiberius let either snake escape? The connection suggested in the diviner's prophecy between the devoted married couple and the pair of snakes may owe something to the belief mentioned by Pliny (*HN* 8. 86) that the snake's only virtue was its conjugal fidelity (see also above, **14. custom to expose their infants ... blood**). The narrative of 8. 86 offers a rationale for the prophetic motif of sparing/killing one rather than both of the snakes. When either of a pair of snakes is killed, the survivor will stop at nothing to gain revenge. The natural historian could, then, have explained

Gracchus' demise as the outcome of a bite inflicted by the surviving snake. In cult, snakes often functioned as guardians (*OCD*³, snakes, 1417–18), and had associations with Asclepius, the god of healing and with household deities. As sacred animals of the Dioscuri at Sparta, the significance of their appearance in pairs may have been enhanced. The more prominent image of the snake in the popular consciousness, however, would have been that of a mysterious creature with ambivalent, sinister, and chthonic connotations (above, **13–20 introd.**), a most appropriate harbinger of unnatural death. While snakes were perhaps not that uncommon in Italian houses (cf. *Div.* 2. 66; *HN* 29. 72), their sinister reputation probably made unexpected appearances more alarming. Not everyone would have shared the robust attitude of the diviner in another of Cicero's anecdotes (*Div.* 2. 62): a snake coiled around a beam is not a portent; a beam coiled around a snake is.

saved . . . country Gracchus' decision displayed *pietas* twice over; to his family and to his country, by saving the wife who bore and reared two of Rome's most famous leaders (above, **57. mother of the Gracchi** and **69. [When females . . . proves]**).

M. Lepidus M. Aemilius Lepidus (*OCD*³, Aemilius Lepidus (2), Marcus, 20) was a follower of Sulla but was elected consul for 78 against the latter's wishes. As proconsul, he attacked the Sullan settlement but was defeated and fled to Sardinia where he died. Gains from the Sullan proscriptions may have financed his house, the most ornate of its day (*HN* 36. 49, 109) and the Basilica Aemilia (*HN* 35. 13). He had earlier divorced his wife, perhaps because she was related to L. Appuleius Saturninus, the ally of Marius, Sulla's enemy. Plutarch (*Pomp.* 16) says he died when he heard that she had been unfaithful, though Appian blames consumption (*BC* 1. 107).

P. Rutilius Cf. Cic. *Tusc.* 4. 17. 40, who also says (*De Amic.* 73) that he was a friend of Scipio and names his brother as Lucius. In fact, the name should be corrected to P. Rupilius Lupus (consul 132 BC), as it has been in the Cicero texts. See Schilling ad loc. and cf. *Inscr. It.* xiii. 1, tab. xxxvii, fr.xxx; Münzer, *RE* I A 1, Rupilius (5), 1229–30.

P. Catienus Philotimus A Greek freedman whose patron was, perhaps, P. Catienus Sabinus (early 1st cent. AD: Hanslik, *RE* suppl. 12, Catienus (1a), 139, cf. Schilling 190). For similarly extreme gestures, cf. the charioteer's fan, below, **186. Felix . . . Reds** and Tacitus, *Hist.* 2. 49. 10 (soldiers of the dead emperor Otho).

123. astrology A Babylonian import, closely linked with astronomy in the ancient world, through the theory that the celestial observations of the latter could be used to make predictions about the course of events in the sublunary world. See *OCD*[3], astrology, 195, and below, **160. those . . . stars, 162. lack of unanimity.**

Berosus Babylonian scholar who dedicated his Babylonian History to Antiochus I of Syria (321–261 BC), cf. *FGH* 3. C, 680. He was priest and interpreter of Belus, the Babylonians' first king and founder, often identified with the god Baal, whom P. calls 'discoverer of the science of the stars' (*HN* 6. 121). The Athenian anecdote is not attested elsewhere, but one tradition made him the bringer of astrology from Babylon to Greece, where he founded a school at Cos (Josephus, *Vs. Apion* 1. 129; Vitruvius, *Arch.* 9. 2, 9. 6. 3, 8. 9. 1). His predictions included the cyclical destruction of the world (Seneca, *NQ* 3. 29. 1, cf. Vitruvius 9. 7). See Schartz, *RE* 3. 1, Berosus, 316; *OCD*[3], 239–40, and below, **160. Epigenes . . . Berosus**.

Apollodorus Learned Athenian scholar and grammarian (*c.*180–to after 120 BC) who also worked in Alexandria. See *OCD*[3], Apollodorus (6), 124.

Amphictyons An amphictyony (from the Greek *amphiktiones*, 'dwellers around') was a Greek league based around a shrine and the maintenance of its cult (see *OCD*[3], 75). The best known were those of Anthela and Delphi, to one of which P. probably refers (perhaps the latter, cf. *HN* 35. 59, where 'an amphictyony' honours Polygnotus, whose painting at Delphi is also mentioned, with free entertainment).

Hippocrates The most famous physician of antiquity (*princeps medicinae*, according to P., below, **171. eyes . . . Hippocrates**, cf. *HN* 18. 75, 22. 136, 26. 10, 29. 4, 30. 10) came from Cos and probably lived in the second half of the 5th cent.; but the biographical tradition is unreliable and it is not certain which, if any, of the treatises and doctrines attributed to him are his. See e.g. G. E. R. Lloyd, 'The Hippocratic Question', *CQ* NS 25 (1975), 171–92 (= *Methods and*

Problems in Greek Science (Cambridge, 1991), 194–223); for recent bibliography, *OCD*[3], 712.

plague . . . assistance   See Soranus, *Biog. Hipp.* 7–8 Ilberg (*CMG* iv, p. 176); Hipp. 9. 400, 418, 420 L; Varro, *RR* 1. 4. 5. The story, which probably originated from Cos no earlier than the mid-4th cent. BC, is part of the generally unreliable biographical tradition on Hippocrates, a late development of which even tried to link him anachronistically with the Athenian plague of 430 (Aetius, *Tetr.* 5. 95, cf. Galen 14. 280–2 K), which came from the south, rather than Illyria in the north (see below, **170. epidemics . . . three months**). The nature of the assistance is unspecified in the Hippocratic references: Varro associates the story with later efforts to deal with a plague threatening the Pompeian army before Pharsalus by shutting out 'infected' winds. Late versions of the story mention the use of fire to correct and purify the air. For a discussion of the story's development, see J. R. Pinault, 'How Hippocrates Cured the Plague', *JHM* 41 (1987), 52–75.

Greeks . . . Hercules   Hercules was honoured widely in Greece as the protector of the community, Heracles Alexikakos, cf. Varro, *LL* 7. 82, K. Galinsky, *The Herakles Theme* (Oxford, 1972), 4, 127.

Cleombrotus . . . King Ptolemy . . . King Antiochus   P.'s story seems irredeemably confused; see Schilling 192–3. Cleombrotus of Ceos (Kind, *RE* 11. 1, Kleombrotus (5), 679) was doctor to Seleucus I Nicator (*c.*358–281 BC, *OCD*[3], 1381). Seleucus' son, Antiochus I (*OCD*[3], 107–8) eventually became co-regent and acquired his father's second wife, Stratonice. A Hellenistic story (Plutarch, *Demetrius* 38, Appian, *Syr.* 11. 10. 59–61; Lucian *De Dea Syria* 17–18; Valerius Maximus 5. 7. 3, ext. 1; Julian, *Misopogon* 347a–348a), based on Euripides' *Hippolytus*, arose from this, attributing Antiochus' life-threatening sickness to desire for his stepmother, but in this version the doctor in attendance was the famous Erasistratus, Cleombrotus' son (Wellmann, *RE* 6. 1, Erasistratus, 333; *OCD*[3], 552–3), which agrees with *HN* 29. 5, where Erasistratus cures Antiochus. It is possible that *HN* 7's mention of Cleombrotus preserves traces of an earlier version, and that the story was later transferred to the more famous son, who would have been very, probably too, young at the time: see M. Wellman 'Zur Geschichte der Medicin im Altertum', *Hermes*, 35 (1900), 380–1. The most confusing aspect of Pliny's stories, both here and in *HN* 29. 5, is the mention of a king Ptolemy, which would naturally suggest the Egyptian dynasty. In the present passage, P.'s language could just be taken to suggest that Ptolemy (I Soter, 367/6–282 BC?) honoured at a joint festival a famous doctor particularly renowned for his cure of another monarch. But Ptolemy is called Antiochus' son in *HN* 29. 5 (although Antiochus of course did not have a son of that name), which does suggest Pliny meant that there was a close, and specifically familial, relationship between rewarder and patient, though we would have expected the rewarder to be Antiochus' father, who gave his wife to his son and was thus closely involved in the cure. Three factors which may have contributed to these inter-dynastic, father-and-son confusions are (*a*) the existence in the mid/late 280s BC of father-and-son co-regencies in both dynasties, (*b*) connections in the sources between the Ptolemaic dynasty and Erasistratus, e.g. Caelius Aurelianus, *M. Chr.* v. 2, Erasistratus pre-scribed a remedy for 'king Ptolemy' (see Wellmann (1900); played down by P. M. Fraser, 'The Career of Erasistratus of Cos', *Ist. Lomb. Rend. Lett.* 103 (1969), 518–37), and (*c*) a later saga involving a marriage which connected a King Ptolemy (II Philadelphus, 308–246 BC) with a king Antiochus (II, son of Antiochus I), narrated in **53** above, see **Laodice**.

Finally, the story itself became a traditional motif (e.g. Aristaenetos, *Ep.* 1. 13 Hercher), linked with other kings and doc-tors (e.g. [Soranus] *Vit. Hipp.* 4, on Hippocrates and Perdiccas of Macedon) and a set-piece for rhetorical exercises (e.g. Seneca the Elder, *Contr.* 6. 7, Ps.-Quint. *Decl.* 291, Calpurnius Flaccus 48). See J. Mesk, 'Antiochus und Stratonike', *RM* 68 (1913), 366–94; A. Mehl, *Seleukos Nikator und sein Reich*, i (Leuven, 1986), 230–68; S. Sherwin-White and A. Kuhrt, *From Samarkhand to Sardis* (London, 1993), 24–5.

Megalensian festival The Roman name for a festival in hon-our of the mother-goddess Cybele (the Roman Magna Mater, above, **120. Claudia**). See *OCD*³, 416–17.

Critobulus . . . Philip's eye Philip II (382–336 BC) of Macedon lost his right eye at the siege of Methone (354 BC), cf. Diodorus Siculus 16. 34. 5. An appropriately damaged skull in tomb II at Vergina (A. J. N. W. Prag, J. H. Musgrave, R. A. H. Neave, 'The Skull from Tomb II at Vergina: King Philip of Macedon', *JHS* 74

(1984), 60–78) is now generally identified as his. A 1983 reconstruction of the face was actually modified in accordance with Pliny's testimony that the scarring was minimal, together with evidence from the Hippocratic Corpus on eye injury treatments (see Prag, 'Reconstructing Philip II: The "nice" Version', *AJA* 94. 2 (1990), 237–47; though the suggestion that the recently invented 'spoon of Diocles' might have been used to extract the arrowhead has now been retracted as medically inappropriate: see Prag and Neave, *Making Faces: Using Forensic and Archaeological Evidence* (London, 1997), 73 and nn., where it is also noted that the alleged example of the 'spoon' from Ephesus has now been proven a forgery). For Critobulus, from Cos (Kind, *RE* 11. 2, Kritobulus, (Kritodemus 3), 1928), cf. Curtius Rufus' praise of his treatment of Alexander, also for an arrow wound (9. 5. 25). P. is the only one of many testimonies to the wound to mention the medical treatment: see A. Swift Riginos, 'The Wounding of Philip II of Macedon: Fact and Fabrication', *JHS* 114 (1994), 103–19. That the lack of disfigurement was worthy of comment might suggest that such an outcome was unusual: see Salazar (2000), 34.

Asclepiades of Prusa　A 1st-cent. BC doctor from Bithynia, who spent some time in Rome and was famous for his non-invasive therapies and physiological theories (*OCD*³, Asclepiades (3), 187; Wellmann, *RE* 2. 2, Asclepiades (39), 1633; J. T. Vallance, *The Lost Theory of Asclepiades of Bithynia* (Oxford, 1990) and *ANRW* 2. 37. 2 (1993), 693–727.

new sect　Asclepiades' theory is mentioned vaguely in *HN* 26. 12, cf. *HN* 29. 6 and a *schola Asclepiadis* in *HN* 14. 76, 20. 42, 22. 128: it was ultimately assimilated to the medical school known as Methodism. Elsewhere, what P. sees as frequent and dramatic changes in Greek medical theory serve to increase his general suspicion of the medical profession (*HN* 29. 5–9; cf. Beagon (1992), 202–40), but his greatest annoyance is reserved for Asclepiades and what he perceived as the glib way in which he made an even more fundamental change—from rhetorician to doctor. E. Rawson, 'The Life and Death of Asclepiades of Bithynia', *CQ* NS 32 (1982), 364–5, argued that this was rooted in a misunderstanding of his successful introductory lectures; cf. Cicero, *De Orat.* 1. 62. See *OCD*³, Asclepiades (3), 187.

Mithridates Mithridates VI, the long-reigning king of Pontus (120–63 BC) and formidable enemy of Rome, had a keen amateur interest in medicine, mainly with the practical purpose of innuring himself to poisoning attempts (cf. *HN* 25. 5–7), in connection with which he tried to persuade Asclepiades to come to Pontus. The latter stayed at Rome but sent the king treatises. *OCD*³, 990–1; R. D. Sullivan, *Near Eastern Royalty and Rome 100–30 BC* (Toronto, 1990), 35–48.

wine Despite his criticism (above, **new sect**), P. has grudging praise (*HN* 26. 12–18) for some of Asclepiades' famous non-invasive treatments, including special baths and the judicious administration of cold water and wine, separately or together (Celsus 4. 26). P. quotes him as saying that the usefulness of wine was barely surpassed by the power of the gods (*HN* 23. 38). A later source (Anon. Londinensis 24. 30) calls him Wine-giver, a nickname clearly alluded to by P. in *HN* 23. 32, where he says Asclepiades composed a book on the medicinal uses of wine, which earned him a *cognomen*; but elsewhere (*HN* 26. 14) he quotes Varro as saying that he preferred the title of Water-giver, since his predecessor Cleophantus was already known for the advocacy of wine. However, textual citations in the *HN* (he was also listed as a source for 12 books) show that he was an important authority for P. on wines and their medicinal uses.

funeral pyre . . . life Cf. *HN* 26. 15; Celsus 2. 6; Apuleius, *Florida* 19; a tale told of many famous doctors and sages. See below, **173–8** on this and other spontaneous revivals.

lose his credibility as a doctor A phrase which may derive extra point from P.'s belief that Asclepiades was originally a rhetorician (above, **new sect**).

125. M. Marcellus . . . Archimedes' . . . ignorance Archimedes of Syracuse (*c*.287–211/10 BC) was a famous inventor and mathematician. See *OCD*³, 146–7. For the story of his inadvertent killing at the Roman capture of Syracuse, see Livy 25. 31. 9–10; Cicero, *Verr.* 4. 131; Plutarch, *Marc.* 14–19; Valerius Maximus 8. 7. 1. The Roman commander M. Claudius Marcellus' (cos. 222 BC) treatment of the Syracusans was otherwise harsh.

Chersiphron . . . Ephesus Architect of the temple of Artemis at Ephesus (*HN* 36. 95–7, Vitruvius 3. 2. 7; 7, *pref.* 12), one of the seven wonders of the world (Martial 1. 1. 3).

Philo   Philo of Eleusis (*OCD*³, Philon (1), 1166), architect of the arsenal of the Piraeus at Athens, destroyed by Sulla, was greatly admired (Cicero, *De Orat.* 1. 62, Val. Max. 8. 12, ext. 2). For his writings, cf. Vitruvius 7, pref. 12 and for the specifications of the arsenal, *IG*² ii. 1668.

four hundred   Pliny's text had '1,000', which has generally been amended with reference to Strabo 9. 1. 15, C395. See Mayhoff 132; Schilling 194.

Ctesibius . . . engines   Ctesibius of Alexandria (fl. 270 BC), employed by Ptolemy II Philadelphus (308–246 BC), invented machines using pneumatics, including a pump (e.g. Vitruvius 10. 7–8) and a catapult (Philo, *Belepoeica* 43). See *OCD*³, 412.

Dinochares . . . Egypt   Cf. *HN* 5. 62, but other authors call him Dinocrates (Valerius Maximus 1. 4., ext. 1; Solinus 32. 41, 40. 5; Vitruvius 2, *pref.* 1). See Fabricius, *RE* 4. 2, Deinochares, 2390–1. For the town and its layout, see *HN* 5. 62 and Strabo 17. 1. 6, C791.

Apelles . . . Pyrgoteles . . . Lysippos   'A rule which, if made, must have been late in his life or ill-applied' (M. Robertson, *A History of Greek Art* (Cambridge, 1975), i. 492). Apelles and Lysippos alone are normally mentioned: Cicero, *Fam.* 5. 12. 7, Horace, *Epod.* 2. 1. 237–42; and Valerius Maximus 8. 11, ext. 2; cf. Pliny, *HN* 35. 85, 37. 8. Apelles of Colophon (fl. 332 BC) was the most highly regarded painter in antiquity with over 40 works named (e.g. Pliny, *HN* 35. 79–97; cf. *OCD*³, 118–19, 1093, Robertson (1975), i. 492–7). Pyrgoteles was an engraver of gems, cf. *HN* 37. 8 and Lysippos of Sicyon (active *c.*370–315 BC) was a famous sculptor of bronzes, prolific, independent, innovatory, and precise, cf. *HN* 34. 61–5, A. F. Stewart, *Greek Sculpture: An Exploration* (New Haven and London, 1990), 186ff., 289ff., *OCD*³, 902–3.

126. King Attalus . . . Aristides   Aristides of Thebes was a 4th-cent. contemporary of Apelles (above, previous note), famous for capturing the emotions in his pictures (*HN* 35. 98–100); there was possibly an earlier painter of the same name (Robertson (1975), i. 432). According to Pliny *HN* 35. 24, Attalus II, king of Pergamum (158–138 BC), bought a painting of Dionysus by Aristides at the sale of booty captured in the Roman sack of Corinth in 146 BC by L. Mummius. The high price alerted Mummius to the painting's true worth and he reclaimed it for dedication in the temple of Ceres (*HN* 35. 100, cf. Strabo 8. 6. 23, C381).

Caesar . . . Timomachus . . . Genetrix. Timomachus came from Byzantium and according to Pliny *HN* 35. 136 (listing these and other works of his), was roughly contemporary with Caesar (Robertson (1975), i. 589–90). For the subject of the paintings, cf. also *HN* 35. 26, Cicero, *Verr.* 4. 135. For the temple of Venus Genetrix, ancestor of the Julii, the centrepiece of the new Forum Julium dedicated on 26 Sept. 46 BC (Dio 3. 22. 2, Appian, *BC* 2. 424, *Fasti* 13. 234–5; 48), and its other dedications and artworks, see Schilling (1954), 309, 313, 328; Richardson (1992), 166. See also above, **94. If I were to list . . . luxury.**

King Candaules . . . Magnesians Candaules of Lydia died *c.*680 BC, murdered by Gyges (Herod. 1. 8–14). P. wrongly dates him to 30 or 40 years earlier, *HN* 35. 56. For Bularchus, an 8th-cent. Ionian, see L. Guernini, *EAA* 152. For the 'destruction' (or 'battle', *HN* 35. 56) see J. M. Croisille, *Pline l'Ancien Histoire Naturelle livre 35* (Paris, 1985), 172. A clash with the Cimmerians seems most likely, cf. Strabo 14. 1. 40, C647 on an early invasion documented by the mid-7th cent. BC poet Callinus of Ephesus.

Demetrius . . . fortifications Demetrius Poliorcetes (the 'Besieger') of Macedon (336–283 BC, *OCD*[3], 449) won his nickname from his epic siege of Rhodes (305–304 BC) which ended in negotiations. According to Pliny *HN* 35. 104, he missed his chance to take the city for fear of damaging the *Ialysos* of Protagoras of Caunus (or Xanthus), a famous contemporary of Apelles, with whom P. records he had a contest in precision-painting (*HN* 35. 81–3). The painting was seen by Cicero in Rhodes (*Orator* 5) but by P.'s day was in the temple of Peace at Rome (*HN* 35. 102). See Robertson (1975), i. 495 ff., *OCD*[3], 1265.

127. Praxiteles . . . Venus at Cnidos Praxiteles of Athens (*OCD*[3], 1242) was a sculptor active *c.*375–330 BC, cf. *HN* 34. 50. His nude *Venus of Cnidos* was his masterpiece and superior to any other statue in the world, according to Pliny, *HN* 36. 20. See Robertson (1975), i. 386–96, esp. 390–4.

notorious . . . man Traces of this encounter were apparently visible on the statue according to Pliny, *HN* 36. 21, cf. the similar fate of Praxiteles' *Cupid*, *HN* 36. 22.

King Nicomedes . . . Cnideans Nicomedes IV Philopater (*c*.94–75/4 BC: *OCD*³, Nicomedes (4), 1043) of Bithynia's offer was all the more remarkable considering his country's impoverished condition. See Sullivan (1990), 34 and n. The Cnideans' debt had arisen in connection with the first Mithridatic war (Appian, *B. Mith.* 63). Cnidos was in north-west Asia Minor, a free city under Roman rule from 129 BC. *HN* 36. 36, an irredeemably corrupt passage, has intermittently been reconstructed to refer to an *Aphrodite* by a Bithynian artist, Daedalsa or Daedalos (cf. Eustathius, *Ad Dion. Perieg.* 793, Overbeck 2045), and a recent theory (A. Corso, 'Nicomede I, Dedalsa e le Afroditi Nude al Bagno', *Numismatica e Antichità Classiche*, 19 (1990), 135–60) makes this a consolatory commission by the thwarted Nicomedes: but see Jex-Blake and Sellers (1896), 293 and J. André, R. Bloch, A. Rouveret (eds.), *Pline l'Ancien, Histoire Naturelle livre 36* (Paris, 1981), 162.

Jupiter . . . Phidias Phidias of Athens (active *c*.465–425 BC: *OCD*³, 1158) was regarded by ancient critics as the greatest Greek sculptor (Quintilian 12. 10. 9; cf. Cicero, *Orator* 2. 8–9; Pliny, *HN* 36. 18). His most famous works were colossal chryselephantine statues of Athene Parthenos for the Parthenon at Athens and an even bigger Zeus for the Panathenaic sanctuary at Olympia (Strabo 8. 3. 30, C353, Pausanias 5. 10. 2ff.: Robertson (1975), i. 311–19), which P. mentions here.

Capitoline . . . Mentor There are a number of references to this engraver in Latin literature, e.g. Martial 3. 41. He was probably active in the first half of the 4th-cent. BC. Finely decorated metalware was highly prized at Rome; P. mentions (*HN* 33. 147) that a pair of chased goblets by Mentor, 'most famous of engravers' (*HN* 33. 154), cost the orator L. Crassus (cos. 95 BC) 100,000 sesterces. Here, P. implies that the vessels dedicated in the temples of Capitoline Jupiter (traditionally consecrated in the first year of the Republic to Jupiter Optimus Maximus, Juno, and Minerva, the city's patron deities, on the Capitol hill, the religious heart of Rome: Richardson (1992), 66–70) and the temple of Diana (i.e. Artemis) at Ephesus (above, **125. Chersiphron . . . Ephesus**) were there in his day. However, in *HN* 33. 154, he says that of four pairs of vessels made by Mentor none survive, owing to the temples' destruction by fire in 83 and 356 BC respectively.

128–9. *Valuable slaves*

After all the examples of human physical, intellectual, and moral achievement, Pliny adds a short section on the most valuable/desirable humans. The examples of the monetary value set on human talent or beauty follow on naturally from the discussion of the artists in the previous paragraphs, whose talents were often measured by the aesthetic appeal of their works, but even more by the high prices paid for them. On slave prices, see above, **56. two hundred thousand sesterces**.

128. Daphnis Probably the Lutatius Daphnis of Suetonius, *Gramm.* 3, bought for this price and then manumitted (hence the acquisition of his ex-master's *nomen*) by Q. Lutatius Catulus (*OCD*³, 893 Lutatius Catulus (1)), the cultured consul of 102 BC (Rawson (1985), 5).

Attius Sometimes identified with the poet and scholar L. Accius (170–*c*.86 BC, *OCD*³, 3) from the same town (D. Detlefsen, 'Emendationem von Eigennamen in Plinius' *Naturalis Historia* B.7', *RM* 18 (1863), 236; contra, F. Marx, *RE* I. I, Accius, 142). See Schilling 197.

Marcus Scaurus, the leading statesman M. Aemilius Scaurus (cos. 115 BC, *OCD*³, Scaurus (1), 22) was a highly skilled politician who amassed great wealth and influence. P. calls him *princeps civitatis*, 'leading citizen of the state', the term *princeps* being used in Republican times of any leading statesman before it was appropriated by the emperors. Scaurus' influence was increased by the official title *princeps senatus*, leader of the senate, a position of great dignity, which allowed the holder to speak first on any motion. Cicero (*De Orat.* 2. 197), emphasizing his power, combines this title with P.'s phrase (for which, cf. also Cic. *Rep.* 5. 7. 9): '*princeps* of the senate and of the state' and said that 'he almost ruled the world by his nod' (*Font.* 24).

actors . . . freedom Actors at Rome were generally slaves or freedmen (Cic. *Fam.* 4. 15. 6, etc.), often of Greek origin. See Balsdon (1969), 279–88.

129. Roscius Q. Roscius Gallus of Solonium (d. before 62 BC), the famous Roman actor, was, unusually, of free birth and was actually made a knight by Sulla, after which he took no more fees (Macr. *Sat.* 3. 14. 12–13; Cicero, *Pro Rosc. Com.* 23 (where an even higher annual income, 600,000 sesterces, is given). See *OCD*³, 1336.

paymaster In the emperor's household, a *dispensator* (treasurer or steward) was responsible for recording, handling, and distributing sums of money on the emperor's behalf. A trusted position, close to the emperor, it could result in considerable wealth as a result of official favour and through embezzlement (e.g. *HN* 33. 145, on the set of massive silver dishes owned by Claudius' slave Drusillanus, *dispensator* of Further Spain) and was highly sought after by imperial slaves and freedmen (Suetonius, *Otho* 5. 2). See Millar (1992), 136. Nero's slave's wealth is less surprising in view of *ILS* 1514 where a *dispensator* of Tiberius is recorded as having sixteen slaves of his own.

Armenian war . . . Tiridates Having been made a Roman protectorate after Pompey's Eastern campaigns, Armenia was at the centre of a protracted power struggle between Rome and Parthia from the 1st cent. BC onwards. In AD 54, Tiridates was placed on the Armenian throne by his brother Vologeses I of Parthia, only to be driven off, reinstated, and finally, in a diplomatic compromise, induced to receive the crown formally from Nero (Tac. *Ann.* 15. 27. 9; 16. 23; Dio 62 (63) 1–7).

value of the war . . . slave himself P. implies that the war provided extremely lucrative pickings (see above, **paymaster**) for the steward, with which he bought his freedom.

Clutorius Priscus . . . Sejanus' eunuchs Clutorius Priscus was the name of a Roman knight who, on the death of Germanicus Caesar in AD 19, had written a poetic lament and had been rewarded by the emperor Tiberius. In AD 21, when Tiberius' son Drusus fell ill, he wrote another in the hope of an even greater reward should Drusus die. His lack of tact led to execution in AD 22 (Tac. *Ann.* 3. 49–51). Lucius Aelius Sejanus (*OCD*³, 19) became praetorian prefect with his father Strabo in AD 14 and, shortly after, sole prefect. He exercised enormous influence after the death of Drusus but was eventually executed on suspicion of imperial ambitions. Two reasons for not identifying the Clutorius in Pliny with the ill-fated poet have been adduced: (i) the manuscript tradition has 'Sutorius' and (ii) the period of mourning mentioned by P. has been identified as the atmosphere prevailing after the fall of Sejanus in 31 (cf. Suetonius, *Tib.* 61), some nine years after Clutorius' execution. See Klebs, *PIR*[1], i. 425, no. 951; Groag and Stein, *PIR*[2], ii. 286, no. 1199. It is also assumed that Pliny is referring to a sale of Sejanus' goods after his fall. However, there is no reason why this might not have been a casual purchase made when Sejanus was alive. On the name, however, see K. Keil, *RM* 16 (1861), 293 for the textual emendation to Clutorius; the name did not escape variation in Dio (57. 20) either. Nor does P.'s phrase have to refer to the state of Rome after Sejanus' fall; the most celebrated period of public mourning in Tiberius' reign was that which followed the death of Germanicus. Tacitus, in addition to the proliferation of honours for the dead Germanicus (*Ann.* 2. 83; cf. Tabula Siarensis) stresses the spontaneous grief of the populace *as a whole* (2. 82, 84, 3. 1–6); whereas the terror following Sejanus' fall would have been less extensive in its scope. It is not impossible that it was at the time of the funeral in AD 20 that Clutorius, enriched with his recent imperial reward, purchased the status symbol of an expensive slave from an already influential and wealthy Sejanus, whose daughter was betrothed to Claudius later that same year (*Ann.* 3. 29).

130–90. *Final assessment of life; longevity; death*

P. now embarks on the final stage of his examination of the human animal from birth to death. A general assessment of the quality of life as a whole, the nature of happiness (**130–52**), is followed by a discussion of longevity, with records and statistics (**153–64**). In sections **165–70**, P. moves from comments on the uncertainties of human destiny (**165–7**) to a discussion of the uncertainties of physical vitality itself (**168–70**). **170** opens the topic of death, with an account of the signs of approaching death. **172–86** examine the uncertainties even of death itself; miraculous revivals, post-death experiences, sudden deaths, happy and unhappy. **187** discusses burial practices and finally, **188–90**, P. airs his scepticism on the subject of life after death. For the paradoxical element in this treatment of life's vicissitudes, see Introd. 5. 4.

130–52. *Happiness and the mutability of human fortunes*

P. begins a long section on the quality of human life, in particular the estimation of human happiness. The argument can be split into sections as follows: (*a*) **130–2**: What is happiness? Is anyone truly happy? (*b*) **133–8**: Examples to show the difficulty of pronouncing anyone truly happy: unique cases of 'triple runs' of good fortune (**133**) but changes of fortune are the norm: some particularly striking cases (**134–6**). The paradox of *Sulla felix* ('Sulla the Fortunate'): this, the most famous claim to happiness, is also the least convincing (**137–8**). (*c*) **139–46**: Detailed case study of fortune's vicissitudes (i): the great republican family of the Metelli. (*d*) **147–50**: Detailed case study (ii): the first and greatest emperor, Augustus. (*e*) **151–2**: Postscript: some famous oracular/divine judgements on human happiness.

130. Of all . . . Roman race   The portrayal of the Roman people as the collective embodiment of a particular quality is to be found elsewhere, especially in Cicero, e.g. *Phil.* 6. 19, where *libertas*, liberty, is said to be their distinguishing feature; cf. *De Orat.* 1. 15 (*ingenium*), 1. 197 (*prudentia*), *Har. Resp.* 19 (*pietas*). The superiority to other peoples implied in that passage is stated explicitly by Pliny with regard to *virtus*, the linchpin of Roman *mos maiorum*, their ancestral moral code. It was *virtus*, according to Cicero (*Verr.* 2. 4. 81) which had made Rome mistress of the world. This belief in the collective superiority of the world's ruling people may also be linked with the generalization in **116. In fact . . . put together**, where Pliny asserts that Rome has produced more outstanding examples of *ingenium*, genius, than all other peoples put together; a statement which may thus be more than an unconvincing Roman retort when faced with Greek intellectual superiority. Pushed to its logical conclusions, this notion of collective superiority might render the highlighting of outstanding individual Roman *exempla* paradoxical; although in the *exemplum* of Cicero himself, which immediately followed this statement, Pliny presented an individual whose pre-eminence was all-embracing, covering the main areas of Roman intellectual and political life. In a sense, Pliny is once again exploring the ideas of unity and totality, variety and versatility, which encourage parallels between the realm of Rome and the realm of nature (see Introd. 4. 2–4, cf. 5. 3). The material structure of Rome, the preeminent city, was, according to Pliny, a composite creation of both time and space; its political structure, according to Cicero (*Rep*. 2. 1. 2), was the product of the composite *ingenium*, exercised over many generations, of its pre-eminent people.

virtue The emphasis is on the moral connotations of *virtus* (see above, **100–29. introd.**; **104. courage . . . fortune**). P. begins by outlining an important philosophical distinction between virtue (*virtus*), in which the Roman people as a whole excel, and happiness/good fortune (*felicitas*). *Felicitas* often denoted luck resulting from the favour of the gods, especially in military affairs, but it could also mean simply 'good luck' and as such was interchangeable with *fortuna* (above, **104. courage . . . fortune**). It is predominantly this latter sense which is evident in P.'s discussion in **130–52**. Hellenistic philosophers believed that undeserved good fortune was inferior, if not actually opposed, to the moral idea of a life spent striving after virtue (leading, in some instances, to the argument that true *felicitas* could be possessed only by the morally worthy, cf. below, **137. Lucius Sulla . . . Felix**), the Stoics denying the relevance of fortune's goods to true virtue-based happiness, though the Academics and Peripatetics allowed them to add to its completeness (Cicero, *Fin*. 5. 71, 78, 81 ff.). The idea developed that virtue could overcome fortune morally if not physically (see above, **106. decorations . . . fortune**; **men . . . fortune**). The Romans were of course, a material as well as a moral success story, but although a successful general possessed both *virtus* and *felicitas* (Cicero, *Pro Leg. Man.* 28), there was often an uneasy alliance between the personal qualities implied by *virtus* and the luck which was outside the individual's control (cf. above, **104. courage . . . fortune**). Rome's preference for attributing her rise to her own efforts is reflected for example in Polybius' occasional attempts to distinguish between success resulting from *tyche-fortuna*, random luck, and that which results from a conscious striving (e.g 1. 13, 18. 28, 36. 17; cf. Walbank (1957–79), comm. ad loc.). The tension was intensified by bad examples such as Sulla (below, **137. Lucius Sulla . . . Felix**). See Erkell (1952), 41–114; Wistrand (1987), 1–62; Kajanto (1981), 502–58. The *virtus/fortuna* antithesis, present already in Cicero, seems to have increased in popularity with the growth of Stoicism in the early empire and is frequently found in the writings of P.'s elder contemporary, Seneca. See Beagon (2002), 120–6.

no human being is happy . . . firm foundation Cf. above, **44. embrace the gifts of fortune . . . true-born child,** and **to achieve a balanced view . . . frailty,** where P. criticizes those who rely too much on shallow assessments of 'good fortune'; and above, **1–3** generally on the basic paradox of human life and its ambiguous relationship with nature the mother-stepmother who has much in common with the fickle blind goddess *fortuna* (cf. *HN* 2. 22–5), her *varietas* often being identifiable with the vicissitudes of *fortuna* (Beagon (1992), 19–23; Kroll, *RE* 21. 1, Plinius (5), 410).

131. What of the saying . . . utterance! This defeatist notion undermines the Stoic belief that the wise man could conquer fortune (above, **130. of all . . . Roman race** and **virtue** and **106. men . . . fortune**) and belief in it as an 'oracular utterance' has similarities with the worship of *fortuna* as a goddess which P. deplores in *HN* 2. 22. Fortune was the mistress of external corporeal things and inferior to *ratio* (Cic. *Tusc.* 2. 11). The wise man must develop inner resources to regard the vicissitudes of fortune with indifference (*SVF* iii. 575; Seneca, *Vit. Beat.* 15, 23. 2) and properly developed *ratio* is true *felicitas* (Seneca, *Ep.* 76. 10, cf. Cic. *Fin.* 3. 26, *SVF* iii. 583–8).

Delusory . . . each individual For the Thracian custom, whereby the pebbles were collected in a quiver, cf. Phylarchus in Zenobius, *Cent.* 6. 13. Using a white stone to mark auspicious days is attested in Latin literature, e.g. Catullus 68. 148, 107. 6; cf. Horace, *C.*1. 36. 10; Martial 9. 52. 5, 8. 45. 2; Pliny, *Ep.* 6. 11. 3.

132. But supposing . . . white stone? The text is uncertain; the translation follows the Budé version: see Schilling, app. crit., p. 87 and p. xxiv.

How many . . . power . . . pleasure? It was a commonplace that fortune's gifts were often illusory, the deception becoming apparent with time; that power and wealth were two-edged swords which would eventually turn against their possessors. (A more complex case is the description, in *HN* 16. 2, of the unconquered

Chauci, happy in their liberty, but bereft of the benefits of Roman civilization: see Beagon (1996), 303–6.) None of these things, as the pun on 'goods' suggests, is a true good in the philosophical sense.

good things . . . smallest grief? Cf. Ovid, *AA* 2. 56. 3.

counting . . . weight Man is given to simplistic calculations of quantity rather than quality when assessing joys and sorrows. Misguided human calculations feature in other contexts in the *HN*, e.g man's tendency to attach exaggerated values to luxury goods (*HN* 33. 4, Beagon (1992), 76–7). By implication, attempts to evaluate happiness in philosophical terms are even rarer, cf. **137. Lucius Sulla . . . *Felix*** below.

133. Lampido Daughter of Leotychides, wife of Archidamus, and mother of Agis, kings of Sparta in the 5th cent. BC (Plato, *Alc.* 1. 18. 123e). She was not unique however. In the 4th cent. BC, Olympias was daughter of Neoptolemus of Molossia, wife of Philip II of Macedon, and mother of Alexander the Great. Others included, in the 3rd cent. BC, Berenice II and several queens of the Ptolemaic dynasty.

Berenice Called Pherenice in some Greek sources, she was daughter of the athlete Diagoras of Rhodes, cf. Pausanias 5. 6. 5, 6. 7. 1; Valerius Maximus 8. 15. 12, ext. 4; Aelian, *VH* 10. 1; Philostratus, *De Arte Gymnastikon* 17. See Kroll, *RE* 19. 2, Pherenice, 2033–4.

Curiones . . . generations They were (i) C. Scribonius Curio, praetor 121 (Cicero, *Brut.* 110, 124; *De Orat.* 2. 98), father of (ii) C. Scribonius Curio, consul 76 (Cicero *Brut.* 216–20, ridiculing his gestures and lack of memory), father of (iii) C. Scribonius Curio, tribune 50 BC. For (ii) and (iii) see *OCD*[3], Scribonius Curio, 1370; for all three, Münzer, *RE* 2 A 1, Scribonius (9), (10), and (11), 861–76.

Fabii . . . Gurges (i) M. Fabius Ambustus, consul 360, 356, and 354 BC, a notable general in Rome's Italian wars; (ii) his son, Q. Fabius Maximus Rullianus, consul in 322, 310, 308, 297, and 295 BC and dictator in 315 BC; (iii) his son, Q. Fabius Maximus Gurges, consul in 292, 276, and 265 BC. For (i) and (ii), see *OCD*[3], 582, 583; for all three, Münzer, *RE* 6. 2, Fabius (44), (114), and (112), 1753–6, 1800–11, 1798–1800.

134. Marcus Fidustius   See Dio 47. 11. 4, where he is L. Filuscius. Sulla's proscriptions were in 81 BC and Antony's 36 years later, in 43 BC.

135. Publius Ventidius . . . Asculum   Surnamed Bassus in Aulus Gellius, *NA* 15. 4. 2 ff., he was a famous example of a rise from humble origins. He came from Picenum and was led as a child (Valerius Maximus 6. 9. 9, Velleius Paterculus 2. 65. 3) or even infant (Gellius loc. cit.) in the triumph of Cn. Pompeius Strabo after the fall of Asculum in the Social War (89 BC). While in the army, he came to Caesar's notice and after serving him in Gaul and entering the senate under his patronage, he became praetor in 43. For helping Antony after Mutina, he got the consulship late in 43, at which time defamatory verses advertised his early humble career as muleteer and foot soldier (Cicero, *Fam.* 10. 18. 3, Gellius 15. 4. 3) which P. mentions here. His two brilliant victories against the Parthians were in 39 and 38 BC (Dio 49. 21. 3). He died soon after his triumph in late 38 and was honoured with a public funeral. See *OCD*[3], 1587; Gundel, *RE* 8 A 1, Ventidius (5), 795–816.

Masurius   Masurius Sabinus was a learned lawyer of the first half of the 1st cent. AD. See *OCD*[3], 935–6. There is no evidence for the assertion about Ventidius mentioned here.

Cicero   See above, **Publius Ventidius . . . Asculum**.

136. Cornelius Balbus . . . Latium   Called Balbus the elder to distinguish him from his nephew, L. Cornelius Balbus, he was born in Gades in Spain but got Roman citizenship through Pompey in 72 BC. When its legality was challenged in 56 BC, its loss would have made him ineligible for the privileges of citizenship such as exemption from certain punishments including flogging (according to the *Lex Porcia* of 195 BC). However, defended by Cicero, he was acquitted. Political acumen and a vast fortune inherited from Theophanes of Mytilene who had adopted him made him very influential: he became Caesar's agent after Pharsalus and in 40 Rome's first foreign-born consul. See *OCD*[3], Cornelius Balbus (1), 392; Münzer, *RE* 4. 1, Cornelius (69), 1266–68.

Lucius Fulvius   As consul in 322 BC (Livy 8. 38), L. Fulvius Curvus triumphed over the Samnites according to the *Fasti Triumphales*, though Livy disputes: see E. Pais (ed.), *Fasti Triumphales*

Populi Romani (Rome, 1920), 55–6. P.'s story of Tusculum and the two consulships is not attested elsewhere. See Münzer, *RE* 7. 1, Fulvius (46), 236–7.

137. Lucius Sulla . . . *Felix* L. Cornelius Sulla took the title *Felix* after the defeat of his Marian opponents at the battle of the Colline gate in 82 BC (Velleius 2. 27. 5; Plutarch, *Sull.* 34; Appian, *BC* 1. 97; Frontinus, *Strat.* 1. 11. 11; *De Vir. Ill.* 75). His belief in his 'luck' also led to the naming of his son and daughter Faustus and Fausta ('blessed', 'fortunate'). See J. P. V. D. Balsdon, 'Sulla Felix', *JRS* 41 (1951), 1–10; S. Weinstock, review of K. Latte, *Römische Religionsgeschichte*, *JRS* 51 (1961), 206–15. For Sulla's 'luck' as a more personal concept than the *felicitas* which accrued to him in his role as a successful general (above, **130. Of all . . . Roman race** and **virtue**), see Wistrand (1987), 29 ff.

a title . . . citizens? For the sarcasm, see also Valerius Maximus 9. 2. 1 and Velleius 2. 27. 5. Casualty figures for the war and proscriptions vary in the sources; Appian says initially 46 senators and 1,600 knights were proscribed, the first time this had been done (*BC* 1. 95); but proscriptions were only instituted after a period of indiscriminate slaughter and illegal killings, and false additions to the lists continued after they had been published (Plutarch, *Sulla* 31; Orosius 5. 21; Cicero, *Pro Rosc.* 130).

What a perverted . . . fortune The title is perverted on several levels. (i) On the philosophical level, *felicitas* is dependent on moral welfare (Cicero, *Fin.* 3. 26, *SVF* iii. 583–8). Sulla's conjunction of the title with such crimes may even have encouraged more emphasis on a moral definition of *felicitas* (Erkell (1952), 41–2, on Cicero's very similar criticism of Caesar's claim to *felicitas*, *Ep. ad Nep.* fr.2. 5). (ii) In Seneca, *felicitas* is connected with the humanitarian ideal, mutual help being the best defence against ill-fortune (*De Clem.* 2. 5. 3). (iii) *Felicitas* in its military sense of the luck of a general (Erkell (1952), 41 ff., Wistrand (1987), 11, 16, 37–8, 57) could of course be associated with killing, but P. links it with i) and ii) and suggests that the general who fights and kills his own countrymen perverts the meaning of *felicitas* in every sense. This is clarified in *HN* 22. 12–13, where P. comments ironically on Sulla's acquisition of the coveted *corona graminea*, the siege-raiser's crown, saying that by his proscriptions which killed more citizens than he had saved, he had effectively torn the crown from his head; he ought to yield both crown and title to Sertorius, who opposed his regime for a number of years in Spain. Sertorius was famous for his military *felicitas* (Plutarch, *Sert.* 15, 20); a moral dimension could perhaps be added through his patriotism. For Seneca, (*Ad Marc.* 6. 12. 6), Sulla's *felicitas* was *deorum . . . crimen*, a crime of the gods themselves.

unfortunate . . . future   The Sullan proscriptions set a precedent for the second triumvirate in 43 BC (above, **134. Marcus Fidustius**).

138. his own death . . . tortures?   Cf. Plutarch, *Sulla* 36; *HN* 26. 138, 11. 114; Val. Max. 9. 3. 8 (Appian 1. 105. 2 merely says that he succumbed to a fever). Aristotle (*HA* 556^{b}21–557^{a}2) describes how certain creatures live on the body, some developing in putrifying matter, others multiplying in the moisture on living animals. The *phtheires* which he describes as emerging from skin eruptions could have been pubic lice (*phthirus pubis*), or even a heavy infestation of *pediculus humanus corporis*, the body louse (although they remain mostly in the clothing), might produce a similar impression while feeding on the body. Ancient writers tend to be vague when describing such infestations. Thus, in *HN* 11. 114, Pliny groups together creatures which are apparently generated from the flesh of the dead and the hair of the living (presumably fly larvae and head lice), and goes on to associate them with the deaths of Sulla and the poet Alcman. Vocabulary is imprecise; the creatures, described as *phtheires* by Plutarch (*Sulla* 36–7) and Aelian (*VH* 5. 2), are simply called *serpentes* by Pliny in **172** below, when describing the similar fate of Pherecydes of Syros. The most detailed description of Sulla's final illness, together with the fullest list of those who suffered similar infestations, is given by Plutarch (*Sulla* 36–7). In all cases, it is likely that the infestation was a secondary factor, vermin multiplying on a body already weakened by disease or neglect. T. F. Carney's argument for syphilis in the case of Sulla ('The Death of Sulla', *Acta Classica*, 4 (1961), 64–79) is not entirely convincing and was rejected as medically unsound by Grmek (1989: 392 n. 3). His rationalization of *phtheires* to 'louse-like sores' seems unlikely in the light of Aelian's description of Pherecydes' similar affliction (below, this note), in which sores are distinguished from *phtheires*. The presence of syphilis in antiquity is in any case debatable. However, Plutarch suggests a long-standing bowel disorder exacerbated rather than caused by promiscuity. The infestation followed upon this neglect and did not respond to washing. Finally, the dictator was killed by a haemorrhage. Even if Sulla's primary problem was not a sexually-transmitted disease, the infestation may well have been pubic lice, especially as these cannot be eradicated by washing alone. We do not have enough information on the other victims listed by Plutarch to identify the nature of their infestation and demise, although a few details about Pherecydes of Syros (see below, **172. Pherecydes . . . body.**) are given by Aelian (*VH* 4. 28 and 5. 2). Once again, infestation was not his initial symptom. He became unwell, at first suffering from a mucus-like sweat, then being attacked by sores and only after that by *ptheires* (5. 2). This does not suggest a louse-borne disease such as typhus or relapsing fever, but rather a secondary infestation of a diseased, weakened, and uncared-for body. It may be no coincidence that two of the other victims listed by Plutarch succumbed to infestation while in the insanitary confines of prison.

final dream . . . glory He died 'the happiest of men, if happiness consists in getting what you want', the evening after dreaming that a divinity was calling him (Appian, *BC* 1. 105). Plutarch (*Sulla* 37) says that in his memoirs, finished two days before his death, he mentioned a recurring dream in which his son begged him to come and live in peace and quiet with him and his mother, and a prophecy foretelling his death 'at the height of his good fortune' after a life 'full of honour'.

one thing . . . Capitol Cf. Tac. *Hist.* 3. 72. 7. Sulla had begun to rebuild the temple of Capitoline Jupiter (above, **127. Capitoline . . . Mentor**) after the fire of 83 BC, but it was not dedicated until 69 BC, by Q. Lutatius Catulus.

139–46. introd. *The fortunes of the Metelli*

The Caecilii Metelli were a high-profile family throughout the late Republic, reaching the peak of their influence in the second half of the 2nd cent. BC with the careers of Macedonicus and his four sons as described by P. here (cf. Velleius 2. 11. 2). For the family generally, see J. van Ooteghem, *Les Caecilii Metelli de la République* (Namur, 1967). Their own family archives would have offered P. a major if biassed (Cicero, *Brutus* 61) source and would have included funeral orations such as that quoted in **139–40** and possibly official papers relating to their terms of office (Rawson (1985), 238–9). They would also have featured prominently in public records. P. was certainly familiar with the *Acta* (above, **95. records** and below, **186. public records**). However, there were also a number of sources from which he could have gleaned his information at second hand; besides histories of the period, the indices alone of book 7 suggest Varro (his *Imagines?*), Atticus (a portrait collection with biographical notes; also family histories of several distinguished families), Nepos (a series of biographies, *De Viris Illustribus*), and Messalla Rufus, the genealogist (cf. *HN* 35. 8 and below, **173**), who wrote a *De Familiis*.

139. Quintus Metellus Q. Caecilius Metellus, consul 206 BC, pontifex (from 216), dictator in 205 BC and a supporter of Scipio Africanus: *OCD*³, Caecilius Metellus, Quintus, 268.

funeral oration The speech was delivered in 221 BC. Lucius Caecilius Metellus apparently reached his hundredth year (see below, **157**). The Roman funeral was a public occasion and the *laudatio* praising the dead person's accomplishments was equally an exhibition of family lineage, status, and tradition. The occasion linked past, present, and future together in a conscious propagation of the continuity of the Roman aristocratic ethos. The presence of the ancestor masks, the memories of the contemporaries of the deceased, and the pattern set before the next generation all contributed, as Polybius appreciated (6. 52. 10; 53. 4, 6; 54. 4). From the late 3rd cent., funeral orations were becoming more structured and rhetorical, though later, Cicero, *De Orat.* 341 suggests that the occasion still curbed the more extravagant displays of artistry. Later still, in the 2nd cent. AD, however, Lucian suggests, albeit humorously, that the givers of funeral orations acted as though they were pleading a case for the deceased with the infernal judges (*De Luctu* 23). The giver of this oration, Quintus Metellus, was a gifted orator, cf. Cicero, *Brutus* 57. Valerius Maximus gives a paraphrase of his later speech on the fate of Carthage at the end of the second Punic war (7. 2. 3). See W. Kierdorf, *Laudatio Funebris: Interpretationem und Untersuchungen* (Meisenheim am Glam, 1980), 10–21; H. Flower, *Ancestor Masks and Aristocratic Power in Roman Culture* (Oxford, 1996), 128–56; O. C. Crawford, 'Laudatio Funebris', *CJ* 37 (1941/2), 17–27; E. Gabba, *Del buon uso della ricchezza* (Milan, 1988), 27–31.

COMMENTARY 337

Lucius Metellus . . . distribution This brief sketch of the deceased man's career may have been paraphrased by Pliny from an earlier part of the *laudatio*. Consul in 251 and 247 BC, Lucius Caecilius Metellus was effectively the founder of the *gens* (Ooteghem (1967), 9). He became *pontifex maximus* in 243, dictator to hold elections in 224 (Cicero, *Sen.* 30), and Master of Horse (for which see below, **147. Master of Horse**) to the dictator Atilius Caiatinus in 249: see Polybius 1. 100–103. The date of his land commission membership is uncertain, cf. Ooteghem (1967), 20; possibly 232 BC, in the wake of the *Lex Flaminia* (J. H. Corbett, 'L. Metellus (cos. 251, 247): Agrarian Commissioner', *CR* NS 20. 1 (1970), 7–8). See *OCD*³, Caecilius Metellus, Lucius, 268; and, in detail, Ooteghem (1967), 7–22.

first . . . procession L. Metellus won a great victory over the Carthaginians at Panormus in 250 BC, capturing many elephants. These evidently made a great impression back at Rome and are mentioned in numerous sources, e.g. Polybius 1. 40. 6–16: see Ooteghem (1967), 11–12. Since Curius Dentatus is credited with the 'first' triumphal elephants (in 275 BC) in *HN* 8. 16, while Metellus is credited with 'a very large number' (240 or 242), some editors have accordingly amended the text here to the latter reading (see Schilling 204 and app. crit.). In *HN* 8. 17, Pliny says they were all transported to Rome from Sicily on rafts. They ended up in the arena, though Pliny's sources disagreed on the question of whether or not they were slaughtered. Elephants thereafter featured frequently on coins of the Metelli (e.g. Crawford (1974), ii. 262. 1–5, pl. 38.5–8; 374. 1, pl. 48.7).

left it in writing The written version of the speech would have been preserved in the family archives. Whether P. used it at first hand or through an intermediate source cannot be determined (see **139–46. introd.**; Kierdorf (1980), 12). For the publication of such speeches, evidently the custom by the late 3rd cent., see Flower (1996), 145–6, who adds a list of later published *laudationes*, including Laelius' on Scipio, Julius Caesar's on his aunt Julia, and Augustus' on Marcellus, Agrippa, and Drusus. Even speeches not actually given, due to their subject's dying abroad for example, might be published. They were important from a literary point of view, providing some of the earliest examples of Latin prose (Cicero, *Brutus* 61). Historically, a permanent record of such a speech was an important contribution to the construction of the family's image and its publication ensured projection of that image into Roman society as a whole.

ten greatest and best objectives In essence, this is a summary of the Roman aristocratic ideal: see Ooteghem (1967), 21; Urlichs (1857), 76 (possible reference to a work of Appius Claudius Caecus); Earl (1967), 24. For similar, if shorter, lists, see above, **100. outstanding . . . senator**, Livy 39. 40 (on Cato the censor), and Aulus Gellius, *NA* 1. 13. 10. The list details (*a*) the vital skills needed to advance a Roman aristocrat's public standing (*dignitas*) in the military and political spheres (warrior, orator, general, statesman); (*b*) the power wielded (*auctoritas*) as a result of this standing and its public recognition (honour, wisdom, distinction); (*c*) the wealth needed to underpin this high profile and the progeny which would preserve the memory (*memoria*) of his achievement and use it as a model (*exemplum*) to ensure the continuation of the family renown.

spend their lives Flower (1996: 139–42) draws attention to this phrase, suggesting that the achievements listed are mentioned in the order they held in his life's career. Early training in war and rhetoric prepared him for positions of power and responsibility as politician and general, the legacy of which was the glory and substantial fortune he handed on to the many descendants who would continue the family tradition.

140. first-rate warrior . . . orator Military and political training were the main areas of aristocratic higher education.

bravest of generals For his military career, see above, **first . . . procession** and Ooteghem (1967), 11–14.

control . . . importance Witness the offices listed above, **Lucius Metellus . . . distribution.**

supreme wisdom For the predominantly practical connotations of *sapientia* in Lucius Metellus' time, see above, **118. wisdom**, and Klima (1971), 56–60. Later, Cicero (*De Orat.* 1. 8) claimed that *consilium* and *sapientia* governed and guided the state. See above, loc. cit.; Earl (1967), 33; J. Hellgouarc'h, *Le Vocabulaire Latin des relations et des partis politiques sous la République* (Paris, 1963), 271 ff.

foremost senator As Flower (1996: 140) notes, this appears to be a general phrase, summing up the effect of all his other positions.

Of the two specific posts which might have merited such a description, the censorship was never held by Metellus, while, as a plebeian, he may have been ineligible for the position of *princeps senatus* (on which see above, **128. Marcus Scaurus . . . leading statesman**).

in an honourable fashion A large fortune added to the family's standing and handing down an increased patrimony was regarded as an important achievement in its own right (Plutarch, *Cat. Mai.* 21. 8). As Pliny's words imply, however, some means of making money were more honourable than others. In the 1st cent. BC, Cicero provides a list (*De Off.* 1. 151), from which it is clear that money made through and invested in land is the only form of wealth totally suited to senatorial status. I. Shatzman, *Senatorial Wealth and Roman Politics*, Collection Latomus 142 (Brussels, 1975), 245, surmises that Lucius Metellus made a fortune in the first Punic war from which, as Gabba (1988: 27–31) suggests, he probably bought more land, perhaps making further acquisitions whilst acting as a Land Commissioner. Commercial activities were engaged in, if indirectly, by senators, even after the restrictions imposed by the *Lex Claudia*, passed in 218 BC, a few years after Metellus' death. In any case, it was risk, rather than dishonour, which characterized such activities even in the first half of the 2nd cent., as the elder Cato (*De Agri.* pref. 1) makes clear. Equally clear, however, is the dishonour Cato attaches to usury and it is doubtless this activity which Lucius avoided.

many children Quintus, the son who gave the funeral oration, is known to have had at least one other brother, disgraced after Cannae. Whether he was called Marcus or Lucius, or whether there were in fact two other brothers, one of each name, is unclear. See Ooteghem (1967), 45–6. Other children, or grandchildren, alive in 221 BC are not mentioned in the sources.

most distinguished individual The climax, as Lucius' life's achievement was recognized by the whole citizen body (Gabba (1988), 29).

no one else since the foundation of Rome A rhetorical flourish which summarizes perfectly the competitive nature of the Roman aristocratic ethos and its embodiment in a testimonial punctuated throughout by superlatives.

141. blindness . . . Vesta The Palladium was a small wooden statue of Athene and the miraculous guardian of Troy, stolen by the Greeks to enable the city's fall. For the powers of such statues, see C. Faraone, *Talismans and Trojan Horses* (New York, 1992), 4, 136–9. However, according to Roman tradition, Aeneas brought it to Italy where, as a pledge of Rome's own fate, it was housed in the innermost sanctuary of the temple of Vesta where only the chief Vestal could enter (Ovid *Fasti* 419–60; Dionysius of Halicarnassus 1. 68–9; Servius, *In Aen.* 2. 162–79; Silius Italicus, *Pun.* 13. 36–70). Some authors tried to reconcile the Roman version with the earlier tradition, e.g. Dion. Hal. 1. 69. 2: see R. G. Austin (comm.), *P. Vergili Maronis Aeneidos, Liber Secundus* (1964, 83–5) on *Aen.* 2. 163. For the question of Metellus' maiming, see Beagon (2002), esp. 116–18, the salient points of which are summarized here. The fire from which Metellus saved the statue occurred in 241 BC (Livy, *Per.* 19; Dion. Hal. 2. 66; Cicero, *Scaur.* 48, Ovid *Fasti* 6. 440–54, Valerius Maximus 1. 4. 5) but, while he may have been burnt in the attempt (Augustine, *CD* 3. 18; from Varro?), the first source to say specifically that he lost his sight is the elder Seneca, *Contr.* 4. 2 (cf. Plutarch, *Mor.* 309f), so the story was possibly an invention for rhetorical purposes (M. Winterbottom, *The Elder Seneca* (Cambridge, Mass., and London, 1974), i. 438; T. P. Wiseman, *Clio's Cosmetics* (Totowa, NJ, 1979), 33, 36), perhaps by Asinius Pollio (O. Leuze, 'Metellus Caecatus', *Philol.* 18 (1905), 95–115). Also, a priest was supposed to be 'whole' (Dion. Hal. 2. 21. 3; Aulus Gellius, *NA* 1. 12. 3; Plutarch, *RQ* 73: see above, **105. infirmity**), and Seneca has Metellus deprived of his priesthood because of his blindness; whereas the evidence suggests that Metellus was still *pontifex maximus* after the incident (Ooteghem (1967), 20; G. Dumézil, *La Religion romaine archaïque* (Paris, 1966), 320–1), as well as dictator (the blinded were allowed to complete their current magistracy but not to stand for further posts: Justinian, *Digest* 3. 1. 1. 5, cf. on disability and secular office generally, Mommsen (1887), i, 494). There may have been more to Metellus' blindness than physical injury. Blindness was traditionally an effect of seeing/revealing the forbidden (e.g. temple-robbers, Valerius Maximus 1. 1, ext. 5; Tiresias; cf. Forbes-Irving (1990), 166–7). It is even possible that his blindness was temporary. Plutarch (*Mor.* 309f) recounts two anecdotes of blindness as a result of touching the Palladium then being reversed by appropriate religious propitiation; and cf. perhaps the story of St Paul.

The uncertain text for the name in the first of these has sometimes been emended to Metellus. For a speculative theory that the story was a myth derived from an unattested gentilician hero, Caecilius (whence *Caecus*, 'blind'), see Ooteghem (1967), 15–20.

chariot Aulus Gellius, *NA* 3. 18. 4, citing Gavius Bassus (1st cent. BC) says that in earlier days this was a privilege of all who had held curule magistracies. The *currus* was a light chariot; similar forms of transport had been prestige vehicles in ancient societies (S. Piggott, *Wagon, Chariot and Carriage: Symbol and Status in the History of Transport* (London, 1992)). They retained ceremonial and ritual uses (*OCD*[3], 1546–7), the *currus* being used as the triumphal chariot. The magisterial privilege was probably already obsolete by the 2nd cent. BC and was revived as a unique honour for Metellus (see Urlichs (1857), 76–7; or (Schilling 205) Metellus may have been conveyed at state expense. Given its connotations, the chariot was a particularly appropriate honour for one whose military and priestly, as well as political, record was so distinguished. Dionysius of Halicarnassus 2. 66. 4 simply refers to 'great honours' from the senate recorded on his statue erected on the Capitol. Later comparisons include the privilege of wearing gold wreaths at public games or ceremonies, granted to Pompey and Caesar (H. S. Versnel, *Triumphus: An Inquiry into the Origins, Development and Meaning of the Roman Triumph* (Leiden, 1970), 130). For outstanding individuals who *spontaneously* adopted distinctive apparel and other features, see Valerius Maximus 3. 6. 1–7.

142. rare ... happiness Cf. Cicero, *Tusc.* 1. 86.

greatest ... Macedonicus Q. Caecilius Metellus Macedonicus gained his *agnomen* from his defeat of Andriscus and settlement of Macedonia in 146, while only of praetorian rank, which was unprecedented. He became consul in 143 (but only after two unsuccessful attempts). He was one of the first pair of plebeian consuls in 131 and augur for at least 25 years, dying in 115. See Ooteghem (1967), 51–78; *OCD*[3], Caecilius Metellus Macedonicus, Quintus, 269.

four sons ... ex-censor The praetorian was C. Metellus Caprarius (Münzer, *RE* 3. 1, Caecilius (84), 1208; Ooteghem (1967), 102–9). He was consul after his father's death in 113. The three consulars were Q. Metellus Baliaricus (*RE* 3. 1, Caecilius (82), 1207;

OCD[3], Caecilius Metellus Baliaricus, Quintus, 268; Ooteghem
87–90), consul 123 BC, Lucius Metellus Diadematus (*RE* 3. 1,
Caecilius (93), 1213; Ooteghem 93–7), consul 117 BC, and M.
Metellus (*RE* 3. 1, Caecilius (77), 1205; Ooteghem 98–101), consul
115 BC. Only one, Baliaricus, had triumphed by the time of his
father's death, after his conquest of the Balearic islands in 121, but
two more, Marcus and Gaius, were to do so in 111. The ex-censor
was Baliaricus (120 BC). See Cicero, *Fin.* 5. 82; Velleius 1. 11. 7;
Valerius Maximus 7. 11 (who attributes it to Fortune) and, briefly,
Cicero, *Tusc.* 1. 85. Pliny does not mention Macedonicus' three
daughters (cf. above, **59. Metellus Macedonicus**), who all
married leading statesmen.

143. Campus Martius . . . deserted   The Campus Martius, a
large area of the Tiber flood plain to the north of the city outside
the religious boundary, held a number of buildings, including the
Villa Publica, a porticoed area used for the census (Richardson
(1992), 65–7; 430–1). The streets were deserted due to the midday
heat.

C. Atinius Labeo   C. Atinius Labeo Macerio, tribune 131 BC
(Klebs, *RE* 2. 2, Atinius (10), 2106). For a summary of the following
events, see also Livy, *Per.* 59, Cicero, *De Domo Sua* 123.

thrown out . . . censor   See Ooteghem (1967), 71–4 and A. E.
Astin, *Scipio Aemilianus* (Oxford, 1967), 237–8, 354, who suggests that
the controversy centred on whether the tribunate conferred auto-
matic membership of the senate.

Tarpeian rock   A cliff on the Capitol from which traitors and
murderers were thrown, cf. Dionysius Halicarnassus 7. 352, 8. 78. 5;
Varro, *LL* 5. 41; Richardson (1992), 377–8.

unlawful . . . sacrosanct tribune   The plebeians, whose
officers they were, swore to guarantee the tribunes' inviolability or
sacrosanctitas while in office.

tribune . . . veto   The tribunes possessed the right of veto (*inter-
cessio*) which could be used against any act of a magistrate or, as in
this case, another tribune, by virtue of their inviolability.

144. property . . . consecrated   *Consecratio bonorum* was an
ancient penalty for serious crimes: the Valerio-Horatian laws

quoted in Livy 3. 55. 7 mentioned harming a tribune, the wrong in this case being the senatorial exclusion of Labeo (cf. below, **condemned**). The goods were sold and the proceeds given to a temple by a magistrate or priest. See Cicero, *De Domo Sua* 123–4 and Nisbet on Cic. loc. cit., pp. 210–11; J. L. Strachan-Davidson, *Problems of the Roman Criminal Law* (Oxford, 1912), i. 185 ff. The laws also mentioned *consecratio* of the condemned person which in Metellus' day was obsolete, but which might be partly behind Atinius' attempt to throw him from the Tarpeian rock. Shatzman (1975: 245) questions whether the father of four sons who ultimately gained consulships could really have suffered so severe a financial penalty as to be left living on charity, as Pliny suggests. Cicero's version, admittedly vague, does say that Metellus suffered no disadvantage as the result of the tribune's activities (*De Domo Sua* 123).

condemned   A reference to Metellus' removal of Labeo from the senate.

vengeance . . . ears!   For similar stories of threats and violence see e.g. Florus 7. 5 and *De Vir. Ill.* 66 on the younger Livius Drusus' (tribune 91 BC) treatment of his opponents.

younger Africanus . . . greater citizen'   P. Cornelius Scipio Aemilianus Africanus (*OCD*[3], 397–8), son of L. Aemilius Paulus but adopted by the son of the elder Africanus; consul 147 BC and destroyer of Carthage in 146 BC. He incurred popular displeasure by approving of Ti. Gracchus' death and his own sudden death in 129 provoked suspicions of foul play. See Livy, *Epit.* 59; Plutarch, *C. Gracchus* 10; Cicero, *Fam.* 9. 21. 3, *QF* 2. 3. 3; and E. Badian, review of H. Malcovati, *Oratorum Romanorum Fragmenta liberae rei publicae iteratis curis recensuit*, *JRS* 46 (1956), 221 on the likelihood of natural death. He had other powerful enemies and his bad relations with Macedonicus became legendary: see Cicero, *De Amic.* 77, *Brutus* 81, *Rep.* 1. 31; Velleius 1. 11. 6. For the latter's reaction to Scipio's death, see Valerius Maximus 4. 1. 12, who says Macedonicus admired his enemy and was shocked at his death; cf. [Plutarch] *Apopth. Caec. Met.* 3. See Astin (1967), 244.

already . . . Baliaricus and Diadematus   Baliaricus did not gain his triumphal *cognomen* until 121 (above, **four sons**). Plut. *Cor.* 11 says the title Diadematus was not honorific at all but gained from prolonged wearing of a bandage on the head for a sore! For a theory as to how it might have become a permanent appellation, see Ooteghem (1967), 93–4.

145. Capitol . . . manner?   The *triumphator* rode in a four-horse chariot to the temple of Jupiter on the Capitol, as part of a procession which included numbers of his prisoners of war, the most prominent of whom were normally executed in the Tullianum near by. The origins of his special costume, the *toga picta* (embroidered toga), the *tunica palmata* (palm-embroidered tunic) and the *corona triumphalis* (triumphal crown), together with a laurel wreath held above his head by a slave (cf. Livy 10. 7. 9–10), may be connected with the ancient kings and/or Jupiter. P.'s 'insignia' accords with the view (Versnel (1970), 56–93) that the accoutrements, often called *insignia* or *ornatus Iovis* by other sources (Livy loc. cit., Suet. *Aug.* 94, Tertullian 13. 1) were literally taken for the occasion from the statue of Capitoline Jupiter. Cf. also *HN* 33. 111 on the red lead once used to colour the *triumphator*'s face and that of the statue at festivals.

146. glorious funeral . . . triumphs   See above, **142. four sons . . . ex-censor.**

glory . . . resentment   Vengeance for a slur on the family's dignity would have been a natural Roman aristocratic reaction; cf., in a later era, the letter of Metellus Celer, bristling with outraged family pride, written to Cicero after the latter had allegedly slighted his brother Metellus Nepos (*Fam.* 1. 1 and 1. 2). However, political prudence (powerful families invite powerful opposition, above, **144. younger Africanus . . . greater citizen'**), rather than noble self-restraint or painful memories may have kept the sons from opening old wounds.

147–50. *The misfortunes of the emperor Augustus*

P. balances his examination of the claim to happiness of Rome's most illustrious Republican dynasty with a consideration of that of the first and greatest of her emperors. The undoubtedly great achievements of Augustus in extracting from a war-torn republic a new and stable system of government, emphasizing at once peace and world-conquest, continuity of tradition and the dawn of a new age, left its mark on the popular consciousness. Augustus' *felicitas* became proverbial (Eutropius 8. 5. 3). Rooted in his military suc-cess, it came to denote an innate personal quality he was born with (Suet. *Aug.* 94. 1; Dio 56. 25. 5 on his birth sign), and which affected his whole reign; his prosperity was Rome's (Suet. *Aug.* 58. 2). Its name and symbols featured in imperial iconography as did that of his personal *fortuna* (see Wistrand (1987), 44–62). But the optimistic view of his reign stemmed in part from the success of his own pub-licity; problems and disasters did not necessarily impinge on the consciousness of his contemporaries, to whom 'an image was more powerful than the reality . . .' (Zanker (1988), 237–8). The more per-ceptive saw the cracks, especially when viewing the Augustan era after a period of time: Tacitus' experience of the misuse of power by some of Augustus' successors served to make him more cynically aware of the darker side of the Augustan achievement (Tac. *Ann.* 1. 1–10). Our closest parallel to P.'s questioning of the appellation *felix* as applied to Augustus is the more overtly philosophical treatment of his older contemporary Seneca in *Brev. Vit.* 4. There, Augustus is depicted as longing for a break from the strains of power, a world-conqueror ironically at his most vulnerable to betrayal at home among his fellow-citizens, friends, and even family (see below, **149–50**). Later, Suetonius (*Aug.* 65) groups together the misfortunes involving death and betrayal in Augustus' own family as an example of the fickleness of fortune. It is perhaps best to see Pliny in this general moralizing tradition, rather than posit irrecoverable 'hostile' historical sources: the only sources Pliny actually mentions are Augustus' friends and advisers, Maecenas and Agrippa (see below, **148. Agrippa . . . Maecenas**). Nor is it necessary to assume that P. is deliberately underplaying Augustus' success so as to flatter the Flavian dynasty. For the positive reson-ances of Augustus for Flavian ideology, see Introd. 4. 4. See also R. Till, 'Plinius uber Augustus', *Wurzburger Jahrbucher*, NS 3 (1977), 127–37; B. Baldwin, 'Emperors in the Elder Pliny', *Scholia*, 4 (1995), 56–78; G. Binder, 'Auguste d'après les informations de la *NH*', in Pigeaud and Oroz (1987), 461–72 . For Augustus in the context of Pliny's treatment of the paradox of the human condition in *HN* 7, see Introd. 5. 4.

147. Master of Horse Octavian, the future emperor Augustus, was Julius Caesar's great-nephew and, from Sept. 45, his adopted son. The *Magister Equitum* was an emergency magistrate, ranking with a praetor, who was appointed as a dictator's deputy. Dio (43. 49. 1) says Antony held the post in 44 but later (43. 51. 7) says two men, one of them, Octavian, had been designated to hold it during the next two years. Appian (*BC* 2. 107) says Lepidus replaced Antony for 44 but later (3. 9) says Octavian was appointed to the position 'for a year'. The fragmentary *Fasti Capitolini* suggest Lepidus held it before he took up a provincial command later in 44. His replacement's name is lost, though the appointee for the following year is named as Cn. Domitius Calvinus. R. Weigel, *Lepidus: The Tarnished Triumvir* (London, 1992), 37–90, suggests the missing name is Octavian's and he was to fill the post only after Lepidus had resigned to take up his provincial post.

proscriptions   The formation of the second triumvirate in Nov. 43, consisting of Antony, Lepidus, and Octavian, was followed by proscriptions. Apologists later excused Octavian as the junior member of the triumvirate overruled by his older, more cynical colleagues (cf. Dio 47. 7). Suet. *Aug.* 27 says he tried to oppose the proscriptions at first, but once begun, he joined in with greater severity than either of his colleagues.

worst citizens . . . predominant   On the balance of power in 43, see Syme (1939), 188–9. Octavian was forced to give up the consulship he had seized after Mutina. Antony, with the most distinguished career and following, held the strategic and militarily vital provinces of Cisalpine Gaul and Gallia Comata. Lepidus retained Gallia Narbonensis and Hither Spain while Octavian had the comparatively modest holding of Africa (still controlled by his opponents), Sicily, Sardinia, and Corsica.

148. illness . . . Philippi   There were two battles at Philippi, in the first of which Brutus' forces took Octavian's camp. The latter was mysteriously absent (Plutarch, *Brut.* 41. 4; Appian, *BC* 4. 463; Dio 47. 41). Velleius (2. 70. 1) and Valerius Maximus (1. 7. 1; and cf. Plutarch, *Ant.* 22. 2, Suet. *Aug.* 91. 1) cite a warning given to his doctor in a dream. His health was poor and he fell ill again on his return to Italy after the eventual victory (Dio 48. 31). Elements of the more favourable interpretations of this murky episode may go back to Augustus' own autobiography (cf. *HN* 2. 24) and those of his supporters (below, **Agrippa . . . Maecenas**).

dropsy   The likeliest interpretation of the text's 'water under the skin', a serious condition: cf. Celsus 2. 7. 5–6, 3. 21, who describes three types.

Agrippa . . . Maecenas Even Augustus' supporters were unable to disguise the less glorious elements of his military career. M. Vipsanius Agrippa, a lifelong friend, became Octavian's military mentor and by 12 BC a partner nearly equal in power to the emperor himself. P. here refers to his lost autobiography though he also uses his geographical commentaries (*OCD*³, 1602; M. Reinhold, *Marcus Agrippa: A Biography* (Geneva and New York, 1933); Hanslik, *RE* 9A, Vipsanius (2), 1270). C. Maecenas was Augustus' trusted friend and agent. A great literary patron, he himself wrote poetry and prose works of which only a few fragments survive. It is not clear to which work P. refers (J.-M. André, *Mécène: Essai de biographie spirituelle* (Paris, 1967), 104–14, 149–50; Syme (1939), 30 and index, Kappelmacher, *RE* 14. 1, Maecenas (6), 224–5).

shipwreck During the protracted struggle with Sextus Pompeius (son of Pompey the Great), from 38–36 BC, Octavian suffered several defeats and shipwrecks, the latter through both enemy action and storm damage (see also below, **178. Sicilian war** and **Gabienus**). See Suet. *Aug.* 16. 1; Appian, *BC* 5. 81 ff. Pliny probably refers to his defeat in 38 BC off Messina, where he was shipwrecked and hid in the mountains (Appian, *BC* 5. 84–7); or possibly to the summer of 36 BC, during an attempt to capture Tauromenium, after which he was discovered in a sorry state at Abala and brought secretly to Messalla's camp (Appian 5. 109–12). Agrippa was responsible for the ultimate victory at Naulochus in Sept. 36 BC. Till (1977) notes the recurrent motif of disaster/hiding, here and in the Philippi episode.

Proculeius C. Proculeius, a knight, was a loyal friend and naval commander (Dio 51. 11. 4, 54. 3. 5; Plutarch, *Ant.* 77–80; Hanslik, *RE* 23. 1, Proculeius (2), 72–4). He had a reputation for blameless character and lack of political ambitions and may once have been considered, if only half-seriously, as a suitable husband for Augustus' daughter, Julia (Tac. *Ann.* 4. 40, cf. *HN* 36. 183). It is not clear to which particular setback in the Sicilian wars the anecdote belongs.

Perusine war As consul in 41, Antony's brother Lucius Antonius, in cooperation with Antony's wife Fulvia, supported the

Italian towns against the post-Philippi land confiscations of Octavian. The latter besieged him at Perusia, sparing his life but plundering the town. Suetonius (*Aug.* 14) talks of occasions of personal danger to Octavian himself during the war.

Actium The aftermath of the famous naval battle of 31 BC against Antony and Cleopatra was protracted. Besides Antony and Cleopatra's survival and escape, Suetonius (*Aug.* 14) also reports threatened mutiny and storms and shipwrecks before Octavian could lay siege to Alexandria. Even after their deaths, he was faced with the problem of their children.

fall . . . Pannonian wars During the siege of Metulum, 35 BC: cf. Suet. *Aug.* 20, Appian, *BI* 20, Dio 49. 35. 2.

149. mutinies . . . illnesses For mutinies, see e.g. Dio 54. 11. 3, 56. 12. 2; Suet. *Aug.* 14, 17. His reforms imposed strict discipline in the army (Suet. *Aug.* 24–5) and there were problems with pay (see below, **shortage . . . army**). For illnesses, see above, **148.** **Agrippa . . . Maecenas** and **shipwreck** and especially Suet. *Aug.* 80–2 (below, **Marcellus' vows**); also *Aug.* 1, 28, and 59.

Marcellus' vows . . . Agrippa Marcellus was the son of Augustus' sister Octavia, was married to his daughter Julia in 25 BC, and to many seemed destined to be Augustus' successor. Pliny's comments may here refer to the dynastic tensions of 23 BC, the year Augustus fell seriously ill. Agrippa disapproved of the honours given to the young man and it was rumoured that he went to the east in disgust (Suet. *Aug.* 66. 3, cf. *Tib.* 10), or at least used the posting as a pretext (Velleius 2. 93. 2), although he was in fact sent officially, perhaps with proconsular power. Syme (1939: 342n.) suspected that Tiberius' retirement to Rhodes 'coloured earlier history'. At all events, it was to Agrippa and not to Marcellus that Augustus gave his signet ring during his illness; nor did he adopt Marcellus officially. The 'vows' of Marcellus may be prayers offered for Augustus' recovery, suspected of insincerity while his chances of succession seemed high. Despite the ambiguities of 23 BC, when he died unexpectedly towards the end of that same year, Marcellus was accorded exceptional honours by Augustus (Dio 53. 30. 5–6) and commemorated by Virgil in book 6 of the *Aeneid* (872ff.) as the lost—and loyal (his *pietas*, 6. 878)—heir.

many conspiracies The list in Suet. *Aug.* 19 includes several attempts involving nine named ringleaders, among them nobles like the grandson of the triumvir Lepidus, the consul of 23 Varro Murena (cf. also Velleius 2. 93. 1; Dio 54. 3. 4), and even a slave, Telephus. Others included C. Cornelius Cinna, grandson of Pompey (Dio 55. 14. 1; Seneca, *De Clem.* 1. 9). Individuals, too, proved treacherous: Salvidienus Rufus (executed, 39 BC: Velleius 2. 76. 4; Dio 48. 33; Suet. *Aug.* 66. 2; Appian, *BC* 5. 66. 278 ff.) and C. Cornelius Gallus (committed suicide, 27 BC: Suet. *Aug.* 66. 3; Dio 53. 23).

accusations . . . bereavement The children were his two eldest grandsons by Julia and Agrippa, Gaius and Lucius Caesar, adopted by him on their father's death in 12 BC. Marked out by honours as potential successors, their premature deaths in AD 2 (Lucius) and AD 4 (Gaius) provoked rumours of foul play on the part of Augustus' wife Livia, eager to secure the succession for her own children, Tiberius and Drusus (Suet. *Aug.* 65. 1; Velleius 2. 96. 1; Tac. *Ann.* 1. 3. 2–5. 3). See below, **150. intrigues . . . life**. Such rumours added to the trauma of Augustus' bereavement, although, according to Suetonius (*Aug.* 65. 2–4), he found his family's misconduct (below, **daughter's adultery . . . father, adultery . . . granddaughter's** and **150. disowning . . . Postumus . . . banishment**) more difficult to bear than their deaths.

daughter's adultery . . . father Julia, born in 39 BC, the daughter of Augustus and his second wife Scribonia, had been a pawn in Augustus' dynastic plans, married in turn to Marcellus, Agrippa, and finally Tiberius (Suet. *Aug.* 63. 1–3). Her alleged adultery (Suet. 65. 2–7; Dio 55. 10. 14; Seneca, *Ben.* 6. 32. 1; Pliny, *HN* 21. 9) resulted in her banishment in 2 BC to the island of Pandateria (*OCD*[3], Julia 4, 777). As for her 'plot', one of her lovers was reputed to be Iullus Antonius, Mark Antony's son, who was suspected of plotting against the Principate and whose punishment, death, went beyond the norm for transgression of the adultery laws (Dio 55. 10. 15; Velleius 2. 100; Seneca, *Brev. Vit.* 4. 6: see Syme (1939), 426–7). Seneca, *Brev. Vit.* 4. 6 describes her liaisons with nobiles 'as if bound by an oath' to harrass Augustus' old age and the attachment to Iullus in particular as a reincarnation of his father's earlier unholy alliance against Augustus with Cleopatra.

insolent retirement . . . Nero In 6 BC, Tiberius Claudius Nero, Augustus' elder stepson, the future emperor Tiberius (*OCD*³, Tiberius, 1523–4) retired to Rhodes where he stayed until 2 BC, pleading a need to rest from his duties, despite Augustus' desire to send him to the east (Suet. *Tib.* 10). The real reason was most likely connected with the positions of Gaius and Lucius Caesar, a refusal to cooperate with Augustus' plans to remove a potential focus of rival loyalties to the east while he consolidated the young princes' positions by promoting them to early honours (Syme (1939), 416–17). Ancient opinions varied, partisan sources interpreting this as a generous rather than sullen withrawal on Tiberius' part (Velleius 2. 99, cf. Suet. *Tib.* 10. 1), a wish to avoid conflict (Dio 55. 9. 7). Others, however, said he was deliberately removed for hostility towards the princes (Tac. *Ann.* 1. 4. 4). Dislike of Julia and disappointment at his own non-preferment were also rumoured (Dio 55. 9. 7, cf. Suet. *Tib.* 10. 1).

adultery . . . granddaughter's Julia, daughter of Julia and Agrippa, was relegated for adultery, then recalled and finally banished permanently in AD 8 for adultery with D. Junius Silanus (Tac. *Ann.* 3. 24; 4. 71, schol. on Juvenal 6. 158, cf. Suet. *Aug.* 65. 1). Shortly before, her husband, L. Aemilius Paulus, had been executed for conspiracy (Suet. *Aug.* 19. 1) and she may have been implicated (Suet. *Claud.* 26).

series of other misfortunes This list divides into two parts; the first series of problems being centred around the Illyricum revolt of AD 6 and the second dealing with the years following Varus' disaster of AD 9. (Although the Agrippa Postumus problem had its beginnings in AD 6, Pliny emphasizes its repercussions on the last years of Augustus' life: see below, **150. Fabius**.)

shortage . . . army The problem of establishing a professional standing army with more detailed provisions than ever before for its pay and conditions of service proved difficult for Augustus to finance. In AD 5, legionaries' regular length of service was increased from sixteen to twenty years because of the expense of discharge payments, hitherto paid from his own funds. In AD 6, he established the *aerarium militare* (Dio 55. 24; Augustus, *RG* 17) with a lump capital sum and an income from taxes on auction sales and inheritances. Even so, mutineers in Pannonia in AD 14 claimed periods of thirty or forty years' campaigning (Tac. *Ann.* 1. 17): see P. A. Brunt, *Italian Manpower* (Oxford, 1971), 332–44; *OCD*³, aerarium, 25, stipendium 1444.

the revolt in Illyricum This started in AD 6 in the wake of troop shortages, 'the most serious of all foreign wars since the Punic wars' (Suet. *Tib.* 16. 1) and was eventually subdued in AD 9 by Tiberius, cf. Dio 55. 29–32; Velleius 2. 109–14.

enlisting of slaves, shortage of manpower In the crisis of the Illyricum revolt (above), freedmen and slaves freed for the purpose were enlisted (Velleius 2. 111; Dio 55. 31. 1; Suet. *Aug.* 25. 2; Macrobius 1. 11. 32; and for similar problems after Varus' disaster, Dio 55. 31. 1). See Brunt (1971), 414, Syme (1939), 458.

plague at Rome, famine in Italy The most serious outbreak of plague was in 22 BC. It indirectly caused a corn shortage through a dearth of agricultural labourers (Dio 54. 1. 1–4: see Garnsey (1988), 21, 227, 219–20). But better documented were the further food shortages in AD 5–9, caused partially by diversion of supplies to the military operations in Illyricum and Germany, though no plague is attested in this case (Dio 55. 26. 1–2; Suet. *Aug.* 42. 3): see Garnsey (1988), 220–2, 228–9. *RG* 18 suggests food shortages occurred in 18 BC and other years.

kill himself . . . death Not attested elsewhere. Illness could depress Augustus, cf. Suet. *Aug.* 28. 1, where, however, the hint is of retirement rather than suicide. He was, of course, famously distraught at the loss of Varus' legions (below). But P. seems to link this attempt with the previous series of disasters, as its climactic result. Syme (1939: 457–8) suggested that, in addition to its significance for foreign policy, the Illyricum revolt was, with its legionary discontent and problems with recruitment, a serious blow to Augustus' patriotic policy.

150. disaster of Varus . . . dignity The destruction in Germany of P. Quinctilius Varus and his three legions by the Cherusci and Arminius prostrated Augustus for several months (Suet. *Aug.* 23; Dio 56. 23). Velleius (2. 119. 1) compared it to the Parthian disaster of 53 BC.

disowning . . . Postumus . . . banishment M. Vipsanius Agrippa Postumus, third son of Agrippa and Julia, was born after his father's death in 12 BC. After the deaths of Gaius and Lucius Caesar, Augustus adopted him as Agrippa Julius Caesar with Tiberius in AD 4. His disowning in AD 6, followed in AD 7 by exile to Planasia, seems to have been caused by a character defect; he was described as wild and intractable (Suet. *Aug.* 65; Dio 55. 32. 2). Stories of Augustus' 'regret' at his loss of the final chance of a Julian successor included rumours of secret visits and reconciliations towards the end of his life (Tac. *Ann.* 1. 5. 2; see below, **Fabius**); but on Tiberius' succession, he was immediately killed, possibly on Augustus' orders (Tac. *Ann.* 1. 6).

Fabius . . . secrets   In Tacitus' account of Augustus' secret visit to the exiled Agrippa Postumus, he was accompanied by a close friend, Fabius Maximus Paulus (cos. 11 BC) , who told the secret to his wife, whence it reached Livia. Tacitus hints that Fabius' death, soon afterwards, was the result of the *princeps'* displeasure at his indiscretion (*Ann.* 1. 5). See Syme (1982), 70; *OCD*[3], 582.

intrigues . . . life   Augustus' wife Livia's ambitions for her son Tiberius led to rumours that she was behind not only the death of Gaius and Lucius Caesar but also the banishment of Agrippa Postumus (Tac. *Ann.* 1. 3) and possibly the death of Augustus himself, shortly after the alleged meeting with Agrippa (*Ann.* 1. 5). Suetonius (*Tib.* 21) rejects the idea that Tiberius' adoption was due solely to Livia's pressure, quoting complimentary letters from Augustus to Tiberius.

god . . . died   P. exploits the paradox of a god succumbing to mortality. Some (e.g. K. Scott, 'The Elder and Younger Pliny on Emperor Worship', *TAPA* 63 (1932), 156–65; Till (1977), 136) see a touch of Flavian bias in the apparent cynicism as to whether Augustus attained divinity through merit or machination: contrast his approbation of Vespasian's own aspirations, *HN* 2. 18. But Pliny may just be elaborating the rhetorical antithesis.

enemy's son   Tiberius' father, Tiberius Claudius Nero (*OCD*[3], 341–2) fought at Perusia with L. Antonius and later with Sextus Pompey before joining Antony, returning to Rome after the pact of Misenum in 39 BC.

151–2.   Having shown that human judgements of human happiness, even when unanimous, as in the case of Augustus, can be very misleading, Pliny finishes this discussion by referring to divine judgements on the matter.

151. Pedius This is essentially the first example of human happiness given by Solon in reply to Croesus of Lydia (*c*.560–546 BC), according to the tale of their anachronistic meeting in Herodotus 1. 30 (who calls the man Tellus). Solon's general sentiment, 'call no man happy until he is dead' , accords with the thrust of P.'s discussion.

Gyges King of Lydia (*c*.680–645 BC). See *OCD*³, 659. According to Herodotus, he had courted the oracle with valuable presents.

Aglaus . . . life An oracle reported at length in Valerius Maximus 7. 1. 2, cf. Pausanias 8. 24. 7, where the link with Croesus is perhaps confusion with the Tellus story (above, **Pedius**).

152. oracle . . . agreement of Jupiter See below, **statue . . . lightning** and **the god . . . offered**.

Euthymus . . . Locri See Pausanias 6. 6. 4. He won the boxing at the 74th, 76th, and 77th Olympic games (484, 476, 472 BC), losing to Theagenes of Thasos in the 75th. Part of the base of his statue at Olympia with an inscription (*Olympia* v. 144) was found in 1878, and it is possible to restore his name on the Oxyrhynchus Victor List (*POxy* 222, i. 12, 25).

The story of his cult is attested only by this passage, which derives from Callimachus (Call. fr. 99 Pfeiffer), but other stories link him with heroic status. Pausanias says that Euthymus' father was not a mortal but the river Caecinus, which would give his son semi-divine status. (But see below, this note.) Heroic status is also suggested and would have been earned, if not already present through birth, by his routing, on his journey home from the games of 472 BC, of the menacing hero of Temesa. According to the legend, which can be pieced together from a number of sources, the hero was said to have been Polites, a sailor of Odysseus, who raped a local girl. Killed and left unburied, he became a revenant and terrorized the populace until the Delphic oracle ordained a cult for him and a yearly tribute of the most beautiful local girl or, in some versions, money (Callimachus frs. 98–9 Pfeiffer; Pausanias 6. 6. 4–11; Strabo 6. 1. 5, C255; Aelian, *VH* 8. 18; *Suda*, s.v. Euthymos; Eustathius on Homer, *Od.* 1. 185). The story may represent the displacing of one local hero cult with another: see Fontenrose (1959), 101–4, cf. 119–20, and 'The Hero as Athlete', *CSCA* 1 (1968), 81 for the assimilation by Euthymos of his predecessor's role. Other examples of this practice include, significantly, the transferral of a cult from an established hero or deity to a living historical person, as, for example, in the case of the Samian Heraia which was renamed Lysandreia for Lysander (Plutarch, *Lys.* 18. 2–4, quoting Duris, *FGH* 76 F 71). The change possibly coincided with a political power-shift: suggestions have ranged from the original Greek conquests in Magna Graecia to 5th-cent. Locrian expansionism (e.g. G. Giannelli, *Culti e miti della Magna Grecia* (Florence, 1924), 261–71; E. Pais, 'The Legend of Euthymus of Locri', in *Ancient Italy* (Chicago and London, 1908), 39–51; F. Bohringer, 'Cultes d'athlètes en Grèce classique: Propos politiques, discours mythiques', *REA* 81 (1979), 5–18). Strabo (6. 1. 5, C255) made Euthymus' arrival coincide with the capture of Temesa by the Locrians, sometime before the mid-5th cent. BC. B. Currie ('Euthymos of Locri: A Case Study in Heroisation in the Classical Period', *JHS* 122 (2002), 24–44), however, has argued for a more proactive role in his heroization on the part of Euthymus himself. From the extant archaeological evidence for Euthymus' cult and the role played by river gods in a prenuptial ritual reception of a bride's virginity, he also identifies the displaced hero with a river deity. The story of Euthymus' divine parentage may therefore be a result rather than a cause of his heroization. Others have emphasized the defeated hero's link with the dead and the chthonic deities (see Rohde (1925), 116, 250 n. 25; M. Visintin, *La vergine e l'eroe: Temesa e la leggenda di Euthymos di Locri* (Bari, 1992)). There are similarities with other stories involving single combat with a chthonic being, including the fight of Heracles with Thanatos (Death) and Coroebus with Poine (Vengeance) (Rohde (1925), 154 n. 119). Fontenrose (1959), 101–5 notes the similarities of the Euthymus legend with other hero combat myths, especially with the Delphian tale of Eurybatos and the monster Sybaris. There are also features in common with a number of other legends concerning hero-athletes (id. (1968), 79–104). Folklorists have identified a large number of traditional motifs: e.g. waiting up for the ghost/monster, cf. the Icelandic *Grettir's Saga* and Anglo-Saxon *Beowulf*; driving the ghost/monster into water (*Beowulf*); rescuing girl from ghost/monster (e.g. legend of Perseus): see W. M. S. Russell, 'Greek and Roman Ghosts', in H. R. Ellis-

Davidson and W. M. S. Russell (eds.), *The Folklore of Ghosts* (Bury St Edmunds, 1981), 195.

Callimachus　A 3rd-cent. BC Alexandrian poet and scholar, from Cyrene. See *OCD*³, 276–7; and above, Introd. 3. 3. The information (fr. 99 Pfeiffer) comes from book IV of his *Aetia*, although the story would also have been appropriate to his works on marvels or athletic contests.

statue . . . lightning　Roman religious custom ordained special funerary rights involving burial rather than cremation for those killed by lightning (*HN* 2. 145). According to Plutarch, their bodies were believed to be incorruptible and to be left untouched by scavengers (*Mor.* 665c; cf. Artemidorus, *Oneirocriticon* 2. 9). In other cultures, too, death by lightning is seen as divinely ordained and marked by special funerary customs and, sometimes, the assignation of the deceased to the restless dead (Hertz (1960), 153 n. 337); and see below, **179. instances . . . after burial**. For the Greeks, being struck by Zeus' lightning bolt could indicate the transition of the victim to a higher state of being, a divine immortality as e.g in the myths of Erectheus, Kapaneus, and Asclepius: see Rohde (1925), app. I, 581–2. Artemidorus, *Oneirocr.* 2. 9 singles out athletes from among those for whom dreaming of a thunderbolt promises the fame they seek, since those struck are revered as gods. Kapaneus' tomb, as well as his body, was called *hieros*, sacred (Euripides, *Suppl.* 935, 981), the same epithet applied to the tomb of the heroized Oedipus (Sophocles, *OC* 1545, 1763: see Garland (2001), 99–100). In Euthymus' case, his statues were substituted for his person, indicating his translation to the status of hero, but apparently leaving him alive (for ambiguity about his death, see below, **nothing surprising**). Another case where divine approval of apotheosis was apparently signalled by lightning striking in an indirect way was that of Lysander. He received cult as a god during his lifetime (see above, **Euthymus . . . Locri** and below **nothing surprising**) and, after his death, his tomb was struck, confirming his exalted status according to Plutarch (*Lys.* 31). At Rome, the striking of statues by lightning was normally regarded as a prodigy requiring expiation, but it is worth noting that, in one case at least, the correct expiation involved the elevation of the statue and its relocation in a more commanding position (Gellius 4. 5. 1–7: the statue was that of the legendary hero, Horatius Cocles).

The indication of Euthymus' elevation through the medium of his statues was particularly appropriate to an Olympic victor: distinguished winners at these and other games were frequently the recipients of hero cults (Fontenrose (1968), 79–104, above, **Euthymus . . . Locri**) and in several cases stories are reported of their statues possessing supernatural powers. That of Theagenes of Thasos killed an opponent of his who insulted it, brought barrenness upon the Thasians when they tried to get rid of it, but after propitiaton and reinstatement, proved, like that of the boxer Polydamas, to be a source of miraculous cures (Pausanias 6. 11. 2–9, 6. 5; Dio Chrysostom 31. 340; Lucian, *D. Conc.* 12; cf. Faraone (1992), chs. 3–5). There may be some connection between the 'living' Euthymus' statues and the role of colossi which could act as doubles of the dead, but especially the unusual dead, e.g. those unburied or missing (see J.-P. Vernant, *Myth and Thought among the Greeks* (London, 1983), 305–20).

the god . . . offered   Delphi played an important role in the promotion of hero cults and Delphic Apollo acted as patron of heroes: see Rohde (1925), 130–3 and 189 n. 82. According to Pausanias and others (refs. above, **Euthymus . . . Locri**), the cult to the original 'hero of Temesa' had also been instituted on the orders of Delphi.

nothing surprising   Worship of a living man would be less surprising to a Roman of Pliny's era, well-used to ruler-worship. The first recorded living individual to receive worship as a god was the Spartan Lysander in 404/3 BC (see above, **Euthymos . . . Locri**), but an earlier cult of Hagnon as hero at Amphipolis in 437–422 is implied by Thucydides (5. 110). Pliny's insistence that Euthymus was worshipped in his lifetime would mean that his cult was established even before Hagnon's, before the middle of the 5th cent. BC (cf. Strabo 6. 1. 5, C225). For the acceptability of Pliny's claim, see now Currie (2002), 33–4.

As time went on, however, one result of Euthymus' heroic accretions may have been to create ambiguity about his living/dead status: Aelian said he disappeared into his father's stream (cf. the disappearance/apotheosis of Romulus), while Pausanias had heard reports that he had eluded death and was still alive in his day: Fontenrose (1959: 120) suggested that this rumour disguises a version of the tale in which the hero fights death for his own life. In addition, the life/death status of his adversary as an embodied ghost, or revenant, is itself ambiguous. While the ordinary dead tended to be regarded as insubstantial, *heroes* and *daimones* were often capable of making their presence felt in more physical ways, cf. Herodotus' stories of heroic military and even sexual activities (6. 117, 6. 69), both of which also characterize Euthymus' adversary. So, too, were the malignant child-killing demons (see above, **42. full moon . . . babies**), who, according to one source, retained some of their corporeality (John Damascenus in Migne, *PG* 94: 1064, discussed in Johnston (1999), 176). For a contrasting view, see Plutarch, *Mor.* 417d–e, where *daimones* are said to demand human sacrifice in order to satisfy sexual desire which they cannot express physically.

153–64. *Longevity*

Ancient interest in longevity took a number of forms. For the basic data, the Roman writers had census records (below, **159, 162–4**) at their disposal, as well as the mythological, anecdotal, and biographical traditions.

Besides their obvious paradoxographical appeal (cf. Phlegon's *Macroboioi*), these data could be used in a rhetorical context (Pseudo-Lucian's *Macroboioi*) or approached from a more scholarly angle, with reference to natural philosophy, astronomy/astrology and chronology (below, **153. places . . . birth, 155. All such . . . 1,000 years, 160–1**). This is the approach taken by Pliny, much of whose material turns up later in Censorinus' *De Die Natali* and derives in particular from Varro (see e.g Rapisarda (1991) on Censorinus, *DN* 19 and 21, pp. 235, 251). The paradoxographical aspect is once again important as an adjunct to his portrayal of human life rather than a literary end in itself.

In **153–5**, he gives examples from mythological fantasies and other apocryphal stories, rationalizing their excesses as being due to variations in the calculation of a 'year'. These are followed by more reliable historical data (**156–9**), culminating in an example from Claudius' reign which the emperor took care to have verified by various means including census records. Astrological/astronomical opinions are then considered (**160–1**) and, finally, the detailed documentary evidence provided by the most recent census (**162–4**).

Pliny's general assumption that the figures' inaccuracy increases in proportion to historical distance is sound. But problems remain even when the mythological and pseudo-historical individuals are left behind. There was a tendency to associate wisdom with great age, which may partially explain the high proportion of philosophers and intellectuals reaching their nineties and beyond, although the consistency of the tradition concerning the sophist Gorgias suggests that some, at least, were genuine cases. In connection with the census figures, Pliny fails to take into account the fact that many very old people would have had no precise notion of their real ages and this, rather than deliberate misrepresentation, probably accounts for the rather high proportion of centenarians and above in the records Pliny uses. See T.R. Parkin, *Demography and Roman Society* (London, 1992), 106–11.

153. place . . . birth 'Place' and 'time' could refer to environmental and historical factors; climate was thought to affect longevity (Aristotle, *On Length and Shortness of Life*, 465ᵃ), though views on e.g. the effects of hot or cold climates could be contradictory (Herodotus 3. 22–3; [Plutarch] *Plac. Philos.* 5. 30, *Mor.* 511b; [Galen] *De Hist. Philos.* 133, 19. 344–5 K). 'Personal destiny' may refer to other factors such as status, health, and physical circumstances, as opposed to the common lot of man (above, **1**). Alternatively, all three could be taken together to indicate the individual fortune predicted by a horoscope, the casting of which had to take into account place and time of birth (below, **160. those . . . stars**). However, the remarks in **162. lack of unanimity**, where P. criticizes the inconsistencies of astrologers, favour the more general interpretation.

Hesiod . . . fantastic One of the earliest Greek poets, he flourished around 700 BC. See *OCD*³, 700. For the fragment from his lost poems which included a genealogical work, see *Frag. Hes.* ed. Solmsen, Merkelbach, West, p. 158, no. 34, cf. Ausonius, *Ecl.* 5. 1–9. That Hesiod may have been referring to generations, that is, the time taken for 'a man to be born and reproduce himself' (Parkin (1992), 187 n. 85), roughly between 27 and 40 years, rather than lifespans (Schilling 216) does not make the calculations any more useful.

154. Anacreon . . . 200 years Fr. 361 *Poet. Mel. Graec.*, ed. Page. He was a lyric poet from Teos, born *c.*575 BC. *OCD*³, 79–80.

Arganthonius, king of the Tartessians Tartessus was an ancient settlement in southern Spain, probably biblical Tarshish. Arganthonius' age is given as 120 years by Herodotus 1. 163, for 80 of which he was king, a figure which fits P.'s statement below, **156** about an Arganthonius of Gades (a settlement which became the port for Tartessus). The two are probably identical. See also Cicero, *Sen.* 19. 69 (120 years), Strabo 3. 2. 14, C151, Valerius Maximus 8. 13, ext. 4 (130 years), Phlegon, *Macrob.* 98 (150 years), Lucian, *Macrob.* 10. 1, p. 118 N (150 years).

Cinyras Legendary king of Cyprus first mentioned in Homer, *Il.* 11. 20 ff. and associated with the cult of Aphrodite at Paphos (Tac. *Hist.* 2. 3).

Aegimius Legendary king and son or father of Dorus, founder of the Dorians. *OCD*[3], 17; Bethe, *RE* 1. 1, Aigimios (1), 963.

Theompompus ... Cnossus *FGH* 2. B, 115, fr. 68c. He was a 4th-cent. historian from Chios. See *OCD*[3], 1505.

Epimenides A late 7th-cent. BC holy man of Crete, he was the subject of a number of miraculous tales besides that of his great age, including a sleep of over 50 years. See below, **175. Epimenides of Cnossus**; also Diogenes Laertius 1. 109–11; *Ath. Pol.* 1; Plato *Laws* 642d; Varro, *LL* 7. 3; Val. Max. 8. 13, ext. 5; Plutarch, *Mor.* 157d, 784a; *OCD*[3], 546; Kern, *RE* 6. 1, Epimenides (2), 173–8.

Hellanicus *FGH* 1.A, 4, fr. 195a. He was a 5th-cent. BC historian and ethnographer from Mytilene: *OCD*[3], Hellanicus (1), 677.

Epii in Aetolia Homer's *Epeioi* (*Il.* 2. 619 ff.), a people originally from Elis whose legendary king Aetolus was forced to flee to Aetolia (Pausanias 5. 1. 4). The Aetolians eventually defeated the Epeians of Elis (Ephorus in Strabo 8. 3. 33, C 357, cf. Pausanias 1. 4. 2; Oberhummer, *RE* 5. 2, Epeioi, 2716–17).

Damastes ... 350 years Cf. *FGH* Damastes fr. 5. He was a historian and geographer from Sigeum, a pupil of Hellanicus (above). See *OCD*[3], 427; Schwartz, *RE* 5. 1, Damastes (3), 2050–1. Valerius Maximus 8. 13, ext. 6 calls the strong man Litorius. Urlichs (1857), 82 identified him with the athlete Titormus of Aelian, *VH* 12. 22, though cf. Schilling 217 on Hardouin's proposal that the name was just a transliteration of the Greek *pyctoraion*, 'fighter without equal'.

155. Ephorus . . . 300 years *FGH* 70, fr. 112b, cf. Censorinus, *DN* 17. 3. Ephorus of Cyme (*c.*405–330 BC) was a historian and pupil of Isocrates: *OCD*³, 529–30.

Alexander Cornelius . . . Illyria *FGH* 273, fr. 17. Valerius Maximus 8. 13, ext. 7 assigns the story to a work on Illyria. Cornelius Alexander Polyhistor (born *c.*105 BC) was a wide-ranging scholar of Miletus who originally came to Rome as a prisoner of war and was given citizenship by Sulla in 82 BC. *OCD*³, Alexander (11), 60; Schwartz, *RE* 9 A 2, Alexander (88), 1449–52.

Periplus, Xenophon . . . 800 Also cited by Valerius Maximus, 8. 13, ext. 7. Xenophon of Lampsacus was a geographer of the late 2nd cent./early 1st cent. BC. See Gisinger, *RE* 9 A 2, Xenophon (10), 2051–5.

Lutmii The name is uncertain: Valerius Maximus has *Latmiorum* and emendations have included *Latriniorum* (Urlichs) or *Latriorum* (Detlefsen) after *HN* 4. 97, which mentions an isle of Latris in the northern seas.

All such . . . 1,000 years A passage reproduced by Augustine, *CD* 15. 12. 80–1; cf. Solinus 1. 34, Macrobius, *Sat.* 1. 12. 2. On the complexities of relative chronology and the concept of the year, see E. J. Bickerman, *The Chronology of the Ancient World* (London, 1980), 52–65. Some differences were caused by calculating a civil year according to terms of office, which would of course vary from place to place. Others, as Pliny suggests here, were a result of the subdivision of the natural year into two or more seasons. While the Egyptians had a clearly-defined official year of 365 days (Macrobius, *Sat.* 1. 12. 2), it existed alongside the popular lunar calendar, in which the important units were the alternating months of 29 and 30 days; cf. Plut. *Numa* 18; Censorinus, *DN* 19. 4, Solinus 1. 34. For the Arcadians, see also Censorinus, *DN* 19. 4; Plut., *Numa* 18; Servius, *G.* 2. 342; Cicero fr. 4. 3, p. 235 Muller; Statius, *Theb.* 4. 275. While Latin *annus* normally referred to the solar year or its civil equivalent, it could sometimes be used of a lunar revolution (G. Rocca-Serra (1980), on Cens. *DN* 19. 6, quoting Macrobius, *Sat.* 1. 14. 4; cf. *OLD*, 'annus' (b), 136, the orbit of an individual planet, as in Lucretius, *RN* 5. 644.

156. Arganthonius of Gades See above, **154. Arganthonius of Tartessus**.

Masinissa For this king of Numidia, celebrated for his longevity (Livy, *Per.* 50; Polyb. 37. 10. 1; Cic. *Sen.* 10. 34; Val. Max. 8. 13, ext. 1); see above, **61. king Masinissa . . . Methimannus**.

Gorgias . . . 108 The great age of Gorgias of Leontini (*c.*485–*c.*380 BC), the influential sophist (*OCD*³, 642–3), is well attested. Estimates varied, but within a narrow margin, suggesting that this celebrated case of longevity, at least, is historically accurate: 105 (Pausanias 6. 17. 5) to 109 (Apollodorus in Diogenes Laertius 8. 58, Quintilian 3. 1. 9, *Suda* s.v. Gorgias), with Cic. *Sen.* 5. 13 and Valerius Maximus 8. 13, ext. 2 giving him 107 years.

Q. Fabius Maximus Q. Fabius Maximus Verrucosus, surnamed Cunctator for his policy of attrition against Hannibal, was consul in 233, 228, 215, 214, and 209 BC and dictator in 221 and 217 BC. His wisdom as augur over 63 (or 62, Livy 30. 26. 7, Valerius Maximus 8. 13. 3) years was praised by Cicero (*Sen.* 4. 10–12). *OCD*³, 583; Münzer, *RE* 6. 2, Fabius (116), 1814–30.

M. Perperna Born *c.*108 BC, consul in 92 BC and censor in 86, he had registered the first of the newly enfranchised Italians. He died in 49 BC (Dio 41. 14. 5, Valerius Maximus 8. 13. 4). *OCD*³, Perperna (2), 1142; Münzer, *RE* 19. 1, Perperna (5), 896–7.

L. Volusius Saturninus see above, **62**.

opinions . . . consul As presiding magistrate chairing a senatorial debate.

157. five-year period . . . lustral sacrifice . . . next pair of censors Censors were normally appointed every five years for eighteen months. During this time their duties included revising the senatorial list (Livy 9. 30. 2, Dio 37. 46. 4; J. Suolahti, *The Roman Censors: A Study in Social Structure* (Helsinki, 1963), 53–6), generally one of their first tasks (Livy 23. 22. 10). They also took the census (see below, **159. Titus Fullonius . . . Claudius, 162. most recent census . . . father and son**), on the successful conclusion of which the lustral sacrifice, a ritual of purification, was performed (Livy 1. 44. 2; R. M. Ogilvie, 'Lustrum Condere', *JRS* 51 (1961), 31–9). P.'s date of 175 BC is wrong: Q. Fulvius Flaccus and A. Postumius Albinus took office as censors in 174 and would not have completed the census and thus performed a *lustrum* until 173 (see Brunt (1971), app. 4, 537 on Livy, *Per.* 41. 10 and *Inscr. It.* xiii.1, 49). Although P.'s wording for the terminus of his five-year period is vague, he clearly means the following *lustrum*, i.e. the end of the next pair of censors' (C. Claudius Pulcher and T. Sempronius Gracchus) term of office rather than the beginning (168 not 169 BC: Livy, *Per.* 43. 14, 45. 15). Schilling's explanation, that Pliny's date of 175 is the date of the censors' election, is based on a misunderstanding: censors took office immediately on election, not in the following year (Soulahti (1963), 78).

M. Valerius Corvinus   Called M. Valerius Corvus in the *Fasti Triumphales* for 301 BC, he held consulships in 348, 346, 343, and 335 BC. The last two, in 300 and 299, may have belonged to M. Valerius Maximus Corvinus, consul 312 and 289 BC, hence the name variant here and in Cic. *Sen.* 17. 60 and Valerius Maximus 8. 13. 1. The span of 46 years rather than the actual figure of 49 may have stuck in the sources because of the correspondence Cicero makes: a prime covering 46 years is equal to the whole lifespan down to the age when men were officially designated *seniores*. See *OCD*[3], 1579; Volkmann, *RE* 7 A 2, Valerius (137), 2413–18.

curule . . . 21   Of the magistracies entitled to use the curule chair, Corvinus possibly held, in addition to his six consulships and two dictatorships (342 BC and reputedly 302/1 BC), six curule aedileships, six praetorships, and a censorship.

the priest Metellus   See above, **139. Lucius Metellus . . . distribution.** He held his priestly office for 22 years (Cic. *Sen.* 17. 61, Valerius Maximus 8. 13. 2) and lived to be 100 (Valerius Maximus loc. cit.)

158. Examples   For Livia, Terentia, and Clodia see Valerius Maximus 8. 13. 6.

Livia . . . Rutilius   L. was probably sister of M. Livius Drusus, consul 112 and enemy of C. Gracchus, and wife of P. Rutilius Rufus, consul 105, enemy of Marius and writer of a history of the period much used by later historians (*OCD*[3], 1340; Münzer, *RE* 1 A 1, Rutilius (34), 1269–80).

Statilia   Perhaps sister or daughter of T. Statilius Taurus, Augustus' great general, consul in 37 and 26 BC (*OCD*[3], 1438; Nagl, *RE* 3 A 2, Statilius (34), 2199–2203). Seneca, *Ep.* 77. 20 says her age was given as 99 on her tombstone (cf. Martial 3. 93. 20, *CIL* vi. 9590 = *ILS* 9434).

Terentia Cicero's first wife, married between 80 and 77 BC and divorced for alleged financial irregularities in 46 (Plutarch, *Cic.* 41). See *OCD*[3], 1484–5; Weinstock, *RE* 5 A 1, Terentius (95), 710.

Clodia Wife of A. Ofilius, jurist and friend of Caesar (Münzer, *RE* 17. 2, Ofilius (4), 2040–1) and possibly niece or granddaughter of Ap. Claudius Pulcher, consul 79 BC.

Lucceia *Mima* was the name for a performance or the performer in a drama form which became very popular in the late Republic and early Empire, producing a number of celebrity actors and actresses including Antony's mistress, Cytheris. See W. Beare, *The Roman Stage: A Short History of Latin Drama in the Time of the Late Republic*[3] (London, rev. edn., 1968), 152, 239–40; Balsdon (1969), 276–8; R. C. Beacham, *The Roman Theatre and its Audience* (London, 1991), 129–39; Münzer, *RE* 13. 2, Lucceia (20), 1562.

Galeria Copiola She was an *embolaria* (from *embolium*, interlude), an actress in entr'actes, cf. Cicero, *Sest.* 116, *CIL* 1949.

age of 104 ... Sulpicius C. Poppaeus Sabinus and Q. Sulpicius Camerinus were consuls in AD 9. She was therefore born in 95 BC.

votive games . . . Augustus Extraordinary games might be held for the emperor's wellbeing (which also ensured the wellbeing of Rome itself), though it became customary to wish him good health at all shows (P. Veyne, *Bread and Circuses: Historical Sociology and Political Pluralism* (London, 1990), 400 n.). From 30 BC, games had been celebrated every five years by one of the priestly colleges or by the consuls in fulfilment of vows to the gods for the emperor's safety (Augustus, *RG* 9; Dio 51. 19. 2, 7: see Weinstock (1971), 217–19). In 13, 8, and 7 BC, special votive games were also held in thanks for his safe return to Rome. The games of AD 9 which P. mentions here may have been held in response to the strains imposed by the Illyricum revolt (above, **149. kill himself . . . death**). They are clearly not the games of Suet. *Aug.* 23. 2, vowed by Augustus himself in the wake of the Varus disaster.

debut ... earlier M. Pomponius was aedile in 82 BC (Gundel, *RE* 21. 2, Pomponius (25), 2333). The consuls of that year were C.

Marius, son and namesake of Sulla's opponent (*OCD*³, Marius (2), 926; Münzer, *RE* 14. 2, Marius (15), 1811–15), and Cn. Papirius Carbo, supporter of and previously consul with Sulla (*OCD*³, 1108; Münzer, *RE* 18. 3, Papirius (33), 1015–21).

as a marvel . . . Pompey . . . theatre   See above, 34.

159. Pedianus Asconius   Q. Asconius Pedianus (*c*.AD 3–88) wrote commentaries on Cicero's speeches for his sons and a number of works now lost, including the one from which this comment is taken, perhaps that mentioned in *Suda* s.v. Apikios, entitled *De Longaevorum Laude* or *Symposium*: *OCD*³, 188–9; Wissowa, *RE* 2. 2, Asconius (3), 1524–5. Sammulla is not attested elsewhere.

Stephanion . . . Roman dancing   Stephanion (Diehl–Stein, *RE* 3A 2, Stephanio (1), 2350), whose punishment and banishment by Augustus is mentioned by Suetonius (*Aug.* 45; he had evidently been recalled by Claudius' reign), is called by him *togatarius*, which is sometimes interpreted as an actor in *fabulae togatae*, comedies with Roman characters, costume, and setting. However, the popularity of this drama form had waned by the 1st cent. AD, although there were revivals (Beare (1968), 237, Balsdon (1969), 280–8, Kroll, *RE* 6A, togata, 1660–2). P. says of Stephanion *primus togatus saltare instituit*, literally 'the first person to introduce dancing in a toga', which does not accord with a dated form of entertainment, unless a revival is meant. Urlichs (1857: 84) suggested that Stephanion had introduced a form of Roman costume to the popular mime, which might be the explanation. A third possibility is that Stephanion was innovative as a pantomime artiste. Although s*altare* could mean 'to portray through dance' (cf. *OLD* s.v. *saltare* 2) and dance played a part in other drama forms (cf. Lucian, *Salt.* 26), it was in pantomime, a sophisticated dramatic ballet normally involving a solo dancer of considerable skill, that this meaning was fully realized. Introduced in 22 BC, it was highly popular in the early Empire. If this were the case, however, we would have to ask why Suetonius distinguished Stephanion as *togatarius* from Hylas as *pantomimus* in the same passage. In what sense was Stephanion *togatus*? Martial later said, understandably, that 'dancing in a toga' was a ridiculous notion (11, proem. 8), though this need not mean that dancing in some form of Roman costume had not been done. But perhaps it was the theme of the pantomime that was Roman. Although pantomime was called 'Italian dance' in the Greek east, the themes were overwhelmingly Greek (Lucian, *Salt.* 35–59; Balsdon (1969), 270–9; cf. Wust, *RE* 18, 833–69). However, a few Roman themes are attested, inspired by the *Aeneid* (Suet. *Nero* 54; Macrobius, *Sat.* 5. 17. 5; Ovid, *Trist.* 2. 519) or even historical matter (Pliny, *Pan.* 54. 1) and it may have been in these that Stephanion distinguished himself.

both . . . secular games . . . Claudius Games and sacrifices were celebrated to mark the end of a *saeculum* (from *senex*, old man, according to Varro, *LL* 6. 11, based on a putative maximum lifespan (cf. below, **160. those . . . stars**): it denoted a period of approximately 100 years in the Republic and 110 from Augustus) and the start of a new one. They had been celebrated in 249 and 146 BC (Censorinus, *DN* 17) but none were held in the 40s. Augustus celebrated them in 17 BC, with an emphasis on the new era, but Claudius was able to celebrate games in AD 47, by adhering to a different cycle probably marking the 800th anniversary of the foundation of Rome. For sources, see G. B. Pighi, *De Ludis Saecularibus*[2] (Amsterdam, 1965); and M. Beard, J. North, S. Price, *Religions of Rome, i: A History* (Cambridge, 1998), 205–6, outlining the problems of chronology.

Mount Tmolus . . . Tempsis A mountain in Lydia to the south of Sardis, famous for its wine (*HN* 14. 74, cf. 5. 110) and precious metals (Herodotus 5. 101, Strabo 13. 4. 5 C625, who calls it 'blessed'). For the similar reputation of Mt. Athos, see above, **27. the inhabitants of Mount Athos**.

Mucianus See above, Introd. 3. 1. 1, 3. 3, 4. 5. 1.

Titus Fullonius . . . Claudius This individual is not attested elsewhere. Claudius' holding of a censorship in AD 47 (Tac. *Ann.* 11. 3, 12. 4, *Hist.* 3. 66, Suet. *Claud.* 16, *Vit.* 2, *HN* 10. 5, *CIL* iii. 6024, v. 8002, vi. 918) with the father of the future emperor Vitellius was, like his secular games, partly a result of his antiquarian interests. Although the occasional use of conscription (Tac. *Ann.* 4. 42) might necessitate an assessment of potential manpower, the practical need for censuses in Italy was diminishing under the empire with the advent of a professional army and the increasing irrelevance of voting and taxation (Suolahti (1963), 509).

emperor . . . tally. Claudius' interest in *mirabilia* (above, **35.**
Claudius Caesar) is in evidence here. For the statistical records
of the population available, see C. Nicolet, *Space, Geography and
Politics in the Early Roman Empire* (Ann Arbor, 1991), 121–39.
Registration of legitimate births only started under Augustus (for
the purpose of proving exemption under laws on emancipation and
inheritance, see Nicolet 132, F. Schulz, 'Roman Registers of Births
and Birth certificates', *JRS* 32 (1942), 78–91) but census records
were kept in the temple of the Nymphs and *atrium libertatis* and
should have been available for Fullonius from the Augustan censuses of AD 14 and of 8 and 28 BC. Going back further would have
been more difficult; censuses had been taken irregularly in the late
Republic. An entry in the last attested Republican census of 69 BC
(Livy, *Per.* 98; Cicero, *Verr.* 1. 34; Phlegon fr. 8) would have had to
assign him an age of 35! Other evidence may have included
remembered past events and possibly documentary or otherwise
corroborated evidence of e.g. an army career.

160. those . . . stars. Astronomical knowledge was used by
astrologers to make predictions about human affairs. Genethli-
alogy, involving the casting of horoscopes, was supposed to foretell
various aspects of an individual's life, including its length. For the
basic principles, see T. Barton, *Ancient Astrology* (London, 1994),
86–162, *OCD*³, astrology, 195. A belief in the links between the
celestial and the terrestrial was widespread and cut across social
divisions, due to the idea of universal sympathy which posited links
between all parts of the universe. This belief was enshrined in
ancient philosophies, including Stoicism, which further supported
astrology by its upholding of divination. Like its adherents, astrology's proponents covered a broad spectrum from the crude to the
highly sophisticated. Its popularity in the early Empire had political repercussions, as the casting of imperial horoscopes in particular was seen as a threat to stability and forbidden, astrologers being
periodically banished (see F. H. Cramer, *Astrology in Roman Law and
Politics* (Philadelphia, 1954), 233–83). P.'s attitude is not surprisingly
ambiguous. He condemns the simplistic notions of the common
people who believe that each man's destiny is attached to a particular star (*HN* 2. 28) but believes that the heavenly bodies exert a
more complex influence on earth (*HN* 2. 30ff., cf. 2. 95, 105ff., 18.
280–9). Here, his researches uncover disagreements between prac-

titioners on the question of maximum life expectancy. See below,
162. lack of unanimity. For other estimates of maximum
longevity in antiquity, see Parkin (1992), 109–10, who notes that the
varying estimates reported by Pliny in the following paragraphs,
ranging from 112 to 124 years, do not exceed too drastically the
present-day estimate of *c*.115 years. The difference between then
and now is that today more individuals are likely to reach such
extremes: see also below, **167. niggardly . . . endowed.** Many
other sources were far more cautious. Pliny's own nephew (*Ep.* 1.
12. 11) said that few people exceeded the age of 67, cf. the view taken
of the 'climacteric' ages (below, **54 years**), in which multiples of
'critical' numbers, such as 7 and 9, played an important role (below
seventh and fifteenth). Upper limits of 100 or 120 years were
popular estimates, the former reflected in the traditional figure of
100 or 110 years for the *saeculum* (above, **both . . . Claudius**).

Epigenes . . . Berosus Cf. Censorinus, *DN* 17. 4. Epigenes of
Byzantium was an astrologer of the late 3rd or early 2nd cent. BC
(Rehm, *RE* 6, Epigenes (17), 65–6). For Berosus (or Berossus) of
Babylon, see above, **123. Berosus**. Both are cited for the antiquity
of Babylonian astrology (below, **193**). For their means of computing longevity, see O. Neugebauer, *A History of Ancient Mathematical
Astronomy* (Berlin and New York, 1975), ii. 721 and below, **theory
of quadrants**. Their figures in fact match today's estimate of
maximum lifespan: see above, **those . . . stars** and below, **167.
niggardly . . . endowed**.

Petosiris and Nechepsos Petosiris, an Egyptian priest who
died before *c*.350 BC, and Nechepsos, a king of the 26th dynasty
(663–522 BC) were the names given to the alleged authors of an
astrological treatise of the 1st cent. BC to give it a spurious antiquity.
See W. and H. G. Gundel, *Astrologoumena* (Wiesbaden, 1966), 27 ff.;
Barton (1994), 26–9.

theory of 'quadrants' . . . anaphore Astrological treatises
offered a number of complicated methods of computing life
expectancy (deliberately obscure, given the political sensitivity of
the issue? Barton (1994), 125–6). Such calculations were often connected with degrees of the zodiac. P. refers to what is essentially the
predecessor of the complex theory of prorogations in Ptolemy, *Tetr.*
3. 10 (see A. Bouché-Leclercq, *L'Astrologie Grecque* (Paris, 1899; repr.

Brussels, 1963), 411–13). The twelve signs of the 360° zodiac are divided into four 90° quadrants of three signs each, with 30 degrees allotted to each sign. Each sign's rising time (the number of degrees of the equator which cross the horizon of a particular place consecutively with that sign), which varies according to historical period and geographical latitude (*HN* 6. 211–18, Censorinus, *DN* 17. 4, Neugebauer (1975), ii. 729), is converted into years, one year per degree. An individual's lifespan was in theory the sum of the rising time of his birth sign and of the next two signs, i.e. his 'ascending measure', or anaphore, of 90 degrees. See Rapisarda (1991) on Censorinus, *DN* 17. 4, Bouché-Leclercq (1899), 411, Neugebauer (1975), ii. 721. A 4th-cent. list of the risings for the signs of the zodiac in various latitudes is recorded by Firmicius Maternus (*Math*. 2. 11). This suggests a maximum of 121 years for Italy, as opposed to Pliny's 124 years, but the figures are in any case problematic (J. Rhys Bram, *Ancient Astrology, Theory and Practice: Matheseos Libri VIII by Firmicius Maternus* (New Jersey, 1975), 308); or else the discrepancy is to be attributed to the time gap between the two authors (Schilling 223). In practice, however, much also depended on the positions of the heavenly bodies at the actual time of birth (see below, **paths . . . sun**). Maternus (*Math*. 8. 2) emphasizes the importance of the ninetieth degree: observation of its sign, the ruler of that sign, and any benefic or malefic planets in aspect to it could offer a summary of the chart as a whole.

paths . . . sun   The zodiacal signs, heavenly bodies, and celestial relationships could produce favourable or unfavourable predictions. In particular, the five known planets, together with the sun and moon, had positive or negative (benefic or malefic) influences depending on their characteristics. Jupiter, Venus, and the moon were basically positive, Saturn and Mars negative, Mercury and the sun mixed. The nature and amount of their influence varied according to the sign they were in, their proximity to the *cardines* (the lines which quadrated the zodiac), and their angular relationships (aspects) with each other or with points within the horoscope (Barton (1994), 96–102). If a malefic is in conjunction with or in aspect to the point determining longevity (*aphetes* or starting point), as it progresses through its 90-degree arc, life can be cut short. Firmicius Maternus occasionally describes the sun's rays as effectively cancelling the effect of otherwise benefic planets by 'hiding' them (e.g. *Math.* 7. 6. 8, 7. 25. 12). In addition, not all degrees are effective and some are more favourable than others (Manilius, *Astr.* 4. 411; Firmicius, *Math.* 4. 22).

school of Asclepius Asclepius became associated with astrology in the 3rd cent. BC. Hermetic writings portrayed Hermes as revealing astrological as well as medical wisdom to Asclepius (A.-J. Festugière, *La Révélation d'Hermès Trismégiste, i: L'Astrologie et les sciences occultés* (Paris, 1950), 136–9), who appears as an astrological source in later writings, e.g. Firmicius Maternus 3. 1. 1, 4. proem 5 (although he is sometimes identified with another early Egyptian astrological sage, Imhotep: see Bram (1975), 310). Pliny says medicine, astrology, and magic were overlapping fields (*HN* 30. 2). Iatromathematics, the application of astrological theory to medical treatment, based on complex correlations between the planets or zodiac and the well-being of various parts of the human body, often appears in general astrological treatises and in specialist works. See Ptolemy *Tetr.* 1. 3. 15–16; E. and L. Edelstein, *Asclepius: A Collection and Interpretation of Testimonies* (Baltimore, 1945; repr. 1998), i. 224, ii. 59; Bouché-Leclercq (1899), ch. 15; Cramer (1954), 188–90, J. Tester, *A History of Western Astrology* (Woodbridge, 1987; repr. 1999), 23–4; also above, **38. Only children . . . no moon** and **39. in Italy**; and below, **lunar days** and **seventh and fifteenth.**

161. lunar days Technically, the 'lunar day' (lundian or lunar diurnal) is, at 24.8 hours, slightly longer than the solar day. But it is likely that, by 'lunar days' Pliny means one of two things. (*a*) He may be distinguishing a period of a day and a night from the hours of daylight alone. The latter definition, he tells us in *HN* 2. 188, was used in popular parlance. For the two different definitions of 'day', see also Gellius, *NA* 3. 2. 4–7; Censorinus, *DN* 23, 3; Geminus 6. 1. For a full list of other references, see J. Beaujeu, *Pline l'Ancien Histoire Naturelle Livre II* (Paris, 1950), 239. The common source was Varro. Different peoples started the day at different times and, in some systems, the length of daylight- and nighttime-hours varied. However, astrologers, when casting horoscopes, divided the day and night into 24 equal (equinoctial) hours, and it is to this astrological 'day' that Pliny refers. (*b*) Alternatively, and more probably, he may be taking for granted the use of the twenty-four-hour day in such a context, and may simply be using the phrase to describe the 'days of the lunar month', as do a number of authors, e.g. Varro, *RR* 1.

37. 1: see Lunais (1979), 26–30; 325–8, when describing the divisions of the lunar month for agricultural purposes. Certain days of the lunar month were regarded as 'critical' in iatromathematics: see below, **seventh and fifteenth**, and above, **38. Only children . . . no moon**, and **39. in Italy**. Here, the same criteria are being applied to the hours of each day.

The emphasis on 'lunar' reflects the fact that the moon was of considerable importance in those areas of applied astronomy which reflected upon destiny and longevity (Préaux (1973), 295–312). According to Firmicius Maternus (*Math.* 4. 1. 1), the moon, as the heavenly body nearest earth, has particular power over earth and all terrestrial life (cf. above, **38. Only children . . . no moon** and **42. full moon . . . babies**), and is closely associated with the growth, shaping, flourishing and decline of the human body. Its important role in iatromathematics has already been mentioned (above, this note and **school of Asclepius**, cf. **38. Only children . . . no moon** and **39. in Italy**; and see below, **seventh and fifteenth**): its position in relation to planets or the signs of the zodiac on the day an illness started determined the 'day' which would predict the disease's nature and outcome: see Barton (1994), 186–7. For its central role in the horoscope, see *Math.* 4 *passim*; Bouché-Leclercq (1899), 524 and nn. Births on particular 'lunar days', in the sense of 'days in the lunar monthly cycle', continued to be regarded as significant into the 16th and 17th cents. and beyond (see Gélis (1991), 196–7).

seventh and fifteenth Odd numbers, especially seven and its multiples, were often regarded as significant. Aulus Gellius (*NA* 3. 10. 1–15) quotes Varro on the significance of seven in celestial and physiological matters and in the medical theory of critical days (*crisimoi*), cf. Celsus 3. 4. 11. The idea that such days could determine the course of an illness for better or worse dated back to at least Hippocrates. See also above, **38. Only children . . . no moon, and 39. in Italy**. From this, astrology developed a number theory with wider applications than the medical crises: certain hours, days, months, and years, usually multiples of 7 or 9, were designated as especially dangerous (not just critical) to other aspects of life in addition to health and longevity (Aulus Gellius, *NA* 3. 10. 1). In more sophisticated systems, these 'climacterics' were determined by planetary courses in the natal chart (Valens 5. 7) but the basic idea was widely known (Pliny, *Ep.* 2. 20). See Censorinus, *DN* 14. 13–15; Firmicius Maternus, *Math.* 4. 20. 3; Bouché-Leclercq (1899), 526–9. Schilling (223) suggested that fifteen was chosen here in preference to the hebdomadal fourteen because it was odd. In any case, Pliny knew that lunar changes could take an hour or so to have an effect on terrestrial life (*HN* 2. 216), so that the hebdomadal pattern would be approximate.

54 years P. chooses a multiple of 9 years (see above, **seventh . . . fifteenth**) as the climacteric year for such people. Augustus regarded 63 (a multiple of both 9 and 7) as the most critical year (Aulus Gellius, *NA* 15. 7. 4; cf. Firmicius Maternus 4. 20. 3, who called it the 'man-weakening' year), while Censorinus mentions 49 (7×7, *DN* 14. 12).

162. lack of unanimity See above, **160. those . . . stars**. Pliny's comments on the *inconstantia* (instability, inconsistency, fickleness) of astrological theory echo his criticism of conflicting medical theories (*nullam artium inconstantiorem*, 'no science is more fickle', *HN* 29. 2). See Beagon (1992), 201. His comments in **165** below on the *inconstantia* of human fortune itself, illustrated by the diverse fates of people with identical birth times, implicitly contradicts the astrological predictions of similar lifespans for such individuals. P. was fundamentally opposed to the passive fatalism which the cult of Fortuna and astrology seemed to him to encourage to the detriment of Roman virtues such as independence and activity (*HN* 2. 22–3; Beagon (1992), 28–9, 96–7). Trust in Fortuna was trust in the inherently uncertain; here he implies that the certainties of astrology, too, are delusory.

most recent census . . . father and son Vespasian and his son Titus assumed the censorship most probably in April AD 73 (see Jones (1984), 83 n. 36 for the evidence) and conducted the last recorded census at Rome (Suet. *Vesp.* 8–11; Pliny, *HN* 3. 9; Aurelius Victor, *Caes.* 9. 9; Dessau iii, pp. 269f. and see above, **159. Titus Fullonius . . . Claudius**), completing the *lustrum* in 74 according to Censorinus (*DN* 18. 14). The use of the traditional office, with its Augustan overtones, partly in order to strengthen a war-weakened senate by adlection, no doubt appealed to the new dynasty. Titus had been his father's partner in government from AD 71, holding tribunician power and sharing the consulship with him seven times.

Pliny refers to them as joint rulers on several occasions (*HN* 2. 58, 3. 66): but see above, Introd. 1. Pliny's examples of longevity, because they include women as well as men, have figured in the debate concerning who was included in the Roman census. In the Republic, it is generally agreed that the census was confined to all male citizens, who declared, among other things, the number of their legitimate children, and the name of their wife (Cicero, *Leg.* 3. 7). A separate register of widows and orphans (who were liable at one time to a special tax, the *aes equestre*) was also taken (Brunt (1971), 22). But the vast discepancy between the last surviving Republican figures (*c.*900,000, in 70–69 BC) and those of the Augustan censuses, in the first of which, conducted in 28 BC, over four million were registered (Augustus, *RG* 8. 2–4), has suggested to some (K. J. Beloch, *Bevolkerung der griechisch-römischen Welt* (Leipzig, 1886), endorsed by Brunt, ch. IX, 113–20), that Augustus, whose marriage laws show a special concern with population figures, registered women and children in addition, perhaps reverting to an ancient custom (Pliny, *HN* 33. 16, see Brunt 113, Nicolet (1991), 131). Others, however, account for the increase by citing other factors, such as the inclusion of the Transpadani, enfranchised by Caesar, increases in slave manumission, and the effects of colonization, and claim that a figure for 28 BC which included women and children would in fact be far higher (see E. Lo Cascio, 'The Size of the Roman Population: Beloch and the Meaning of the Augustan Census Figures', *JRS* 84 (1994), 23–40). In fact, there seems to be no certainty either way on this issue. Moreover, the present passage does not, in fact, add anything to the debate. Although Pliny's evidence has been taken to imply that Vespasian's census included women, these particular ones, being old and therefore probably widows, could have been included even in the Republic on the special register, as Brunt points out (114–15).

last four years   P. was therefore writing this *c.* AD 77. Mommsen (1887, ii. 352 n. 3) advocated this meaning of *intra quadriennium* as opposed to the interpretation that the censorship had been held 'during four years', which was inconsistent with the bulk of the evidence; see previous note.

all the archives   From at least the time of Caesar and probably before (*Tab. Her.* ll. 142–55; Brunt (1971), 38–40; Nicolet (1991), 127–32), information for the census had been gathered locally in

Italian towns as well as at Rome. The Tablet of Heraclea stipulated that the information should be deposited in the local archives and a copy sent to Rome. An increasing tendency to arrange census material geographically rather than by tribe may have been the result (Nicolet (1991), 202 n.). That Augustus' division of Italy into 11 regions (*HN* 3. 46: see below, **area . . . Po**), probably in 7 BC (cf. Suet. *Aug.* 30), provided the statistical and archival framework for the census by the time of Vespasian is clearly suggested by the present passage. Pliny is able to select records from just one area, the eighth region (below, **area . . . Po**), which was close to his own home district of Cisalpine Gaul, the tenth region, but whether he examined them at first hand is unclear; the same source was evidently used by Phlegon (*Macrob.* 1–97), who gives a similar but fuller list of examples from the same region. Phlegon also has material from Spain, Macedonia, and Bithynia-Pontus, suggesting the common ultimate source was, or derived from, the central records in Rome rather than the local ones of the eighth region.

area . . . Po This area is identified in **164** as the eighth region of Italy. Pliny is the only author to mention the Augustan regional divisions. *HN* 3's description of Italy is arranged by region, though its relationship to an original work by Augustus himself (cf. *HN* 3. 46) has been much debated (R. Thomsen, *Italic Regions from Augustus to the Lombard Invasions* (Copenhagen, 1947; repr. 1984), 2; Nicolet (1991), ch. 8). *HN* 3. 115–22 deals with the eighth region, describing its boundaries as Ariminium, the Po, and the Apennines. The description here, 'midway between the Po and the Apennines', is apt for the towns mentioned in **163–4**. With the exception of Veleia (*c.*35 k. south of Placentia) and Brixillum (some 20 k. northeast of Parma), they all lie on the great Via Aemilia which bisected the region from Ariminium in the south-east, going north-west through Faventia, Bononia, and Parma to Placentia on the Po, and gave it the name Aemilia (Martial 3. 4. 1). For Placentia, see above, **105. Cremona . . . Placentia**. Parma and Bononia were originally 2nd-cent. BC colonies, Roman and Latin foundations respectively. See Thomsen (1984), 112–20.

163. L. Terentius son of Marcus Named also in Phlegon, *Macrob.* 96.

of the Galerian tribe Even if the practical significance of the 35

Roman tribes had declined, it was a proof of citizenship even for provincial citizens and still stated in census returns (Nicolet (1991), 198, 203).

164. eighth region   See above, **area . . . Po**. This summary of the statistics by age rather than town is similar to Phlegon's lists of centenarians: those aged 100 (*Macrob.* 1–68), between 100 and 110 (*Macrob.* 69–94), between 110 and 120 (*Macrob.* 91–5), etc. There are discrepancies between Pliny's and Phlegon's figures but this may be due partly to breaks in the latter's text.

165–6. *Uncertainties of human destiny*

The examples in **165** follow on from the previous discussion on horoscopes (the same birth date does not entail the same fate). Those in **166** hark back to the discussion of longevity (the extraordinary reversals of health or success described there make estimations of longevity even more uncertain), but they also look forward to the ensuing discussion of dying, death, and the afterlife (**167–90**), since they are equally examples of the unpredictability of sickness and death.

165. Hector and Polydamus   See *Iliad* 18. 249–52, where Homer contrasts the careful counsellor Polydamus with the rash warrior Hector.

M. Caelius Rufus and L. Licinius Calvus . . . paths
Caelius, a protégé of Cicero had a political career (tribune 52, aedile 50, and praetor 48 BC, before his death in the war between Caesar and Pompey). His rhetorical style was clever, witty, and devastating, especially in prosecutions. He defended himself at a trial in 56 BC at which Cicero delivered the *Pro Caelio*. See *OCD*[3], 271; Münzer, *RE* 3. 1, Caelius (35), 1266f. Calvus was a drier, more severe, but respected speaker in 'Attic' style (see esp. Cicero, *Brut.* 279ff.). He was a friend of the poet Catullus and was himself remembered as a poet rather than politician, dying, prematurely, before 47 BC. See *OCD*[3], 857; Münzer, *RE* 13. 1, Licinius (113), 429. For C. Marius and Cn. Carbo, consuls in 82 BC, see above, **158**.
debut . . . earlier. The year is too late for Caelius' birth which was probably *c*.88–87 BC.

identical birth-times . . . basis. See above, **162. lack of unanimity.**

166. P. Cornelius Rufus . . . Jason . . . Q. Fabius Maximus. See above, **165–6. uncertainties . . . destiny.** P. Cornelius Rufus (or Rufinus, Münzer, *RE* 4. 1, Cornelius (302), 1422–4), consul in 290 BC but removed from the senate, despite a distinguished career, for extravagance (Valerius Maximus 2. 9. 4; Aulus Gellius, *NA* 4. 8. 7; Pliny, *HN* 18. 39, 33. 142), was inexplicably blinded in the apparent security of sleep; while Jason, tyrant of Pherae in Thessaly (d. 370 BC: *OCD*³, Jason (2), 793–4) and Q. Fabius Maximus (cos. 121 BC, *OCD*³, 583; Münzer, *RE* 6. 2, Fabius (110), 1794–9) found cures amid the perils of battle. For the story of Jason's abscess, burst by his attacker, see also Cicero, *ND* 3. 70, Valerius Maximus 1. 8., ext. 6. Q. Fabius Maximus defeated the Allobroges and Arverni in 121 BC (Livy, *Per.* 61, cf. Valerius Maximus 3. 5. 2). According to Pliny, he had a malarial fever, but, in his case, too, the cure may have coincided with and therefore was attributed to, a wound he had received: see Appian, *Celt.* 2.

quartan fever A fever which recurred every third day (Celsus 2. 1. 20; Cicero, *Fam.* 16. 11. 1, *ND* 3. 24; *HN* 22. 150). See below, **169. The rest of mankind . . . quartan fevers.**

167–90. introd. *Dying, death, the afterlife*

Uncertainty is a recurrent theme in P.'s description of the final phase of human existence, a pessimistic corollory of the *varietas* which characterized the multifaceted achievements of the human animal in the prime of life. From the uncertainties of life-expectancy (**153**), of attempts to predict it (**162**), and of the course of individual destinies (**165–6**), P. passes to those of death itself. In spirit he returns to his opening idea of nature the mother/stepmother (**1**) whose gift of life had a number of disadvantages from the outset (**4–5, 44**) which are now reiterated (**167. precarious and fragile**). Even at its close, she has some unpleasant surprises in store: general debility (**168**) and countless illnesses (**169–70** and **172**). Then, even the blessing of death itself can be illusory, the spirit apparently or actually (though P. is sceptical of claims to the latter) absenting itself temporarily from the body (**173–9**). Where death is genuine, it can be sudden and unexpected (**180–6**). A brief discussion of burial practices follows (**187**). Finally, although the oblivion of death is a blessing, irrational *vanitas* leads humanity to propose a life in death for itself alone of all animals (**188–90**), cf. above, **5. unbounded appetite for life** and **burial . . . dead**.

167. precarious and fragile See above, **5. precarious** and **43–4**.

niggardly and short . . . endowed Even the examples of longevity (above) are insignificant in the overall context of time. Although maximum lifespan was similar to today's limit of *c*.115 years (above, **160. those . . . stars** and **Epigenes . . . Berosus**), fewer individuals attained anything close to it: to reach 80 was exceptional, and the average age at death was far lower than today's (see Parkin (1992), 4–66; *OCD*³, age, 38).

time spent asleep . . . unable to sleep *HN* pref. 19, *vita vigilia est*, 'life is being awake' sums up P.'s thoughts here. He himself managed on comparatively little sleep: see Introd. 1. Moralists linked sleep with luxury and idleness (Sallust, *Cat*. 2. 8; Cicero, *Sest*. 66, 138, Tac. *Hist*. 2. 90), but P. does also acknowledge, as here, the problem of insomnia, suggesting remedies in *HN* 23. 42, 48 (traditional use of wine) and 30. 140.

years of our infancy See above, **4**.

old age . . . torment. By forgetting to stipulate eternal youth when asking Zeus to make her consort Tithonus immortal, Eos condemned the latter to an everlasting old age which was effectively a living death. The happiness of living into old age was very much dependent on quality of life, in which physical health played a vital role. The possible 'torments' were many and are listed below (**168. The truth . . . life**). Old age is vilified because of its debility, according to Plutarch, who adds to these physical disadvantages the spiritual degeneration consequent upon prolonged immersion in earthly matters (*Mor*. 611e). Ancient medicine offered little help and most ancient testimonies echo Plutarch's (e.g. Cicero, *Phil*. 8. 31, *Fin*. 5. 33; Virgil, *Aen*. 6. 275; Tac. *Ann*. 13. 30; Horace, *Ep*. 13. 5; Valerius Flaccus 6. 283), though contrast Cicero, *De Senectute* and Pliny, *Ep*. 3. 1. Physical degeneration could set in before 30 (see Garland (1995), 11–27 and *OCD*³, 38); and, despite the complaints voiced by the upper-class minority as represented in the written sources, the process of degeneration was likely to be quickest among the least privileged, as is implied in Seneca's comments (*Ep.* 12. 3) on the decrepit old slave who turns out to have been his child-favourite from many years earlier. Yet, even among the affluent elderly, quality of life could vary enormously; witness the younger Pliny's comments on the hedonistic Ummidia Quadratilla (*Ep.*7. 24) and the bedridden cripple Domitius Tullus (*Ep.* 8. 18). See M. Harlow and R. Lawrence, *Growing Up and Growing Old in Ancient Rome* (London, 2001), 117–31; K. Cokayne, *Experiencing Old Age in Ancient Rome* (London, 2003); A. van Hooff, *From Autothanasia to Suicide: Self-Killing in Classical Antiquity* (London, 1990), 30–9, 123–5, 149.

accidents, illnesses, fears and worries Cf. *HN* 25. 23, where P. bemoans man's lot, for whom, besides every kind of unexpected accident, 'there are thousands of diseases to be feared', and *HN* 26. 9, where the fear is said to have been increased in the last fifty years by an influx of new illnesses (though not all ancient commentators were willing to admit that such novelties were truly new; see M. Grmek, *Diseases in the Ancient Greek World* (Baltimore and London, 1989), 170; R. Sallares, *The Ecology of the Ancient Greek World* (London, 1991), 240). See above, **4. diseases . . . maladies**. Lack of predictability was a facet of disease as well as of accident, since the causes of illness were often unknown and enhanced the 'fear and worry' of those under threat: for man's fear and feebleness generally, see above, **4–5**.

pleas for death . . . prayers See below, **The truth**.

168. The truth . . . life. For this commonplace and its variants, see above, **4. not to be born at all**. The failure of the senses elaborated on here was regarded as an inevitable consequence of growing old, cf. *HN* 11. 277 and above, **old age . . . torment**. Pliny stresses elsewhere that man has the power to escape by his own efforts, through a self-inflicted death: in *HN* 28. 9, a timely death is described as nature's best gift to man, especially as each person has the ability to administer it himself: suicide is an advantage man holds over god (*HN* 2. 27). Cf. Seneca, *Ad Marc.* 20. 1. Bodily suffering could precipitate an aversion to life and this *taedium vitae* was a legally recognized motive for suicide: see van Hooff (1990), 84. In

HN 25. 23, Pliny selects as the most unbearably painful diseases those affecting the bladder, the stomach, and the head. These, he says, account for nearly all instances of such suicides. Old age increased the likelihood of physical suffering. Use of suicide to escape its tribulations was a feature of the Hyperborean Utopia (*HN* 4. 89) and a number of Roman examples feature in the *HN* (20. 199; 25. 24). For others, see D. Gourévitch, 'Suicide among the Sick in Classical Antiquity', *BHM* 43 (1969), 501–18 and *Le Triangle Hippocratique dans le monde Greco-Romain: Le Malade, sa maladie et son médecin*, BEFAR 251 (Paris, 1984), 169–216; van Hooff (1990), 33–9, 42–5, 122–6. Cf. also Y. Grisé, *Le Suicide dans la Rome antique* (Montreal and Paris, 1982), 68–72; M. T. Griffin, 'Philosophy, Cato and Roman Suicide', *G&R* ns 33 (1986), 64–77, 192–202; and below, **190. seductive illusions . . . death**. The stress in P. on physically rather than ideologically motivated suicide may be a facet of his practical view of life (see Beagon (1992), 239 and n.). But in any case, the distinction was not necessarily clear-cut. The Stoics and Epicureans could condone suicide in cases where incurable illness made it impossible to live 'well': e.g. Cic. *Fin.* 1. 49, 62; Diogenes Laertius 7. 130; Seneca, *Ep.* 58. 35; and tradition held that a number of prominent philosophers had availed themselves of this escape for reasons of physical or mental debility: Lucretius, *RN* 3. 1039–41; Lucian, *Long.* 19; cf. van Hooff (1990), 36–7. Pliny's practical reasons for extolling brevity of life contrast with the moral-philosophical exhortations of Seneca in *De Brevitate Vitae* (life is long enough if lived well) to those who complain that it is too short.

The senses grow dull . . . life.   See above, **old age . . . torment**.

Xenophiles   A 4th-cent. Pythagorean and musician from Chalcis in Thrace. For his vigorous old age, see Valerius Maximus 8. 13, ext. 2.

169. The rest of mankind . . . quartan fevers   Pliny gives an accurate description of some of the symptoms of malaria in humans. Other species of malaria are known to infect many animals, including birds. Ancient writers tended, wrongly, to regard all diseases as common to both men and animals, having observed that some animal diseases were transmittable to humans (e.g. anthrax, cf. Virgil, *G.* 3. 563–6), and that many human diseases were similar to those seen in animals (see Sallares (1991), 287–90; also below, **170. illnesses . . . classes**). It is therefore interesting that, although he knew that 'fevers' could occur in animals (e.g. *HN* 36. 117), the periodicity which characterizes malarial fevers is regarded by Pliny as unique to humans. Three forms of the human variety were endemic in the ancient Mediterranean world. Infection from *plasmodium vivax* involved a cyclical fever recurring every other day (= tertian fever). In the case of *plasmodium malariae*, fever occurred every third day (= quartan fever). The more severe and often fatal *plasmodium falciparum* (malignant tertian) was also present in the Graeco-Roman period. Although they may exhibit tertian periodicity, both *plasmodium vivax* and *plasmodium falciparum* frequently exhibit a quotidian periodicity, especially in primary infections, due to infection with different generations of parasites: see P. F. Burke, 'Malaria in the Graeco-Roman World: A Historical and Epidemiological Study', *ANRW* 2. 37. 3 (1996), 2254–5; R. Sallares, *Malaria and Rome* (Oxford, 2002), 11. In his description of the various types of fever (3. 3–18), Celsus noted that the prescribed intermissions were frequently not observable (3. 3. 5). Infections can last for a considerable time; in particular, *plasmodium vivax* can last from three to six years, while there is evidence to suggest that *plasmodium malariae* can persist for life (Sallares (2002), 12). Taking both these factors into account, together with the possibility of reinfection and the seasonal nature of the disease (below, **170. quartan . . . months**), it is possible to account for the long-term persistent fever of Maecenas and the even longer-term periodic fevers of Antipater, below, **172**. For the regularity of the *hours* at which malarial fever can recur, see Bede, *HE* 3. 12 on the miraculous cure of a child sufferer. Presumably, it was when his 'hour' did not arrive that the embattled Q. Fabius Cunctator realized that his fever had left him: see above, **166. P. Cornelius Rufus . . . Q. Fabius Maximus.**

Pliny's highlighting of 'fever' as a prime cause of human disease and suffering is in line with its deleterious effect on life expectancy and mortality levels in those communities in malarial areas. Although W. H. S. Jones's theory that malaria was a primary causative factor in Graeco-Roman history is now generally discounted, the evolution and impact of malaria in the Mediterranean world is a matter of considerable debate: see e.g. Burke (1996), 2252–81, with bibliography; Brunt (1971), 611–24 (app. 3.18

'Malaria in Ancient Italy'); J. Zulueta, 'Malaria and Mediterranean History', *Parasitologia*, 15 (1973), 1–15; Grmek (1989), 275–83, and 'La Malaria dans la Méditerranée orientale préhistorique et antique', *Parasitologia*, 36 (1994), 1–6. In the most recent and detailed study, R. Sallares (2002, esp. chs. 3–5) has argued for the antiquity of malaria, including the dangerous *plasmodium falciparum* (ibid. 12–22; 23–42; 140–5), in the Mediterranean and emphasized the considerable demographic effects of the disease in ancient Italy. Its depredations would have made an even greater impression, given that medicine could offer no effective treatments.

The ancients were apparently unaware of the exact connection between malaria and mosquitoes. Marshes were connected with ill-health, including enlarged spleens, and mosquitoes, but any sickness was attributed not to mosquito bites but to imbibing the water or inhaling the air in such areas (e.g. Hipp. *Airs* 7. 24, i. 28–9 L; Columella, *RR* 1. 5. 3, 1. 5. 6), although Varro did portray the air as infested with invisible disease-bearing 'creatures' (*animalia, RR* 1. 12. 2) which could be breathed in, while Columella described earth-bound but similarly pestiferous creatures as brought forth from the swamp by the summer heat (*RR* 1. 5. 6). See F. Borca, 'Towns and Marshes in the Ancient World', in V. M. Hope and E. Marshall (eds.), *Death and Disease in the Ancient City* (London, 2000), 75–6. Instead, malaria and fevers generally were thought to be caused by imbalances in the four bodily humours (Grmek (1989), 291–2; W. D. Smith, 'Implicit Fever Theory in Epidemics 5 and 7', in W. F. Bynum and V. Nutton (eds.), *Theories of Fever from Antiquity to the Enlightenment, Medical History* suppl. 1 (London, 1981), 10). In the case of quartans, Galen mentions black bile (14. 745, 15. 369, 16. 15, 17. B. 659 K). This was also associated with the enlarged spleen (Cato, *RR* 157. 7), which was a recognized side-effect of such infections (Galen 11. 18 K). Yellow bile was implicated in tertians, phlegm in quotidian fevers (7. 350, 16. 14, 17. A. 113, 17. B. 737 K). Explanations as to how such imbalances occurred varied; see e.g. I. M. Lonie, 'Medical Theory in Heraclides of Pontus', *Mnemosyne*, 18 (1965), 126–32, on those of Erasistratus and Asclepiades of Bithynia (Sextus Empiricus, *Adv. Math.* 8. 220). According to some theories, excess humour overloaded the blood vessels and overheated the body, causing fever (Celsus, *De Med.* pref. 13–16; Ps.-Arist. *Prob.* 1. 8. 860ª5: see P. Pellegrin, 'L'Imaginaire de la fièvre dans la médecine antique', *History and Philosophy of the Life Sciences*, 10 (1988), 109–20).

Conventional medical treatments, such as the blood-letting advocated by Celsus (3. 6. 13, 3. 7. 1, 3. 8. 2), may have done more harm than good. Although he lists some herbal remedies for tertian, quartan, and other fevers (*HN* 26. 114–17), Pliny himself states that ordinary medicines are more or less useless for a quartan fever (*HN* 36. 98), a statement which apparently holds good for malaria generally, since he reluctantly ('so much does suffering love to hope against hope', *HN* 30. 104) offers magical recipes for all types of fever. Many of these remedies take the form of amulets (*HN* 28. 114–15; 30. 98–104; 32. 113–16, cf. Q. Serenus Sammonicus, *Lib. Med.* 48–51, 895–946), and incantations and spells might be used (e.g. Ammianus 29. 2. 26). Ingredients which were particularly repellent or fearsome and therefore powerful, such as bedbugs (*HN* 29. 63, cf. Diosc. *MM* 2. 34, Serenus, *Lib. Med.* 921–2, cf. 900) and menstrual blood (*HN* 28. 83–4), also featured and survived in the remedies of later ages: see Sallares (2002), 134; and above, **64. It . . . menstrual flow**, and **65. since it sticks . . . tainted**. If all else failed, and much to Pliny's disgust, recourse might be had to transference: nail parings, in wax, should be surreptitiously placed on a neighbour's door before sunrise. Less controversially, the disease may be transferred to an ant (*HN* 28. 86). It was perhaps in a similar frame of mind that patients with splenomegaly came to be healed by the sacrifice of a white cock and the magical touch of king Pyrrhus' foot (see above, **20. right toe . . . temple**). Then, as later (Burke (1996), 2266–71; M. W. Dickie, 'Bonds and Headless Demons in Graeco-Roman Magic', *GRBS* 40 (1999 = 1999*b*), 99–104), even divine aid was sought to combat the disease. Prayers were offered for Pompey when he was stricken with fever (Juv. *Sat.* 10. 283; Vell. 2. 48; cf. Cicero, *Tusc.* 1. 86, *Att.* 8. 16. 1). Like Cicero, Pliny disapproved of the shrine to Fever on the Palatine (*HN* 2. 16, cf. Cic. *ND* 3. 63, *Leg.* 2. 28; Aelian, *VH* 12. 11; Theod. Prisc. *Phys.* 4. 3), but the divinity was evidently popular, as Valerius Maximus mentions two more shrines at Rome (2. 5. 6), and there may have been more (see Burke (1996), 2268–71). Dedications to Tertiana and Quartana have also been found. The tried and tested remedies said by Maximus to have been displayed at these shrines perhaps afforded some more practical inspiration to petitioners. They, too, however, like the remedies in Pliny and Serenus mentioned earlier, were probably amulets, since they are said to have been 'applied' or 'attached'—*adnexa*—to the bodies of sufferers. Most curious of all were the statues credited with effecting cures, including fever cures, cf. above, **152. statue . . . lightning**. Of these, the most bizarre was the statue of the pot-bellied Corinthian general with protruding veins, in Lucian's *Philopseudes* 18–20. Presumably its swollen abdomen and veins were taken to be representations of the splenomegaly and overloaded blood vessels of the malaria victim (see above, this note: 'prominence of the vessels' is listed in Sextus Empiricus, *Adv. Math.* 8. 219 as a sign of fever).

even at intervals of a whole year. This seems to be the most likely meaning of Pliny's *etiam toto anno*, and accords e.g. with the case of Antipater of Sidon, **172** below.

septenary . . . disease Numerous editors and commentators have tried, with little success, to make sense of P.'s *morbus est aliquis per sapientiam mori*, with or without emendations. Thus, for example, by understanding death 'through wisdom' as a sort of scholarly neglect of more mundane needs; by translating as 'death of the mind', i.e. senility; and even by translating as death 'in a state of lucidity' (but see below, **171. in dementia . . . bedclothes**). Emendations include *per senectutem*, 'through old age' for *per sapientiam*, endorsing Pliny's pessimistic comments in **167** above; and *morbus est aliquantisper* ('for a time') *sapientiam mori*, i.e. bouts of insanity. All these and more are discussed by Ajasson de Grandsagne in the 1827 Lemaire edition. For further references, see Schilling, 226, who highlights Littré's (*Histoire Naturelle de Pline, avec la traduction en français* (1865), 316–17) proposal that *per sapientiam* referred to an illness affecting the seat of the reason, on the basis of the symptoms, described by Hippocrates and Celsus, of those who, when moribund, pick at the bedclothes and who, according to Pliny, suffer *sapientiae aegritudine*. See below, **171. In dementia . . . delirium . . . bedclothes**. However, I have tentatively adopted an emendation of J. Pigeaud ('Un *locus desperatus* chez Pline l'Ancien', *Helmantica*, 44 (1993): *Thesauramata Philologica Iosepho Orozio Oblata*, 467–76), for whom *sapientiae aegritudine* in **171** is a red herring in the context of the present passage. Reading *mori per septenarium* ('death involving a period of seven', 'septenary death') instead of *mori per sapientiam* is still rather cryptic, but has the distinct advantage of re-establishing Pliny's remark as a more logical comment in the overall context of **169–72**, namely, the regular laws regarding incidence, duration, and recurrence frequently observed in cases of human illness. For the importance of periods of seven in the context of life rhythms, including those of human health and longevity, see above, **161. seventh and fifteenth, 38. Only children . . . no moon**, and **39. in Italy**. On this reading, P. moves from illnesses recurring at particular hours, to those recurring at intervals of days or even a whole year, before mentioning one which involves death in a period of seven days/years.

170. quartan . . . months. Ancient authors noted that fevers were particularly common in the late summer and autumn: e.g. Theophrastus, *Caus. Plant.* 1. 13. 5–6; Ps.-Arist. *Prob.* 862^{b}27; Galen 7. 470 K. The prevalence of fevers and some other infectious diseases in summer, and the occurrence of more serious fevers in autumn had been noted in the Hippocratic corpus, *Aph.* 3. 21–2, 4. 495–7 L, cf. 3. 9, 4. 489 L), though the reasoning in some parts of that work may have been a simple analogy between dry, hot weather and a 'hot' fever, with 'wet' diseases like catarrh and pleurisy occurring in the cold, wet winter months (*Aph.* 3. 7. 23, 4. 496 L). The Dog Days in late July were regarded as particularly unhealthy and would be a likely time for the start of *plasmodium falciparum*, which needs higher temperatures, with cases extending well into the autumn: see Sallares (2002), 20–2; 61–3; 130–3. A crop of cases around March might be a result of *plasmodium vivax*, which could flourish at lower temperatures. Spring relapses after primary infection in autumn were common (Sallares (2002), 21). Pliny's statement that a quartan fever will not start in the winter months is likely to be correct but, as Sallares (132) points out, a fever contracted earlier may continue throughout the winter (cf. Ps.-Arist. *Prob.* 862^{b}29), as was the case with his friend Atticus' quartan fever which was documented in some detail in Cicero's letters. Having fallen ill in September, Atticus was not finally rid of his fevers until the following April (*Att.* 6. 9. 1, 7. 1. 1, 7. 2. 2, 7. 5. 1, 5, 7. 7. 2, 7. 8. 2, 8. 6. 4, 9. 2, 9. 5. 1, 9. 4. 3, 9. 8. 2, 10. 9. 3, 10. 15. 5, 10. 16. 5). Both Celsus (2. 8. 42) and Galen (9. 561 K) expected the quartan fever which started in the autumn to last a particularly long time.

Some . . . 60. Susceptibility to certain diseases was often regarded as age-related and/or sex-related in the ancient medical texts (e.g. Hipp. *Aph.* 3. 24–31, 4. 496–502 L; *Progn.* 502, 5. 700 L, *De Morbis* 22, 6. 182–8 L). For the greater resistence to disease generally of the elderly, see Hipp. *Aph.* 2. 39, 4. 481 L. Acquired immunities would have helped. Galen agreed that, in general, the elderly were less prone to disease. Being drier, colder, and more bloodless than younger people (1. 582 K), they were less likely to suffer from fevers in particular. However, he also thought they were less likely to survive long illnesses (16. 352, 17. B. 253, 414, 538 K).

puberty . . . women. The particular susceptibility of infants and children to a range of potentially fatal illnesses may have encouraged the idea that puberty was a milestone in the acquisition of resistance to disease. In addition, the onset of puberty was supposed to alleviate certain childhood conditions, including epilepsy (e.g. Hipp. *Aph.* 5. 7, 4. 534 L). Aristotle (*HA* 581^{b}25 ff.) says that the disharge of semen or menses can rid the adolescent of excess residues and improve their general health and fitness, although those with no excess can suffer by the loss. Pliny says that 'many types of illness are cured by the first sexual intercourse and the first menstruation' (*HN* 28. 44). This would have particularly favoured women, who would normally menstruate on a regular basis from the onset of puberty and also marry earlier than men. Perhaps by association with these medically significant rites of passage, menstrual blood, always a powerful substance in its own right, was even more effective at the menarche, or in the first period after intercourse (*HN* 28. 80, 85). The medical efficacy of the two processes, intercourse and menstruation, combines with the inherent powers of the menses in *HN* 28. 84, where intercourse with a menstruous woman is said to cure quartan fevers in a man (see above, **169. The rest . . . quartan fevers; 64. It . . . menstrual flow; 66. This amazingly . . . occurs at all**). In general, this bleeding had a beneficially purgative effect and its passage, dangerous if blocked (Hipp. *On the Nature of the Child* 15, 7. 494 L), might be aided by intercourse. More specifically, spontaneous as well as medically applied bleeding was advocated as a cure for malarial and other fevers. But, whereas a man might be cured of a fever by a fortuitous nosebleed (Hipp. *Epid.* 1. 3. 8, 2. 642 L), women once again had an advantage over men since their moister bodies shed blood on a regular monthly basis. The Hippocratic corpus has a number of examples of women whom the onset of menstruation relieved of fever. The author of the Hippocratic treatise *Epidemics* noted the recovery from fever of girls who menstruated during their illness (*Epid.* 1. 3. 8, 2. 646–8 L), and the same work includes a number of case studies: see King (1989), 24–5, for a discussion of some of these, including *Epid.* 1. 2. 8, 2. 640–50 L; 1. 2. 9, 2. 658 L; 3. 17. 7, 3. 122 L; and 3. 17. 12, 3. 136 L. This theory may have been strengthened by the observation of pregnant women whose malarial infection caused them to abort, while they themselves survived. Modern studies have shown that the rate of miscarriage in malaria epidemics can be extremely high. In one American study, the maternal mortality rate was 4%, while infant mortality was 60% (R. Torpin, 'Malaria Complicating Pregnancy', *Am. J. Obstet. Gyn.* 41 (1941), 882–5). See Sallares (2002), 66–8, 125–6, with a discussion of the ancient evidence provided by the foetal burials in a child cemetery at Poggio Gramignano in southern Umbria.

The more enclosed lifestyle of Greek women was also thought to make them less susceptible to catching illnesses (*Ep.* 6. 7. 1, 5. 334. 14–18 L), but modern scholarship disagrees. See Dean-Jones (1994), 136–47; H. King, 'Bound to Bleed: Artemis and Greek Women', in A. Cameron and A. Kuhrt (eds.), *Images of Women in Antiquity* (London, 1983), 113–14. However, it may have made a difference in certain circumstances: Sallares (2002: 55) mentions early 19th-cent. observations concerning the greater frequency of malarial infection among men in the town of Sezze (Setia) in Lazio, due to the fact that they, unlike the women, would leave the comparative safety of their hillside home to farm the malarial plain below. To some extent, it may also have been the case that fewer women than men were treated by doctors.

Old men   See above, **170. Some . . . 60.** That women aged more quickly than men was a consequence of their inferior nature according to Aristotle: see further above **37. Girls . . . quickly**. However, the singling out of men may be due to the fact that, as often in preindustrial societies, more men than women did in fact survive into old age (see *OCD*[3], 38; Parkin (1992), 103–5, who urges against exaggerating this trend). Women were at greater risk due to the risks arising from childbirth, and from pregnancies while very young or in excessive numbers (Aristotle, *Pol.* 7. 16. 7, 1335[a]; J.-M. Lassère, *Ubique Populus* (Paris, 1977), 560–2; D. Gourévitch, 'La Mort de la femme en couches et dans les suites de couches', in F. Hinard (ed.), *La Mort, les morts et l'au-delà dans le monde romain* (Caen, 1987), 187–94). But in addition to the dangers of childbirth itself, more women may have succumbed at an earlier age due to their vulnerability to diseases such as 'plague' during pregnancy, when such immunities as have been acquired may weaken or break down.

illnesses . . . classes For the susceptibility of particular groups or classes to infectious diseases, see e.g. Hipp. *Ep.* 1. 1. 1, 2. 602 L. Obviously, any group of people living in close proximity to each other was at risk, especially in the cramped and unhygienic conditions of the urban poor. Such conditions may explain references to armies struck down by disease, especially invading ones, which were also unaccustomed to local conditions: see Grmek (1989), 150–61 and Sallares (2002), 36–7 on the plight of the Athenian army at Syracuse in 413, probably caused by malaria. Sicily also brought disease to the Carthaginians in 397 BC (Diod. 14. 70. 4–71. 4), the Romans in 262 BC (Polyb. 1. 19. 1), and to both Romans and Carthaginians in 212 BC (Livy 25. 26; Sil. Ital. 4. 580–626). The majority of diseases were believed to be common to both humans and animals (see above, **169. The rest . . . quartan fevers**), so epidemics were sometimes portrayed as starting in livestock and spreading primarily to farm-workers, initially at least: e.g. Livy 4. 30. 7–9. Many slaves were also vulnerable, due to overcrowded living-quarters, and were the main victims of another pestilence described by Livy (41. 21. 5–11). Cf. also Dion. Hal. 9. 67. 1–2; 10. 53. 1. However, conditions at all levels of society would have encouraged infection; and a general increase in the incidence of infectious diseases in the Roman empire may have been the result of an increase in population density: see Grmek (1989), 98–9, 169–71; Sallares (1991), 43–4. In *HN* 26. 2–4 Pliny mentions that particular diseases strike the poor or children or adults (for age-specific diseases, see above, **Some . . . 60** and **puberty . . . women**), singling out a new skin disease from the east which particularly affected the upper classes in the reign of Tiberius, being spread by their social custom of kissing, cf. also Martial 12. 98. This is one of the more specific references relating to the notion of contagion in the ancient sources. The risks involved in proximity to the sick in the case of certain diseases was recognized, as Thucydides and his fellow-citizens observed in the case of the Athenian 'plague' (Thuc. 2. 47. 4, 51. 5, 58. 2). See J. Longrigg, 'Death and Epidemic Disease in Athens', in V. M. Hope and E. Marshall (eds.), *Death and Disease in the Ancient City* (London, 2000), 57–8. However, there was uncertainty as to how contiguity was to blame and explanations of the spread of disease were equally likely to be couched in terms of polluted air or individual susceptibility. See V. Nutton, 'Did the Greeks have a word for it? Contagion and Contagion Theory in Classical Antiquity', in L. I. Conrad and D. Wujastyk (eds.), *Contagion: Perspectives for Pre-Modern Societies* (Aldershot, 2000), 137–62.

epidemics . . . southern . . . three months   Pliny uses the word *pestilentia*, pestilence, which, like plague, was a term used of infectious epidemics, e.g. smallpox and typhus, as well as of plague proper, *yersinia pestis*. See *OCD*³, plague, 1188. That epidemics come from the south is suggested by Thucydides 2. 47 in the famous description of the plague of Athens (430 BC), which was said to have started in Ethiopia and spread to Egypt and the Persian empire. Lucian (*How to Write History* 15) was to criticize some later writers for simply copying this detail from Thucydides. Others doubtless worked on theoretical assumptions about disease and climate, as had the author of the Hippocratic *Airs, Waters, Places*. Pliny himself, when describing Egypt (*HN* 26. 4, cf. 26. 8) as the parent of skin diseases, may have in mind the negative aspect of the heat and moisture which gave it a reputation for fertility (above, **21. So great . . . water**; **33. In Egypt . . . septuplets** and **portentous . . . fertility**; and **39. In Egypt . . . eighth month**). Galen, *Mixtures* I.529–30 K describes extreme heat and moisture as the worst possible climatic conditions and a breeding ground for disease, while Theophrastus had specifically associated the Nile with disease (fr. 159). Even the flying snakes which allegedly invaded Egypt periodically from further south in Africa (cf. Pliny, *HN* 10. 75) were said by Cicero to be a health hazard, not only because of their bite, but also because of the miasma produced by their rotting flesh (*ND* 1. 101). The tendency to see pestilence as emanating from the south is also suggested by Celsus' rules for avoiding such diseases, 'especially one brought by the south wind' (1. 10). Sallares (1991: 253–5), however, thinks that the evidence on density-dependent infectious diseases bears out Pliny's general rules for southern origins and westward movement. The areas of greatest population-density in antiquity were the Near East and Egypt. In addition, like the Athenian plague whose westerly movement may have been responsible for the pestilence which struck Rome in the 430s and

420s BC (cf. e.g. Livy 4. 25), the Antonine plague, too, moved westwards from the Near East. True plague in Egypt is attested by Rufus of Ephesus (Oribasius, *Coll. Med.* 43. 41, 44. 14 Raeder), as are a number of other infectious diseases, including smallpox. For summer as the main season for infectious diseases, see above, **170**. **quartan . . . months**. The ideas underlying the treatment of pestilence by Roman writers are considered by J.-M. André, 'La Notion de *pestilentia* à Rome: Du tabou religieux a l'interprétation prescientifique', *Latomus*, 39 (1980), 3–16.

171. signs of approaching death Descriptions in ancient medical sources of many, though not all, of these symptoms of imminent death go back to the Hippocratic corpus. The classic Hippocratic *facies* was first described in Hipp. *Progn.* 2–4 (2. 112–24 L). For other references, see M. Grmek 'Les *indicia mortis* dans la médecine gréco-romaine', in F. Hinard (ed.), *La Mort, les morts et l'au-delà dans le monde romain* (Caen, 1987), 132–5. Cf. also Celsus 2. 6, Galen 1. 364–5 K, 9. 567 K.

in dementia . . . delirium . . . bedclothes Some translators and commentators have wished to make a contrast between *furoris morbo* and *sapientiae aegritudine*, namely, 'in a state of dementia/delirium . . . in a state of lucidity'. However, the symptoms of the patient *sapientiae aegritudine* (literally, 'in sickness of wisdom'; or 'in sickness of mind', cf. *HN* 23. 41, where P. quotes the proverb *sapientiam vino obumbrari*, 'wine befuddles the wits') are close to those ascribed in Celsus 2. 6. 6 to a patient 'in a fever or mad with pain', cf. also Hipp. *Progn.* 4, 2. 116–24 L, Ajasson De Grandsagne, 20. It is therefore more likely that a distinction is being made between illness involving *furor*, Greek *mania*, a chronic state of mental imbalance (translated here as dementia), and an acute feverish illness affecting the mind, phrenitis (translated here as delirium), whose recognized symptoms Pliny goes on to describe. See also Pigeaud (1993), 471–2.

lack of response . . . incontinence See Celsus 2. 6. 5.

eyes . . . Hippocrates The facial changes are those of the Hippocratic *facies*, *Progn.* 2–4, 2. 122–4 L, cf. Celsus 2. 6. 1. For Hippocrates, see above, **123. Hippocrates**.

fluttering pulse *Formicante*, here translated as 'fluttering', is derived from *formica*, an ant. A number of Greek medical writers had used the term *myrmekizon*, the originator perhaps being Herophilus (H. von Staden, *Herophilus: The Art of Medicine in Early Alexandria* (Cambridge, 1989), 286 n.161) from *myrmex*, ant. Its characteristics are described by Galen, *De Diagn. Puls.* (8. 553 K 8. 826–8 K, 8. 835K) as small, faint, and frequent (but not 'fast'), and as a sign of mortal danger (9. 506 K).

Cato . . . oracular . . . death'. For Cato, see above, **100. Cato and outstanding . . . senator.** For the oracular tone of his sayings, see Horace, *Sat.* 1. 2. 32; Plutarch, *Cato* 23. This is probably from the *Ad Filium*, quoted in *HN* 29. 13–4: see above, **112. Cato the Censor.** Youthful precocity was believed to shorten life: see Seneca the Elder, *Contr.* 1. 2 on mental, and above, **75. infants . . . three**, on physical precocity.

172. infinite . . . diseases See above, **167–90. introd.**

Pherecydes . . . body. The first Greek prose writer, according to Pliny (below, **205. Pherecydes**), and 6th-cent. philosopher from Syros, who wrote a work on theogony and cosmogony. See *OCD*³, 1157; Fritz, *RE* 19. 2, Pherecydes (4), 2025–33. For his death, see Aristotle, *HA* 557ª1–2; Aelian, *VH* 4. 28 and 5. 2; Pausanias 1. 20. 7. The same complaint caused the death of the dictator Sulla. See above, **138. his own death . . . tortures**.

Maecenas See above, **148. Agrippa . . . Maecenas** For chronic fever, see above, **169. The rest of mankind . . . quartan fevers.** For his insomnia, Seneca, *Prov.* 3. 10.

Antipater of Sidon A 2nd-cent. BC writer of epigrams who spent his last years in Rome (Cicero, *De Orat.* 3. 194): *OCD*³, Antipater (3), 111. For his fever, see Valerius Maximus 1, ext. 16 and above, **169. even at intervals of a whole year**.

173–8. introd. Cases of amazing returns to life (apparent deaths, out-of-body and near-death episodes, ghost stories) exercised a perennial fascination and occur in a variety of literary sources. The most famous was the story of Er, told in book 10 of Plato's *Republic*, who lay on a battlefield for ten days before recovering on his funeral pyre and recounting the wondrous experiences he had had while dead. For his, and other ancient descriptions of near-death experiences, see J. Bremmer, *The Rise and Fall of the*

Afterlife (London, 2002), 87–102. The entertainment value of such stories made them increasingly popular from the Hellenistic period (see also below, **179. instances . . . after burial**), and they were collected as *mirabilia* by a number of writers, including Phlegon and the 5th-cent. AD philosopher Proclus (*In Rep.* 2. 109–16), who drew on Aristotle's pupil Clearchus' work *On Sleep* and mentions other collectors: see Rohde (1925), 338, Bolton (1962), 148–56, Hansen (1996), 65–112, esp. 65–8 and app. 1. The revival of the apparently lifeless corpse was an inherently dramatic scenario which appealed to ancient novelists (see D. W. Admundsen, 'Romanticising the Ancient Medical Profession: The Characterisation of the Physician in the Graeco-Roman Novel', *BHM* 43 (1974), 320–37; Grmek (1987), 140; E. Bowie, 'Apollonius of Tyana: Tradition and Reality', *ANRW* 2. 16. 2 (Berlin and New York 1986), 1665; and G. W. Bowersock on the 'resurrection' motif in imperial literature, *Fiction as History: Nero to Julian* (California and London, 1994 = 1994*b*), 99–109). Similar anecdotes were related of historical sages and doctors (e.g. Apollonius of Tyana, in Philostratus, *Vit. Apoll.* 4. 45; Asclepiades, above, **124. funeral pyre . . . life**; Empedocles, below, **175. Heraclides**) and, although rational explanation might focus on superior medical powers of observation (cf. Celsus 2. 6, on Asclepiades), there was often an aura of mystical power and miracle-working (below, **175. Heraclides**). Such exalted claims were not necessarily discouraged by a medical profession in which showmanship was inherent. Moreover, such returns to life had serious socio-religious consequences. The consternation of the revived man's heirs when they realize that the *post-mortem* redistribution of roles and property has been thrown into disarray is exploited in Apuleius' (*Florida* 19) anecdote to comic effect. However, *deutero-potmoi* or 'second-fated ones', a term applied both to those who revived en route to the tomb and those presumed dead abroad who returned unexpectedly, were in a potentially dangerous position, having been conveyed out of the world of the living but then rejected by the land of the dead. According to Roman custom, those falsely thought dead could not return to their homes through the normal mode of entry, the door, but had to be let down through the roof (Plutarch, *Mor.* 264e–f, quoting Varro). The reason for this is made clearer by Plutarch's description of the special rites prescribed in Greece for one such survivor, which involved what was effectively an enactment of a rebirth into this world (*Mor.* 264f–

265b). Re-entry through the door was forbidden because feet-first exit across the threshold was the final mode of exit for the dead and was a one-way journey. For reintegration into the world of the living, a different mode of entry was needed, symbolizing rebirth rather than the unnatural reversal of death. See also above, **46. It is the law of nature . . . feet first**; and Garland (2001), 100–1. However, as Pliny claims in **173**, death in the ancient world really could be deceptive. Although medical writers discussed signs of imminent death (see above, **171. signs of approaching death**), far less attention was paid to indications that death had actually occurred. Lack of bodily warmth, absence of pulse, and, in particular, lack of respiration were commonly cited, but Galen, in his discussion of the case of the woman cited by Heraclides (below, **175. female sex . . . turning of the womb** and **Heraclides**), recognized that respiration might not always be visually perceptible (8. 414–16 K). Pliny's stories of Aviola, Lamia, and Tubero are particularly interesting, as these are historical figures who enhance the factual basis of the phenomenon. Death-like comas from which the victims recovered had been described in the Hippocratic corpus (*Epid.* 5. 2, 5. 204 L). Plato (*Laws* 959a) implied that one purpose of the exhibition of a body after death was to ascertain that death had really occurred. It is also possible that the ritual *conclamatio*, or calling on the deceased, which was a feature of Roman funerary practice in the period between death and burial, served a subsidiary function as a means of checking for signs of life, as would the washing of the body in warm water: see Lindsay (2000), 162–3. That the danger of mistaken assumptions of death was real is only emphasized by similar occurrences even in the context of the sophisticated tests available to modern medicine. A recent press report (*Daily Mirror*, 22 Jan. 2003) concerns an Italian who revived at his own wake, an occurrence greeted by the hospital which had been treating him with the insistence that 'when he was released [for burial] he was clinically dead'.

173. Aviola   Called Acilius Aviola in the more elaborate version of this anecdote in Valerius Maximus 1. 8. 12, without mention of his consular status (Klebs, *RE* 1. 1, Acilius (19), 253). He has been identified (by Schilling, 227) with the legate in the Gallic revolt of AD 21 mentioned in Tac. *Ann.* 3. 41 (Klebs, *RE* 1. 1, Aviola (20), 253) though this cannot hold if Syme's (*The Augustan Aristocracy* (Oxford,

1986), 378) identification of the legate with the consul of AD 24 (Groag, *RE* 3. 1, Calpurnius (21), 1366) is correct: see Wardle (1998), 269; the latter bore a different *nomen* (C. Calpurnius Aviola) and died too late to be Valerius Maximus' Aviola.

Lamia   Valerius Maximus 1. 8. 12 mentions a L. Lamia, possibly L. Aelius Lamia, praetor 42 BC (Klebs, *RE* 1. 1, Aelius (75), 522. cf. Cic. *De Orat.* 2. 262); see Schilling 227.

C. Aelius Tubero   P.'s details (Klebs, *RE* 1. 1, Aelius (149), 534) do not fit any of the known members of this family; though a *P.* Aelius Tubero (Klebs, *RE* 1. 1, Aelius (152), 535) was praetor in 201 and 177 BC.

Messala Rufus   M. Valerius Messala Rufus, consul 53 BC, wrote a genealogical work much used by P. (cf. above, **139–46. introd.**) and other writers: *OCD*[3], 1579.

Such ... death   See above, **167–90. introd.**

174–5. Among other examples   Pliny turns to apparent examples of out-of-body experiences in which the soul of an individual appears temporarily to leave the body. Some of those mentioned, e.g. Hermotimus and Epimenides, entered this state at will, while others, such as the unnamed woman in Heraclides' treatise, fell into it involuntarily. Hermotimus, Aristeas, and Epimenides were all Greek seers of the late Archaic era, whose spiritual exploits (death-like trances, bilocation, out-of-body experiences) were reminiscent of the shamans of Scythia and Thrace, areas with which Aristeas and a similar figure, Abaris, had connections. Direct northern influence was therefore posited by K. Meuli ('Scythica', *Hermes*, 70 (1935), 121–76) and E. R. Dodds (*The Greeks and the Irrational* (Berkeley, 1951), 140–2), though others have more cautiously suggested that traditions of wandering souls could equally well have roots in indigenous Greek belief (J. Bremmer, *The Early Greek Concept of the Soul* (Princeton, 1983), 14–69: a primitive dualistic concept of the soul). cf. also Rohde (1925), 299–303, and Bolton (1962), 119–75, who saw Pythagorean (for Pythagoras' similar feats, see below, **177. come from his brother**) shaping in the tradition. More recently, Bremmer (2002: 27–40) has argued that the attribution of psychic excursions to the Greek seers of the Archaic period was a post-Pythagorean interpretation of their activities, a result of later philosophical doctrines about the soul. Whatever its origins, the idea of a free wandering soul which could leave its body and later return to it was long-lived. The Peripatetics were interested in the powers of the soul when the body was unconscious: see M. Détienne, 'De la catalepsie à l'immortalité de l'âme', *Nouvelle Clio*, 10–12 (1958–60), 123–35, and below, **177. come from his brother**. Aristotle's pupil, Clearchus of Soli, told a story of a slave-boy whose soul was drawn out of his body while he lay unconscious and later recounted its wanderings (fr. 7 Wehrli). Plutarch (see below, **174. Hermotimus**) attempted to explain the phenomenon. The motif has occurred in many periods and cultures (Thompson E 720–2; Hertz (1960), 46–7), including later traditions connected with European witchcraft. In 16th-cent. Italy, for example, both alleged witches and their declared antagonists, the Benandanti, claimed to attend nocturnal gatherings in spirit, having left their bodies behind in a sort of cataleptic trance (Ginzburg (1983), 16–20). See also below, **174. Aristeas ... raven**. The causes of such 'separation' remain mysterious; drugs, epilepsy, and certain ecstatic techniques have been suggested. Both ancient and later sources, however, agree in suggesting that it was risky: see below, **burnt.**

174. Hermotimus of Clazomenae Philosopher and supposed reincarnation of Pythagoras; see Diogenes Laertius 8. 5. For the wanderings of his soul, see Plutarch, *Mor.* 592c; Lucian, *Muscae Encomium* 7; Origen, *Contra Celsum* 3. 32; Tertullian, *De Anima* 44; and Apollonius, *Mir.* 3, the fullest version of the story. The two last said that his wife gave his enemies access to his body. See Bremmer (1983), 27–8, 39–43. See also Rohde (1925), 300 and 331 n. 112 for other refs. According to Plutarch, it was just the purest part (*nous*) of the soul which wandered in such cases, leaving its owner unconscious rather than completely bereft of life. Aristotle (*Met.* 984^b fr. 61 Rose) had connected Anaxagoras' theory of *nous* with Hermotimus, implying that the latter referred to the soul which left his body as *nous*: see Bremmer (1983), 40–1.

comatose Pliny's *corpore ... seminanimi* is sometimes translated as 'semi-conscious', but it is clear from the descriptions of similar conditions (see above, **174–5. Among other examples** and **174. Hermotimus**) that a complete lack of consciousness was often the case. Bremmer (1983), 29–30 quotes a 16th-cent. traveller's tale of a shaman's death-like trance and similar stories from other traditions, cf. Dodds (1951), 140–2.

Cantharidae Bolton (1962: 199 n.3) thinks Hermotimus may originally have been a local hero-prophet, destroyed by the clan of a rival. Bremmer (1983), 42, suggests that a rival Dionysiac organization with similar interests in the soul at that time is referred to. Dionysus was often represented with a *cantharos* (drinking cup) in his hand.

burnt The prevention of the soul's return to the body by covering the mouth was a common feature of western folk tradition (Thompson E 721. 1. 2, 721. 1. 2. 4), but Bremmer can find only an Indian parallel to match this 'more ruthless' solution , as he puts it, of Hermotimus' enemies (1983: 39–40 and nn.; app. 2). Later evidence, such as the records of the Italian witch trials (cf. Ginzburg (1983), 53, 59, cf. 16–20, and Thompson E 721. 1. 2. 3), also suggests that far less interference than outright destruction was sufficient to jeopardize the soul's safe return. Even turning the body over (and thereby perhaps obstructing the mouth?) could make the soul's re-entry more difficult. Delaying the re-entry for too long effectively condemned the soul never to return and the body to be disposed of as dead. The soul would then wander as one of the restless dead until the time came when the body would have died naturally (see Ginzburg 59).

like a sheath Cf. Apollonius, *Mir.* 3.

Aristeas . . . raven See above, **10**, and Bremmer (1983), 25–38. For his shamanistic feats, see Herodotus 4. 13–15, according to whom he reappeared in southern Italy 240 years after disappearing and informed the people of Metapontum that he had been accompanying his god, Apollo, in the form of a raven (Apollo's bird: see Bremmer (1983), 35 and n. 57, though Dodds (1951), 162 and n. 38, sees parallels with the idea of the bird-soul in northern shamanism, cf. Bolton (1962), 126). In the western European folk tradition, the wandering soul is frequently endowed with corporeal qualities, leaving the body through the mouth in the form of a small animal or insect. The motif appears from the 8th-cent. AD, in Paul the Deacon's *History of the Lombards* (3. 34), to the present day: see Thompson E 721. 1. 2, 721. 1. 1. 2. 4, 721. 5, 721. 5. 1, G 251. 1; K. M. Briggs, *A Dictionary of British Folklore*, vol. B pt. 2 (London, 1971), 524,

582; Bremmer (1983), 63–6 and app. 2, 132–5; E. Le Roy Ladurie, *Montaillou, the Promised Land of Error*, trans. B. Bray (New York, 1978), 351; Ginzburg (1983), 19–20.

tall . . . tale What Pliny sees as the fanciful detail of the raven and the exaggerated length of the sleep attributed to Epimenides in the following tale arouse his scepticism. Otherwise, he seems to be able to accept tales of apparent deaths or near-death episodes, so long as they are not too prolonged. See below, **176. Corfidius . . . indicated** and **179. supernatural . . . phenomena**.

(175) Epimenides of Cnossus See above, **154. Epimenides**. For the long sleep, compared by Dodds (1951) to a shamanistic initiation, see Varro, *LL* 7. 3; Diogenes Laertius 1. 109–11, 111; Plutarch, *Mor.* 784a; Pausanias 1. 14. 4. Estimates of its length varied from over forty to over fifty years. A reference in a late source (*Suda* s.v. Epimenides) mentions an ability to leave his body and return to it at will, linking him with the other individuals discussed in this section and suggesting that the 'sleep' may have been an enhanced trance. Cf. Plutarch, *Mor.* 157d on his asceticism. See also J. Svenbro, *Phrasikleia: Anthropologie de la lecture en Grèce ancienne* (Paris, 1988), 150–61; Bolton (1962), index, s.v. Epimenides, esp. 160–1.

female sex . . . turning of the womb Belief that the womb could move around the body (cf. Plato, *Timaeus* 91c) dated back to the Hippocratic corpus (cf. above, **63. It is mobile**) and was blamed for a number of medical complaints. Even those who, like Aristotle, did not believe that it could wander freely, believed that it could be pushed upwards and impede breathing (*GA* 719^{a}21–2) and *pnix hysterike*, hysterical suffocation, is a condition found in a number of sources. See Lonie (1965), 138–43; Grmek (1987), 141–3; King (1993), 3–90, esp. 34–5, and sources quoted above, **63. It is mobile**. Cf also above, **43. smell . . . abortion** and **64. It . . . bizarre . . . menstrual flow**. For other references to the condition in the *HN*, see Vons (2000), 141–5. Galen (8. 414 K) discussed a kind of hysteria which left women apparently lifeless, citing Heraclides' case study (below, **Heraclides**). It may be no coincidence that many of the stories of miraculous returns to life featured young women (see Grmek (1987), 141).

Heraclides Heraclides was a 4th-cent. BC philosopher of wide interests including history, astronomy, and eschatology. See *OCD*^{3},

686. The work Pliny mentions was probably called the *peri tes apnou* (Diogenes Laertius proem. 12; F. Wehrli, *Die Schule des Aristoteles*, vol. vii (Basel, 1953; 2nd edn. 1969), fr. 76–89). The story about the woman involved the philosopher Empedocles, who was apparently responsible for explaining her condition: see Galen (8. 414–15 K) and Diogenes Laertius (8. 60–1, 67). Cf. also Origen, *Cels.* 2. 16; *Suda* s.v. *apnous*. For its relation to other tales of 'wandering souls', see Détienne (1958–60), 123–35; Grmek (1987), 141–3. In connection with the case, Empedocles described himself as both doctor and seer (Diog. Laert. 8. 61), suggesting that he recognized the metaphysical as well as the physiological aspects of the case. See Lonie (1965), 134–8. It is therefore likely that Heraclides' work discussed out-of-body experiences (Bolton (1962), 156–7) as well as the physical causes and symptoms of the condition (H. B. Gottschalk, *Heracleides of Pontus* (Oxford, 1980), 13–22). Heraclides' own interest in the soul, together with a tendency to showmanship, is suggested by other stories. He had, for example (Diogenes Laertius 5. 89–90), arranged for a snake, a creature with chthonic and divine associations, to appear at his funeral as an indication of his translation to the afterlife, but it mis-cued, emerging from the shroud too early and causing panic. According to Diogenes, the woman exhibited neither breath nor pulse, but in Galen's account (8. 414–15 K) Empedocles was able to deduce she was not dead when he detected some warmth in her body.

seven days Other sources, e.g. Diogenes Laertius, suggest she had been in a coma for 30 days (fr. 77, 79 Wehrli).

176. Varro See Introd. 4.5.1.

Board of Twenty ... Capua See *Fr. Ant. Rer. Hum.* 1, fr. 10 ed. Mirsch (1882). Caesar's second land bill of 59 BC authorized land distribution in Campania, with a colony at Capua. A commission of twenty was in charge (Broughton, *MRR* ii. 191 ff.; Varro, *RR* 1. 2. 10; Suet. *Caes.* 20. 3; Appian, *BC* 2. 10; Dio 38. 7. 3; Velleius 2. 44): see Brunt (1971), 313–18. Aquinum was about 80 k. north-west of Capua.

176–7. Corfidius ... indicated This (for which see also Granius Licinianus 28, 17–21 Criniti), and the following story of Gabienus, are P.'s most detailed examples of the uncertainty of death. The tale of the Corfidii perhaps attracted the normally sceptical (see below, **178. life . . . false**) P.'s attention because, unlike the Greek tales above, it was vouched for by a respected Roman authority who actually claimed to be related to the protagonists. It is not easy to reconcile these stories with the extreme scepticism P. expresses later on (**188–90**) about any kind of life after death. However, there are two possible explanations for their inclusion. First, it may be that, in keeping with his other stories of amazing returns to life (above), P. regards both cases as apparent or near death episodes: i.e. he does not believe that the elder Corfidius or Gabienus were really dead, and so their recoveries are within the laws of nature. This could fit the case of Corfidius, but Gabienus is more problematic; it is true that, unlike Plato's Er, he had lain 'dead' for only one day, but the severity with which Pliny says his throat was severed implies a more or less instantaneous death. The second possibility revolves around the question of burial. Corfidius and Gabienus have not yet been buried. Therefore, they are not apparitions from beyond the grave, the phenomenon which Pliny specifically distinguishes in **179** from his other examples as being unnatural and therefore outside the scope of his work. The period between death and burial was popularly regarded as a time of transition (see below, **179. instances . . . after burial**) and it is possible that Pliny felt able to accept 'returns to life' within this ambiguous, post-death but pre-burial, period.

177. come from his brother An apparent case of bilocation, a familiar folk-tale motif of an individual asleep, in a trance, or dying, who is simultaneously seen in a different place (Thompson E 721. 1, 721. 2, 723. 4. 1, cf. Briggs B. 2 (1971), 587; Thompson E 723. 6, cf. Briggs (1971), 588; also the stories of Pythagoras and Apollonius of Tyana in Aelian, *VH* 2. 26, 4. 17; Apollonius, *Mir.* 6; Philostratus, *Vit. Apoll.* 4. 10). Those in sleeping, unconscious, and semiconscious states have long been regarded as particularly prone to the projection and perception of visions and apparitions. According to Hipp. *De Victus Ratione* 486, 6. 640–1 L, the soul in effect worked overtime when the body was unconscious, performing the functions of both body and soul. For Peripatetic interest in the soul's potential at such times, see Détienne (1958–60), 123–35. Aelian (*VH* 3. 11) attributes to the Peripatetics a belief in the soul's enhanced mantic powers during sleep, while Sextus Empiricus quotes Aristotle as comparing these powers of the soul to those it possesses when it is separating from the body at death (*Adv. Dogm. 3. 20–2*). Bremmer (1983), 31–4 sees in the notion of bilocation the remnants of a dualistic concept of the soul (above, **174–5. Among other examples**). He classes Aristeas' (see above, **174. Aristeas . . . raven**) appearance on the road to Cyzicus when lying apparently dead in the fuller's shop as another example (Herod. 4. 15), and also mentions Augustine, 18. 18: a philosopher dreamed he was expounding his theories; at the same time he was seen and heard at his discourse in another man's house.

178. Life . . . false Varro's *auctoritas* may have allowed the Corfidii story into *HN* 7, but P. proceeds to illustrate the general falsity of such predictions by an example which subsequent history had discredited.

Sicilian war The war between Octavian and Pompey's son Sextus, fought for control of the Mediterranean 38–36 BC, ended with victory for Octavian's side at Naulochus. See above, **148. shipwreck**.

Gabienus Otherwise unknown. Apparent death on the battlefield has obvious similarities with the earlier story of Er (above, **173–8. introd.**), and battlefields generally, being productive of violent and premature deaths (and consequentially of restless ghosts, see below, **179. instances . . . after burial**), were popular settings for tales of hauntings (e.g. Pausanias 1. 32 on Marathon). But as a whole, the story of Gabienus has its most striking parallel in the tale of Bouplagos (Phlegon 3. 1–15), in which a Syrian cavalry commander fighting for Antiochus III the Great against Rome at the beginning of the 2nd cent. BC apparently dies of wounds in the battle of Thermopylae. He returns temporarily to life to deliver a vague but threatening prophecy to the victorious Romans. See Hansen (1996), 102–12. Although the Romans were victorious in the war against Antiochus, the prophecy was too vague to be discredited: see E. Gabba, 'P. Cornelio Scipione Africano e la leggenda', *Athenaeum*, 53 (1975), 3–17; J.-D. Gauger, 'Phlegon von Trallis, mirab. III: zu einem Dokument geistigen Widerstandes gegen Rom', *Chiron*, 10 (1980), 225–49 and Hansen 102. The Bouplagos story is likely to be a piece of anti-Roman resistance literature, whose author has placed its prophecies in a narrative framework which makes use of the motif, already in the myth of Er, of a dead soldier who revives to deliver a message from the underworld. The Gabienus story uses the same motif, putting it to a similar use as a vehicle for war propaganda. This time, however, the prophecy is unambiguous in its support for Sextus Pompey and would seem to emanate from opponents of Octavian during the Sicilian war between 38 and 36 BC, before the outcome of the conflict was known. This war may offer another motif in common with the Bouplagos episode: a fleeting remark, in Appian, *BC* 5. 79, that Antony's opposition in 38 BC to the war against Sextus was increased by a prodigy, in which a wolf devoured one of his guards at Brundisium, leaving only his face. This is an eery echo of the sequel to the Bouplagos story, in which the Roman general Publius (Scipio Africanus? see Gabba, Gauger, Hansen, above, this note), after prophesying in a state of divine possession, is devoured by a wolf, apart from his head, which continues to prophesy (Phlegon, *Mir.* 3. 8–15). There is obvious similarity to the legend of Orpheus' head and cf. necromantic/prophetic uses of skulls, *PGM* iv. 1928–2144 discussed by F. Graf, *Magic in the Ancient World*, trans. F. Philip (Harvard, 1997), 198–204; Hippolytus, *Ref. Her.* iv. 41. For more examples, see D. Ogden, *Greek and Roman Necromancy* (Princeton, 2001), 208–15, who also points to the near-severing of Gabienus' head and, like F. M. Ahl (*Lucan: An Introduction* (Ithaca and New York, 1976), 133–7), notes the apparent significance, in a number of 'whole body' necromancy tales, of the cutting of throat and neck. In turn, the Gabienus story may well have been the inspiration behind Latin literature's most famous description of necromancy, in Lucan's *Pharsalia*, which also involved Sextus Pompey; see below, **Sextus Pompey**.

It is difficult to date the Gabienus story more precisely. One possibility is the early part of the Sicilian war, when it was by no means obvious that Octavian would be the winner (Syme (1939), 230–1; and above, **148. shipwreck**), and a bad defeat, followed by a destructive storm, provoked riots at Rome against him. M. Hadas (*Sextus Pompey* (New York, 1930), 137–8), however, dated it to 36 BC, around the time of Sextus's successes against Octavian after Mylae (cf. Appian, *BC* 5. 110–12), when popular support for the Pompeian cause was still evident to the point of causing unrest at Rome (Appian, *BC* 5. 112, cf. 99); and when the nature of the fighting meant that Sextus was most likely to have been present to hear the prophecy; though the stylized nature of the story suggests that its details need not be matched too literally to the historical actuality.

The story does not appear elsewhere in extant literature. It may have survived as part of an anti-Octavian/Augustus literary tradition (or was it preserved with the victorious tradition precisely because it proved to be false?), but was likely to have been incorporated, like the Bouplagos story, into *mirabilia* collections.

Octavian   See above, **147–50.**

Sextus Pompey   The younger son of Pompey the Great (above, **95–9**), born *c.*67 BC, who, following his father's death, continued fighting for his cause, ultimately against Octavian. He was eventually put to death shortly after his defeat at the battle of Naulochus (36 BC). See *OCD*³, Pompeius Magnus, Sextus, 1216–17; Hadas (1930); E. Gabba, 'The Perusine War and Triumviral Italy', *HSCP* 75 (1971), 153–6. Lucan's *Pharsalia* (6. 670–825) included a detailed and dramatic depiction of necromancy performed in the presence of the young Sextus (who was in fact probably left in Lesbos with his stepmother during the campaign: see Hadas (1930), 21–35 with refs.), with a view to obtaining a prediction of Republican fortunes in the earlier civil war with Caesar. The two stories are not exact parallels: Lucan describes a deliberate summoning of the dead man's spirit which matches the procedures described in other accounts of necromancy, e.g. Heliod. *Aeth.* 6. 14. 3–15. 5; Apuleius, *Met.* 11. 28–30; *PMG* IV. 2145–77, XII. 278, whereas Gabienus revives spontaneously. They are, however, similar enough to arouse interest, and a number of scholars have suggested that the Gabienus story was the inspiration for Lucan: see esp. R. Grenade, 'Le Mythe de Pompée et les Pompéians sous les Césars', *REA* 52 (1950), 28–63; F. M. Ahl, 'Appius Claudius and Sextus Pompey in Lucan', *C&M* 30 (1967), 331–46: see above, **Gabienus**. The connection of two necromantic stories and the bizarre little anecdote in Appian (above, **Gabienus**) with the same figure may be no more than coincidence: a dramatic reflection of the embattled fortunes of the losing side in Lucan's poem and the adoption in the Gabienus story, with a reflection in Appian, of a motif already utilized in earlier resistance literature (see above, **Gabienus**). However, other possible links have been suggested. Grenade (1950: 31–2) had noted accusations of magical practices against Pompey's descendants in the early Empire, but the extent of intermarriage among the leading aristocratic families makes the concept of a 'Pompeian' tradition in this instance of limited validity. More intriguing, when taken together with the tales already discussed, are the following traditions: (i) that Pompey the Great prophesied to his son on the eve of his death (*Phars.* 6. 814 and schol.; Grenade (1950), 31–2; Ogden (2001), 151); (ii) that a number of *deuteropotmoi* (above, **173–8 introd.**), were reported from the Sicilian wars (Plutarch, *Mor.* 264d–e; Grenade, 38); (iii) that Agrippa's building activities at Avernus during the war laid to rest the supernatural tales told of the area (Strabo 5. 4. 5, C245; Ogden (2001), 151). Lastly, we should not forget the active support for the Pompeian cause of the abstruse scholar and alleged dabbler in necromancy and magic, Nigidius Figulus, which may well have given some encouragement to the formation of these narratives.

179. who . . . side P. uses the adjective *pius, pii*, from *pietas*, loyalty to gods, family and country (see above, **121. devotion**). It was claimed as a principle by other civil war factions (Syme (1939), 157) but in the case of Sextus' followers it had particular resonance, having been the Pompeian war cry in their final battle against Caesar at Munda in 45 BC (Appian, *BC* 2. 104, 430) and later appropriated as *cognomen* by Sextus to symbolize his continuation of his father's cause (e.g. *ILS* 8895). Popular at Rome, Sextus also advertised himself as the protégé of the sea god Neptune (Horace, *Epod.* 9. 7; Dio 48. 31. 5, 48. 5; Appian, *BC* 5. 100).

This . . . predicted Pliny refers ironically to the occurrence of Gabienus' death, not to the fulfilment of the prophecy which he had claimed his death would guarantee, but which events proved false.

instances . . . after burial In contrast to the cases dealt with in **173–8,** P. refers here to sightings of those who have unequivocably died and been buried; ghosts and revenants. Popular religious belief held that the spirits of the unburied, murder victims, and those who had died untimely deaths were most likely to be restless (Rohde (1925), 181; Bremmer (1983), 101–8, Johnston (1999), *passim*: for other cultures/eras, e.g. Hertz (1960), 85; J. Pentikäinen, 'The Dead without Status', *Temenos*, 4 (1969), 92–102). There was also a primitive belief, found in many cultures, ancient and modern, that the soul after death remained for a time in between two worlds

(Garland (2001), 38–41; Bremmer, (1983), 93–4; other cultures/ eras: Hertz (1960), 34–7, 42, 45–6, 52, 61; P. Ariès, *The Hour of Our Death* (New York and Oxford, 1981), 354–61; Johnston (1999), 9–10, with more anthropological references; Thompson E 722. 2. 8. 1, 722. 2. 8. 2, 722. 3. 1. 1, 722. 3. 2). Sometimes, the transitional period extended for a time after burial: Plato (*Phaedo* 81c–d, below; cf. also Cicero, *Somn. Scip.* 29) suggested that the souls of the insufficiently virtuous lingered for a while around their tombs; and, according to Servius, *In Aen.* 3. 68, Stoics believed that the soul remained with its body in the tomb until the body had decomposed, cf. Hertz (1960), 34–7, 45–6; Thompson E 722. 3. 2, the soul wanders until the corpse decays, a motif found in various cultures, e.g. Lawson (1964), 485–8 on modern Greece. The process of becoming one of the dead may be by no means instantaneous, starting with recognition that a person is dying and not ending until the completion of a period of funerary rites: see S. C. Humphreys, 'Death and Time', in S. C. Humphreys and H. King (eds.), *Mortality and Immortality: The Anthropology and Archaeology of Death* (London, 1981), 263; Garland (2001), 39; cf. Ogden (2001), 260–2; the dying bridge two worlds). Normally, however, in Roman belief, burial was supposed to literally fetter the dead and prevent their reappearance (cf. [Quintilian] *Decl. Mai.* 10. 1–2, ultimately secured in this case by iron bands). Servius (*In Aen.* 3. 68) claimed that the *anima* was lured into the tomb by the funerary offerings. P. may have felt able to accommodate stories of revivals and appearances in this ambiguous transitional period (see above, **176–7. Corfidius . . . indicated**), while regarding those which occurred after the disposal or destruction of the body as breaking the laws of nature. It is clear from Cicero, *Tusc.* 1. 18–22 that there were considerable differences of opinion, not only on the nature of the soul, but also on the question of its ability to survive the body and, if so, for how long and where. See also R. Lattimore, *Themes in Greek and Latin Epitaphs* (Illinois, 1942), 13–48. The atomist Democritus, who considered that death was a process involving the gradual dispersal of atoms rather than an instantaneous separation of body and soul, was able to explain apparent returns to life, but his remained a minority view: see Proclus, *In Remp.* I, p. 113 Kroll; Celsus 2. 6. 14, cf. Cicero, *Tusc.* 1. 22.

The souls of the dead featured in Graeco-Roman literature from Homer onwards. From the Archaic Greek period, the dead may have been increasingly articulated as individuals (see C. Sourvinou-Inwood, 'To die and enter the House of Hades: Homer, Before and After', in J. Whaley (ed.), *Mirrors of Mortality* (New York, 1981), 15–39 and *'Reading' Greek Death to the End of the Classical Period* (Oxford, 1995), 106–7 and index s.v. 'shades'). From the same period, fear of the dead may have increased in line with a physical and metaphysical separation from them (Sourvinou-Inwood (1995), 413–44; I. Morris, *Burial and Ancient Society* (Cambridge, 1987), 192–3; Johnston (1999), 95–9). Stories of ghosts and revenants haunting tombs (cf. Plato, *Phaedo* 81c–d, a passage influential on later literature: see P. Courcelle, 'L'Âme au tombeau', in *Mélanges d'histoire de religion offerts à H.-Ch. Puech* (Paris, 1974), 331–6) and appearing to the living became popular in Hellenistic literature and embedded in popular belief (cf. Lactantius, *Inst.* 2. 26). See L. Collison-Morley, *Greek and Roman Ghost Stories* (London, 1912); Rohde (1925), index, s.v. 'ghosts', 'souls', 'conjuration of the dead'; F. Cumont, *Lux Perpetua* (Paris, 1949), 78–109; M. P. Nilsson, *Greek Religion* (Oxford, 1925; 3rd edn. 1949), 100, 182–4; E. R. Dodds, 'Supernormal Phenomena in Classical Antiquity', in *The Ancient Concept of Progress and other Essays on Greek Literature and Belief* (Oxford, 1973), 156–210; J. Winkler, 'Lollianos and the Desperadoes', *JHS* 100 (1980), 155–81; Russell (1981), 193–213; Bremmer (1983), 89–124; W. Burkert, *Greek Religion: Archaic and Classical* (Oxford, 1985), 300, 317; A. Bernstein, *The Formation of Hell: Death and Retribution in the Ancient and Early Christian Worlds* (London, 1993), 84–106; Hansen (1996), 66 with biblio.; D. Felton, *Haunted Greece and Rome: Ghost Stories from Classical Antiquity* (Texas, 1999); Johnston (1999); Ogden (2001). Extant collections in Phlegon and Lucian attest their entertainment value by the first two centuries AD (J. R. Morgan, 'The Fragments of Ancient Greek Fiction', *ANRW* 34. 4 (1998), 3293–3390, esp. 3296), while a well-known letter of Pliny's nephew (*Ep.* 7. 27) offers three stories (see below, **supernatural . . . phenomena**).

supernatural . . . phenomena Things or events which seemed alarmingly unnatural might be termed *prodigia*, portents, prodigies, and be deemed to require religious expiation; see above, **33. portentous . . . fertility; 34. once . . . pets**. However, P. also uses the term without religious overtones to describe the extraordinary and monstrous, and the fact that he includes in his account of nature creatures which he calls *prodigia*, such as the monstrous races (above, **32. individual creations . . . miracles**) suggests that he normally considered them to be within the range of nature's amazing versatility (see above, **7–8**), even if they seemed to stretch her laws to breaking point. But in the present passage, he specifically contrasts *prodigia* with the natural phenomena which are the proper subject of his work. Here, in fact, *prodigium* seems to mean 'supernatural'. Why does Pliny draw the line at ghosts and revenants? Probably because to go from death to life is the inversion of one of the most basic laws of nature; the progression from vitality to degeneration and death. Another topic where Pliny's use of *prodigium* seems to step over the boundary from extraordinary to unnatural is magic, which aims to control and in some cases invert natural processes (Beagon (1992), 100–1, 106–10). It is true that Pliny has already suggested that the natural antithesis between life and death is less clearly delineated than is normally believed. But the temporary ambiguities of **173–8** did not fundamentally disrupt the one-way progression from the former to the latter and were distinguished from reappearances *post sepulturam*: see above, **176. Corfidius . . . indicated**, and **179. instances . . . after burial**. On the whole, then, Pliny cannot be said to believe in ghosts. They are excluded from the *HN* since they defy the laws of nature and it is the magicians' attempts to defy those same laws that Pliny dismisses as *vanitas*. The two combine in *HN* 30. 15, where Nero's attempts to summon ghosts by magic are also an example of *vanitas*. Other aspects of the supernatural arouse doubts (*HN* 28. 10–29 on the effectiveness of prayer) and outright scepticism (*HN* 2. 14–27 on the existence of gods) as does the whole idea of an afterlife (below, **188–90**). His nephew inclined to the idea that ghosts were real, referring to the theory of Democritus of Abdera that they were lingering physical emanations or *eidola* which penetrated the pores of a dreamer (Diels, *Fr. Vorsok.* ii (1959), Democritus 166, quoted by Sherwin-White (1966), comm. *Ep.* 7. 27. 21) an idea elaborated by Lucretius (*RN* 1. 127–35, 4, esp. 26–109, 724–818) whose *rerum simulacra* can produce waking as well as sleeping visions. Pliny himself may have preferred the Aristotelian theory that ghosts were merely a result of mental or physical disturbance in the perceiver (*Div. p. Somn.* 463^{a}ff.), and thus a product of the weakness and *vanitas* of man himself which he so frequently notes.

180–90. introd.   Pliny's survey of the human animal from birth to death closes with examples of sudden deaths (**180–6**), followed by some comments on burial practices (**187**) and speculations on the afterlife (**188–90**). Sudden deaths are 'life's greatest joy' (**180**), being devoid of pain or fear. They are also sure (unlike the near-deaths of **173–9**) and peaceful (**185**), forming an appropriate transition to P.'s view of death itself, as a state of unambiguous non-being, a regaining of prenatal oblivion, rather than a shadowy repetition of former life (see **188–90**nn. on his philosophical influences). However, P. reminds readers that the transition is not always as happy as those in **180–5**. **186** offers three examples of the 'innumerable' unhappy instances, in which the wretchedness of a suffering victim's fate is increased by a final hitch: the unhappy suicide who repents his attempt and the indignities inflicted on the funeral pyre itself in the case of the racing fan whose devotion is passed off as an accident and in that of Lepidus and his makeshift cremation. The mention of cremation leads into a brief factual discussion of burial customs, then to the speculations on the afterlife. It is noticeable that the last five sections, (**186–90**), return to a number of the themes of the first five sections of book 7, where P. expounded the paradox of the weaknesses of man, the most exalted of animals. See also Introd. 5.4. The inauspicious deaths (**186**) mirror the inauspicious birth (**2**) of the naked, weeping infant. The unreasonable hunger (*vanitas*, **188**, **189**; *dementia, credulitas*, **190**) for a life after death (**188–90**), is named in section **5** as unique to man, whose illogicality in thus distinguishing himself from other animals is emphasized in **188. mode of breathing . . . animals**; and above, **43–4.**

180. frequent . . . natural   A contrast is intended with the prodigies of **179**. It is not entirely clear how Pliny 'shows' that sudden death is natural. Schilling renders 'show to have natural causes', but P. does not offer causes: the point of the stories is that there are no obvious causes, as he specifically states in **181**. Probably it is their frequency, which Pliny emphasizes here ('frequent'; 'scores of examples') which enhances the likelihood that they are natural occurrences. Pliny's list was of particular interest to the 16th-cent. essayist Michel de Montaigne, who repeated it with additions (*Essays* I. xix). His brother had suffered a similarly unexpected demise, suddenly collapsing six hours after having been struck on the temple, without apparent damage, by a tennis ball.

Verrius   See above, Introd., 4.5.1. These examples are probably from his *Res Memoriae Dignae*; see Münzer (1897), 324ff. Many of the names cannot be certainly identified with known individuals, but those which can be suggest an overall context of the last two centuries BC.

Chilo   See above, **119. Chilo of Sparta**.

Sophocles . . . contest   For Sophocles, see above, **109. Sophocles . . . father Liber**. For his death, from joy following anxiety as to the contest's result, Diodorus Siculus 13. 103. 4, 15. 74. 2; Valerius Maximus 9. 12, ext. 5. For Dionysius, see above, **110. Dionysius . . . Plato**. He presented *The Ransom of Hector* at the Lenaea in 367 BC, and, according to Diodorus 15. 73. 5, won first prize despite his lack of talent, but died from the effects of a celebratory drinking binge.

the mother . . . Cannae . . . report   For this anecdote of the aftermath of Cannae, 216 BC (above, **106**), see Aulus Gellius, *NA* 3. 15. 4. Livy (22. 7. 13) and Valerius Maximus 9. 12. 2 place it after Trasimene (217 BC) and add a further story about a mother who died embracing her returned son.

Diodorus   Diodorus 'Cronos' of Iasus (d. *c*.284 BC: *OCD*³, Diodorus (2), 472; Nator, *RE* 5. 1, Diodorus (42), 705–7) was a leading member of the Dialectical school, a branch of the Megarian school, and a noted dialectical performer (Cicero, *De Fato* 12). Diogenes Laertius sets this clash with Stilpo, head of the Megarian school (*OCD*³, 1444) in 307 BC at Megara, in the presence of Ptolemy I, who had captured the town.

181. two Caesars . . . Pisa   The praetor was L. Julius Caesar, who died suddenly as praetor in 166 BC (Münzer, *RE* 10. 1, Iulius (28), 111). The father of the dictator was C. Julius Caesar, who died at Pisa in 85 BC (Münzer, *RE* 10. 1, Iulius (130), 185–6).

Q. Fabius Maximus . . . replace him.   Q. Fabius Maximus (Münzer, *RE* 6. 2, Fabius (108), 1791–2) was given the consulship for the last three months of 45 BC by Julius Caesar in return for his role in the battle of Munda (March 45). His sudden death on the last day of December led to the impromptu election, engineered by Caesar and deplored as a constitutional sham by Cicero (*Fam.* 7. 30), of another loyal partisan, C. Caninius Rebilus (Münzer, *RE* 3. 2, Caninius (9), 1478–9; *OCD³*, 285), to a consulship of just a few hours; cf. Dio 43. 46. 2.

C. Volcatius Gurges Otherwise unknown: Gundel, *RE* 9A 1, Volcatius (5), 742.

Q. Aemilius Lepidus Probably the consul of 21 BC: von Rohden, *RE* 1. 1, Aemilius (78), (79), 564.

stubbed his toe The founder of the Stoa, Zeno of Citium, had, in his old age, apparently regarded a similar accident as a hint to leave this world. According to Diogenes Laertius (7. 28–9), he struck the ground with his fist, saying 'I come; why do you call me?' He then held his breath and died. No fewer than 3 of Pliny's examples (Lepidus and the two who follow him) stumble, while a further 4 die in the act of 'going out'. Presumably such departures attracted attention as symbolizing the passage over the threshold of life into death.

C. Aufustius Otherwise unknown: Klebs, *RE* 2. 2, Aufustius (2), 2299.

Comitium The main venue for political assemblies in the late Republic, at the foot of the Capitoline hill; Nash (1981), i. 287–9; Richardson (1992), 97–8.

182. ambassador . . . Curia This may be the Rhodian admiral, Theaidetos, who headed an embassy in 167 BC, after Rhodes' equivocal attitude to Rome in the Third Macedonian war. Polybius, however, while mentioning his embassy and subsequent death at Rome (30. 21. 1) does not hint at the immediate and dramatic demise described here.

Curia The senate house; in this period, the Curia Hostilia, on the north side of the Comitium: Richardson (1992), 102–3.

Cn. Baebius Tamphilus Possibly the praetor of 168 BC, cf. Livy 44. 17. 4–5: Klebs, *RE* 2. 2, Baebius (42), 2732.

Aulus Pompeius Possibly one of several individuals of that name, e.g. father or brother of the consul of 141 BC or the son of the tribune of 102 BC; see Miltner, *RE* 21. 2, Pompeius (1), (2), (4), 2053–4.

M'. Iuventius Thalna Consul of 163 BC (Groag, *RE* 10. 2, Iuventius (30), 1371). For his death, cf. Valerius Maximus 9. 12. 3.

C. Servilius Pansa . . . Publius . . . Baebius . . . Corax. All otherwise unknown. Corax was possibly a freedman of M. Terentius Varro: see Münzer, *RE* 5 A 1, Terentius (42), 652; Münzer and Stein, *RE* 2 A 1, Servilius (70), 1802.

183. ivory statue . . . Augustus The forum of Augustus, dedicated in 2 BC, was dominated by the temple of Mars Ultor. As well as the treasures kept in the temple (cf. *HN* 34. 48, 141; Pausanias 8. 46. 4–6), individual artworks were on view in the forum itself, including paintings by Apelles (*HN* 35. 27, 93–4), as well as its famous statue of Augustus in a chariot and series of Roman gods and heroes (Richardson (1992), 162; Zanker (1988), 291).

doctor C. Julius Otherwise unknown.

probe . . . ointment For this procedure, see Varro, *LL* 6. 82.

ex-consul . . . Torquatus Probably A. Manlius Torquatus, consul 164 BC: Münzer, *RE* 14. 1, Manlius (73), 1193.

L. Tuccius Valla Detlefsen (1867: 41) emended *medicus Valla* to *medicus Sullae*, 'doctor of Sulla' (cf. Münzer, *RE* 7 A 1, Tuccius (4), 766) but neither reading produces an individual mentioned elsewhere.

Appius Saufeius . . . Decimus Saufeius The Saufeii were prominent in Praeneste (Münzer, *RE* 2 A 1, Saufeius and Saufeius (2), 256), so Schilling (231) attributed their mention to Verrius Flaccus' (above, **180. Verrius**) links with that town (cf. his compilation of the *Fasti Praenestini, Inscr. It.* xiii. 2, 107 ff.).

P. Quintius Scapula . . . Aquilius Gallus C. Aquilius Gallus (*OCD*[3], 34; Klebs, *RE* 1. 1, Aquilius (23), 327–8), a Roman jurist, pupil of Q. Mucius Scaevola, was praetor with Cicero in 66 BC. For his luxury house, see *HN* 17. 2. His guest, Scapula, is not otherwise known.

184. ex-praetor Cornelius Gallus Possibly father of C.

Cornelius Gallus, poet and prefect of Egypt, who committed suicide in 27 BC (Münzer, *RE* 4. 1, Cornelius (163), 1342).

while making love Ovid's ideal end, according to *Am.* 2. 10. 29–36. Montaigne added to Pliny's list at this point 'Tigillinus, Captaine of the Romans Watch, Lodowicke, sonne of Guido Gonzaga, Marquis of Mantua. . . . And of a farre worse example, Speusippus the Platonian philosopher and one of our Popes . . .' (*Essays* 1. xix, trans. J. Florio). Tigellinus' death was in fact a forced suicide rather than a sudden collapse (Tac. *Hist.* 1. 72), but committed 'in the midst of his concubines' embraces and kisses'. Montaigne's version of Speusippus' death seems to go back no further than a polemical passage of Tertullian attacking pagan philosophers (*Apol.* 46).

Hetereius Not otherwise known.

recent . . . pantomime . . . Mysticus P.'s 'recent' (*nostra aetas* = 'our age/era') is vague, usually referring to events within the last thirty years but occasionally going back further: see Introd. 4.5.2. The phrase does, however, suggest that this is an insertion of Pliny's own into the examples gathered from Verrius. For pantomime, see above, **159. Stephanion . . . costume.** The individuals named are not otherwise known.

artistically contrived . . . Hilarus P.'s *operosissima securitas*, 'painstaking serenity' has been slightly amplified in translation to bring out the idea of a staged death, the actor's final tableau. Death invited dramatic simile, which was further encouraged by literary treatments, as did life (e.g. Augustus' death-bed quotation of the closing lines of a play, Suet. *Aug.* 99. 1; Cicero's projected 'dramatic' biography, *Fam.* 5. 12. 2) and indeed nature (Beagon (1992), 153). This was especially the case with deliberately staged death in the form of a stylish suicide (Griffin (1986), 64–77, 192–202). Petronius, who so managed his suicide that he was able to appear at dinner 'so that his death, even if coerced, should appear natural' (Tac. *Ann.* 16. 19) is a useful comparison with Ofilius, the real actor, whose death at dinner actually was natural. Pliny was also doubtless conscious of the appropriateness of the *cognomen* Hilarus, 'cheerful, happy'. This anecdote's position as the finale and culmination of the list of happy deaths paves the way for P.'s description of the oblivion of death as a happy state of serenity.

ancient sources Münzer (*RE* 17. 2, Ofellius (11), 2042) assumed this story came from Verrius, who was himself quoting an older source. It is, however, possible that P. derived it from elsewhere, perhaps directly from the 'early writers', as it is likely that he has already broken away from the Verrius material in the previous anecdote (see above, **recent . . . Mysticus**). In either case, Münzer's projected date, late 2nd cent. or early 1st cent. BC, for the setting is plausible.

185. without anyone noticing Other examples of 'happy' deaths frequently involved slipping gently and imperceptibly away, cf. the famous story of Cleobis and Biton (Herod. 1. 31) who, after a conspicuous act of piety, fell asleep in a temple, never to wake again. The death of the aged Bion of Priene (Diogenes Laertius 1. 84) has some similarities to Hilarus'. After speaking for a client in court, Bion dozed off, leaning against his grandson. His client was acquitted, but when an attempt was made to rouse the old man at the end of the case, he was found to be dead.

186. happy . . . unhappy See above, **180–90 introd**.

L. Domitius . . . Julius Caesar L. Domitius Ahenobarbus (*OCD*³, Domitius Ahenobarbus (1), 492; Münzer, *RE* 5. 1, Domitius (23), 1328–31), consul 54 BC, a leading opponent of Caesar, was forced to surrender to him at Corfinium at the start of the Civil War but was pardoned and released (Caesar, *BC* 1. 16–23). He then took part in the defence of Massilia but escaped before its capture (*BC* 1. 34. 2, 36. 1, 2. 22. 3–4) and fought at Pharsalus (48 BC), where he was killed trying to escape in the aftermath (*BC* 3. 99. 4). The earlier suicide attempt is unflatteringly elaborated in Suet. *Nero* 2. 3, where his change of mind is attributed to personal cowardice, for which his physician had already made allowance by giving him a non-fatal dose in the first place, cf. Seneca, *Ben*. 3. 24.

public records See above, **60. In the public records**. These, the *acta diurna*, together with the *acta senatus*, were originally published by Caesar in 59 BC, according to Suetonius (*Jul*. 20), which might make their inclusion of an event which occurred shortly after a death of 77 BC, and which is apparently the earliest reliable reference to circus colours, problematic. This, and the apparent lack of evidence that the *acta diurna* contained anything other than official notices before the imperial era, led Rawson ('Chariot-Racing in the

Roman Republic', *PBSR* 49 (1981), 8) to follow O. Hirschfeld (*Kleine Schriften* (Berlin, 1913), 685) and make the Lepidus whose death (**122** and below) slightly pre-dated Felix's the husband of an Appuleia Varilla condemned for adultery in AD 19. Felix's own demise was thus placed within the early imperial era, for which non-official events appearing in the *acta* are well attested and was no longer the first reliable reference to faction colours (J. H. Humphrey, *Roman Circuses: Arenas for Chariot-Racing* (London, 1986), 137; see below, **Felix . . . Reds**). However, the name of Appuleia Varilla's husband is not mentioned; and if lack of evidence is no barrier to the acceptance of this theory, it can equally well allow of the possibility that non-official events were recorded in the *acta* before the Augustan era. As for the time lapse between the 59 BC introduction of the *acta* and the chronological proximity of Felix's death to that of Lepidus in 77 BC, it is (*a*) quite possible that 'Caesar may have regularised and expanded what had hitherto appeared occasionally and in more restricted physical form' (Baldwin (1979), 190), and (*b*) dangerous to interpret too exactly Pliny's temporal phrases (see above, **recent . . . pantomime . . . Mysticus**).

Felix . . . Reds Chariot races were the most popular of the public spectacles at Rome, the most important venue, the Circus Maximus, holding up to 250,000 spectators. Stables, of which the Reds, together with the Whites, were probably the oldest (Humphrey (1986), 137: but see above, **public records**), engendered extreme loyalties among their fans (cf. Pliny, *Ep.* 9. 6). Individual charioteers could become stars (cf. Diocles, *CIL* vi. 10048, Sherk (1988), no. 167, whose inscription mentions a number of other past champions, though not a Felix) but risked injury and death, possibly the fate of Felix here: see *ILS* 5277–5316, Sherk (1988), no. 168; Balsdon (1969), 314–24; R. Auguet, *Cruelty and Civilisation: The Roman Games* (London, 1994), 120–48, 161–6, 170–7; Humphrey (1986), 137; Rawson (1981), 1–16.

perfumes Lavish provision of such luxuries as the myrrh, frankincense, and other spices that were Arabia's chief exports (*HN* 12. 51 ff.) indicated a high-status funeral. Nero 'burnt more spices than Arabia produced in a year' at the funeral of his wife Poppaea, according to P. (*HN* 12. 83). As Poppaea was embalmed (see below, **189. preservation . . . Democritus**), these may have been burnt as incense (cf. J. M. C. Toynbee, *Death and Burial in the Roman World*

(London, 1971), 45) or in a mock pyre connected with a deification ceremony (H. Furneaux, *The Annals of Tacitus* (Oxford, 1896), ii. 436, on Tac. *Ann.* 16. 6). Otherwise, gums and scented woods (cf. *HN* 12. 76, 81) may also have been burnt in the pyre at a cremation, and other sources (e.g. Juvenal 4. 108–9, Persius 3. 103–5) suggest the body itself was heavily anointed with perfumes and ointments.

not long before   Lepidus (above, **122**) died in 77 BC, giving a lower limit for the date of Felix's death. But see above, **public records**.

187. Cremation . . . dead   Archaeological excavation suggests that both cremation and inhumation were current in early Rome and there was always a variety of practices. See G. Davies, 'Burial in Italy up to Augustus', in R. Reece (ed.), *Burial in the Roman World* (London, 1977), 13–19; I. Morris, *Death Ritual and Social Structure in Classical Antiquity* (Cambridge, 1992), ch. 2. Greek influence may have encouraged inhumation from the 8th cent. BC but later, cremation grew in popularity and came to predominate by the 1st cent. BC. Cicero, like P., considered that inhumation was the more ancient practice (*Leg.* 2. 56), adding that it was also the more natural, since the body was being returned to its 'mother', earth; and it was probably this idea, rather than any factual evidence, which encouraged the perception of inhumation as the more primitive method. The choice between burial and cremation may in some instances have been decided by the classification of the deceased, cf. P.'s comment (above, **72. Among . . . through**) that children whose teeth had not yet come through were not cremated.

Cornelian . . . Marius   The Cornelii were an ancient and aristocratic family with their own traditions (see Macrobius, *Sat.* 1. 16–17). For their conservatism on the matter of burial, see also Cicero, *Leg.* 56. For Sulla, see above, **137–8**. He was said to have exhumed Marius' remains and thrown them in the river Anio (Cicero, *Leg.* 2. 57; Valerius Maximus 9. 2. 1). For his own cremation, see Appian, *BC* 1. 105–6.

[Sepulture . . . earth.]   Generally regarded as a later gloss on vocabulary by editors, this statement contradicts Cicero, *Leg.* 2. 58.

188. variety . . . spirits of the dead.   The spirits of the dead, *Manes*, were referred to as a collective divine entity, *Di Manes*, and were the objects of religious rituals at public festivals and privately. See *OCD*³, 916–17; Cumont (1949), 392 ff. P.'s 'variety of vague theories' reflects the diversity of speculation in 1st cent. AD Rome, which was not assimilated into any coherent theory. To traditional beliefs in *Manes* and popular notions of an underworld inhabited by weak, insubstantial ghosts which went back to Homer (*Od.* 11. 23 ff; 24. 5 ff.), had been added the Hellenistic deification of outstanding individuals and Greek philosophical theories of the soul's immortality, Pythagorean beliefs in transmigration, and promises held out by mystery cults of a blessed afterlife. See below, **immortality . . . transformation** and **making a god . . . man.**

After . . . birth   P.'s sentiment is closely paralleled in Seneca, *Ep.* 57. 4: death is simply not being, a state we were previously in before birth; although Stoic theory could also entertain the idea that the soul survives the body, at least until the next periodic conflagration, and that the souls of the truly wise might be assumed into a state of eternal blessedness (*SVF* ii. 809–22; cf. Cumont (1949), 113–15). It was the Epicureans who expressed most strongly a belief in the mortality of the soul and hence in ultimate oblivion: see Lucretius, *RN* 3. 450–end and Bailey (1947), comm. ad loc.

human vanity   For *vanitas*, see above, **5** and **180–90. introd**. Here, as with the far-fetched spells of the Magi in Pliny (Beagon (1992), 74), it is in opposition to rational thought, as demonstrated by Pliny's arguments against the afterlife in **189**. See also below, **189. preservation . . . Democritus**, on the *vanitas* of the resurrection beliefs of Democritus, also credited with magic knowledge by Pliny; cf. **190. what is . . . serenity** and above, **5**, where worry about what will happen after death is one of the emotional weaknesses which endanger human *ratio*.

immortality . . . transformation   That the soul was separate from and possibly capable of surviving the body was well established in Greek thought by the 5th cent. BC (Bremmer (1983), 70–124). It was an important component of Pythagoreanism and the theory of transmigration of souls (metempsychosis, P.'s 'transformation') was attributed to Pythagoras himself (J. Barnes, *The Presocratic Philosophers*, i: *Thales to Zeno* (London, 1979), 103–4; W. Burkert, *Lore and Science in Ancient Pythagoreanism* (Cambridge, Mass. 1972), 120–36). Arguably the most influential philosophical exposition of the soul's immortality, including transmigration, was Plato's *Phaedo*, while similar ideas existed at a more popular level in literature associated with Orphic religion.

or else   P. turns from ideas inspired by Greek philosophical thought to those belonging more specifically to popular Roman religious belief and public cult.

sensation . . . spirits   see above, **188. variety . . . spirits of the dead**.

making a god . . . man.   A reference to the cult of the Manes (above, **188. variety . . . spirits of the dead**); or possibly to ruler cult, though P. was aware of the latter's political role (*HN* 2. 18–19, 2. 94). His attitude to gods generally was one of extreme scepticism, attributing 'divine' attributes to nature alone (*HN* 2. 14–27; Beagon, (1992), 92–102).

mode of breathing . . . animals   P. may simply mean that the physiological similarity of man and other animals should extend to their dead as well as their living state. But the etymology of Greek *psyche*, 'soul', was connected with *psychein*, 'to breathe', and originally denoted the physical aspect of the soul, as opposed to the 'free' soul denoting personality and individuality (Bremmer (1983), 22–4). Animals were thought to possess only this physical aspect of soul, not the 'free' soul which could survive death (Bremmer, app. 1, 125–31), sometimes identified with *nous*, mind, reason and emotion (Lucretius, *RN* 3. 94–135, with Bailey (1947), pp. 1005–6). So, despite his belief in the uniqueness of human mental and moral attributes (above, **1–7**nn.) P. may also be implying that there is nothing so unique about the human soul as to allow of a post-mortem survival not granted to animals.

creatures . . . lifespans   For animals believed to have longer lifespans than man, see above, **153. Hesiod . . . fantastic**, and *HN* 8. 28, 47.

189. Taken on its own . . . touch?   Pliny's language echoes Lucretius' Epicurean arguments. Lucretius did give the spirit a structure, of atoms, but it was delicate (*RN* 3. 180–235). Its atoms were so small and mobile that it would disintegrate more quickly than smoke when deprived of its corporeal home (3. 25–44). The senses only function when body and spirit are combined (3.

560–79). As the spirit on its own cannot possess the vehicles of the senses (eyes, ears, etc.), 'it canot be sentient, or so much as exist' (3. 625–33).

fabrications of childish fancy P. gives a twist to the commonplace: rather than fears (Plato, *Phaedo* 77; Lucretius, *RN* 2. 55–61, 87–93, 6. 35–41; cf. Seneca, *Ep.* 106. 6), his adults entertain childish hopes.

mortality greedy for immortality See **5** above, **unbounded appetite for life**. Lucretius too condemned 'lust for life'; though rather as a clinging to this life through fear of death and what it might bring (*RN* 3. 1076), than as a desire to believe in a second life after death.

vanity See above, **188. human vanity.**

preservation . . . Democritus The attribution of such an idea to Democritus of Abdera (b. 460–57 BC) is surprising. He was creator with Leucippus of the atomic theory adopted by Epicurus who, as Lucretius' exposition shows, asserted the soul's, as well as the body's, mortality. However, a fragment of Varro's Menippean Satire *peri psyches*, cited by Nonius Marcellus (p. 342 L) was noted by Hardouin (Ajasson de Grandsagne 222) and repeated by Schilling (234), attributing to Democritus the preservation of bodies in honey (cf. above, **35. honey**). Democritus' reputation was considerably clouded in antiquity by the existence of spurious alchemical and magical literature, some by the Egyptian Bolus. P. on several occasions condemns Democritus for magical, 'eastern' material (especially *HN* 30. 9–10), a connection which may explain the present remark. Embalmment, although mentioned in Lucretius, *RN* 3. 890–3 as one of three methods of disposal of the dead, was not much used at Rome and was regarded as foreign: Cicero (*Tusc.* 1. 45–108) connects it specifically with Egypt and Persia, Tacitus (*Ann.* 16. 6, see above, **186. perfumes**) with Eastern kings. Toynbee (1971: 32–3) suggested that occasional embalmments found in Italy may have been connected to the Egyptian mystery cults of Isis or Serapis, and later Christian burials sometimes employed methods of preservation such as embalming or plaster-packing (C. J. S. Green, 'The Significance of Plaster Burials for the Recognition of Christian Cemeteries', in R. Reece (ed.), *Burial in the Roman World* (London, 1977), 48).

190. What is . . . serenity. A final rhetorical elaboration built around what P. sees as the perversity of the notion of life in death.

What peace . . . ? This reflects a popular theme on funerary monuments (F. Cumont, *Recherches sur le symbolisme funéraire des Romains* (Paris, 1942), 355–9; id., *Afterlife in Roman Paganism* (New Haven, 1922 repr. New York, 1959), 190–3): peace (*pax, quies*), tranquillity (*securitas*, cf. above, **185. artistically contrived . . . Hilarus**) and freedom from trouble and care (*taedio/cura solutus*) were frequently inscribed. Ideas which remove the possibility of post-mortem freedom from life's cares double the sorrow of those facing death, already burdened with the sufferings of this life.

seductive delusions . . . death refers not only to the paradox of prolonging life into death but also to the initial false premiss that life is entirely desirable (for its tribulations and death as a blessed release, see **167–8** above and **4. not to be born at all**).

if life is . . . sweet? The paradox of life in death is here represented by present and perfect tenses of *vivere*, to live. The perfect, *vixisse*, 'to have lived' could be used euphemistically to mean 'to be dead', and was allegedly used by Cicero to announce the execution of the Catilinarian conspirators (Plutarch, *Cic.* 22). Cf. also Plautus, *Bacch.* 1. 2. 43.

prenatal . . . serenity P. reiterates the statement (**188. After . . . birth**) with which he began this discussion of death.

191–215. *Postscript: a list of discoverers and discoveries*

191–215. introd. This section, a catalogue of inventions and discoveries, is in many ways an appendix to P.'s main account of the natural history of man from birth to death. It appears to have been added as an afterthought, 'Before we leave the subject of man's nature' (**191**). The treatment is distinctly cursory; discoverers and discoveries are rarely more than names, packed in with little or no elaboration. Yet the list is by no means totally irrelevant to the *HN*'s portrayal of man in nature, which includes his cultural achievements in art, agriculture, commerce, etc. (see above, Introd. 5.5) and their use of and impact on his natural environment. The catalogue is overwhelmingly Greek in content and inspiration, a compilation arising out of a number of cultural strands. These included (i) the Greek interest in origins, which led to the construction of genealogies tracing back the descent of both individual families and cities, as well as the ascribing of significant inventions and cultural developments to specific gods and heroes. Ritual, cult, and magical practices might be assigned a divine origin (see Faraone (1992), 28–9). (ii) Cultural origins were the subject of increased scrutiny in the 5th century BC, due to the anthropological preoccupations of some of the Sophists, most notably Prodicus of Ceos, whose interest in the origins and progress of human culture led to a lost work, *On the Original State of Man* and the suggestion that such benefactor gods as Dionysus and Demeter (cf. **191**) were originally human beings deified as a result of their cultural gifts to mankind. (iii) Although political origins were a topic of particular concern to the philosophers, the wide-ranging researches of the Peripatetics into every branch of knowledge clearly threw up a correspondingly wide range of material on cultural origins, as P.'s quotations of the first two heads of the school, Aristotle and Theophrastus (cf. Diogenes Laertius 5. 47), on inventions ranging from writing to metalwork, quarrying, fortifications, and painting (**193, 195, 197, 205**) suggest. Theophrastus' successor, Strato (cf. fr. 144–7 Wehrli), is mentioned in the index to *HN* 7 for his polemic against Ephorus' work *On Discoveries* (see below, (vii): cf. Diogenes Laertius 5. 60). (iv) An enhanced emphasis in Hellenistic religion upon gods and heroes as saviours and wonder-workers further highlighted the figure of the divine and semi-divine culture-bringer, as did (v) increased interest in antiquarian and local history which produced more inventors and discoverers from specific towns and cities, in some ways continuing an earlier tradition, found in e.g. Pindar, of featuring local culture-heroes in literature praising particular Greek states. P.'s list frequently names not only the individual inventor but also his native city. (vi) The growing influence of Hellenistic monarchs and ruler-cult also led to more frequent depiction of culture-bringers as kings and royal benefactors. Euhemerus of Messene (early 3rd cent. BC), following Prodicus, made the mythical figures of the Hesiodic *Theogony*, Uranus, Cronos, and Zeus, into a dynasty of mortal kings who were bringers of many different aspects of culture and encouraged other benefactors (*FGH* 63 F 20: see A. Henrichs, 'The Sophists and Hellenistic Religion: Prodicus as the Spiritual Father of the Isis

Aretologies', *HSCP* 88 (1984), 147–9). (vii) Culture-hero material offered scope for the compilations and handbooks which formed one of the interests not only of the Peripatetics but also of 4th-cent. and Hellenistic scholarship generally. The 4th-cent. BC historian Ephorus' lost work *On Discoveries* may have been one such product and was used, at least indirectly, by P., who lists Ephorus as a source for book 7, together with 'Strato's reply to Ephorus' work *On Discoveries*' (*HN* 1, index 7). Another was *On Discoveries* (cf. Clement of Alexandria, *Strom.* 1. 308a) by the 3rd-cent. BC scholar and paradoxographer (above, Introd. 3.3) Philostephanus of Cyrene, quoted by Pliny in (**208**) as an authority for a naval invention and listed in the index to book 7. Handbooks of mythology, often thematically arranged, were another potential repository of such material (cf. Hyginus' *Fabulae*, below). Such collections and compilations played a part in the formation and preservation of a cultural tradition: see Introd. 4.2. Writers of ethnography and universal history were also preoccupied with such matters as the relative antiquity of Egypt, which had already been explored by Herodotus, and the cultural significance of the Phoenicians.

From as early as the 5th cent. BC, the culture-bringer tradition was being parodied by Aristophanes and others. It continued to influence later writings well into the Christian era: brief catalogues appear in works of Tatian, Clement of Alexandria, and Gregory of Nazianzus and references can be found in works as late as the *Variae* of the 6th-cent. AD writer Cassiodorus and the *Origines* of Isidore of Seville.

Although the preoccupation with culture-bringers was mainly Greek, the Roman poet Ennius had by his translation introduced Euhemerus' ideas to a Latin-speaking audience. The late 2nd-cent. BC historian Gnaeus Gellius also seems to have been interested in this aspect of Hellenistic scholarship: his *Annals*, a large-scale history of Rome, are largely lost, but he is cited on three occasions by Pliny for discoveries as diverse as writing (**192**), building in clay (**194**), and medicinal uses of metals (**197**).

A philosophical interest in cultural origins is also discernible in the 1st cent. BC, not only in the famous account of man's general cultural progress in book 5 of Lucretius' poem on Epicurean doctrine, *De Rerum Natura*, but in the ideas of the Stoic polymath Posidonius, as preserved in Seneca's 90th *Moral Letter*. These seem to have included accounts of the invention of most of the techniques P. mentions, including building, metallurgy, mining, agriculture, weaving, ship-building, and pottery-making. Such techniques became common motifs of the ancient accounts of cultural origins, where basic needs for fire, shelter, food, and clothing were moved on a stage by the discovery of metallurgy and the subsequent invention of metal tools to further develop basic skills and evolve new ones (see T. Cole, *Democritus and the Sources of Greek Anthropology* (Cleveland, Philological Monographs 25, 1967), 25–6). Significantly for P.'s inclusion of inventors and inventions in *HN* 7, Posidonius was apparently interested, as the Sophists had been, in inventions both as the result of man's interaction with and imitation of nature and also as a result of man's intellectual superiority, which he stressed to the point of suggesting that philosophers were the inventors of all the basic cultural breakthroughs (Seneca, *Ep. Mor.* 90. 20–6; 31–3).

Besides the Christian examples mentioned earlier, a catalogue of inventions featured in Hyginus' *Fabulae*, an unreliable handbook of mythology probably of the 2nd cent. AD (see H. D. Rose's edition (1934), Henrichs (1984), and id., 'Three Approaches to Greek Mythography', in J. Bremmer (ed.), *Interpretations of Greek Mythology* (London, 1987), 252, 272 n. 47), but the most extensive extant example is P.'s, which draws on a variety of Greek sources, including the Peripatetic tradition, as well as Gellius and Varro. The rationale behind all the attributions made by P. and by other writers is often far from clear; problems with e.g. relative chronology of inventor and invention were apparent even to ancient commentators, cf. Seneca on Posidonius' attribution of the potter's wheel to Anacharsis and the arch to Democritus (*Ep.* 90. 31, 32). Many of P.'s have an etymological (e.g. Arachne, Closter (**195**), Pyrodes (**198**)) or aetiological (e.g. Curetes (**204**), Chalcos (**200**)) basis or rest on early usage as preserved in mythological traditions (e.g. Bellerophon (**202**), Theseus (**202**)), or famous geographical locations (e.g. Athens and silver (**197**)). See A. Kleingünther, 'Protos Heuretes', *Philologus* suppl. 26. 1 (1933); K. Thraede, *Reallexicon für Antike und Christentum*, ed. T. Klauser, v (1962), 'Erfinder', 1191–1278; Cole (1967), 1–24 (heuristic literature in the general context of ancient *Kulturgeschichte*); Henrichs (1984), 139–58; S. Blundell, *The Origins of Civilisation in Greek and Roman Thought* (London, 1986), 165–202; *OCD*[3], culture-bringers, 412.

In later centuries, histories of inventions were to become a recurrent feature of popular literature: see J. Ferguson, *Bibliographical Notes on Histories of Inventions and Books of Secrets*, 2 vols. (London, 1959), a catalogue of various printed editions of such works dating from the 16th to the 19th cents., some written much earlier and some utilizing material from the classical tradition (cf. Ferguson, vol. i, pt. III, 8–9).

191. Mercury ... Father Liber ... Ceres ... Rhadamanthus
For the rationalization of gods as being originally benefactors of mankind, see above, **191–215. introd**.

Mercury   The Roman god was, like the Greek Hermes, connected with circulation and movement (*OCD*[3], Mercurius, 962) and in particular with the buying, selling and transportation of merchandise (*merx*).

Father Liber   The old Italian god of fertility and wine (*OCD*[3], Liber Pater, 854; A. Bruhl, *Liber Pater* (Paris, 1953)) became associated and identified with Greek Dionysus (*OCD*[3], Dionysus, 479–82), some of whose attributes he shared, even in the context of the latter's eastern triumph (Solinus, 52. 5; see below, **diadem ... triumph**).

diadem ... triumph   Dionysus had been associated with eastern travels in the 5th cent. BC (Euripides, *Bacch.* 13–17), but the legend of his triumphs, especially over India, was built up by association with the exploits of Alexander the Great (as Strabo recognized, 15. 1. 9, C688) and later became the prototype for the triumphs of Roman *imperatores* (Diodorus Siculus 4. 5. 2 and see above, **95. Hercules ... Bacchus, 96. triumphal chariot**, and *HN* 8. 4). It was a major theme on Roman imperial sarcophagi (R. Turcan, *Les Sarcophages romains à représentations dionysiaques: Essai de chronologie* (Paris, 1966), 441–72) and formed the centrepiece of the 5th-cent. AD epic *Dionysiaca* by Nonnos: see Bowersock (1994*a*); H. Jeanmaire, *Dionysos: Histoire de la culte de Bacchus* (Paris, 1951), 351–6. The diadem was essentially a band of white cloth tied around the head, which became the mark of Hellenistic kingship on its adoption by Alexander the Great. Legend (e.g. Diodorus Siculus 4. 4. 4) connected the diadem with the headdress—*mitra*—worn by Dionysus and his followers (see E. R. Dodds (ed. and comm.), *Euripides Bacchae*[2] (Oxford, 1960; repr. 1977), 831–3), which was otherwise normally worn only by women and connected by a number of authors with the East (e.g. Herodotus 1. 195, Babylonians; Juvenal 3. 66; Athenaeus 535a, Persia); though the diadem was not necessarily part of Persian (Diodorus 17. 77. 6, see *OCD*³, diadem, 460) or Indian (Strabo 15. 1. 58, C712) royal regalia. See Schuppe, *RE* 15. 2, mitra (1), 2217–20. Dionysus' association with exotic headgear is also seen in the myth of Ariadne, to whom he presented a crown 'made of gold and stones from India' (Diodorus Siculus 16. 4, cf. Tertullian, *De Corona* 7. 4).

Ceres . . . Sicily The Italian goddess of growth, Ceres, was identified with Greek Demeter, who, in gratitude for assistance rendered in her search for her daughter Persephone who had been carried off by Hades, taught the art of agriculture to various communities in Greece (cf. Hyginus 277, 153 Rose); in particular, to Eleusis in Attica, site of the famous Mysteries. Sicily, too, was especially sacred to her and was popular as the setting for the Persephone story in Hellenistic and Roman times, cf. Cicero, *Verr.* 4. 108. For acorns as man's earliest food, see e.g. *HN* 16. 1, cf. 15; Ovid, *Fasti* 4. 401–2.

Because . . . goddess. See above, **Mercury . . . Rhadamanthus**.

She . . . laws. Demeter, with Persephone, was given the title *Thesmophoros*, lawgiver, which was reflected in the title of one of her festivals, the Thesmophoria. It has been suggested that the laws of her title were those of religious rite, rather than political constitution (A. C. Brumfield, *The Attic Festivals of Demeter and their Relation to the Agricultural Year* (New Hampshire, 1985), 70–2); but in any case, her protégé, Triptolemus (*OCD*³, 1553), an Attic prince to whom she taught her rites, and who was also regarded as a lawgiver, eventually became a judge in the Underworld (Plato, *Apol.* 41a); a position also held by the wise and just Rhadamanthus (Pindar, *Ol.* 2. 75), son of Zeus and Europa, together with his brothers, Minos and Aeacus (see *OCD*³, Rhadamanthys, 1311).

192. Assyrians . . . Egypt . . . Syria For appreciation of the antiquity of the civilizations of Egypt and the Near East, see e.g. Herodotus 1. 1; 2. 2–3, 44, 49–54. Assyrian or Akkadian cuneiform script dated back to the mid-3rd millennium BC, when it began to supersede the oldest known script, Sumerian, which dated back to the 4th millennium. By the 2nd millennium, it was used throughout the civilized Near East. See *OCD*[3], Akkadian, 48, cuneiform, 413, Sumerian, 1456; *CAH* I. I[3], 135–8, 145, 226–8. Egyptian hieroglyphs, which dated back to the first dynasty (3100 BC), were morphologically distinct, although a very general influence from the Mesopotamian developments is not impossible: see *CAH* I. 2[3], 43–4, 90; S. E. Thompson, 'Egyptian Language and Writing', in K. A. Bard (ed.), *Encyclopaedia of the Archaeology of Ancient Egypt* (London, 1999), 274–7 and J. Baines, 'Writing: Invention and Early Development', ibid. 882–5; I. Shaw and P. Nicholson, *British Museum Dictionary of Ancient Egypt* (London, 1995), s.v. 'Hieratic', 'Hieroglyphs', 'Demotic'; W. V. Davies, *Egyptian Hieroglyphs* (London, 1987), 21–4; and below, **193. Anticleides–records**.

writing   *Litterae* can mean the alphabet (Cicero, *Part. Or.* 2. 26; Tac. *Ann.* 11. 13) but, as in the present passage, it often denotes prealphabetic scripts such as cuneiform and hieroglyphs, as well as the alphabetic form.

Gellius   Cn. Gellius, an historian of the later 2nd cent. BC, wrote a large-scale history of Rome, the *Annales*: see *OCD*[3], 628; Münzer, *RE* 7, Gellius (4), 998–1000; Wiseman (1979), 20ff.; and above, **191–215. introd.**

Mercury   The Egyptian god Thoth was identified with Greek Hermes and with Mercury by the Romans. He was credited with the introduction of writing to Egypt: see Cicero, *ND* 3. 56 and Rusch, *RE* 6A 1, Thoth, 358.

Cadmus   The legendary son of Agenor and brother of Phoenix, eponymous hero of Phoenicia, who founded Boeotian Thebes. His own origins were often ascribed to Phoenicia, but other traditions mentioned Egypt: see *OCD*[3], Cadmus, 267; Lenschau, *RE* 10. 2, Kadmos (4), 1459–73; R. B. Edwards, *Kadmos the Phoenician: A Study in Greek Legends and the Mycenaean Age* (Amsterdam, 1979), 47–8 and ch. 3. He featured as a culture-hero in various contexts and locations: see below, **195. quarries . . . Phoenicia, 197. Cadmus . . . Mount Pangaeus**, and Edwards 32 for other refs.

brought . . . Phoenicia   Pre-alphabetic scripts (probably influenced by, though not derived from, Near Eastern cuneiform and Egyptian hieroglyphs) existed in Greece: see *OCD*[3], prealphabetic scripts (Greece), 1243. But the various forms of the

Greek alphabet were derived from Phoenician, a language known from the late 2nd millennium BC, in the 8th cent. BC: see *OCD*³, Alphabet, Greek, 66. The Phoenician origin of the alphabet proper was frequently mentioned in the classical sources; see e.g. Herodotus 5. 58; Tac. *Ann.* 11. 14. 1–3 (below, **193. writing . . . Egypt**); Lucan 3. 220.

sixteen See below, **These were . . . Θ**

Palamedes A legendary Greek hero who fought at Troy, Palamedes' name meant, literally, 'handyman'. Together with Prometheus ('Forethought'; see below, **199**), he was one of the most frequently-cited culture-heroes. His contriving cleverness (Aristophanes, *Frogs* 1451) resulted in the attribution of various other inventions (e.g. **198, 202** below and Pausanias 2. 20) as well as alphabet letters (Hyginus, *Fab.* 277, Euripides, *Palam.* fr. 3) to him. See *OCD*³, Palamedes, 1099. According to Tacitus (*Ann.* 11. 14), some traditions attributed the bulk of the alphabet to him, or to Linus (Diodorus Siculus 3. 67, see below, **204. Linus**) or Cecrops, with Simonides (below, **Simonides . . . poet**) mainly responsible for the later additions.

These were . . . Θ Needless to say, there are a number of textual variants for these two groups of letters (see e.g. Schilling app. crit., p. 113 and 237); the corresponding lists in Hyginus 277 are also unreliable (see Rose ad loc.). The translation follows Schilling's text, which offers a plausible reflection of the actual additions and modifications made by the Greeks to the original set of letters they acquired from the Phoenicians. The Phoenician alphabet was consonantal, so the significance of the letters aleph, he, yod, and ayin was altered to express the Greek vowels *A, E, I,* and *O,* to which *Y,* the original form of wau, was added. *H* in the first group is Schilling's emendation of MSS *N*, part of the original group. *H,* too, was a Phoenician letter but from being an aspirate it was modified to long *E* in dialects such as the ultimately predominant East Ionic. Not all Greek states adopted the letter *Ξ* from Phoenician; hence, perhaps, its status as an 'addition' here. *Φ, X,* and *Ψ* were all Greek additions, but *Θ* was taken from the Phoenician and P. may have included it by analogy with these aspirates (G. D. Buck, *Comparative Grammar of Greek and Latin* (Chicago and London, 1933), sect. 66, p. 71). *Ω* originated in East

Ionic (Buck (1933), 19). Hyginus (*Fab.* 277) lists as additions *Ω, E, Ξ, Φ, Ψ*, and *Π*; all but the last fitting in with the pattern of development just outlined. See generally Buck (1933), sects. 64–8, pp. 68–73.

Simonides ... poet   The 6th-cent. poet from Ceos had a reputation for wisdom and was credited with the invention of mnemonics (above, **89. Simonides**) and notes for the lyre (below, **204. Simonides . . . eighth**), as well as alphabet letters. Hyginus attributes *Ω, E, Ξ*, and *Φ* to him: see above, **These were ... Θ**

sounds ... alphabet   Even if the Greek letter was not represented in the Latin alphabet, its sound could be represented by another letter or combination of letters: e.g. *Θ* could be transcribed *th*, *Φ ph* and *X ch*. See Buck (1933), sect. 130, p. 119.

Aristotle ... Epicharmus   The Aristotle passage is not extant (fr. 501 Rose). Epicharmus was an early 5th-cent. BC comic poet from Sicily. A number of factual works were also dubiously attributed to him; see *OCD*[3], 532. Hyginus attributed *Ψ* and *Π* to him: see above, **These were ... Θ**

193. Anticleides   Anticleides of Athens was a 3rd-cent. BC historian, interested in antiquities. His history of Alexander included a long digression on those of Egypt. See *OCD*[3], 104; *FGH* 2.B, 140.

writing ... Egypt   As Pliny, unlike Tac. *Ann.* 11. 14. 1–3, does not distinguish between alphabetical and non-alphabetical writing in his use of *litterae* in **192**, he is probably referring to hieroglyphs, which dated back to c.3100 BC (see above, **Assyrians ... Egypt ... Syria**). According to Tacitus, the Egyptians also claimed the invention of *litterae* as well as hieroglyphs, probably a reference to hieratic and demotic scripts, cursive modifications of hieroglyphs. Demotic did not develop until the 7th cent. BC, but hieratic appeared as early as the first dynasty. See Herodotus 2. 36–9 with How and Wells (1912), i. 182; and citations above, **192. Assyrians ... Egypt ... Syria**.

Menon   The name in the text is uncertain.

Phoroneus   Ancient king of the whole Peloponnese in Argive legend, according to which he discovered fire (Pausanias 2. 19. 5)

and created communities (Pausanias 2. 15. 5); see below, **194.**
Argos . . . Phoroneus; *OCD*³, 1175.

records   P. uses *monumenta*, which can refer to written records.
He probably means inscriptions, cf. Tacitus (*Ann.* 11. 13), who talks
of Egyptian hieroglyphs as 'the oldest *monumenta* . . . impressed on
stone'.

Epigenes   See above, **160. Epigenes . . . Berosus.**

astronomical . . . 490,000 years   In fact, Sumerian went back
to about 3000 BC.

bricks   This refers to the clay tablets on which cuneiform script
was created by making wedge-shaped indentations with a reed.
Many of the cuneiform tablets which have been preserved are
mathematical or astronomical in content.

Berosus   See above, **123, 160. Epigenes . . . Berosus.**

Critodemus   An astrological writer of the Hellenistic period:
Boll, *RE* 9. 2, Kritodamus (1), 1928–30.

Latium . . . Pelasgians   Writing, in the form of the Greek
alphabet, reached Italy via Greek settlers in the 8th cent. BC. The
Etruscans were intermediaries for and a subsequent influence on its
development in a number of areas including Latium; though some
southern areas adopted it directly from the Greeks and all regions
made variations and modifications to suit their particular requirements. See *OCD*³, Alphabets of Italy, 66–7; T. J. Cornell, 'The
Tyranny of the Evidence: A Discussion of the Possible Uses of
Literacy in Etruria and Latium in the Archaic Age', *JRA* suppl. 3
(Ann Arbor, 1991), 17.

Pelasgians   Pelasgians were a legendary people in Homer
whose name came to be applied more generally to pre-Hellenic
peoples of Greece. They featured as settlers in Italy in Hellenizing
accounts of Rome's origins and some traditions may have
identified them with the Arcadians (see J. Bayet, 'Les Origines de
l'arcadisme romaine', *MEFRA* 38 (1920), 63–143), whose legendary
leader Evander was often credited with the introduction of the
alphabet to Italy (e.g. *FGH* 3.C, 809, fr. 23, 810, fr. 6; Livy 1. 7; Tac.
Ann. 11. 14; Hyginus, *Fab.* 277; Dionysius of Halicarnassus 1. 33: see
below, **210. ancient Greek . . . today's Latin**). See *OCD*³, 1131;

D. Briquel, *Les Pélasges en Italie: Recherches sur l'histoire de la légende* (Rome, 1984), 449–54.

194–209. After the introductory examples of divine gifts and the digression on an invention, writing, so ancient that it 'always existed' (**192, 193**), P. begins the main part of his list of inventors and inventions. He starts with the material basics of civilization: the creation of shelters and communities, water supply and basic clothing; tools, metalwork, woodwork, and fire (not in fact mentioned until **198**, despite earlier listings of fire-based crafts); agriculture and political constitutions. These are followed by developments in the arts of war, augury, music, poetry, prose, games, and painting.

194. Euryalus and Hyperbius Legendary architects: see Kroll, *RE* suppl. 5, Euryalos, 56. A Pelasgian called Hyperbius is mentioned with Agrolas as the builder of the Acropolis walls (Pausanias 1. 28. 3). Another, Corinthian, Hyperbius, is mentioned in **198** below.

Gellius See above, **191–215. introd.**, **192. Gellius**, and, for this passage, Peter, *HRR*[2] i. 149, fr.4. Toxius and Caelus are not mentioned elsewhere.

Cecrops . . . Athens Mythical autochthonous king of Athens, whose name was attached to the old royal citadel on the Acropolis. He was credited with other civilizing inventions: see *OCD*[3], Cecrops, 305; Eitrem, *RE* 11. 1, Kekrops, 119–25.

Argos . . . Phoroneus For Phoroneus, see above, **193**. The foundation of Argos, chief city of the eastern Peloponnese, was normally attributed to the son of his daughter Niobe and Zeus, Argos. See *OCD*[3], Argos (1) and (2), 154–5; Wernicke, *RE* 2. 1, Argos (18), 790.

Sicyon Situated west of Corinth, Sicyon's origins remain obscure, the site of its original citadel having been lost. *OCD*[3], 1403–4.

Egyptians . . . Diospolis Diospolis was the name in the Roman period for Thebes, the ancient capital of Pharaonic Egypt, modern Luxor (*OCD*[3], Thebes (2), 1496). It was already famous in the Roman period for its ancient monuments, including the temple of Ammon at Karnak and the pharaohs' tombs.

195. Cinyra son of Agriopas An otherwise unattested individual, whose name is similar but not identical to the long-lived king of Cyprus (above, **154. Cinyras**). He should perhaps be identified with this, or another Cypriot king, since the monopoly of the important Cypriot copper mines (below, **mining . . . Cyprus**) was closely controlled by the native monarchs: see R. J. Forbes, *Studies in Ancient Technology²*, ix (Leiden, 1972), 79.

mining . . . Cyprus See *HN* 34. 2. Mining had its beginnings in the Palaeolithic period, but more sophisticated techniques were the product of the bronze age in Egypt, an early source of gold, and the Near East: see J. F. Healy, *Mining and Metallurgy in the Greek and Roman World* (London, 1978), 70. Cyprus possessed important copper ore deposits (cf. Strabo 14. 6. 5, C684) which were exploited from prehistoric times. Homer refers to Cyprian copper (see H. D. F. Gray, 'Metal-Working in Homer', *JHS* 74 (1954), 1–15), and it was a prolific exporter of the metal *c*.1250–1050 BC. Production continued into the Roman empire. Its late Bronze Age metalwork was famous (*HN* 34. 2). It also had ancient deposits of silver (Strabo 12. 3. 19, C549). See *OCD³*, Cyprus, 420; Forbes ix (1972), 75–80.

wells . . . Danaus . . . Argos Danaus was the eponymous hero of the Danaans, a word used by Homer and others for Greeks. He was brother of Aegyptus, eponymous hero of Egypt, who came to Argos with his fifty daughters (cf. Aeschylus, *Suppliants*), where he or the daughters (Strabo 8. 6. 10, C372) were regarded as the inventors of irrigation. Argos had the epithet *polydipsion*, thirsty, in Homer (*Il.* 4. 171). See *OCD³*, Danaus 428.

quarries . . . Cadmus . . . Thebes . . . Phoenicia For Cadmus, see above, **192**. He was founder of Thebes in Boeotia and had links with both Phoenicia and Egypt. Theophrastus' reference to Phoenicia in such a context is not extant but in *De Lapid.* 1. 6ff, he mentions famous quarries 'at Thebes' which is usually identified with Egyptian Thebes, home to famous limestone quarries and close to sources of sandstone and granite (the 'Egyptian stone' of *HN* 31. 157). It may also have been a distribution point for oriental alabaster: see A. Dworakowska, *Quarries in Ancient Greece* (Wrocław, 1975), 46 and nn. Egyptian quarrying dated back to the 3rd millennium BC. Greece had lost quarrying techniques after the Mycenaean collapse and may have relearned them from Egypt; though because Greek techniques and equipment were more advanced than the contemporary Egyptian equivalents, some scholars now suggest an alternative source of influence, perhaps Asia Minor (see M. Waelkins, P. de Paepa, L. Moens, 'Patterns of Extraction and Production in the White Marble Quarries of the Mediterranean: History, Present Problems and Prospects', in .J. Clayton Fant (ed.), *Ancient Marble Quarrying and Trade: Archaeological Institute of America Colloquium 1987, San Antonio, Texas*, BAR suppl. ser. 483 (Oxford, 1988), pp. 88–9). In either case, an intermediary role might explain Phoenicia's mention here.

Theophrastus   He is cited on several occasions as an authority on inventions (**195, 197, 205**): see above, **191–215 introd**.

Thrason   Otherwise unattested.

towers . . . Cyclopes . . . Theophrastus   The Cyclopes were one-eyed giants, children of Ouranos and Gaia. See above, **9. Cyclopes**. They were credited with constructing various cities' walls, including those of Mycenae (Pausanias 2. 16. 5; Seneca, *Thyestes* 407) and Tiryns (Pausanias 2. 25. 8; Strabo 8. 6. 10–11, C372–3), celebrated for their size by Homer (*Il.* 2. 559): hence the second tradition, ascribed to Theophrastus here.

196. woven fabrics . . . Egyptians   Woven materials were made in the Near East from prehistoric times. Pliny's tradition reflects the fine reputation of Egyptian textiles, especially linen, from early times to the Ptolemaic period and later. Martianus Capella (*Nupt.* 2. 158) attributed the invention of growing flax and weaving linen to Isis, cf. Firmicius Maternus, *De Errore* 16. 1. Ptolemaic Egypt was noted for the breeding of fine-woolled sheep (Diogenes Laertius 6. 41: *OCD*[3], wool, 1626). See *OCD*[3], linen, 683, textile production, 1490; *CAH* i. 1[3], 310, 485; Forbes iv (1964), 27ff.

wool-dyeing . . . Sardis   'Blankets of Sardian red' are mentioned by Athenaeus (*Deipn.* 2. 48). Ovid's story of Arachne (*Met.* 6. 5–145, see below, **Arachne**) made her the daughter of a Lydian dyer from Colophon, skilled in the use of dye from Phocaea, the renowned mercantile city, northernmost of the Greek cities of Asia Minor. This area of Asia Minor was noted for its textiles and fine wool; approximately sixty miles south-west of Sardis was the Greek city of Miletus, whose reputation for the best quality wool was surpassed in the Roman period by Laodicia-Lycus, some sixty miles south-east of Sardis and an important centre for linen manufacture as well. P.'s mention of Sardis here led to an emendation of Hyginus' reference to Lydian wool-dyeing (*Fab.* 274. 17; see Rose, comm. ad loc.; Ajasson de Grandsagne 234).

spindle . . . Closter The name, unattested elsewhere, means 'Spinner'.

thread *Linum* is flax or something made from it, such as linen or sails; but also rope, fishing-line, net, or the yarn or thread itself (see *OLD* s.v. 'linum', 1034). This last is the most appropriate translation here, as the invention of the 'spider' (see below, **Arachne**) in conjunction with *retia*, 'nets', her web.

Arachne Arachne, 'spider', for whose parentage see above, **wool-dyeing . . . Sardis**, challenged Athene to a weaving contest. The goddess, annoyed at being outdone, turned her into a spider (Ovid, *Met.* 6. 5–145), forever doomed to spin her threads into webs. See *OCD*³, Arachne, 135; Wagner, *RE* 2. 1, Arachne (1), 367.

fulling . . . Nicias of Megara Nicias is otherwise unknown. Fulling (removing impurities with water, old urine, and fullers' earth, then rinsing) was a process used both in the manufacture of woollen cloth and in the laundering of clothes in the ancient world: see *OCD*³, textile production, 1490.

shoemaking . . . Tychius of Boeotia Tychios from Hyle in Boeotia was the famous leather-worker who made Ajax's shield of 'sevenfold ox-hide' according to Homer, *Il.*7. 220, cf. Ovid, *Fasti* 3. 824.

The Egyptians . . . Apollo Apart from evidence of neolithic trephining techniques, the earliest evidence of medical practice comes from Egypt and Mesopotamia. Papyri such as the Ebers papyrus (*c.*1570 BC) detail cures both pharmacological and surgical, copied from older sources. Mesopotamian physicians' seals from the 3rd millennium have survived and the Code of Hammurabi dates back to *c.*1950 BC. Egypt was probably more important for medical theory and for its influence on the development of Greek medicine. As for the alternative tradition given here, there is no mention elsewhere of a son of Apollo called Arabus; though Apollo's own connection with healing was well established. Strabo

(1. 2. 34, C42) says Hesiod and Stesichorus mentioned an Arabus, eponym of Arabia, who was son of Hermes and Thronia, daughter of Belus, Babylonian deity and legendary king/founder, cf. above **123. Berosus**, and *OCD*³, Belus, 238. See Tumpel, *RE* 1, Arabios (2), 363; Baumstark, *RE* 2. 1, 'Babylon' (4), 2700. Eastern connections here, together with the name Babylon in Pliny's version, might suggest that his Arabus tradition reflects some Near Eastern, especially Babylonian, influences on Greek medicine. See *OCD*³, medicine 1. 3, 945; J. B. de C. M. Saunders, *The Transitions from Ancient Egyptian to Greek Medicine* (Lawrence, 1963); Singer and Underwood (1962), 1–15; D. Guthrie, *A History of Medicine*² (London, 1958), 17–38.

Chiron   The wise Chiron was an exception among the normally savage, uncivilized centaurs. Tradition made him tutor of heroes such as Achilles and Jason. His skill in pharmacy was attested in Homer: he taught Achilles the remedy he used to treat Patroclus' wound (Homer, *Il.* 11. 822–32) and was the teacher of the healer Machaon, son of Asclepius, and of Asclepius himself (*Il.* 4. 200–19). Cf. Hyginus 274, 141 (Rose). See *OCD*³, centaurs 308–9; D. Phillips, *Greek Medicine* (London, 1973), ch. 1.

197. Aristotle . . . Theophrastus   See above, **191–215. introd.**

Lydian . . . Phrygian   For the evolution of copper metallurgy see Forbes ix (1972), 29–48. Copper and gold were the metals involved in the earliest metallurgy in the mountains of Anatolia and Armenia but by 4000 BC, copper was being smelted and worked in western Asia. Asia Minor became an important metallurgy centre, which is reflected in the mention of Lydian Scythes and Phrygian Delas (both otherwise unknown) here and makes the alternative translation, 'Lydus the Scythian' (cf. Lamer, *RE* 13. 2 Lydos (5), 2209) unlikely. This importance probably gave rise to legends of the Telchines and Dactyli (see below, **Hesiod . . . Dactyli . . . Crete**). Cf. also, **bronze . . . Chalybes**, below. Pausanias (7. 14. 8, 9. 41. 1) mentioned Samians Theodorus (below, **198. Theodorus the Samian**) and Rhoikus, usually dated to the early 6th cent. BC, as inventors of bronze-casting: possibly they refined an art which had been in existence well before this period.

bronze . . . Chalybes   Bronze was the earliest and most widely used alloy (basically copper and tin) in the ancient world (Healy (1978), 208–14, cf. 237–53). The Chalybes were a people on the south-east coast of the Black Sea, also famous in legend as the first workers of iron (cf. Aeschylus, *Prom. Vinct.* 714–15; Strabo 11. 14. 5, C528). There were important mineral deposits in that area, together with evidence of early metal-working around Trapezus. See *OCD*[3], 316–17.

Cyclopes   See above, **9**, and **195. towers . . . Cyclopes . . . Theophrastus**; and below, **Hesiod . . . Dactyli . . . Crete.**

Hesiod . . . Dactyli . . . Crete.   The Dactyli (ancient sources usually derive their name from their manual dexterity) were a legendary daimonic race credited with supernatural/magical powers and renowned as metal-workers. (For magic and metallurgy, see M. Delcourt, *Héphaistos: ou, La Légende de magicien* (Paris, 1959) and, for correspondence between the metallurgist's polymorphic mind and the elements he worked with, M. Détienne and J.-P. Vernant, *Cunning Intelligence in Greek Culture and Society* (Hassocks, 1978), 259–75.) They were one of several such peoples, including the Telchines, Cabiri, Cyclopes, Curetes, and Centaurs, associated with inventions (cf. above, **195**, **197**; below, **198**, **202**, **204**) and in the case of the first three, with metal-working in particular and the divine smith-magician Hephaestus. Some ancient writers placed them near Mount Ida in Crete (e.g. Diodorus Siculus 5. 64. 5) and made them kinsmen of another legendary race of metal-workers, the Telchines (Diodorus Siculus 5. 55. 2, Strabo 10. 3. 3 C464), who came to Crete from Cyprus and thence to Rhodes (Strabo 14. 2. 7, C653–4). Strabo said that the Dactyli were the first workers of iron and worked on Mount Ida *in Phrygia* (10. 3. 72). Forbes (ix (1972), 194–5, cf. 271) suggested that it was the sources' confusion between the Phrygian and Cretan Mount Ida which led to the placing of legendary iron-workers in Crete, where native iron deposits are poor and few; whereas Asia Minor had an ancient and flourishing iron industry in the Phrygian mountains and elsewhere (cf. Pliny, *HN* 36. 28, Strabo 13. 4. 17, C631; and for early iron-working in the Pontic area, home of the mythical Chalybes, see above, **bronze . . . Chalybes**); or the legends of daimonic metal-workers may have travelled west via the islands from Phrygia with the new, magical-seeming skill. Metallic items, possibly votive offerings, have been found in Cretan caves; see Dasen (1993), 196 n. 145. See generally

Dasen 194–200, 203–4; *OCD*³, 745–6; Forbes, ix (1972), 186–287 (on iron); B. Hemberg, 'Die Idaiischen Daktylen', *Eranos*, 50 (1952), 41–52 collects relevant texts on the Dactyli.

Erichthonius A hero-king of Athens, connected with the Acropolis and the institution of various cult practices. See *OCD*³, 555. For his discovery of silver, cf. Hyginus, *Fab.* 274. 4 and below, **silver**.

Aeacus Son of Zeus and the nymph Aegina, he was an ancient hero of the island of Aegina. See *OCD*³, 15. Other sources attributed the discovery of gold to him (Hyginus 274. 4 (Rose); Cassiodorus, *Var.* 4. 34. 3) as does Pliny below. Aegina was famous for her manufacturing from, rather than her deposits of, metals, as Pliny specifically says with regard to its famous bronze-ware (*HN* 34. 9–10). Her silver coinage was famous but the silver was imported, probably from Siphnos.

silver The origins of silver metallurgy were in Asia Minor (Forbes viii (1971), 196) but one of the largest mining areas in Greece was at Laurion in Attica, where the primary product was silver-lead and evidence of exploitation at Thorikos goes back to at least the 3rd millennium BC; see *OCD*³, mines and mining (Greek), 984; Laurium, 822. Hence, perhaps, a tradition placing the discovery of silver in Attica. Erichthonius' manner of birth may have made him a particularly appropriate discoverer of a metal: he was literally 'earth-born' (as are metals, cf. P.'s imagery in *HN* 33. 3), having been conceived by earth from the spilt semen of Hephaestus, divinity of fire and metal-working.

Cadmus . . . Mount Pangaeus Early Greek sources of gold may have included Egypt and possibly the Danube valley, though ancient deposits existed in northern Greece and some of the islands: see Healy (1978), 45, Forbes viii (1971), 161–8. Many of the Greek sites were exhausted by the classical period but in archaic times, the deposits of Macedonia and Thrace were famous, especially at Mount Pangaeus in northern Thrace (cf. Strabo 14. 5, C680, who also mentions Cadmus as discoverer, as does Clement, *Strom.* 1. 16; Xenophon, *Hell.* 5. 2. 17; Herodotus 6. 46, 7. 112, 9. 75). Hyginus 274 (Rose) connects him with copper or bronze. Cadmus' city of Thebes in northern Greece had good access to Thrace. See *OCD*³, Pangaeus, 1105.

Thoas Son of Dionysus and Ariadne and king of Lemnos, an island well situated for the mines of both Macedonia/Thrace and Asia Minor and the Hellespont. See Modrze, *RE* 6A 1 Thoas (2), 297–9.

Aeacus See above, **Aeacus**.

Panchaia An utopian island in the Indian ocean which featured in Euhemerus' (see above, **191–215. introd.**) writings (*FGH* 1. 301ff.). It was supposedly rich in minerals (Diodorus Siculus 5. 46. 4); cf. Hyginus 274. 4 (Rose).

Sol . . . Oceanus Sol, identified with the Greek sun-god Helios (see *OCD*[3], Sol, 1420–1 and Helios, 676–7) was said by Hesiod, *Theog.* 371ff. and 134ff. to be the child, together with the moon and dawn, of the Titan Hyperion and his sister Theia. The usual offspring of the god Oceanus, depicted as a river encircling the world in Homer, were the river gods and Oceanides, but the sun and stars were believed to rise and set in Ocean (Homer, *Od.* 3. 1, 12. 4), which may account for the genealogy here. For the euhemeristic interpretation of Sol as inventor, see Hertze, *RE* 17. 2, Okeanos, 2318.

Gellius see above, **192**.

medicinal uses of metals Graeco-Roman medicine included remedies derived from metals. *Medicina metallica* forms a substantial part of *HN* 34–5, since Pliny supplies details of the medicinal uses of metals and their by-products in his description of metals and metallurgy: e.g. *HN* 34. 100–5, 109–16, 126–7, 131–2, 135–6, 151–5, 166–78, cf. 33. 105–10. For some of these, see above, **64. smell . . . bronze**.

Tin Similarities in colour meant that tin was often classed as lead in antiquity, together with antimony and lead proper; hence P.'s reference here to 'lead' and elsewhere to 'white lead' (cf. Caesar, *BG* 5. 12. 4): see Forbes ix (1972), 166–7.

Cassiterris Herodotus (3. 115) did not know where the Cassiterrides were but knew tin came from the ends of the earth. There were three important European tin fields on the Atlantic coast: in Spain, Brittany, and Cornwall. Diodorus (5. 38. 4, 5. 22. 5) said the Cassiterrides were islands off the Spanish coast. Originally, the term probably referred to the European tin fields generally (see Forbes ix (1972), 146), and various authors then narrowed it down to particular islands involved in the trade (e.g. Hesiod 258; Strabo 3. 2. 9, C147, 3. 5. 11, C175–6; Pomponius Mela 3. 6. 2; [Aristotle] *De Mir. Ausc.* 81). See Forbes's bibliography, ix (1972), 182 nn. 20–1.

Midacritus   Possibly a mistake for Midas, the mythical Phrygian king whose golden touch was supposed to be the origin of the gold dust in the river Pactolus (*OCD*[3], Midas (1), 978). Both Hyginus (*Fab.* 274. 6) and Cassiodorus (*Var.* 3. 31. 4) named Midas as the discoverer of tin and Hardouin (Ajasson De Grandsagne 237) proposed emending P. accordingly: see Gisinger, *RE* suppl. 8, Midacritus, 353–4.

198. Iron-working . . . Cyclopes   See above, **195. towers . . . Theophrastus**.

pottery . . . Coroebus   Production of pottery in Greece was widespread but Attic pottery had emerged as the most accomplished following the Mycenaean collapse and its aftermath, in the Protogeometric period, and from the late 6th cent. reached an artistic high point. See M. Robertson, *The Art of Vase Painting in Classical Athens* (Cambridge, 1992), 1–2. Coroebus is otherwise unknown.

Anacharsis the Scythian   A semi-legendary Scythian prince, sage, and traveller of the 6th cent. BC (Herodotus 4. 76ff.; *OCD*[3], 79). For his role as culture-bringer, see Plato, *Rep.* 10. 600a; for the potter's wheel in particular, see Seneca, *Ep.* 90. 31 (above, **191–215. introd.**). See also below, **209**.

Hyperbius the Corinthian   According to a scholiast on Pindar 13. 27, this attribution was made by Theophrastus in his last work, *peri heurematon*. Corinth had been the leading producer of decorated pottery before she was eclipsed by Athens around 600 BC. An Athenian Hyperbius and a son of Mars of the same name also feature in P.'s catalogue (above, **194**, below, **209**).

Daedalus . . . isinglass.   Daedalus, 'artful', was originally associated with Crete, whence he famously escaped the wrath of king Minos with his son Icarus by flying on waxen wings. All kinds of wonderful objects and edifices were attributed to his handiwork. From the 5th cent., he was associated more with Athens (Plutarch,

Theseus 19) and acquired an Athenian genealogy, becoming the son of Erechtheus' son Metion and a patron of artisans: hence the inventions here, and legends such as Apollodorus 3. 15. 8 which assigned to Daedalus' nephew Talos the invention of the saw, for which his jealous uncle murdered him: see Hyginus 274. 14 (Rose), who calls him Perdix; Diodorus Siculus 4. 76; *OCD*³, Daedalus, 425–6.

Theodorus the Samian The 6th-cent. BC architect, sculptor, and innovator in bronze-casting techniques (Pliny, *HN* 35. 153, 36. 90, cf. above, **197**; Pausanias 8. 14. 8, 9. 41. 1, 10. 38. 6) is credited here with the invention of some of the tools of his trade. See *OCD*³, Theodorus (1), 1501; Lippold, *RE* 5 A 2, Theodoros (195), 1920.

Phaedon of Argos The tradition that this early 7th-cent. king of Argos, whose building up of Argive power culminated in the defeat of Sparta at Hysiae (669/8 BC), established weights and measures in the Peloponnese goes back to Herodotus (6. 127). See *OCD*³, Pheidon, 1157.

Gellius See above, **192**.

Palamedes See above, **192**.

Pyrodes . . . Cilix Pyrodes is otherwise unattested and clearly bears a name ('Fire-form') derived from his discovery. Cilix was a son of the king of Phoenicia, Agenor, and brother of Phoenix and Cadmus (above, **192**): *OCD*³, Agenor, 39; Geisau, *RE* 11. 1, Kilix (1), 390–1. He was founder of the Cilicians. Schilling suggested play on the similarity of Cilix to *silex*, flint.

Prometheus The son of the Titan Iapetus brought fire to men against the will of Zeus, hiding the flame in a fennel rod (Hesiod, *WD* 5; cf. Aeschylus, *Prom. Vinct.* 190ff.). Aeschylus' Prometheus is a culture-bringer in a more general sense (442–525), providing 'all mortal skills and crafts', including religious rituals (such as sacrifice: see below, **209. [Hyperbius . . . ox]**), medicine and minerals; the last mentioned perhaps connected with his association with Hephaestus (see above, **197. Hesiod . . . Dactyli . . . Crete**) as well as with fire. Some sources even attribute to him the creation from clay of the human race itself (refs. in Détienne and Vernant (1978), 83–4 and n. 120). See *OCD*³, 1253–4 and below, **209. [Hyperbius . . . ox]**.

199. Phrygians . . . vehicle   The earlest four-wheeled vehicles were probably Mesopotamian (*c*.3000 BC) rather than Phrygian, but were soon widespread, first in the Danubian cultures and then in Greece and Asia Minor. For the problems of origins and transmission, see S. Piggott, *The Earliest Wheeled Transport: From the Atlantic Coast to the Caspian Sea* (London, 1983), 60–4. They were slightly earlier than two-wheeled carts and also pre-dated chariots, which appeared *c*.1600 BC: see L. Casson, *Travel in the Ancient World* (London, 1974/94), 23.

Carthaginians . . . commerce   Carthage was traditionally a colony (probably 8th cent.) of the sea-trading Phoenicians and in turn became the maritime trading state *par excellence* in the ancient world until her destruction in 146 BC. See *OCD*³, 295–6.

Eumolpus . . . arboriculture   Eumolpus was a son of Poseidon and ruler of Eleusis (where he was ancestor of the priestly Eumolpidae) and instructed in the Mysteries. See *OCD*³, Eumolpus, 568. Here he is given an agrarian culture-bringing role similar to Demeter's (above, **191. Ceres . . . Sicily**) and Triptolemus' (below, **The ox . . . Triptolemus**).

Staphylus . . . water   Once again, the name, 'grape-cluster' is derived from the discovery; see *OCD*³, Staphylus (1), 1438. The mythology surrounding him is confused but links him to wine (as discoverer of the vine, Probus on Virgil, *G*. 1. 9) and Dionysus, sometimes as the latter's son (Plutarch, *Thes*. 20) or as the son of Dionysus' companion, Silenus, as here (cf. Sallust, fr. 87). Hyginus (274. 1 Rose) attributes the invention to Cerasus.

Aristaeus . . . honey.   The Greek demi-god, a son of Apollo, was connected with various parts of Greece and his role as a culture-bringer was predominantly agrarian and pastoral (eg. Pindar, *Pyth*. 9. 59). See *OCD*³, Aristaeus, 158. P. refers to honey, oil-presses and the oil for which Aristaeus was worshipped in Ceos (Apollonius Rhodius 2. 500. 27). His apiculture was the subject of the end of Virgil's fourth Georgic.

The ox . . . Triptolemus   Buzyges, 'yoker of oxen' was an Athenian hero and ancestor of the priestly Buzygae. He was celebrated as a bringer of agriculture and inventor of the plough, the original of which was preserved on the acropolis (Toepffer, *RE* 3. 1,

Buzyges (1), 1095–7) For Triptolemus, see above, **Eumolpus** . . . **arboriculture**; the Athenians said he was taught the arts of agriculture but then in turn set out to transmit them to other nations (cf. Hyginus, *Fab.* 277. 4; Ovid, *Fasti* 4. 507, 550–60; Cic. *Tusc.* 1–98). For the ox as attendant of Demeter and Triptolemus, see Columella 6, pref. 7.

200. Egyptians . . . **monarchy** The Pharaonic system of government was formed in the periods of the first and second dynasties (*c.*3200–2700 BC) and was the oldest monarchic system known to the Greeks.

Athenians . . . **Theseus** The mythical king of Athens was credited with the synoecism and initial political unification of Attica. There was then a long process of development in which the reforms of Draco (7th cent.) and Solon (6th cent.) and the tyranny of Peisistratus and his sons were particularly regarded as landmarks before the actual democratization of the constitution. This occurred well within the historical period, starting with the reforms of Cleisthenes in 508/7 BC. See *OCD*[3]; democracy, Athenian 451–3; Theseus, 1508–9; Cleisthenes (2), 344.

tyrant . . . **Phalaris of Agrigentum** Strictly speaking, a tyranny was a monarchy set up by a usurper and was not necessarily cruel or repressive; its negative connotations were in part due to Plato and Aristotle's condemnation of it as a form of government. Phalaris of Agrigentum (*c.*570–549 BC), the first important tyrant in Sicily, was typical in that he seized power from a ruling aristocracy and ruled with the help of mercenaries. He was, however, notorious for his cruelty and must therefore have contributed to tyranny's poor image. See *OCD*[3], Phalaris of Acragas, 1153.

Spartans . . . **slavery** Slavery of various types was endemic in the ancient world. Sparta may have been singled out, not because she 'invented' slavery but because she was the most singular example of a relatively uncommon system whereby a state enslaved an entire national group communally. Additionally, in Sparta's case, her unique political system was entirely dependent upon the military and economic obligations of her helots who also, unlike chattel slaves, possessed some limited property and family rights and considerably outnumbered their masters. See *OCD*[3], slavery, 1415–17; helots, 680.

capital trial . . . Areopagus   The ancient Athenian council which met on the hill of the same name, north-west of the Acropolis (*OCD*³, 151–2), had some powers of jurisdiction, including homicide cases, from early times. Many of its judicial powers were removed by the reforms of Ephialtes (462/1 BC), but it kept control of murder trials. Aeschylus' *Eumenides* (487–9) gave this function a mythological beginning with the trial of Orestes for his mother Clytaemnestra's murder. Another tradition (Hellanicus, *FGH* 1.A, 4, fr. 169a) traced it back to the trial of Ares himself for murder.

phalangae   Phalangae or *palangae* were heavy logs, poles, or rollers, especially those used for ships (*OLD* 1371). For this primitive battle, see Hyginus, *Fab.* 274. 22 (Rose). According to Herodotus (2. 63), ritual violence using wooden clubs was practised at the Egyptian temple of 'Ares' at Papremis. For ancient rivalry between the Egyptians and their Ethiopian neighbours, see Herodotus 2. 29 ff., reflecting the actuality of clashes between Egyptians and Kushites as early as the first dynasty (3100–2890 BC): see Snowden (1983), 21–6. The Ethiopians were, like the Egyptians, seen as an ancient source of civilization; cf. Herodotus 2. 104, Pliny, *HN* 2. 189, Plutarch, *Mor.* 151b–c: see Snowden 52.

Proetus . . . Acrisius   These mythological twin brothers quarrelled in their mother's womb and on the death of their father, king Abas of Argos, fought for the succession, inventing the shield in the process. Acrisius eventually won Argos, Proetus becoming the first king of Tiryns. See *OCD*³, Acrisius, 9; Proetus 1253.

Chalcus . . . Athamas   Chalcus ('copper', 'bronze', so a personification? cf. the tradition that associated Chalcis with the introduction of the sword and breastplate: P. Cartledge, 'Hoplites and Heroes: Sparta's Contribution to the Technique of Ancient Warfare', *JHS* 97 (1977), 21) is not otherwise attested among the children of the mythical king of Boeotian Orchomenos, Athamas. See *OCD*³, Athamas, 201. The hoplite shield was made from bronze and leather and even the Mycenaean shields of hide may have had some metal reinforcements and accessories such as bosses, at least in the late period: see A. M. Snodgrass, *Arms and Armour of the Greeks* (Ithaca, 1967), 19, 32–3.

Midias . . . breastplate   Midias is otherwise unknown. The traditions of Messenia in the south-west Peloponnese were obscured by Spartan domination and some of the surviving mythology may have been invented on the refounding of the Messenian state in 370/69 BC. See *OCD*³, Messenia, Messenian Cults and Myths, 964–5. However, it may have been links with the Spartan war-machine which gave rise to this particular story: see below, **Spartans . . . spear**.

Spartans . . . spear These items as such were common to most ancient fighting forces from early times, and pre-hoplite Sparta is not known to have had weapons or equipment any different from those of the rest of her Greek contemporaries (see J. F. Lazenby, *The Spartan Army* (Warminster, 1985), 70). Stories of the invention of individual weapons by particular states may have been based on the fact that they produced a particularly effective version of the item in question (see Cartledge (1977), 21). While Sparta is not associated elsewhere with a particular item (cf. the 'Corinthian' helmet; though another type, the Illyrian, may have been a Peloponnesian development; see Snodgrass (1967), 52), P.'s attribution of several to her may be a result of her well-known supremacy in hoplite fighting with its distinctive arms and armour.

Carians . . . plumes The Carians were a non-Greek people who became Hellenized. According to Herodotus 1. 171, they were originally islanders subject to Minos of Crete and well-known fighters in his fleet, who invented helmet plumes, as well as heraldic devices and handles for shields. cf. 2. 152; also Diodorus Siculus 1. 66; Ephorus fr. 12; Strabo 14. 2. 77, C661. Pliny is the only source to mention greaves specifically. It has been suggested (A. M. Snodgrass, 'Carian Armourers: The Growth of a Tradition', *JHS* 84 (1964), 110) that the literary tradition making them inventors of armour was based on their popularizing the items due to their well-documented and widespead mercenary activities.

201. Scythes . . . arrow Eponymous hero of Scythia whom Herodotus makes the youngest son of Heracles, rather than Jupiter, and Echidna, half snake and half woman (Herodotus 4. 10; Kretschmer, *RE* 2 A 1, Scythae, 926). He became Scythia's first king because he alone of the brothers was able to draw his father's bow. The Scythians were renowned as mounted, ambidextrous, archers, cf. Herod. 4. 47. Perses (Wust, *RE* 19. 1, Perses (3), 974) was the son of Perseus, killer of the gorgon Medusa, and Andromeda according to Herodotus 7. 61, cf. 150. He was eponym of the Persians, a race also distinguished by use of the bow and arrow (Herodotus ibid.).

Light spears ... Mars The wild and rugged terrain of Aetolia, in central west Greece encouraged the deployment of lightly armed and mobile troops who made much use of throwing spears, cf. Thucydides 3. 94–8, describing their defeat of the Athenian general Demosthenes in 427/6 BC. Aetolus was the eponymous hero of the Aetolians (*OCD*[3], 32), whose father was normally given as Endymion, king of Elis, Pliny alone naming Mars, god of war.

Tyrrhenus ... Phoenicians Some manuscripts have 'Syrophoenicians' rather than 'Syrians ... Phoenicians'. Reading 'Syrophoenicians', the punctuation of this passage is altered and *eundem* ('the same person') added after *Tyrrhenum* by Mayhoff to give the following: 'the skirmishing spear by Tyrrhenus (the same person invented the javelin), the axe by the Amazon Penthesilea, hunting spears and the Scorpion, one of the missile engines, by Pisaeus, the catapult by the Cretans, the ballista and sling by the Syrophoenicians . . .'. In terms of the attributions of the various weapons, there is little to choose between the two readings (though see below, **javelin ... Penthesilea**). Reasons for re-establishing 'Syrians ... Phoenicians' are given by Schilling 246 (for the textual variants, see his app. crit., p. 116): note in particular that P. elsewhere distinguishes between Syrians and Phoenicians (e.g. **192** above) and between Phoenicia itself and the territory of Syria around it (*HN* 5. 67).

Tyrrhenus There are several variants of Tyrrhenus' genealogy. Some made him the son, others the grandson, of king Atys of Lydia. He settled in Italy, becoming the eponymous ancestor of the Tyrrhenians (the Etruscans); see Herodotus 1. 94ff.; Dion. Hal. *Ant. Rom.* 1. 27. 1; *OCD*[3], Tyrrhenus, 1568. Herodotus 7. 72 described them as carrying javelins hardened by fire in Xerxes' army as it was marshalled for his invasion of Greece.

javelin ... Penthesilea Penthesilea was the daughter of Ares and queen of the Amazons, killed by Achilles at Troy. Amazons, a mythical race of warrior women, inhabiting the Pontic region, were said to have removed their right breasts (hence the derivation of Amazon from Greek *maza*, breast) to facilitate their javelin throwing (e.g. Strabo 11. 5. 1, C504). The basic historicity of the

Amazon legend is suggested by numbers of female warrior graves found in the north Pontic and Steppe regions, in which the weaponry most commonly includes spears and javelins (see Rolle (1989), 86–91). Although early representations show them with Greek-style weapons, Greek vase iconography often portrays them as exotic foreign warriors, light-armed archers in eastern or Scythian style. However, the alternative reading, attributing the axe to Penthesilea (see above, **Tyrrhenus . . . Phoenicians**) is also plausible. Some representations show them carrying battle-axes (J. Boardman, *Athenian Black Figure Vases* (London, 1974), 231–2; *Athenian Red Figure Vases of the Archaic Period* (London, 1975), 233), regarded as a non-Greek weapon used by the Scythians (Snodgrass (1967), 85); or even as a woman's weapon against men (W. Blake Tyrrell, *Amazons: A Study in Athenian Myth-Making* (Baltimore and London, 1984), 49–52, quoting Aeschylus, *Cho.* 889). See *OCD*³, Penthesilea, 1137; Amazons, 69–70.

Pisaeus Pisaeus is mentioned again below as the son of Tyrrhenus (above, **Tyrrhenus**) and inventor of the trumpet, which some (Diodorus Siculus 5. 40; Hyginus, *Fab.* 274. 20; cf. Athenaeus 4. 184a: Radke, *RE* 7A 2, Tyrrhenus (1), 1938–9) ascribed to Tyrrhenus himself.

scorpion . . . catapult . . . ballista These were all items of ancient artillery, mechanical devices powered by springs to hurl bolts or shot. Such weapons are first attested in Greece in 399 BC in the possession of Dionysius I of Syracuse (Diodorus Siculus 14. 41–2). Some historians (e.g. W. W. Tarn, *Hellenistic Military and Naval Developments* (Cambridge, 1930), 102ff.) have suggested that the Assyrians, and then the Phoenicians and Carthaginians, possessed such devices at an earlier date, which would fit in with P.'s statements here. More recently, however, E. W. Marsden (*Greek and Roman Artillery: Historical Development* (Oxford, 1969), 48–55) argued that Dionysius' were in fact the first, relatively unsophisticated, non-torsion artillery devices; and that earlier evidence is either misleading or does not in fact refer to artillery proper.

scorpion The scorpion was a type of arrow-throwing catapult which could vary in size (Livy 26. 47). Archimedes devised one with a particularly powerful blow during the siege of Syracuse (213–211 BC): see above, **125. M. Marcellus . . . ignorance**) and ancient authors generally described it as possessing an exceptionally good range. See Marsden (1969), app. 1.

catapult . . . ballista Catapult was a generic term for any arrow- or bolt-throwing machine. The ballista was the other main type of artillery device, more powerful than the catapult and used mainly for throwing stones. The definitions changed in the later imperial period. See Marsden (1969), 1, 48–64, index s.v. 'ballista'.

bronze trumpet See above, **Pisaeus**.

tortoise . . . Artemon A siege-machine (Caesar, *BG* 5. 42. 5) rather than the shield formation (Caesar, *BG* 5. 9. 7) is meant. Artemon of Clazomenae was a Greek engineer who assisted Pericles in the use of a number of siege-engines at the siege of Samos in 440/39 BC (Plutarch, *Per.* 27, quoting Ephorus; Diodorus Siculus 12. 28. 3: see Toepffer, *RE* 2. 1, Artemon (1), 1446). Some scepticism has been expressed about the story; later sieges were apparently conducted without these machines; though there are other references to such devices in this period (e.g. Aristophanes, *Clouds* 478–90): see A. W. Gomme, *A Historical Commentary on Thucydides*, i: *Introduction and Commentary on Book 1* (Oxford, 1945), 354.

202. the horse . . . Epius Epius, son of Panopeus, was the builder of the famous Trojan horse (Homer, *Od.* 8. 493, cf. Virgil, *Aen.* 2. 264): see *OCD*[3], 527. Hence, probably, the idea (a rationalization?) of a horse siege-engine, otherwise unattested, as the alleged precursor of the ram, the iron-tipped beam used to pound and smash enemy walls (cf. Pausanias 1. 23. 8; Servius, *In Aen.* 2. 15). A relatively simple and early device, it may have been portrayed on Assyrian reliefs (Marsden (1969), 50–4). In the 5th cent. BC it featured, together with siege-towers and flame-throwers, in the Peloponnesian war: Thucydides 3. 51, 4. 110, and 4. 115; cf. Diodorus Siculus 13. 54.

Horse-riding . . . Bellerophon Bellerophon, son of Glaucus, was a Corinthian hero (Homer, *Il.* 6. 152–262). He rode the ultimate horse, the winged Pegasus, as he accomplished various tasks, including killing the Chimaera and fighting the Amazons, and finally tried to fly on him to Olympus. See *OCD*[3], Bellerophon, 237.

reins . . . Pelethronius Pelethronium was an area to the west of Mount Pelion (Virgil, *G.* 3. 115). P. refers to its eponymous hero, king of the Lapiths (Krischan, *RE* 19. 1, Pelethronios, 270–1), to whom Virgil ascribed invention of the reins and equine manoeuvres, cf. Hyginus, *Fab.* 274. 2 (Rose).

fighting . . . Pelion   For centaurs, see above, **196. Chiron**, cf. **35. hippocentaur**. They inhabited the wilder, wooded parts of northern Greece, in particular Thessaly, where Mount Pelion was situated. Thessaly was famous for its horses; hence the connections of the Lapiths, a Thessalian clan, as well as the centaurs, half man and half horse, with the equestrian arts. Rationalization of centaurs as men on horseback came later: see Pease on *ND* 3. 51, 1088; and above, **35. hippocentaur**.

Phrygian   Use of the horse as a draft animal started in the Near East in the late 3rd millennium BC and by the mid-2nd millennium the horse-drawn chariot was in widespread use in the east, Greece, and northern Europe. The tradition here could relate to the skilled chariot-fighting of the Hittites, the pre-classical inhabitants of Asia Minor. See Casson (1974/94), 23–4; 26; Piggott (1992).

Erichthonius   See above, **197**. For his invention of the *quadriga*, see Virgil, *G.*3. 113.

Palamedes   See above, **192**.

Sinon   The Greek spy, posing as a deserter, who deceived the Trojans into bringing the wooden horse within the walls of Troy. See *OCD*[3], 1412. Later, under cover of darkness, Sinon released the Greeks inside the horse after receiving a fire signal from the Greek fleet (Virgil, *Aen.* 2. 57–256); hence his role here as an inventor of signals in war.

Lycaon   Among the complex of legends attached to Lycaon, son of Pelasgus and king of Arcadia, are those of a culture-bringer: see *OCD*[3], Lycaon (3), 894; though Schilling's suggestion, a reference to Lycaon, son of Priam, killed by Achilles after pleading in vain for his life (*Il.* 21. 46ff.), is possible. Indeed, P. or his source may have conflated the two.

Theseus   See above, **200. Athenians . . . Theseus**. He was portrayed by the 5th-cent. Athenian democracy as the embodiment of idealized Attic attributes, including those involving government and statecraft.

203. Car The eponymous hero of Caria, brother of Lydus and Mysus, eponyms of the Lydians and Mysians (Herodotus 1. 171). See Eitrem, *RE* 10. 2, Kar (1), 1924. He does not feature in Cicero's list of early exponents of this art (*Div.* 1. 87–8).

Orpheus The son of Apollo and a muse. His song possessed the supernatural power to charm animals and even rocks and he visited the underworld to bring back his wife, Eurydice. From this, the scope of his expertise gradually widened into a religious, prophetical, and mystical role. See *OCD*[3], Orpheus, 1078; Ziegler, *RE* 17. 1, Orpheus, 1262–3.

Delphus King of Parnassus and eponymous hero of Delphi when Apollo arrived there (Waser, *RE* 4. 2, Delphos, 2700): see Aeschylus, *Eum.* 16. See Fontenrose (1959), 47, 394, 421. Hence his connection here with an art of divination. Divination by sacrifice was practised in Greece, but P. uses the word *aruspicia*, which properly referred to the art of Etruscan diviners, the *haruspices*, who interpreted unusual occurrences and thunderbolts but especially *exta*, entrails. See *OCD*[3], divination, 487–8; haruspices, 668.

Amphiaraus A descendant of the seer Melampus, Amphiaraus was part of the expedition of the Seven against Thebes. According to one tradition, he was killed fighting, but in another version (cf. Pausanias 1. 34) he fled and was swallowed up when a chasm was created in the ground by Jupiter's thunderbolt; a motif apparently connected with his underground oracular associations: see *OCD*[3], Amphiaraus, 75. His oracle at Oropus was consulted by incubation and it is with the institution of oracular dreaming that he is credited by Pausanias (1. 34). While Cicero (*Div.* 1. 88) associates him with the 'interpretation of birds and signs', Pliny is the only source to mention pyromancy, perhaps connected with the thunderbolt legend.

Tiresias The legendary blind seer of Thebes (*OCD*[3], Tiresias, 1530) observed birds by listening to their cries and having their appearance described by his daughter (Sophocles, *Ant.* 1000ff.), who is also depicted aiding his interpretation of pyromantic signs and perhaps entrails in Statius, *Theb.* 10. 667. Her assistance explains Tiresias' description by P. as an expert in the entrails of birds, despite their fineness and intricacy (Cicero, *Div.* 2. 29).

Amphictyon . . . dreams The mythical founder of the amphictyony of Anthela and Delphi had a temple at Anthela near Thermopylae. Oracles may have been received there through incubation. See Wagner, *RE* I. 2, Amphictyon (2), 1904 (*NP* I, 611).

Astronomy . . . Atlas . . . Libya A Titan, son of Iapetus and brother of Prometheus, Atlas held the pillars separating earth and heaven. According to Homer, *Od.* I. 52–4, he knew the depths of the whole sea and was evidently well placed to know the heavens in equal detail. He was father of a number of constellations, especially the Pleiades and, for his invention of astronomy, see Diodorus Siculus 3. 60, 4. 27, cf. Pliny, *HN* 2. 31; Vitruvius 6. 10. 6; Augustine, *CD* 18. 39. Pliny is the only source to mention Libya, a personification of the country Libya (Herodotus 4. 45), rather than Clymene, as his mother. Her genealogy included connections with Egypt and perhaps Babylon (see *OCD*³, Libya, 856); countries whose connections with astronomy (above, **123. astrology,** **Berosus,** and **160. those . . . stars, Epigenes . . . Berosus,** and **Petosiris and Nechepsos**) may have suggested this particular parentage for Atlas. See Wernicke, *RE* 2. 1, Atlas, 2119–33; Bouché-Leclercq (1899), 576 ff. The connection between Libya and astronomy may, however, be more direct: Lucian (*De Astronomia*) credited the 'Ethiopians' with giving this art to the Egyptians.

Egyptians . . . Assyrians For the early contribution of Babylon (often confused with Assyria by ancient writers) and Egypt, see above, **123. astrology** and **Berosus** and **160. those . . . stars, Epigenes . . . Berosus,** and **Petosiris and Nechepsos**.

Anaximander . . . sphere Anaximander of Miletus (d. *c*.547 BC) was a pupil of Thales and wrote the first prose work on the nature of the universe. See *OCD*³, 86. His *sphairos*, mentioned also by Diogenes Laertius II. 112, was perhaps a simple solid model or even a flat chart, portraying the universe as a system of concentric circles: see C. H. Kahn, *Anaximander and the Origins of Greek Cosmology* (New York, 1960, Indianapolis and Cambridge, 1994), 89.

Aeolus . . . winds Aeolus was the name of the ruler of the winds in Homer (*Od.* 10. 1–79). It was also the name of the eponym of the Aeolians, the son of Hellen, and of a son of Poseidon. These individuals were often confused, as here. Diodorus (4. 67) linked them in a single genealogy, cf. Hyg. *Fab.* 125. 6. See *OCD*[3], Aeolus (1), (2), (3), 24.

204. Amphion The son of Zeus and Antiope, Amphion founded, together with his brother Zethus, seven-gated Thebes. He was said to have walked around the site playing his lyre and charmed the stones into a wall (Homer, *Od.* 11. 260; Hesiod fr. 182 M–W). See *OCD*[3], Amphion, 75–6. As well as music generally, Pliny says he invented the lyre itself, the Lydian mode, and singing to the lyre (see below). See Plutarch, *Mor.* 1131f, Pausanias 9. 5. 8.

Pan . . . single oboe Pan, half man and half goat, was the pastoral god of Arcadia and son of Hermes and a nymph. His distinguishing instrument was the shepherd's pipe or syrinx, made of reeds of equal lengths plugged to different depths with wax (the Roman version had stepped reeds: Ovid, *Met.* 1. 711–2). The aulos, or pipe sounded with a reed, was normally played in pairs; here, a single one (*monaulos*, cf. Euphorion, cited by Athenaeus, 4. 184a) is referred to. A single end-blown shepherd's pipe was known from the 4th cent. BC. See *OCD*[3], music (3): instruments, 1005.

Midas . . . transverse flute For Midas, see above, **197. Midacritus**. According to one legend, he was asked to judge a musical contest between Apollo and Pan (or Marsyas, see below) and chose Pan, whereupon Apollo caused him to grow donkey's ears, which he hid under a turban. (The historical king (*OCD*[3], Midas (2), 978) who probably lies behind the legendary figure may have had an hereditary condition causing hair growth on the upper and outer edges of the ear: see A. J. N. W. Prag, 'Reconstructing King Midas: A First Report', *Anat. Stud.* 39 (1989), 159–65 and Prag and Neave (1997), 96–104.) But reeds whispered his secret (uttered by his barber) forever (Ovid, *Met.* 11. 90–193). This connection of Midas with music, reeds, and Pan may account for his particular contribution here to musical history: for the single, side-blown shepherd's flute, *photinga plagiaulon*, see Athenaeus 4. 184a.

Marsyas . . . double oboe. Marsyas was a satyr or silenus who invented the double oboe or appropriated one discarded by Athene. He rashly challenged Apollo with his lyre to a musical contest and, upon losing, was flayed alive by the god. See *OCD*[3], Marsyas (1), 930.

Lydian . . . Phrygian Ethnic names were used early to distinguish different kinds of music, including structural differences of attunement. A late source, Aristides Quintilianus 18. 5–19 (1. 9), gives details of six *harmoniai*, including Lydian, Dorian, and Phrygian. See further, *OCD*³, music (6): melodic structure, 1010.

Amphion See above.

Thamyras or Thamyris boasted that he could outplay the Muses and was deprived of his skill and blinded as a result, cf. Homer, *Il.* 2. 594 ff. See *OCD*³, Thamyras, 1492. Hence, besides his invention of the Dorian mode, the invention of singing without an instrumental accompaniment (see below) is attributed to him.

Marsyas See above, **Marsyas . . . double oboe.**

lyre . . . Amphion For Amphion, see above. The earliest type of lyre found in the Greek world was the box-lyre which featured in Minoan and Mycenaean wall-paintings. The Homeric *phorminx* was of this type. See *OCD*³, music (3. 1), 1004.

Orpheus See above, **203**.

Linus A son of Apollo, Linus was, according to one version of his myth, killed by the god for claiming to play as well as he (Pausanias 9. 29. 6). Others said he was tutor to Heracles and the latter killed him (Apollodorus 2. 63); also that Orpheus was his brother (Apollodorus 2. 4. 9. 1). He was connected with the ancient Linus song. See *OCD*³, Linus, 868.

Terpander . . . seven-stringed lyre For Terpander, see below, **Terpander . . . voice.** By classical times, lyres normally had seven or eight strings.

Simonides . . . eighth For Simonides, see above, **192.**
Simonides . . . poet. Other sources say he discovered the lyre's third note (Callimachus fr. 64; *Suda*).

Timotheus . . . ninth Timotheus of Miletus (*c*.450–360 BC) a famous lyre-player and poet, emerges from the comic poet Pherecrates' fr. 155 as the foremost musical innovator of his time. For his increasing the number of lyre strings, see Cicero, *Leg.* 2. 39. See *OCD*³, Timotheus (1), 1529; Maas, *RE* 6A 2, Timotheus (9), 1333.

Thamyris   See above, **Thamyras**.

Amphion . . . singing   For Amphion, see above. The Homeric bard sang to his own accompaniment on the *phorminx*.

Terpander . . . voice   The art of singing to one's own accompaniment on the lyre—*kithariodia*—was established as an element in competitive festivals. The development of the latter was popularly attributed to Terpander, the first musician who is an attested historical figure. He came to Sparta around 680 BC from Lesbos, a contemporary centre of excellence for citharodes, and was responsible for the canon of set pieces known as citharodic nomoi. A number of other musical innovations, including the *barbiton* and the seven-stringed lyre (see above, **Terpander . . . seven-stringed lyre**) were attributed to him. See *OCD*³, Terpander, 1486.

Ardalus of Troezen   See Plutarch, *Mus.* 5, 1333a for his invention. Others attributed aulodic *nomoi* to Clonas, a contemporary of Terpander. See Hirschfeld, *RE* 2. 1, Ardalos, 611; Wernicke, *RE* 2. 1, Ardalides, 610–11.

Curetes . . . armour   The Curetes, Cretan divine warriors, the male equivalent of nymphs, were given charge of the infant Zeus in their cave on Mount Dicte to protect him from being eaten by his father, Cronos. See *OCD*³, Curetes, 413–14. To drown his cries, or to frighten off Cronos, they danced, clashing their spears against their shields (Diodorus Siculus 5. 70; Dionysius of Halicarnassus 7. 72. 7, Strabo 10. 3. 11, C480), thus inventing the armed dance. Such dances existed from early times in Crete, Greece, and Asia Minor (cf. the similar story told of the Phrygian Dactyli), but the Curetes' was supposed to be the oldest and the origins of armed dances elsewhere were consequently attributed to Crete. The nature of the Curetes legend and other early associations of such dances suggests that their origins lay in fertility ritual rather than military connections: see S. Lonsdale, *Dance and Ritual Play in Greek Religion* (Baltimore and London, 1993), 137–68; L. B. Lawler, *The Dance in Ancient Greece* (Middletown, 1964), 106–8; and below, **Pyrrhus . . . Pyrrhic dance**.

Pyrrhus . . . Pyrrhic dance   A Greek armed dance, which in historical times played a part in military training, especially at Sparta. For its supposed Cretan origin (Plato, *Laws* 815a; Strabo

10. 3. 11, C480; Solinus 11. 5), see above, **Curetes . . . armour**. It was often attributed to an eponymous Pyrrhus or Pyrrhicus or to various other founders (see Warnecke, *RE* 4A 2, Tanzkunst, 2237); though Aristotle derived its name from *pur*, fire (fr. 519 R), connecting it with Pyrrhus' father, Achilles', obsequies before Patroclus' funeral pyre. While clearly military in character by Plato's time, its early origins may have been more complex: see Lonsdale (1993), 168, and above, **Curetes . . . armour**.

205. epic . . . oracle Greek oracles in surviving literature are in hexameter verse, which was also the format for epic poetry. The oracle of Apollo at Delphi, whose origins dated back to 800 BC, was the most important of the Greek oracles and its antiquity suggests the possibility of some truth in P.'s claim: see J. Fontenrose, *The Delphic Oracle* (Berkeley and London, 1978), 186. The divine responses were given by the Pythia but were then modified in some way by the *prophetai*, or interpreters. Exactly how is unclear, but Strabo (9. 3. 4–5, C419) says that some prophecies were in verse but others were not and these latter had to be put into verse by the *prophetai*. By Plutarch's day, all responses were in prose (*Mor.* 396c, 392d). See *OCD*³, Delphic oracle 445; Parke and Wormell (1956), vol. ii, pp. xxix–xxx; H. W. Parke, *Greek Oracles* (London, 1967), 84–5; R. Flacelière, *Greek Oracles* (London, 1976), 51–2.

debate There was much disagreement from the 5th cent. BC as to whether Homer or Hesiod was the oldest Greek poet (cf. Herodotus 2. 53; Aulus Gellius, *NA* 3. 11). Homer's claim came to predominate and modern scholarship gives the Homeric epics dates of *c.*750 and 725 BC, while Hesiod probably wrote around 700 BC.

before the Trojan war The Homeric epics relate the events of the Trojan war and its aftermath which happened about 450 years before their likely date of composition. P. is no doubt referring to the fact that the epics depicted bards as an established part of the social milieu of the war period, from which it would be reasonable to assume that they had existed before that time.

Pherecydes See above, **172. Pherecydes . . . body.**

Cadmus of Miletus Cf. *HN* 5. 112. Cadmus of Miletus, son of Pandion, was supposed to have written works on the foundation of

Miletus and Ionia, but his historicity is suspect and there may be some confusion with the mythical Phoenician of the same name (see above, **192**, **195. quarries . . . Phoenicia**, and **197. Cadmus . . . Mount Pangaeus**). See Jacoby, *RE* 10. 2, Kadmos (6), 1474–5 and Edwards (1979), 83 n. 77.

Lycaon . . . Arcadia For Lycaon, see above, **202**. According to Pausanias (8. 2. 1–7, cf. 8. 38. 5), he instituted the festival known as the Lycaea in honour of Zeus (cf. Pindar, *Ol.* 9. 97) which took place on Mt. Lycaea, near the temple of the god.

Acastus . . . Iolcus Acastus, one of the Argonauts, organized funeral games in honour of his father Pelias, king of Iolcus, killed when Medea tricked his daughters into believing that he would be regenerated if he were chopped up and boiled. The games were a popular subject in vase painting and archaic epic. Acastus, together with Theseus and Hercules (below, **Theseus . . . Isthmus** and **Hercules . . . Olympia**) featured as part of a more extensive list of games founders in Hyginus 273 (Rose). See *OCD³*, Acastus, 3; Scherling, *RE* 19, Pelias, 317–26.

Theseus . . . Isthmus The Isthmian games were held near Corinth in honour of Poseidon and from 582 BC were a Panhellenic festival held biennially and organized by Corinth. According to Athenian legend, they were founded by Theseus (see above, **200. Athenians . . . Theseus**) after he killed the robber Sinis, a son of Poseidon, who attacked travellers at the Isthmus (Bacchylides 18. 19–22). See *OCD³*, Isthmian games, 772.

Hercules . . . Olympia According to one tradition (Pindar, *Ol.* 10. 24–77, cf. *Ol.* 2, 5), the Olympic games, the most important in Greece, held every four years from 776 BC in the precinct of Zeus at Olympia, were founded by Heracles. See *OCD³*, Olympian Games, 1066.

Pythian god *Pythius* is Schilling's emendation, on the grounds that it was the cult name of Apollo, credited with founding the Pythian games which included athletic contests (cf. Ovid, *Met.* 1. 446–7; Hyginus, *Fab.* 140. 5). An older reading is *Pythus*, explained by Ziegler (Ziegler and Schneider, *RE* 24, Pythus, 618) as a corruption of Pythagoras, who is named in *HN* 23. 121 as the inventor of a special diet for athletes. Mayhoff's emendation was *Pittheus* (cf.

König and Winkler, 240) though this legendary king of Troezen (*OCD*³, Pittheus, 1187) is not linked elsewhere with games. In favour of *Pythius*, the Pythian games were the most important after the Olympic games and a reference next to the Olympic and Isthmian games would be appropriate (cf. *OCD*³, Pythian Games, 1285).

ball game . . . Gyges For Gyges, see above, **151**; and cf. also **126. King Candaules . . . Magnesians**. In fact, the ball game was at least as old as Homer. Other sources attribute its invention to the Spartans, where it formed part of athletic training. Athenaeus (1. 14, 1. 15c) quotes a Spartan treatise on the subject. See *OCD*³, ball games, 232.

Egyptians . . . painting Modern archaeology has dated cave paintings to as early as 25,000–17,000 BC (the Chauvet cave in the Ardèche valley, discovered in 1994). However, the ancients did not possess reliable means of assessing the relative antiquity of ancient art and artefacts. Egyptian painting, the basics of which can be seen even in the pre-dynastic period (before 3200 BC) was the product of a civilization whose claim to extreme antiquity was familiar to them (refs. above, **192. Assyrians . . . Egypt**). Ancient painting was believed to have existed in other areas as well, however, and in his main history of painting in *HN* 35, Pliny leaves the question open. He is sceptical of Egypt's claim to have introduced painting to Greece (*HN* 35. 15), though he names an Egyptian as well as a Corinthian as possible inventors of line-drawing. Overall, he places the origins of painting in Corinth or Sicyon. Painted temple walls from *c*.690–650 BC have been found at Corinth, while her neighbour Sicyon's painting and sculpture were highly regarded by the Classical period. Much of Pliny's information on art comes from a Sicyonian, Xenocrates. P. was also aware of the antiquity of Etruscan tomb painting (*HN* 35. 17–18). The art of painting had in fact been known in Greece in Mycenaean times but was lost until the early Archaic period after the fall of palace culture, *c*.1200 BC. Hence Pliny's belief that 'painting did not exist at the time of the Trojan war' (*HN* 35. 18). More sophisticated techniques, such as light and shade, perspective, etc. do seem to have been Greek developments. See generally Jex-Blake and Sellers (1896), 84–7; Croisille (1985), 139–40 with bibliography.

Aristotle . . . Daedalus Euchir 'skilled hand', son of Daedalus, is clearly a personification, cf. a Euchir of Corinth, named together with Eugrammus, 'skilled drawer' and dated to the 7th cent. BC (*HN* 35. 152), i.e. the time of the late Archaic rediscovery of painting (see above, **Egyptians . . . painting**).

Theophrastus . . . Polygnotus   Although regarded as a primitive because he did not use shading, Polygnotus of Thasos was acknowledged by ancient critics to be the first great painter. He did much of his work in or near Athens soon after 480 BC and was particularly famous for his variable groundline to denote depth (cf. *HN* 35. 58) and the expressiveness and grandeur (*ethos*) of his figures. See *OCD*³, Polygnotus, 1212–13; Robertson (1975), i. 242–70; R. M. Cook, *Greek Art: Its Development, Character and Influence* (London, 1972), 62–3. For Theophrastus, see above, **191–215. introd**.

206. Danaus   See above, **195. wells . . . Danaus . . . Argos**, and below, **boat . . . Red Sea** for his voyage. For his connection with ships, see Hyginus 277. 5.

boat . . . Red Sea   Erythras (Tumpel, *RE* 6. 1 Erythras (4), 592) was the eponymous legendary king of the Persian Gulf (cf. *HN* 6. 107, 153). The term Erythraean Sea could refer to all eastern waters but especially the present-day Red Sea and Persian Gulf (see above, **97. the Red Sea**). Strabo, quoting Agatharchides (16. 4. 20, C779; cf. Agatharchides fr. 101, Muller, *GGM* i. 189), mentions two versions of the Erythras legend. According to one, he was a Persian who built a raft and crossed to an offshore island in pursuit of some cattle, later returning with others to colonize this and other islands. According to the other version, he was a son of Perseus and ruled the region. Strabo also describes (16. 4. 18, C777) how the Nabataeans, living on the coast and the islands of the Red Sea, used rafts to plunder Egyptian shipping, and (16. 4. 19, C778) how the Sabaeans would sail across to Ethiopia in 'skin boats' (*dermatinois ploiois*) on trading expeditions. Although there is no direct evidence for boats other than log-boats before the Bronze Age, simple rafts and boats of hide and reed bundles could theoretically have been used from much earlier: see S. McGrail, *Boats of the World* (Oxford, 2002), 10–12; L. Casson, *Ships and Seamanship in the Ancient World*² (Baltimore and London, 1995), 3–10. While the earliest activity would have been on inland waters, Pliny's reference to Danaus' (above, **Danaus**) voyage from Egypt to Greece suggests he is thinking of early maritime activity. As far as the Red Sea/Persian Gulf area is concerned, there is evidence for small Babylonian trading vessels using the Persian Gulf in the 3rd millennium BC. There is evidence of boats or rafts of hide or reed at least a millennium earlier, some of which could have been used in coastal voyages (Casson (1995), 23–4; McGrail (2002), 54–8). The date and extent of early maritime activity on the part of Egypt, Danaus' country of departure, is disputed. Reed boats had probably been employed on the Nile from earliest times, but in the 3rd millennium, commercial voyages to Lebanon, Cyprus, and Asia Minor and then military expeditions to the eastern Mediterranean seem to have taken place (Casson (1995), 20–1; McGrail (2002), 16–17; S. Wachsmann, *Seagoing Ships and Seamanship in the Bronze-Age Levant* (Texas, 1998), 9–38). Evidence for very early maritime activity in his country of destination, Greece, and the Aegean is clearer. The many islands and harbours aided navigation. Melian obsidian dating from the 10th millennium found in southern Greece points to early overseas trade. A number of islands were settled by the late Neolithic period, with those on Cyprus and Crete probably dating to as early as the 9th and early 7th millennia respectively. See Casson (1995), 30–9; Wachsmann (1998), 69–82; McGrail (2002), 97–100.

Mysians . . . Trojans . . . Hellespont . . . Thracians   The narrow strait of the Hellespont separating Europe and Asia had obvious attractions as a quick sea-route, despite its strong current, and traffic to and fro, both mercantile and military, enhanced the prosperity of the cities on either side. For evidence of early shipping in the eastern Mediterranean, see above, **boat . . . Red Sea**.

Even today   For the antiquity of simple reed and hide boats, see above, **boat . . . Red Sea**. The two types are also paired by Lucan (*Phars.* 4. 130–6), again with the implication that they are survivors from an earlier era. The use of both types of craft has continued from Pliny's time until the present day: see below, **British Ocean . . . coracles** and **Nile . . . reeds**.

British Ocean . . . coracles   Caesar had seen coracles in Britain (*BC* 1. 54) and Solinus describes coracles used by the Irish in a similar manner (22. 7), cf. Dio 48. 18. 19, *HN* 4. 104, 34. 156. Hide boats were also used, both inland and at sea, elsewhere in Atlantic Europe (e.g. Strabo 3. 3. 7, C155) and in many other parts of the world. Representations of hide boats in Mesopotamia date from the 5th millennium BC, and at Babylon Herodotus (1. 194) saw round boats made of hides stretched over withies which had come from Assyria down the Euphrates. See M. C. de Graeve, *The Ships of the Ancient Near East c.2000–500BC* (Leuven, 1981), 85–9. Lucan mentions them in the Po valley (*Phars.* 4. 131–2). For Strabo's account of hide craft in the Red Sea, see above, **boats . . . Red Sea**. They have been used, in various periods, in places as far afield as China, the Americas, and the Nile delta (Wachsmann (1998), 9 n. 2). In modern times they could still be seen in Mesopotamia, India, and Tibet, and they are in use today off the west coast of Ireland and on some rivers in Wales. See Casson (1995), 5–7 and nn; McGrail (2002), 67–8, 181–3.

Nile . . . reeds   In *HN* 13. 72, Pliny mentions such boats built from papyrus reeds, the inner fibres of the plant being used to weave matting and sails. Papyrus boats were among the earliest vessels and dated back to the 4th millennium BC, appearing in paintings from early Dynastic times. Reed vessels were also used by the civilizations of Mesopotamia. See Casson (1995), 11–13; McGrail (2002), 17–22; de Graeve (1981), 89–93. As with hide boats, their use has been widespread and long-lasting, both at sea and on inland waters. The tradition lasted into the 20th cent. on the Nile itself (Wachsmann (1998), 9) and in India (McGrail (2002), 263). It continues in parts of the Americas, such as Lake Titicaca in Peru, and in Morocco, the Lake Tana region of Ethiopia, and the area of Lake Chad. For modern reconstructions and associated problems, see T. Heyerdahl, *The Ra Expeditions* (Harmondsworth, 1970), 1–153 and *The Tigris Expedition* (Harmondsworth, 1980), 11–74.

207. Philostephanus   A 3rd-cent. BC scholar, friend or pupil of Callimachus, from Cyrene, who wrote geographical and antiquarian works in which wonders were prominent; also a *peri heurematon* (cf. Clement, *Strom.* 1. 308–1): see above, **191–215. introd**. See *OCD*[3], Philostephanus, 1171.

Jason . . . warship   A reference to the legendary ship *Argo* in which the Argonauts, led by Jason, sailed to the east to find the Golden Fleece. See especially Apollonius Rhodius' *Argonautica*. See *OCD*[3], Jason (1), 793. Oared longships are represented in art from the 3rd millennium BC. They were originally used for transporting armed men, as in the Homeric poems, rather than as combat vessels. From the 9th cent., Athenian vases show oared longboats, many probably representing triakonters (single rows of fifteen rowers aside) and pentekonters (25 men aside). Ships with decks and a second bank of oars begin to appear by the 8th cent. (see below, **bireme**). See Casson (1995), 43–52, 61–3; J. S. Morrison, J. F. Coates, N. B. Rankov, *The Athenian Trireme*² (2000), 25–30; McGrail (2002), 127–8.

Hegesias Hegesias of Magnesia was a historian and orator who wrote a history of Alexander. See *OCD*³, Hegesias (2), 674.

Parhalus An Attic hero and son of Poseidon, Parhalus was probably the eponym of the Athenian state trireme *Paralus* (cf. *HN* 35. 101). See H. T. Wallinga, *Ships and Sea-Power before the Great Persian War* (Brill, 1993), 18–19; Lenschau, *RE* 18. 3, Paralos (3), 1208–9.

Ctesias See above, **23, 28**.

Samiramis A warrior queen, based on the historical figure, Sammu-ramat, who was wife of Shamshi-Adad of Assyria and campaigned with her son against Commagene in 805 BC. Greek legend made her the daughter of the Syrian goddess Derketo and wife of Ninos, king of Nineveh, and assigned various conquests to her. For her fleet, see Diodorus Siculus 2. 16–17. See *OCD*³, Semiramis, 1383.

Archemachus A 3rd-cent. BC historian who wrote a history of his native Euboea. See Schwartz, *RE* 2. 1, Archemachus (4), 455.

Aegaeon Aegaeon was a hundred-armed monster who had a cult at Carystus on the east side of Euboea and was one of the eponyms of the Aegean sea (another was Theseus' father, Aegeus). See Tumpel, *RE* 1. 1, Aigaion (1), 945.

Damastes See above, **154. Damastes . . . 350 years**.

bireme *Dieres*, the Greek equivalent of Latin *bireme*, does not appear until the 2nd cent. AD (Pollux 1. 82 Bethe). Before that, a ship pulled by two banks of oars might be referred to as *dikrotos naus*, or with reference to the number of its oarsmen e.g. triaconter and pentekonter (Morrison, Coates, Rankov (2000), 28). Representations of fighting vessels with oars at two levels appear from the 8th cent. BC, and Homer's description of the Boeotian ships with '120 men' might suggest a similar system (*Il.* 2. 509–10). The fully-developed bireme, with its two banks of oars was probably the work of the Phoenicians and appears on Assyrian reliefs of the evacuation of Tyre in 701 BC (Casson (1995), 56–9). The ships known as pentekonters were normally two-banked according to Casson (1995: 59), while Wallinga (1993: 46–51) argues that the term came to refer exclusively to the two-banked vessels which were the standard Greek warships before the introduction of the trireme. Doubling the oar banks could lead to a decrease in length and increase in speed and agility, considerable advantages for a combat ship involved in the new ramming tactics: see Casson (1995), 56; Morrison, Coates, Rankov (2000), 28–32.

Erythraeans Erythrae was an Ionian coastal city of Asia Minor, opposite the island of Chios. See *OCD*[3], Erythrae, 557.

Thucydides The Athenian historian (*c*.460–400 BC), author of an eight-book history of the Peloponnesian war, in which he served for a time as general. See *OCD*[3], Thucydides (2), 1516–21.

trireme . . . Corinth Cf. Thucydides 1. 13. 3. Thucydides' 'Archaeology', chapters 1–20 of the *History of the Peloponnesian War*, emphasizes the importance of sea-power as the backdrop to the struggle and stresses the antiquity of Corinthian sea-power. Thucydides says that the first triremes to be built in Greece (for the question of the vessel's invention, see below, same note) were built in Corinth, whose position on the Isthmus well suited her for a leading maritime role and ensured her mercantile prosperity. Ameinocles is named by Thucydides as an early Corinthian shipwright who built four ships for Samos in the last quarter of the 8th cent. BC, suggesting that Corinth was the leading *polis* in terms of technical expertise and the development of the state navy (Wallinga (1993), 13–32). The trireme was the standard classical warship from the 5th cent. BC to the 4th cent. AD. Its oarsmen were arranged in groups of three, one above the other, producing three banks of oarsmen using oars of equal length. Speed and manoeuvrability were its qualities, especially in the hands of skilled practitioners like the fifth-century BC Athenians, the object being to disable and sink enemy ships using the bronze ram on the prow of the ship. The actual invention of the trireme is a matter of considerable debate among scholars. The view (e.g. Casson (1995), 81) that it was primarily a Greek invention, probably Corinthian, is based mainly on Thucydides 1. 13 (discussed above). Thucydides, however, talks of triremes having been built 'first at Corinth in Greece', perhaps implying that they were built outside Greece as well. Clement of Alexandria, possibly quoting Philostephanus (above, **207. Philostephanus**), said that the Sidonians invented a *trikrotos naus* (*Strom.* 1. 16. 76), and some have suggested that a prototype of a ship with three banks of oars appears on the Nineveh relief. This depicts the evacuation fleet of king Luli of Sidon in 701 BC (J. S. Morrison in R. Gardiner and J. S. Morrison (eds.), *The Age of the Galley* (London, 1995), 54–7; Morrison, Coates, Rankov (2000), 32–6). The ships built for the Samians by Ameinocles according to Thucydides appear in the context to be triremes. The question of priority, however, is problematic. Ameinocles' ships are dated to 'three hundred years' from the end of the war; either 721 BC if the Peace of Nikias is meant, or 704 BC if Thucydides is referring to the surrender of Athens in 404 BC. Greek iconographic evidence for, and specific literary references to, the trireme, however, do not appear until the 6th cent. BC. Thucydides' chronology has been questioned and the date for the ships put forward towards the middle of the 7th cent. BC (e.g. J. B. Salmon, *Wealthy Corinth* (London, 1984), 218). Questions of priority aside, it may well be that two leading sea-powers were each independently working on their own design of three-banked warship as early as the end of the 8th cent. (Morrison, Coates, Rankov (2000), 38). Such early developments were rejected by J. A. Davidson ('The First Triremes', *CQ* 41 (1947), 20–2) and, more recently, by Wallinga (1993: 106–8), who has suggested that, amongst other things, the trireme's size and the financial demands of naval warfare made it an unlikely innovation of the archaic Greek *polis* and argued that the initial move was the creation of three-banked ships by the bigger powers of the east, particularly Egypt and (in the face of politico-military pressures) Phoenician Carthage, in the later 6th cent., before the Greek adoption of the trireme. A gap between their initial development and the widespread deployment of triremes by Greek navies has been advocated by A. J. Papalas ('The Development of the Greek Trireme', *Mariner's Mirror*, 83 (1997), 259–71) on the grounds of insufficient tactical development before the last quarter of the 6th cent. BC.

208. Aristotle   See Introd. 4.2, 5.21.

quadrireme . . . forty   Warships larger than a trireme were largely a product of the Hellenistic era, in particular the power-struggle between Dionysius I of Syracuse and Carthage, and that which ensued among Alexander's successors. The manner in which such large ships were oared is problematic. Extra banks of rowers each with a single oar would be impossible beyond five or six banks. The theory that there were multiple rowers to oars arranged in a single bank would not work beyond sweeps of about eight rowers per oar. For boats of up to 'sixteen', Casson proposed a combination of the two theories, e.g. a 'nine' with two banks of oars and five men to each upper and four men to each lower oar (100–6) and for those up to the massive 'forty', a catamaran-type construction in addition (107–16). The reasons for the gradual supercession of the trireme by ships of larger denominations is unclear. A dearth of skilled rowers has been suggested (e.g. Morrison, Coates, Rankov (2000), 48). Higher denomination ships probably had more than one man to an oar, but only one skilled rower would have been necessary per oar. Tactical foundations of naval warfare also began to change, but how far this was in response to the problem outlined is uncertain.

quadrireme . . . Carthaginians   The quadrireme was attested in the Athenian and Sidonian navies and that of Alexander (see Casson (1995), 97nn. for references) by the latter part of the 4th cent., but already by 399 BC was being built by Dionysius I of Syracuse (Diodorus Siculus 14. 42. 2). Dionysius was involved in a power struggle with the Phoenician colony of Carthage, eager for Sicilian grain, and the tradition that Carthage originated the quadrireme, found also in Clement, *Strom.* 1. 75. 10, is plausible given the maritime competition of the two powers. They were swift and some may have had fewer oars than a trireme, with two men to an oar (see Casson 101 and n.).

Mnesigiton . . . quinquereme   The quinquereme was attested in Greek navies from the later 4th cent. BC (below, **Salaminians**). It was possibly equipped with three banks of oars, with two rowers per oar on the upper banks and one on the lower. It was the main warship of the Roman republican navy from the time of the Punic wars: see Casson (1995), 101–2, 105, and index; *OCD*[3], 1290.

Mnesigiton was a Hellenistic scholar and grammarian (Bux, *RE* 15. 2, Mnesigiton, 2275).

Salaminians Most probably a reference to the city of Salamis in Cyprus. The city had wielded considerable sea-power under its king, Evagoras, from 411 to 374/3 BC (see *OCD*³, Evagoras, 578). Later, when Alexander moved against Phoenician cities after Issos (333 BC), quinqueremes were among the ships of the Cypriot kings who joined him, as well as in the Tyrian fleet he fought (Diod. 16. 44. 6; Arrian 2. 21. 9, 22. 2). However, Diodorus Siculus (14. 41. 3, 42. 2, 44. 7) attributes the invention of the quinquereme to Dionysius I (see above, **quadrireme ... Carthaginians**), as part of the naval rivalry with Carthage, which also resulted in the 'six' (below, **Syracusans**).

Xenagoras A 2nd-cent. BC historian and geographer who wrote a chronology and a work on islands. See *OCD*³, 1628.

Syracusans ... six rows A Syracusan origin is corroborated by Aelian, *VH* 6. 12, who refers to the possession of such ships by Dionysius II (367–344 BC), son of Dionysius I of Syracuse.

Mnesigiton See above, **Mnesegiton ... quinquereme.**

Alexander ... ten Alexander was said to have been planning a great fleet of ships 'bigger than triremes' to fight Carthage, but died before his plans came to fruition (Diod. 18. 4. 4). Diodorus (19. 62. 8) instead assigns the 'ten' (and indeed the 'seven'), to the period during which Alexander's successors fought for supremacy, attributing them to the navy of Antigonus 'the One-eyed' (*c.*382–301 BC): his fleet, in 315 BC, consisted of some 240 ships of which ten were quinqueremes, three were 'nines', and ten were 'tens'. The 'ten' may have been abandoned early: see Casson (1995), 140; ch. 6, app. 2.

Philostephanus Above, **207. Philostephanus**.

Ptolemy Soter Ptolemy (I) Soter (367/6–282 BC), friend and general of Alexander the Great, eventually gained control of Egypt in the power struggles after Alexander's death, taking the title of king in 305 BC. See *OCD*³, Ptolemy I Soter, 1271–2.

twelve Other sources concentrate on Ptolemy's rival, Demetrius Poliorcetes (see below), as the originator of the polyremes of this period; though not specifically for the 'twelve'. For this Hellenistic arms race, see Casson (1995), 137–40 and below, **fifteen**. A 'thirteen' is attested in Demetrius' possession in 301 BC (Plut. *Dem.* 31. 1) and Theophrastus mentions the wood cut for his 'eleven' (*Hist. Plant.* 5. 8. 1).

Demetrius son of Antigonus Demetrius Poliorcetes of Macedon (336–283 BC) was the son of Antigonus I 'the One-eyed' (above) and took part with his father in the power-struggles which followed Alexander the Great's death. See above, **126**. **Demetrius . . . fortifications**; *OCD³*, Demetrius (4), 448–9.

fifteen For Demetrius' 'fifteen' and the 'sixteen', his biggest yet and launched in 288 BC, see Plutarch, *Dem.* 43. 4–5. Ptolemy I (above) may have got both after Demetrius' fall: see Casson (1995), 139.

Ptolemy Philadelphus Ptolemy II Philadelphus (308–246 BC), son of Ptolemy I Soter succeeded his father to the throne of Egypt in 282 BC. See *OCD³*, Ptolemy II Philadelphus, 1272.

thirty Ptolemy's navy outshone all others and included a 'twenty' and two 'thirties', according to Athenaeus 5. 203d, cf. *OGIS* 39.

Ptolemy Philopater . . . Tryphon Ptolemy IV Philopater (*c*.244–205 BC), son of Ptolemy III, became king of Egypt in 221 BC. The surname Tryphon was in fact given to Ptolemy VIII Euergetes II (also called Physcon, 'Pot-belly'). See *OCD³*, Ptolemy IV Philopater, 1272; Volkmann, *RE* 23. 2, Ptolemaios (22), 1678–92.

forty According to Plutarch (*Dem.* 43. 5), this ship was only for display. It moved unsteadily and with difficulty.

Hippus of Tyre Otherwise unknown. Tyre was a major Phoenician trading city, an appropriate home for a merchant vessel: see *OCD³*, 1568.

freight carrier The *oneraria* was a ship of burden or merchant vessel; cf. Cicero, *Att.* 16. 12. 2, where Cicero plans a clandestine escape on one at the outbreak of civil war in 49 BC. See Casson (1995), 169–70.

Cyrenaeans . . . Phoenicians . . . Rhodians . . . Cypriots.

These peoples all had maritime trade interests. Rhodes and Cyprus were islands: Rhodes was an important trading centre in the east Mediterranean, especially in the Hellenistic era (see Casson (1995), 135–6), while Cyprus had long been of economic and strategic importance (Casson 419–20). For Phoenician trade- and sea-power, see above, **Hippus of Tyre, 192. brought . . . Phoenicia, and 195. quarries . . . Phoenicia.** Cyrene in Africa, although a few miles inland, had a dependent port, Apollonia, through which a profitable trade exporting silphium was conducted.

cutter . . . skiff . . . yacht . . . yawl. The *lembus*, 'cutter', was a small, quick, sharp-prowed vessel, which, according to Polybius 5. 109, was developed by Illyrian pirates. It served as an auxiliary naval boat (Casson (1995), 125–7, 162). However, like the other boat names given here, it could be used more generally, of fishing-boats (Theocritus 21. 12) or even dinghies (Plautus, *Merc.* 193, 259). *Cumba*, Greek *cymbe*, 'skiff', was a term often used quite vaguely to mean boat (cf. Virgil, *G.* 4. 195–6), normally a small one (Ovid, *Met.* 293, rowed by a single man), such as the craft used by Charon to transport the souls of the dead in the underworld (Virgil, *Aen.* 6. 303; Horace, *Odes* 2. 3. 28). The *celes* (*keles*), yacht, was a small sailing boat built for speed and used as a dispatch vessel in Greek navies (Herodotus 8. 94; Xenophon, *Hell.* 1. 6. 36) and sometimes, like the *lembus*, by pirates (Thucydides 4. 9. 1; Livy 38. 27), as well as serving as a small merchant vessel. The *cercyrus* or *cercurus* (Greek *kerkouros*), 'yawl', was a large cargo boat whose name may derive from the Assyrian *qurqurru*. It was in general use in Mediterranean fleets by the 3rd cent. BC and used as a grain carrier on the Nile but it was attested in the Persian fleet as early as 480 BC (Herodotus 7. 89, 97): see Casson (1995), 163–6; Wallinga (1993), 109–10. These eastern connections perhaps explain P.'s citation of Cyprus, with her links to Egypt, the Near East, and western Asia, for the origins of this boat.

209. Phoenicians . . . stars For the Phoenicians, see above, **192. brought . . . Phoenicia, 195. quarries . . . Phoenicia, 208. Cyrenaeans . . . Cypriots.** For their practical astronomical skills exercised in sailing at night, see Strabo 16. 2. 24, C757.

Copae . . . blade Copae and Plataea were towns in Boeotia.

Strabo (9. 2. 17, C406) derived the name Copae from *kope*, oar handle and Plataea from *plate*, oar blade.

Icarus . . . sail-yard. The son of Daedalus (see above, **198. Daedalus . . . isinglass**), according to the well-known legend, fell into the sea and drowned after flying too close to the sun and melting the waxen wings made by his father for their escape from Minos. However, another tradition had the pair making their escape by boat (Diodorus Siculus 4. 77; Pausanias 9. 11. 4); hence their connection with sails and masts here. Sails (and ships) were also attributed, via the legend of her search for Osiris, with the Egyptian goddess Isis. See Rose on Hyginus 277. 5.

Samians   The Aegean island of Samos was close to the coast of Asia Minor. Its tyrant Polycrates (*c*.550–522 BC) had a powerful fleet (cf. Thuc. 1. 13) and later it was a prominent ship-contributing member of Athens' Delian league. See *OCD*³, Samos, 1351.

Pericles   The famous Athenian statesman (*c*.495–429 BC: see *OCD*³, Pericles (1), 1139–40) is suggested as an inventor of the horse-transport and grappling hooks (see below, **Pericles . . . claws**), items of naval warfare, probably as a result of his building-up of the Athenian fleet: cf. Thucydides 1. 107. 1, 1. 143. 5, 2. 13. 2, 2. 65. 7.

horse-carrier   The *hippagos* or *hippagogos* (Herod. 6. 48, 7. 21; Aristophanes *Knights* 595f.) was not a custom-built transporter but any vessel which could be suitably adapted. In 430 BC, when Pericles led an expeditionary force against the Peloponnese, old triremes were used for the first time by Athens (Thuc. 2. 56), and this may account for the attribution of a newly invented form of transport to the Athenian leader. The oarsmen were reduced to sixty (*IG*2² 1628. 154) to make room for about thirty horses: see J. Morrison and R. Williams, *Greek Oared Ships* (Cambridge, 1968), 248–9; Casson (1995), 93–4; Wallinga (1993), 139, 171.

Thasians   Thasos in the north Aegean was famous for its timber and precious metals and its commercial interests made it a very prosperous sea-power (cf. Herod. 6. 46. 2) which the Athenians took two years to subdue when it seceded from the Delian league *c*.465 BC (Thuc. 1. 100. 1).

decks . . . stern   Thucydides (1. 10. 4) talks of the undecked ships of the Homeric fleet as an old-fashioned feature. These 'aphracts' might have fighting decks at either end only, whereas from around the 8th cent. BC, a galley with a superstructure was developed which, in addition to a raised deck at either end, had full-length (but not full-width: cf. Thuc. 1. 14. 3) decking in between. This decking became more substantial as time went on and side-screening could be hung from it, eventually creating the enclosed 'cataphract' galley. An early Greek fighting deck is depicted on the Aristonothus vase (675–650 BC). See Casson (1995), 51–3.

Pisaeus See above, **201.**

beaks The *rostrum*, 'beak' or 'snout', was the end of the ship's prow and in particular the ram, which, from sometime after 1000 BC, the prow carried at sea-level. In the early days, this was a single prong designed to hole the enemy ship. In the 6th cent., blunt-ended rams intended to spring the planking started to appear; while from around 400 BC, the trident ram, with its three fin-like plates arranged horizontally, became standard. Towards the end of the 1st cent. AD, this began to disappear in favour of a single, blunt or pointed, ram. Changes in naval warfare, in particular the use of fire, eventually resulted in the ram's disappearance. See L. Casson and E. Lindor, 'The Evolution in Shape of the Ancient Ram', in L. Casson and J. R. Steffy (eds.), *The Athlit Ram* (Texas, 1991), 67–75.

Eupalamus Eupalamus, 'skilled handiman', was the father of Daedalus: Gaertringen, *RE* 6. 1, Eupalamos (1), 1159.

anchor . . . two-pronged anchor Early anchors, such as those featured in Homer (*Il.* 1. 436; 14. 77, etc.) were made entirely of stone, the simplest form being a flat slab (Casson (1995), 252). By the 5th cent. BC, more sophisticated anchors, some made wholly or partly from iron, the majority from wood weighted with lead or stone, were in use. These had wooden arms with metal tips, but not flukes, which don't appear until the late imperial era (Casson 253 and n.). It seems therefore that P.'s 'two-pronged' (*bidens*, lit. 'with two teeth') refers to these metal-tipped arms.

Anacharsis See above, **198. Anacharsis the Scythian**. Strabo 7. 3. 9, C303 also assigns this invention to Anacharsis, citing Ephorus as his source.

Pericles . . . claws For Pericles, see above, **209.** *Harpagones,* grappling hooks, and manus, literally 'hands' (the full term was 'iron hands': cf. Caesar, *BC* 1. 57) were in use by the 5th cent. BC (cf. Diodorus Siculus 13. 50. 5 on Alcibiades) and probably before. More sophisticated grappling tools, like Agrippa's (above, **45**) *harpax* (Appian, *BC* 5. 118), might be fired from catapults. See Casson (1995), 121–2.

Tiphys　was the steersman of the *Argo* (see above, **207. Jason . . . warship**): see Wust, *RE* 6A 2, Tiphys (1), 1426–9.

tiller　Literally, 'means of steering'. Mycenaean ships had a single steering oar but from the 8th cent. BC, double oversized oars were used as side-rudders on either side of the ship near the stern, operated by a tiller socketed into their upper shafts (Casson (1995), 46, 224–8).

Minos . . . battle　Various writers, including Herodotus (1. 171), Thucydides (1. 4. 1), and Diodorus Siculus (4. 79. 1) cite the mythical king of Crete (*OCD*³, 987) as the first to rule the seas with his fleet; a reflection of Minoan sea-power in the Bronze Age.

[Hyperbius . . . ox.]　This line was bracketed by Mayhoff because it appears to be out of context at the end of a long section devoted to ships and therefore possibly an interpolation, but it may simply have been a hasty afterthought, better suited, perhaps to section **199**, where arts connected with human sustenance (viticulture, agriculture) are mentioned; or, if the killing of animals is thought of in a sacrificial context, at the head of section **203**, where the origins of prophecy from animals and animal sacrifice are mentioned. Hyperbius (for the name, see also above, **194, 198**) son of Mars, is not mentioned elsewhere; although for the tradition which predictably linked his war-god father with early human killing, see above, **200. capital trial . . . Areopagus**. For Prometheus as culture-bringer, see above, **198**. His connection with the slaughter of animals generally, for both food and sacrifice, probably originates from a tradition that the division of a sacrifical victim between men and gods was the result of a trick played by Prometheus on the gods, by which the latter received only the fat and bones (see Hesiod, *Theog.* 506–616; a myth whose ultimate origins West (1966), 306, places in a purely human meal from which the inedible was ritually conserved). As a result, he is the originator of this form of animal sacrifice in Aeschylus, *Prom. Vinct.* 496–7, though he is not

specifically connected with the slaughter of an ox. Killing this particular animal had ambiguous overtones. The ox drawing the
plough was regarded as man's partner in labour and traditionally
its killing for food was regarded as one of the steps in man's moral
decline; thus Cicero (*ND* 2. 159), quoting his own translation of
Aratus' *Phaenomena*, links it with the development of weapons of
war, as mankind descended into the age of Iron (see above, **73**); cf.
Virgil, *G.* 2. 537 and Columella 6, pref. 7, who says that it was once
as serious a crime as killing a man (cf. Hyperbius' parentage).
Cicero's reference to weapons and Columella's comment on
human killing both lead back to Hyperbius' father, Mars, and help
to explain the attribution here.

210. The first . . . nations. Pliny finishes with three examples
of the widespread adoption of particular customs by the Graeco-
Roman world. These take the process of human civilization a step
further on from the initial stage of inventions by individual persons
or cities to the history of its spread and development. In each example, the move is from the Greek past to the Roman present. In the
first, P. suggests that the present-day Latin alphabet is the most
recent link in a continuous chain of development. In the latter two
examples, the emphasis is on the comparative lateness of the
Romans in making the requisite changes.

Ionian letters Of the various forms of the Greek alphabet
developed from the Phoenician (see above, **192–3**), one from the
mainly eastern group, east Ionic, came to predominate and by
*c.*370 BC was current throughout the Greek world. See Buck (1933),
68 ff.; *OCD*³, alphabet, Greek, 66.

ancient Greek . . . today's Latin The development of the
Italian alphabets from the Greek was a complex one. Ancient
sources such as the fragmentary *De Origine Linguae Latinae* (*De
Gramm. Libr.* fr. 6) by Varro and Tac. *Ann.* 11. 14. 4 connect the Latin
alphabet with the Arcadian hero Evander who was supposed to
have settled on the site of Rome, bringing the Aeolic dialect, cf.
Dionysius of Halicarnassus 1. 31, though Pliny (above, **193.
Latium . . . Pelasgians**) names the Pelasgians. Tacitus implies
that it developed separately from the Etruscan alphabet. Modern
scholarship suggests, however, that the Latin alphabet was based
on a southern Etruscan one (see above, **193**), the Etruscan perhaps

being an adaptation of the Greek alphabet via the trading settlements at Pithecoussae and Cumae. See *OCD*[3], alphabet, Latin, 67 and refs. in **192–3** above.

confirmed . . . dedication A similar 'proof', three cauldrons in the temple of Ismenian Apollo in Boeotian Thebes, was used by Herodotus to demonstrate the similarities between Ionian and Phoenician letters (5. 59).

Delphic . . . dedication *Delphica* often referred to a three-legged table, reminiscent of the Delphic tripod (see *OLD* 510, s.v. *delphica*); though an actual tripod may be meant here (O. Rossbach, 'Agroecius et Plinius de Delphica', *RM* 57 (1902), 473–4).

Palatine . . . library The complex of palace buildings built by Augustus on the Palatine included Greek and Latin libraries: Suet. *Aug.* 23, 72, 29. 3; Velleius 2. 81. They may have been used frequently for senate meetings in the early imperial period (D. L. Thompson, 'The Meetings of the Roman Senate on the Palatine', *AJA* 85. 3 (1981), 335–9; cf. Richardson (1992), 58–9; Nash (1981), i. 202–4). Elsewhere in the *HN*, Pliny uses the plural *principes*, emperors, when referring to Vespasian and Titus, so this would be its natural interpretation here. It has, however, been inferred from references in Tacitus, Dio, and Suetonius that the library was destroyed by fire in AD 64 and not restored until the reign of Domitian. The phrase 'in the library', which appears in all manuscripts, was thus deleted by Mayhoff (p. 75). However, the library is never specifically named in accounts either of the conflagration or the restoration. The libraries adjoined the temple of Apollo, close to the house of Augustus (Suet. *Aug.* 29. 3; Velleius 2. 81). Tacitus (*Ann.* 15. 39) says that Nero's palace, the *Domus Transitoria*, 'and all around it' was engulfed in AD 64 and in *Ann.* 15. 41 implies (*monumenta ingeniorum antiqua* 'ancient records of genius') that a library had suffered. Dio (62. 18. 2) says simply that the whole *palation* was burned. The inferred reference to the library's restoration, however, Suet. *Dom.* 20, does not identify either the libraries Domitian restored or the fire which destroyed them. We know, for example, from Dio 66. 24. 2, that the library in the Porticus Octaviae was among buildings destroyed in the fire of AD 80. While it is difficult to believe that the Palatine libraries had escaped the AD 64 fire, restoration may well have been earlier than Domitian and prior to

P.'s reference here. Nero was responsible for various building projects on the Palatine both before the 64 fire and afterwards, when rebuilding generally seems to have been energetic and prompt (Tac. *Ann.* 15. 43). References in Tacitus, Suetonius, and Dio suggest that Nero's successors, from Galba to Vespasian and Titus, were all using buildings on the Palatine, including the *Domus Tiberiana* (Darwall-Smith (1996), 182). Suetonius' (*Vesp.* 8. 5) reference to areas of dereliction due to earlier fires and fallen buildings in Vespasian's reign seems to refer to private property. As far as public buildings are concerned, he documents Vespasian's painstaking restoration of the Capitol and its ancient records, destroyed in the fighting of AD 69: the first steps were taken in 70 (Tac. *Hist.* 4. 53; Dio 65. 10. 2). On balance, it would seem that any damage to the Palatine libraries had been repaired by Nero, or possibly Vespasian. Some of the contents may have been saved in 64 if, as Tacitus' account suggests, the hill was not immediately assailed by the flames (cf. the rescue of the Sibylline books from the temple in the fire of AD 363 (Ammianus Marcellinus 23. 3. 3). Treasures in the adjoining temple of Apollo are mentioned several times, nearly always in the present tense, by Pliny (*HN* 36. 13, 24, 25, 32; 37. 11). A gift by Vespasian and Titus (as part of the refurbishment?) would be in keeping with Vespasian's generosity especially to the arts (Suet. *Vesp.* 17, 18), which included a library by his new temple of Peace, and with Titus' personal generosity after the later fire of AD 80 (*Titus* 8. 4).

Nausicrates ... tithe   The text is extremely uncertain. Various reconstructions were attempted in the 19th and early 20th cents.: see e.g. Mayhoff 75, Schilling 120. The dedication may have had an Athenian provenance, but was probably not as old as Pliny thought (F. Beuchelar, 'Coniectanea', *RM* 37 (1882), 336–7); cf. How and Wells (1912) on Herodotus 5. 59). Even if Pliny is wrong about its antiquity, specific identification of Nausicrates with a 4th-cent. BC playwright of that name (Korte, *RE* 16. 2, Nausicrates (1), 2020; Bonaria, *RE* suppl. 10, Nausicrates (2), 412) seems unwarranted.

211. barbers   The *tonsor* was responsible for cutting the hair and also for trimming and shaving the beard, a task which the individual did not perform for himself. See J. Carcopino, *Daily Life in Ancient Rome* (London, 1941, repr. 1963), 160–70; and below, **Before ... norm**.

later ... Varro In Greece, the practice of shaving dated back to the time of Alexander (Athenaeus 564f–565a). P.'s description of its introduction follows Varro (*RR* 2. 11. 10) who dates it to 301 BC and mentions an inscription at Ardea commemorating the event.

Before ... norm Varro mentions statues of bearded ancestors (*RR* 2. 11. 10). Roman portraiture was notably realistic (*OCD*[3], portraiture, Roman, 1229). Literary sources also refer to the Romans' bearded ancestors, e.g. Cicero, *Pro Caelio* 33, contrasting the full, long beards of old with the neatly trimmed little beards of his fashionable younger contemporaries (cf. *Pro Sestio* 18). Where these references are more specific, e.g. Horace, *Odes* 2. 15. 10 on the elder Cato, they show that the practice of shaving did not become the norm at Rome before the mid-2nd cent. BC. A similar picture is presented by coins of the period and by P.'s reference to the younger Africanus (below, next note). See Carcopino (above, **211. barbers**), R. G. Austin, *Cicero: Pro Caelio*[3] (Oxford, 1960), 91–2.

younger Africanus P. Cornelius Scipio Aemilianus' (*c.*185/4–129 BC: *OCD*[3], 397) habit of regular shaving was noted by Aulus Gellius as a general feature of his generation (*NA* 3. 4).

Augustus Cf. Suet. *Aug.* 79. 1.

(212) time-keeping Ancient sundials used a pointer or gnomon to mark the hours of daylight on an engraved network of hour lines and day curves (cf. Vitruvius 9. 7). The day was divided into twelve equal divisions, the length of which varied according to the season and the engraved day curves normally allowed the sundial to function as a crude calendar (see S. L. Gibbs, *Greek and Roman Sundials* (New Haven and London, 1976), 4–5). Their construction involved both astronomical and mathematical expertise, as Vitruvius' (9. 8) list of designers, including Aristarchus of Samos (*OCD*[3], 159), Berosus (above, **123** and **160**), and Eudoxus of Cnidus (*OCD*[3], 565–6), suggests: see Gibbs 8–11. Pliny's account in **212–14**, especially **the lines ... hours**, shows that, while sundials may have been introduced into Greece in the 6th cent. BC (below, **1 ... Greece**), it took the Romans a considerable length of time to work out the theory behind the accurate functioning of the gnomon; though the number and variety of sundials uncovered at Pompeii (Gibbs 90–2) suggests that by Pliny's day it was taken for granted.

I . . . Greece In *HN* 2. 187, Pliny claims that Anaximenes of Miletus (fl. second half of the 6th cent. BC) set up the first sundial at Sparta, though according to Diogenes Laertius it was Anaximenes' predecessor, Anaximander: see KRS nos. 94–5 and pp. 100–4, who think P. is mistaken as he occasionally is elsewhere on early astronomy. They also suggest (p. 83) that the gnomon could have been known to Anaximander's predecessor, Thales. Herodotus had attributed the twelve-part division of the day and some form of time-keeper to the Babylonians (though see Gibbs (1976), 6 and nn.). The earliest surviving sundials are from the 3rd cent. BC, when greater mathematical expertise had made the divisions more accurate. See *OCD*³, clocks, 350; Gibbs (1976).

Twelve Tables . . . midday was added. The Twelve Tables, traditionally compiled by a board of ten men with consular powers in 451–449 BC (*OCD*³, Twelve Tables, 1565–6) were regarded as the basis for the development of Roman law and frequently cited. According to Censorinus (*DN* 23. 8), they did not mention the individual hours but he does not mention the recording of sunrise and sunset either. However, he does mention a differentiation between afternoon and morning which implies that midday was already recognized (cf. Aulus Gellius, *NA* 17. 2. 10, who, like Varro, *LL* 6. 5, also mentions sunset). It may have been just the public announcement of midday which came later.

consuls' attendant The *accensi* were salaried officials, the personal assistants of the consuls. They were chosen by the latter and served for their year of office. See *OCD*³, *apparitores*, 129; Purcell (1983), 125–73.

senate house . . . prison The original senate-house, *Curia Hostilia* (Richardson (1992), 102–3), must have been orientated on cardinal points on the north side of the *comitium*, so that when the *accensus* looked from the building due south for midday, the *rostra*, or speaker's platform (*OCD*³, *rostra*, 1336; Nash ii. (1981), 272; Richardson (1992), 334–5), was to the south-east and the *graecostasis*, where foreign embassies waited to be received by the senate (Richardson 182–3), an equal distance to the south-west. When he looked due west, to sunset, the prison (Nash i., 206–7; Richardson 71–2) was to the north-west and the Maenian column (dedicated to C. Maenius, consul 338 BC: Pliny, *HN* 34. 20; *OCD*³, 998;

Richardson 945) to the south-west: for a possible reconstruction, see F. B. Sear, *Roman Architecture* (1982), 14–15. However, the positions of P.'s *rostra* and *graecostasis* are problematic, according to Richardson (102–3, 182–3, 334–5), who identifies the former with the *rostra Antiana* in the forum, rather than the one in the *comitium*, and the latter with a different, earlier, *graecostasis* to that known from other sources, or possibly a forerunner of the *graecostadium*. He points out that several of the landmarks Pliny mentions were no longer visible in his day.

first Punic war 264–241 BC.

213. Fabius Vestalis Nothing is known about this author, mentioned only in Pliny's reference here and his listing in the indices of books 34–6: cf. Peter, *HRR²*, fr. 158 and cvii–cviii; Stein, *RE* 6. 2, Fabius (156), 1872; Münzer (1897), 353–6.

eleven . . . Pyrrhus Pyrrhus' (*OCD³*, 1283) invasion of Italy and famous defeat of the Romans at Heraclea happened in 280 BC, but elsewhere (*HN* 8. 16) Pliny gives the date of the invasion as 282 BC. This would appear to be the date he is thinking of here, since eleven years before 282 BC would be 293 BC, the date given elsewhere (Livy 10. 46. 7) for the dedication of the temple of Quirinus (see below, **L. Papirius Cursor . . . vow**.)

L. Papirius Cursor . . . vow Consul in 293 BC, L. Papirius Cursor defeated the Samnites at Aquilonia (Livy 10. 38. 42). His father (also L. Papirius Cursor, five times consul and at least twice dictator) was a famous hero of the second Samnite war, winning notable victories in 320 and 319 BC: see *OCD³*, Papirius Cursor (1) and (2), 1109. The temple of Quirinus replaced an old shrine to the god on the Quirinal and was adorned with spoils from the Samnite war (Livy 10. 46. 7) The origins and function of the god are unclear. He was eventually assimilated with Romulus and may have been a deity of the citizen body: see *OCD³*, 1291.

However . . . source P.'s reservations about Fabius' information may reflect the fact that the tradition was not unanimous. Censorinus, *DN* 23. 6–8 mentions the Capitol and the temple of Diana on the Aventine as alternative sites for the first sundial; according to him the only certainty was that there was no sundial in the forum before the one imported from Sicily (below, **214. Messalla . . . 263 BC**).

Varro His *Antiquitates Rerum Humanarum* seems to have been the main source for the discussion of the divisions of day and its measurement in Pliny. There are parallels with Censorinus. *DN* 23–4 and Aulus Gellius, *NA* 3. 2. 1–11 and 17. 2. 10. See Mirsch (1882), 121–5. Pliny's information on the sundial may be from book xv, *de temporum descriptionibus* (Mirsch 121) or *de diebus* (Rocca-Serra (1980), 68).

214. Messalla . . . 263 BC. During the first Punic war, M.' Valerius Maximus Messalla, as consul in 263 BC, secured the surrender of Catania and other Sicilian communities and peace with Hiero II of Syracuse: see *OCD*[3], 1579. This sundial was evidently part of the spoils of war. For the *rostra*, see above, **212. senate house . . . prison.**

The lines . . . hours Censorinus, *DN* 23. 7 explains that this was because it was made for the latitude of Sicily rather than of Rome. On this problem, see Vitruvius 9. 7. 1. There is a difference of more than four degrees between Rome (41.53° N) and Sicily (37.31° N). Gibbs (1976: 91 n. 25) calculated that the greatest error could only have been .07 Roman summer hours, which would explain why it went apparently unnoticed for so long. The calendrical error, however, especially at the solstices, would have been more obvious, unless the dial had been inadvertently tilted, cancelling out the difference. Even the great sundial constructed by the emperor Augustus, using as gnomon an obelisk transported to Rome to commemorate his victory at Actium in 31 BC, was not immune from problems: see Pliny, *HN* 13. 72–3.

Q. Marcius Philippus . . . L. Paulus As consul in 186 BC, Q. Marcius Philippus had, with his colleague, crushed the Bacchanalia and was consul again in 169 at the outbreak of the war with Perseus. He was censor in 164 BC with L. Aemilius Paulus (consul 182 and 168 BC): see *OCD*[3], Marcius Philippus, Quintus, 923; Aemilius Paulus (2), Lucius, 21–2.

215. Even then . . . *lustrum* For the *lustrum*, see above, **157. five-year period . . . next pair of censors.** A sundial was, of course, useless in dull weather.

Scipio . . . Laenas For P. Cornelius Scipio Nasica Corculum, see above, **118. surnames . . . Corculum.** With M. Popillius Laenas (Volkmann, *RE* 22. 1, Popillius (24), 61–2), he was censor in

159, the *lustrum* following Philippus and Paulus; cf. Censorinus, *DN* 23. 7.

the first . . . day. The 5th-cent. philosopher Empedocles (fr. 100) had described a device known as a *klepsydra* in a famous simile. This could be used to measure a given length of time, but without subdividing it (A. G. Drachmann, *Ktesibios, Philon and Heron: A Study in Ancient Pneumatics* (Copenhagen, 1948) 16), and simple versions were used as time-keepers in the late 5th-cent. Athenian lawcourts: see P. J. Rhodes, *A Commentary on the Aristotelian Athenaion Politeia* (Oxford, 1981), 719–20. Water-clocks which accurately marked the hours were perfected by Ctesibius (above, **125. Ctesibius . . . engines**), with a device to control water flow (Drachmann (1948), 17–21); cf. Vitruvius 9. 8. 4–6. See Drachmann (1948), 16–41.

He dedicated . . . 159 BC   Varro (*LL* 6. 4) says a clock was placed 'by Cornelius' in the *Basilica Aemilia et Fulvia* (a public hall built in 179 BC on the north side of the forum and according to Pliny (*HN* 36. 101–2) still one of the three most beautiful buildings of his day). He refers to it in the context of the word *solarium* but as Censorinus explains, the term came to be used generically of water-clocks as well. Scipio and his colleague had, according to Pliny, *HN* 34. 30, been responsible for reorganizing and clearing the forum, by removing unauthorized statues.

For so long . . . day!   According to Censorinus (*DN* 23. 6), the introduction of divisions of the day and night post-dated the introduction of the sundial at Rome; and accurate division of the night would not be possible without a water-clock (for possible early arrangements, see Drachmann (1948), 17): cf. also above, **212. Twelve Tables . . . midday was added**.

Now . . . land.   The rather abrupt ending is typical of many books in the *HN* (on the use of introductions and conclusions to individual books of the *HN*, see above, Introd. 4.5.3 and n. 107). The most elaborate conclusion is that of book 37, where the rhetorical valediction to Nature serves to conclude the whole work. In certain respects, section **190** marked a more natural end to the description of the human animal (but see above, **191–215. introd.** and Introd. 5.5).

BIBLIOGRAPHY

ADAMS, J. N., 'The Uses of *neco*' I, *Glotta*, 68 (1990), 230–55.
——, 'The Uses of *neco*' II, *Glotta*, 69 (1991), 94–123.
ADMUNDSEN, D. W., 'Romanticising the Ancient Medical Profession: The Characterisation of the Physician in the Graeco-Roman Novel', *BHM* 43 (1974), 320–37.
AHL, F. M., 'Appius Claudius and Sextus Pompey in Lucan', *C&M* 30 (1967), 331–46.
——*Lucan: An Introduction* (Ithaca and New York, 1976).
ALLERS, R., 'Macrocosmos: From Anaximandros to Paracelsus', *Traditio*, 2 (1944), 319–407.
ANDERSON, G., *Sage, Saint and Sophist: Holy Men and their Associates* (London, 1994).
ANDRÉ, J., *La Vie et l'œuvre d'Asinius Pollion* (Paris, 1949).
——*Pline l'Ancien Histoire Naturelle livre 21* (Paris, 1969).
——and FILLIOZAT, J., *Pline l'Ancien Historie Naturelle livre 6, 2e partie* (Paris, 1980).
——, BLOCH, R., ROUVERET, A., *Pline l'Ancien, Histoire Naturelle livre 36* (Paris, 1981)
ANDRÉ, J.-M., *Mécène: Essai de biographie spirituelle* (Paris, 1967).
——'La Notion de *pestilentia* à Rome: Du tabou religieux a l'interprétation prescientifique', *Latomus*, 39 (1980), 3–16.
ANTONACCIO, C. M., *An Archaeology of Ancestors: Tomb Cult and Hero Cult in Early Greece* (Maryland and London, 1995).
ARIÈS, P., *The Hour of Our Death* (New York and Oxford, 1981).
ARNAUD, P., 'L'Image du globe dans le monde Romain: Science, iconographie, symbolique', *MEFRA* 96, pt. 1 (1984), 53–116.
ARRIGHETTI, G., *Epicuro*[2] (Turin, 1973).
ASTIN, A. E., *Scipio Aemilianus* (Oxford, 1967).
——*Cato the Censor* (Oxford, 1978).
AUBERT, J.-J., 'Threatened Wombs: Aspects of Ancient Uterine Magic', *GRBS* 30. 3 (1989), 423–5.
AUGUET, R., *Cruelty and Civilisation: The Roman Games* (London, 1994).
AUSTIN, R. G. (ed. and comm.), Cicero: *Pro Caelio*[3] (Oxford, 1960).
——(ed. and comm.), *P. Vergili Maronis Aeneidos, Liber Secundus* (Oxford, 1964).
AXTELL, H. L., *Deification of Abstract Ideas in Roman Literature and Inscriptions* (New Rochelle and New York, 1907; repr. 1987).
BADIAN, E., 'The Date of Pompey's First Triumph', *Hermes*, 83 (1955), 107–18.

474 BIBLIOGRAPHY

BADIAN, E., review of H. Malcovati, *Oratorum Romanorum Fragmenta liberae rei publicae iteratis curis recensuit, JRS* 46 (1956), 221.

BAILEY, C., *Epicurus: The Extant Remains* (Oxford, 1926).

——— *Titi Lucreti Cari De Rerum Natura*, 3 vols. (Oxford, 1947).

BAINES, J., 'Writing: Invention and Early Development', in Bard (1999), 882–5.

BALDRY, H. C., *The Unity of Mankind in Greek Thought* (Cambridge, 1965).

BALDWIN, B., 'The Acta Diurna', *Chiron*, 9 (1979), 189–203.

——— 'The Composition of Pliny's *Natural History*', *Symbolae Osloenses*, 70 (1995 = 1995*a*), 72–81.

——— 'Emperors in the Elder Pliny', *Scholia*, 4 (1995 =1995*b*), 56–78.

BALSDON, J. P. V. D., *The Emperor Gaius* (Oxford, 1934).

——— 'Sulla Felix', *JRS* 41 (1951), 1–10.

——— *Life and Leisure in Ancient Rome* (London, 1969).

——— 'The Principates of Tiberius and Gaius', *ANRW* 2. 2 (Berlin and New York, 1975), 86–94.

——— *Romans and Aliens* (London, 1979).

BARNES, J., *The Presocratic Philosophers*, i: *Thales to Zeno* (London, 1979).

BARRATT, A. A., *Caligula: The Corruption of Power* (London, 1989).

BARTON, T., *Ancient Astrology* (London, 1994).

BAUMAN, R. A., *Crime and Punishment in Ancient Rome* (London, 1996).

BAYET, J., 'Les Origines de l'arcadisme romaine', *MEFRA* 38 (1920), 63–143.

BEACHAM, C., *The Roman Theatre and its Audience* (London, 1991).

BEAGON, M., *Roman Nature: The Thought of Pliny the Elder* (Oxford, 1992).

——— 'Plinio, la tradizione enciclopedica e i mirabilia', in *Storia della Scienza*, i: *La Scienza Antica* (Istituto della Enciclopedia Italiana, Rome, 2001), 735–45.

——— 'Beyond Comparison: M. Sergius, *Fortunae Victor*', in G. Clarke and T. Rajak (eds.), *Philosophy and Power in the Graeco-Roman World: Essays in Honour of Miriam Griffin* (Oxford, 2002), 111–32.

——— 'Situating Nature's Wonders in Pliny's *Natural History*', forthcoming.

BEARD, M., NORTH, J. and PRICE, S., *Religions of Rome*, 2 vols. (Cambridge, 1998).

BEARE, W., *The Roman Stage: A Short History of Latin Drama in the Time of the Late Republic*[3] (London, rev. edn., 1968).

BEAUJEU, J., *Pline l'Ancien Histoire Naturelle livre II* (Paris, 1950).

BEHRENS, L. H., and BARR, D. P., 'Hyperpituitarism Beginning in Infancy: The Alton Giant', *Endocrinology*, 16 (1932), 120–8.

BELMONT, N., *Les Signes de la naissance: Étude de représentations symboliques associées aux naissances singulières* (Paris, 1971).

BELOCH, K. J., *Bevolkerung der griechisch-römischen Welt* (Leipzig, 1886).

BERGMANN, M., *Die Strahlen der Herrscher: Theomorphes Herrscherbild und politische Symbolik im Hellenismus und in der römischen Kaiserzeit* (Mainz, 1998).

BERNSTEIN, A., *The Formation of Hell: Death and Retribution in the Ancient and Early Christian Worlds* (London, 1993).

BEUCHELAR, F., 'Coniectanea', *RM* 37 (1882), 321–42.

BEVAN, E., *Representations of Animals in Sanctuaries of Artemis and other Olympian Deities*, BAR ser. 315 (i) (Oxford, 1986).

BIANCHI, E., 'Teratologia e geografia, l'homo monstruosus in autori dell'antichità classica', *Acme*, 34 (1981), 227–49.

BICKERMAN, E. J., *The Chronology of the Ancient World* (London, 1980).

BICKNELL, P. J., 'The Dark Side of the Moon', in A. Moffatt (ed.), *Maistor: Classical, Byzantine and Renaissance Studies for Robert Browning* (Canberra, 1984), 67–75.

BIDEZ, J., and CUMONT, F., *Les Mages Hellénisés: Zoroastre, Ostanes et Hystaspe d'après la tradition greque*, i (Paris, 1938; repr. 1973).

BIEBER, M., *The History of the Greek and Roman Theater* (Princeton, 1961).

BINDER, G., 'Auguste d'après les informations de la *NH*', in Pigeaud and Oroz (1987), 461–72.

BLIQUEZ, L. J., 'Greek, Etruscan and Roman Prosthetics', *ANRW* 37. 3 (Berlin and New York, 1996), 2640–76.

BLOCH, R., *Les Prodiges dans l'antiquité classique* (Paris, 1963).

BLUMENFELD-KOSINSKI, R., *Not of Woman Born: Representations of Caesarian Birth in Medieval and Renaissance Europe* (Cornell, 1990).

BLUNDELL, S., *The Origins of Civilisation in Greek and Roman Thought* (London, 1986).

BOARDMAN, J., *Athenian Black Figure Vases* (London, 1974).

——*Athenian Red Figure Vases of the Archaic Period* (London, 1975).

BOEDEKER, D., 'Hero Cult and Politics in Herodotus: The Bones of Orestes', in C. Dougherty and L. Kurke (eds.), *Cultural Poetics in Archaic Greece* (Cambridge, 1993), 164–77.

BOHRINGER, F., 'Cultes d'athlètes en Grèce classique: Propos politiques, discours mythiques', *REA* 81 (1979), 5–18.

BOLTON, J. D. P., *Aristeas of Proconnesus* (Oxford, 1962).

BONNER, J., *Education in Ancient Rome* (London, 1977).

BORCA, F., 'Towns and Marshes in the Ancient World', in V. M. Hope and E. Marshall (eds.), *Death and Disease in the Ancient City* (London, 2000), 74–84.

BORST, A., *Das Buch der Naturgeschichte: Plinius und seiner Leser im Zeitalter des Pergaments* (Heidelberg, 1994).

BOSWORTH, A. B., *Conquest and Empire: The Reign of Alexander the Great* (Cambridge, 1988).

BOUCÉ, P.-G., 'Imagination, Pregnant Women and Monsters in Eighteenth-Century England and France', in G. S. Rousseau and

476   BIBLIOGRAPHY

R. Porter (eds.), *Sexual Underworlds of the Enlightenment* (Manchester, 1987), 86–100.

Bouché-Leclercq, A., *L'Astrologie Grecque* (Paris, 1899, repr. Brussels, 1963).

Bowersock, G. W., *Hellenism in Late Antiquity* (Michigan, 1990).

—— 'Dionysus as Epic Hero', in N. Hopkinson (ed.), *Studies in the Dionysiaca of Nonnos* (Cambridge, 1994 = 1994*a*), 156–64.

—— *Fiction as History: Nero to Julian* (California and London, 1994 = 1994*b*).

Bowie, E., 'Apollonius of Tyana: Tradition and Reality', *ANRW* 2. 16. 2 (Berlin and New York 1986), 1652–99.

Bradley, K., *Suetonius' Life of Nero* (Brussels, 1978).

Bram, J. Rhys, *Ancient Astrology, Theory and Practice: Matheseos Libri VIII by Firmicius Maternus* (New Jersey, 1975).

Brand, J., *Observations on Popular Antiquities, illustrating the Origin of our Vulgar Customs, Ceremonies and Superstitions*, rev. H. Ellis, 3 vols. (London, 1841–2).

Breguet, E., 'Urbi et orbi: un cliché et un thème', in J. Bibauw (ed.), *Hommages à Marcel Renard*, i (Brussels, 1969), 140–52.

Bremmer, J., *The Early Greek Concept of the Soul* (Princeton, 1983).

—— *The Rise and Fall of the Afterlife* (London, 2002).

Brenk, F. E., 'In the Light of the Moon: Demonology in the Early Imperial Period', *ANRW* 2. 16. 3 (Berlin and New York, 1986), 2008–2145.

Briggs, K. M., *A Dictionary of British Folklore*, vol. B, pt. 2 (London, 1971).

Briquel, D., *Les Pélasges en Italie: Recherches sur l'histoire de la légende* (Rome, 1984).

Briscoe, J., *A Commentary on Livy Books xxi–xxxiii* (Oxford, 1973).

Brosius, M., *Ancient Archives and Archival Traditions: Concepts of Record-Keeping in the Ancient World* (Oxford, 2003).

Bruhl, A., 'Le Souvenir d'Alexandre le Grand et les Romains', *MEFRA* 47 (1930), 202–21.

—— *Liber Pater: Origine et expansion du culte Dionysiaque à Rome et dans le monde Romain* (Paris, 1953).

Brumfield, A. C., *The Attic Festivals of Demeter and their Relation to the Agricultural Year* (New Hampshire, 1985).

Brunt, P. A., *Italian Manpower 225 BC–AD 14* (Oxford, 1971).

—— 'Cicero's *Officium* in the Civil War', *JRS* 76 (1986), 12–32.

—— review of H. D. Meyer, *Die Aussenpolitik des Augustus*, *JRS* 53 (1963), 170–6 (= *Roman Imperial Themes* (Oxford, 1990), 96 ff.).

Bryan, E. M., *Twins and Higher Multiple Pregnancies: A Guide to their Nature and Nurture* (London, 1992).

Buck, G. D., *Comparative Grammar of Greek and Latin* (Chicago and London, 1933).

BUNBURY, E. H., *A History of Ancient Geography*, vol. ii, (London, 1879).

BURKE, P. F., 'Malaria in the Graeco-Roman World: A Historical and Epidemiological Study', *ANRW* 2. 37. 3 (Berlin and New York, 1996), 2252–81.

BURKERT, W., *Lore and Science in Ancient Pythagoreanism* (Cambridge, Mass., 1972).

—— *Greek Religion: Archaic and Classical* (Oxford, 1985).

BUXTON, R., 'Wolves and Werewolves in Greek Thought', in J. Bremmer (ed.), *Interpretations of Greek Mythology* (London, 1987), 60–79.

CAIRNS, F., and FANTHAM, E. (eds.), *Caesar against Liberty? Perspectives on his Autocracy*, Papers of the Langford Latin Seminar 11, ARCA 43 (Cambridge, 2003).

CAPLAN, H., *Of Eloquence: Studies in Ancient and Medieval Rhetoric* (Ithaca and London, 1970).

CARCOPINO, J., *Daily Life in Ancient Rome* (London, 1941; repr. 1963).

CAREY, S., *Pliny's Catalogue of Culture: Art and Empire in the Natural History* (Oxford, 2003).

CARNEY, T. F., 'The Death of Sulla', *Acta Classica*, 4 (1961), 64–79.

CARRUTHERS, M., *The Book of Memory: A Study of Memory in Medieval Culture* (Cambridge, 1990).

CARSWELL, J., 'The Port of Mantai, Sri Lanka', in V. Begley and D. de Puma (eds.), *Rome and India: The Ancient Sea Trade* (Wisconsin and London, 1981).

CARTLEDGE, P., 'Hoplites and Heroes: Sparta's Contribution to the Technique of Ancient Warfare', *JHS* 97 (1977), 11–27.

CASSON, L., *Travel in the Ancient World* (London, 1974, repr. 1994).

—— *Ships and Seamanship in the Ancient World*² (Baltimore and London, 1995).

—— and LINDOR, E., 'The Evolution in Shape of the Ancient Ram', in L. Casson and J. R. Steffy (eds.), *The Athlit Ram* (Texas, 1991), 67–75.

CAVEN, B., *Dionysius I: Warlord of Sicily* (London and Yale, 1990).

CÉARD, J., *La Nature et les prodiges: L'Insolite au 16e siècle en France* (Geneva, 1977).

CHARPIN, F. (ed. and comm.), *Lucilius: Satires*, vol. ii (Paris, 1978).

CHESNUT, G. F., 'The Ruler and the Logos in Neopythagorean, Middle Platonic and Late Stoic Political Philosophy', *ANRW* 2. 16. 2 (Berlin and New York, 1978), 1310–32.

CHIBNALL, M., 'Pliny's *Natural History* and the Middle Ages', in T. A. Dorey (ed.), *Empire and Aftermath* (London, 1975), 57–78.

CHURCHILL, J. BRADFORD, '*Ex qua quod vellet facerent*; Roman magistrates' Authority over *praedia* and *manubiae*', *TAPA* 129 (1999), 85–116.

—— review of E. M. Orlin, *Temples, Religion and Politics in the Roman Republic*, Bryn Mawr Classical Review (1999.07.02).

CICHORIUS, C., *Römische Studien, Historisches, Epigraphisches, Literargeschicht-liches* (Leipzig, 1922).

CITRONI MARCHETTI, S., *Plinio il Vecchio e la tradizione del moralismo Romano* (Pisa, 1991).

CLERC, J.-B., *Homines Magici* (Bern, 1995).

COARELLI, F., 'Il Complesso Pompeiano del Campo Marzio e la sua decorazione scultorea', *Rend. Pont.* (1971–2), 99 ff.

—— 'Roma, i Volsci e il Lazio Antico', in *Crise et transformation des sociétés archaïques de l'Italie antique au Ve siècle av. J.-C.*, Coll. Ec. France de Rome, 137 (Rome, 1990), 135–54.

COKAYNE, K., *Experiencing Old Age in Ancient Rome* (London, 2003).

COLE, T., *Democritus and the Sources of Greek Anthropology* (Cleveland, Philological Monographs 25, 1967).

COLEMAN, R. (ed. and comm.), *Virgil: Eclogues* (Cambridge, 1977).

COLLISON-MORLEY, L., *Greek and Roman Ghost Stories* (London, 1912).

CONGER, G. P., *Theories of Macrocosms and Microcosms in the History of Philosophy* (New York, 1922).

CONTE, G. B., 'The Inventory of the World: Form of Nature and Encyclopaedic Project in the *HN* of Pliny the Elder', in *Genres and Readers*, trans. G. W. Most (Baltimore, 1994), 67–104.

COOK, R. M., *Greek Art: Its Development, Character and Influence* (London, 1972).

CORBETT, J. H., 'L. Metellus (cos. 251, 247): Agrarian Commissioner', *CR* NS 20. 1 (1970), 7–8.

CORNELL, T. J., 'The Formation of the Historical Tradition of Early Rome', in I. S. Moxon, J. D. Smart, A. J. Woodman (eds.), *Past Perspectives* (Cambridge 1986), 67–86.

—— 'The Tyranny of the Evidence: A Discussion of the Possible Uses of Literacy in Etruria and Latium in the Archaic Age', *JRA* suppl. 3 (Ann Arbor, 1991), 7–33.

—— *The Beginnings of Rome: Italy and Rome from the Bronze Age to the Punic War* (London, 1995).

CORSO, A., 'Nicomede I, Dedalsa e le Afroditi Nude al Bagno', *Numismatica e Antichità Classiche*, 19 (1990), 135–60.

COURCELLE, P., 'L'Âme au tombeau', in *Mélanges d'histoire de religion offerts à H.-Ch. Puech* (Paris, 1974), 331–6.

COXON, A. H., *The Fragments of Parmenides* (Assen and New Hampshire, 1986).

CRAMER, F. H., *Astrology in Roman Law and Politics* (Philadelphia, 1954).

CRAWFORD, M. H., *Roman Republican Coinage*, 2 vols., (London, 1974).

—— 'Hamlet without the Prince', review of E. S. Gruen, *The Last Generation of the Roman Republic*, *JRS* 66 (1976), 214–17.

CRAWFORD, O. C., 'Laudatio Funebris', *CJ* 37 (1941/2), 17–27.

CRAWFORD, P., 'Attitudes towards Menstruation in Seventeenth-Century England', *P&P* 91 (1981), 47–73.

CROISILLE, J. M., *Pline l'Ancien Histoire Naturelle livre 35* (Paris, 1985).

CUMONT, F., *Afterlife in Roman Paganism* (New Haven, 1922; repr. New York, 1959).

—— *Recherches sur le symbolisme funéraire des Romains* (Paris, 1942).

—— *Lux Perpetua* (Paris, 1949).

CURRIE, B., 'Euthymos of Locri; A Case Study in Heroisation in the Classical Period', *JHS* 122 (2002), 24–44.

DARAB, A., 'Cicero bei Plinius dem Älteren', *ACD* 31 (1995), 33–41.

DARWALL-SMITH, R., *Emperors and Architecture: A Study of Flavian Rome* (Brussels, 1996).

DASEN, V., *Dwarfs in Ancient Egypt and Greece* (Oxford, 1993).

—— 'Multiple Births in Graeco-Roman Antiquity', *OJA* 16. 1 (1997), 49–63.

DAVID, D. J., HEMMING, D. C., and COOTER, R. D., *Craniofacial Deformities* (New York, 1990).

DAVIDSON, J. A., 'The First Triremes', *CQ* 41 (1947), 18–24.

DAVIES, G., 'Burial in Italy up to Augustus', in R. Reece (ed.), *Burial in the Roman World* (London, 1977).

DAVIES, W. V., *Egyptian Hieroglyphs* (London, 1987).

DEAN-JONES, L., 'The Cultural Construct of the Female Body in Classical Greek Science', in S. B. Pomeroy (ed.), *Women's History and Ancient History* (Chapel Hill, NC, 1991), 111–37.

—— *Women's Bodies in Classical Greek Science* (Oxford, 1994).

DE GRAEVE, M. C., *The Ships of the Ancient Near East c.2000–500BC* (Leuven, 1981).

DELCOURT, M., *Stérilités mystérieuses et naissances maléfiques dans l'antiquité classique* (Liège and Paris, 1938).

—— *Hermaphrodite: Mythes et rites de la bisexualité dans l'antiquité classique* (Paris, 1958).

—— *Héphaistos: ou, la légende de magicien* (Paris, 1959).

DENCH, E., *From Barbarians to New Men* (Oxford, 1995).

DEONNA, W., 'Monokrepides', *RHR* 12 (1935), 50–72.

—— *Le Symbolisme de l'oeil* (Berne, 1965).

DESANGES, J., *Pline l'Ancien Histoire Naturelle V.1–46* (Paris, 1980).

DÉTIENNE, M., 'De la catalepsie à l'immortalité de l'âme', *Nouvelle Clio* 10–12 (1958–60), 123–35.

—— *Dionysus mis à mort* (Paris, 1977).

—— and Vernant, J.-P., *Cunning Intelligence in Greek Culture and Society* (Hassocks, 1978).

DETLEFSEN, D., 'Emendationem von Eigennamen in Plinius' *Naturalis Historia* B.7', *RM* 18 (1863), 227–40.

DEUTSCH, M. E., 'Pompey's Three Triumphs', *CPh.* 19 (1924), 277–9.

480 BIBLIOGRAPHY

DICKIE, M. W., 'Talos bewitched', *Papers of the Leeds International Latin Seminar*, 6 (1990), 267–96.
—— 'Heliodorus and Plutarch on the Evil Eye', *CPh*. 86 (1991), 17–29.
—— 'The Learned Magician', in D. R. Jordan, H. Montgomery, and E. Thomassen (eds.), *The World of Ancient Magic* (Bergen, 1999 = 1999*a*), 168–72.
—— 'Bonds and Headless Demons in Greco-Roman Magic', *GRBS* 40 (1999 = 1999*b*), 99–104.
—— *Magic and Magicians in the Greco-Roman World* (London, 2001).
DODDS, E. R., *The Greeks and the Irrational*, Sather Classical Lectures vol. 25 (Berkeley, 1951).
—— 'Supernormal Phenomena in Classical Antiquity', in *The Ancient Concept of Progress and other Essays on Greek Literature and Belief* (Oxford, 1973), 156–210.
—— (ed. and comm.), *Euripides Bacchae*² (Oxford, 1960, repr. 1977).
DRACHMANN, A. G., *Ktesibios, Philon and Heron: A Study in Ancient Pneumatics* (Copenhagen, 1948).
DUCHESNE-GILLEMIN, J, *The Western Response to Zoroaster* (Oxford, 1958).
DUMÉZIL, G., *La Religion romaine archaique* (Paris, 1966).
DUNBABIN, K. M. D., and DICKIE, M. W., '*Invida rumpantur pectora*: The Iconography of *phthonos / invidia* in Greco-Roman Art', *Jahrbuch für antike und Christentum*, 26 (1983), 7–27.
DUNBAR, N., (ed. and comm.), *Aristophanes Birds* (Oxford, 1995).
DUNDES, A., 'Wet and Dry, the Evil Eye, an essay in Indo-European and Semitic Worldviews', in A. Dundes (ed.), *Interpreting Folklore* (Indiana UP, 1980), 93–133.
DWORAKOWSKA, A., *Quarries in Ancient Greece* (Wrocław, 1975).
EARL, D., *The Moral and Political Tradition of Republican Rome* (Ithaca, 1967; repr. 1984).
ECKSTEIN, A. M., 'Human Sacrifice and Fear of Military Disaster in Republican Rome', *AJAH* 7 (1982), 69–95.
EDELSTEIN, E. and EDELSTEIN, L., *Asclepius: A Collection and Interpretation of Testimonies*, 2 vols. (Baltimore, 1945; repr. 1998).
EDELSTEIN, L., *The Idea of Progress in Classical Antiquity* (Baltimore, 1967).
EDWARDS, R. B., *Kadmos the Phoenician: A Study in Greek Legends and the Mycenaean Age* (Amsterdam, 1979).
ELWORTHY, F. T., *The Evil Eye* (London, 1895).
—— 'Evil eye', in J. Hastings, *Encyclopedia of Religion and Ethics*, vol. v (Edinburgh, 1912), 608–15.
ENDRES, K. P., and SCHAD, W., *Moon Rhythms in Nature: How Lunar Cycles affect Living Organisms*, trans. C. Von Arnim (Edinburgh, 2002).
ERKELL, W. D., *Augustus, Felicitas, Fortuna: Lateinische Wortstudien* (Göteborg, 1952).

ERNOUT, J., *Pline l'Ancien Histoire Naturelle livre 1* (Paris, 1950).
—— *Pline l'Ancien Histoire Naturelle livre 28* (Paris, 1962).
EWBANK, W. W., *The Poems of Cicero* (London, 1933, repr. Bristol, 1977).
FARAONE, C., *Talismans and Trojan Horses* (New York, 1992).
FARNELL, L. R., *Cults of the Greek States*, vol. v (Oxford, 1909).
FELTON, D., *Haunted Greece and Rome: Ghost Stories from Classical Antiquity* (Texas, 1999).
FERGUSON, J., *Bibliographical Notes on Histories of Inventions and Books of Secrets*, 2 vols. (London, 1959).
FESTUGIÈRE, A.-J., *La Révélation d'Hermès Trismégiste*, i: *L'Astrologie et les sciences occultés* (Paris, 1950).
FIEDLER, L., *Freaks: Myths and Images of the Secret Self* (London and New York, 1978).
FLACELIÈRE, R., *Greek Oracles* (London, 1976).
FLEMMING, R., *Medicine and the Making of Roman Women* (Oxford, 2000).
FLOWER, H., *Ancestor Masks and Aristocratic Power in Roman Culture* (Oxford, 1996).
FONTENROSE, J., *Python* (Berkeley, 1959).
—— 'The Hero as Athlete', *CSCA* 1 (1968), 73–104.
—— *The Delphic Oracle* (Berkeley and London, 1978).
FORBES, R. J., *Studies in Ancient Technology*² 9 vols. (Leiden, 1964–72).
FORBES, T. R., 'The Social History of the Caul', *Yale Journal of Biology and Medicine*, 25 (1953), 495–508.
—— *The Midwife and the Witch* (Yale, 1966).
FORBES-IRVING, P. M. C., *Metamorphosis in Greek Myth* (Oxford, 1990).
FÖRSTER, R. (ed.), *Scriptores Physiognomici Graeci et Latini*, 2 vols. (Lipsiae, 1893).
FRASER, P. M., 'The Career of Erasistratus of Cos', *Ist. Lomb. Rend. Lett.* 103 (1969), 518–37.
FRENCH, R., *Ancient Natural History: Histories of Nature* (London, 1994).
FRIEDLÄNDER, L., *Roman Life and Manners under the Early Empire*, 4 vols. (London, 1909–13).
FRIEDMAN, J. B., *The Monstrous Races in Medieval Art and Thought* (Harvard, 1981).
FROST, F. J., and BADIAN, E., 'The Dubious Origins of the "Marathon" ', *AJAH* 4 (1979), 159–66.
FURNEAUX, H. (ed. and comm.), *The Annals of Tacitus*, 2 vols. (Oxford, 1896).
GABBA, E., 'The Perusine war and Triumviral Italy', *HSCP* 75 (1971),
—— 'P. Cornelio Scipione Africano e la leggenda', *Athenaeum*, 53 (1975), 3–17.
—— 'True History and False History in Classical Antiquity', *JRS* 71 (1981), 50–62.

GABBA, E., *Del buon uso della ricchezza* (Milan, 1988).

GAGÉ, J., 'Pyrrhus et l'influence religieuse de Dodone dans l'Italie primitive', *RHR* 164 (1954), 137–65.

—— *Apollon romain* (Paris, 1955).

GALINSKY, K., *The Herakles Theme* (Oxford, 1972).

GARDEN, A. E., *Paediatric and Adolescent Gynaecology* (London, 1998).

GARDINER, R., and MORRISON, J. S. (eds.), *The Age of the Galley* (London, 1995).

GARLAND, R., *The Eye of the Beholder: Deformity and Disability in the Graeco-Roman World* (London, 1995).

—— *The Greek Way of Death*[2] (Bristol, 2001).

GARNSEY, P. A., *Famine and Food Supply in the Graeco-Roman World: Responses to Risk and Crisis* (Cambridge, 1988).

GAUGER, J.-D., 'Phlegon von Trallis, mirab. III: zu einem Dokument geistigen Widerstandes gegen Rom', *Chiron*, 10 (1980), 225–49.

GÉLIS, J., *History of Childbirth: Fertility, Pregnancy and Birth in Early Modern Europe*, trans. R. Morris (Cambridge, 1991).

GELZER, M., *Pompeius* (Munich, 1949).

—— *Caesar: Politician and Statesman* (Oxford, 1968).

GIANNELLI, G., *Culti e miti della Magna Grecia* (Florence, 1924).

GIBBS, S. L., *Greek and Roman Sundials* (New Haven and London, 1976).

GIL, L., *Therapeia* (Madrid, 1969).

GINZBURG, C., *The Night Battles: Witchcraft and Agrarian Cults in the Sixteenth and Sevententh Centuries*, trans. J. and A. Tedeschi (Baltimore, 1983).

GOMME, A. W., *A Historical Commentary on Thucydides*, i: *Introduction and Commentary on Book 1* (Oxford, 1945).

——, ANDREWES, A., DOVER, K. J., *A Historical Commentary on Thucydides*, v: *Book 8* (Oxford, 1981).

GOODENOUGH, E. R., 'The Political Philosophy of Hellenistic Kingship', *YCS* 1 (1928), 55–102.

GOODYEAR, F. R. D., *The Annals of Tacitus books 1–6* (Cambridge, 1981).

GORDON, R., 'Aelian's Peony: The Location of Magic in the Graeco-Roman Tradition', *Comparative Criticism*, 9 (1987), 59–95.

GOTTSCHALK, H. B., *Heracleides of Pontus* (Oxford, 1980).

GOURÉVITCH, D., 'Suicide among the Sick in Classical antiquity', *BHM* 43 (1969), 501–18.

—— *Le Triangle Hippocratique dans le monde Greco-Romain: Le Malade, sa maladie et son médecin*, BEFAR 251 (Paris, 1984).

—— 'La Mort de la femme en couches et dans les suites de couches', in Hinard (1987), 187–94.

GOWERS, E., 'The Anatomy of Rome, from Capitol to Cloaca', *JRS* 85 (1995), 23–32.

GRAF, F., *Magic in the Ancient World*, trans. F. Philip (Harvard, 1997).

GRANT, M., *Gladiators: The Bloody Truth* (London, 1967; rev. edn. Harmondsworth, 1971).

GRAY, E. W., 'The *Imperium* of M. Agrippa', *ZPE* 6 (1970), 227–38.

GRAY, H. D. F., 'Metal-Working in Homer', *JHS* 74 (1954), 1–15.

GREEN, C. J. S., 'The Significance of Plaster Burials for the Recognition of Christian Cemeteries', in R. Reece (ed.), *Burial in the Roman World* (London, 1977), 46–53.

GREENHALGH, P., *Pompey the Republican Prince* (London, 1981).

GRENADE, R., 'Le Mythe de Pompée et les Pompéians sous les Césars', *REA* 52 (1950), 28–63.

GRIFFIN, M. T., *Nero: The End of a Dynasty* (London, 1984).

—— 'Philosophy, Cato and Roman Suicide: I and II', *G&R* NS 33 (1986), 64–77, 192–202.

—— 'Philosophy, Politics and Politicians at Rome', in M. T. Griffin and J. Barnes (eds.), *Philosophia Togata: Essays on Philosophy and Roman Society* (Oxford, 1989), 1–37.

—— *Seneca: A Philosopher in Politics*, rev. edn. (Oxford, 1992).

—— 'The Flavians', in A. K. Bowman, P. Garnsey, D. Rathbone (eds.), *The Cambridge Ancient History* ², xi (Cambridge, 2000), 23–5.

—— '*Clementia* after Caesar: From Politics to Philosophy', in Cairns and Fantham (2003), 157–82.

GRIMAL, P., *Les Jardins Romains* ² (Paris, 1969).

GRISÉ, Y., *Le Suicide dans la Rome antique* (Montreal and Paris, 1982).

GRMEK, M. D., 'Les *indicia mortis* dans la médecine gréco-romaine', in Hinard (1987), 129–44.

—— *Diseases in the Ancient Greek World* (Baltimore and London, 1989).

—— 'La Malaria dans la Méditerranée orientale préhistorique et antique', *Parasitologia*, 36 (1994), 1–6.

GROS, P. (ed. and comm.), *Vitruve De l'Architecture 3*, Coll. Univ. France (Paris, 1990).

GUNDEL, W., and GUNDEL, H. G., *Astrologoumena* (Wiesbaden, 1966).

GUTHRIE, D., *A History of Medicine* ² (London, 1958).

GUZMÁN ARIAS, C., 'Nota a Plinio *Naturalis Historia* VII.2.16–8', *Faventia*, 12–13 (1990–1), 437–42.

HADAS, M., *Sextus Pompey* (New York, 1930).

HAGENDAHL, H., *Augustine and the Latin Classics* (Göteborg, 1967).

HALSBERGHE, G. H., *Sol Invictus* (Leiden, 1972).

HANSEN, W. (trans. and comm.), *Phlegon of Tralles' Book of Wonders* (Exeter, 1996).

HANSON, A. E., 'The Eighth Month Child: *Obsit Omen*', *BHM* 61 (1987), 589–602.

—— 'Continuity and Change: Three Studies in Hippocratic Gynecological Therapy and Theory', in S. B. Pomeroy (ed.), *Women's History*

484   BIBLIOGRAPHY

and Ancient History (Chapel Hill, NC, 1991), 73–110.

—— 'Conception, Gestation and the Origin of Female Nature in the *Corpus Hippocraticum*', *Helios*, 19 (1992), 31–71.

HARLOW, M., and LAWRENCE, R., *Growing Up and Growing Old in Ancient Rome* (London, 2001).

HARRIS, H. A., *Greek Athletes and Athletics* (London, 1964).

HARRIS, W. V., 'Towards a Study of the Roman Slave Trade', *MAAR* 36 (1980), 117–40.

—— *Ancient Literacy* (Cambridge, Mass., 1989).

HARTOG, J., *The Mirror of Herodotus* (Berkeley, 1988).

HEALY, J. F., *Mining and Metallurgy in the Greek and Roman World* (London, 1978).

—— *Pliny the Elder on Science and Technology* (Oxford, 1999).

HELLGOUARC'H, J., *Le Vocabulaire Latin des relations et des partis politiques sous la République* (Paris, 1963).

HEMBERG, B., 'Die Idaiischen Daktylen', *Eranos*, 50 (1952), 41–52.

HENRICHS, A., 'The Sophists and Hellenistic Religion: Prodicus as the Spiritual Father of the Isis Aretologies', *HSCP* 88 (1984), 139–58.

—— 'Three Approaches to Greek Mythography', in J. Bremmer (ed.), *Interpretations of Greek Mythology* (London, 1987), 242–77.

HERDT, G., 'Mistaken Sex: Culture, Biology and the Third Sex in New Guinea' in G. Herdt (ed.), *Third Sex, Third Gender: Beyond Sexual Dimorphism in Culture and History* (New York, 1994).

HERTZ, R., *Death and the Right Hand* (Oxford, 1960).

HEURGON, J., 'Les Sortilèges d'un avocat sous Trajan', *Scripta Varia* (Brussels, 1986), 99–104.

HEYERDAHL, T., *The Ra Expeditions* (Harmondsworth, 1970).

—— *The Tigris Expedition* (Harmondsworth, 1980).

HILL, D. E., 'The Thessalian Trick', *RM* 116 (1973), 221–8.

HINARD, F. (ed.), *La Mort, les morts et l'au-delà dans le monde romain* (Caen, 1987).

HORDEN P. and PURCELL, N., *The Corrupting Sea: A Study of Mediterranean History* (Oxford, 2000).

HORNBLOWER, S., *Thucydides* (London, 1987).

HORSFALL, N., *Cornelius Nepos: A Selection, including the Lives of Cato and Atticus* (Oxford, 1989).

—— 'Statistics or States of Mind?', in *Literacy in the Ancient World*, JRA suppl. ser. vol. 3 (Ann Arbor, 1991), 59–76.

HOW, W. W., and WELLS, J., *A Commentary on Herodotus with Introduction and Appendixes*, 2 vols. (Oxford, 1912).

HOWE, N. P., 'In Defense of the Encyclopedic Mode: On Pliny's Preface to the Natural History', *Latomus*, 44 (1985), 561–76.

HOWELL, P., 'The Colossus of Nero', *Athenaeum*, 46 (1968), 292–9.

HOWEY, M. O., *The Horse in Magic and Myth* (London, 1923).

HUGHES, D., *Human Sacrifice in Ancient Greece* (London, 1991).

HUMPHREY, J., 'The Three Daughters of Agrippina Maior', *AJAH* 4 (1979), 128–43.

HUMPHREY, J. H., *Roman Circuses: Arenas for Chariot-Racing* (London, 1986).

HUMPHREYS, S. C., 'Death and Time', in S. C. Humphreys and H. King (eds.) *Mortality and Immortality: the Anthropology and Archaeology of Death* (London, 1981), 261–84.

—— 'Fragments, Fetishes and Philosophies: towards a History of Greek Historiography after Thucydides', in G. W. Most (ed.), *Collecting Fragments: Fragmente Sammeln* (Göttingen, 1997), 207–24.

HURLEY, D. W., *An Historical and Historiographical Commentary on Suetonius' Life of Caligula* (Atlanta, 1993).

HUXLEY, G., 'Bones for Orestes', *GRBS* 20. 2 (1979), 145–8.

INWOOD, B., *Ethics and Human Action in Early Stoicism* (Oxford, 1985).

ISAGER, J., *Pliny on Art and Society: The Elder Pliny's Chapters on the History of Art* (London, 1991).

JEANMAIRE, H., *Dionysos: Histoire de la culte de Bacchus* (Paris, 1951).

JEX-BLAKE, K., and SELLERS, E., *The Elder Pliny's Chapters on the History of Art* (London and New York, 1896).

JOHNSTON, S. I., 'Crossroads', *ZPE* 88 (1991), 217–24.

—— *Restless Dead* (California, 1999).

JONES, B., *The Emperor Titus* (London, 1984).

JONES, C. P., 'Stigma: Tatooing and Branding in Graeco-Roman Antiquity', *JRS* 77 (1987), 139–55.

KAHN, C. H., *Anaximander and the Origins of Greek Cosmology* (New York, 1960, and Indianapolis and Cambridge, 1994).

KAJANTO, I., *The Latin Cognomina* (Helsinki, 1965).

—— 'Fortuna', *ANRW* 11. 17. 1 (Berlin and New York, 1981), 502–58.

KEELING, J. W. (ed.), *Foetal and Neo-natal pathology*² (London, 1992).

KEIL, K., 'Zur Lateinische Onomatologie', *RM* 16, (1861), 290–5.

KELLER, O., *Die Antike Tierwelt* (Hildesheim, 1909; repr. 1963).

KERENYI, K., *Apollon; und Niobe* (Munich, 1980).

KEYNES, G. (ed.), *The Works of Sir Thomas Browne*, 4 vols. (London, 1928, repr. 1964).

KIDD, I. G., 'Stoic Intermediates and the End for Man', in A. A. Long (ed.), *Problems in Roman Stoicism* (London, 1971), 200–15.

KIERDORF, W., *Laudatio Funebris: Interpretationem und Untersuchungen* (Meisenheim am Glam, 1980).

KING, H., 'Bound to Bleed: Artemis and Greek Women', in A. Cameron and A. Kuhrt (eds.), *Images of Women in Antiquity* (London, 1983), 109–27.

—— 'The Daughter of Leonides: Reading the Hippocratic Corpus', in A. Cameron (ed.), *History as Text* (London, 1989), 13–32.

KING, H., 'Once upon a Text: Hysteria from Hippocrates', in S. L. Gilman, H. King, R. Porter, G. S. Rousseau, E. Showalter, *Hysteria beyond Freud* (California, 1993), 3–90.

KIRK, G. S., *Heraclitus: The Cosmic Fragments* (Cambridge, 1954).

KITTREDGE, G. L., *Witchcraft in Old and New England* (New York, 1958).

KLEINGÜNTHER, A., 'Protos Heuretes', *Philologus* suppl. 26. 1 (1933).

KLIMA, U., *Untersuchungen zu dem Begriff Sapientia von der republikanischen Zeit bis Tacitus* (Bonn, 1971).

KRAUSS, F. B., *An Interpretation of the Omens, Portents and Prodigies recorded by Livy, Tacitus and Suetonius* (Pennsylvania, 1930).

KRENKEL, W. A., 'Cursores Maiores Minoresque', *Classical World*, 70 (1976), 373–4.

LADURIE, E. LE ROY, *Montaillou, the Promised Land of Error*, trans. B. Bray (New York, 1978).

LAISTNER, M. L. W., *The Intellectual Heritage of the Early Middle Ages* (Ithaca, 1957).

LAQUEUR, T., *Making Sex: Body and Gender from the Greeks to Freud* (Harvard, 1990).

LASSÈRE, J.-M., *Ubique Populus* (Paris, 1977).

LATTIMORE, R., *Themes in Greek and Latin Epitaphs* (Illinois, 1942).

LAURAND, L., *Études sur le style des discours de Cicéron*[3], 3 vols. (Paris, 1926).

LAWLER, L. B., *The Dance in Ancient Greece* (Middletown, 1964).

LAWSON, J. C., *Modern Greek Folklore and Ancient Greek Religion* (New York, 1964).

LAZENBY, J. F., *The Spartan Army* (Warminster, 1985).

LEACH, J., *Pompey the Great* (London, 1977).

LE BONNIEC, H., *Pline l'Ancien Histoire Naturelle livre 34* (Paris, 1953).

LEFKOWITZ, M., *The Lives of the Greek Poets* (London, 1981).

LEIGH, M., 'Lucan and the Libyan Tale', *JRS* 90 (2000), 95–109.

LESKY, A., 'Aithiopika', *Hermes*, 87 (1957), 27–38.

LEUZE, O., 'Metellus Caecatus', *Philol.* 18 (1905), 95–115.

LÉVÊQUE, P., *Pyrrhos* (Paris, 1957).

—— and VIDAL-NAQUET, P., 'Épaminondas Pythagoricien: ou le problème tactique de la droite et de la gauche', *Historia*, 9 (1960), 294–308.

LEVI, D., 'The Evil Eye and the Lucky Hunchback', in *Antioch-on-the-Orontes*, iii: *The Excavations of 1937–9* (Princeton, 1941), 220–32.

LEVICK, B., *Claudius* (London, 1990).

LIMBERIS, V., 'The Eyes Infected by Evil: Basil of Caesarea's Homily, *On Envy*', *H. Th. R.* 84. 2, (1991), 163–84.

LINDSAY, H., *Suetonius Life of Caligula* (Bristol, 1992).

—— 'Death Pollution and Funerals in Rome', in V. M. Hope and E. Marshall (eds.) *Death and Disease in the Ancient City* (London, 2000), 152–73.

LLOYD, G. E. R., 'Right and Left in Greek Philosophy', *JHS* 82 (1962), 56–66.

—— 'The Hippocratic Question', *CQ* NS 25 (1975), 171–92 (= *Methods and Problems in Greek Science* (Cambridge, 1991), 194–223).

—— *Science, Folklore and Ideology* (Cambridge, 1983).

LO CASCIO, E., 'The Size of the Roman Population: Beloch and the Meaning of the Augustan Census Figures', *JRS* 84 (1994), 23–40.

LOCHER, A., 'The Structure of the *Natural History*', in R. French and F. Greenaway (eds.), *Science in the Early Roman Empire: Pliny the Elder, his Sources and Influence* (London, 1986), 20–9.

LONG, A. A., and SEDLEY, D., *The Hellenistic Philosophers*, 2 vols. (Cambridge, 1987).

LONGRIGG, J., 'Death and Epidemic Disease in Athens', in V. M. Hope and E. Marshall (eds.) *Death and Disease in the Ancient City* (London, 2000), 55–64.

LONIE, I. M., 'Medical Theory in Heraclides of Pontus', *Mnemosyne*, 18 (1965), 126–43.

LONSDALE, S., *Dance and Ritual Play in Greek Religion* (Baltimore and London, 1993).

LOVEJOY, A. O., *The Great Chain of Being: A Study of the History of an Idea* (Harvard, 1932; repr. 1970).

—— and BOAS, G., *Primitivism and Related Ideas in Antiquity* (New York, 1935).

LUCE, G. G., *Body Time* (London, 1972).

LUFKIN, A. W., *A History of Dentistry*[2] (London, 1948).

LUNAIS, S., *Recherches sur la lune*, i: *Les Auteurs Latins de la fin des guerres Puniques à la fin du règne des Antonins* (Leiden, 1979).

MACBAIN, B., *Prodigy and Expiation: A Study in Religion and Politics in Republican Rome*, Coll. Lat. 177 (Brussels, 1982).

McCARTNEY, E. S., 'Praise and Dispraise in Folklore', in A. Dundes (ed.), *Interpreting Folklore* (Indiana UP, 1980), 9–38.

McDANIEL, W. B., 'The *pupula duplex* and Other Tokens of an Evil Eye in the Light of Opthalmology', *CPh.* 13 (1918), 335–46.

—— *Conception, Birth and Infancy in Ancient Rome and Modern Italy* (Florida, 1948 = 1948*a*).

—— 'The Medical and Magical Significance in Ancient Medicine of Things Connected with Reproduction and its Organs', *JHM* III (1948 = 1948*b*), 525–46.

McDONALD, B., 'The Special Senses: The Eyes', in Keeling (1992), 667–82.

McGRAIL, S., *Boats of the World* (Oxford, 2002).

MACHIN, G. A., 'The Pathology of Twinning', in Keeling (1992), 223–37.

MAJNO, G., *The Healing Hand* (Cambridge, Mass., 1975).

MALONEY, C., 'Don't say "Pretty baby" lest you Zap it with your Eye: The Evil Eye in South Asia', in C. Maloney (ed.), *The Evil Eye* (Colombia, 1976), 102–47.

MANCHESTER, K., and ROBERTS, C., *The Archaeology of Disease*[2] (Stroud, 1997).

MARSDEN, E. W., *Greek and Roman Artillery: Historical Development* (Oxford, 1969).

MARSHALL, B. A., 'Pompey's Temple of Hercules', *Antichthon*, 8 (1974), 80–4.

MARTIN, D. E., BENARIO, H. W., GLYN, R. W. H., 'Development of the Marathon from Pheidippides to the Present, with Statistics of Significant Races', in 'The Marathon: Physiological, Medical, Epidemiological and Psychological Studies', *Ann. N.Y. Ac. Sci.* 301 (1977), 821–52.

MATTHEWS, J., *The Roman Empire of Ammianus* (London, 1989).

MATTHEWS, V. J., 'The *Hemerodromoi*: Ultra Long-Distance Running in Antiquity', *Classical World*, 68 (1974), 161–9.

MATTIEU, A., 'Lithopedion developed from Extrauterine Gestation in Intrauterine and Extrauterine Pregnancy', *Am. J. Obstet. Gyn.* 37 (1939), 297–302.

MAXFIELD, V. A., *The Military Decorations of the Roman Army* (Berkeley, 1981).

MAXWELL-STUART, P. G., 'Studies in the Career of Pliny the Elder and the Composition of his *Naturalis Historia*' (Ph.D. diss., St Andrews, 1996 = 1996*a*).

—— 'Dating by African Figs', *Mus. Helv.* 53 (1996 = 1996*b*), 256–8.

MAYOR, A., *The First Fossil Hunters* (Princeton, 2000).

MEHL, A., *Seleukos Nikator und sein Reich*, vol. i (Leuven, 1986).

MEIGGS, R., *Trees and Timber in the Ancient Mediterranean World* (Oxford, 1982).

MELYUKOVA, A. I., 'The Scythians and Sarmatians', in D. Sinor (ed.), *The Cambridge History of Early Inner Asia* (Cambridge, 1990), 97–117.

MESK, J., 'Antiochus und Stratonike', *RM* 68 (1913), 366–94.

MEULI, K., 'Scythica', *Hermes*, 70 (1935), 121–76.

MIKALSON, J., *The Sacred and Civil Calendar of the Athenian State* (Princeton, 1975).

MILLAR, F., *The Emperor in the Roman World*[2] (London, 1992).

MIRSCH, P., 'De M. Terenti Varronis Antiquitatum rerum humanarum libris XXV', *Leipziger Studien*, 5 (1882), 1–144.

MOMIGLIANO, A., 'Livio, Plutarco e Giustino su virtù e fortuna dei Romani contributo alla ricostruzione della fonte di Trogo Pompeo', *Athenaeum*, ns 12 (1934), 45–56.

—— *On Pagans, Jews and Christians* (Connecticut, 1987).

MOMMSEN, T., 'Die Familie des Germanicus', *Hermes*, 13 (1878), 245–65.

—— *Römisches Staatsrecht*[3], 3 vols. (Leipzig, 1887).

MONTEVECCHI, O., 'Poson menon estin', *ZPE* 34 (1979), 113–17.

MOORE, I. E., 'Macerated Stillbirth', in Keeling (1992), 182–97.

MORGAN, J. R., 'The Fragments of Ancient Greek Fiction', *ANRW* 34. 4 (Berlin and New York, 1998), 3293–3390.

MORRIS, I., *Burial and Ancient Society* (Cambridge, 1987).

—— *Death Ritual and Social Structure in Classical Antiquity* (Cambridge, 1992).

MORRISON, J., and WILLIAMS, R., *Greek Oared Ships* (Cambridge, 1968).

——, COATES, J. F., RANKOV, N. B., *The Athenian Trireme*[2] (Cambridge, 2000).

MOSS, L. W. and CAPPANNARI, S. C., 'Mal'occhio, Ayin ha ra, Oculus fascinus, Judenblick: The Evil Eye Hovers Above', in C. Maloney (ed.), *The Evil Eye* (Colombia, 1976), 1–15.

MOYNIHAN, R., 'Geographical Mythology and Roman Imperial Ideology', in R. Winkes (ed.), *The Age of Augustus* (Louvain, 1986), 148–57.

MÜLLER, K., *The Fragments of the Lost Historians of Alexander the Great* (Paris, 1846; repr. Chicago, 1979).

MUNRO FOX, H., 'Lunar Periodicity in Reproduction', *Proc. Roy. Soc. B.* 95 (1924), 523–50.

MÜNZER, F., *Beiträge zur Quellenkritik der Naturgeschichte des Plinius* (Berlin, 1897).

NAAS, V., 'Réflexions sur la méthode de travail de Pline l'Ancien', *Rev. Phil.* 70. 2 (1996), 305–32.

—— 'L'Histoire Naturelle de Pline l'Ancien: est-elle une œuvre scientifique?', in *Science antique, science médiévale (Actes du colloque international Mont-Saint-Michel, 4–7 Septembre, 1998)* (Hildesheim and New York, 2000), 255–71.

—— *Le Projet encyclopédique de Pline l'Ancien*, Coll. Ec. France de Rome, 303 (Rome, 2002).

NADEAU, Y., 'Ethiopians', *CQ* NS 20 (1970), 339–49.

NASH, C., *Pictorial Dictionary of Ancient Rome*[2], 2 vols. (New York, 1981).

NEEDHAM, J., *A History of Embryology*[2] (Cambridge, 1959).

NÉRAUDAU, J.-P., 'La Loi, la coutume et le chagrin: Réflexions sur la mort des enfants', in Hinard (1987), 195–208.

NEUGEBAUER, O., *A History of Ancient Mathematical Astronomy*, 3 vols. (Berlin and New York, 1975).

NICHOLSON, F. W., 'The Saliva Superstition in Classical Literature', *HSCP* 8 (1891), 23–40.

NICOLET, C., *Space, Geography and Politics in the Early Roman Empire* (English trans., Ann Arbor, 1991).

—— 'A la recherche des archives oubliées: une contribution à l'histoire de la bureaucratie Romaine', in *La Mémoire perdue: a la recherche des archives oubliées, publiques et privées, de la Rome antique* (Paris, 1994), v–xvii.

490 BIBLIOGRAPHY

NIEKIRK, W. A. van, *True Hermaphroditism: Clinical, Morphological and Cytogenetic Aspects* (New York and London, 1974).

NILSSON, M. P., *Greek Religion* (Oxford, 1925; 3rd edn. 1949).

NOIVILLE, J., 'Les Indes de Bacchus et d'Heraclès', *Rev. Phil.* 55 (1929), 245–69.

NUTTON, V., 'Did the Greeks have a word for it? Contagion and Contagion Theory in Classical Antiquity', in L. I. Conrad and D. Wujastyk (eds.), *Contagion: Perspectives for Pre-Modern Societies* (Aldershot, 2000), 137–62.

OAKLEY, S., *Commentary on Livy VI–X* (Oxford, 1997).

O'DONOVAN, J., *Annals of the Kingdom of Ireland*, 4 vols. (Dublin, 1856).

OGDEN, D., *Greek and Roman Necromancy* (Princeton, 2001).

OGILVIE, R. M., '*Lustrum Condere*', *JRS* 51 (1961), 31–9.

—— *Commentary on Livy books 1–5* (Oxford, 1965).

OLIVEIRA, F. DE, *Les Idées politiques et morales de Pline l'Ancien*, Estudos de Cultura Clássica, 5 (Coimbra, 1992).

OOTEGHEM, J. VAN, *Pompée le Grand, bâtisseur d'Empire* (Namur, 1954).

—— *Les Caecilii Metelli de la République* (Namur, 1967).

OPPENHEIM, L. A., 'A Caesarian Section in the Second Millennium BC', *JHM* 15 (1960), 292–4.

ORLIN, E., *Temples, Religion and Politics in the Roman Republic* (Leiden, 1997).

OUTRAM, D., *Georges Cuvier* (Manchester, 1984).

PAIS, E., *Ancient Legends of Roman History*, trans. M. E. Cosenza (London, 1906).

—— 'The Legend of Euthymus of Locri', in *Ancient Italy* (Chicago and London, 1908), 39–51.

—— *Fasti Triumphales Populi Romani* (Rome, 1920).

PAPALAS, A. J., 'The Development of the Greek Trireme', *Mariner's Mirror*, 83 (1997), 259–71.

PAPARAZZO, E., 'Pliny the Elder on the Melting and Corrosion of Silver with Tin in Solders: *prius liquescat argentum . . . ab eo erodi argentum* (*HN* 34.161)', *CQ* 53. 2 (2003), 523–9.

PARÉ, A., *Des monstres et prodiges*, ed. J. Céard (Geneva, 1973).

PARK, K., and DASTON, L. J., 'Unnatural Conceptions: The Study of Monsters in Sixteenth- and Seventeenth-Century France and England', *P&P* 92 (1981), 20–54.

PARKE, H. W., *Greek Oracles* (London, 1967).

—— *Sibyls and Sibylline Prophecy in Classical Antiquity*, ed. B. C. McGing (London, 1988).

—— and Wormell, D. E. W., *The Delphic Oracle*², 2 vols. (Oxford, 1956).

PARKER, R., *Miasma: Pollution and Purification in Early Greek Religion* (Oxford, 1983).

PARKIN, T. R., *Demography and Roman Society* (London, 1992).

PAVÓN, P., 'La Pietas e il carcere del Foro Olitorio: Plinio NH 7.121',
    MEFRA 109. 2 (1997), 633–57.
PEARSON, L., *The Early Ionian Historians* (Oxford, 1939; repr. Connecticut,
    1979).
—— *The Lost Historians of Alexander the Great* (New York, 1960).
PEASE, A. S. (ed. and comm.), *M. Tulli Ciceronis De Natura Deorum*, 2 vols.
    (Cambridge, Mass., 1955).
—— *M. Tulli Ciceronis de Divinatione libri duo* (Darmstadt, 1973).
PELLEGRIN, P., 'L'Imaginaire de la fièvre dans la médecine antique',
    History and Philosophy of the Life Sciences, 10 (1988), 109–20.
PENTIKÄINEN, J., 'The Dead without Status', *Temenos*, 4 (1969), 92–102.
PENTOGLOS, G. E. and LASCARATOS, J. C., 'A Surgical Operation
    Performed on Siamese Twins during the Tenth Century', *BHM* 58. 1
    (1984), 433.
PFLAUM, H. G., *Les Carrières procuratoriennes equestres sous le Haut-Empire
    Romain* (Paris, 1960).
PHILLIPS, D., *Greek Medicine* (London, 1973).
PHILLIPS, E. D., *The Royal Hordes: Nomad Peoples of the Steppes* (London,
    1965).
PICARD, G.-C., *Les Trophées Romains: Contribution à l'histoire de la religion et de
    l'art* (Paris, 1957).
—— 'Le Monument qui réconforta Neron', *CRAI* (Jan.–Mar. 1990),
    659–66.
PICCALUGA, G., 'I Marsi e gli Herpi', in P. Xella (ed.), *Magia: Studi in mem-
    orie R. Garosi* (Rome, 1976), 207–31.
PIGEAUD, J., 'Un *locus desperatus* chez Pline l'Ancien', *Helmantica*, 44 (1993):
    Thesauramata Philologica Iosepho Orozio Oblata, 467–76.
—— and OROZ, J. (eds.), *Pline l'Ancien: Témoin de son temps*, Conventus
    Pliniani Internationalis, Nantes, 22–26 Octobre 1985 (Salamanca and
    Nantes, 1987).
PIGGOTT, S., *The Earliest Wheeled Transport: from the Atlantic Coast to the
    Caspian Sea* (London, 1983).
—— *Wagon, Chariot and Carriage: Symbol and Status in the History of Transport*
    (London, 1992).
PIGHI, G. B., *De Ludis Saecularibus*² (Amsterdam, 1965).
PINAULT, J. R., 'How Hippocrates Cured the Plague', *JHM* 41 (1987),
    52–75.
PLATNER, S. B., and ASHBY, T., *A Topographical Dictionary of Ancient Rome*
    (London and Oxford, 1929).
POLLINI, J., '*Damnatio memoriae* in Stone: Two Portraits of Nero Recut to
    Vespasian in American Museums', *AJA* 88 (1984), 547–55.
PRAG, A. J. N. W., 'Reconstructing King Midas: A First Report', *Anat.
    Stud.* 39 (1989), 159–65.

492   BIBLIOGRAPHY

PRAG, A. J. N. W., 'Reconstructing Philip II: The "nice" Version', *AJA* 94. 2 (1990), 237–47.

—— and Neave, R. A. H., *Making Faces: Using Forensic and Archaeological Evidence* (London, 1997).

——, Musgrave, J. H., Neave, R. A. H., 'The Skull from Tomb II at Vergina: King Philip of Macedon', *JHS* 74 (1984), 60–78.

PRÉAUX, C., *La Lune dans la pensée Grecque* (Brussels, 1973).

PUNDEL, J., *L'Histoire de l'opération Césarienne* (Brussels, 1969).

PURCELL, N., 'The Apparitores: A Study in Social Mobility', *PBSR* 51, NS 38 (1983), 125–73.

—— review of C. Nicolet, *L'Inventaire du monde: Géographie et politique aux origines de l'Empire Romain, JRS* 80 (1990), 178–82.

RABENHORST, M., *Der ältere Plinius als Epitomator des Verrius Flaccus: Eine Quellenanalyse des siebenten Buches der Naturgeschichte* (Berlin, 1907).

RAMAGE, E. S., 'Denigration of Predecessor under Claudius, Galba and Vespasian', *Historia*, 32 (1983), 201–14.

RAMIN, J., *Mythologie et géographie* (Paris, 1979).

RANKIN, H. D., *Archilochus of Paros* (Parke Ridge, NJ, 1977).

—— *Celts and the Classical World*² (London, 1996).

RAPISARDA, A., *Censorini De Die Natali liber ad Q. Caerellium, prefazione, testo critico* (Bologna, 1991).

RAWSON, E., 'Chariot-Racing in the Roman Republic', *PBSR* 49 (1981), 1–16.

—— *Intellectual Life in the Late Roman Republic* (London, 1985).

—— 'Roman Rulers and the Philosophic Advisor', in M. T. Griffin and J. Barnes (eds.), *Philosophia Togata: Essays on Philosophy and Roman Society* (Oxford, 1989), 233–57.

REEVE, M., 'Conceptions', *PCPS* 215 (1989), 81–112.

REINHOLD, M., *Marcus Agrippa: A Biography* (Geneva and New York, 1933).

RENEHAN, R., 'The Greek Anthropocentric View of Nature', *HSCP* 85 (1981), 239–59.

RHODES, P. J., *A Commentary on the Aristotelian Athenaion Politeia* (Oxford, 1981).

RICHARD, J. C., 'Alexandre et Pompée: à propos de Tite-Live IX.16.19–19.7', in *Mélanges de philosophie, de littérature et d'histoire ancienne offerts à Pierre Boyancé*, Coll. Ec. France de Rome, 22 (Rome, 1974), 653–69.

RICHARDSON, L., *A New Topographical Dictionary of Ancient Rome* (Johns Hopkins, 1992).

RIGINOS, A. SWIFT, 'The Wounding of Philip II of Macedon: Fact and Fabrication', *JHS* 114 (1994), 103–19.

RIJK, L. M. DE, *'enkuklios paideia*: A Study of its Original Meaning', *Vivarium*, 3 (1985), 24–93.

RIPOLL, F., 'Aspects et function de Néron dans la propagande impériale

Flavienne', in J. M. Croisille, R. Martin, and Y. Perrin (eds.), *Néron: Histoire et légende: Notes du Ve Colloque International 2–6 Novembre 1994* (Brussels, 1999), 137–51.

RIST, J. M., *Stoic Philosophy* (Berkeley and London, 1978).

RIVES, J., 'Human Sacrifice among Pagans and Christians', *JRS* 85 (1995), 65–84.

ROBERTS, C. H., and SKEAT, T. C., *The Birth of the Codex* (Oxford and British Academy, London, 1987).

ROBERTSON, M., *A History of Greek Art*, 2 vols. (Cambridge, 1975).

—— *The Art of Vase Painting in Classical Athens* (Cambridge, 1992).

ROCCA-SERRA, G., *Censorinus, Le Jour Natal; traduction annotée* (Paris, 1980).

RODDAZ, J.-M., *Marcus Agrippa*, BEFAR 252 (Paris, 1984).

ROHDE, E., *Psyche*, trans. W. B. Hillis (London and New York, 1925).

ROLLE, R., *The World of the Scythians* (London, 1989).

ROLLER, M. B., *Constructing Autocracy: Aristocrats and Emperors in Julio-Claudian Rome* (Princeton, 2001).

ROMER, F., 'Die Plinianische Anthropologie und der Aufbau de *HN*', *WS* NS 17 (1983), 104–8.

ROMM, J. S., *The Edges of the World in Ancient Thought: Geography, Exploration and Fiction* (Princeton, 1992).

RONCORONI, A., 'Plinio Tardoantico', in *Plinio il Vecchio; sotto il profilo storico e letterario: Atti del convegno di Como 5–7 Ottobre, 1979* (Como, 1982), 151–68.

ROSSBACH, O., 'Agroecius et Plinius de Delphica', *RM* 57 (1902), 473–4.

ROSUMEK, P., and NAJOCK, D., *Concordantia in C. Plinii Secundi Naturalem Historiam*, 7 vols. (Zurich, 1996).

ROTTLÄNDER, R. C. A., 'The Pliny Translation Group of Germany', in R. French and F. Greenaway (eds.) *Science in the Early Roman Empire: Pliny the Elder, his Sources and Influence* (London, 1986), 11–19.

ROUVERET, A., 'Toute la mémoire du monde: La Notion de collection dans la *NH* de Pline', in Pigeaud and Oroz (1987), 431–49.

RUSSELL, W. M. S., 'Greek and Roman Ghosts', in H. R. Ellis-Davidson and W. M. S. Russell (eds.), *The Folklore of Ghosts* (Bury St Edmunds, 1981), 193–214.

SABBAH, G., 'Présence de la *HN* chez les auteurs de l'Antiquité tardive; l'exemple d'Ammien Marcellin, de Symmaque et d'Ausone', in Pigeaud and Oroz (1987), 519–37.

SAINTYVES, P., *Le Guérison des verrues* (Paris, 1913).

—— *L'Astrologie populaire: Étudiée spécialement dans les doctrines et les traditions relatives à l'influence de la lune* (Paris, 1937).

SALAZAR, C., *The Treatment of War-Wounds in Graeco-Roman Antiquity* (Brill, 2000).

SALLARES, R., *The Ecology of the Ancient Greek World* (London, 1991).

494   BIBLIOGRAPHY

SALLARES, R., *Malaria and Rome: A History of Malaria in Ancient Italy* (Oxford, 2002).

SALLER, R., 'Anecdotes as Historical Evidence of the Principate', *G&R* 27 (1980), 69–83.

—— *Patriarchy, Property and Death in the Roman Family* (Cambridge, 1994).

SALMON, J. B., *Wealthy Corinth* (London, 1984).

SAUNDERS, J. B. DE C. M., *The Transitions from Ancient Egyptian to Greek Medicine* (Lawrence, 1963).

SCARCIA, R., 'Fragmentum Agrippinae: Ipotesi di un ricupero (e un riscontro Shakespeariano)', *GIF* 43 (1991), 243–63.

SCHILLING, R., *La Religion romaine de Vénus depuis les origines jusqu'au temps d'Auguste* (Paris, 1954, repr. 1982).

SCHMIDT, J., *Vie et mort des esclaves* (Paris, 1973).

SCHULZ, F., 'Roman Registers of Births and Birth Certificates', *JRS* 32 (1942), 78–91.

SCOTT, J. H., and SYMONS, N. B. B., *Introduction to Dental Anatomy*⁵ (Edinburgh and London, 1967).

SCOTT, K., 'The Elder and Younger Pliny on Emperor Worship', *TAPA* 63 (1932), 156–65.

SEAR, D. R., *The History and Coinage of the Roman Imperators* (London, 1998).

SEAR, F. B., *Roman Architecture* (London, 1982).

SEDLAR, J. W., *India and the Greek World: A Study in the Transmission of Culture* (New Jersey, 1980).

SERBAT, G., 'Il y a Grecs et Grecs! Quel sens donner au prétendu antihellénisme de Pline?', in Pigeaud and Oroz (1987), 589–98.

SHATZMAN, I., 'The Roman General's Authority over Booty', *Historia*, 21 (1972), 177–205.

—— *Senatorial Wealth and Roman Politics*, Coll. Lat. 142 (Brussels, 1975).

SHAW, I., and NICHOLSON, P., *British Museum Dictionary of Ancient Egypt* (London, 1995).

SHERK, R. K., *The Roman Empire: Augustus to Hadrian* (Cambridge, 1988).

SHERWIN-WHITE, A. N., *The Letters of Pliny: An Historical and Social Commentary* (Oxford, 1966).

SHERWIN-WHITE, S., and KUHRT, A., *From Samarkhand to Sardis* (London, 1993).

SINGER, C., and UNDERWOOD, R. A., *A Short History of Medicine* (New York and Oxford 1962).

SKUTSCH, O. (ed., introd., comm.), *The Annals of Quintus Ennius* (Oxford, 1985).

SMALL, J. P., *Wax Tablets of the Mind: Cognitive Studies of Memory and Literacy in Classical Antiquity* (London, 1997).

—— and Tatum, J., 'Memory and the Study of Classical Antiquity', *Helios*, 22 (1995), 149–77.

SMITH, C. S., 'Clinical Features of Growth Hormone Deficiency', in P. E. Belchetz (ed.), *The Management of Pituitary Disease* (London, 1984), 461–86.

SMITH, K. F., 'Pupula duplex', in *Studies in Honour of Basil L. Gildersleeve* (Baltimore, 1902), 287–310.

SMITH, W. D., 'Implicit Fever Theory in Epidemics 5 and 7', in W. F. Bynum and V. Nutton (eds.), *Theories of Fever from Antiquity to the Enlightenment*, Medical History suppl. 1 (London, 1981), 1–18.

SNODGRASS, A. M., 'Carian Armourers: The Growth of a Tradition', *JHS* 84 (1964), 107–18.

—— *Arms and Armour of the Greeks* (Ithaca, 1967).

SNOWDEN, F., *Before Color Prejudice: The Ancient View of Blacks* (London and Harvard 1983).

SOAMES, J. V., and SOUTHAM, J. C., *Oral Pathology* 3 (Oxford, 1998).

SOURVINOU-INWOOD, C., 'To die and enter the House of Hades: Homer, Before and After', in J. Whaley (ed.), *Mirrors of Mortality*, (New York, 1981), 15–39.

—— *'Reading' Greek Death to the End of the Classical Period* (Oxford, 1995).

STEWART, A. F., *Greek Sculpture: An Exploration* (New Haven and London, 1990).

STIBBE, C. M., 'Satricum e Pometia: Due nomi per la stessa città?', *Mededelingen van het Nederlands Instituut te Rome*, 47 (1988), 7–16.

STRACHAN-DAVIDSON, J. L., *Problems of the Roman Criminal Law*, 2 vols. (Oxford, 1912).

STRASBURGER, H., 'Poseidonius on the Problems of the Roman Empire', *JRS* 55 (1965), 40–53.

SULLIVAN, R. D., *Near Eastern Royalty and Rome 100–30 BC* (Toronto, 1990).

SUOLAHTI, J., *The Roman Censors: A Study in Social Structure* (Helsinki, 1963).

SVENBRO, J., *Phrasikleia: Anthropologie de la lecture en Grèce ancienne* (Paris, 1988).

SYDENHAM, E. A., *The Coinage of the Roman Republic* (London, 1952).

SYME, R., *The Roman Revolution* (Oxford, 1939).

—— *Tacitus*, 2 vols. (Oxford, 1958).

—— 'Pliny the Procurator', *HSCP* 73 (1969), 201–36 (= E. Badian (ed.), *Roman Papers*, ii (Oxford, 1979), 742–73).

—— 'Domitius Corbulo', *JRS* 60 (1970), 27–39 (= E. Badian (ed.), *Roman Papers*, ii (Oxford, 1979), 805–24).

—— 'Tacitus: Some Sources of his Information', *JRS* 72 (1982), 68–82.

—— 'Correspondents of Pliny', *Historia*, 34 (1985), 324–59 (= E. Badian (ed.), *Roman Papers*, v (Oxford, 1988), 440–77).

—— *The Augustan Aristocracy* (Oxford, 1986).

—— 'Carrière et amis consulaires de Pline', in Pigeaud and Oroz (1987), 539–47.

SYME, R., 'Consular Friends of the Elder Pliny', in A. R. Birley (ed.), *Roman Papers*, vii (Oxford, 1991), 496–511.

SZULMAN, A. E., 'Trophoblastic Disease: Pathology of Complete and Partial Moles', in G. B. Reed, A. E. Claireaux, and F. Cockburn (eds.), *Diseases of the Fetus and Newborn*² (London, 1995), 187–99.

TARN, W. W., *Hellenistic Military and Naval Developments* (Cambridge, 1930).

T.E.C., Jr., 'The Power of Maternal Impression Causes the Alleged Father's Name to Appear in Legible Letters in his Infant Son's Right Eye (1817)', *Pediatrics* 58 (1976), 901.

TESTER, J., *A History of Western Astrology* (Woodbridge, 1987; repr. 1999).

THOMAS, K., *Religion and the Decline of Magic* (London, 1971).

THOMPSON, D. L., 'The Meetings of the Roman Senate on the Palatine' *AJA* 85. 3 (1981), 335–9.

THOMPSON, S. E., 'Egyptian Language and Writing', in K. A. Bard (ed.), *Encyclopaedia of the Archaelogoy of Ancient Egypt* (London, 1999), 274–7.

THOMSEN, R., *Italic Regions from Augustus to the Lombard Invasions* (Copenhagen, 1947; repr. 1984).

THOMSON, J. O., *History of Ancient Geography* (Cambridge, 1948).

THRAEDE, K., 'Erfinder', in T. Klauser (ed.), *Reallexicon für Antike und Christentum*, v (1962), 1191–1278.

TILL, R., 'Plinius uber Augustus', *Wurzburger Jahrbucher*, NS 3 (1977), 127–37.

TOHER, M., 'Julius Caesar and Octavian in Nicolaus', in Cairns and Fantham (2003), 132–56.

TORPIN, R., 'Malaria Complicating Pregnancy', *Am. J. Obstet. Gyn.* 41 (1941), 882–5.

TOYNBEE, J. M. C., *Death and Burial in the Roman World* (London, 1971).

TOZER, H. F., *A History of Ancient Geography*² (Cambridge, 1935).

TROLLE, D., *The History of Caesarian Section* (Copenhagen, 1982).

TUPET, A.-M., *La Magie dans la poèsie Latine* (Paris, 1976).

—— 'Rites magiques dans l'antiquité romaine', *ANRW* 2. 16. 3 (Berlin and New York, 1986), 2591–675.

TURCAN, R., *Les Sarcophages romains à représentations dionysiaques: Essai de chronologie* (Paris, 1966).

TYRRELL, W. BLAKE, *Amazons: A Study in Athenian Myth-Making* (Baltimore and London, 1984).

UNDERWOOD, E. A., *A Short History of Medicine* (Oxford, 1962).

URLICHS, L., *Chrestomathia Pliniana* (Berlin, 1857).

VALLANCE, J. T., *The Lost Theory of Asclepiades of Bithynia* (Oxford, 1990).

VAN HOOFF, A., *From Autothanasia to Suicide: Self-Killing in Classical Antiquity* (London, 1990).

VEGETTI, M., 'Zoologia e antropologia in Plinio', in *Plinio il Vecchio sotto il profilo storico e letterario: Atti del convegno di Como 5–7 Ottobre 1979* (Como, 1982), 117–31.

VENDRYES, J., 'Agrippa et Vopiscus', *Miscelânea Scientifica e Literaria dedicado ao Doutor J. Leite de Vasconcelos*, i (Salamanca, 1934), 428–33.

VERDIER, Y., *Façons de dire, façons de faire* (Paris, 1979).

VERNANT, J.-P., *Myth and Thought among the Greeks* (London, 1983).

VERSNEL, H. S., *Triumphus: An Inquiry into the Origins, Development and Meaning of the Roman Triumph* (Leiden, 1970).

——'Historical Implications', in C. M. Stibbe, G. Colonna, C. de Simone, and H. S. Versnel (eds.), *Lapis Satricanus: Archaeological, Epigraphical, Linguistic and Historical Aspects of the New Inscription from Satricum*, (Rome, 1980), 95–150.

——'IUN]IEI, A New Conjecture in the Satricum Inscription', *Mededelingen van het Nederlands Instituut te Rome*, 56 (1997), 177–200.

VEYNE, P., *Bread and Circuses: Historical Sociology and Political Pluralism* (London, 1990).

VISINTIN, M., *La vergine e l'eroe: Temesa e la leggenda di Euthymos di Locri* (Bari, 1992).

VONS, J., *L'Image de la femme dans l'œuvre de Pline l'Ancien*, Coll. Lat. 256 (Brussels, 2000).

VON STADEN, H., *Herophilus: The Art of Medicine in Early Alexandria* (Cambridge, 1989).

——'Women and Dirt', *Helios*, 19 (1992), 7–30.

WACHSMANN, S., *Seagoing Ships and Seamanship in the Bronze-Age Levant* (Texas, 1998).

WAELE, J. A. K. E. DE, 'The Lapis Satricanus and the Chronology of the Temples of Mater Matuta at Satricum', *Ostraka*, 5 (1996), 231–42.

WAELKINS, M., DE PAEPA, P., MOENS, L., 'Patterns of Extraction and Production in the White Marble Quarries of the Mediterranean: History, Present Problems and Prospects', in J. Clayton Fant (ed.), *Ancient Marble Quarrying and Trade: Archaeological Institute of America Colloquium 1987*, San Antonio, Texas, BAR suppl. ser. 483 (Oxford, 1988), 81–116.

WAGENWOORT, H., *Roman Dynamism* (Oxford, 1947).

WALBANK, F. W., *An Historical Commentary on Polybius*, 2 vols. (Oxford, 1957–79).

WALCOT, P., *Envy and the Greeks: A Study of Human Behaviour* (Warminster, 1978).

WALLACE-HADRILL, A., *Suetonius: The Scholar and his Caesars* (London, 1983).

——'Pliny the Elder and Man's Unnatural History', *G&R* NS 37 (1990), 80–96.

WALLINGA, H. T., *Ships and Sea-Power before the Great Persian War* (Brill, 1993).

WARDLE, D. (ed., trans., comm.), *Valerius Maximus' Memorable Deeds and Sayings Book 1* (Oxford, 1998).

498   BIBLIOGRAPHY

WARMINGTON, E. H., *The Commerce between the Roman Empire and India*[2] (London, 1974).

WEHRLI, F., *Die Schule des Aristoteles*, vol. viii (Basel, 1953; 2nd edn. 1969).

WEIGEL, R., *Lepidus: The Tarnished Triumvir* (London, 1992).

WEINSTOCK, S., review of K. Latte, *Römische Religionsgeschichte*, *JRS* 51 (1961), 206–15.

——*Divus Julius* (Oxford, 1971).

WELLMAN, M., 'Zur Geschichte de Medicin im Altertum', *Hermes*, 35 (1900), 349–84.

WEST, M. L. (ed. and comm.), *Theogony* (Oxford, 1966).

——(ed. and comm.), *Hesiod: Works and Days* (Oxford, 1978).

WHEELER, E. L., 'Sapiens and Stratagems: The Neglected Meaning of a cognomen', *Historia*, 37 (1988), 166–95.

WINKLER, J., 'Lollianos and the Desperadoes', *JHS* 100 (1980), 155–81.

WINTERBOTTOM, M., *The Elder Seneca*, 2 vols. (Cambridge, Mass., and London, 1974).

WISEMAN, T. P., 'Legendary Genealogies in Late Republican Rome', *G&R* 21 (1974), 153–64.

——*Clio's Cosmetics* (Totowa, NJ, 1979).

WISSOWA, G., *Religion und Kultus der Römer* (Munich, 1902).

WISTRAND, E., *Felicitas Imperatoria* (Göteborg, 1987).

WITTCOWER, R., 'Marvels of the East: A Study in the History of Monsters', *JWCI* 5 (1942), 159–97.

WOLVERTON, R. E., 'The Encomium of Cicero in Pliny the Elder', in C. Henderson (ed.), *Classical, Medieval and Renaissance Studies in Honor of B. L. Ullman*, vol. i (Rome, 1964), 159–64.

WOODSIDE, A., 'Vespasian's Patronage of Education', *TAPA* 73 (1942), 123–9.

WRIGHT, M. R., *Cosmology in Antiquity* (London, 1995).

YATES, F., *The Art of Memory* (London, 1966).

YOUNG, J. H., *Caesarian Section: The History and Development of the Operation from Earliest Times* (London, 1944).

ZANKER, P., *The Power of Images in the Age of Augustus* (Ann Arbor, 1988).

ZULUETA, J., 'Malaria and Mediterranean History', *Parasitologia*, 15 (1973), 1–15.

INDEX

Roman emperors and many Roman authors are indexed under the popular anglicised forms of their names; thus Cicero, not Tullius Cicero; Vespasian, not Flavius Vespasianus